西南政法大学校级规划教材

英美刑法学

Anglo - American Criminal Law

英汉双语版

主编 | 姜敏
副主编 | 李立丰 肖敏 郭旨龙
参编者 | 朱晓华 胡树琪 叶宁 詹惟凯 秦长森 饶克瑾 张文馨

法律出版社
——北京——
始创于1954年

图书在版编目（CIP）数据

英美刑法学：汉、英 / 姜敏主编. -- 北京：法律出版社，2024. -- ISBN 978-7-5197-9597-9

Ⅰ. D956.14;D971.24

中国国家版本馆 CIP 数据核字第 20245JA358 号

英美刑法学(英汉双语版)
YINGMEI XINGFAXUE
(YINGHAN SHUANGYU BAN)

姜 敏 主编

责任编辑 吴 昉 胡佳文
装帧设计 鲍龙卉

出版发行 法律出版社
编辑统筹 法律教育出版分社
责任校对 晁明慧
责任印制 刘晓伟
经　　销 新华书店

开本 710 毫米×1000 毫米 1/16
印张 27.25 **字数** 508 千
版本 2024 年 12 月第 1 版
印次 2024 年 12 月第 1 次印刷
印刷 三河市龙大印装有限公司

地址：北京市丰台区莲花池西里 7 号(100073)
网址：www.lawpress.com.cn
投稿邮箱：info@lawpress.com.cn
举报盗版邮箱：jbwq@lawpress.com.cn

销售电话：010-83938349
客服电话：010-83938350
咨询电话：010-63939796

书号：ISBN 978-7-5197-9597-9　　**定价**：65.00 元

编者简介及分工

主　编

姜　敏

西南政法大学法学院教授，博士生导师，博士后合作导师。本科毕业于四川外语学院，英语专业（通过专业英语八级）；于西南政法大学取得硕士和博士学位，专业为刑法学；北京师范大学刑事法律科学院博士后；北京大学法学院中青年骨干教师访问学者；国家留学基金委公派美国宾夕法尼亚大学法学院学习1年。现已发表论文80余篇，被人大复印资料转载10余篇；出版专著4部；翻译专著7部，主持国家社科基金项目2项（重点项目1项）；司法部项目3项；博士后基金项目2项（特别基金项目和一般项目各1项）；重庆市教委人文社科重大课题1项，其他课题10余项；积极从事教学、教育研究和课程改革，获西南政法大学首届旭焰巾帼教学奖（2022年），研究生和本科生的“英美刑法（双语）”，分别被认定为重庆市一流课程（2019年）和重庆市一流本科课程（2022年）。现为中国刑法学会理事，重庆市法学会首席法律咨询专家，重庆市刑法学会常务理事，副秘书长。负责撰写本书第2章。

副主编

李立丰

吉林大学匡亚明特聘教授，吉林大学理论法学研究中心、法学院博士生导师，兼任中国犯罪学会常务理事、中国刑法学会理事、吉林省法学会刑法学研究会副会长、吉林省法学会环境法治研究会常务副会长、吉林省法学会东北亚法治研究会副会长、上海法院特聘教授、吉林省高级人民法院研修学者、日本早稻田大学访问学者、日本关西学院大学法学部客员教授等学术职务，曾任浙江省金华市人民检察院副检察长（挂职）。曾全奖赴美攻读法学硕士（LLM）学位。先后主持国家社科基金、教育部社科基金、吉林省社科基金项目多项，在CSSCI期刊、辑刊发表相关论文、译文50余篇，其中多篇被《新华文摘》《中国社会科学文摘》《人大报刊复印资料》全文转载，使用日语、英语在日本、英国、俄罗斯等国家的学术刊物发表论文，已出版个人专著5部,英文、日文译著40余部。2018年当选第三届吉林省十大杰出中青年法学家。负责撰写本书第9章、第10章、第11章。

肖　敏

西南政法大学法学院副教授,硕士生导师,昆士兰科技大学访问学者。主要研究方向为刑法学、犯罪学和英美刑法学等。法学博士,曾在《政治与法律》等期刊发表学术论文几十余篇,主持国家社科基金一般项目1项,主研国家社科基金重点项目、国家重点实验室开放项目、教育部人文社科基金项目及省部级课题四项,出版专著3部。负责撰写本书第4章、第7章、第8章;部分撰写第1章。

郭旨龙

中国政法大学刑事司法学院副教授,博士生导师(刑法学学术学位与刑事法治专业学位),刑事辩护创新发展研究中心研究员。英国格拉斯哥大学法学博士。研究数字刑法、比较刑法、智慧法治、法与社会。参与法律、规章起草论证。多次参加联合国有关公约谈判会议建言献策,接受中央电视台、中国国际电视台、《人民日报》(海外版)等媒体采访。在《法学研究》、《中外法学》、*Legal Studies*、*Computer Law & Security Review*、*Artificial Intelligence and Law* 等刊物发表论文71篇,被《高等学校文科学术文摘》《人大复印报刊资料》等文摘全文转载10篇,被《中国社会科学文摘》《检察日报》论点摘要3篇。出版独著、合著著作4部,主编、参编教材5部。在《中国社会科学报》、《法治日报》、光明网、人民网等媒体发文23篇。主持国社科青年项目、教育部后期项目、司法部青年项目、京社科青年项目等课题11项。负责撰写本书第6章、第12章。

参编者

朱晓华

曾留学美国蒙大拿大学。主要从事法律语言学和法律翻译研究及实务。参译《中华人民共和国最高人民法院案例选》(第二辑、第三辑、第四辑),编撰及参编《法律英语教程》《法律英语泛读教程》《法律英汉大词典》等教材和工具书。讲授中国慕课网"法律英语"在线课程;"法律英语""高级法律英语""法律经贸英语翻译""法律英汉语言对比与翻译""公民权""公平与正义""高级英语""英语语法"等在校课程。2023年指导学生获华政杯全国法律翻译大赛一等奖;法律英语大赛西南片区一等奖,全国三等奖,2024年指导学生法律英语大赛西南片区一等奖,全国一等奖及三等奖,2024指导学生获重庆市优秀毕业论文。部分撰写本书第1章。

胡树琪

国家法官学院讲师,北京师范大学刑法学博士。曾在《法学评论》等刊物发表文章,赴英国牛津大学、澳大利亚昆士兰大学交流学习,参与国社科一般项目、国社科青年项目等。负责撰写本书第5章。

叶　宁

西南政法大学法学院讲师,西南政法大学与苏黎世大学联合培养法学博士,来华留学硕士生导师;东盟等国的司法机关法律人员高级研修班导师;讲授"中国司法制度""中国刑事法律制度"等来华留学生课程和"英美刑法(双语)"课程;参与培养七届约90名"一带一路"共建国家法学研究生。负责本书部分英文内容的校对。

詹惟凯

西南政法大学刑法学博士研究生。于西南政法大学获法学学士学位、四川外国语大学获英语文学学士二学位、西南大学法学院获法学硕士学位。发表论文近10篇,参研省部级课题2项,参与翻译、校对外文专著2部。负责撰写本书第3章。

秦长森

东南大学法学院博士研究生,英国格拉斯哥大学访问研究员,江苏省泰兴市检察院第五检察部副主任(挂职)。研究方向为中国刑法学、比较刑法学、公共政策与法治。在《中国法学(英文版)》《北方法学》《刑法论丛》等刊发表学术论文35篇,获中国刑法学研究会、中国行为法学研究会、中国警察法学研究会等一级学会奖励7次,主持中国法学会自选项目、江苏省检察院青年项目、河南省法学会一般项目等各类课题7项。部分撰写本书第13章。

饶克瑾

西南政法大学刑法学硕士研究生。本科毕业于西安外国语大学翻译专业,通过英语专业八级。拥有扎实的英语语言基础、法律基础和翻译实践经验;曾在律所实习和工作;多次参与外国语大学丝绸之路语言服务协同创新中心翻译项目。负责本书部分英文内容的校对。

张文馨

中国政法大学刑法学硕士研究生,在《人民检察》《犯罪学研究》发表学术论文2篇。部分撰写本书第13章。

Content

目　录

Chapter 1　Criminal Law：An Overview
第 1 章　刑法概述

■ The Learning Objectives（学习目标）

1. To define and understand what behavior deserves criminal punishment.
界定并了解哪些行为应受到刑事处罚。

2. To understand different crimes and the standards for the classification thereof.
了解不同的犯罪行为及其分类标准。

3. To comprehend the general and special parts of criminal law.
理解刑法的总则和分则。

4. To identify the main sources of criminal law.
了解刑法的主要法律渊源。

5. To analyze case rulings and apply them in the study of criminal law.
了解案例裁判文书及其运用。

6. To acquire some legal terminologies frequently used in this filed.
掌握一些本章的常用刑法术语。

■ Chapter Outline（本章内容概要）

This chapter provides an overview of criminal law, focusing on the behaviors deserving criminal punishment, the classification of crimes, the general and special parts of criminal law, the sources of law, and the case – based study method.

本章是刑法概述，重点介绍犯罪（何种行为该受刑罚惩罚）、犯罪分类、刑法总则与分则、刑法渊源和案例裁判文书阅读的方法。

■ The Purpose of Curriculum Ideology and Politics for this Chapter (本章的课程思政目标)

Students should through the study of Anglo – American criminal law enhance their knowledge system of criminal law. The Anglo – American criminal law is an important part of criminal law, which has its own characteristics and special knowledge points in addition to the common knowledge elements of criminal law. Chinese students should not only grasp Chinese criminal law in depth, but also have an international perspective and understand the Anglo – American criminal law and other extra – territorial criminal law knowledge, to broaden their professional horizons and improve the knowledge structure of criminal law that they have mastered.

学生通过研习英美刑法,完善刑法知识体系。英美刑法是重要的刑法内容,其除具有刑法学共同的知识要素外,还具有自己的特征和特色知识点。中国学生不仅应深度把握中国刑法,还应具有国际视野,了解英美刑法等域外刑法知识,拓展自己的专业视野,完善刑法知识结构。

The common law is the main source of law in Anglo – American criminal law. The common law principle of "following decisis" makes it important for legal practitioners to be familiar with the relevant precedent or precedent. The precedent in Anglo – American criminal law can present the facts of the case, the issues in dispute and the principles of law, as well as to demonstrate its judicial practice. In addition, it also allows the views of dissenting judges to be presented in the judgement. Therefore, the study of precedents in Anglo – American criminal law can not only help students to know the relevant legal provisions and application of legal principles of Anglo – American criminal law, understand the value and significance of judges' reasoning, and allow judges to express different opinions, but also cultivate the ability to analyze and solve practical legal problems.

普通法是英美刑法的主要法律渊源。普通法秉承"遵循先例"原则,使法律人士必须熟悉相关先例或判例。英美刑法的判例能呈现案件事实、争议问题和法律原则,并且能展现司法实践情况。不仅如此,其在判决书中还允许呈现持不同意见的法官的观点。因此,研阅英美刑法判例,不仅能够帮助学生知晓英美刑法的相关法律规定及法律原则的运用,领悟和了解法官的推理、说理以及允许法官表达不同意见的价值和意义,而且还能培养学生分析和解决实际法律问题的能力。

■ Terminologies（专业术语）

criminal law	刑法
crime	犯罪
tort	侵权
felony	重罪
misdemeanor	轻罪
malum in se crime	自然犯
malum prohibitum crime	法定犯
common law	普通法
modern statutes	现代成文法
Bill of Rights	《人权法案》
American Law Institute	美国法学会
Model Penal Code	《模范刑法典》
majority opinion	大多数意见
concurring opinion	协同意见
dissent	异议

1.1 What Behavior Deserves Criminal Punishment?（何种行为应被刑罚惩罚?）

Defining crime is not easy, even in Anglo – American criminal Law. Generally, crimes refer to any behavior that legislators define as criminal. Under common Law system, there is no clear societal "consensus" on what should be deemed criminal, nor is there any clear underlying moral evaluation criteria to what is criminal. Many crimes are defined as such simply because the overwhelming majority of people feel they should be. Crimes, then, are little more than behaviors that lawmakers, who in the United States are our elected representatives, consider illegal.[1]

要给犯罪下定义并不容易,这在英美刑法中也不例外,但一般而言,犯罪是指任何被立法者规定为犯罪的行为。在英美法系中,对于哪些行为应被认定为犯罪,社会并没有明确的共识,对于哪些行为属于犯罪,也没有明确的道德评价标准。许多犯罪之所以被定义为犯罪,仅仅是因为绝大多数人认为它们应该被视为犯罪。因此,犯罪不过是立法者(在美国,立法者是被选出的代表)所认为具有非法性质的行为。

The concept of crime is perhaps more easily understood by looking to state penal

[1] Jennifer L. Moore & John L. Worrall, *Criminal Law*, 2nd editon, Pearson Education Inc. ,2018,p. 1 – 2.

codes and their stated purpose for the criminal law in U. S. For example, in Pennsylvania, the stated purposes of the criminal law, according to Section 104 of that state's Crimes Code, are as follows: (1) To forbid and prevent conduct that unjustifiably inflicts or threatens substantial harm to an individual or public interest. (2) To safeguard conduct that is without fault from condemnation as criminal. (3) To safeguard offenders against excessive, disproportionate, or arbitrary punishment. (4) To give fair warning of the nature of the conduct declared to constitute an offense, and of the sentences that may be imposed on conviction of an offense. (5) To differentiate on reasonable grounds between serious and minor offenses, and to differentiate among offenders for just individualization in their treatment. Crimes need to be distinguished from torts. Generally speaking, that difference is that even though many offences are committed against other individuals, the criminal law treats them as offenses against society as a whole, torts, are not characterized as such.[1]

通过研究美国各州的刑法及其阐明的刑法目的,也许更容易理解犯罪的概念。例如,在宾夕法尼亚州,根据该州刑法第 104 条的规定,刑法的既定目的如下:(1)禁止和预防对个人或公共利益造成或威胁造成重大损害的行为;(2)保护无过错的行为免受刑事处罚;(3)保障犯罪者免受过度、不相称或任意的惩罚;(4)对被宣布构成犯罪的行为的性质以及定罪后可能判处的刑罚给予公平警示;(5)以合理的理由区分严重犯罪和轻微犯罪,并区分罪犯,以便对其进行公正的个别化处理。从这个阐述来看,犯罪需要与侵权行为区分开来。一般而言,这区别就是:尽管许多犯罪行为是针对个人实施的,但刑法将其视为对整个社会的危害,而侵权行为却不具有这样的特点。

This is why most criminal law cases are named with the charged person and the governing authority responsible for prosecution. Cases such as People v. Smith, Commonwealth v. Jones, and State v. Wallace reflect this arrangement. In contrast, a tort is a private wrong or injury. In tort cases, a court will provide a remedy through an "action", that is a lawsuit between the two parties, the victim and the alleged tort - feasor. Tort actions are brought by victims seeking compensation them for their injuries, usually in the form of financial restitution. In contrast, criminal cases are brought for the purpose of punishing wrongdoers, I. e., its thrust is not on compensation.[2]

这就是为什么大多数刑法案例的名称都包含被指控者的姓名以及负责指控罪犯的管理机构。人民诉史密斯案(People v. Smith)、联邦诉琼斯案(Commonwealth

[1] Jennifer L. Moore & John L. Worrall, *Criminal Law*, 2nd editon, Pearson Education Inc. ,2018, p. 2.

[2] Jennifer L. Moore & John L. Worrall, *Criminal Law*, 2nd editon, Pearson Education Inc. ,2018, p. 2.

v. Jones)和州诉华莱士案(State v. Wallace)等案件都反映了这一特征。相比之下,侵权行为是一种私人过失或伤害行为。在侵权的场合,法院将以诉讼的形式提供救济,即在被害人和所谓的侵权者之间发生诉讼。侵权诉讼是由被害人提起的,旨在赔偿其所受伤害。这种赔偿通常是经济赔偿。相比之下,刑事案件的目的是惩罚不法行为人,即其主旨不在于赔偿。

1.2 The Classification of Crimes(犯罪分类)

Although there is greatdispute as to what constitutes a crime and what kind of conduct should be punished, one common approach is that crimes are defined as such by legislative bodies. While there is no consensus over what should be illegal, there is a certain measure of agreement when it comes to more harmful types of behavior, such as murder. With this backdrop, we can begin to make sense of criminal law by classifying crimes.[1] In general, crimes can be categorized as felonies or misdemeanors based on the severity of the crime, while crimes can be categorized as *malum in se* crime versus *malum prohibitum* crime based on the degree of viciousness of the crime. The next section will focus on these two major classifications.[2]

尽管人们对何为犯罪及何种行为应该受到惩罚的认识有很大分歧,但在涉及谋杀等危害性较大的行为时,人们还是会在某种程度上达成一致意见。在此背景下,我们可以通过对犯罪进行分类来理解刑法。一般而言,根据罪行轻重可以将犯罪分为重罪和轻罪,而根据罪行恶性性质则可以将犯罪分为自然犯和法定犯。接下来的部分将重点介绍这两大分类。

1.2.1 Felonies and Misdemeanors(重罪和轻罪)

The classification of crimes into felonies and misdemeanors is age - old, popular, and found in nearly every penal code. In general, a felony is a crime punishable by death or confinement in prison for more than 12 months. Obviously, death is reserved for the most serious felonies, such as first - degree murder. Lesser felonies, such as theft of goods valued at a certain threshold, may result in imprisonment rather than capital punishment. A misdemeanor, by contrast, is a crime punishable by a fine or a period of incarceration less than 12 months. Importantly, a crime is defined as a felony or amisdemeanor based on possible, not actual, punishment. For example, in one case,

---

[1] Jennifer L. Moore & John L. Worrall, *Criminal Law*, 2nd editon, Pearson Education Inc. ,2018, p. 2.

[2] Jennifer L. Moore & John L. Worrall, *Criminal Law*, 2nd editon, Pearson Education Inc. ,2018, p. 5.

a woman was sentenced to one year in prison for driving under the influence, but the judge "probated" her sentence (which means that he suspended it) and instead required her to serve 120 days in home confinement. She later argued she was a misdemeanant, not a felon, but an appeals court said that "a person whose... felony sentence is reduced... does not become a misdemeanant by virtue of the reduction but remains a felon".[1]

将犯罪分为重罪和轻罪的做法由来已久且广受欢迎,其见诸美国很多州的刑法。一般来说,重罪是指可判处死刑或监禁 12 个月以上的罪行。显然,死刑只适用于最严重的重罪,如一级谋杀罪。情节较轻的重罪,如行为人盗窃价值一定数额的物品,会被判处监禁而非死刑。相比之下,轻罪是指可处以罚款或监禁时间少于 12 个月的罪行。重要的是,一项罪行被定义为重罪或轻罪是基于可能而非实际的惩罚。例如,在某个案例中,一名妇女因酒后驾车被判处 1 年监禁,但法官对她判决了缓刑(缓期执行),并要求她在家中禁闭 120 天。该妇女后来辩称自己是轻罪犯,而不是重罪犯,但上诉法院表示:"重罪减刑的人……不会因为减刑而成为轻罪犯,其仍然是重罪犯"。

Why is the distinction between felonies and misdemeanors significant, beyond the punishments that can be imposed? A key reason is that trial procedures differ for felonies and misdemeanors. For example, jury trials are not required in misdemeanor cases where the punishment does not exceed six months' confinement. Also, felony trials tend to be longer and more complex due to the potential severity of the punishment, which can include capital punishment in serious cases. Another important reason for classifying crimes in this way is because certain crimes necessitate it. For example, some statutes define burglary in terms of unlawful entry with intent to commit a felony inside. If a misdemeanor is committed inside, then the crime is not burglary.[2] It is worth noting that the Model Penal Code categorizes crimes according to the severity of their penalties: felony, misdemeanor, petty misdemeanors, and violations.

为什么我们关心重罪和轻罪之间的区别,而不关注施加的刑罚呢?一个重要原因是重罪和轻罪的审判程序不同。例如,处罚不超过 6 个月监禁的轻罪案件,不需要陪审团审判。此外,重罪审判往往会因其涉及的利害关系,而经历更加冗长和复杂的程序,严重的案件可能包括对罪犯处以极刑。以这种方式对犯罪进行分类的另一个重要原因是,某些犯罪需要这样做。例如,有些法规将夜盗罪定义为非法侵入并意图于室内实施重罪。如果在室内实施的是轻罪,则不属于夜盗罪。值得注意的

[1] Jennifer L. Moore & John L. Worrall, *Criminal Law*, 2nd editon, Pearson Education Inc. ,2018, p. 5.

[2] Jennifer L. Moore & John L. Worrall, *Criminal Law*, 2nd editon, Pearson Education Inc. ,2018, p. 5.

是,《模范刑法典》按照刑罚轻重将犯罪分为:重罪、轻罪、微罪及违警罪。

1.2.2 Malum in Se Crime versus Malum Prohibitum Crime(自然犯与法定犯)

Malum in se (or the plural form, mala in se) is a Latin phrase meaning wrong or evil in itself. In contrast, malum prohibitum (or mala prohibita) refers to something that is wrong or evil because it is defined as such. Certain crimes which are simply wrong in themselves are called *Malum in Se Crime*. For example, it is all but impossible to convince someone that an unjustified and inexcusable murder is acceptable. Other examples of *mala in se* offenses include robbery, larceny (theft), and rape, among others. However, the line between what is wrong in itself(*malum in se crime*) and what is wrong because legislators defined it that way (*malum prohibitum crime*) is difficult to draw. Is drug possession wrong in itself? What about speeding? Speeding arguably poses risks to other drivers, so is it inherently wrong? If not, could it be wrong once a driver exceeds a certain speed, such as 100 miles per hour? There are no easy answers. The distinction between *malum in se crime* and *malum prohibitum crime* is largely academic these days because for the majority of offenses it is difficult to objectively place them in one category.[1]

自然犯的英文表达是 malum in se,malum in se(或复数形式,mala in se)是一个拉丁短语,意思是本身就是错误或邪恶的。与此对应,法定犯的英文表达是 malum prohibitum,malum prohibitum(或 mala prohibita)的意思是,某件事之所以是错误或邪恶的,是因为它被规定为不法或邪恶。某些本身就是错误的罪行被称为自然犯,例如,几乎不可能让人相信无理且不可原谅的谋杀是可以被接受的。其他自然犯还包括抢劫、盗窃和强奸等。但是,很难区分哪些行为本身是错误的(自然犯),哪些行为是因为立法者这样规定才是错误的(法定犯)。持有毒品本身是错误的吗?那超速驾驶呢?超速会给其他司机带来风险,但它本身就是错误的吗?如果不是,那么一旦驾驶者超过一定的速度,比如每小时100英里[2],是否就是错误的呢?答案并不简单。这导致如今,自然犯和法定犯很大程度是一种学术性的分类,因为对于大多数非法行为而言,很难客观地将它们归为一类。

1.3 The General and Special parts of Criminal Law (刑法的总则和分则)

As mentioned earlier, criminal law defines the behavior that deserves criminal punishment, which is the essence of criminal law. In terms of its form, criminal law

---

[1] Jennifer L. Moore & John L. Worrall, *Criminal Law*, 2nd editon, Pearson Education Inc. ,2018, p. 5.

[2] 约为161千米。

consists of two parts: a general part and a special part. The general part of criminal law consists of principles that apply to more than one crime. Most state criminal codes today include a general part. The special part of criminal law defines specific crimes and categorize them into groups according to the protected legal interests. All states include definitions of at least some specific crimes, and most classify them based on the criminal object.[1] Next, we'll discuss the general and special parts of the criminal law.

如前所述,刑法规定了哪些行为是应受惩罚的,这是刑法的实质内容。从形式来看,刑法由两部分组成:总则部分和分则部分。一般而言,刑法的总则部分是关于使用一种以上犯罪的原则。如今,美国大多数州的刑法都有总则部分。刑法的分则部分规定具体的罪行,并根据犯罪客体将其分为若干组。所有州的刑法都至少包括一些规定具体罪行的法条,大多数州根据犯罪客体将其分组。接下来,本书将分别介绍刑法的总则和分则。

1.3.1 The General Part of Criminal Law (刑法总则)

The general part of criminal law includes the general principles, offenses of general applicability, and the principles of justification and excuse. Some general principles apply to all crimes, others to all felonies; and still others apply only to only certain some crimes. In addtion to the general principles, the general part of criminal law where includes two categories of "offenses of general applicability". The first is complicity, where one person is held criminally liable for someone else's conduct. The second category comprises in complete crimes such as attempt, conspiracy, and solicitation. Lastly, the general part of criminal law includes the principles of justification and excuse, the principles that govern most defenses to criminal liability.[2]

总则规定的内容有一般性原则、总则性犯罪和抗辩事由。一般而言,在总则规定的原则中,某些一般性原则适用于所有犯罪,一些原则适用于所有重罪,还有一些原则仅适用于某些犯罪。除了一般性原则外,总则规定了两种被称为总则性的犯罪。第一种是共犯,即让一个人对其他人的行为承担刑事责任的罪行。第二种是未完成犯罪,其主要包括未遂罪、共谋罪和教唆罪。[3] 最后,刑法的总则部分还规定了正当化事由和可宽恕事由,这些事由适用于大多数刑事责任的辩护。

---

〔1〕 Joel Samaha, *Criminal Law*, 10th edition, Wadsworth Cengage Learning, 2011, p. 12.

〔2〕 Joel Samaha, *Criminal Law*, 10th edition, Wadsworth Cengage Learning, 2011, p. 12.

〔3〕 对于总则性犯罪的范畴,英美法系的教材有所不同。有些教材只把未完成犯罪(未遂罪、共谋罪和教唆罪)作为总则性犯罪,而有些教材则把共同犯罪、未完成犯罪(未遂罪、共谋罪和教唆罪)视为总则性犯罪。——笔者注

1.3.2 The Special Part of Criminal Law (刑法分则)

The special part of criminal law defines specific crimes, based on the principles set out in the general part. Specific crimes vary across common Law Jurisdictions, but in general, they are divided into four groups: crimes against persons; crimes against property; crimes against public order and morals; and crimes against the state. The definitions of specific crimes consists of the elements prosecutaors have to prove beyond a reasonable doubt to convict defendants. From the standpoint of understanding how general principles relate to specific crimes, each definition of a specific crime is an application of one or more general principles.[1]

刑法分则部分根据总则部分规定的原则对具体犯罪进行规定。在英美法系,各个国家的刑法分则规定的犯罪有所区别,但一般而言,分则一般都规定了以下四类犯罪:侵犯人身罪、侵犯财产罪、违反公共秩序和道德罪以及危害国家安全罪。从理解总则原则与具体犯罪关系的角度来看,每一个具体犯罪的规定都是一个或多个刑法总则基本原则的应用。

1.4 Sources of Criminal Law(刑法渊源)

We have already mentioned the essence, form and some moral foundations of criminal law, but we have not yet to explore its origins. What does criminal law come from? There are many sources—some ancient and others more modern. Here, we examine the primary sources of criminal law: common law, modern statutes, the Model Penal Code, and constitutional provisions. Each is best viewed as a piece of the criminal law puzzle.[2]

我们已经谈到刑法的本质和形式,也论及刑法具有道德基础,但还没有讨论刑法的渊源。刑法的渊源是什么?英美法系国家的刑法有很多渊源,有些是古代的渊源,也有些是现代的渊源。在此,我们将探讨刑法的主要渊源,即普通法、现代成文法、《模范刑法典》以及宪法渊源。这些渊源都是组成刑法拼图的一部分。

1.4.1 Common Law(普通法)

Common law developed before legislatures existed and evolved through centuries of history. After the Norman Conquest of England in 1066, King William and his Norman dukes and barons moved quickly to consolidate their control over their new territories.

---

〔1〕 Joel Samaha, *Criminal Law*, 10th edition, Wadsworth Cengage Learning, 2011, p. 12.

〔2〕 Jennifer L. Moore & John L. Worrall, *Criminal Law*, 2nd editon, Pearson Education Inc., 2018, p. 6.

One method was to take charge of the preexisting legal and court system. Once this was alone, judges not only issued decisions but also recorded them in writing. These decisions were subsequently shared with other judges, a resulting in a measure of uniformity from one court to the next. This was literally the law "common" to England, and it came to be known as the common law. The United States is a common law country since it inherited its legal system from England.[1]

普通法诞生于立法机关设立之前,是经过了悠久的历史逐渐演变而来的。在诺曼人征服英格兰(1066 年)后,威廉国王和他的诺曼公爵、男爵们迅速采取行动,以巩固他们对新占领土的控制。他们所采取的其中一个措施就是控制原有的法律和法院系统,使法庭上的法官不仅要作出判决,还要将判决记录下来。这些判决随后分发给其他法官。如此一来,各法院之间就具备某种程度的统一性。这就是全英国通用的法律,后来被称为普通法。美国就是一个普通法国家,且其继承了英国的普通法。

Under the reign of Henry Ⅱ (1154 – 1189), national law was introduced, but not through legislative authority as is customary today. Rather, Henry Ⅱ implemented a system where judges from his own central court traveled to the countryside to preside over disputes. They resolved these disputes based on what they perceived as local custom. The judges effectively created law, as there was no democratic law – forming process in place at the time. As more and more judges began to record their decisions, the principles of stare decisis and precedent were developed. Precedent refers, generally, to some prior action that guides current action.[2]

在亨利二世统治时期(1154—1189 年),国家法律被引入,但当时国家法律并不如同现在惯常那样是由立法权所确定。相反,亨利二世实施了一项制度,即委派中央法院法官前去乡村解决纠纷,这些法官根据自己认可的习俗来解决纠纷。由于当时没有民主的法律制定程序,法官们的行为实际是创造法律。随着越来越多的法官开始记录他们所作的判决,"遵循判决"和"先例"原则逐渐形成。先例一般是指导当前诉讼的某些先前诉讼的判决。

In the common law context, this meant that judges' decisions were guided by earlier decisions. Thus, precedent ensured continuity and predictability of judicial decisions. If decisions changed radically from one judge to the next, from place to place, or both, the "common" law would be anything but common. It was also easier

---

〔1〕 Jennifer L. Moore & John L. Worrall, *Criminal Law*, 2nd editon, Pearson Education Inc. ,2018, p. 6.

〔2〕 Jennifer L. Moore & John L. Worrall, *Criminal Law*, 2nd editon, Pearson Education Inc. ,2018, p. 6.

for judges to rely on earlier decisions; otherwise, they would have to continually reinvent the wheel.[1]

在普通法背景下,这意味着法官判决需以先前的判决为指导。因此,先例确保了司法判决的连续性和可预测性。如果不同法官、不同地方或两者的判决发生根本性的变化,那么"普通"法就不是普通法了。此外,法官也更易依赖先前的判决,否则,他们将不得不不断地"重新发明轮子"。[2]

While the common law is usually viewed as a legal concept, it also had social implications: Medieval judge were entrusted with the collective wisdom, values, and morals established by the community and were trusted to apply them to solve disputes between citizens. Even when appointed by the king, the medieval judge represented the community and applied the community's (not the king's) law, thereby maintaining its age - old customs and values.[3]

尽管普通法通常被视为一个法律概念,但它也具有社会意义:中世纪的法官被赋予社区的集体智慧、价值观和道德观,并被信任以解决公民之间的纠纷。即使由国王任命,中世纪法官也代表社区,适用社区(而非国王)的法律,从而维护其古老的习俗和价值观。

1.4.2 Modern Statutes(现代成文法)

Modern statutes exist at different levels of government (federal and state) and come in several different forms. United States Code contains "Crimes" section, know as the "Federal Criminal Code". States have their respective codes, and other units of government, such as counties and cities, often have their own ordinances, which all include criminal provisions. States such as California list criminal offenses in more than one code. There, most crimes are spelled out in the Penal Code, but the Health and Safety Code criminalizes drug law violations. The state has 29 separate legal codes! In today's world, the laws of various countries are made by the legislature, and the United States makes laws by the elected representatives at the state and local levels. Every year, without fail, members of Congress and state legislatures enact laws of all sorts, including those that make criminal offenses of specific behaviors. Sometimes they even decriminalize certain actions, such as marijuana legalization. It is also important to note

---

[1] Jennifer L. Moore & John L. Worrall, *Criminal Law*, 2nd editon, Pearson Education Inc. ,2018, p. 6.

[2] 此处意指法官重新创造跟先例一样的判例。

[3] Jennifer L. Moore & John L. Worrall, *Criminal Law*, 2nd editon, Pearson Education Inc. ,2018, p. 6 - 7.

that there is considerable overlap in the criminal laws of various jurisdictions.[1]

现代法规存在于不同级别的政府(联邦政府和州政府),并采用不同的形式。《美国联邦法典》就包含了"犯罪"部分,这就是"联邦刑法"。而各州有各自的法律,郡和市等其他政府单位通常也有各自的条例,在这些法律或条例中也包含了犯罪条款。比如,加利福尼亚州等在不止一部法典中列出刑事犯罪。一般而言,大多数罪行都规定于州刑法典之中,但其《健康与安全法》也将违反毒品法的行为规定为刑事犯罪。加利福尼亚州共有 29 部独立的法律。在现代社会,各个国家的法律都是由立法机构制定,美国是由所在的州和地方一级选出的立法代表制定法律。每年,国会议员和州立法机构都会制定各种法律,包括将特定行为规定为刑事犯罪的法律。有时,他们甚至会将某些行为非犯罪化,譬如大麻合法化。还需要注意的是,不同司法管辖区的刑法有相当多的重合之处。

1.4.3 The Model Penal Code(《模范刑法典》)

In American federal system of government, each state is free—within certain constitutional limitations—to develop its own common and statutory law. This led to considerable variation in law from state to state. In 1962, however, the American Law Institute, a private organization of lawyers, judges, and legal scholars, adopted the Model Penal Code. The Code was intended to serve as, a "model" for states to follow. Since 1962, several states have adopted the Model Penal Code, either in full or in part. This is beneficial in at least two respects. First, it promotes consistency across the states. Second, it makes the study of criminal law more manageable. But bear in mind that the federal system has not adopted it, nor has California, the nation's most populous state.[2] Despite this, Judges also invoke its provisions in their reasoning or ruling give it conciderable influence on the practice of criminal law in the United States.

在美国联邦政府体系中,每个州都可以在一定的宪法限制范围内自由制定自己的普通法和成文法。这导致各州之间的立法差异相当大。然而在 1962 年,由律师、法官和法律学者组成的民间组织——美国法学会,通过了《模范刑法典》。该法典旨在作为各州效仿的范本。自 1962 年以来,已有多个州全部或部分采用了《模范刑法典》。这至少在两个方面是有益的:首先,它促进了各州之间的一致性;其次,它使刑法研究更具可控性。但需要注意的是,联邦系统尚未采用《模范刑法典》,美国人口最多的州——加利福尼亚州,也没有采用《模范刑法典》。尽管如此,《模范刑法典》

[1] Jennifer L. Moore & John L. Worrall, *Criminal Law*, 2nd editon, Pearson Education Inc. ,2018, p. 7.
[2] Jennifer L. Moore & John L. Worrall, *Criminal Law*, 2nd editon, Pearson Education Inc. ,2018, p. 7.

的规定仍会被法官在推理或判决中援引,因此其对美国的刑法实践具有很大的影响力。

1.4.4 Constitutional Sources(宪法渊源)

Constitutions are the most significant source of law, especially as they provide the foundation for certain principles of criminal law, such as the principle of legality. Unlike penal codes, constitutions generally do not prohibit actions on the part of private citizens. Rather, constitutions generally place limits on government authority. They define, in broad terms, government structure and organization; they also spell out various rights that people enjoy, how government officials will be selected, and what roles various government branches will take on. The U. S. Constitution and constitutional documents are so important to the criminal law, especially the prohibition of expost facto laws in criminal law, the concept of equal protection under the law, issues of vagueness and overbreadth in the criminal law.[1]

宪法是最重要的法律渊源,尤其是刑法某些原则的重要渊源,比如合法性原则。但其与刑法不同,宪法一般不禁止公民个人的行为,反而通常限制刑法。宪法从广义上定义了政府的结构和组织;宪法还规定了人民享有的各种权利、政府官员的选拔方式以及政府各部门的职责。美国宪法及宪法性文件对刑法非常重要,尤其是刑法的禁止事后法的规定、法律平等保护原则、刑法的模糊性和过度宽泛性的禁止等,都是由宪法及宪法性文件规定的。

The Bill of Rights, an important constitutional document consisting of the first ten amendments to the Constitution, also set important limitations on government authority with respect to the investigation and prosecution of crime. The Fourth Amendment, for example, spells out warrant requirements, and the Fifth Amendment protects people, in part, from being forced to incriminate themselves. The Eighth Amendment prohibits cruel and unusual punishment. While the federal Constitution receives the most attention due to its status as the supreme law of the United States, it is important to note that each state has its own constitution. These often mirror the federal Constitution, but they often go into much more detail. Some states have used their constitutions to more clearly spell out what they consider prohibited action.[2]

《权利法案》是重要的宪法性文件,其是由宪法前十条修正案组成的。《权利法

---

〔1〕 Jennifer L. Moore & John L. Worrall, *Criminal Law*, 2nd editon, Pearson Education Inc. ,2018,p.7.

〔2〕 Jennifer L. Moore & John L. Worrall, *Criminal Law*, 2nd editon, Pearson Education Inc. ,2018,p.7.

案》宣布了在调查和起诉犯罪方面对政府权力的重要限制。例如,第四修正案规定搜查令要求,第五修正案在一定程度上保护人们不会被迫自证其罪,第八修正案禁止残忍和不寻常的惩罚。尽管联邦宪法因其具备美国最高法律地位而受到最多关注,但必须指出的是,每个州都有自己的宪法。这些宪法通常照搬联邦宪法,但往往更加详细。有些州则利用本州宪法,更明确地规定了其认为应该禁止的行为。

State constitutions can be more restrictive than the U. S. Constitution, but no state Constitution can undermine protections spelled out in the U. S. Constitution. For example, the Fourth Amendment spells out search warrant requirements, but is vague in terms of whether a warrant is required in all circumstances. In theory, a state could require warrants for all searches, but as a practical matter, most states have followed the U. S. Constitution's lead (and the U. S. Supreme Court's interpretation of it).[1]

州宪法可以比《美国宪法》更具限制性,但任何州宪法都不能触犯《美国宪法》规定的保护性规范。例如,《美国宪法》第四修正案规定了搜查令要求,但对于是否在所有情况下都需要搜查令却含糊其词。理论上,一个州可以对所有搜查都要求出示搜查令,但实际上,大多数州都遵循《美国宪法》的规定以及美国最高法院对《美国宪法》的解释。

In addition to these main sources described above, there are also municipal ordinances and administrative agency rule. Municipal ordinances are made by city, town and village governments, which possess broad powers to create criminal laws govering drugs, violence, public disorder, and other quality of life offence that violate community standards of good manners in public. But municipal ordinances have two limits – constitutional limits and the power of states to preempt municipalities.[2] Administrative crimes means violations of these federal and state agency rules. Both federal and state legislatures frequently grant administrative agencies the authority to make rules. For example, state legislatures commonly authorize the state highway patrol agencies to make rules regarding safety inspections,[3] and some violations of the above safety inspections rules are suspected to constitute an offence.

除了前面介绍的这些主要渊源,刑法渊源还包括了市政条例和行政法规。市政条例中的犯罪条款是由市、镇和村政府制定的,市政当局拥有制定刑法的广泛权力,并利用这种权力来处理毒品、暴力、公共秩序扰乱和其他违反社区良好公共生活秩

---

〔1〕 Jennifer L. Moore & John L. Worrall, *Criminal Law*, 2nd editon, Pearson Education Inc., 2018, p. 7.

〔2〕 Joel Samaha, *Criminal Law*, 10th edition, Wadsworth Cengage Learning, 2011, p. 17 – 19.

〔3〕 Joel Samaha, *Criminal Law*, 10th edition, Wadsworth Cengage Learning, 2011, p. 19.

序的犯罪。但其受到两个限制:宪法限制和各州权力优先于市政当局的限制。而行政犯罪是指违反联邦和州行政机构所制定法规的行为。联邦和州立法机构经常授予行政机构制定法规的权力。例如,州立法机构通常授权州高速公路巡逻机构制定有关安全检查的法规,违反上述安全检查法规的行为就涉嫌构成犯罪。

1.5 The Framework of A Case Text(案例判决文书的框架)

The criminal law of common law countries is based on case law, making precedent an important part of their criminal law. Reading or studying the judgments of cases in Anglo – American law countries helps to understand the basic content of the judgments, the application of law, and the practice of criminal justice, as well as the style of the judges' judgments. Therefore, reading or studying judgments is an important part of learning Anglo – American criminal law. However, there are both similarities and differences between the criminal judgments in the judicial practice of the Anglo – American countries and China. Therefore, the study of Anglo – American criminal law begins with an understanding of the basic components and structure of its judgments.

英美法系国家的刑法属于判例法,判例是其刑法的重要的组成部分。阅读或研究英美法系国家案件的判决书,可以了解其判决书的基本内容、法律适用情况等,而且还能了解刑事司法的实践情况、法官判案的风格等。因此,阅读或研究英美法系国家判决书,是学习英美刑法的重要内容。但是,英美国家司法实践中的刑事判决书,与中国司法实践的刑事判决书既有相同之处,也有不同之处。因此,学习英美刑法首先就应了解其判决书的基本组成部分和结构。

In general the basic components of a criminal judgment in Anglo – American criminal law countries include the case title, citation, trial information (mainly the date of the judgment and the name of judge, etc.), facts, the main issue, the court decision, and the holding. However, depending on the level of the trial, whether there are dissents, the judgment often also includes sections such as the writ of certiorari, procedural history, concurrences and dissents. In the common law system, the writ of certiorari is a writ of request from the higher court for access to the case file by the lower court when the judgment of the lower court is dissented. The procedural history is the judicial opinion of the appellate trial will also state the information of each court in the course of the appeal, the decision of the legal dispute, and the result of the judgment. A concurrence opinion is when some judges agree with a decision based on the majority opinion, but reach the same conclusion for different reasons. A dissenting opinion means that a minority of judges have a different view of the majority judge's opinion, and may write a dissenting opinion explaining why they disagree with the majority judge's decision.

一般而言,英美国家的刑事判决书的基本组成部分包括案例名称、案例引证号、审判信息(主要包括判决日期和主审法官姓名等信息)、案情、主要争议、法院判决、裁判理由,但除此之外,因为审判级别、是否有异议等因素存在,判决书除了上述基本组成部分,通常还会包括调卷令号、审理历史、协同意见和异议意见等部分。英美法系的调卷令是下级法院的判决受到异议时,上级法院向下级法院要求调阅有关案卷的令状。审理历史是指上诉审的司法意见书在案情部分还会陈述上诉过程中各法院的信息,对法律争议的认定以及判决结果。协同意见是指某些法官虽然同意基于多数法官意见作出的判决结果,但其是基于不同的推理而得到的同样结论。异议意见指少数法官对于多数法官意见持有不同看法,可以书写异议意见,解释为何不同意多数法官的判决结果。[1]

To help illustrate the structure of the judgment, attached below is a copy of the judgment. The judgment was in Griswold v. Connecticut, which established that "privacy is a constitutionally protected right". The basic framework is as follows:

下面附一份判决书以介绍判决书的构成。这份判决书是格里斯沃尔德诉康涅狄格州案(以下简称 Griswold v. Connecticut)的判决书,其是确立"隐私权是受宪法保护的权利"的案例,判决书基本框架如下所示:

Griswold v. Connecticut, 381 U. S. 479 (1965)

HISTORY

Estelle Griswold and others were convicted in a Connecticut trial court. They appealed, and the intermediate appellate court affirmed their conviction. They appealed to the Connecticut Supreme Court of Errors, which affirmed the intermediate appellate court's judgment. They appealed to the U. S. Supreme Court. The Supreme Court reversed, holding that the Connecticut law forbidding use of contraceptives unconstitutionally intrudes upon the right of marital privacy.

DOUGLAS, J., joined by WARREN, CJ., and CLARK, HARLAN, BRENNAN, WHITE, and GOLDBERG, JJ.

---

[1] 参见叶小琴:《我的第一本法律英语学习指南——比较刑法的路径》,北京大学出版社 2020 年版,第 105-107 页。

FACTS

[The facts are taken, in part, from the Connecticut Supreme Court of Errors, 400 A2d 479, 480.] In November, 1961, The Planned Parenthood League of Connecticut occupied offices at 79 Trumbull Street in New Haven. For ten days during that month, the league operated a Planned Parenthood center in the same building. The defendant, Estelle T. Griswold, is the salaried executive director of the league and served as acting director of the center. The other defendant, C. Lee Buxton, a physician, who has specialized in the fields of gynecology and obstetrics, was the medical director of the center. The purpose of the center was to provide information, instruction, and medical advice to married persons concerning various means of preventing conception. In addition, patients were furnished with various contraceptive devices, drugs, and materials. A fee, measured by ability to pay, was collected from the patient. At the trial, three married women from New Haven testified that they had visited the center, had received advice, instruction, and certain contraceptive devices and materials from either or both of the defendants and had used these devices and materials in subsequent marital relations with their husbands. Upon these facts, there is no doubt that, within the meaning of [the statute]… the defendants did aid, abet, and counsel married women…

…

Section 54 - 196 provides: Any person who assists, abets, counsels, causes, hires or commands another to commit any offense may be prosecuted and punished as if he were the principal offender. The appellants were found guilty as accessories and fined $100 each, against the claim that the accessory statute as so applied violated the Fourteenth Amendment. The Appellate Division of the Circuit Court affirmed. The Supreme Court of Errors affirmed that judgment.

OPINION

We are met with a wide range of questions that implicate the Due Process Clause of the Fourteenth Amendment. We do not sit as a superlegislature to determine the wisdom, need, and propriety of laws that touch economic problems, business affairs, or social conditions. This law, however, operates directly on an intimate relation of husband and wife and their physician's role in one aspect of that relation. The association of people is not mentioned in the Constitution or in the Bill of Rights. The right to educate a child in a school of the parents' choice—whether public or private or parochial—is also not mentioned. Nor is the right to study any particular subject or any foreign language. Yet the First Amendment has been construed to include certain of those rights. We protected the "freedom to associate and privacy in one's associations", noting that freedom of association was a peripheral First Amendment right. In like context, we have protected forms of "association" that are not political in the customary sense but pertain to the social, legal, and economic benefit of the members. Those cases involved more than the "right of assembly"—a right that extends to all irrespective of their race or ideology. The right of "association," like the right of belief, is more than the right to attend a meeting; it includes the right to express one's attitudes or philosophies by membership in a group or by affiliation with it or by other lawful means. Association in that context is a form of expression of opinion; and while it is not expressly included in the First Amendment, its existence is necessary in making the express guarantees fully meaningful.

…

The very idea is repulsive to the notions of privacy surrounding the marriage relationship. We deal with a right of privacy older than the Bill of Rights—older than our political parties, older than our school system. Marriage is a coming together for better or for worse, hopefully enduring, and intimate to the degree of being sacred. It is an association that promotes a way of life, not causes; a harmony in living, not political faiths; a bilateral loyalty, not commercial or social projects. Yet it is an association for as noble a purpose as any involved in our prior decisions.

Reversed.

DISSENT

STEWART, J., joined by BLACK, J.

Since 1879 Connecticut has had on its books a law, which forbids the use of contraceptives by anyone. I think this is an uncommonly silly law. As a practical matter, the law is obviously unenforceable, except in the oblique context of the present case. As a philosophical matter, I believe the use of contraceptives in the relationship of marriage should be left to personal and private choice, based upon each individual's moral, ethical, and religious beliefs. As amatter of social policy, I think professional counsel about methods of birth control should be available to all, so that each individual's choice can be meaningfully made.

…

At the oral argument in this case we were told that the Connecticut law does not "conform to current community standards." But it is not the function of this Court to decide cases on the basis of community standards. We are here to decide cases agreeably to the Constitution and laws of the United States. It is the essence of judicial duty to subordinate our own personal views, our own ideas of what legislation is wise and what is not. If, as I should surely hope, the law before us does not reflect the standards of the people of Connecticut, the people of Connecticut can freely exercise their rights to persuade their elected representatives to repeal it. That is the constitutional way to take this law off the books.

From Griswold v. Connecticut, the basic framework is:

从 Griswold v. Connecticut 案的判决书来看,其基本框架就是:

Griswold v. Connecticut	(1) title(案件名称)
381 U. S. 479 (1965)	(2) citation(案例引证号)
DOUGLAS, J., joined by…	(3) judges(法官名字)
HISTORY	(4) procedural history(审理历史)
FACTS	(5) facts(案件事实)
OPINION	(6) opinion(审判意见)
REVERSED	(7) judgment(案件判决结果)

These different components carry different content and play different functions. The following is a brief introduction to the significance and function of each component of the judgment.

这些不同的部分承载的是不同的内容,发挥的是不同的功能。下面分别对判决书各个部分的意义和功能进行简要介绍。

1.5.1 Title(案件名称)

The case title is the official name of the case and usually consists of the names of the plaintiff and the defendant. For example, in Griswold v. Connecticut, v. is an abbreviation for versus, which means "v.". Griswold v. Connecticut is the title of an appellate case and is typical of criminal cases. The case title of the first trial in that case was Connecticut v. Griswold. Griswold is a personal name, and Connecticut is a state name, and the state versus an individual represents the state as an organ of authority to prosecute the individual, and the individual versus against the state means that the individual is not satisfied with the outcome of the first instance trial and appeals to the state. The main function of this part is to introduce the names of the parties involved in the case, such as personal names, such as company names, such as a state in the United States, or even the federal government, and according to the order of the parties, you can also know whether the case is a trial case or an appellate case.

案件名称是指案件的正式名称,通常由原告和被告的名字组成。例如在"Griswold v. Connecticut"中,"v."是versus的缩写,是"诉"的意思。"Griswold v. Connecticut"是指格里斯沃尔德诉康涅狄格州,这是典型的刑事案件名称,而且是上诉案件。该案一审的案名是康涅狄格州诉格里斯沃尔德案。"Griswold"是人名,而"Connecticut"是州名。州起诉个人,代表着作为权力机关的州向个人提起公诉;而个人对州提起诉讼,意味着个人不满意第一审审判结果而对州提起上诉。这部分的主要功能就是介绍案件涉及的当事人名称,比如个人名称、公司名称、美国某个州甚至联邦政府的名称,而且根据当事人的排序,还能够了解该案是初审案还是上诉案。

1.5.2 Citation(案例引证号)

A case citation number can indicate how to locate the case text of a particular case in a vast number of legal publications. For example, the citation number 381 U. S. 479 (1965), 381 is the volume number, i. e., Volume 381, 479 is the starting page number of the case, U. S. is the abbreviation for the case collection United States Reports, and 1965 is the year of the decision in which the opinion was rendered. The case citation indicates the specific location where the case judgment, guiding the reader to the source further reference can be found.

案例引证号能够指示如何在数量繁多的法律出版物中查找特定案例的判决文

书。例如在前述的 Griswold v. Connecticut 判决书中,“381 U. S. 479 (1965)”为其引证号,“381”是卷号,即“Volume 381”;“479”是案例的起始页码;“U. S.”是案例集“United States Reports”的缩写;“1965”是司法意见书的判决年份。案例引证号标明了该案例判决书被收录在纸本案例汇编中的具体位置,能够指引需要进一步查阅的读者,寻找到其出处。

1.5.3 Procedural history(案件审理历史)

The procedural history is to explain, at the appellate hearing, the basic information about the courts at all levels of the appellate process, the decision of legal disputes by the courts at all levels, and the results of the judgments rendered. For example, in Griswold v. Connecticut, in the "HISTORY" part, the history of the case was introduced through four levels of trial proceedings, including the Connecticut Trial Court, the Intermediate Court of Appeals, the Connecticut Supreme Court, and the U. S. Supreme Court, which ultimately overturned the guilty verdict. The trial history of a case helps the litigants and the public understand how many levels of trial the case has gone through and the outcome of each level of court.

案件审理历史的作用主要是在上诉审时说明上诉过程中各级法院的基本信息、各级法院对法律争议的认定以及作出的判决结果。例如,Griswold v. Connecticut 的判决书中,“HISTORY”这部分介绍了案件审理历史:该案历经康涅狄格州初审法院、中级上诉法院、康涅狄格州最高法院及美国最高法院四级审判程序,最终由美国最高法院推翻有罪判决。案件审理历史能够向诉讼当事人及公众说明该案件经历了几级审判程序以及每一级法院的审判结果。

1.5.4 Judge(法官名字)

The name of the judge refers to the judge who wrote the opinion and issued the court's judgment in the case. If there is a concurring or dissenting judge in the decision, the names of the judges holding the concurrence or dissenting opinion are also indicated. For example, in Griswold v. Connecticut, the judges listed are DOUGLAS, J. WARREN, CJ., and CLARK, HARLAN, BRENNAN, WHITE, and GOLDBERG, JJ. The name of the judge is the basic information of the trial, allowing the litigants and the public to understand which judges made the decision.

法官名字是指撰写司法意见书并发布法院判决的法官姓名。如果该判决还有持有协同意见或异议意见的法官,也会标明这些法官的姓名。例如,在 Griswold v. Connecticut 的判决书中,审理法官就是 DOUGLAS, J. WARREN, CJ., CLARK, HARLAN, BRENNAN, WHITE, 和 GOLDBERG, JJ.。法官名字属于审判的基本信息,可以向诉讼当事人和公众展示该判决是由哪些法官作出的。

1.5.5　Fact(案件事实)

The facts of the case refer to the legal facts found by the court on the basis of the evidence. For example, in Griswold v. Connecticut, the defendants did aid, abet, and counsel married women... The statutes whose constitutionality is involved in this appeal are Sections 53 - 32 of the General Statutes of Connecticut. It provides: Any person who uses any drug, medicinal article or instrument for the purpose of preventing conception shall be fined not less than fifty dollars or imprisoned not less than sixty days nor more than one year or be both fined and imprisoned. The case fact mainly states the time and place of the incident, the acts taken by the defendant, and the crimes that the defendant is accused of, so that the litigants and the public can have a comprehensive and clear understanding of the case as a whole.

案件事实是法院根据证据所认定的法律事实。例如,在 Griswold v. Connecticut 案中,被告被认定实施了帮助、唆使和建议妇女避孕的行为,该行为违反了《康涅狄格州一般法规》第 53 - 32 条规定:任何人使用任何药物、药用物品或器械以防止受孕,应处以不少于 50 美元的罚款,或处以不少于 60 天、不超过 1 年的监禁,或同时处以罚款和监禁。案件事实部分主要阐明案件发生的时间地点、被告所实施的行为以及被告涉嫌触犯的罪名,使诉讼当事人和公众能够全面清晰地认识和了解案件整体情况。

1.5.6　Opinion(审判意见)

The court backs up its judgment by explaining how and why the court applied the law to the facts of the case. It includes three essential ingredients: (1) the court's holding—the legal rule the court has decided to apply to the facts of the cases. (2) the court's reasoning—the reasons the court gives to support its holding.[1] (3) In Griswold v. Connecticut, the judge found that he General Statutes of Connecticut directly invade the intimate relationship between husband and wife and the role of physicians in that relationship. Such relationships, the court ruled, fell within the scope of the right of privacy under constitutional guarantees. Therefore, the General Statutes of Connecticut were unconstitutional laws. On this basis, the statute is invalid and therefore the defendant cannot be convicted under the invalid statute. An opinion is a process by which the court analyzes and argues on the points of legal issues, and finally draws a

---

[1] Joel Samaha, *Criminal Law*, 10th edition, Wadsworth Cengage Learning, 2011, p. 34.

conclusion in accordance with the relevant law, which is also a process of showing the court's reasoning to the litigants and the public.

法院通过解释如何以及为何将法律适用于案件事实来支持其判决。它包括两个基本要素:(1) 法院的裁决——法院决定适用于案件事实的法律;(2) 法院的推理——法院为支持其裁决而给出的理由。在 Griswold v. Connecticut 案中,美国最高法院法官认为《康涅狄格州一般法规》直接涉及夫妻之间的亲密关系以及医生在这种关系中的作用,而这种亲密关系属于宪法保障的隐私权范围,因此,认定《康涅狄格州一般法规》系违宪法律。基于此,该法规无效,因而不能根据该无效法规判定被告有罪。审判意见是法院对法律争议点进行分析和推理并根据相关法律规定得出结论的过程,也是一个向诉讼当事人和公众展示法院说理的过程。

1.5.7 Judgment(法院判决)

The court's judgment (sometimes referred to as the court's "decision") is how the court resolves the case. A trial court's decision result in a verdict of guilty or not guilty, followed by sentencing. An appellate court's decision usually results in a decision to reverse, remand, or affirm. For example, in Griswold v. Connecticut, the judgment was "Reversed". The court judgment presents a legally binding decision of the court to the litigants and the public, and the litigants have the option of appealing or accepting the decision, except the decision of the Court of Final Appeal.

法院的判决(有时称为法院的"决定")是法院处理案件的方式。一审刑事案件的判决结果是:无罪或有罪(以及量刑)。上诉法院对上诉案件作出的判决通常有:撤销判决、发回重审、维持原判。例如,Griswold v. Connecticut 一案中的判决结果是撤销判决。法院判决向诉讼当事人和公众展示了法院具有法律效力的裁决结果,如果该判决非终审判决,则诉讼当事人可以选择上诉或者接受该裁决。

1.5.8 Concurrences and Dissents (协同意见或者异议意见)

In addition, there may be concurring or dissenting opinions of different judges regarding the judgment. A concurring opinion is one in which some judges, while agreeing with the judgment based on the majority opinion, reach the same conclusion for different reasons. Dissenting opinions are written by a minority of judges who disagree with the majority opinion and provide explanations for their dissenting opinion. For example, in Griswold v. Connecticut, Justices STEWART, J., and BLACK, J., filed a dissenting opinion, arguing that although the statues enacted by the state of Connecticut to prohibit the use of contraceptives by any person was very stupid, the Constitution did not explicitly state that the statues were unconstitutional, therefore, it would take the people of Connecticut to convince their legislative representatives that repealing the law was the constitutional way. Concurring or dissenting opinions can present the opinions of different judges to the litigants and the public, allowing people to treat important issues from different perspectives and reasoning approaches.

此外,还有不同法官对于判决结果的协同意见或异议意见。协同意见是指某些法官虽然同意基于多数法官意见作出的判决结果,但其是出于不同的理由而得出的同样结论。异议意见指少数法官在对多数法官意见持有不同看法时,可以书写的,解释为何不同意多数法官的判决结果的意见。例如,Griswold v. Connecticut 案中,大法官 STEWART, J. 和 BLACK, J. 提出异议意见,认为虽然康涅狄格州颁布禁止任何人使用避孕药具的法律非常愚蠢,但宪法并未明文规定该项法规违宪,因此,需要康涅狄格州人民说服其立法代表废除该项法规,才是合宪的处置方案。协同意见或者异议意见可以向诉讼当事人和公众展示不同法官的意见,使人们能从不同角度和不同推理方式来看待和处理重要问题。

In general, the case text of the common law system mainly explains the legal matters at issue and provide detailed and clear jurisprudence for legal practitioners and legal researchers to better understand the background of the cases, the legal issues, and the reasoning behind the judgment, and then study and analyze the legal reasoning and principles in depth and apply them in practice.

总体而言,英美法系的裁判文书通过阐释案件的法律事宜,为法律从业者和法律研究者提供了详尽而清晰的判例,使其能更好地理解案件的背景、法律问题和判决理由,进而深入学习和分析法律推理和法律原则并运用于实践。

■ Curriculum Ideology and Politics(课程思政)

Common law judgments often include "dissenting opinions" and "concurring opinions" where judges express disagreements with the content or reasoning of the judgment, they will express it through one of these two parts. "Dissenting opinions" and "concurring opinions" can not only show the different understandings of each judge on the facts, reasoning, and application of law in the case, but also illustrate the responsibilities of judges. Although the final judgment is based on the opinion of the majority, "dissenting opinions" and "concurring opinions" illustrate alternative views and reasonings. In the event of a wrongful conviction, etc., the judge's reasoning, opinion, position, understanding and application of the law can be used to identify the fault of the judge. In - depth understanding of this meaning and analyzing its practical significance can cultivate a sense of responsibility.

英美法系的判决书有“异议意见”和“协同意见”部分，即法官如果对判决内容或推理等有不同意见，可以选择通过这两个部分中的一种进行表达。“异议意见”和“协同意见”不仅能展示各个法官对案件事实、推理、法律适用等内容的不同认识，更能喻示法官的责任。尽管最后的判决意见是按照多数人的意见作出的，但不同的意见、推理和对法律的适用，可以通过“异议意见”和“协同意见”显示出来。由是，如果出现错案等情况，通过查询判决书的法官的推理、观点、立场、对法律的理解和适用等内容，即可明辨出是谁的错误。深度认知这层意义，并分析其具有的实践意义，能培养责任精神。

1.6 Exercise(课后练习)(答案请扫描右侧二维码获取)

1.6.1 Test of Terminologies(术语考查)

①crime ②tort

③felony ④misdemeanor

⑤*malum in se crime* ⑥*malum prohibitum crime*

⑦common law ⑧modern statutes

⑨Bill of Rights ⑩American Law Institute

⑪Model Penal Code ⑫majority opinion

⑬dissent

1.6.2 True or False(判断题)

1. The sources of criminal law in the United States include mainly the common law, modern statutes, the Model Penal Code, and constitutional sources.

普通法、现代成文法、《模范刑法典》和宪法，均是美国刑法的渊源。

2. The principle of legality is an important source of certain principles of criminal law.

合法性原则是刑法原则的重要渊源。

3. The Model Penal Code categorizes crimes, according to the severity of their penalties, into: felony, misdemeanor, petty misdemeanors, and violations.

《模范刑法典》按照刑罚轻重将犯罪分为：重罪、轻罪、微罪及违警罪。

4. If a judge hearing a case agrees with the majority decision but disagree with the reasoning behind it, he/she will write a dissenting opinion to be included in the case file.

如果某个审案法官同意大多数法官的决定，但不同意其背后的推理，他/她会在案件判决中写一份异议意见。

5. Dissenting opinions are written by a minority of judges who disagree with the majority opinion and write an opinion explaining why they disagree with the majority's opinion.

异议意见指少数法官在对多数法官意见持有不同看法时,可以书写的,解释为何不同意多数法官的判决结果的意见。

1.6.3　Short – answer Questions (简答题)

1. Smith kills Betty and is prosecuted and sentenced to two year in jail. Did Smith commit a felony or a misdemeanor?

史密斯杀死了贝蒂,被起诉并被判处监禁2年。史密斯犯的是重罪还是轻罪?

2. How are crimes classified?

如何给犯罪分类?

3. What is common law?

什么是普通法?

■ Curriculum Ideology and Politics(课程思政)

Question: How do you evaluate thecase law of Anglo – American criminal law? (Please scan the QR code on the right to get the answer)

如何评价英美刑法的判例法?(答案请扫描右侧二维码获取)

■ Summary (总结)

1. From the legislative perspective, the crime is what lawmakers define as criminal.

从立法规定看,犯罪是指立法者规定为犯罪的行为。

2. Crimes can be classified in many ways, more important and substantive of which is the severity of punishment. Whereby crimes are generally graded into two categories: felonies, misdemeanors.

犯罪可以按照多种方式进行分类,其中更为重要和实质性的分类标准是刑罚的严重程度。因此,犯罪通常被分为两类:重罪和轻罪。

3. The sources of criminal law in Anglo – American law are mainly the common law, modern statutes, the Model Penal Code, and the constitution, among others.

英美刑法渊源主要包括普通法、现代成文法、《模范刑法典》和宪法等。

4. A case text is a judgement of precedent legal matters.

案例裁判文书就是一份关于先例法律事宜的判决书。

Chapter 2 Constitutional Limits on Criminal Law
第 2 章 宪法对刑法的限制

■ The Learning Objective(学习目标)

1. To have a basic understanding of the constitutional limits on criminal law.

了解宪法对刑法的限制。

2. To understand the principle of legality and equal protection of the laws.

了解合法性原则、法律平等保护原则。

3. To understand the constitutional significance and consequences of principle of proportionality in criminal punishment.

了解刑事处罚中比例原则的宪法意义和后果。

4. To understand the importance of the right to trial by jury in the process of sentencing and conviction.

了解陪审团审判权在定罪和量刑过程中的重要性。

5. To learn terminologies in this chapter.

掌握本章的专业术语。

■ Chapter Outline(本章内容概要)

This chapter is to study the constitutional limitations on criminal law, in particular those imposed by some of the important principles and constitutional acts, i. e., the principle of legality, the principle of equal protection of the law, the link between the Bill of Rights and criminal law, the link between the Constitution and sentencing, the right to trial by jury on criminal law. This chapter presents the definition and importance of each principle, as well as relevant landmark cases.

本章节的学习内容为宪法对刑法的限制,尤其是一些重要原则和宪法性法案对刑法的限制,即合法性原则、法律平等保护原则、人权法案与刑法的联系、宪法与量刑的联系、陪审团审判权对刑法的限制。本章介绍了各个原则的定义、重要性以及相关的经典案例。

■ The Purpose of Curriculum Ideology and Politics for this Chapter (本章的课程思政目标)

1. To enhance internationalization competence. This chapter involves the English expression of criminal law's terminologies, the path of constitutional restriction of criminal law in Anglo - American criminal law, etc., and these contents involve important internationalization competence in the repertoire of professional competence of criminal law. The English expression of the terminology will be learned in this chapter and students can understand how the Constitution limits the criminal law in Anglo - American criminal law, which not only improves the English ability of criminal law, but also expands the knowledge system of criminal law, so as to improve internationalization ability.

提升国际化能力。本章主要内容为刑法专业术语的英语表达、英美刑法中宪法限制刑法的路径等知识,这些内容涉及刑法专业能力中重要的国际化能力。学习本章的专业术语的英语表达,了解宪法如何限制英美刑法,既能提升刑法专业英语能力,也可以拓展刑法知识体系,提高国际化能力。

2. To understand the value of rule of law of constitutional limitations on criminal law. In modern civilized countries under the rule of law, the main embodiment of the rule of law spirit in criminal law is the constitutional limitation on criminal law, and the compliance of criminal law with the Constitution, etc. The principle of *nulla poena sine lege* in Chinese criminal law and the principle of legality in Anglo - American criminal law, the principle of proportionality, and the right to trial by jury which is unique to Anglo - American criminal law, are also all manifestations of the spirit of the rule of law in the field of criminal law. Mastering these principles, students can deepens their understanding of the spirit of the rule of law in the field of criminal law, and be inspired to revere its spirit.

了解宪法限制刑法的法治价值。在现代文明法治国家,刑法的法治精神主要体现在宪法对刑法的限制,以及刑法对宪法的遵守等方面。罪刑法定原则(中国刑法)和合法性原则(英美刑法)、罪刑均衡原则以及英美刑法特有的陪审团审判权等内容,也均是刑事法领域的法治精神的体现。通过掌握这些原则,学生能够加深对刑法领域法治精神的理解,激发对法治精神的崇尚。

3. To recognize the common phenomenon that both Anglo – American criminal law and Chinese criminal law are limited by the Constitution. The constitution is the mother law and fundamental law of the legal system of modern countries under the rule of law. Chinese criminal law is based on the constitution, therefore there are constitutional restrictive effects on criminal law. By linking to the constitutional limits on China's criminal law, students will be guided to compare the similarities and differences of the constitutional limits on Anglo – American and China's criminal laws and understand the commonality between them.

认识英美刑法和中国刑法均受宪法限制这一共同现象。宪法是现代法治国家法律体系中的母法和根本法。中国刑法根据宪法制定,宪法对刑法具有限制作用。学生比较英美刑法和中国刑法受宪法限制的不同,并认识二者共性。

■ Terminologies(专业术语)

Constitutional limits	宪法限制
The Supreme Court	最高法院
rule of law	法治
nulla poena sine lege	法无明文规定不处罚
fair notice	合理告知
misdemeanor	轻罪
felony	重罪
clarity	明确性
amendment	修正案
ex post facto law	溯及既往法
Appellate Court	上诉法院
amnesty	大赦
pardon	赦免
life imprisonment	终身监禁
Congress	国会
void – for – vagueness doctrine	模糊即无效原则
unconstitutional	违宪的
equal protection of the laws	法律平等保护
recidivist	累犯
Bill of Rights	《权利法案》

expressive conduct	表达性行为
justify	证明……正当性
right to privacy	隐私权
free speech	言论自由
due process	正当程序
power of punishment	刑罚权
barbaric punishments	残暴的惩罚
electrocution	电刑
Chief Justice	首席大法官
criminal sentencing	量刑
impeachment	弹劾
principle of proportionality	相称性原则,合比例原则
convict	定罪;宣判……有罪
jury	陪审团
execution	处决,执行
murder	谋杀
death penalty	死刑
capital punishment	死刑
defendant	被告人

2.1　The Principle of Legality(合法性原则)

2.1.1　Outline(概述)

The Principle of Legality in Anglo – American criminal law is referred to as the*nulla poena sine lege* in the Latin maxim, which means no act should be made criminal or punished without advance warning in the form of legislative act.[1] As the most fundamental principle of criminal law, it takes precedence over all other theories of criminal law and is dedicated to preserving and safeguarding the foundations of a country's legal system.

英美刑法中的合法性原则,在拉丁文格言中被表述为"法无明文规定不为罪,法无明文规定不处罚"。合法性原则是刑法的最基本原则,它优先于其他所有刑法

〔1〕 See Thomas J. Gardner & Terry M. Anderson, *Criminal Law*, 11th edition, Wadsworth Cengage Learning, 2020, p. 12.

理论，致力于维护和保障一个国家法律制度的根基。

The principle of legality is one of the fundamental concepts of criminal law, whose basic meaning is that a person cannot be punished for an act that is not defined as a crime by the law. In criminal law and criminal punishment, there is an old proposition based on the principle of legality: "No crime without criminal law, no punishment without criminal law." This means that no one can be convicted or punished for an act unless the law defines it as a crime before it is committed. The principle of legality is also known as the "first principle of criminal law".

合法性原则是刑法的基本概念之一。合法性原则的基本含义是：一个人不能因为法律未定义为犯罪的行为而受到惩罚。在刑法和刑事处罚中，有一个基于合法性原则的古老命题："无法无罪，无法无罚。"这意味着，除非在某个行为被实施之前，法律就把其规定为犯罪，否则任何人都不能因该行为被定罪或受到惩罚。合法性原则，也被称为"刑法第一原则"。

The principle of legality implies that fair warning must be given to the actor first by the legislation. From the definition of the principle of legality, whether an act is a crime or not must be preceded by legislation in order to give citizens fair warning that the act is illegal. Fair warning includes both substantive and procedural considerations. Firstly, from the substantive perspective, the legislature must, on the basis of careful consideration, express through legislation that the act is prohibited by criminal law and that citizens may not do it. Secondly, from the procedural perspective, when criminal law legislation prohibits an act and treats it as a crime, it must be done through due process.

合法性原则意味着立法必须首先给予行为人合理警告。从合法性原则的定义看，某个行为是否为犯罪，必须先对其进行立法，以该行为不可为而给公民合理警告。合理警告包括实体和程序两个维度的考量。第一，从实体内容角度看，立法机关必须在审慎考虑的基础上，通过立法表示该行为是被刑法禁止的，公民不可为。第二，从程序内容角度看，刑法立法禁止某个行为，把其视为犯罪，必须通过正当的程序进行。

There is also a cost to follow the principle of legality: following this principle allows certain morally reprehensible and dangerous people to go unpunished and get away with it.[1] This is illustrated below by the case of Hughes v. State:

---

[1] Joel Samaha, *Criminal Law*, 10th edition, Wadsworth Cengage Learning, 2011, p. 40.

遵循合法性原则也有代价:遵循这一原则,会让某些在道德上值得指责的、危险的人不受惩罚而逍遥法外。下面以休斯诉州政府案为例进行说明。

In 1990, Hughes was driving drunk when he collided with Reesa Poole's automobile, killing Poole's fetus, while Poole was expected to give birth in four days after the accident. After a jury trial in the District Court for the District of Oklahoma, Hughes was convicted of first – degree manslaughter and sentenced to eight years in prison. Meanwhile, Hughes was also sentenced to six months' probation for driving while under the influence of intoxicating liquor causing injury to another person. Hughes then appealed, seeking the Appellate Court to have his conviction for manslaughter overturned.

1990年,休斯醉酒驾驶汽车,与丽萨·普尔驾驶的汽车相撞。该起事故导致普尔腹中的胎儿死亡,而普尔预计将在事发4天后分娩。本案件经俄克拉何马州地区法院陪审团审理,休斯被判一级过失杀人罪,判处8年有期徒刑。同时,休斯还因为在酒后受到影响的情况下驾车致使他人受到伤害被判处6个月缓刑。随后休斯提出上诉,要求上诉法院推翻对他过失杀人罪的定罪。

The appellate court later reversed Hughes' conviction for manslaughter. The court held that the scope of "person" under Oklahoma Statute 691 did not specify that it included unborn fetuses, so that the legislation did not provide Hughes with fair notice.[1] Therefore, the interpretation of Oklahoma's section 691 to include fetuses was unforeseeable, as was Hughes' expectation of the particular consequences of his conduct and the possibility of increased penalties as a result.

上诉法院后来推翻了对休斯过失杀人罪的定罪。法庭认为,俄克拉何马法规第691条规定的"人"的范围未曾说明过包含未出生的胎儿,因此立法没有向休斯提供合理告知。所以,行为人对俄克拉何马州第691条包含胎儿的解释是不可预见的,休斯对其行为的特定结果和因此而加重处罚的可能性也是不可预见的。

The appellate court was also aware of the negative effects resulting from the principle of legality, but it still had to adhere to the principle of legality in order to uphold the rule of law. Finally the court wrote in the decision: "That Hughes will go unpunished for having taken the life of another is frustrating. There are, however, basic principles upon which this country is founded which compel the result we reach… The retroactive application of criminal law… is so abhorrent that we must occasionally endure

[1] See Joel Samaha, *Criminal Law*, 10th edition, Wadsworth Cengage Learning, 2011, p. 41.

some frustration in order to preserve and protect the foundation of our system of law."[1]

上诉法院也意识到了合法性原则导致的负面效果,但为了维护法治原则,法院仍必须遵守合法性原则。上诉法院最终在判决中写道:"休斯因夺取他人的生命而没有受到惩罚,这令人沮丧。然而,这个国家所依据的基本原则迫使我们得出这样的结果……刑法的追溯适用……是如此令人憎恶,以至于我们必须偶尔忍受一些挫折,以维护和保护我们法律体系的基础。"

While compliance with the principle of legality has costs, violations of the principle of legality are even more costly. Violations of the principle of legality infringe on the principle of the rule of law, leading to abuses of judicial power. Again, in Hughes v. State, for example, Hughes' conduct did kill an unborn fetus, but more importantly, Hughes could not be prosecuted or convicted under the ex post facto law because he was not prohibited by the law made before the criminal conduct from killing or injuring the "fetus". In other words, Hughes cannot be punished for acts that were not expressly criminalized by law at the time they were committed. Therefore, to punish Hughes for that would violate the principle of legality. Although Hughes' committed act is wrong and seriously harmful, the court adhered to the principle of legality. The principle of legality plays a crucial role in ensuring, among other things, that the government and its officials cannot punish people arbitrarily or without justification. The principle of legality is not only a safeguard against abuse of power, but also ensures that citizens are treated fairly.

尽管遵守合法性原则会有代价,但如违反合法性原则,代价更大。违反合法性原则会侵害法治原则,导致司法权力的滥用。同样以休斯诉州政府案为例,休斯的行为确实杀死了一个未出生的胎儿,但更重要的是,事前法没有针对杀死或伤害"胎儿"的罪名以禁止其实施该行为,因此,休斯不能被事后法起诉或定罪。换言之,休斯不能因行为当时法律没有明文规定为犯罪的行为而受惩罚。若因此惩罚休斯,将违背合法性原则。尽管休斯实施的行为是错的,且有严重危害性,但法院还是遵守了合法性原则。合法性原则在确保政府及其官员不能任意或无正当理由地惩罚人们等方面,具有至关重要的作用。合法性原则不仅是防止权力滥用的屏障,更是公民受到公平待遇的保证。

The principle also requires that warning is clear. It means that a warning must be

---

〔1〕 See Hughes v. States (1994).

given in language that the average person can understand. But it does not necessitate that the statute includes an itemized list of all the prohibited actions that may result in wrongdoing. Criminal homicide, for instance, can be carried out through numerous illegal means, including the use of firearms, vehicles such as a truck or a car, and various other methods such as by strangulation. However, the murder statute does not need to provide a full enumeration of the numerous ways in which murder can be committed, but only needs to outlaw the wrongful act and provide clear notice of the prohibited conduct.[1]

除合理警告外,该原则还要求,警告必须明确。明确警告的意思是警告应以普通人能够理解的语言发出。但这并不意味着法规必须列出所有应被禁止的行为。例如,刑事谋杀可以通过许多非法手段进行,包括使用枪支、使用卡车或者汽车之类的交通工具,以及使用其他方法,如勒死。然而,谋杀罪法规并不需要对众多的谋杀方式进行全部列举,只需将不法行为定为非法,并明确提供关于被禁止的行为的告知。

2.1.2　The Ban on Ex Post Facto Laws(禁止溯及既往原则)

Ex post facte law is one that permits liability for innocent acts committed prior to the enactment of the law. The ban on doctrine of retroactivity is explicitly stated in the U.S. Constitution, which provides in Article 1, Section 9 that "No bill of attainder or ex post facto law shall be passed"; and in Article 1, Section 10, which provides that "No state shall... pass any bill of attainder, ex post facto law, or law impairing the obligation of contracts."[2] Also, some states include the ban on Ex post facte laws in their state constitutions.

事后法就是许可对该法律颁布以前的无罪行为追究责任的法律。《美国宪法》对禁止溯及既往原则有明确规定,《美国宪法》第1条第9款规定:"不得通过任何褫夺公权的法案和溯及既往的法律";《美国宪法》第1条第10款规定:"各州不得……通过任何褫夺公权的法案、溯及既往的法案和损害契约义务的法律。"而且,大多数州的宪法也规定了对事后法的禁止。

The Ban on retroactivity is a legal principle that prohibits the government from passing laws that retroactively punish people for actions that were not illegal at the time

---

〔1〕 See Thomas J. Gardner & Terry M. Anderson. *Criminal Law*, 11th edition, Wadsworth Cengage Learning, 2020, p.13.

〔2〕 See Joel Samaha, *Criminal Law*, 10th edition, Wadsworth Cengage Learning, 2011, p.41.

they were committed. In simpler terms, it means that a person cannot be punished for doing something that was legal when they did it, even if the government later decides to make it illegal.

禁止溯及既往是一项法律原则,它禁止政府通过法律,追溯性地惩罚那些在实施时并不违法的行为。换句话说,这意味着一个人不能因为做了当时合法的事情而受到惩罚,即使政府后来决定将其定为非法行为。

Specifically, *the ban on ex post facto laws* forbids the following contents: (1) Creating a criminal law and making it retroactive so as to make conduct before the enactment of the law a criminal violation; (2) Laws that aggravate a crime retroactively (e. g., making a misdemeanor a felony as of a date six months before the enactment of the legislation); (3) Laws that increase the punishment for a crime retroactively; (4) Laws that alter the legal rules related to evidence and permit conviction on less or different evidence than the law required at the time of the commission of the offense.[1]

具体而言,禁止溯及既往原则禁止以下内容:(1)制定一项刑法并使其具有追溯力,从而使法律颁布前的行为成为犯罪行为;(2)追溯性地加重犯罪的法律(例如,法律规定从立法颁布前6个月的某一天起,将轻罪变成重罪);(3)追溯性地加重对犯罪的惩罚的法律;(4)改变证据的相关法律规则,允许以低于或不同于犯罪时法律要求的证明标准的证据定罪的法律。

In order to better understand the principle of the ban on ex post facto laws, it is quite important to elaborate on the two necessary conditions for the prohibition of ex post facto laws: "the law must be retrospective—that is, it must apply to events occurring before its enactment; it must disadvantage the offender affected by it."[2] Criminal law provisions in the above circumstances will violate the ban on ex post facto laws. Conversely, there is no violation of the prohibition against ex post facto principles if the retroactivity is favorable to the defendant.

为了更好理解禁止事后法原则,阐述事后法的两个必要条件是非常重要的:"法律必须具有追溯性——也就是说,它必须适用于其颁布前发生的事件;法律必须对受其影响的罪犯不利。"符合上述条件的刑法规定,就违反了禁止溯及既往原则。如果溯及既往对被告人有利,则不违反禁止事后法的原则。

From the previous analysis, it is clear that *retroactivity* has the following

---

〔1〕 Thomas J. Gardner & Terry M. Anderson. *Criminal Law*, 11th edition, Wadsworth Cengage Learning, 2020, p. 16.

〔2〕 Joycelyn M. Pollock, *Criminal Law*, 10th edition, Routledge, 2015, p. 19.

drawbacks: Firstly, *retroactivity* lacks fair notice. To know the commands of law provides individuals with the opportunity to comply with the law and avoid punishment, but *retroactive laws* do not provide citizens with this opportunity. Secondly, *retroactivity* undermines the concepts of autonomy and dignity. While informing citizens in advance of what is and is not permissible under criminal law and promotes the values of human autonomy and dignity. Thirdly, *retroactive laws* can lead to judicial arbitrariness. If there is no prior legislation, but retroactive laws are allowed, it will lead to judges to punish what they believe to be wrongful acts, which leaves the opportunity for arbitrariness. To summarize, *retroactive laws* infringe on the principle of the rule of law.

从前面的分析可以看出,事后法存在以下弊端:第一,事后法缺乏公正告知。了解法律命令为个人提供了遵守法律和避免被惩罚的机会,但是事后法却没有给公民提供此机会。第二,事后法损害了自治和尊严理念。事先告知公民什么是刑法允许的,什么是刑法所不允许的,能促进人的自主和尊严的价值。第三,事后法会造成司法擅断。若事先没有立法,但允许法律溯及既往,会导致法官对其认为是错误的行为进行惩罚,这就给擅断和专断留下了机会。概言之,溯及既往法侵害了法治原则。

It can be seen from the drawbacks of the *retroactive laws* that the Ban on *Ex Post Facto Laws* is significant. Firstly, it protects individuals from being punished for actions that were not illegal at the time they were committed. Secondly, this principle helps to ensure that laws are applied fairly and that people have notice of what actions are illegal. Thirdly, it also prevents the government from abusing its power by passing retroactive laws to punish individuals for actions that were not previously considered illegal. Without this ban, the government could unfairly punish individuals for past actions with no warning. In summary, the principle of *retroactivity* upholds the principle of the rule of law and safeguards the rights and interests of citizens.

从事后法的弊端可以看出,禁止溯及既往原则有重要意义:第一,禁止溯及既往原则使个人不会因为在实施时并不违法的行为而受到惩罚;第二,这一原则有助于法律的公平适用,确保人们知道哪些行为是非法的;第三,这一原则可以防止政府滥用权力,通过追溯性法律来惩罚个人以前不被认为是非法的行为,如果没有这项禁令,政府可以不公正地对个人过去的行为进行惩罚,而没有任何警告。概言之,禁止溯及既往原则能维护法治原则,保障公民权益。

2.1.3 Void-for-Vagueness Doctrine(模糊即无效原则)

The Void-for-Vagueness Doctrine, which comes from the Fifth and Fourteenth

Amendments,[1] states that a law is invalid if it lacks adequate clarity or fails to provide a person with fair notice of what is prohibited. This doctrine ensures that laws and regulations are not used to unfairly punish individuals for conduct that they could not reasonably understand to be illegal. It protects against arbitrary and discriminatory enforcement of vague laws.

模糊即无效原则的意思是,如果一项法律缺乏充分的明确性,或没有向公民提供关于被禁止事项的合理告知,那么该法律就是无效的。这一原则确保法律和法规不会被用来对个人无法合理地理解为非法的行为进行不公正的惩罚。该原则可以防止任意地和歧视性地执行模糊的法律。

It is noteworthy that the lawmakers will never be able to eliminate the ambiguity in all laws, which are written in words, not figures, and several factors have coincided to generate vagueness of the law itself, including the inherent ambiguity in language, the diversity of human behavior and the limited imagination of the lawmakers. It also dictates that not all laws that are semantically ambiguous will be declared invalid. Consequently, laws are presumed to be constitutional. If someone argues that a law or its semantics in the law vague, the "heavy burden of proof" is on the challenger.[2] That is, "the challenger must show that upon examining the statute, an individual of ordinary intelligence would not understand what he is required to do under the law".[3]

需要注意的是,立法者并不能消除所有法律中的模糊性,因为法律是用文字而不是数字写成的。有几个因素共同导致了法律本身的模糊性,包括语言中固有的模糊性、人类行为的多样性和立法者有限的想象力。这也决定了不是所有语义模糊的法律,都会被宣布无效。因此,法律被推定具备合宪性。如果有人提出某个法律或法律中语义是模糊的,"沉重的举证责任"则由质疑者来承担。也就是说,"质疑者必须证明,在查询法规时,一个智力正常的人不能理解法律要求他做什么"。

The void - for - vagueness doctrine is explicitly enshrined in the Constitution, namely, the due process clauses of the Fifth and Fourteenth Amendments to the United States Constitution. The Fifth Amendment to the United States Constitution provides that "no person shall be… deprived of life, liberty, or property, without due process"; and the Fourteenth Amendment to the United States Constitution provides that "…nor shall any State deprive any person of life, liberty, or property, without due process of law".

---

[1] Joycelyn M. Pollock, *Criminal Law*, 10th edition, Routledge, 2015, p. 17.

[2] See Joel Samaha, *Criminal Law*, 10th edition, Wadsworth Cengage Learning, 2011, p. 44.

[3] See State v. Anderson (1991).

The Due Process Clause requires legislatures to provide sufficiently explicit standards of judgment for law enforcement officials and the public when enacting laws, and if a law does not clearly specify what people should or should not do, then the law violates due process and is therefore unconstitutional.[1]

“模糊即无效原则”是由宪法明文规定的，即美国《宪法第五修正案》和美国《宪法第十四修正案》的正当程序条款。美国《宪法第五修正案》规定：“未经正当程序，不得剥夺任何人的生命、自由和财产”；美国《宪法第十四修正案》规定：“无论何州，未经正当程序均不得剥夺任何人的生命、自由或财产”。正当程序条款要求立法机关在制定法律时，为执法人员和民众提供足够清晰的判断标准。如果一项法律没有清晰地规定人们应当做什么或者不得做什么，那么该项法律就违反了正当程序，因而是违宪的。

Generally, the following requirements are made by the void – for – vagueness doctrine：

一般来说，“模糊即无效原则”提出了以下要求：

1. Fair and adequate notice must be given of the conduct that is forbidden or required.

必须对所禁止或要求的行为给予公平和充分的告知。

2. A precise standard of conduct must be specified in terms of results that can reasonably be expected.

必须在可以合理预期的结果方面规定准确的行为标准。

3. The statute or ordinance cannot permit or encourage arbitrary and discriminatory law enforcement that may result in erratic and arbitrary arrests and convictions.

法规或条例不能允许或鼓励任意和歧视性的执法，这可能会导致不稳定和任意的逮捕和定罪。

4. The statute or ordinance cannot violate or infringe on rights that are secured or granted by the U. S. Constitution.[2]

法规或条例不能违反或侵犯美国宪法所保障或授予的权利。

The void – for – vagueness doctrine is considerably significant. Firstly, the doctrine ensures that laws and *regulations* are not too vague or ambiguous to provide fair notice of prohibited conduct to individuals. Secondly, it guarantees that laws and *regulations* are

---

〔1〕 Cliff Roberson, *Constitutional Law and Criminal Justice*, CRC Press, 2009, p. 10.

〔2〕 Thomas J. Gardner & Terry M. Anderson, *Criminal Law* ,11th edition, Wadsworth Cengage Learning, 2020, p. 20.

not used to unfairly punish individuals for conduct that they could not reasonably understand to be illegal. Thirdly, it protects against arbitrary and discriminatory enforcement of vague laws, which is a strong guarantee of the fundamental rights of citizens.

"模糊即无效原则"具有重要的意义。第一,该法律原则确保法律和法规不会过于模糊或模棱两可,以至于无法向个人提供关于被禁止行为的合理告知。第二,该原则保证法律和法规不被用来不公正地惩罚不能被合理地理解为非法行为的个人行为。第三,该原则可以防止随意性和歧视性地执行模糊的法律,是公民基本权利的有力保障。

■ Case Study(案例学习)

Lanzetta v. State of New Jersey, 306 U.S. 451 (1939)(兰泽塔诉新泽西州案)

Facts(基本案情)

An act of New Jersey declared: "Any person not engaged in any lawful occupation, known to be a member of any gang consisting of two or more persons, who has been convicted at least three times of being a disorderly person, or who has been convicted of any crime in this or any other State, is declared to be a gangster…" "Every violation was punishable by fine not exceeding $10,000 or imprisonment not exceeding 20 years, or both." (§ 4, c. 155, Laws 1934)

新泽西州的一项法案规定:"任何没有合法职业且已是由两人或两人以上组成的任何帮派的成员,若其至少三次被定为扰乱治安的人,或在本州或其他州被判任何罪,则应被视为黑帮分子。"每项违法行为都可被处以不超过10,000美元的罚款或不超过20年的监禁,或两者并罚。

The defendants were accused of violating the act mentioned above. A judgment of conviction was rendered against defendants, and each was sentenced to be imprisoned in the state prison for not more than ten years and not less than five years, at hard labor. On June 12, 16, 19, and 24, 1936, the four challengers were "declared to be gangsters" for "not being engaged in any lawful occupation," "being known to be members of a gang, consisting of two or more persons," and "having been convicted of a crime in the State of Pennsylvania." The accused, Ignatius Lanzetta, Michael Falcone, and Louie Del Rossi, challenged the constitutionality of the provision, alleging that its vagueness and uncertainty violated the due process clause of the Fourteenth Amendment.

有四名被告被指控违反上述法案,因此被定罪,每个人被判处不超过10年的监禁并处不少于5年的苦役。1936年6月12日、16日、19日和24日，这四位被“宣布为黑帮分子”，因为他们“没有从事任何合法的职业”，“已知是由两个或更多人组成的团伙的成员”，以及“曾在宾夕法尼亚州被定罪”。被告伊格内修斯·兰泽塔、迈克尔·法尔科内和路易·德尔·罗西质疑该条款的合宪性，声称其模糊性和不确定性违反了美国《宪法第十四修正案》的正当程序条款。

Dispute(主要争议)

The dispute in Lanzetta v. New Jersey was whether the New Jersey enactment, which declared any person not engaged in any lawful occupation and known to be a member of any gang consisting of two or more persons, a gangster, was repugnant to the due process clause of the Fourteenth Amendment. The appellants were accused of violating this clause and were convicted and sentenced to imprisonment and hard labor.

在兰泽塔诉新泽西州案中，争议在于新泽西州所颁布的法令是否与美国《宪法第十四修正案》的正当程序条款相抵触，该法令宣布任何不从事任何合法职业和已知是由两人或多人组成的任何团伙成员的人都是黑帮分子。上诉人被指控违反了这一条款，被定罪并被判处监禁和苦役。

Conclusion(结论)

The conclusion was that the challenged provision was repugnant to the due process clause because it was too vague, indefinite, and uncertain to inform people of what conduct would render them liable to its penalties and thus violated the principle of due process of law. The phrase “consisting of two or more persons” was the provision's only definition of “gang”, while the definitions of that word from dictionaries and historical and sociological writings were numerous and varied. Furthermore, the statute failed to provide specifications of details of the offense intended to be charged to validate it. Therefore, it was unconstitutional.

结论是，被质疑的条款与正当程序条款相抵触，因为它过于含糊、不明确和不确定，无法告知人们哪些行为会使他们受到惩罚，所以它违反了正当法律程序原则。短语“由两个或两个以上的人组成”是该条款对“帮派”的唯一定义，但字典、历史及社会学著作对该词的定义是多种多样的。而且，该法规未能提供其欲指控的犯罪行为的具体细节，以使其生效。因此，它是违宪的。

Questions:1. What was the New Jersey enactment that Lanzetta v. New Jersey challenged? (Please scan the QR code on the right to get the answer)

兰泽塔诉新泽西州案所质疑的新泽西州法令是什么？（答案请扫描右侧二维码

获取）

2. Why did the court declare the challenged provision unconstitutional?（The way to obtain the answer is the same as above）

法院为什么宣布被质疑的条款违宪？（答案获取方式同上）

■ Curriculum Ideology and Politics（课程思政）

Strengthening the significance of the rule of law in the principle of legality (*nulla poena sine lege*). The principle of legality is the basic principle of criminal law in modern countries under the rule of law, and it is also an important manifestation of the spirit of the rule of law in the field of criminal law, and it has even been held as the first principle of criminal law. Therefore, the principle of legality must be observed in criminal legislation and practice to ensure the implementation of the spirit of the rule of law in the field of criminal law. (1) The principle of legality in the United States is stipulated in the Constitution and other constitutional documents, which gives the principle of legality the status of a constitutional principle. The principle of "*nulla poena sine lege*" in Chinese criminal law is stipulated in Article 3 of the Criminal Law, which means it is a basic principle of Chinese criminal law. (2) Practically, the principle of legality restricts the criminal law, including the restriction on both the legislation and the judiciary in the United States' criminal law. Restrictions on legislation are realised through the "void - for - vagueness doctrine" and are guaranteed by due process. Limitations on the judiciary are achieved through the "*ban on ex post facto law*". The principle of "*nulla poena sine lege*" in Chinese criminal law is supported by the derived principles of prohibition of retroactivity, prohibition of customary law, prohibition of absolute indeterminate sentences and prohibition of analogy. (3) The principle of legality (*nulla poena sine lege*) is the result of the continuous progress in the construction of the rule of law, limiting the abuse of penal power in both the legislative and judicial dimensions and guaranteeing citizen's legitimate rights and interests.

强化合法性原则（在我国，为罪刑法定原则）的法治意义。合法性原则是现代法治国家刑法的基本原则，也是法治精神在刑事法领域的重要体现，其甚至被誉为刑法第一原则。因此，刑事立法与实践必须遵守合法性原则，以保证法治精神在刑法领域得到贯彻。(1)美国的合法性原则由《美国宪法》和其他宪法性文件予以规定，这赋予合法性原则以宪法性原则的地位。中国刑法的罪刑法定原则由《刑法》第3条规定，其是刑法的基本原则。(2)从实践层面看，美国刑法的合法性原则对刑法的限制包括对立法和司法的限制。对立法的限制通过模糊即无效原则实现,且以正当程序予以保障。对司法的限制通过禁止溯及既往原则实现。中国刑法的罪刑法定原则通过派生原则禁止溯及既往、禁止习惯法、禁止绝对不定期刑和禁止类推来保证实现。(3)合法性原则(罪刑法定原则)是法治建设不断推进的结果,其从立法和司法两个维度限制刑罚权的滥用,切实保障公民的合法权益。

2.2 The Principle of Equal Protection(平等保护原则)

The principle of Equal Protection of the Laws is stipulated by the Fourteenth Amendment to the United States Constitution to guarantee equal protection of the law to citizens. The Fourteenth Amendment declares: "No state shall... deny to any person within its jurisdiction the equal protection of the laws." This amendment extends many of the protections of the Bill of Rights to the states, and ensures that criminal defendants are treated fairly regardless of where they live.

法律平等保护原则由美国《宪法第十四修正案》规定,以保障法律对公民的平等保护。美国《宪法第十四修正案》规定:"任何州都不得……拒绝其管辖范围内的任何人获得法律的平等保护。"该修正案将《权利法案》的许多保护措施扩展到各州,并确保刑事被告人受到公平对待。

The basic meaning of the principle of Equal Protection of the Laws is thatall individuals are entitled to the equal protection and treatment under the law, regardless of their race, gender, religion, national origin, or any other characteristic. This principle ensures that everyone is treated fairly and without discrimination by the government. No one should be discriminated against based on their personal characteristics. For example, Virginia's miscegenation laws criminalized intermarriage between people of different races. However, they were invalidated in 1967 by the U. S. Supreme Court. The Supreme Court found that it lacked sufficient justification to treat differently between those who wished to marry someone from a different race and those who wished to marry within their own race. Consequently, the Supreme Court held that Virginia's miscegenation laws were invalid because they were against the principle of equal protection of the laws. The Supreme Court's decision had a broad impact, making miscegenation laws in other states also invalidated later.[1]

平等保护原则的基本含义是:所有人都有权得到法律的平等保护和对待,无论

[1] Joycelyn M. Pollock, *Criminal Law*, 10th edition, Routledge, 2015, p. 18.

其种族、性别、宗教、民族血统或任何其他特征。这一原则确保每个人都得到政府的公平对待,不受歧视。任何人都不应因其个人特征而受到歧视。例如,弗吉尼亚州通婚法规定了不同种族的人之间通婚是犯罪,该通婚法后于1967年被美国最高法院宣布无效。美国最高法院认为,区别对待希望异族通婚的人和希望同族通婚的人,缺乏充分的理由。因此,美国最高法院认为弗吉尼亚州的通婚法违背了平等保护原则,该法律是无效的。最高法院的裁决产生了广泛的影响,使其他州的禁止异族通婚法也在后来被宣布无效。

However, equal protection does not imply that the government must treat everyone precisely the same. Statutes can do categorize specific categories of persons and behaviors for special treatment. Premeditated homicides, for instance, are considered more severe than negligent homicides; recidivists are penalized harsher than first – time offenders.[1] Another example is consanguinity laws present in most states that prohibit marriages between close relatives to prevent potential genetic defects.[2] These special treatments are necessary because they are beneficial for the realization and maintenance of more important social interests.

不过,平等保护并不意味着政府必须完全相同地对待每个人。法规可以将特定类别的人和行为归入特殊对待的范畴。例如,预谋杀人被认为比过失杀人更严重;对累犯的惩罚比初犯更严厉。又如,大多数州的血缘关系法禁止近亲结婚,以防止胎儿出现基因缺陷。这些特殊对待是必要的,因为其有利于实现和维护更重要的社会利益。

■ Curriculum Ideology and Politics(课程思政)

Develop students' moral qualities and legal professionalism in treating people equally. Equality is not only a legal concept and a constitutional principle, but also a kind of life literacy and moral cultivation. Both the U. S. Constitution and Chinese law reflect this result of the civilised progress of the rule of law. Article 33 of the Constitution of P. R. C expressly provides that "All citizens of the People's Republic of China are equal before the law." Article 4 of the Criminal Law also states, "All persons are equal in the application of the law to any offence. No one is allowed privileges

---

〔1〕 See Joel Samaha, *Criminal Law*, 10th edition, Wadsworth Cengage Learning, 2011, p. 46.

〔2〕 Thomas J. Gardner & Terry M. Anderson, *Criminal Law*, 11th edition, Wadsworth Cengage Learning, 2020, p. 23.

beyond the law." Understanding and comprehending the principle of equality before the law or the criminal law enhances the following virtues:(1) Legal literacy. Whether in legislation or in the administration of justice, whether poor, rich, old, young, female or male, legal professionals should treat every citizen equally and protect their rights and interests; (2)Moral literacy in life. The legal priniciples are the response to the life, which also reflects the basic requirements of human society that the constitution or criminal law treats everyone equally. Serious comprehension and observance of this principle will enhance the basic moral literacy as a citizen.

培养学生平等待人的道德素养和法律职业素养。平等不仅是法学理念、宪法原则,更是一种生活素养和品德修为。《美国宪法》和中国法律均体现了这一法治文明进步的结果。我国《宪法》第 33 条明文规定:"中华人民共和国公民在法律面前一律平等。"《刑法》第 4 条也规定:"对任何人犯罪,在适用法律上一律平等。不允许任何人有超越法律的特权。"理解、参悟法律或刑法面前人人平等原则,能提升:(1)法律素养。无论是在立法还是在司法中,无论是贫穷、富贵、年老年幼、性别差异,法律职业者都应平等对待每个公民,保障每个公民的权益。(2)生活道德素养。法律原则是生活的反映,宪法或刑法把平等对待每个人作为基本原则,这也是人类社会基本要求的反映。认真领悟和遵守该原则,能提升作为公民的基本道德素养。

2.3 The Bill of Rights and the Criminal Law(《权利法案》和刑法)

In 1689, because of numerous violations of personal liberty, the Parliament of the United Kingdom forced King James Ⅱ to abdicate, and Parliament produced a Bill of Rights(1689). Later, this document served as a guide for Americans to formulate the Bill of Rights(1791).

1689 年,由于国王詹姆斯二世多次侵犯人身自由,英国议会迫使其退位,并制定了英国《权利法案》。后来,这份文件成为美国人制定美国《权利法案》的指南。

The first ten Amendments to the Constitution of the United States are known as the Bill of Rights (1791), and many provisions of it relate to criminal law. The Bill of Rights prohibits the criminalization of certain acts, first, those relating to the rights of speech, religion and association; and second, those relating to the constitutional right to privacy, which has been established by the jurisprudence of the United States Supreme Court. In summary, it is prohibited to criminalize conduct related to freedom of speech, the rights of religion and association, the right to privacy and other rights, which are protected by the United States Constitution.

《美国宪法》的前10个修正案被称为《权利法案》。《权利法案》的很多规定均与刑法有关。《权利法案》禁止法律将某些行为规定为犯罪:一是禁止将言论、宗教和结社权利相关的行为规定为犯罪;二是禁止将与美国最高法院的判例设立的隐私权这一宪法性权利有关的行为规定为犯罪。概言之,言论自由、宗教和结社权利、隐私权等权利受《美国宪法》保护,与其有关的行为被禁止规定为犯罪。

2.3.1 The Right of Free Speech(言论自由权)

Every citizen has the right of freedom of expression. The First Amendment provides that "Congress shall make no law abridging the freedom of speech, or of the press." Moreover, courts of the United States have repeatedly pointed out that "freedom to speak one's mind is not only an aspect of individual liberty—and thus a good unto itself—but also is essential to the common quest for truth and the vitality of society as a whole."[1]

公民享有言论自由由美国《宪法第一修正案》规定,"国会不得制定剥夺言论或新闻自由的法律"。除此之外,美国法院也一再指出:"表达自己想法的自由不仅是个人自由的一个方面,其对自身有利,且对共同追求真理和整个社会的活力至关重要。"

Human communications take many forms. Pure speech encompasses verbal exchanges that take place in person or across a variety of mediums. Books, newspapers, magazines, billboards, bumper stickers, and other written media are examples of written communication. Besides, it should be recalled that, in addition to these forms of speech mentioned above, there is also "expressive speech", which is neither spoken nor written, but a type of message or symbolic gesture. Symbolic speech, such as uniforms, religious garments, black armbands, and hand gestures, express messages and ideas, and are also protected by the First Amendment.

人类言论有多种形式。纯言语包括面对面或通过多种媒体发表的言论。书面交流则通过书籍、杂志、报纸、广告牌、保险杠贴纸等形式进行。除此之外,特别需要提醒的是,除了前面这些言论方式,还有一种"表达性言论",即既不是口头语言,也不是书面语言,而是一种信息或象征性动作。比如,制服、宗教服装、黑色臂章和手势等象征性言论表达信息和思想。这些也受美国《宪法第一修正案》保护。

However, speech and other forms of communication are not absolute rights, as they can seriously clash with the rights of others and the need for public order. The U. S.

---

[1] See Hustler Magazine v. Falwell(1988).

Supreme Court has pointed out that such regulation is necessary or these rights could be "lost in the excesses of unrestrained abuse".[1] Citizens having these freedoms of speech granted by the First Amendment does not mean that they are permitted to express themselves freely anywhere, at any time, on any subject, and in any way. In general terms, the following five types of speech are not protected by the First Amendment: (1) Obscenity Material whose predominant appeal is to nudity, sexual activity, or excretion. (2) Profanity Irreverence toward sacred things, particularly the name of God. (3) Libel and slander Libels are damages to reputation expressed in print, writing, pictures, or signs; slander damages reputation by spoken words. (4) Fighting words Words that are likely to provoke the average person to retaliation and cause a "breach of the peace." (5) Clear and present danger Expression that creates a clear and present danger of an evil, which legislatures have the power to prohibit.[2]

言论和其他形式的交流不是绝对的权利,因为其可能与他人的权利和公共秩序的需要发生冲突。美国最高法院指出,这样的限制是必要的,否则这些权利可能会"在过度的无限制滥用中丧失"。公民拥有美国《宪法第一修正案》赋予的这些言论自由,但并不意味着公民可以在任何地方、任何时间,以任何主题、任何方式表达自己。一般而言,下列五类言论不受《宪法第一修正案》保护:(1)淫秽性言论,以裸体、性活动或排泄物为主要吸引力的材料。(2)亵渎性言论,对神圣事物的不敬,尤其对上帝的名字的不敬。(3)诽谤和流言性言论,诽谤是指以印刷品、文字、图片或标志表达的对名誉的损害;诽谤通过言语损害名誉。(4)挑衅性言论,这些话可能会激起普通人的报复,并导致"破坏和平"。(5)明确而现实的危险言论,立法机构有权禁止制造明显和现实的邪恶、危险的表达。

Depending on the manner, time, and place of expression, the government has the power to deem the aforementioned speeches illegal, and prohibits them under criminal law. In other words, federal or state government in the United States cannot restrict or suppress speech unless the speech is likely to cause injury to individuals or property. The principal test used for restriction of speech based on its content is the "clear and present danger", that is, criminal law may prohibit a person's speech when the content of the speech causes a real and imminent danger. U. S. Supreme Court Justice Oliver Wendell Holmes pointed out, "The most stringent protection of free speech would not protect a

---

〔1〕 See Cox v. Hampshire(1941).

〔2〕 See Joel Samaha, *Criminal Law*, 10th edition, Wadsworth Cengage Learning Press, 2011, p.47.

man in falsely shouting fire in a theatre and causing a panic."[1]

根据表达的方式、时间和地点,政府有权将上述言论视为非法言论,并予以禁止。换言之,除非言论可能对个人或财产造成伤害,否则美国联邦政府或州政府不能限制或压制言论。基于内容的言论限制的主要标准是"明确和现实的危险",即当一个人言论的内容会引起现实的紧迫危险,刑法就可以予以禁止。美国最高法院大法官奥利弗·温德尔·霍姆斯指出:"对言论自由最严格的保护并不能保护一个在剧院里谎称起火并引起恐慌的人。"

■ Curriculum Ideology and Politics(课程思政)

Develop an awareness of the legitimate and proper exercise of the right to free speech:(1) Citizens should realize that their right to free speech is protected by the Constitution. Article 35 of the Constitution of the People's Republic of China protects this right, which states: Citizens of the People's Republic of China shall have freedom of speech, of the press, of assembly, of association, of procession and of demonstration. Therefore, citizens should bravely defend their own rights under the law against any infringement of the right to free speech. (2) Citizens should be aware of the boundaries of the right to free speech. The laws of each country not only give citizens the right to free speech, but also set the boundaries for such freedom. For example, they cannot provoke or insult others, use vulgar and indecent language, or cause serious danger with their words, etc. Citizens should establish a correct concept of freedom of speech. Citizens are required to establish a correct view of free speech, forming habits of civilised, courteous, lawful and proper speech.

培养合法和正当行使言论自由权的意识:(1)公民要意识到自己的言论自由权受宪法保护。《中华人民共和国宪法》第35条保护公民的言论自由,其规定:中华人民共和国公民有言论、出版、集会、结社、游行、示威的自由。因此,对于侵害自己言论自由的行为,公民应用法律勇敢捍卫自己的权利。(2)公民应意识到言论自由权的边界。各国法律在赋予公民言论自由权的同时,也为言论自由设置了边界。比如,不能挑衅、辱骂他人,不能使用低级下流的语言,不能以言辞引发严重危险等。公民要树立正确的言论自由观,培养文明、礼貌、合法和正当的言论习惯。

2.3.2 The Right to Privacy(隐私权)

The right to privacy is not expressly provided for in the United States Constitution,

[1] See Schenck v. U. S. (1919).

but the U. S. Supreme Court has inferred that citizens' right to privacy is constitutionally protected based on its provision and interpretation of other constitutional rights made by Framers. Griswold v. Connecticut established the principle that the right to privacy is constitutionally protected, which had landmark significance.

隐私权在《美国宪法》中没有明确规定,但美国最高法院根据制宪者对其他宪法权利的规定和解释,推断出公民的隐私权是受宪法保护的。格里斯沃尔德诉康涅狄格州案确立了隐私权受宪法保护原则,这一案件具有里程碑意义。

A Connecticut law from 1879 that banned citizens from counseling or using birth control medicine, even by married couples, was at issue. In *Griswold v. Connecticut*, 381 U. S. 479 (1965), the Director of Planned Parenthood Griswold, a physician, was penalized under the law for providing married couples with birth control instructions and birth control pills, a practice prohibited by Connecticut law at the time. Griswold appealed to the state appellate court, which affirmed. Griswold appealed again, and the Connecticut Supreme Court also upheld the Appellate Court's decision. Griswold then appealed to the United States Supreme Court. The Supreme Court ruled that the Connecticut legislation prohibiting the use of contraceptives violated citizen's right to privacy. However, the right to privacy is a constitutional right of citizens, which bans "all governmental invasions of the sanctity of a man's home and the privacies of life". According to the Federal Supreme Court, the right to privacy is not only a fundamental right, but also a constitutional right. Ultimately, it not only reversed the original decision, but also struck down the law enacted by the State of Connecticut.[1]

1879 年,康涅狄格州制定了一项法律,该法律规定禁止公民咨询或使用避孕药具,即使是已婚夫妇也不例外。在格里斯沃尔德诉康涅狄格州案中,计划生育主任格里斯沃尔德是一名医生,他为已婚夫妇提供了节育指导和避孕药,而当时的康涅狄格州法律禁止他的这种做法,因此他受到法律的处罚。格里斯沃尔德向州上诉法院提出上诉,州上诉法院维持了原判。格里斯沃尔德再次提出上诉,康涅狄格州最高法院也维持了上诉法院的裁决。随后格里斯沃尔德向美国联邦最高法院提出上诉。联邦最高法院的裁决指出康涅狄格州禁止公民使用避孕药具的立法侵犯了公民隐私权,而隐私权是公民享有的宪法性权利。这项权利禁止"所有政府侵犯人类的神圣性和生活的隐私"。根据联邦最高法院的观点,隐私权不仅是一项基本权利,而且还是一项宪法权利。最终,美国联邦法院不仅推翻了原判,还推翻了康涅狄格

---

〔1〕 See Joel Samaha, *Criminal Law*, 10th edition, Wadsworth Cengage Learning Press, 2011, p,52.

州制定的这项法律。

It is noteworthy that the "right to privacy" is not expressly provided in the Constitution or constitutional documents, but the United States Supreme Court has held that a citizen's right to privacy is protected by the Constitution and is a constitutional right. The conclusion is based on the following six amendments: (1) The First Amendment: rights of free speech, religion, and association; (2) The Third Amendment: prohibition against the quartering of soldiers in private homes; (3) The Fourth Amendment: prohibition against unlawful searches and seizure; (4) The Fifth Amendment: guarantees against self - incrimination; (5) The Ninth Amendment: the enumeration in the Constitution, of certain rights, shall not be construed to deny or disparage others retained by the people; (6) The Fourteenth Amendment: due process principle.

值得注意的是,"隐私权"并没有宪法及宪法性文件的明确规定,但美国联邦最高法院认为公民享有的隐私权是受宪法保护的,这是一项宪法性权利。该结论的得出,是以以下6个修正案作为根据的:(1)第一修正案:言论、宗教和结社自由的权利;(2)第三修正案:禁止士兵在私人住宅中居住;(3)第四修正案:禁止非法搜查和扣押;(4)第五修正案:防止自证其罪的保障;(5)第九修正案:宪法对某些权利的列举,不得被解释为否认或贬低人民保留的其他权利;(6)第十四修正案:正当程序原则。

Based on the analysis above, it can be seen that in the United States, although the "right to privacy" is protected by the Constitution and is a constitutional right, it is not expressly provided in the United States Constitution and other constitutional documents, but was established by the famous Griswold v. Connecticut case. It can be said that Griswold v. Connecticut established that the right to privacy enjoyed by American citizens is protected by the Constitution.

从上述分析可以看出,在美国,尽管"隐私权"受宪法保护,且是一项宪法性权利,但其不是由《美国宪法》以及其他宪法性文件明文规定的,而是由著名的格里斯沃尔德诉康涅狄格州案确立的。可以说,格里斯沃尔德诉康涅狄格州案确立了美国公民享有的隐私权是受宪法保护的。

Another famous case related to the right to privacy is Roe v. Wade, 410 U. S. 113, 153 (1973). Roe was a single woman living in Texas who claimed that Texas' criminal abortion law was unconstitutional and deprived her of her personal right to privacy. In that case, the U. S. Supreme Court ultimately declared the Texas abortion law unconstitutional and a violation of a woman's right to privacy. The U. S. Supreme Court stated that this right of privacy, whether it be based on the concept of personal liberty and limitations on state action found in the Fourteenth Amendment, as we believe it is, or, as the District Court found, on the reservation of rights to the people found in the Ninth Amendment, is broad enough to cover a woman's right to decide to terminate a pregnancy. However, the Court also held that the right was not absolute: "We, therefore, conclude that the right to personal privacy includes the right to decide to have an abortion, which means that the constitutionally – protected right to privacy includes a woman's right to an abortion, but this right is not unqualified and must be considered against important state interests when exercising it. "[1]

与隐私权相关的著名案例还有罗伊诉韦德案。[2] 罗伊是一名居住在得克萨斯州的单身女性,她主张得克萨斯州的刑事堕胎法违宪,剥夺了她的个人隐私权。在该案中,美国最高法院最后宣布得克萨斯州的堕胎法违反宪法,侵犯了妇女的隐私权。美国最高法院提出:这种隐私权,无论是建立在我们认为的第十四修正案的个人自由和对国家行动的限制的概念中,还是建立在地区法院认定的第九修正案对人民权利的保留中,都足以涵盖妇女决定终止妊娠的权利。但是,美国最高法院也认为,这项权利不是绝对的:"因此,我们得出结论,个人隐私权包括决定堕胎的权利,这意味着,受宪法保护的隐私权包括妇女的堕胎权。但这项权利并非无条件的,行使时必须考虑到重要的国家利益。"

It should also be noted that the six amendments cited by the Federal Supreme Court in Griswold v. Connecticut express the implied but strong belief that citizens have the right to be let alone by the government. The Ninth Amendment acknowledges that citizens have rights not named in the Constitution. As mentioned above, when the U. S. Supreme Court overturned the Connecticut law, it marks that the United States has explicitly recognized the constitutional protection of citizens' right to privacy.[3] Nevertheless, in the year 2022, the Supreme Court overturned the verdict in Roe v. Wade (1973), mainly on the grounds that the Constitution did not mention or protect abortion, and the ruling of Roe v. Wade(1973) was incorrect and the argument at that time was not adequately convincing.

---

[1] See Thomas J. Gardner & Terry M. Anderson, *Criminal Law*, 11th edition, Wadsworth Cengage Learning Press,2012,p. 243 – 244.

[2] See Roe v. Wade, 410 U. S. 113, 153 (1973).

[3] See Joel Samaha, *Criminal Law*, 10th edition, Wadsworth Cengage Learning Press, 2011, p. 53.

还需指出的是,美国联邦最高法院在格里斯沃尔德诉康涅狄格州的案件中使用的6个修正案,表达了一种隐含但强烈的信念,即公民有权被政府放任不管。美国《宪法第九修正案》承认公民拥有宪法中没有提到的权利。前述提及,当美国最高法院推翻康涅狄格州的法律时,就标志着美国已明确承认公民的隐私权受宪法保护。但是,当历史的车轮辗转到2022年,美国最高法院又推翻了罗诉韦德案的判决,其主要理由是:宪法本身没有提及和保护堕胎权,当时的判决是错误的以及当时的论证不够有说服力。

2.3.3 The Right to Bear Arms(持有武器权)

The Second Amendment to the U. S. Constitution states "A well regulated Militia, being necessary to the security of a free State, the right of the people to keep and bear Arms, shall not be infringed." The law on controlling the use of weapons and how to interpret the meaning and scope of the Second Amendment have always been controversial. This debate intensified after the assassination of President Reagan. One side believes that holding weapons for legitimate purposes is a constitutional right protected by the Constitution, and Congress shall not pass laws to violate this right of citizens; The other party believes that controlling firearms is necessary and reasonable for the state to exercise its security power.

美国《宪法第二修正案》规定:出于维护自由国家安全的必要,人民持有和携带武器的权利不受侵犯。控制使用武器的法律以及如何解释第二修正案的含义和范围,一直存在争议。这种争论在里根总统遇刺后更加激烈。一方认为,以合法目的为由持有武器是受宪法保护的权利,国会不得通过法令来侵犯公民的这一权利;另一方认为,管控枪支对于国家行使治安权是必要的和合理的。

The National Rifle Association of America (NRA) spends a great deal of money each year to defend the right of individuals to own firearms, while other public interest organizations also spend a lot of money to promote the idea of limiting the supply of firearms. It seems obvious that states have the right to regulate guns regulation. Regardless of public opinions on gun control, few people, if any, would advocate no restrictions on gun control, even the NRA supports it. Thus, when discussing gun control, the core issue is not the gun control, but rather that children under the age of eight and psychiatric patient should not have guns.〔1〕

美国全国步枪协会每年都会花费大量资金来捍卫个人拥有枪支的权利,而其他公共利益组织也会花费大量金钱来宣传限制枪支供应的想法。很明显,各州有权对

---

〔1〕 See Cliff Roberson, *Constitutional Law and Criminal Justice*, CRC Press, 2009, p. 4.

枪支进行监管。不管大家对枪支管制有什么看法,但很少有人会主张对枪支不加限制。即使是全国步枪协会也支持对枪支进行一定的限制。因此,当社会讨论枪支管制问题时,真正的问题不是枪支管制,而是8岁以下儿童及精神病人不应持有枪支。

In 2008, in District of Columbia v. Heller, 128 S. Ct. 2783 (2008), the U. S. Supreme Court recognized for the first time that gun right, as described in the Second Amendment to the Constitution, is an individual right that cannot be unduly infringed by the government under other handgun control statutes. Heller was a police officer in the District of Columbia. Under District of Columbia law, as a police officer, Heller can carry a gun in a federal government building, but cannot bear a gun in his home. Heller challenged the District of Columbia's ban on handgun, starting with a lawsuit in the lower courts and working his way up to the federal Supreme Court. Ultimately, the Federal Supreme Court ruled that the District of Columbia's handgun law was unconstitutional, and therefore, Columbia could not prohibit its citizens from owning or possessing handguns. However, the Court indicated that the District of Columbia could enact reasonable firearm regulations, such as prohibiting convicted felons from possessing guns, or enacting laws designed to control sales of firearms.[1]

2008年,在哥伦比亚特区诉海勒案中,美国最高法院第一次承认了《宪法第二修正案》所描述的枪支权利是个人权利,政府不能根据其他的手枪控制法规不当地侵犯该权利。海勒是哥伦比亚特区的一名警官。根据哥伦比亚特区的法律,海勒作为一名警官,可以在联邦政府大楼持枪,但不可以在家中持有枪支。海勒对哥伦比亚特区的手枪禁令提出了质疑,并从低级法院开始起诉,一路上诉至联邦最高法院。最终联邦最高法院裁定哥伦比亚特区的手枪法违宪,因此,哥伦比亚不能禁止公民持有或拥有手枪。然而,法院表示哥伦比亚特区可以制定合理的枪支法规,例如禁止被定罪的重罪犯持有枪支,或颁布旨在控制枪支销售的法律。

2.4 The Constitution and Criminal Sentencing(宪法和量刑)

The Eighth Amendment to the U. S. Constitution provides that "excessive bail shall not be required, nor excessive fines imposed, nor cruel and unusual punishments inflicted".

美国《宪法第八修正案》规定:"不得要求过多的保释金,也不得处以过多的罚款,禁止残酷和不寻常的惩罚。"

---

[1] See Thomas J. Gardner & Terry M. Anderson, *Criminal Law*, 11th edition, Wadsworth Cengage Learning Press, 2012, p. 240.

Included in the Eighth Amendment to the Constitution is the prohibition of "cruel and unusual punishment". Henceforth, in the United States, the prohibition of "cruel and unusual punishment" has a constitutional basis. In United States judicial practice, and according to the philosophy of the United States Supreme Court, there are two types of cruel and unusual punishment: "barbaric" punishment and punishment that is disproportionate to the crime committed.[1] These will be analyzed in detail in the following paragraphs.

《宪法第八修正案》包含了禁止"残酷和不寻常的刑罚"。因此,在美国,禁止"残酷和不寻常的刑罚"有宪法作为根据。在美国的司法实践中,依据美国联邦最高法院的理念,残忍和不平常的惩罚可被分为两种:"野蛮"的惩罚和与所犯罪行不合比例的惩罚。下面的内容将对此进行详细的分析。

2.4.1 Barbaric Punishments(酷刑)

Barbaric punishments usually refers to excessively severe, cruel, inhumane, or degrading treatment and punishment, which are considered unacceptable to civilized society. This is the case, for example, with capital punishment and hanging.

残酷的惩罚通常是指过分严厉、残忍、不人道或有辱人格的待遇和处罚,是被认为不为文明社会所接受的惩罚。

The Eighth Amendment to the Constitution was added to the U.S. Constitution in 1791 as part of the Bill of Rights. It prohibits the imposition of excessive bail or fines and cruel and unusual punishment. The provisions of the Eighth Amendment to the Constitution were alerted by the English legal tradition that preceded the American Revolution. In England, it was common for defendants to be subjected to harsh and barbaric punishments such as torture, mutilation, and public execution. Recognizing the evils of cruel and barbaric punishments, the American founding fathers sought to protect citizens from the abuses of these cruel punishments by limiting the government's power to impose them.

《宪法第八修正案》于1791年作为《权利法案》的一部分被纳入美国宪法。《宪法第八修正案》禁止征收过高的保释金或罚金,禁止残忍和不寻常的惩罚。《宪法第八修正案》的规定受美国革命之前的英国法律传统所警醒。在英国,被告人受到严酷和野蛮的惩罚是很常见的,如酷刑、残害和公开处决。美国开国者认识到残酷和野蛮刑罚的弊端,就试图通过限制政府实施惩罚的权力来保护公民免受这些残酷刑

[1] See Solem v. Helm (1983).

罚的虐待。

The protections provided by the Eighth Amendment are a critical component of the American legal system and have been the subject of numerous Supreme Court cases. The prohibition against cruel and unusual punishment has been interpreted to prohibit practices such as the death penalty for juveniles and individuals with intellectual disabilities, as well as the use of certain forms of physical punishment in prisons.

《宪法第八修正案》提供的保护是美国法律制度的一个重要组成部分,也是最高法院众多案件的主题。禁止残忍和不寻常惩罚的规定被解释为禁止对青少年和智障人士判处死刑,以及禁止在监狱中使用某些形式的体罚等做法。

Overall, the Eighth Amendment reflects the importance that the framers placed on protecting citizens from arbitrary and excessive government actions by preventing cruel and unusual punishments and making sure that financial penalties are not disproportionately harsh.

总的来说,《宪法第八修正案》反映了制定者对保护公民不受政府任意和过度行为影响的重视,禁止了残忍和不寻常的惩罚,并确保经济处罚不会过分严厉。

For more than a hundred years after the adoption of the Bill of Rights, no "cruel and unusual" punishment cases reached the U. S. Supreme Court because these medieval forms of execution weren't used in the United States. The use of hanging as a method of execution was questioned by the governor of the state of New York in 1885, who said: "The present mode of executing criminals by hanging has come down to us from the dark ages, and it may well be questioned whether the science of the present day can provide a means of taking life in a less barbaric manner." The legislature then established a commission to study the issue. The committee's study described electrocution as the most humane and practical method of execution known to modern science. Then, the legislature replaced the hangman's noose with the electric chair in 1888.[1]

在《权利法案》通过后的一百多年里,没有任何"残忍和不寻常"的惩罚案件提交美国最高法院,因为这些中世纪的处决形式在美国没有被使用。但是,1885年,纽约州州长在给立法机构的年度致辞中,质疑将绞刑作为处决方法:"目前绞死罪犯的模式是从黑暗时代传下来的,我们很可能会思索当今的科学是否能提供一种手段,以一种不那么野蛮的方式处决生命。"立法机关随后成立了一个委员会来研究这个

[1] See Joel Samaha, *Criminal Law*, 10th edition, Wadsworth Cengage Learning Press, 2011, p. 59.

问题。委员会研究称电刑是为现代科学所知的最人道和实用的处决方式。1888 年，立法机构用电刑取代了绞刑。

Kemmler was sentenced to death for the murder of his mistress at a time when New York State passed a new law making the electrocution an alternative to hanging as a method of execution. Therefore, in 1890, Kemmler became the first person to be executed by electrocution. When the unusualness and cruelty of electrocution was again challenged, the U. S. Supreme Court stated that electrocution was certainly unusual, but not cruel. In this case, the Supreme Court explained what constitutes a death sentence that is not cruel: First, death has to be both instantaneous and painless. Second, it can't involve unnecessary mutilation of the body. So, according to the Court, beheading is cruel because it mutilates the body. Crucifixion is doubly cruel because it inflicts a "lingering" death and mutilates the body.[1]

凯姆勒因杀害自己的情妇而被判处死刑,而当时纽约州通过了一项新的法律,将电刑作为替代绞刑的死刑执行方式。因此,在 1890 年,凯姆勒成为第一个被执行电刑处死的人。当有人又质疑电刑的不寻常性和残酷性时,美国最高法院表示,电刑当然不寻常,但并不残忍。在该案中,最高法院解释了何为并不残忍的死刑:首先,死亡必须是即时的和无痛的;其次,死刑不能涉及不必要的身体残缺。因此,根据最高法院的观点,斩首是残忍的,因为它会肢解尸体。钉十字架是双重残忍的,因为它会造成"挥之不去"的死亡,并残害身体。

Chief Justice Warren stated in a judgment in 1958 that "this court rarely explains the precise content of the Eighth Amendment. This content is not static, but rather draws its meaning from the constantly evolving standards. The basic meaning of this amendment is to protect human dignity, with the aim of upholding the principle of civilized treatment".

首席大法官沃伦在 1958 年的一个判决意见中说:"本法院很少解释《宪法第八修正案》的精确内容,此内容不是静态的,而是从不断发展的标准中汲取它的意义,这条修正案的基本意思是保护人的尊严,目的是维护文明处置的原则"。

2.4.2 Disproportionate Punishments(不合比例刑罚)

The proportionality concept, which states that the penalty should be proportionate for the crime, has a long history. In Weems v. U. S. (1910), the U. S. Supreme Court recognized the proportionality concept as a principle safeguarded by the Eighth

---

[1] See In re Kemmler, 136 U. S. 436 (1890).

Amendment. Weems was convicted of falsifying a public document. The trial court first sentenced him to 15 years in prison at hard labor in chains and then took away all of his civil rights for the rest of his life. The penalty was deemed "cruel and unusual" by the Supreme Court because it was out of proportion to his offence. The case prohibited disproportionate punishments under federal criminal law.[1]

相称性原则,即刑罚应与罪行相适应,该原则有着悠久的历史。1910 年,美国最高法院在威姆斯诉美国案中首次将相称性原则设置为《宪法第八修正案》所保护的原则。保罗·威姆斯因伪造公共文件而被定罪。初审法院首先判处他 15 年有期徒刑、戴着镣铐进行苦役,然后剥夺了他余生的所有公民权利。美国最高法院裁定,这种惩罚是"残忍和不寻常的",因为这与他的罪行不成比例。该案禁止在联邦刑事司法中实施过度惩罚。

Historically, the term "proportionality" has been employed in the context of a deductive assessment of the appropriateness of a sentence for a certain crime. The principle of proportionality takes into account the seriousness of the offense, the severity of the penalty, the sentences imposed for similar crimes and the sentencing practices of other jurisdictions. Therefore, the Supreme Court has occasionally invalidated punishments as being inherently disproportionate to the crime and thus cruel and unusual when applied to a specific crime or category of crimes.

从历史上看,"相称性"一词一直被用于对某一犯罪施加的刑罚是否适当而进行的评估。相称性原则要考虑到犯罪的严重性、刑罚的严重程度、对类似犯罪的判决以及其他司法管辖区的量刑做法。据此,最高法院偶尔会宣布某些判决的刑罚无效,因为这些刑罚本质上与罪行是不相称的,因此在适用于特定犯罪或犯罪类别时是残忍和不寻常的。

The death penalty has received more attention in the United States than any other criminal sanction. The primary dispute concerning the death penalty is whether it violates the prohibition against the cruel and unusual punishment clause of the Eighth Amendment. As for whether the death penalty is inherently cruel, the Supreme Court of the United States has not made a clear explanation. Capital punishment must be limited to those offenders who commit a narrow category of the most serious crimes and whose extreme culpability makes them the most deserving of execution.[2] The Court's own knowledge and interpretation of the language, history, meaning, and purpose of the

[1] See Weems v. U. S. (1910).

[2] See Joel Samaha, *Criminal Law*, 10th edition, Wadsworth Cengage Learning Press, 2011, p. 62.

Eighth Amendment, as well as the standards outlined by governing cases, will determine whether the death penalty is disproportionate in comparison to the offense committed.

在美国,死刑比其他任何刑事制裁都更受关注。关于死刑的主要争议是它是否违反了《宪法第八修正案》中禁止残忍和不寻常的惩罚条款。至于死刑是否具有内在的、固有的残忍性,美国联邦最高法院并未作出明确的解释。死刑必须仅限于犯了最严重罪行的罪犯,因为罪犯的极端罪责使他们应该被判处死刑。法院自身对《宪法第八修正案》的语言、历史、含义和目的的了解与解释,以及管辖案件的标准,会决定死刑刑罚与罪犯所犯罪行是否相称。

In the case of Coker v. Georgia (1977), Coker had served time in prison for murder, rape, kidnapping and aggravated assault, and he committed rape and kidnapping after he escaped from prison. After his arrest, he was charged with various crimes, including rape, for which he was also sentenced to death. Coker appealed, and the Georgia Supreme Court upheld the trail court's conviction and sentence. The case was later appealed to the Federal Supreme Court.[1] The Federal Supreme Court rules that the death penalty for the rape of an adult woman is a disproportionate punishment. In fact, it looked as if a majority of the Court agreed on the proposition that death is always disproportionate, except in some aggravated murders. In America, while many people insist that rape should undoubtedly be severely punished, it cannot be compared to murder in terms of its moral evil and the harm it does to both individuals and the public, as the former merely infringes on sexual autonomy while the latter unjustly ends a person's life. Therefore, the death penalty is a disproportionate penalty for rape and violates the Eighth Amendment to the Constitution.

在科克诉佐治亚州案中,科克曾因谋杀、强奸、绑架和严重伤害罪在监狱服刑,他越狱后又犯下强奸、绑架等罪行。被捕后,他被指控犯有包括强奸在内的各种罪行,他也因强奸罪被判处死刑。科克提出上诉,佐治亚州最高法院维持了初审法院的定罪和量刑。后该案上诉至联邦最高法院,联邦最高法院裁定,因强奸成年妇女而被判处死刑是与罪行不相称的惩罚。事实上,法院的大多数成员似乎都认同这样一个主张,即判处死刑总是不合适的,除非是在一些严重的谋杀案中。在美国,很多人认为强奸毫无疑问应当加以严重的惩罚,但是就其道德恶性与对个人和公众的伤害而言,它无法与谋杀相比,因为前者仅仅侵害了性自主权,而后者不正当地夺走了一个人的生命。因此,对于强奸犯来说,判处死刑是过度的惩罚,违反了宪法第八修正案。

---

〔1〕 See Coker v. Georgia, 433 U. S. 584 (1977).

■ Case study(案例学习)

Kennedy v. Louisana 554 U. S. 945(2008)(肯尼迪诉路易斯安那州案)

Fact(基本案情)

Patrick Kennedy was convicted of the aggravated rape of his eight - year - old stepdaughter under a Louisiana statute that provided capital punishment for the rape of a child under 12 years of age and was sentenced to death. Kennedy appealed to the Louisiana Supreme Court, claiming that according to the Supreme Court's 1977 ruling in Coker v. Georgia, "rape is a serious crime, but it is different from murder that illegally deprives others of their lives." Therefore, "imposing the death penalty on rapists is an extremely excessive and excessive punishment, and belongs to the 'cruel and abnormal punishment' prohibited by the Eighth Amendment of the Constitution. The Louisiana Supreme Court responded that the Corker case only prohibits the death penalty for raping adult women, but young children are a group that needs special protection, and the rape of young children poses great harm to both victims and society. Therefore, the punishment for Kennedy is not bound by the Cook case. The Louisiana Supreme Court also reviewed the laws of other states and found that there are five other states that allow the death penalty for raping young children. The Louisiana Supreme Court believed that this indicates that there is already a "national consensus" on the issue of executing rapists of young children, and therefore ruled to refute Kennedy's appeal and uphold the original verdict.

根据路易斯安那州的一项法令,帕特里克·肯尼迪因强奸8岁继女而被定罪。该法令规定强奸12岁以下儿童的人可能被判处死刑。肯尼迪向路易斯安那州最高法院提出上诉,表示根据最高法院在1977年库克诉佐治亚州案中的裁决,"强奸是一种严重的犯罪,但它不同于非法剥夺他人生命的谋杀"。因此,"对强奸犯判处死刑是一种极其残忍和过度的惩罚,属于《宪法第八修正案》所禁止的'残忍和不正常的惩罚'"。路易斯安那州最高法院回应称,科克案只禁止对强奸成年妇女的人判处死刑,而幼儿是一个需要特殊保护的群体,强奸青少年、儿童的行为对受害者和社会都造成了巨大的伤害。因此,对肯尼迪的惩罚不受库克案的约束。路易斯安那州最高法院还查阅了其他州的法律,发现还有5个州允许对强奸幼童的人判处死刑。路易斯安那州最高法院认为,这表明在处决强奸犯的问题上已经有了"全国共识",因此裁定驳回肯尼迪的上诉,维持原判。

Dispute(争议点)

The controversial point of this case is whether the death penalty for raping young children is unconstitutional. Justice Kennedy believed that as long as the rapist had no intention of killing and had no fatal consequences, whether the victim was a child or not, the death penalty could not be imposed. Moreover, since 1964, no one in the United States has been sentenced to death for rape, which demonstrates what is truly a "national consensus". Not imposing the death penalty on rapists is a result of the continuous evolution of social ethics standards and a necessary requirement of a mature society. Justice Alito proposed that all five states mentioned above have passed laws for the execution of child rapists shortly before the case occurred, which precisely indicates that this is a trend of public opinion and the direction of the "evolution of social morality standards". And why did they do this? It is because the precedent in 1977 did not allow the execution of rapists, so states amended their legislation to avoid this precedent.

本案的争议点在于对强奸幼童的人判处死刑是否违宪。肯尼迪大法官认为,只要强奸犯没有杀人意图,也没有致命后果,无论受害者是否为儿童,都不能判处死刑。而且,自 1964 年以来,美国没有人因强奸罪被判处死刑,这表明了什么是真正的"全国共识"。不对强奸犯判处死刑是社会伦理标准不断演变的结果,也是成熟社会的必然要求。阿利托大法官提出,前述 5 个州在该案案发前不久才通过了处决儿童强奸犯的法律,这恰恰表明这是一种民意趋势,也是"社会道德标准演变的方向"。它们为什么这么做?正是因为 1977 年的先例不允许处决强奸犯,因此各州修改了立法以避免这一先例。

Conclusion(结论)

On June 25, 2008, the federal Supreme Court announced its decision in Kennedy v. Louisiana, in which the justices voted 5 to 4 to invalidate the state law that made rape of young children punishable by death as unconstitutional. The Supreme Court's ruling had led to a public outcry. Even many politicians came out to denounce the Supreme Court's decision.

2008 年 6 月 25 日,联邦最高法院宣布了其在肯尼迪诉路易斯安那州案中的裁决,法官们以 5 票对 4 票的投票结果宣布该州法律无效,该法律规定强奸幼童者可被判处死刑是违宪的。最高法院的裁决引起了公众的强烈抗议。甚至许多政客也站出来谴责最高法院的裁决。

Questions:1. Is Louisiana the only state in the United States that allows the death penalty for raping young children? (Please scan the QR code on the right to get the answer)

路易斯安那州是美国唯一允许对强奸幼童者判处死刑的州吗?

（答案请扫描右侧二维码获取）

2. Why to the Louisiana Supreme Court, considers death is a proportionate penalty for child rape? (The way to obtain the answer is the same as above)

路易斯安那州最高法院为什么认为死刑是对强奸儿童者的相称惩罚？（答案获取方式同上）

2.5 The Right to Trial by Jury（陪审团审判的权利）

The jury system originated in England. Whether it is a grand jury or a small jury, it may have existed during the Anglo – Saxon era. In 1791, the United States passed the Sixth Amendment to the Constitution, which stipulated that "defendants have the right to a prompt and public trial by a fair jury in the place where the criminal act occurred". Article 3 (2) of the Constitution stated that "all crimes except for impeachment shall be tried by a jury". This is one of the few provisions of the 1789 Constitution that guarantees individual rights.

陪审制源于英国。无论是大陪审团还是小陪审团，在盎格鲁－撒克逊时代就已经存在。1791年美国通过的《宪法第六修正案》规定："被告享有由犯罪行为发生地的公正陪审团予以迅速和公开审判的权利。"《美国宪法》第3条第2款则规定："除弹劾案外一切犯罪由陪审团审判。"这是美国《1789年宪法》规定的为数不多的个人权利保障条款。

There are grand juries and petit juries, with grand juries generally consisting of 23 people and petit juries generally consisting of 12 people. The jury in Anglo – Amerian legal system is not a member determined by collegiate bench; the jury is responsible only for the factual part of the case, and the judge is responsible for the legal part. Jurors do not speak in court, they just listen to both sides and their witnesses and then decide on the facts of the case. While the judge controls the process of questioning by the attorneys and points out what evidence that comes before the court was obtained illegally or what testimony is not credible to alert the jury that it is inadmissible. In the United States, many people believe that the jury system can avoid professional bias or abuse of power by judges or prosecutors, as well as preventing defendants from being charged or punished unreasonably, and that even if the verdicts are unsatisfactory, they can be considered as a reflection of public opinion rather than a manipulation of power. Therefore, the majority of the people in the United States have always trusted the jury even though the jury has many shortcomings in handling cases.

陪审团有大陪审团和小陪审团之分,大陪审团一般由 23 人组成,小陪审团一般由 12 人组成。英美法系的陪审团不是合议庭成员,陪审团只负责认定案件的事实部分,法官则负责认定案件的法律部分。陪审团成员在法庭上不发言,只倾听双方及其证人的发言,然后就案件事实进行裁决。而法官会控制律师的询问过程,并指出法庭上出现的哪些证据属于违法获得或者哪些证言不具有可信度,以提醒陪审团不能采用。在美国,许多人认为陪审制可以避免法官或检察官的专业偏见或滥用职权,也可以防止被告人受到不合理的指控或惩罚,即使裁决结果不尽如人意,也可以认为是民意的体现,而不是权力的操控。所以,即使陪审团在处理案件时还有许多不足,美国大多数人民仍始终信赖陪审团。

District courts hear cases using the jury system, where the jury is responsible for finding out the facts of the case, and if the defendant is deemed to have committed a crime, the judge decides on the sentencing range. The Federal Appellate Courts do not have juries when hearing cases. and cases are generally heard by a panel of judges. The Federal Appellate Courts only hear cases of improper application of the law by the court of first instance, and do not hear appeals on questions of fact.

地区法院审理案件采用陪审团制度,由陪审团负责查明案件的事实,如果认为被告人构成犯罪,则由法官决定量刑的幅度。联邦上诉法院审理案件时没有陪审团,一般由法官组成合议庭审理案件,联邦上诉法院仅受理一审法院适用法律不当的案件,不受理对于事实问题提出上诉的案件。

2.6 Exercise(课后练习)(答案请扫描右侧二维码获取)

2.6.1 Test of Terminologies(术语考查)

①ex post facto law　　②void – for – vagueness doctrine

③barbaric punishments　　④principle of proportionality

⑤convict　　⑥Bill of Rights

⑦death penalty　　⑧jury

2.6.2 True or False(判断题)

1. In order to punish those morally blameworthy, dangerous people, the criminal law can be applied retroactively.

为了惩罚那些在道德上值得谴责的、危险的人,刑法可以被溯及既往地适用。

2. No crime without law; no punishment without law; no one can be punished for a crime that did not exist at the time they engaged in the behavior.

没有法律就没有犯罪;没有法律就没有惩罚;没有人可以因为在他们行为当时

不存在的罪行而受到惩罚。

3. The law must be adequately explicit and reasonably understood by average people.

法律必须具备充分的明确性,能被普通人合理地理解。

4. In the United States, the death penalty can still be imposed by courts on juveniles and mentally disabled people.

在美国,法院仍然可以对青少年和智障人士判处死刑。

5. The Second Amendment protects citizen's right against the government's restriction on the individual right to use handguns to protect us in homes.

《宪法第二修正案》保护公民在家中持有枪械,以保护自身的权利不受政府的限制的权利。

2.6.3 Short – answer Questions(简答题)

1. What is the connotation of ex post facto laws?

溯及既往法的内涵是什么?

2. What is the definition of the void – for – vagueness doctrine?

模糊即无效原则的含义是什么?

3. List the speech that is not protected by the First Amendment.

列出不受美国《宪法第一修正案》保护的言论。

4. Explain the meaning of barbaric punishment.

解释野蛮刑罚的含义。

■ Curriculum Ideology and Politics(课程思政)

Develop students' objective knowledge of China's practice and China's wisdom in the death penalty system. The United States has not completely abolished the capital punishment. While China's criminal law also retains the death penalty, it sets strict restrictions. From the perspective of China's criminal law and criminal procedure, its death penalty system is very distinctive. China's death penalty in Chinese criminal law provides a valuable Chinese Paradigm for the death penalty system in the world's criminal law.

培养学生客观认知死刑制度的中国实践和中国智慧。美国没有全面废止死刑,中国刑法也保留了死刑,但设置了严格的限制条件。从中国刑法和刑事程序看,中国的死刑制度非常具有特色。中国死刑制度为世界刑法的死刑制度,提供了有价值的中国范式。

■ Summary(总结)

1. The Principle of Legality requires that a criminal offense and its corresponding punishment must be clearly defined in advance by law, and that no one can be punished if his conduct was not considered a crime at the time it was committed, or if the law is so vague that it could not be understood by ordinary people.

合法性原则要求刑事犯罪及其相应的惩罚必须事先由法律明确规定,任何人都不能因为在实施时未被规定为犯罪的行为而受到惩罚,也不能因为过于模糊以至于普通人无法理解其意义的法律规定而被惩罚。

2. The ban on ex facto laws prohibits the retroactive application of criminal laws, that is, an act cannot be punished if it was not a crime at the time it was committed.

禁止溯及既往法这一原则禁止追溯性适用刑事法律,如果一个行为在实施时不属于犯罪,就不能对其进行惩罚。

3. The Void – for – vagueness Doctrine requires that criminal laws must be clear and specific enough to give ordinary people fair notice of what is prohibited, and that vague or overly broad laws will be considered unconstitutional and unenforceable.

模糊即无效原则要求刑事法律必须足够明确和具体,以合理地向普通人告知被禁止的行为,模糊或过于宽泛的法律被视为是违宪的和不可被执行的。

4. The Principle of Equal Protection of the Laws ensures that all individuals are entitled to equal treatment under the law, and that no person or group can be given preferential treatment or discriminated against based on any irrelevant factors, such as race, religion, gender, or social status. Nevertheless, it is noticeable that special protection for the disadvantaged groups is still constitutional.

法律平等保护原则确保所有个人都有权得到法律的平等对待,任何个人或群体都不能因为任何不相关的因素,如种族、宗教、性别或社会地位而受到优惠待遇或歧视。然而,需要注意的是,对弱势群体的特殊保护仍然是合宪的。

5. The Second Amendment states "A well regulated Militia, being necessary to the security of a free State, the right of the people to keep and bear Arms, shall not be infringed." The law on controlling the use of weapons and how to interpret the meaning and scope of the Second Amendment have always been controversial.

《宪法第二修正案》规定:出于维护自由国家安全的必要,人民持有和携带武器的权利不受侵犯。控制使用武器的法律以及如何解释《宪法第二修正案》的含义和范围,一直存在争议。

6. The Eighth Amendment guarantees that no one is given an excessive amount of

punishment and establishes the principle that “punishment should fit the crime”.

《宪法第八修正案》保证任何人都不会受到不相称的惩罚,并确立了“惩罚应与罪行相适应”的原则。

7. The Supreme Court ruled that any fact that increases the penalty for the crime charged must be submitted to the jury and proved beyond a reasonable doubt.

最高法院认为,任何能够增加对所指控罪行刑罚的事实都必须提交给陪审团确认,并在排除合理怀疑的情况下予以证明。

Chapter 3 The General Principles of Criminal Liability(Ⅰ): *Actus Reus*

第 3 章 刑事责任一般原则 I :客观行为

■ The Learning Objective(学习目标)

1. To know the elements of criminal liability.

了解刑事责任的构成要素。

2. Appreciate the importance of the *actus reus*(criminal act) as the first principle of criminal liability.

认识客观要件(犯罪行为)作为刑事责任第一原则的重要性。

3. Understand the voluntariness requirement, as well as its significance and applicability.

了解行为的自愿性要件及其意义和适用。

4. Explore three special situations of *actus reus*: criminal status, criminal possession, and criminal omissions.

探究客观行为要件的三种特殊情形:状态犯、持有型犯罪、不作为犯。

5. To learn some terminologies related to this chapter.

掌握本章中的专业术语。

■ Chapter Outline(本章内容概要)

This chapter mainly introduces the elements of criminal liability and the *actus reus* (criminal act) as the first principle of criminal liability, as well as four relevant issues about the *actus reus*: firstly, the voluntariness requirement that people are responsible only for their voluntary acts; secondly, the status as a criminal act and its challege from the constition; thirdly, the possession as a criminal act and its incompatibility with the act requirement; fourthly, the omissions and the duties making the omissions as criminal acts.

本章主要介绍刑事责任成立的构成要素和作为刑事责任成立第一原则的客观要件(犯罪行为),以及与客观要件相关的四个主题:第一,行为的自愿性要件,即行为人只能对其自愿做出的行为负责;第二,被视作犯罪行为的状态,及其背后的合宪性疑虑;第三,持有型犯罪,及其与行为要件的不兼容性;第四,不作为及使不作为成为犯罪行为的义务。

■ The Purpose of Curriculum Ideology and Politics for this Chapter (本章的课程思政目标)

1. Expand students' academic horizons and train their ability to compare and analyze. *Actus reus* involves some certain specific issues, and there are both connections and differences in the handling methods of such issues between Anglo – American criminal law and Chinese criminal law. Therefore, studying the content of this chapter can not only cultivate students to form an academic attitude that combines rational evaluation and reasonable reference, but also help them fully understand the commonalities and differences of *actus reus* in Chinese and Anglo – American criminal laws.

扩宽学生学术视野,训练其比较分析的能力。客观要件涉及诸多具体议题的探讨,而英美刑法和我国刑法对此形成了既有联系又有区别的认识。通过学习本章内容,既可培育学生形成理性评判和合理借鉴相结合的学术态度,也能助其充分认识客观要件在中国和英美刑法中的共通性和差异性。

2. Cultivate students' initiative to contemplate frontier and international legal issues. The connotation of *actus reus* is sometimes broadened to cope with complex criminal situations and special problems, and thus encounters doubts about rationality, which is also a contemporary issue that Chinese criminal law cannot avoid in the process of crime governance. Thus, by knowing the *actus reus* and its special situations will help to stimulate students' enthusiasm to broaden their horizons, practice divergent thinking, and explore cutting – edge issues.

培育学生关注前沿问题、共性问题的主动性。客观行为要件的内涵有时会被扩宽以应对复杂多变的犯罪形势和特殊问题,并由此遭遇正当性质疑,而这也是我国刑法在犯罪治理过程中所必需直面的当代议题。因此,通过了解客观行为要件及其特殊情形,有助于激发学生开阔视野、发散思维、发掘前沿问题的积极性。

3. Understand the rule – of – law significance contained in *actus reus*, and cultivate studens' own concepts of rule of law. The *actus reus*, as the basic prerequisite for

initiating punishment, eliminate the punishment for ideology, and constitute a barrier to protect individual freedom, which has important legal significance. Accordingly, students could prompt them to shape their own rule – of – law awareness and humanistic spirit, and prevent them from making presumption of guilt based only on the actor's personal situation and mental states in future law practical.

了解客观行为要件的法治意义,培养学生自身的法治思维。客观行为要件作为发动刑罚的基本前提,杜绝了思想入罪,构成了保障个人自由的一道屏障,这具有重要的法治意义。学生可借此积极形塑自身的法治意识和人文精神,在今后可能从事的实践工作中,防止仅根据行为人的个人状况和主观想法就作出有罪推定的行为出现。

■ Terminologies(专业术语)

actus reus	客观要件
mens rea	主观要件
criminal liability	刑事责任
elements of criminal liability	刑事责任的构成要素
the general principles of criminal liability	刑事责任成立的一般原则
criminal act	犯罪行为
act requirement	行为要件
attendant circumstances	附随情状
result	结果
defense	抗辩事由
conduct crimes	行为犯
result crimes	结果犯
"voluntary" act requirement	"自愿性"行为要件
status	状态
possession	持有
legal fiction	法律拟制
actual possession	实际持有
constructive possession	推定持有
knowing possession	明知的持有
mere possession	事实上的持有
criminal omissions	不作为犯罪

duties to act　　　　　　　　　　　　　作为义务

3.1　The Elements of Criminal Liability(刑事责任的构成要素)

When writing the definitions of the thousands of crimes, the drafters may have several building blocks at their disposal. These building blocks are the elements of a crime that the prosecution has to prove beyond a reasonable doubt. Normally, these building blocks include criminal act (*actus reus*), criminal intent (*mens rea*), attendant circumstances and a criminal harm (result).

立法者定义的各种各样的犯罪往往会由几个组成要素构成。这些组成要素就是犯罪成立所需的构成要素。在诉讼中,如果要认定被告构成犯罪,就需要以排除合理怀疑的证明标准来证明这些构成要素的齐备。通常,这些组成要素包括犯罪行为(客观要件)、犯罪意图(主观要件),并可能同时包括附随情状和结果。

3.1.1　*Actus Reus* and *Mens Rea*(客观要件和主观要件)

It has become orthodox to divide the constituent elements of a crime into two parts, which are called *actus reus* and *mens rea*. The *mens rea* is a state of mind, while the *actus reus* is the "external element" that may be simply defined negatively as those elements left over when the mental element (*mens rea*) is subtracted from the whole prohibition, and it chiefly describes a certain type of conduct. Notice that the *actus reus* and *mens rea* of all the offences can only be fully unpacked by identifying certain enduring features within offence definitions.[1] Referring to the *actus reus*, those features typically contain a statement of the act (act requirement), circumstance and result. For instance, in murder, manslaughter and other homicide offences' there must be an unlawful killing mainly manifesting some form of homicidal act like the shooting in practice. And sometimes the accused must cause the victim's death and needs causality linking the defendant's act with this result. Besides, the killing should be unlawful, and this is a certain circumstance constitutive of the crime. The attendant circumstances element isn't an act or a result; rather, it's a "circumstance" connected to an act or a result, such as the "intoxicated" in the case of "driving while intoxicated". In sum, "sometimes the *actus reus* and the *mens rea* are jointly called the definitional elements of a crime. For ease of analysing offences, it is usual to divide them into the various constituent ingredients, some of which are *actus reus* elements and some of

---

〔1〕 See William Wilson, *Criminal Law*, 7th edition, Pearson Education Limited Press, 2020.

which are *mens rea* elements. Add together all the elements and the definition of that, offence is reached".[1]

一项完整的犯罪定义(犯罪构成)一般会被分为客观要件(*actus reus*)和主观要件(*mens rea*)两个方面。其中,主观要件体现为一种主观心理状态,而客观要件则是犯罪定义排除主观要件之后所剩下的那些"外部要素",它主要是对某种行为特征的描述。而各种犯罪的客观和主观要件都需要展现出犯罪的核心和典型特征。就客观要件而言,这些特征则需要以行为方式(行为要件)、附随情状和结果等要素来体现。例如,谋杀、非预谋杀人以及其他杀人犯罪,均要求客观上具备"非法杀人"行为,其在实践中通常体现为枪击等杀人手段。此外,有时还需要具备死亡结果,以及行为与死亡结果间具备确实的因果关系。再者,杀人行为必须出于"非法",这即是成立犯罪所需的附随情状。附随情状并不是一种行为或结果,它只是与行为或结果相关的某种客观情况,比如醉酒驾驶中的醉酒。总之,"通常以犯罪的构成要素来指称客观要件和主观要件的结合体,而为了方便分析和解释犯罪,这些主、客观要件会被细分为各种组成元素,其中一些元素构成了客观要件要素,而其他的则构成主观要件要素。将所有这些要素集合在一起,就形成了某项犯罪的完整定义"。

Here are some issues that should be noted:

此外,还需要注意以下问题:

1. The establishment of a crime requires the *actus reus* and *mens rea* do not exist separately, they must be contemporaneous meaning that a criminal intent has to trigger the criminal act (which is called the concurrence).

犯罪的成立要求客观要件和主观要件同时存在,二者不能被割裂,即"同时性",客观行为需要被相对应的主观意图所驱动和支配。

2. The *mens rea* qualifies the *actus reus*, and each external element may have a different *mens rea* attached to it. For example, in the offence of rape, the "penetration", "woman" and "not consent" points constitute the *actus reus*, and the accused must "intentionally" commit the penetration, knowing that the woman does not consent.

主观要件修饰和限定客观要件,并且不同客观要件要素会对应不同的主观要件。例如,强奸罪的客观要件要素是"性行为"、"妇女"和"违背妇女意志",而行为人则是在"明知"妇女不同意的情况下"故意"实施性行为。

3. The *actus reus* differs from crime to crime. Although all crimes have an *actus*

---

[1] Michael Jefferson, *Criminal Law*, 12th edition, Pearson Education Limited Press, 2015, p. 36.

reus, yet what the *actus reus* is in each offence can only be determined by specific prohibition.

不同犯罪有不同的客观要件。所有犯罪都需要具备客观要件,但客观要件的具体内容则只能根据具体犯罪进行确定。

4. Notice the difference between conduct crimes and result crimes. The former requires a criminal act triggered by criminal intent while the latter further requires causation and criminal harm.

注意行为犯和结果犯的不同。前者只需要一定主观意图驱动下的客观行为,而后者则进一步要求因果关系和犯罪结果。

5. *Actus reus* could encompass all objective material elements including act, circumstance and result. But in certain context, *actus reus* may be used in a narrow sense, in other words, it may equals to the criminal act or act requirement.

actus reus(客观要件)可以囊括行为、附随情状和结果等所有客观物质要素。但在特定语境下,*actus reus*(客观要件)这一术语会被狭义地使用,并可以与 criminal act(客观行为)或者 act requirement(行为要件)具有同等意义。

3.1.2　Defence(抗辩事由)

(The absence of) defences may be regarded as the third element in criminal liability in addition to *actus reus* and *mens rea*. Among them, the *actus reus* and *mens rea* are the positive elements that constitute a crime, while the defense is the negative one. Defences are the facts and reasons used to block the establishment of a crime and criminal responsibility when the *actus reus* and *mens rea* in the definition of a crime are proven to be satisfied. In practice, the court can only convict a defendant when his conduct satisfies the *actus reus* and *mens rea* without any grounds for defense. However, there is a type of defence called "failure of proof defence", which negates either the *actus reus* or *mens rea* or both, only to indicate that the various elements in the crime definition have not been proven beyond a reasonable doubt by the prosecution. Therefore, Anglo – American criminal law generally holds that this kind of defense is not a true defense.

(不具备)抗辩事由,可以成为除客观要件和主观要件之外的,施加刑事责任(犯罪构成)的第三个独立构成要素。其中,客观要件和主观要件是构成犯罪的积极要素,而抗辩事由则是消极条件,它是在犯罪定义中的主、客观要素(在形式上)被证明齐备的情况下,用以阻却犯罪成立和刑事责任的事实和理由。在实践中,当被告的行为符合了主、客观要件而又不具备抗辩事由时,法院才能对其定罪。不过,在抗辩事由中,有一种情形属于"证据不足辩护",它的作用是否定客观要件或主观要件本身的成立,其效果只是表明,犯罪定义中各个要素的齐备,并未被控方以排除合理怀疑的标准所证明。也因此,英美刑法一般认为这种情形下的抗辩事由并不是"真正的抗辩"。

(The true) defenses can be further divided into justifications (such as self - defense) and excuses (such as duress). The former indicates that although the elements required by the definition are proven, the act itself does not have the wrongfulness, while the latter suggests that even if the act is still wrong, the actor is not culpable. In Anglo - American criminal law, justifications and excuses constitute the mainstay and research focus of defense, and the relevant content will be specifically discussed in the related chapters. As for the theme of this chapter, the following content will mainly revolve around *actus reus* as the first principle of criminal liability.

(真正的)抗辩事由可进一步分为正当化事由(如正当防卫)和可宽恕事由(如胁迫)。前者表明,虽然犯罪定义要求的各个要素已齐备,但行为本身却不具备不法性,而后者则表明,即使行为不正当,但行为人却不具备主观上的可谴责性。在英美刑法中,正当化事由和可宽恕事由构成抗辩事由的主体和研究重点(相关内容会在相应章节中予以专门探讨)。就本章主题而言,后文内容将主要围绕作为刑事责任第一原则的客观行为所展开。

3.1.3 The First Principle of Criminal Liability(刑事责任的第一原则)

The *actus reus* (act requirement) is the first principle among the constituent elements of criminal responsibility, because in a free society we punish people only for what they *do*, but not for their anti - social ideas, desires or intentions. Without doubt, thoughts cannot be punished. Punishing thoughts stretches the reach of the criminal law too far, an accused might be punished even he is too irresolute even to begin to translate into action. Thus, the general aim of modern criminal law is to forbid certain types of conduct, which is of great significance for human rights protection and preventing arbitrary punishment. So, to *wish* someone die, or to *think about* taking someone's wallet when he's not looking would not be a crime, because it is only a mental state and lacks act requirement. Attitudes have to turn into deeds, this requirement is called manifest criminality. Manifest criminality leaves no doubt about the criminal nature of the act.[1] The bottom line: we don't punish thoughts because it's impractical,

---

[1] For more details, see George Fletcher, *Rethinking Criminal Law*, Little, Brown, 1978, p. 115 - 116.

inequitable, and unjust.[1]

在刑事责任的构成要素中,客观要件(行为要件)是其中的第一原则,因为在一个自由社会中,行为人只能基于其做了什么,而不能基于其反社会的想法、愿望、意图而受到惩罚。毫无疑问,思想不能构成犯罪,因为惩罚思想将使刑罚的范围过度延伸,即使是并没有下定决心要真正付诸行动的人都会被纳入刑法的打击范围。因此,现代刑法普遍将行为作为评价中心,这对于人权保障和防止刑罚恣意具有重要意义。由此,"希望他人去死",或者"想要趁着他人不备而拿走他的钱包",这些都不是犯罪,因为其只是主观心态,而欠缺行为要件。主观心态必须外化为实际行动,这样才能表明存在明显的不法性(manifest criminality),以征表行为的犯罪性质。因此,我们应坚守这样的底线:不惩罚思想,因为这既不现实,也不公平,更不正当。

Here arethe reasons to further explain why there must be an act to impose criminal liability: First, it's impossible to prove a mental attitude by itself. We can only infer the state of mind from actions, so acts help to prove intent. Second, it's terribly hard to separate day dreaming and fantasy from true criminal intent. Few angry thoughts like "I' m gonna kill you for that!" turn into actual killing. Punishment has to wait for practical action to prove the actor really intends to commit a crime. Third, a mental attitude by itself doesn't hurt anybody. Unlike the moral law, the criminal law demands actual criminal acts. Fourth, it reserves the harsh sanction of the criminal law for cases of actual danger. Fifth, it protects the privacy of individuals. The law doesn't have to pry into the thoughts of individuals unless the thinker crosses "the threshold of manifest criminality."[2]

施加刑事责任必须具有客观行为的理由为:第一,主观态度本身很难被证明。犯罪意图无法被观测,其只能通过行为被推断,因此只有行为才能说明犯意真实存在。第二,真正的犯罪意图和普通的幻想很难被精确地区分。诸如"我要杀了你"等愤慨想法,在现实中很少被转化为真正的行动,只有当行为人通过实际行动证明其有真实的犯罪意图,刑罚才能被施加。第三,主观心态本身不会产生任何危害。不同于道德评判,刑法只有基于实际的犯罪行为才能被适用。第四,刑罚是最严厉的制裁措施,所以只能用于有实际危险性的情形。第五,这有助于保护个人的隐私。法律并不窥探人们的内心想法,除非行为人"跨过了迈向明显犯罪行为的门槛"。

Criminal acts include action and inaction (omission). The former is manifested as positive physical movements, which is a typical act, while the latter does not require

---

[1] See Glanville Williams, *Criminal Law*, 2nd edition, Stevens and Sons, 1961, p. 1 – 2.

[2] See Joel Samaha, *Criminal Law*, 11th edition, Wadsworth Cengage Learning Press, 2014, p. 97.

bodily movements and is a negative act. With the development of criminal law, there are also criminal possessions which punish the control and domination of things. The theory of Anglo – American criminal law generally believes that possession is neither a physical movement nor an omission,[1] but still considers it as a form of act. Besides, some crimes regard the individual's state as the *actus reus*. Therefore, *actus reus* or act requirement sometimes may not be directly translated as "act", because criminal omissions, criminal possessions, and criminal status could broaden the connotation of act. And regardless of the form of act, perpetrator must be voluntary, which is the voluntariness requirement. The following will provide specific discussions on these contents.

客观行为可以分为作为和不作为,前者表现为积极的身体动作,是典型意义上的行为,而后者无须肢体运动,表现为一种消极的行为。随着刑法的发展,还出现了持有型犯罪这种行为类型,"持有"表现为对物的控制和支配。英美刑法理论一般认为它既不是作为(肢体运动)也不是不作为,但仍然将其视作一种行为形式。一些犯罪还会将个人所处的状态当作犯罪的客观行为。所以,客观要件(*actus reus*)或者说行为要件(act requirement)有时难以被直接理解为一种"行为(act)",因为不作为犯、持有型犯罪和状态犯会将行为的内涵扩宽。而不管对行为作何种形式的把握,它都必须是行为人自愿发出的,这便是行为的自愿性要件。下文将针对这些内容展开具体论述。

3.2 The "Voluntary" Act Requirement("自愿性"行为要件)

Only *voluntary* acts qualify as criminal *actus reus*. "An act is a muscular contraction, and something more. The contraction of muscles must be willed".[2] According to the Model Penal Code (MPC), "A person is not guilty of an offense unless his liability is based on conduct that includes a voluntary act". The rationale that explain the reason why only voluntary acts qualify as criminal acts goes like this: Criminal law only punishes people should be blamed, and we can only blame people who are responsible for their acts, and people can only be responsible for their voluntary acts.

只有自愿行为才能被视作行为要件中的行为,因为"一个行为不仅是肌肉收缩,这样的肌肉收缩还应是具备意愿的"。《模范刑法典》规定:"行为人不构成犯

[1] See Wayne R. Lafave, *Criminal Law*, 3rd edition, West Group, 2002, p. 211.
[2] Oliver Wendell Holmes, *The Common Law*, Little, Brown, 1963, p. 46 – 47.

罪,除非行为人的举止包括一个自愿的行为”。之所以只能将自愿行为视作犯罪行为当中的行为,主要是基于以下理由:刑罚惩罚的是应当被谴责的人,而只有应当对其行为负责的人才是可以被谴责的,人们只能对其自愿行为负责。

The MPC, as well as many state criminal codes, define “voluntary” by naming involuntary acts. The drafters seemed to be content with listing acts which are not voluntary, and did not attempt to explicitly define “voluntariness”. Generally, the list includes movements during various forms of automatism (reflexes or convulsions; sleepwalking; unconsciousness; actions under hypnosis). The MPC adds a fourth catchall category that (to a certain extent) defines voluntary acts. Here is the MPC scheme: “The following are not voluntary acts within the meaning of this Section: (a) a reflex or convulsion; (b) a bodily movement during unconsciousness or sleep; (c) conduct during hypnosis or resulting from hypnotic suggestion; (d) a bodily movement that otherwise is not a product of the effort or determination of the actor, either conscious or habitual.”

《模范刑法典》以及许多州刑法典都未明确界定“自愿”的定义,仅止步于列举出非自愿的行为有哪些,来反向解释何为“自愿”。一般而言,对非自愿行为的列举包括各种不受控制的身体举动(反射性动作或抽搐、痉挛;梦游;无意识的举动;催眠状态下的行动)。《模范刑法典》在此之外还增加了第四种兜底的类型,而该兜底条款的表述在一定程度上也暗示和反证了何为自愿行为。以下是《模范刑法典》的规定:“下列动作不属于本条规定的自愿行为:(a)反射动作或痉挛;(b)在无意识或者睡眠中的身体动作;(c)处于催眠状态中的动作或者由催眠中的暗示所引起的动作;(d)非基于行为人的意思活动或意思决定而作出的有意识或者习惯性的其他身体动作。”

Notice that according to the MPC, conduct only has to “*include* a voluntary act”, hence not all “bodily movements” have to be voluntary. Therefore, voluntary act requirement does not necessarily demand that every act up to the moment the crime is completed be voluntary (the act directly causing a criminal result can be involuntary), in so far as there’s one voluntary act, other acts surrounding the crime may be involuntary. For example, a person who’s subject to frequent fainting spells voluntarily drives a car and faints while he’s driving, then loses control of the car and hits a pedestrian. The driver’s voluntary act is the one that counts, so the fainting spell doesn’t relieve the driver of criminal liability.[1] The MPC's one – voluntary – act – is – enough definition is followed by most statutes.

并且,《模范刑法典》并不要求所有的身体举动都必须出于自愿,其只是说整个行动过程中必须"包括一个自愿的行为"。因此,自愿性要件并不要求犯罪完成前的各个环节都是自愿的(直接引起危害结果的行为可以不具有自愿性),只要其中包括了一个自愿的行为,那么整个犯罪过程中的其他行为也可以是非自愿的。例如,一个经常晕厥的人自愿驾驶汽车,并在驾驶过程中出现晕厥,导致汽车失控并撞向了行人。其中就具有一个自愿行为(自愿驾驶汽车),所以撞人时处于晕厥并不能成为驾驶人的免责事由。许多借鉴了《模范刑法典》的州刑法典也采用了"一个自愿行为即充要"的模式。

Moreover, the voluntariness requirement may be used in two senses. One is that it only refers to the willingness and control to drive bodily movements, which is only a factor that constitutes *actus reus*. Another involves the subjective culpability of the perpetrator, which is often used in practice as a defense against subjective guilt. For example, if the perpetrator is forced to rape others under strong threats, then the act of rape is entirely due to his conscious control over his own body. However, he can raise defenses such as duress to demonstrate that the act was not done voluntarily, thereby achieving the effect of being excused. The latter form of voluntariness is also clearly reflected in *Tippetts* mentioned below. As for the act requirement, voluntariness should be understood in the first sense, as an element of the act itself.

此外,行为的"自愿性"要件会在两种含义上被使用。一种含义是,它仅指驱动身体动作的意愿和控制力,其只是构成客观行为的一个因素。而另一种含义则涉及行为人的主观可责罚性,它常在实践中被当作一种阻却主观罪过的抗辩事由。例如,行为人在强力威胁下被迫强奸他人,其强奸行为完全出于他对自己身体的意识支配和控制,但他可以提出胁迫这类抗辩事由,来表明强奸并不是他自愿所为,从而达到免责的效果。后一种含义的"自愿性"在下文提及的蒂皮茨案中也有明显体现。而就行为要件而言,"自愿性"则应在第一种含义上予以把握,它是行为本身的一个要素。

[1] See Brown v. State(1997).

■ Case Study(案例学习)

State v. Tippetts, Court of Appeals of Oregon, 180 Or. App. 350, 43 P.3d 455 (2002)(州诉蒂皮茨案)

Fact(基本案情)

The police officers searched defendant's house, and found methamphetamine and a weapon. The officers arrested and took the defendant to the Washington County Jail, where the prison guard searched him and found a small bag of marijuana in his pants pocket. Based on the marijuana, the state charged defendant with supplying contraband. A person commits the crime of supplying contraband if "the person knowingly introduces any contraband into a correctional facility, youth correction facility or state hospital." [Ore. Rev. Stat. § 162.185(1)(a)]

警方搜查了被告的住所,并在房屋中搜出了甲基苯丙胺类药物和一把武器。警方遂逮捕了被告,随后将其带至华盛顿县监狱。之后,狱警对被告进行了检查,并在被告的裤子口袋里发现了一小包大麻。据此,控方指控被告成立供应违禁品罪(Supplying Contraband)。根据俄勒冈州刑法[Ore. Rev. Stat. § 162.185(1)(a)],"若行为人明知地(knowingly)将违禁品带入矫正机构、青少年矫正机构或州立医院",将成立供应违禁品罪。

Dispute(主要争议)

At trial, defendant argued that he could be found guilty of that crime only if he voluntarily introduced the contraband into the jail. He contended that no reasonable juror could find that he acted voluntarily, once he was arrested, he could not avoid taking the marijuana with him into the jail. On appeal, defendant renews his argument based on Ore. Rev. Stat. § 161.095(1), which provides: The minimal requirement for criminal liability is the performance by a person of conduct which includes a voluntary act or the omission to perform an act which the person is capable of performing.

在初审中,被告认为只有当其自愿地将违禁品带入监狱时才构成本罪,但是由于其被逮捕,其不可避免地将大麻携带在身,故其并不是自愿地实施这一行为。在上诉中,被告援引俄勒冈州刑法[Ore. Rev. Stat. §161.095(1)]进一步重申其主张。该条文规定:只有当行为人实施了包含一个自愿行为在内的行为举止,或者怠于履行一个其本可以履行的作为义务,其才应当承担刑事责任。

The state defend that Ore. Rev. Stat. § 161.095(1) requires (1) that the act that gives rise to criminal liability be performed or initiated by the defendant and (2) that the act be voluntary. Ore. Rev. Stat. §161.085(2) defines the phrase "voluntary act" as "a bodily movement performed consciously." The state reasons that the word "consciously" means "aware" and that an act will be voluntary as long as the defendant is aware that it is occurring. Besides, the Oregon Revised Statutes requires "the performance by a person of conduct which includes a voluntary act", which means, even if defendant did not voluntarily introduce the marijuana into the jail after the police arrested him, he voluntarily possessed it before he was arrested, and that is sufficient to hold defendant criminally liable for the later involuntary act of introducing the marijuana into the jail.

俄勒冈州刑法[Ore. Rev. Stat. §161.095]要求:(1)能够引起刑事责任的行为应由被告实施或发起,并且(2)该行为应出于自愿。该条第(2)项进一步将"自愿行为"定义为"有意识的身体举动"。本案控方据此认为,"有意识的"(consciously)代表"知道"(aware),所以,只要被告知道某行为正在发生,那么他就是自愿的。此外,俄勒冈州刑法要求"整个行为过程中包括一个自愿行为"即可。这意味着,即使被告由于被逮捕而并不是自愿将大麻带进监狱,但他却自愿在被逮捕前就持有大麻,这就足以使其为后续的将大麻带入监狱的行为承担责任。

Conclusion(结论)

The court of appeals reversed the conviction for supplying contraband. Applied to the charge of supplying contraband, it requires: (1) that defendant either initiate the introduction of contraband into the jail or cause it to be introduced; (2) that he do so consciously. Defendant did not initiate the introduction of the contraband into the jail or cause it to be introduced in the jail. Rather, the contraband was introduced into the jail only because the police took defendant (and the contraband) there against his will. A voluntary act requires something more than awareness. It requires an ability to choose which course to take—i. e., an ability to choose whether to commit a crime. For example, a person may be aware that a particular act is being committed during a seizure or during a reflexive act, but that fact alone does not make the act voluntary. Moreover, a prior voluntary act may be regarded as sufficiently for liability to be imposed, however, this need to base on the entire course of conduct, to measure the specific conduct that resulted in the injury. Therefore, the mere fact that defendant voluntarily possessed the drugs before he was arrested is insufficient to hold him criminally liable for the later act of introducing the drugs into the jail. Rather, to satisfy Ore. Rev. Stat. §161.095(1), the involuntary act must, at a minimum, be a reasonably foreseeable consequence of the prior voluntary act. On these facts, no reasonable juror could find that the introduction of contraband into the jail was a reasonably foreseeable consequence of possessing it.

上诉法院最终撤销了对被告的定罪。成立供应违禁品罪,需要:(1)被告发起将大麻带入监狱的行为,或者由他造成大麻被带入监狱的局面;(2)以上都是有意识的举动。但被告并没有发起这样的行为,也并不是由他造成了这样的局面。相反,是警方以违背被告意愿的方式将他(连同违禁品)带入了监狱。自愿行为不仅是“明知”,更代表着一种选择能力——选择是否要实施犯罪行为的能力。例如,在癫痫发作期间或者在反射性动作中,行为人也可能知道正在发生什么,但这并不代表行为就是自愿的。此外,虽然前期的自愿行为的确可能使行为人承担刑事责任,但这却需要站在整个行为过程的维度来衡量后续实际造成结果的行为。因此,仅仅因为被告在被逮捕前自愿持有毒品,并不足以使其为将毒品带入监狱的行为承担责任。要满足俄勒冈刑法[Ore. Rev. Stat. § 161.095(1)]的要求,则需要后续实施的非自愿行为至少应是前期自愿行为的合理预期结果。但基于本案事实情况,无法认为被告将违禁品带入监狱的行为是前期自愿持有行为的合理预期结果。

Questions: **1.** Dose the voluntariness equal to the awareness according to the court of appeals in *Tippetts*? (Please scan the QR code on the right to get the answer)

根据该案中上诉法院的说理,解释“自愿”和“知道”是否等同?(答案请扫描右侧二维码获取)

2. How to comprehend the one - voluntary - act - is - enough rule according to the court of appeals in *Tippetts*? (The way to obtain the answer is the same as above)

根据该案中上诉法院的说理,如何理解“一个自愿行为即充要”规则?(答案获取方式同上)

■ Curriculum Ideology and Politics(课程思政)

Understand the importance of voluntary act requirement in safeguarding personal freedom, and recognize the connections and differences between Chinese and Anglo - American criminal laws. (1) The voluntariness requirement avoids punishment for acts that individuals cannot control and reasonably expect, and has important practical significance in safeguarding personal freedom. (2) Chinese criminal law does not directly express the voluntariness requirement, but both the theory and practice will limit the act in criminal law to exclude punishment for involuntary act. Besides, “One -

voluntary – act" in Anglo – American criminal law is similar to the logic of "free preceding act" adopted by Chinese criminal law theory. So, even though the specific approaches are different, the two systems achieve the same goals.

使学生明白自愿性要件对保障个人自由的重要作用,并认识中美刑法的联系和差异。(1)自愿性要件避免了刑法对个人无法控制和合理预期的行为进行处罚,在保障个人自由上具有重要的实践意义。(2)我国《刑法》条文并没有直接表达行为的自愿性要求,但理论和实践都会对刑法意义上的"行为"予以限制,以排除对非自愿行为的处罚。而英美刑法"一个自愿行为即充要"原则,与我国刑法理论所采取的"原因自由行为"也具有相通的逻辑。

3.3 Status as a Criminal Act(犯罪行为的状态)

The *actus reus* of certain offences requires proof not of some form of act but simply of the defendant being in a situation which the law forbids him to be or continue to be in. Being drunk when driving is a well – known instance of this form of (situational) liability, conviction for which does not depend upon any act of taking charge of the vehicle. It is based on that the person is in charge and is drunk. Status can be formed in two ways. One results from priory voluntary acts – drug or alcohol addicts are caused by taking drugs and drinking voluntarily. However, another results from no act at all, and we have no control over them, such as the characteristics we're born with like sex, age, and race. Obviously, the latter form of status cannot qualify as *actus reus* or act requirement.

一些犯罪的成立并不要求具备某种形式的行为,只需要被告处于或持续处于某种被法律禁止的状态。在驾车过程中处于醉酒状态就是典型事例,此时责任的施加并不基于任何实际的驾驶行为,而是基于汽车处于行为人的控制下而行为人又处于醉态。状态可以由两种方式形成,一种是源于之前的自愿行为,比如自愿吸毒和自愿饮酒使行为人成为药物和酒精成瘾者。而另一种则不来自任何行为,并且行为人对其也无法控制,例如我们生来就具有的特质:性别、年龄、民族和种族。显然,至少就后一种情形而言,其难以被视作成立犯罪所需的客观要件或者行为要件。

3.3.1 Doubts about Punishing Status(处罚状态的争议)

As the first principleof criminal liability, the *actus reus* (act requirement) requires that punishment can only be imposed for what people did. But punishing a certain state is somehow punishing the person who is in this state. Consequently, Punishing status has always been difficult to dispel doubts about the legitimacy, allowing for criminal conviction in the absence of any wrongdoing. However, in so far as an offence sets a standard of behaviour to which the accused is capable of conforming by appropriate avoiding action, there may no ethical reason to limit the substance of such offences to acts, that is, the accused should be responsible for the situation he has caused. Thus, the problem with situational liability is less the fact that it is objectionable *per se*, but rather that it may stray too far from the criminal law's paradigm of culpable wrongdoing, which can be used for objectionable purposes (such as punishing the individuals' potential propensity to engage in certain harmful conducts to maintain the social stability and order at the cost of personal autonomy).[1] Some scandalous examples are criminalizing addiction to narcotics and membership of a certain party. It is easy to see the value an authoritarian government might reap from such offences. Therefore, in order to prevent the excessive expansion of state power, there needs to be sufficient reasons in legislation to reflect the necessity of using criminal law to prohibit a certain status, manifesting that the status prohibited by law is not only something that the accused is able to avoid, but also something that he should avoid.

行为要件作为刑事责任成立的第一原则,它要求刑罚只能针对行为。而处罚某种状态实则就是在惩罚处在这种状态中的人。所以,对状态予以惩罚,始终难以摆脱刑罚施加的正当性疑虑,因为它使刑法在没有行为的情况下介入。不过,如果法律禁止的状态是行为人有能力去合理避免的,那么处罚这种状态就未必不具有合理性,即行为人应对他造成的状态负责。所以,虽然对状态施加刑罚令人生疑,但这并不意味着"状态犯"本身一定要被反对,之所以对其抱有疑虑,是因为它极大地偏离了刑法只针对"不法行为"的核心观念,从而可能被用来推行某些令人警惕的目的与诉求(比如,将个人可能实施某些危害行为的潜在倾向作为刑罚适用对象,以牺牲个人自治空间为代价,换取社会的稳定有序)。试图对药物成瘾状态和某种组织身份进行犯罪化,就是典型的例子,将这类状态定义为犯罪,会轻易促成专制政府推行其国家意志和政策诉求。因此,要防止国家权力的过度膨胀,立法就需要有充分的理由来体现用刑法禁止某种状态的必要性,以表明法律禁止的状态不光是行为人能够避免的,也是其应当避免的。

3.3.2 The Constitutional Concerns about regarding status as the actus reus(将状态视为客观行为的合宪性疑虑)

Punishing status may violate the Eighth Amendment to the U. S. Constitution

〔1〕 See William Wilson, *Criminal Law*, 7th edition, Pearson Education Limited Press, 2020.

commanding that "cruel and unusual punishments" shall not be "inflicted", because punishment is inflicted only on a condition rather than an act. This violation was confirmed by the U. S. Supreme Court in *Robinson v. California* (1962). In *the case*, Robinson was convicted for violating a California statute making it a misdemeanor "to be addicted to" narcotics. The Supreme Court agreed that punishing Robinson solely for his addiction to heroin was cruel and unusual punishment, and expressed the ban on status crimes in various ways: The statute created a crime of personal condition, punishing Robinson for who he was (heroin addict), not for what he did; the statute punished the sickness of heroin addiction; the statute punished a condition that may be "contracted innocently and involuntarily".

处罚某种状态有违美国《宪法第八修正案》,因为仅仅处罚某种状态而不是行为,涉嫌违背该修正案不得"施加残忍的和非常的刑罚"的要求。对此,美国联邦最高法院在罗宾逊案(Robinson v. California, 1962)的审理中予以了确认。在该案中,罗宾逊因为违反了一项加利福尼亚州法规而被定罪,根据该州法规,药物"成瘾"行为构成一项轻罪。最高法院认为,仅仅因为对海洛因成瘾就处罚罗宾逊,这构成残酷的和非常的刑罚。最高法院以多种表达方式阐明了这种状态犯为什么要被禁止:该法律将个人的状况规定为犯罪,并仅仅因为罗宾逊是谁(一个海洛因成瘾者)而非其做了什么而施加刑罚;该法规处罚的是海洛因成瘾这种"疾病";该法规很可能处罚一种"无辜和非自愿形成"的状况。

A comparable case is *Powell v. Texas* (1968). In *Powell*, Powell was arrested and charged under a Texas statute, which provided: Whoever shall get drunk or be found in a state of intoxication in any public place, or at any private house except his own, shall be fined not exceeding one hundred dollars. Powell appealed to the U. S. Supreme Court, his argument to Court was that "the disease of chronic alcoholism" destroyed "his will power to resist drinking and appearing drunk in public", so the statute, which "criminally punishes an ill person for conduct" he can't control, violates the ban on cruel and unusual punishment. However, *Robinson* was distinguished on the ground that *Powell* was not convicted for being a chronic alcoholic, but for being in public while drunk. Unlike *Robinson*, the sanctions of the statute were not directed at "mere status", but at a socially offensive behavior: the actor appears in public drunk, which means the statute includes the requirement of some act in addition to the condition.

与罗宾逊案具有比较意义的是鲍威尔案(Powell v. Texas,1968)。在鲍威尔案中,鲍威尔基于一项得克萨斯州法律而被逮捕和起诉,根据该州法律,任何人在公共场所和非本人的私人住所醉酒或被发现处于醉态,将被处以最高100美元的罚金。鲍威尔向最高法院上诉,主张"酒精成瘾这种疾病"摧毁了他"抵抗饮酒和在公共场所醉酒的意志力",因此,该法规将"一个无法控制其举止的病人予以了刑罚",这有违禁止施加残酷的和非常的刑罚的宪法性要求。但鲍威尔案与罗宾逊案的不同之处在于,鲍威尔案的定罪并不仅是基于行为人是一个酒精成瘾者,而是基于其在醉态下出现在了公共场所中。不同于罗宾逊案中的情形,该项法规并不是针对单纯的状态,而是针对一种具有社会意义的冒犯举动:行为人醉酒出现在公共场所中,其相当于在状态本身之外还额外要求具备某种行为。

Therefore, the U. S. Supreme Court did not consider the Texas statute unconstitutional and upheld Powell's conviction. The further issue that may be raised by the *Powell* is, is the principle of *actus reus* a constitutional command? Or, how far the U. S. Constitution goes into the principle of *actus reus*? In *Powell*, the U. S. Supreme Court further concluded: *Robinson* brings this Court but a very small way into the substantive criminal law, and the Constitution bans only pure status as a basis for criminal liability, which means that the Supreme Court should not broadly place constitutional review in the substantive criminal laws of the states under the aegis of the Cruel and Unusual Punishment Clause. Finally, the Court invoked federalism to support its hands - off position regarding the principles of criminal liability. How to establish *actus reus* of crimes falls within the scope of the province of the States.

所以,美国联邦最高法院并未认为鲍威尔案中的得克萨斯州法规违宪,并维持了对鲍威尔的定罪。而该案引申出的问题是,客观要件(行为要件)是否本身就构成一项宪法性要求?或者说,即使客观要件(行为要件)是一项宪法性要求,那么这对实体刑法的建构又能产生多大的影响?对此,联邦最高法院在鲍威尔案的说理中进一步总结道:只有罗宾逊案中的情形才会真正涉及某些合宪性疑虑,即宪法禁止的只是将纯粹的状态犯罪化,除此之外并无更多,而联邦最高法院也不应该轻易地凭借"禁止残酷和非常的刑罚"这样的宪法条款,来广泛地将合宪性审查置于各州的实体刑法之上。由此,联邦最高法院基于联邦制度,采取了针对刑事责任成立的一般要素的不介入立场,也即,如何设立犯罪的客观要件,属于各州自治的范畴。

Most Anglo - American criminal law booksand criminal law classes, spend lots of time or space on the Constitution and the general principles of criminal liability. At the time the cases were decided, there was a saying that an "activist" Supreme Court would use the "cruel and unusual punishment" ban and other provisions in the U. S. Constitution to write a constitutional doctrine of criminal liability and responsibility. It never happened. Real cases in courts since *Powell* haven't tried to bring the constitutional review further into the principles of criminal liability than *Robinson* brought it in 1962. It's left in the hands of legislatures to adopt general principles of liability and elements of specific crimes in criminal codes. It's left in the hands of courts to interpret and apply the code's provisions in decisions involving individual defendants.[1]

许多英美刑法教科书和刑法课程会花较多的篇幅或时间来谈论宪法与刑事责任成立的一般原则。在上述两案发生的时期,美国社会普遍存在一种看法,即联邦最高法院会积极地利用"禁止残酷和非常的刑罚"以及其他宪法条款来为刑事责任的成立设定宪法性教义,但这其实从未发生。自鲍威尔案之后,基本没有法院会直接将合宪性审查介入刑事责任成立的一般要素当中,即使有,也不会超越罗宾逊案中的那种情形。责任成立的一般原则,以及法典中具体犯罪的成立要素,这些都是交由立法者决定的事项,而法院的工作只是解释和适用具体的刑法条款。

■ Case Study(案例学习)

People v. Davis, Court of Appeals of New York, 33 N. Y. 2d 221, 306 N. E. 2d 787 (1973)(人民诉戴维斯案)

Fact(基本案情)

The officer searched a house, and observed the defendant about to inject himself with a syringe later determined to contain heroin. In effecting the arrest, the officer found fresh needle marks on defendant's right arm. Defendant admitted that he had been using heroin for about a year and a half. In the end, the defendant has been convicted of criminal possession of a dangerous drug in the sixth degree and criminal possession of a hypodermic instrument.

警员对某处房屋进行了搜查,发现被告正准备向自己注射海洛因。在对其进行逮捕时,警员发现被告右臂上有新鲜针孔。被告承认一年半以来他一直持续使用海洛因。最终,被告被认定构成六级持有毒品罪(criminal possession of a dangerous drug in the sixth degree)和持有药物注射器罪(criminal possession of a hypodermic instrument)。

Dispute(主要争议)

At trial, the defendant offered evidence which showed that he was, in fact, a

[1] See Joel Samaha, *Criminal Law*, 11th edition, Wadsworth Cengage Learning Press, 2014, p. 104 – 106.

narcotic addict. The defendant's argument implicates that it constitutes cruel and unusual punishment to impose a criminal penalty upon an addict who possesses narcotics and associated paraphernalia for his own use. It is logically appealing that if an addict cannot, consistent with the Federal and State Constitutions, be punished for being in the status or condition of addiction, he cannot be punished for the acts of possessing for his personal use narcotics and associated instruments. After all, drug addiction leads to the prossession of narcotic, which acts are realistically inseparable.

在初审中,被告出示证据表明自己的确是一个药物成瘾者。如果一个药物成瘾者,由于持有药物和供自己吸食药物的工具而被处罚,那么这将构成残忍的和不同寻常的惩罚。其中暗含的逻辑是,如果法院处罚一个成瘾者的成瘾状态本身是有违联邦和州宪法的话,那么法院也不能因为该成瘾者持有药物和相关物品而对其施以处罚,毕竟,正是因为药物成瘾才会持有药品等相关物品,这二者是不可分割的。

Conclusion(结论)

The Court of Appeals of New York affirmed the conviction of state court in this case. According to the appellate court, there is no square holding for defendant's position that acts incident to addiction may not be punished. Actual behavior may be punished even the condition or status of addiction itself cannot. And strong reasons of public policy militate against recognition of defendant's constitutional claim and the drug dependence defense. Firstly, recognizing the defense of drug dependence may be extended to other crimes which can be shown to arise from the compulsive craving for drugs like robberies and burglaries. Secondly, if "mere purchase or possession" by the addict for his own use is protected, then what about the "mere sale" to the same addict? Thirdly, if punish an addict who, out of a compulsive craving for drugs, merely purchases or possesses illicit drugs for his own use is unreasonable, then why an addict who, out of the same craving, steals to fund his habit is blameworthy ? Fourthly, we should not lose sight of the utility of such penalties to law enforcement. For example punishments can facilitate the policy of elimination of the drug traffic, persuade addicts to undertake rehabilitation, and prevent the addict from being the witting or unwitting tool of the drug trafficker.

但在本案中,上诉法院认可了州法院的定罪。根据上诉法院的说理,被告的主张不能得到支持,因为不得处罚某种状态本身,并不代表不能处罚实际存在的关联行为。上诉法院进一步指出,公共政策上的有力理由也反对被告提出的抗辩。首先,诸如抢劫和偷盗等犯罪也可能是由于毒品成瘾而实施,关于药物依赖的抗辩可能会被过度用至这些犯罪。其次,如果成瘾者的“购买和持有”是不该被惩罚的行为,那么向该成瘾者的“贩卖”是否也不能被处罚?再次,该成瘾者基于其药物成瘾而仅购买和持有毒品供自己使用,如果认为此时对其施加刑罚是不合理的,那么,为什么对通过盗窃资金来供给自己的成瘾者,就一定施以盗窃罪处罚?毕竟二者都是同样的药物成瘾。最后,审理法院应该认识到对药物成瘾者施加处罚在促进执法上的功效,比如,处罚可以帮助落实消灭毒品交易的政策,促使成瘾者进行矫治,并防止成瘾者在不经意间沦为毒贩的“工具”。

Questions:1. What is the defendant's argument? (Please scan the QR code on the right to get the answer)

被告的主要主张是什么?(答案请扫描右侧二维码获取)

2. Why the Court of Appeals of New York affirmed the conviction? (The way to obtain the answer is the same as above)

为什么上诉法院最终认可了一审法院对被告的定罪?(答案获取方式同上)

3.4 Possession as a Criminal Act(作为犯罪行为的“持有”)

Anglo – American criminal law establishes a number of offences concerned with the possession of prohibited objects and substances. In line with the general pattern of situational liability, the possession of certain contraband does not impose any requirement upon the prosecution to establish any act of (voluntarily) taking possession. Simply in possession of the item is enough. So, possession is a state of affairs, not a way of action. The most common criminal possession crimes in Anglo – American criminal law include possession of weapons, illegal drugs, and drug paraphernalia.

在英美刑法中,许多犯罪规制的是对某些违禁物的持有。持有型犯罪的认定并不要求被告具有某种(自愿)占有的行为,其只需被告对某种违禁品处于实际的持有状态,因此和状态犯一样,“持有”并不是一种直接的行为。英美刑法中比较常见的持有型犯罪包括持有武器、持有毒品、持有吸毒用具。

3.4.1 Incompatibility with the Act Requirement(与行为要件的不兼容)

Precisely because criminal possession manifest as a passive condition, it also appears inconsistent with the act requirement. MPC §2.01(4) provides, “possession is an act… if the possessor knowingly procured or received the thing possessed or was aware of his control thereof for a sufficient period to have been able to terminate his possession.” According to this wording, the *actus reus* may include possession only by means of a legal fiction (pretending something is a fact when it's not, based on a "good" reason for pretending).[1] But no obvious injustice arises by requiring the accused to remedy the possession situation if he is in a position to be able to avoid falling foul of the proscription. Thus, as in the case of situational offences, this is not an argument against possession offences *per se*, only against stretching the connotation of *actus reus* and the net of responsibility too far.[2]

正因为持有型犯罪表现为一种状态,因此其同样面临与行为要件的冲突。《模范刑法典》§2.01(4)规定,"如果持有人明知其获得或者接受该持有物,或者在能够终止其持有的充足时间内,认识到其支配该持有物时,该'持有'构成本条所称的行为"。根据这种措辞,显然只能以法律拟制(legal fiction)的方式(基于某种合理的理由,将原本不是某种事物的东西直接视作这种事物),才能将"持有"纳入客观(行为)要件之中。只要被告处在一种可以避免违反禁令的情况下,那么要求他去消除这种境况就是合理的。所以,和状态犯一样,这种观点不是要反对持有犯罪本身,而是反对把客观行为的内涵和刑事责任范畴扩张得太大了。

For example, a good reason for criminalizing possession as an act is the powerful pull of the idea that "an ounce of prevention is worth a pound of cure". Better to nip the bud of possession before it grows into an act of doing drugs or shooting someone.[3] Also, criminal possession can skillfully relief the burden of proof on the prosecution, facilitating the crime combat, namely, either possession is punished in lieu of prior or future acts by the offender which are closer to harm but harder to prove.[4] And these may explain why it is often thought that "possession does the crime war's dirty work."[5] Therefore, how a principled approach to the issue of possession (and wider situational offences) can be constructed concerns reconciling punishment's protective function with maintaining a basic minimum responsibility for criminal liability to be incurred.[6]

例如,持有型犯罪可明显体现出"高成本的矫治不如小成本的预防"这种极具诱

[1] See Joel Samaha, *Criminal Law*, 11th edition, Wadsworth Cengage Learning Press, 2014, p.115.

[2] See William Wilson, *Criminal Law*, 7th edition, Pearson Education Limited Press, 2020.

[3] See Joel Samaha, *Criminal Law*, 11th edition, Wadsworth Cengage Learning Press, 2014, p.116.

[4] Markus D. Dubber & Tatjana Hörnle, *Criminal Law: A Comparative Approach*, Oxford University Press, 2014, p.206.

[5] Markus D. Dubber, *Policing Possession: The War on Crime and the End of Criminal Law*, 91 Journal of Criminal Law and Criminology 856(2001).

[6] For analysis see M. Dubber, *The Possession Paradigm: The Special Part and The Police Power Model of The Criminal Process*, in R. A. Duff and S. P. Green eds., Defining Crimes, Oxford University Press, 2005.

惑力的超前预防理念,也即,最好在持有毒品或枪支的状况真正演变成吸毒或枪击行为之前,就让刑法介入以防患于未然。此外,持有型犯罪也能巧妙减轻控方的证明负担,以方便国家严密刑事法网。具体而言,真正值得处罚的是之前已经造成实害结果的行为(比如持有贪贿所得的巨额财产),或者是之后可能造成实害结果的行为(比如为了杀人而持有枪支),但要证明前、后行为显然不如证明持有本身容易,故就以处罚持有作为替代。所以,持有型犯罪常被认为承担了"打击犯罪的脏活"。也因此,构建起持有型犯罪(或者说状态犯)的合理根据,实际上就在于调和刑法的社会保护机能(protective function)与其谦抑性之间的张力,也即,究竟是利用刑法的高压来积极管控社会一切问题,还是将刑法的适用范围控制在最小限度内,以体现刑法的最后手段性。

3.4.2 The Types of Possession(持有的类型)

There is adistinction between actual and constructive possession. Actual possession means items are"on you", such as drugs in your pocket, while constructive possession means items are not on your person but in places under your control like your car or apartment. Whether actual or constructive, possession can be either "knowing" or "mere". Knowing possession means you are aware of what you possess (you know you are possessing a weapon), and knowing doesn't mean you have to know it's a crime to possess the item. Mere possession means you don't know what you possess (you got a briefcase and you don't know the fact that it is filled with drugs, then you may be in mere possession of the drugs). All but two states (North Dakota and Washington) require knowing possession. Also, almost all the cases in the court reports are constructive possession cases, and they're almost all drug and/or weapons cases.[1]

持有包括两种类型:实际(actual)持有和推定(constructive)持有。实际持有意味着物品确实处于本人身上,比如本人口袋里的大麻。推定持有指物品并不实际处于本人身上,但却处于能被本人支配的地方,比如本人的汽车和公寓。而无论是实际持有还是推定持有,都可能构成明知的持有(knowing possession)和事实上的持有(mere possession)。明知的持有意味着持有人知道他所持有的是何物(如持有人知道他正在持有一把武器),当然,明知并不意味着持有人必须知道持有武器构成犯罪。事实上的持有意味着持有人并不知道他持有的是什么(如持有人得到了一个公事包,但不知道里面装有毒品,那么他可能对这些毒品构成事实上的持有)。几乎所有的州(除了北达科他和华盛顿)都要求持有具有明知条件。此外,几乎所

[1] Joel Samaha, *Criminal Law*, 11th edition, Wadsworth Cengage Learning Press, 2014, p. 117.

有诉诸法庭的持有型犯罪涉及的都是推定持有,而且一般都是持有药物或者武器。

3.5　Omissions as Criminal Acts(作为犯罪行为的不作为)

Although the principle remains that generally a person cannot be guilty for omitting to do something and the law traditionally does not force a person to do so, there are exceptional cases where the accused should still be liable. When the criminal law imposes a duty to act and the accused does not perform that act, he may be guilty. This is the criminal omission. Accordingly, criminal omissions satisfy the *actus reus* (act requirement) only when the perpetrator has a legal duty to act actively but not to do. However, to what extent could the exceptional cases that can establish the criminal omission be defined should be based on principle and policy. Besides, it is the values the criminal law ought to incorporate which should be discussed and the clash of values is between interpersonal duties and personal autonomy. This is the reason why liability for omissions remains a controversial topic.[1] Consequently, the list of exceptional cases where the accused is liable for failing to act (i. e. where there is a duty to act) is not closed and remains open to the changes of social concepts.

原则上,行为人不会因为他没有做什么而招致处罚,法律也不会强迫他必须做出某种行为。但在例外情形中,如果法律赋予行为人某种作为义务,而他又没有履行这种义务,那么他将构成犯罪,并为不作为承担责任,这就是不作为犯。据此,只有在具备相应的作为义务又未履行时,不作为才能被认为是成立犯罪所需的客观要件(行为要件)。不过,究竟应当在多大范围内划定不作为犯的内涵,涉及理念和政策的选择,也关涉刑法中的多元价值对立以及由此带来的价值取舍,以及个人的自治权应在多大程度上向人与人之间的相互义务妥协。正是这些宏观的问题,使不作为犯始终充满争议。也因此,能够成立不作为犯的情形(或作为义务的来源)并不是恒定不变的,而是会随着社会观念的变化而变化。

3.5.1　How *Actus Reus* Incorporates Omission(能以不作为实施犯罪的情形)

Here are some specific situations in which we could argue that the offences may be (or may not be) committed by an omission,[2] and they correspond to the two types of omission in Anglo – American criminal law. One type is offenses of failing to act, that

---

〔1〕 See Michael Jefferson, *Criminal Law*, 12th edition, Pearson Education Limited Press, 2015, p. 72, 73.

〔2〕 See Michael Jefferson, *Criminal Law*, 12th edition, Pearson Education Limited Press, 2015, p. 61 – 64.

is directly stipulated by criminal law, with the content of not committing a certain act. Another type is that the crime is usually committed by action, but the accused committed it by omission.

在以下情形中,可以认为法律规定的犯罪能够以(或不能够以)不作为的方式实施,它们对应了英美刑法中不作为犯的两种类型。一种类型是刑法直接规定的,以不实施某种行为为内容的犯罪。另一种类型则是通常由作为的方式施行,但行为人却通过不作为的方式实施的犯罪。

First, because of legislative supremacy, legislator can change the general law that a person is not guilty for omitting to do something and create offences which can be committed only by omissions. In each of these offences it should be noted on whom the duty is imposed. Usually liability is imposed on a certain type of person, since the duty is restricted to a certain class of persons.

第一,基于立法机关的立法权,立法者可以直接改变"行为人不会因为他们没做什么而受到处罚"的原则,并规定一些只能由不作为方式构成的犯罪。但在这些犯罪中也需要明确,究竟是哪些人需要承担作为义务(通常这只关涉少部分处于特定情形中的人)。

Second, in some offences the language of the statute can be read as imposing liability for not doing something, such as permitting one's drivers to break the law if one does not take reasonable steps to prevent breaches, or obstructing the highway by not removing a collapsed wall after being given notice to remove it. But if a statute states "act", that term cannot be construed as including an omission. Legislator stipulated "act", if what the accused did cannot sensibly be described as an "act", he should not be guilty. Some wording of the definition of crime is considered to directly exclude the application of omission, for example, it is impossible to conceive of a person's committing robbery or burglary, which includes "enters" (or "having entered") a building by omission.

第二,某些犯罪定义的措辞可以被认为涵盖了不作为的方式。例如,行为人以不采取阻止措施的方式来允许其驾驶员违法驾驶,又如,行为人在收到告知后,以不移除倒塌物的方式来妨碍交通。不过,如果法规明确以"作为"(act)来表述,那么相应的犯罪就不能被认为包括了不作为。由于立法者直接以"作为"来措辞,所以,如果被告的举止不能被合理地认为是一种"作为",那么他就不构成犯罪。一些犯罪定义的措辞可以被认为是直接排除了不作为的适用,比如,很难想象行为人可以通过不作为的方式"进入"房间进行偷盗或抢劫。

Third, sometimes the courts construe offences as imposing liability for omissions. If the *actus reus* of murder and manslaughter is "causing death", one can cause death by failing to prevent death occurring. "Causing" is therefore sometimes read as requiring an act but sometimes as covering an omission. However, when the offence consists of "causing or permitting", "permitting" covers a failure to act but here "causing" does not.

第三,法院可以通过法律解释,将不作为囊括进犯罪的实施方式中。假如杀人罪的客观要件是"造成死亡",那么"造成"就既可以来自作为也可以来自不作为,因为不阻止死亡发生也能成为造成死亡结果的方式。然而,如果犯罪的客观要件是"造成或允许死亡",由于"允许"本身就体现出不作为,所以此时的"造成"就只能是作为。

3.5.2 The Duties to Act(作为义务的来源)

Although offences, which are normally committed by an act, are capable of being committed by an omission, there must be a duty to act. Notice that this kind of duty should not be understood in a moral sense (duties enforced by conscience, religion, and social norms), omissions are criminal omissions only if defendants had a legal duty to act,[1] because a bystander should not be imposed a duty to help imperiled strangers (even if this is morally noble), otherwise, it is disguised as using the power of criminal law to regulate the individual conscience, and all who did nothing would cause the *actus reus* to happen. Therefore, normally it is for the judge to rule whether such a duty exists. Juries cannot expand and contract the various duties to act,[2] for it might lead to a jury saying that because of the serious harm and their simple emotions, there must have arisen a duty to prevent that result. And here is a list that states when a person is under a such duty:[3]

虽然犯罪也能够以不作为的方式构成,但这需要以作为义务为前提。并且,这种作为义务必须是法律上的作为义务,而不能仅仅停留在道德层面(比如个人良知、宗教信仰或社会风评上的要求),因为一个旁观者或者局外人不应当被强迫去帮助处在险境中的陌生人(即使这在道德上是高尚的),否则就是将公民的个人良知交由刑法的强力来调控,这会轻易地让社会公众面临成立不作为犯罪的可能。也因此,

〔1〕 See, Joel Samaha, *Criminal Law*, 11th edition, Wadsworth Cengage Learning Press, 2014, p. 106.
〔2〕 See, Michael Jefferson, *Criminal Law*, 12th edition, Pearson Education Limited Press, 2015, p. 61.
〔3〕 See, Michael Jefferson, *Criminal Law*, 12th edition, Pearson Education Limited Press, 2015, p. 64 – 70.

一般只能由法官来释明作为义务是否存在,陪审团不能随意扩张或限缩作为义务的成立范围,因为陪审团有可能基于实际出现的严重后果,并出于其朴素的情感,来倒推被告应当具备相应的作为义务以阻止该严重后果的发生。以下情形描述了行为人何时具有作为义务:

1. Duty based upon voluntary assumption. Liability is imposed for failing to perform a duty one has undertaken voluntarily. In other words, no duty will arise if the accused refused to accept the obligation to take care of another but it will arise if he does so and performs it poorly. This head of liability might be extended in the future to cover, for example, joint participation in dangerous sports such as potholing. One problematical question concerns whether, and if so how, a person can give up a duty once he has undertaken it. Another question concerns how far, once one has voluntarily embarked on a duty, one must perform it.

自愿承担的义务。如果某人自愿承担起某项义务而他又未能履行,那么他将有可能构成不作为犯。换言之,如果某人一开始就没有照顾他人,那么他可能并不会承担相应的作为义务。这种情形下的作为义务有可能扩展至共同实施危险活动的场合,比如探险活动。不过,是否可以(以及如何)放弃已承担起的作为义务,以及自愿承担了某种义务后,必须要履行到何种程度才不至于构成相应的不作为犯,这尚有讨论空间。

2. Contractual duty. If one fails to perform a duty imposed by contract, one may be guilty. The contractual duties need not be owed to the victim. Presumably a lifeguard employed by a local authority at a pool or a seaside resort, or a doctor whether employed by the NHS or privately, would be guilty of manslaughter under this exception.

基于合同承担的义务。如果某人未能履行基于合同的义务,那么他可能构成不作为犯罪。不过,合同双方并不一定是被告和受害人。例如,受雇于地方当局的泳池或海边的救生员,或者是受雇于国民医疗机构或私立医院的医生,如果未能履行他们的雇用职责而导致被害人死亡,那么他们有可能构成非预谋杀人罪。

3. Statutory duty. Liability will be imposed if one fails to perform a duty imposed by law. Responsibility may arise out of a blood or marital relationship or be generated by common law in other ways. The main illustration of a duty based upon statute is the obligation of a parent to feed his young child.

法律规定的义务。作为义务也可以源于法律的赋予,比如亲属关系或夫妻关系,或者是普通法上确认的其他情形。法律上的作为义务的一个典型事例即是父母对子女的抚养义务。

4. Duty based upon creation of the peril. If one creates a dangerous situation, one is under a duty to put it right provided that to do so is not dangerous. A passer – by would not be under this duty to act, which is followed by nearly all jurisdictions in America. It is uncertain whether an accused is guilty if it was his omission to act which led to the dangerous situation. One yet unresolved point is whether this principle applies where the original act is justified, such as when the accused acts lawfully in self – defence but then refuses to call the medical services.

基于造成险境的义务。如果某人造成了某种险境,那么他应承担相应的作为义务以排除致害危险(前提是不会把他自身也置于险境当中)。一个偶然出现的路人不具有这样的作为义务,这也是美国绝大多数州所秉持的态度。不过,如果是之前的某种不作为造成了这种险境,那么是否还会产生相应的作为义务,这尚无定论。此外,先前的正当行为能否产生作为义务这也有讨论的余地,比如,正当防卫之后是否有义务为对方寻求医疗帮助。

5. Duty to control conducts of others. Where a person has a right of control over the action of another, he is liable for failing to exercise that control when the other commits an offence.

监管义务。如果某人对他人具有某种监管义务,而其未能履行这种监管义务导致他人实施了犯罪,那么其可能成立不作为犯。

■ Case study(案例学习)

State v. Miranda, Supreme Court of Connecticut, 245 Conn. 209, 715 A. 2d 680 (1998)(州诉米兰达案)

Fact(基本案情)

The defendant lived with his girlfriend and her two children (a 2 – year – old son and the victim of this case, a 4 – month – old daughter). Although he was not the biological father of either child, the defendant took care of them and considered himself to be their stepfather. On that very evening, the victim was taken for treatment of her injuries following a 911 call by the defendant that the child was choking on milk. Upon examination at the hospital, it was determined that the victim suffered from multiple injuries. The trial court found that the injuries, many of which created a risk of death, had been caused by great and deliberate force and that the defendant had been aware of the injuries. The defendant was charged with not preventing the child's mother from inflicting the injuries. The defendant appealed to the Appellate Court, which reversed the assault convictions concluding that the defendant had no legal duty to act under the circumstances of this case.

被告和他的女友以及女友的两个孩子(2 岁的儿子和本案受害人,4 个月大的女儿)同居。虽然被告和两个孩子并无血缘关系,但直至案发时,被告一直照料这两个小孩,并以父亲的身份自居。案发当晚,被告报警称受害人被牛奶呛到,随后受害人被送往医院,并被检查出有多处伤痕。初审法院认定,受害人的多处伤痕均是被严重和有意的暴力造成的,且对其具有死亡危险,而被告对此是知情的。被告被指控没有制止孩子的母亲对孩子实施伤害。上诉法院认为被告不具有相应的作为义务,故撤销了定罪。

Dispute 1(争论点 1)

The Connecticut Supreme Court started by turning attention to the question of whether, even if we assume such a duty exists, the failure to act can create liability under the statute. In other words, by failing to act in accordance with a duty, does a defendant commit a crime, that is not specifically defined by statute in terms of an omission to act but only in terms of "cause and result"? The trend of Anglo – American law has been toward enlarging the scope of criminal liability for failure to act in those situations in which the common law or statutes have imposed an affirmative responsibility for the safety and well – being of others. Criminal liability of parents based on a failure to act in accordance with common – law affirmative duties to protect and care for their children is well recognized in many jurisdictions. Criminal conduct can arise not only through overt acts, but also by an omission to act when there is a legal duty to do so. Omissions are as capable of producing consequences as overt acts. The special relationship exception to the "no duty to act" rule represents a choice to retain liability for some omissions, which are considered morally unacceptable. Therefore, had the defendant been the victim's parent—someone with an undisputed affirmative legal obligation to protect and provide for his minor child—we would conclude that his failure to protect the child from abuse could constitute a violation of the statute.

康涅狄格州最高法院首先讨论了,即使被告具有相应的作为义务,但如果法条只是表述为"造成和导致"(cause and result)而没有直接表明犯罪可以由不作为构成,那么被告是否可以成立不作为犯这一问题。英美刑法的趋势是,如果普通法或实定法规确认应对他人的安全和福利承担确实的责任,那么此时是可以成立不作为犯的。父母如果没有履行得到普通法确认的保护和照顾其孩子的作为义务,将可能承担相应的刑事责任,这得到了许多司法管辖区的认可。犯罪行为不仅可以表现为明显的作为,也可以表现为未履行相应作为义务的不作为。同直接的作为一样,不作为也可以产生危害结果。虽然一般而言,人们并不会被苛求承担相应的作为义务,但一些具有特别关系的情形构成例外,在这些例外情形中,刑事责任依然可能施加给不作为,因为这些不作为在道德上同样是不可接受的。因此,如果被告是受害人的父母,即其具备保护和供养未成年子女的无可争议的法定义务,那么就可以认为,他未能为孩子提供保护以避免孩子遭受虐待,这样的不作为处在法规的规制范围之中。

Dispute 2(争论点 2)

Then the Court turn to the issue of whether the duty to protect can be imposed on the defendant, an adult member of the household unrelated to the child. According to the Court, it is undisputed that parents have a duty to provide food, shelter and medical aid for their children and to protect them from harm. In addition to biological and adoptive parents and legal guardians, there may be other adults who establish familial relationships with and assume responsibility for the care of a child, thereby creating a legal duty to protect that child from harm. Such duties may be regarded as derived from the nature of the circumstances, in other words, the nature of the relationship of the defendant to the victim and whether the defendant, as part of that relationship, had assumed a responsibility for the victim. The Court also recognize the continuing demographic trend reflecting a significant increase in non – traditional alternative family arrangements. Consequently, more and more children will be living with or may depend upon adults who do not qualify as a natural or adoptive parent. To distinguish among children in deciding which ones are entitled to protection based upon whether their adult caregivers have chosen to have their relationships officially recognized hardly advances the public policy of protecting children from abuse.

康涅狄格州最高法院随后探讨了,与被害人并无法律关系的被告是否能够具备相应的作为义务这一问题。根据州最高法院的意见,父母具有保护子女免受伤害的作为义务,这并无争议。但除具有血缘关系和收养关系的父母,以及其他法定监护人之外,可能还会有其他成年人与孩子建立起类似家庭的关系,并承担起照顾孩子的责任,这些成年人因此就同样具有了保护孩子免受伤害的作为义务。在这种情形下,作为义务可以被认为来自特定的事实情况,也即来自被告和受害人的实质性关系,以及被告在这样的关系中是否担负起了对受害人的责任。该州最高法院同样谈到了非传统家庭关系逐步增多的趋势,在这种现实情况下,会有越来越多的孩子和与其不具有血缘关系或收养关系的成年人生活在一起,如果一定要以具有官方确认的关系为依据,那么保护儿童免受伤害的公共政策将得不到有效落实。

Conclusion(结论)

Therefore, the Court conclude that, based on the trial court's findings that the defendant had established a family – like relationship with the mother and her two children, that he had voluntarily assumed responsibility for the care and welfare of both children, and that he had considered himself the victim's stepfather, there existed a common – law duty to protect the victim from her mother's abuse. The judgment of the Appellate Court is reversed.

因此,康涅狄格州最高法院的结论是,被告与两个孩子以及孩子的母亲建立起了家庭关系,他自愿承担起照顾孩子的责任,并将自己视作孩子的继父,所以应当认可其具有保护孩子免受其母亲虐待的普通法上的作为义务。故上诉法院的判决被撤销。

Question:On what basis does the Supreme Court affirm the duty to act of the defendant?(Please scan the QR code on the right to get the answer)

问题:州最高法院基于什么理由认可了被告的作为义务?(答案请扫描右侧二维码获取)

3.6 Exercise(课后练习)(答案请扫描右侧二维码获取)

3.6.1 Test of Terminologies(术语考查)

①criminal liability ②elements of criminal liability

③*actus reus* ④*mens rea*

⑤criminal act ⑥act requirement

⑦"voluntary" act requirement ⑧status

⑨possession ⑩criminal omissions

⑪duty to act

3.6.2 True or False(判断题)

1. Not all the crimes require a *actus reus*.

不是所有犯罪的成立都需要客观(行为)要件。

2. Thoughts can be punished.

思想也可以被施加刑罚。

3. The MPC define the "voluntariness".

《模范刑法典》明确定义了什么是"自愿性"。

4. The MPC, and many state criminal codes, define "voluntary" by naming involuntary acts.

《模范刑法典》以及美国许多州刑法典,都通过列举什么是非自愿行为来反向界定什么是自愿行为。

5. One – voluntary – act – is – enough definition means that conduct only has to include a voluntary act.

"一个自愿行为即充要"原则意味着,只要有一个行为是自愿的即可成立犯罪。

6. Constitutional concerns may arise if punishing status.

处罚状态可能会带来某些合宪性质疑。

7. Actual possession means items not on my person but in places I control, for example, my car or apartment.

如果持有物不在本人身上,但处于本人实际控制的场所中,比如其公寓和汽车里,那么他将构成实际的持有。

8. Omissions are criminal omissions only if defendants had a duty to act.

只有当被告具有作为义务而又未履行时,他才会构成不作为犯罪。

9. If there is a dangerous situation, a passer – by would under a duty to act to put it right.

如果存在某种危险情境,那么即使是偶然路过的路人也应当承担排除危险的作为义务。

3.6.3　Short – answer Questions(简答题)

1. Why only voluntary acts qualify as criminal acts?

为什么只能处罚基于自愿的行为?

2. How does the MPC reflect the voluntariness requirement?

《模范刑法典》是如何体现行为的自愿性要求的?

■ Curriculum Ideology and Politics(课程思政)

Appreciate the significance of the *actus reus* as the first principle of criminal responsibility. *Actus reus*, as the basic prerequisite for initiating punishment, constitutes a barrier to protect individual freedom, which is of great importance for the construction of the society based on the rule of law.

充分领会行为要件作为刑事责任第一原则的重要意义。客观行为要件作为发动刑罚的基本前提,构成了保障个人自由的一道屏障,这对法治社会的构建具有重要作用。

Question: How the Anglo – American criminal law and Chinese criminal law value and reflect the *actus reus*? What enlightenment can we draw from it? (Please scan the QR code on the right to get the answer)

英美刑法和中国刑法都是如何重视和体现行为要件的？我们可以从中得到何种启示？（答案请扫描右侧二维码获取）

■ Summary(总结)

1. The elements of criminal liability include *actus reus* (act, attendant circumstances, result), *mens rea*, and (the absence of) defenses.

刑事责任的构成要素包括客观要件(行为、附随情状和结果)、主观要件和(不具备)抗辩事由。

2. The criminal act is the first principle of criminal liability because there must be an act for a crime to have occurred. Mere thoughts can never be crimes. All crimes include, at a minimum, a criminal act (*actus reus*).

客观行为是成立刑事责任的第一原则,因为是否存在犯罪必须要以行为来体现,仅具有某些想法并不能构成犯罪。所有犯罪的成立都必须要有客观行为(客观要件)。

3. The importance of the voluntary act requirement is that the law punishes people who are responsible for their acts, and people are responsible only for their voluntary acts. However, not all the acts need to be voluntary to satisfy the requirement; conduct has to include only one voluntary act.

"自愿性"要件的意义在于,法律只能处罚能对自己行为负责的人,而人只能对自己的自愿行为负责。要满足"自愿性"要件,并不需要行为过程中的所有行为都是自愿的,只要求其中有一个行为是自愿的即可。

4. The *actus reus* of certain offences requires proof not of some form of act but simply of the defendant being in a situation which the law forbids him to be or continue to be in. Possession may be regarded as a passive condition. However, this is not an argument against status (possession) offences *per se*, only against stretching the net of responsibility too far.

某些犯罪的客观(行为)要件并不是某种形式的行为,而是一种被禁止的状态。持有型犯罪也可被视作一种被动的状态。但是,这不是反对状态犯(持有犯)本身,而是反对把刑事责任范畴扩展太宽了。

5. Status can arise in two ways: a prior voluntary act, or result from no act at

alllike our characteristics. And there are different types of possession according to the law：actual，constructive，knowing，and mere.

状态可能由两种方式形成，一种来自之前的自愿行为，另一种来自我们本身就具有的某些特征。而持有型犯罪也可被分为实际持有、推定持有、明知的持有和事实上的持有。

6. The Constitution bans pure status as a basis for criminal liability. Yet the U. S. Supreme Courtis not willing to expand their interpretation of criminal liability and responsibility beyond that into what has traditionally been the decisions of the courts.

《美国宪法》禁止处罚纯粹的状态。但是，除纯粹的状态，美国联邦最高法院并不热衷于将合宪性讨论广泛介入刑事责任成立的一般要素当中。

7. Omissions are criminal omissions only if defendants had a legal duty（not just a moral duty）to act. Where there is a duty to act comprise blood relationships，contractual relationships，voluntary assumption of a duty of care，statutory duties，and dangerous situations which the accused has created.

如果被告具有某种作为义务（并且不能仅仅是道德上的义务），那么其不作为也可构成犯罪。作为义务一般包括血缘关系、合同关系、先前自愿承担的某种义务，法定义务，以及造成某种险境的先行行为引起的义务。

Chapter 4 The General Principles of Criminal Liability(Ⅱ): Mens Rea, strict liability, mistake, and intoxication

第4章 刑事责任一般原则Ⅱ:主观心态、严格责任、错误和醉态

■ The Learning Objective (学习目标)

1. To understand the modes of mens rea in Model Penal Code.

理解《模范刑法典》规定的主观心态的类型。

2. To understand strict liability, mistake, and intoxication.

理解严格责任、错误和醉态。

3. To compare the difference between mens rea in common law and mens rea in civil law.

比较英美法系和大陆法系的主观心态。

4. To learn some terminologies in this chapter.

掌握本章中的专业术语。

■ Chapter Outline(本章内容概要)

This chapter primarily covers the following aspects of general principles of criminal liability: mens rea, strict liability, mistake, and intoxication, with particular emphasis on the four types of mens rea established by the Model Penal Code. The chapter also introduces the definition and importance of general principles of criminal liability, and elucidates and illustrates them with the help of some classic cases.

本章主要介绍刑事责任一般原则中的以下内容:主观心态、严格责任、错误和醉态,尤其是《模范刑法典》所确定的四种主观心态。本章介绍了刑事责任一般原则的定义及其重要性,并借助一些经典案例予以阐述和说明。

■ Terminologies(专业术语)

mens rea	主观心态
purpose	蓄意
knowledge	明知
recklessness	轻率
negligence	疏忽
strict liability	严格责任
mistake of fact	事实认识错误
mistake of law	法律认识错误
self - induced intoxication	自我诱发性醉态
pathological intoxication	病理性醉态
voluntary intoxication	自愿性醉
involuntary intoxication	非自愿性醉态
American Law Institute(ALI)	美国法学会
Model Penal Code(MPC)	《模范刑法典》

■ The Purpose of Curriculum Ideology and Politics for this Chapter (本章的课程思政目标)

1. Through studying this chapter, students will enhance their international literacy and improve their knowledge system of criminal law. This chapter primarily covers the professional knowledge regarding the general principles of criminal liability in Anglo - American criminal law, as well as the English expressions of criminal law terminology. This content not only improves students' understanding of the criminal law knowledge system but also enhances their legal English skills, thereby cultivating an international perspective and the ability to interact on a global stage.

通过本章学习,使学生提升国际化素养,完善刑法知识体系。本章主要涉及英美刑法刑事责任一般原则的专业知识和刑法专业术语的英语表达。该内容既能完善学生刑法知识体系,又能提升学生法律英语能力,培养其国际视野及国际交往能力。

2. Anglo - American criminal law encompasses unique issues, such as the distinctive concept of strict liability. A rational analysis of the advantages and disadvantages of strict liability in this legal system can enable students to develop a mindset for rational thinking and objective evaluation of criminal law principles.

英美刑法的刑事责任具有一些特别的议题,譬如较为独特的严格责任,理性分析英美刑法严格责任的利弊得失,可以使学生形成理性思考和客观评价刑法知识的思维。

4.1 Mens rea(主观心态)

Mens rea is called "mental element", "mental attitude", "guilty mind", "criminal intent", or "subjective state of mind". In Anglo – American criminal law, a crime has two sides: actus reus and mens rea. So far, we have dealt with one side of actus reus, now it is time to have a look at the other side of mens rea. In fact, it is the other side, that of mens rea or subjective offence elements, that tends to attract far more attention than the first. It is the mens rea that turns the actus reus into a crime, as the old common law put it. When the Model Penal Code drafters went to work, they focused much of their attention on the question of mens rea, not only because they thought that the law on this subject was particularly rife with inconsistencies and irrationalities, but also because the problem of mens rea lay at the heart of the inquiry into criminal liability.[1] The Model Penal Code delineates four levels of mental states, ordered from the most to the least culpable: purpose, knowledge, recklessness, and negligence. Additionally, there exists a special circumstance concerning mens rea that, while not explicitly provided for in the Model Penal Code, is recognized in judicial practice as the doctrine of transferred mens rea. Furthermore, the discussion will proceed to cover the four types of mens rea outlined in the Model Penal Code as well as the doctrine of transferred mens rea.

Mens rea 被称为"主观要件""主观态度""主观罪过""犯罪意图""主观心态"。在英美刑法中,犯罪包含了两个层面:客观行为和主观心态。到目前为止,我们已经研究了客观行为,现在是时候看看主观心态这方面的内容了。事实上,与客观行为相比,主观心态往往会引起更多的关注。恰如传统普通法所言,正是主观心态将客观行为变成了犯罪。《模范刑法典》起草者开始起草工作时,将大部分注意力集中于主观心态方面,不仅是因为起草者认为关于这一主题的法律尤其充斥着不一致和不合理的地方,而且还因为主观心态是追究刑事责任的核心部分。《模范刑法典》列举了4种主观心态,根据受谴责程度由高到低的排序是:蓄意、明知、轻率和疏忽。此外,还有一种涉及主观心态而《模范刑法典》并未明文规定的特殊情形,即犯意转移。接下来的部分将具体探讨《模范刑法典》所规定的4种主观心态以及犯意转移。

---

〔1〕 Markus D. Dubber & Tatjana Hörnle, *Criminal Law: A Comparative Approach*, Oxford University Press, 2014, p. 223.

4.1.1　Purpose(蓄意)

As provided in the Model Penal Code §2.02(2), a person acts purposely with respect to a material element of an offense when: (i) if the element involves the nature of his conduct or a result thereof, it is his conscious object to engage in conduct of that nature or to cause such a result; and (ii) if the element involves the attendant circumstances, he is aware of the existence of such circumstances or he believes or hopes that they exist.[1] According to the Model Penal Code, purpose represents the most culpable state of mind. For example, Mike shoots John with the intention of killing him but misses, Mike will still be guilty of attempted murder, regrardless of whether he is standing next to John or one hundred meters away. This intention is called purpose.

《模范刑法典》第 2.02(2)条规定,在存在下列情形时,行为人对于犯罪本体要件实施的行为具有蓄意:(i)犯罪本体要件中包括特定行为或者特定行为的结果,行为人以有意识的目的实行该行为或者引起该结果;以及(ii)犯罪本体要件中包括附随情状,行为人认识到该情状存在,或者,相信或希望该情状存在。根据《模范刑法典》的规定,蓄意是最值得谴责的主观心态。例如,迈克向约翰开枪,想要杀死约翰却没射中,无论迈克是站在约翰身边还是距其一百米之遥,迈克都构成谋杀未遂罪。这种谋杀意图就是“蓄意”。

4.1.2　Knowledge(明知)

According to the Model Penal Code §2.02(2), a person acts knowingly with respect to a material element of an offense when: (i) if the element involves the nature of his conduct or the attendant circumstances, he is aware that his conduct is of that nature or that such circumstances exist; and (ii) if the element involves a result of his conduct, he is aware that it is practically certain that his conduct will cause such a result.[2] Knowledge means awareness, no matter what the offense element type. Knowledge with respect to result, however, requires awareness of a "practical certainty," so a likelihood close, but not equal, to 100 percent.[3] Even if a person does not necessarily want it to happen, he may be aware of the consequences of his

---

〔1〕 Markus D. Dubber & Tatjana Hörnle, *Criminal Law: A Comparative Approach*, Oxford University Press, 2014, p. 226.

〔2〕 Larry Alexander, Kimberly Kessler Ferzan & Stephen J. Morse, *Crime and Culpability: A Theory of Criminal Law*, Cambridge University Press, 2009, p. 32.

〔3〕 Markus D. Dubber & Tatjana Hörnle, *Criminal Law: A Comparative Approach*, Oxford University Press, 2014, p. 236.

conduct because he knows that the consequences will virtually certainly happen. For example, a person bombs a plane for cargo insurance premiums, not concerned about whether or not the pilot is killed. However, he pursues the goal of claiming compensation and, while not desiring the pilot's death, is aware that it is practically certain. Thus, he has knowledge of the virtual certainty of the pilot's death.

《模范刑法典》第2.02(2)条规定,在存在下列情形时,行为人对于犯罪本体要件实施的行为具有明知:(i)犯罪本体要件中包括特定行为或者附随情状,行为人知道该行为的性质或者该情状存在时;以及(ii)犯罪本体要件中包括行为的结果,行为人知道行为引起结果具有现实的确定性。无论在哪种犯罪类型中,明知都意味着知道。然而,对结果的明知只需具备"现实的确定性",无须100%的确定性,只要极有可能导致结果的发生即可。某人不一定希望某种危害结果的发生,但知道自己行为几乎肯定会引起某种结果的发生。如果某人为索赔货物保险费而炸毁一架飞机,但他不在乎飞行员是否死亡。其所追求的目标是索赔,并不是飞行员的死亡,不过,他也知道飞行员死亡结果几乎是肯定会发生的,所以,其对飞行员死亡结果是明知的心态。

4.1.3 Recklessness(轻率)

The Model Penal Code §2.02(2) provides: "a person acts recklessly with respect to a material element of an offense when he consciously disregards a substantial and unjustifiable risk that the material element exists or will result from his conduct. The risk must be of such a nature and degree that, considering the nature and purpose of the actor's conduct and the circumstances known to him, its disregard involves a gross deviation from the standard of conduct that a law-abiding person would observe in the actor's situation." In everyday language, "recklessness" means taking a substantial and unjustified risk.[1] For example, if Mike knows that it is unsafe to drive 100 miles per hour in torrential rain but does so anyway. Mike is consciously aware of the substantial and unjustifiable risk but disregards it, he has acted recklessly.

《模范刑法典》第2.02(2)条对轻率行为的定义如下:"轻率是指对于犯罪要件本体存在或者其将由行为人的行为引起,有不合理的实质危险时,行为人有意识地无视该危险,对于犯罪本体要件实施的行为具有轻率。对行为人的行为性质、目的和行为人知道的情况予以考虑,危险的性质和程度必须达到行为人无视行为严重背离基于行为人处境之下守法者所应遵守的行为标准。"在日常用语中,"轻率"意味

---

〔1〕 Catherine Elliott & Frances Quinn, *Criminal Law*, Pearson Education Limited, 2016, p. 37.

着承担重大且不合理的风险。例如，如果迈克知道在大暴雨中以161千米/时的速度行驶是非常不安全的，却仍然高速驾驶。迈克有意识地知道重大且不合理的风险存在却无视该风险，那么，迈克就实施了一种轻率行为。

4.1.4 Negligence(疏忽)

The Model Penal Code section 2.02(2) defines negligence, the least culpable state, in this way: "A person acts negligently with respect to a material element of an offense when he should be aware of a substantial and unjustifiable risk that the material element exists or will result from his conduct. The risk must be of such a nature and degree that the actor's failure to perceive it, considering the nature and purpose of his conduct and the circumstances known to him, involves a gross deviation from the standard of care that a reasonable person would observe in the actor's situation." Negligence requires that one is unreasonably unaware of a substantial and unjustifiable risk that the forbidden result may occur or that the relevant circumstances exist.[1] In negligence, the defendant is not aware of the risk but should have been aware of it.[2] The existence of negligence is traditionally determined according to an objective test, which asks whether the defendant's conduct has fallen below the standards of the reasonable person.[3]

《模范刑法典》第2.02(2)条对罪责最小的疏忽是如此定义的："对于犯罪本体要件存在或者其将由行为人的行为引起，有不合理的实质危险时，行为人应当认识该危险但没有认识，对于犯罪本体要件实施的行为具有疏忽。对行为人的行为性质、目的和行为人知道的情况予以考虑，危险的性质和程度必须达到其未能认识该危险严重背离在行为人处境之下的正常人所应遵守的注意标准。""疏忽"要求一个人不合理地不了解可能发生某种禁止的结果或存在相关情况的重大且不合理的风险。在疏忽犯罪中，被告应当知道存在风险，却因疏忽而没有认识到该风险的存在。传统上，根据客观标准来确定疏忽的存在，即考虑被告人行为是否低于普通理性人的标准。

4.1.5 Transferred Mens Rea(犯意转移)

A general principle, well established in the case law, though sometimes criticised by academics and not specified in the Model Penal Code, is the doctrine of transferred

[1] Larry Alexander, Kimberly Kessler Ferzan & Stephen J. Morse, *Crime and Culpability: A Theory of Criminal Law*, Cambridge University Press, 2009, p. 23-24.

[2] Jens David Ohlin, *Criminal Law: Doctrine, Application, and Practice*, Wolters Kluwer, 2016, p. 141.

[3] Catherine Elliott & Frances Quinn, *Criminal Law*, Pearson Education Limited, 2016, p. 30.

mens rea.[1] Transferred mens rea means that the defendant's mens rea is "transferred" from the one object to the other, allowing the courts to treat the defendant as though he had intended to harm the object which he actually harmed. Some commentators argue that the doctrine of transferred mens rea is too broad: people should not be liable for unexpected and unforeseeable consequences. They argue that the correct accusation is an attempt on the intended victim. Transferred mens rea, however, is limited to results that create the same type of harm as was actually intended. Transferring the intention to injure a person did not enable the conviction to stand, because the mens rea transferred has to be the correct mens rea for the offence.[2] Fro example, Mary throws a stone at Jim and hits John, the intent is said to transfer, and Mary will be convicted of intentionally hitting John. If, however, the stone misses Jim and breaks a plate glass window behind him, the intent is not transferred.[3]

虽然时有学术界的批评,且《模范刑法典》未有明文规定,但判例法还是确立了犯意转移学说。犯意转移意味着在被告的犯罪意图从一个对象"转移"到另一个对象时,法院可认定被告犯有其原有计划伤害对象之罪行。某些评论家认为,犯意转移学说过于宽泛:人们不应对意外和不可预见的后果承担责任,正确的指控应是对原来受害者的犯罪未遂。然而,犯意转移仅仅限于造成与实际预期相同类型的危害后果。伤害他人的犯意转移并不一定成立犯罪,转移的犯罪意图必须和原本计划实施的犯罪意图相同才能成立犯罪。例如玛丽向吉姆投掷石头却击中约翰,这意味着犯意转移,玛丽将被判故意攻击约翰。然而,如果石头没击中吉姆,而是打碎了他身后的平板玻璃窗,那么玛丽故意攻击他人的犯罪意图就没有转移。

■ Curriculum Ideology and Politics(课程思政)

Mens rea plays a crucial role in the criminal legislation and theory of all jurisdictions. The theoretical challenges and judicial dilemmas encountered in Anglo - American criminal law regarding mens rea are likely to be mirrored in Chinese criminal law as well. In Anglo - American jurisprudence, there is significant dispute over the definition and types of mens rea, with the existence of mens rea often decided by the jury in judicial practice. The United States' Model Penal Code simplifies mens rea into

[1] Jonathan Herring, *Crininal Law*, Macmillan Publishers Limited, 2011, p. 75.

[2] Jonathan Herring, *Crininal Law*, Macmillan Publishers Limited, 2011, p. 75 - 76.

[3] Shima Baradaran Baughman, Richard G. Singer & John Q. La Fond, *Criminal Law: Examples and Explanations*, Wolters Kluwer, 2022, p. 71.

four types, but it is not legally binding; rather, it serves as an authoritative reference for the judiciary across various states. Although Chinese criminal law contains explicit clauses for criminal intent and criminal negligence, these concepts remain somewhat abstract. In judicial practice, the understanding and application of mens rea typically depend on normative documents, such as judicial interpretations. The Chinese criminal law community often refers to these normative documents for guidance in understanding and applying mens rea (subjective state of mind). Therefore, clarifying the connotation and types of mens rea and determining how to ascertain it in judicial practice is an inescapable issue in Chinese criminal law. Studying the criminal legislation and case law on mens rea in Anglo – American criminal law can broaden students' international perspectives and enable them to deeply consider universal global issues.

主观心态在各国刑事立法及理论中都有着至关重要的地位。英美刑法主观心态所遇到的理论维谷与司法困境,中国刑法大概率也会遭遇。英美刑法对主观心态的内涵界定及类型划分,存在较大争议,甚至其在司法实务中将如何认定行为人的主观心态交由陪审团决定。美国《模范刑法典》将主观心态简化为 4 种类型,但《模范刑法典》毕竟不是具有实际效力的法律规范,其只能作为各州司法的权威参考指南。我国《刑法》虽有犯罪故意和犯罪过失的明文规定,但较为抽象,司法实务对于如何理解和运用主观心态,通常依赖司法解释等规范性文件。因此,厘清主观心态的内涵、类型以及在司法实务中如何认定主观心态,是中国刑法无法回避的课题。学习英美刑法主观心态的刑事立法及判例理论,可以拓宽学生国际视野,使其深度思考全球共性课题。

4.2　Strict Liability(严格责任)

4.2.1　Introduction (概述)

Strict liability offence means a crime in which a defendant can be convicted without proof of the defendant's state of mind. In other word, the strict liability crime refers to criminal offences which do not require mens rea.[1] Most are created by statutes. Over half of all offences in Anglo – American law are crimes of strict liability. These statutory offences are the result of a massive expansion of state regulation over commercial and public welfare activities since the end of the Second World War. They exist in the areas of health and safety, environmental health, pollution, licensing, motoring, public

[1] Jonathan Herring, *Crininal Law*, Macmillan Publishers Limited, 2011, p. 87.

transport, consumer protection, copyright, financial services, food safety, trade and industry.〔1〕

严格责任犯罪是指被告可以在没有证据证明其主观心态的情况下被定罪的罪行。换言之,严格责任犯罪就是不需要考虑主观心态的刑事犯罪,其大多是由法规所规定的。英美刑法中,超过一半的罪行是严格责任犯罪。这些严格责任犯罪是第二次世界大战结束以后英美法系国家对商业和公共福利活动大规模监管的结果,其主要存在于健康和安全、环境健康、污染、许可、驾驶、公共交通、消费者保护、版权、金融服务、食品安全、贸易和工业等领域。

Which crimes are crimes of strict liability? Unfortunately, statutes are not always so obliging as to state"this is a strict liability offence". Occasionally the wording of an Act does make this clear, but otherwise the courts are left to decide for themselves.〔2〕Two important decisions of the House of Lords (B. v. DPP [2000]〔3〕 and R. v. K. [2002]〔4〕) have emphasized the "presumption of mens rea". The presumption means that if there is any doubt about whether an offence requires mens rea, it should be presumed that it does. In other words, there is a presumption against an offence being one of strict liability.〔5〕 The Model Penal Code does not prohibit the application of strict liability, but it establishes a presumption of the mens rea in section 2. 02 (3) to avoid considering crimes that do not be prescribe the culpability by law as strict liability.

哪些行为构成严格责任罪行?遗憾的是,法律条文并不总是明确标注"此为严格责任罪行"。有时,法律文本的措辞能够直接指明这一点,但除此之外,法院必须自行判断。英国上议院在两项重要判决(B. v. DPP [2000 年]〔6〕和 R. v. K. [2002 年]〔7〕)强调了"主观心态的推定"。这就意味着,如果对某种犯罪是否需要

---

〔1〕 Janet Loveless, *Criminal Law Text, Cases, and Materials*, 3rd edition, Oxford University Press, 2012, p. 170.

〔2〕 Catherine Elliott & Frances Quinn, *Criminal Law*, London, Pearson Education Limited, 2016, p. 41.

〔3〕 Basic brief: A 14 – year – old boy asked a 13 – year – old girl (who he believed to be 14) to perform oral sex on him. He was charged with inciting a child under 14 to commit an act of gross indecency. He was convicted, his appeal rejected, but his final appeal allowed by the House of Lords.

〔4〕 Basic brief: A man had sex with a 14 – year – old girl, genuinely, though not reasonably, believing that she was 14. The House of Lords quashed conviction.

〔5〕 Jonathan Herring, *Crininal Law*, Macmillan Publishers Limited, 2011, p. 89.

〔6〕 基本案情简介:一名 14 岁的男孩要求一名 13 岁的女孩(他认为她 14 岁)与他口交。男孩被指控煽动一名 14 岁以下儿童做出严重猥亵行为,因而被判有罪。男孩的上诉被驳回,但最终上诉得到了上议院的批准。

〔7〕 基本案情简介:某男与一位 14 岁的女孩发生了性关系,男人真诚地,尽管不合理地,相信女孩是 14 岁。上议院撤销了有罪判决。

主观心态存有疑问,则应推定该罪行需要主观心态。换言之,通过推定主观心态的存在以否认该犯罪系严格责任罪行。美国《模范刑法典》虽不禁止适用严格责任,但在其第2.02(3)条设置了一项关于主观心态推定存在的规定,以防止将没有规定可责性要件的犯罪理解为严格责任罪行。

4.2.2 Evaluation: Arguments for and against Strict Liability(评价:支持或反对严格责任)

In fact, the Anglo - American criminal law community generally holds two different views on strict liability crimes: one is in favor of strict liability crimes, and the other is against strict liability crimes, which will be discussed separately.

事实上,对于严格责任犯罪,英美刑法学界通常持有两种截然不同的观点,一种观点是支持严格责任犯罪,另一种观点是反对严格责任犯罪,接下来将分而述之。

Proponents argue that strict liability crimes should be upheld for the following reasons:

支持者认为应该坚持严格责任犯罪,具体理由如下:

1. The argument for strict liability is social protection. The argument that society needs protecting from certain types of harm is a utilitarian one: that the greatest happiness of the greatest number should be protected by the law, even at the risk of convicting a few innocent people. It would not in many cases be possible to prove mens rea if it were required, and so the object of promoting public welfare would be circumvented. Therefore, criminal law should focus primarily on social protection, adhering to the principle of strict liability to safeguard the interests of the majority of society.

支持严格责任的理由是社会保护。主张社会需要免受特定伤害的观点基于功利主义理念:大多数人的最大幸福应该受到法律保护,即使冒着给少数无辜者定罪的风险。许多案件不可能证明行为人的主观心态,如果需要证明主观心态就会背离公共福利的目标。因此,刑法应该主要关注社会保护,为了维护社会大多数人的利益,坚持严格责任原则。

2. The main argument in favour of strict liability is that it can be justified for minor, quasi - criminal offences. Offences subject to strict liability are not real crimes and may, in fact, be regulated not by police prosecution but by regulatory enforcement processes, such as compliance and warning notices. Only those who are blameworthy

will be prosecuted.[1]

支持严格责任的主要论点在于,对于轻微的准刑事犯罪实施严格责任是合理的。严格责任犯罪并不是真正的犯罪,实际上其可能不是由警方起诉而是由监管执法程序予以规制,例如合规和警告通知。仅仅那些应受严重谴责者才会被提起公诉。

3. One of the principal arguments for strict liability is the ease of proof. It is easier for the prosecution to establish strict liability offenses because there is no need to present evidence of the defendant's mental state. The prosecution can establish a case by simply proving that the defendant acted in a certain manner.

严格责任的主要支持理由是易于举证。检方更容易证明严格责任犯罪,因其没有必要出示被告主观心态的证据。检方确定案件,只需证明被告以某种方式行事即可。

The main reasons for the disagreers are as follows:

反对者主要理由如下:

1. Strict liability leads to individual unfairness, especially when applied to offences which are not minor and which carry a custodial penalty. This is morally unjustifiable. The social protection arguments in favour of strict liability cannot justify punishment for anything other than minor offences, especially where it leads to imprisonment. The criminal law should be reserved for behaviour which deserves the stigma of criminal conviction because it is seriously culpable, poses a serious risk of harm or demonstrates moral failing.

严格责任会导致个人不公平,特别是在适用非轻微且可被判处监禁的罪行时。这在道德上是不合理的。支持严格责任的社会保护论不能证明对轻微罪行以外的其他犯罪行为的惩罚是正当的,尤其是惩罚将导致监禁的情况下。刑法应该保留给那些应受到刑事定罪的行为使用,那些行为具有严重的伤害危险或表现出极度的道德败坏,理应受到严厉谴责。

2. Strict liability will do nothing to deter offending nor prevent recurrence, especially when the actor has taken all reasonable precautions to prevent its commission. If liability is to be imposed, even in the absence of negligence, it will not encourage greater vigilance since liability will be incurred no matter how much effort and expense has been put into preventing accidental harm. Strict liability will therefore achieve

---

[1] Janet Loveless, *Criminal Law Text, Cases, and Materials*, 3rd edition, Oxford University Press, 2012, p. 196 – 197.

nothing that could not be achieved without the requirement of negligence.[1]

严格责任无法阻止或防止犯罪再次发生,尤其是行为人已采取一切合理谨慎措施防止犯罪发生。追究主观上不具备疏忽罪过的行为人的刑事责任,不会鼓励行为人提高警惕,因为无论其为防止意外伤害而付出多少努力和代价都毫无意义,最终都要承担刑事责任。因此,严格责任不能在行为人没有疏忽罪过的情况下实现阻吓和威慑犯罪的目标。

■ Curriculum Ideology and Politics(课程思政)

In Anglo – American criminal law, strict liability offenses do not require consideration of the actor's mens rea, or even negligence—the least blameworthy state of mind. An act constitutes a crime as long as the actus reus conforms to legal provisions or results in a legal consequence. From the perspective of criminal law norms, Chinese criminal law lacks strict liability clauses. Section 16 of the Chinese criminal law illustrates this, stipulating that an actus reus that objectively causes damage is not considered a crime if it is due to irresistible or unforeseeable reasons beyond the actor's intention or negligence. This contrasts sharply with the strict liability in Anglo – American law, which does not require mens rea. Furthermore, the clauses on force majeure or accidents in section 16, intentional crimes in section 14, and negligent crimes in section 15 of the Chinese criminal law collectively reflect that criminal law targets the actor's mens rea. In contrast, strict liability in Anglo – American law does not capture the essence of such criminal punishment. Therefore, students should develop a dialectical, reflective, and objective mindset when considering foreign criminal laws.

英美刑法的严格责任不须考虑行为人的主观心态,甚至无须考虑"疏忽"这种受谴责程度最低的主观心态,只要行为人的客观行为符合法律规定,或导致某种法定结果,即构成犯罪。从刑法规范层面来看,中国刑法并无严格责任的规定,《刑法》第16 条即是明证,其规定行为人之行为在客观上虽然造成了损害结果,但因缺乏故意或过失,是由于不能抗拒或者不能预见的原因所引起的,不是犯罪。这和英美刑法无须主观心态的严格责任形成鲜明对比。并且,更为重要的是,我国《刑法》第 16 条不可抗力或意外事件的规定与第 14 条故意犯罪及第 15 条过失犯罪的规定共同体现了刑法所打击和惩罚的就是犯罪人的主观心态,而英美刑法的严格责任无法体现

[1] Janet Loveless, *Criminal Law Text, Cases, and Materials*, 3rd edition, Oxford University Press, 2012, p. 198.

这种刑法惩罚的本质。由此,学生应培养辩证、反思、客观地对待域外刑法的思维。

4.3 Mistake(认识错误)

4.3.1 Introudction(概述)

Mistake refers to the actor's misunderstanding of the legal significance or factual circumstances of the act he has committed. In general, mistake comes in two forms: a mistake of law (ignorance of the law) and a mistake of fact. The latter type of mistake is by far the more interesting, and controversial, of the two. These will be discussed below.

认识错误是指行为人对自己实施的行为的法律意义或者事实情况发生的错误认知。一般而言,认识错误具有两种形式:对法律的认识错误(对法律的无知)和对事实的认识错误。后一种类型的认识错误是迄今为止两者中更有趣和更具争议性的类型。接下来将分而述之。

4.3.2 Mistake of Law (Ignorance of the Law)(法律认识错误/法律无知)

Few criminal law rules are as widely known as "ignorance of the law is no excuse". In brief, people should be aware of the law and have a responsibility to avoid acting in certain situations without checking whether they will violate the law. In other words, everyone has an obligation to "inquire" about the legality of this actions. There is no doubt that in many cases it is impossible for the criminal to know that he has broken the law. However, ignorance or mistake can be used as a defense for criminal liability mainly in some situations. First, in some circumstances, a person may be able to depend on an interpretation of the law that includes relying on one's own understanding, relying on the advice of a lawyer, or relying on the interpretation of other officials, which later proves to be mistake. Model Penal Code section 2.04(3) provides that a defendant has a defense to a charge if he can show that (a) the statute or other enactment defining the offense is not known to the actor and has not been published or otherwise reasonably made available prior to the conduct alleged; or (b) he has acted in reasonable reliance on an official statement of the law, afterward determined to be invalid or erroneous, contained in (i) a statute or other enactment; (ii) a judicial decision, opinion or judgment; (iii) an administrative order or grant of permission; or (iv) an official interpretation of the public officer or body charged by the law with responsibility for the interpretation, administration or enforcement of the law defining the offense.

“对法律的无知不是逃避法律责任的借口”是一条广为人知的法律原则。简言之，人们应该了解法律，有责任先检查自己行为是否违反法律后再采取行动。换句话说，每个人都有“咨询”其行为合法性的义务。毫无疑问，在很多情况中，犯罪者不可能知道其行为违反了法律。不过，对法律的无知或认识错误可以在某些情形下作为免除刑事责任的辩护理由。《模范刑法典》第2.04(3)条规定，被告可以对指控进行抗辩，如果：(a)行为人不知道规定犯罪的制定法或其他成文法，并且在实施被起诉的行为之前，该法律尚未被公布或不能被合理地知悉；或者(b)被告能够证明他“合理地依赖”法律的官方声明而行事，但后来该法律被确定为无效或错误的（该法律包括(i)法规或其他法令；(ii)司法决定、意见或判决；(iii)行政命令或许可；(iv)对规定犯罪的法律负责解释、实施或执行的公职人员或机构所作的官方解释）。

4.3.3 Mistake of Fact（事实认识错误）

Mistake of fact means that the actor is mistaken about a fact which is an aspect of the actus reus, that is, the actor's understanding of his own behavior is inconsistent with the objective facts. This misunderstanding may affect whether the actor has criminal intent, and then affect whether the actor is willful or negligent, or innocent.

事实的认识错误意味着行为人对犯罪行为某方面事实存有错误的理解，即指行为人对自己行为的认识与客观事实不一致。这种对事实的认识错误可能影响行为人主观上是否存有犯罪故意，进而影响行为人承担故意责任还是过失责任，抑或不负刑事责任。

Consider an example of Tom, who went to the grocery store, picked 10 items from the shelves, and had the cashier start scanning the items. Tom was talking on his cell phone and didn't notice that the cashier missed an item. while leaving the store, a security guard noticed Tom leaving with an item for which he had not paid. Tom was charged with theft. It seemed that he made an honest mistake. We can safely assume that he was aware that stealing was unacceptable, but he just didn't notice what the cashier missed.

以汤姆案为例，汤姆去一家商店购物，从货架上挑选了10件物品，交给收银员扫描这些物品的标签。此时，汤姆正用手机通话，没注意到收银员漏扫了一件物品。离开商店时，保安发现汤姆拿了一件未付款的物品。汤姆被指控实施盗窃行为。看起来汤姆犯了一个诚实的错误。我们可以有把握地假设汤姆肯定知道盗窃是错误的，他只是没注意到收银员漏扫了某件物品。

Tom made a mistake of fact. He mistakenly left the store with an item unpaid. However, he was likely to be acquitted, because he did not form the necessary mens rea to support a criminal conviction. If the crime for which he was charged did not require elements of mens rea, such as in strict liability offences, then his mistake may be irrelevant and could lead to a conviction.

汤姆具有事实认识错误,错误地拿着一件未付款的物品准备离开商店。然而,汤姆很可能会被无罪释放,因为其没有形成盗窃罪所必要的犯罪意图。如果汤姆被指控的罪行不要求具备犯罪意图,譬如严格责任犯罪,那么他的认识错误就是无关紧要的,其仍有可能被定罪。

4.4 Intoxication(醉态)

4.4.1 Introduction (概述)

Intoxication is formally defined as a disturbance of mental or physical capacities resulting from the introduction of any substance into the body. Note that this definition does not distinguish between alcohol and drugs. It is possible to become intoxicated from a substance that is neither alcohol nor a drug (e. g., paint). Indeed, most of the popular intoxication cases referenced in criminal law books focus on alcohol intoxication. Intoxication is important in criminal law because it impairs decision - making capabilities and affects judgment. For example, a person who is under the influence of alcohol may not be able to form the requisite mens rea to commit a crime. And even if an intoxicated person can form intent, he may not act the same way in a sober state.[1] Anglo - American criminal law reflects a general reluctance to recognize intoxication as a defense, or as a reason for mitigating liability in general. At best, and in extreme cases, intoxication may negate some, but not all.[2]

醉态被正式定义为"将任何物质引入体内而导致的精神或身体能力的干扰"。这一定义没有区分酒精和毒品,且也有可能是由既不是酒精也不是毒品的物质(如油漆)所引发的醉态。事实上,刑法书籍中所提到的大多数流行的醉态案例都集中于酒精中毒方面。醉态在刑法中居于重要地位,因为它会损害行为人的决策能力并影响其判断力。例如,受酒精影响的人可能无法形成犯罪所需的主观心态,即便一个醉酒者具有犯罪故意,但可能他在清醒状态下是不会实施该行为的。英美刑法普遍不愿承认醉态可以作为无罪辩护的理由,或者作为减轻刑事责任的理由。至多在

[1] Jennifer L. Moore & John L. Worrall, *Criminal Law* (*Justice Series*), Pearson Education, 2018, p. 80 - 81.

[2] Markus D. Dubber & Tatjana Hörnle, *Criminal Law: A Comparative Approach*, Oxford University Press 2014, p. 277.

极端情况下,醉态可以否定部分但不是全部的刑事责任。

4.4.2　Intoxication Serves as a Defense(醉态作为辩护理由)

How intoxication serves as a defense to criminal liability primarily depends on the type of intoxication. It is crucial to determine whether the intoxication is voluntary or involuntary. Voluntary intoxication occurs when a person knowingly introduces a substance into his body, knowing or reasonably foreseeing that the substance is likely to cause intoxication, such as through the use of alcohol or drugs. A person who voluntarily becomes intoxicated may find it significantly more difficult to have his conduct "excused". If a person who voluntarily consumes alcohol or drugs enters an aggressive state, loses awareness of his action, and then commits a vicious assault, it is hardly arguable that his action is purely accidental and should exempt him from criminal liability. This perspective is adopted by English common law, which is grounded in common sense and experience rather than strict logic.[1]

醉态如何作为刑事责任的辩护理由主要取决于醉态的类型,究竟是自愿醉态还是非自愿醉态。自愿醉态是指行为人明知自己主动摄入体内物质,并且其知道或应当知道该物质导致醉态的可能性,譬如行为人饮酒、吸毒等。自愿醉态者的行为是很难被免责的。一个自愿饮酒和吸毒的人,使自己进入一种不知道自己所作所为的侵略性状态,然后实施恶毒的攻击,很难说其攻击行为纯属意外,从而免除其刑事责任——这是普通法所采用的构建于常识和经验而非严格逻辑之上的观点。

Involuntary intoxication refers to a situation where a person does not knowingly take alcohol, illegal drugs, or other substances capable of impairing mental or physical faculties. It typically encompasses pathological intoxication and intoxication due to other involuntary causes. Pathological intoxication often constitutes a strong defense, but the impact of other forms of involuntary intoxication on criminal liability hinges on the jury's assessment. However, if the jury, after considering evidence of involuntary intoxication alongside other relevant factors, determines that the defendant possessed the necessary mens rea, the defense of involuntary intoxication fails to exonerate the defendant.

非自愿醉态是指某人不是故意服用酒精、非法药物或其他可能导致精神或身体能力紊乱的物质。非自愿醉态通常包括病理性原因导致行为人出现的醉态以及其他原因导致的醉态。病理性醉态通常都是被告有力的辩护理由,但其他的非自愿醉态能否成为辩护理由则取决于陪审团的态度。如果陪审团在斟酌其他非自愿醉态

---

〔1〕 Jennifer L. Moore & John L. Worrall, *Criminal Law*, 2nd editon, Pearson Education, Inc., 2018, p. 81.

的证据之后,裁定被告确实具有相关的犯罪意图,则被告不能以非自愿醉态作为辩护理由。

■ Case study(案例学习)

People v. Lawson 155 Cal. Rptr. 3d 236 (Cal. App. 2013)(加利福尼亚州诉劳森案)

Fact(基本案情)

William Gibson was working as a loss prevention agent at the Walmart store in Rancho Cucamonga. On October 28, 2010, at approximately 10:00 a. m., Gibson was doing paperwork and watching video surveillance of the store from inside his office next to the customer service registers. Around 10:10 a. m., the defendant walked into the store and proceeded directly to the customer service area, where he returned some items and was issued a gift card. After he received a call from the customer service desk that the defendant was leaving the area, Gibson left his office and began following the defendant inside the store. Gibson observed the defendant as he went to the jewelry department, returned a pair of earrings, and received another gift card. The two gift cards the defendant received were for approximately $104 and $124. The defendant then proceeded to the menswear department, selecting a purple sweater with a hoodie. After the defendant selected the hoodie, he walked to an empty space in the center of the store that customers walk through. There, the defendant took the hoodie off its hanger, put the sales tag inside the hoodie, threw the hoodie over his shoulder, and walked to the cash registers. The price of the hoodie was $20, and its sales tag had a bar code that is scanned at the register. Defendant first walked to the area of register No. 15. He then proceeded to register No. 11 where he selected a pack of gum, and returned to register No. 15. At register No. 15, he had the cashier select some cigars or cigarettes for him. The cashier scanned the gum and cigarettes and the defendant paid for them. Defendant did not take the hoodie off his shoulder or present it to the cashier. Five or six minutes passed between the time defendant selected the hoodie in the menswear department and the time he purchased the other items at the register. After paying for the gum and cigarettes, the defendant walked out of the store. As soon as he was outside the store, Gibson stopped him. The hoodie was still on the defendant's left shoulder. Gibson identified himself and asked the defendant to come back inside the store. Defendant cooperated. He walked back into the store with Gibson and did not try to run away. The jury was shown surveillance videotapes and still photographs of the defendant's movements inside the store.

威廉·吉布森在兰乔库卡蒙加的沃尔玛商店担任防损员。2010 年 10 月 28 日上午 10 时左右，吉布森一边做文书工作，一边在客户服务收银台旁边的办公室内观看商店的视频监控。10 时 10 分左右，被告走进店内，直接前往客服区，退回了一些物品，并获得了礼品卡。吉布森接到客户服务台的电话，得知被告要离开该区域，吉布森就离开办公室，开始在商店内跟踪被告。吉布森观察被告前往珠宝部门，归还了一对耳环，并收到另一张礼品卡，其所收到的两张礼品卡价值分别是 104 美元和 124 美元。被告随后前往男装部门，选择了一件紫色毛衣和卫衣。选好卫衣后，被告走到商店中间的空地，从衣架上取下卫衣，将销售标签放在卫衣内，然后将卫衣扔到肩膀上，走到收银台前。卫衣价值 20 美元，销售标签上有一个供收银台扫描的条形码。被告先走到 15 号收银台处，然后又走到 11 号收银台，挑选了一包口香糖，最后又返回 15 号收银台。在 15 号收银台处，被告让收银员为其挑选一些雪茄香烟。收银员扫描了口香糖和香烟，被告支付了费用。但被告没有把卫衣从肩膀上拿下以交给收银员扫描收费。从被告在男装部选择卫衣到其在收银处购买其他物品，有五六分钟的时间。在支付口香糖和香烟费用之后，被告走出商店，刚到店外，吉布森就拦住他。此时，卫衣仍然挂在被告左肩上。吉布森向被告表明自己身份，要求其回到商店里。被告配合地和吉布森一起回到商店，并没有试图逃跑。监控录像带和被告在商店内行动的静态照片皆展示给陪审团以供参考。

Dispute（争议点）

At trial, the defendant claims his conviction for petty theft must be reversed because the trial court erroneously failed to instruct the jury, sua sponte, on the defense of mistake of fact. He argues that the jury could have reasonably inferred that he simply forgot about the hoodie, which was draped over his shoulder as he passed through the checkout line, paid for other items, and walked out of the store. And given that he forgot about the hoodie, he argues that the jury could have reasonably inferred that he did not intend to steal it when he walked out of the store with it.

在庭审中，被告声称其犯有轻微盗窃罪的定罪必须被撤销，因为初审法院没有就事实认识错误的辩护指示陪审团。他辩称，陪审团本可以合理地推断出：他只是忘记了那件卫衣。当他经过收银台时，将卫衣披在肩上，买了其他东西，然后走出了商店。考虑到自己是忘记了那件卫衣而没付款，被告辩称，陪审团可以合理地推断出，当他拿着卫衣走出商店时，并没有打算偷走卫衣。

Conclusion（结论）

The Court of Appeals of California affirmed the order of the appellate term in this case. The defense of mistake of fact does not apply to the present facts. The defendant was charged with petty theft. The elements of theft are well settled: the offense is committed by every person who (1) takes possession (2) of personal property (3) owned or possessed by another, (4) by means of trespass, and (5) with intent to steal the property, and (6) carries the property away. The act t of taking personal property from the possession of another is always a trespass unless the owner consents to the taking freely and unconditionally or the taker has a legal right to take the property. And the particular defense of mistake of fact requires, at a minimum, an actual belief in the existence of circumstances, which, if true, would make the act with which the person is charged an innocent act. In all cases, however, the defendant's mistaken belief must relate to a set of circumstances which, if existent or true, would make the act charged an innocent act. Defendant's alleged mistake of fact was that he forgot the hoodie was on his shoulder when he walked out of the store without paying for it. The act of forgetting about the hoodie does not amount to a mistaken belief in a set of circumstances which, if true, would have made the defendant's act of walking out of the store with the hoodie lawful. In sum, the defense of mistake of fact is inapplicable to the present facts.

但在本案中,加利福尼亚上诉法院认可了对被告的定罪。对事实认识错误的辩护不适用于目前情况。被告人被控轻微盗窃罪。盗窃罪要件已得到很好的确认:盗窃罪是由行为人实施的,其要件为:(1)占有;(2)财产;(3)由他人拥有或占有;(4)以非法侵入的方式;(5)意图窃取财产;以及(6)将财产拿走。从他人手中夺取个人财产的行为始终是非法侵占,除非财物所有者同意行为人自由或无条件地占有该财产或行为人有合法权利取得该财产。对事实认识错误的特别辩护至少需要行为人实际相信存在某种情况,如果该情况属实,则使其被指控的盗窃行为成为无罪行为。然而,在所有案件中,被告的错误认知必须与一系列情况相关联,如果这些情况存在或真实,将使被指控的行为变为无罪。被告所谓的事实认识错误是,当他没付钱走出商店时,忘记卫衣还搁在自己肩膀上。忘记卫衣并不构成对一系列情况的错误认知,如果错误认知是真实的,被告带着卫衣走出商店的行为就是合法的。综上所述,事实认识错误的辩护不适用于目前的事实。初审法院没有义务就事实认识错误或任何类似辩护理由予以指示,这种辩护只会否定盗窃的主观心态。即使证据支持关于事实认识错误的指示,初审法院也没有义务对辩护自发进行指示。

Questions 1. Explain why the defense of mistake of fact is available? (Please scan the QR code on the right to get the answer)

为什么可以对事实认识错误进行辩护?(答案请扫描右侧二维码

获取)

2. Why is the defense of mistake of fact not applicable to the defendant in this case?(The way to obtain the answer is the same as above)

为什么在该案中,对事实认识错误的辩护不适用于该案被告?(答案获取方式同上)

Morissette v. United States Supreme Court of the United States 342 U. S. 246 (1952)(莫里塞特诉美国最高法院案)

Fact(基本案情)

On a large tract of uninhabited and untilled land in a wooded and sparsely populated area of Michigan, the government established a practice bombing range over which the Air Force dropped simulated bombs at ground targets. These bombs consisted of a metal cylinder about forty inches (about 1 meter) long and eight inches (about 0.2 meters) across, filled with sand and enough black powder to cause a smoke puff by which the strike could be located. At various places about the range signs read "Danger—Keep Out—Bombing Range." Nevertheless, the range was known as good deer country and was extensively hunted. Spent bomb casings were cleared from the targets and thrown into piles "so that they will be out of the way". They were not sacked or piled in any order but were dumped in heaps, some of which had been accumulating for four years or upwards, were exposed to the weather, and rusting away. In December of 1948, Morissette went hunting in this area but did not get a deer. He thought to meet the expenses of the trip by salvaging some of these casings. He loaded three tons of them on his truck and took them to a nearby farm, where they were flattened by driving a tractor over them. After expending this labor and trucking them to market in Flint, he realized $84. Morissette, by occupation, is a fruit stand operator in summer and a trucker and scrap iron collector in winter. An honorably discharged veteran of World War Ⅱ, he enjoys a good name among his neighbors and has had no blemish on his record more disreputable than a conviction for reckless driving. The loading, crushing and transporting of these casings were all in broad daylight, in full view of passers-by, without the slightest effort at concealment. When an investigation was started, Morissette voluntarily, promptly and candidly told the whole story to the authorities, saying that he had no intention of stealing but thought the property was abandoned, unwanted and considered of no value to the Government. He was indicted, however, on the charge that he "did unlawfully, wilfully and knowingly steal and convert" property of the United States of the value of $84, in violation of 18 U. S. C. § 641, which provides that "whoever embezzles, steals, purloins, or knowingly converts" government property is punishable by fine and imprisonment. Morissette was convicted and sentenced to imprisonment for two months or to pay a fine of $200. Morissette appealed. The court of appeals affirmed the conviction because, "As we have interpreted the statute, appellant was guilty of its violation beyond a shadow of doubt, as evidenced even by his own admissions."

美国政府在密歇根州的一大片无人居住和开垦的林地上建立了一个模拟轰炸靶场,空军在其上空向地面目标投掷模拟炸弹。这些炸弹由一个长约40英寸(约1米),直径8英寸(约0.2米)的金属圆柱体组成,里面装满了可以引起烟雾的沙子和足够分量的黑火药。射程内的不同位置都用标语写着"危险—远离—轰炸靶场"。尽管如此,该场地仍被人们广泛当作狩鹿的区域。为了不挡路,使用过的炸弹外壳会被人们清理成一堆,但不会依序堆放,而是被成堆倾倒,其中一些炸弹外壳已经积累了4年或更长时间,暴露在空气中生锈。1948年12月,莫里塞特前去这个区域打猎,但没有找到一头鹿。他想拿走其中一些废弃炸弹外壳来支付旅行费用,就将3吨重的废弃炸弹外壳装上卡车,带到附近的一个农场。莫里塞特先用拖拉机压扁炸弹外壳,并费力地将这些外壳运到弗林特市场销售,获利84美元。莫里塞特在夏季时是水果摊贩卖者,在冬季时是卡车司机和废铁收集者。作为一名光荣退伍的"二战"老兵,莫里塞特在邻居中享有盛誉,在其记录中,没有比轻率驾驶罪名更不光彩的瑕疵。对废弃炸弹外壳的装载、碾碎和运输没有丝毫掩饰,是在光天化日、众目睽睽之下进行的。当调查开始时,莫里塞特自愿、迅速和坦率地将整件事情的来龙去脉都告诉当局,并解释自己无意偷窃,以为该财产是被遗弃,不受欢迎,且对政府没有价值的。然而,他被起诉的罪名是"非法、故意窃取和转换"价值84美元的美国财产,他的行为违反了《美国法典》第18编第641条规定,相关法律规定,"任何人贪污、偷盗、窃取或故意转换"政府财产,可处以罚款和监禁。莫里塞特被定罪并被判处2个月的监禁或支付200美元的罚款。莫里塞特提出上诉。上诉法院确认了定罪,因为"按照我们对法规的解释,上诉人违反法规的行为是毫无疑问的,这甚至可以从他自己的供述中得到证明"。

Dispute(争议点)

At trial, Morissette testified, as he at all times did, to investigators that from appearances he believed the casings were abandoned and discarded, that he had no intention of stealing the property, and took it with no wrongful or criminal intent. And the trial court ruled："He took it because he thought it was abandoned and he knew he was on government property. That is no defense." The court refused to submit or to allow counsel to argue to the jury whether Morissette acted with innocent intention. It charged："The question on intent is whether or not he intended to take the property. Morissette says he did. Therefore, he is guilty."

在审判中，莫里塞特一如既往地向调查人员说，从表面上看，其相信这些废弃炸弹外壳是被遗弃的，其无意偷走美国财产，并且没有不法或犯罪意图。初审法院裁定："莫里塞特拿走这些自认为被遗弃的弹壳，而且知道这是政府财产，故无法成立抗辩理由。"法院拒绝提交或允许律师向陪审团论证莫里塞特的行为是否具有无辜意图，法院指示说："关于故意的争议焦点是，莫里塞特是否故意拿走这些财产，其承认是故意拿走这些弹壳的。因此，他就是有罪的。"

Conclusion（结论）

The Supreme Court reversed the judgment of conviction because the trial judge wrongly instructed the jury and did not allow consideration of Morissette's honest belief that he believed the casings were discarded as a defense. Strict liability legislation does not specify intent as a necessary element. Section 641 at issue here is such a statute for what has been aptly called "public welfare offenses." However, Stealing, larceny, and its variants and equivalents were among the earliest offenses known to the law that existed before legislation and state courts have retained the requirement of intent in larceny-type offenses. Congressional silence as to the mental element in § 641 will not be interpreted as removing that element from the condemned offense. Moreover, in this case, the presumption concluded that there was an intent to steal casings based merely on the fact that the defendant took them. The only question the court found was, "Did he intend to take the property?" That the removal of them was a conscious and intentional act was admitted. But that isolated fact is not an adequate basis on which the jury should find the criminal intent to steal, that is, wrongfully to deprive another of possession of the property. Whether that intent existed, the jury must determine, not only from the act of taking but from that together with the defendant's testimony and all of the surrounding circumstances.

最高法院推翻了定罪判决，因为初审法官错误地指示陪审团，不允许陪审团考虑莫里塞特的诚实信念，即让他以"认为这些废旧弹壳属于被丢弃的"作为辩护理由。严格责任立法没有规定主观要件是必备要素。本案所涉及的《美国法典》第641 条就是这样一条被恰当地称为公共福利犯罪的法规。然而，偷窃、盗窃及其变体是已知最早的罪行之一,州法院一直要求在盗窃类犯罪中行为人具有犯罪意图。国会对第641条中主观心态的沉默不会被解释为在这种被谴责的罪行中无须犯罪意图。此外,在本案中,推定得出的结论是莫里塞特意图窃取废弃弹壳,依据仅仅是其拿走了这些废弃弹壳。法院认为唯一的问题是"他打算拿走财产吗?"。陪审团承认,将废弃弹壳带走是一种有意识的故意行为。但是,这一孤立的事实并不是陪审团认定莫里塞特具有偷窃犯罪意图的充分依据,即其不正当地剥夺他人所拥有的财产的充分依据。无论是否存在这种犯罪意图,陪审团不能仅仅依据被告拿走废弃弹壳行为本身,而是还需从被告的证词和所有周围情况一起予以确定莫里塞特的犯罪意图。

Questions:1. What is the distinction between so – called "public welfare" offenses and traditional crimes? (Please scan the QR code on the right to get the answer)

所谓的"公共福利"犯罪和传统犯罪有什么区别?(答案请扫描右侧二维码获取)

2. Why did the Supreme Court reverse the judgment of conviction? (Please scan the QR code on the right to get the answer)

为何最高法院推翻了有罪判决?(答案请扫描右侧二维码获取)

4.5 Exercise(课后练习)(答案请扫描右侧二维码获取)

4.5.1 Test of Terminologies(术语考查)

①Mens Rea ②Strict liability

③Mistakes of fact ④Intoxication

⑤Purpose ⑥Knowledge

⑦Recklessness ⑧Negligence

⑨Self – induced intoxication ⑩Pathological intoxication

4.5.2 True or False(判断题)

1. A person is possibly punishable even if he does not have the intent to commit a crime.

即使一个人没有主观心态,他也可能受到刑罚处罚。

2. Ignorance or mistake can serve as a criminal law defense insome situations.

对法律的无知和认识错误可以在某些情况下作为辩护理由。

3. The core of the term "negligence" lies in the actor's possession of direct intent during thc commission of the act.

"疏忽"一词的核心是行为人施行行为时具有直接目的。

4.5.3 Short – answer Questions(简答题)

1. The accused, Mme Larsonneur, came from France to England and was deported to Dublin. The Irish police sent her back. On arrival at Holyhead, she was charged with being an illegal immigrant in violation of the Aliens Order 1920. Her appeal from conviction was dismissed. Was Mme Larsonneur guilty? why?

被告拉森诺夫人从法国来到英国,后被英国驱逐到爱尔兰的都柏林。爱尔兰警方又将拉森诺夫人遣送回英国。抵达英国的霍利黑德后,拉森诺夫人因违反1920年英国《外国人令》,被指控为非法移民。拉森诺夫人的上诉被驳回。拉森诺夫人有罪吗?为什么?

2. Under the United Kingdom Licensing Act 1872, Section 13, it is an offense for any licensed person to sell intoxicating liquor to a person who is drunk. The question arises whether Mike should be convicted despite his lack of knowledge that the person he served was in a state of intoxication?

英国《1872年许可法》第13条规定,任何酒馆持牌人向醉酒者出售酒精均构成犯罪。那么,售酒者迈克不知道顾客已经喝醉,则其是否应当被定罪?

3. Lisa's parents were incredibly wealthy entrepreneurs who earned hundreds of millions of dollars through the course of their careers. After her mother passed away recently, her father's health began declining rapidly. It was no secret that he likely would not make it much longer. Lisa secretly anticipated his death. Her relationship with her parents was always turbulent, and she assumed she had half of a large fortune coming her way. Lisa visited her father one day and found his will, which left most of his and his wife's estate to their son— Tom — and a modest sum to Lisa. The will stipulated that if either child was not alive upon the will's execution, the living child would inherit everything. Furious, Lisa ran home and began plotting to kill Tom. She knew his wife would be out of town that weekend, so she bought a gun and made plans to stage a robbery gone wrong. That weekend, she broke into his house, snuck into his room, and shot in the direction of his bed. Unfortunately for Lisa, she missed Tom entirely. Also unfortunate was that she struck and killed Tom's wife, who had cancelled her weekend plans. What result if Lisa is charged.[1]

---

[1] Shima Baradaran Baughman, Richard G. Singer & John Q. La Fond, *Criminal Law: Examples and Explanations*, Wolters Kluwer, 2022, p. 95.

丽莎的父母是非常富有的企业家，他们在职业生涯中赚了数亿美元。最近，丽莎母亲去世了，丽莎父亲的健康状况也开始迅速恶化，很可能不会活得太久，这也不是什么秘密。丽莎已经暗中预料到自己父亲的死亡。她与父母的关系一直不是很好，但她以为自己至少能获得父母一半的巨额财富。一天，丽莎去看望父亲，发现了父亲的遗嘱，遗嘱安排是将大部财产留给儿子汤姆，而丽莎只能得到一笔微薄的钱款。遗嘱还说，如果汤姆和丽莎中任意一位在执行遗嘱时已死亡，那么，活着的另一位将继承所有财产。丽莎愤怒地跑回家，开始筹划杀死汤姆。她知道汤姆的妻子周末会出门，就买了一把枪，计划上演一桩抢劫案。周末，她闯进汤姆的房子，偷偷溜进房间，朝床上开枪射击。不幸的是，射中的不是汤姆，而是汤姆的妻子，她恰好取消了周末外出计划。如果丽莎被起诉，结果会怎样？

4. Mike, a 25 – year – old man, is out at a 21 – and – over bar with some friends. He meets and begins talking to a girl named Jenna. Jenna has her driver's license out and Mike notices they were born in the same year. When he mentions this, Jenna confirms that she is 25. At the end of the night, Jenna invites Mike back to her apartment, where they engage in consensual sexual acts. Eventually, Mike learns that Jenna is actually a 17 – year – old high school student who regularly goes to bars using her fake ID. "Her" apartment is actually her older sister's apartment, which she uses when her sister is out of town. Mike is arrested for statutory rape, which criminalizes an adult engaging in any sexual acts with a minor under the age of 18. Mike argues that he sincerely believed — based on the facts that Jenna was in a bar, had an ID that showed she was 25, and seemed to have her own apartment — that Jenna was an adult. Please analyze this case.[1]

迈克是一位25岁的男子，和朋友前去一家只招待21岁以上人士的酒吧玩耍。他遇到一位名叫珍娜的女孩并与之交谈。珍娜还拿出了自己驾照，迈克发现他们俩出生于同一年。当迈克提及年龄这一点时，珍娜确认自己就是25岁。晚上酒吧打烊时，珍娜邀请迈克去她的公寓，在那里他们发生了双方都同意的性行为。最终，迈克得知珍娜实际是一名17岁的高中生，她经常使用假身份证去酒吧，她所拥有的公寓实际是她姐姐的，当她姐姐出城时，珍娜就会使用该公寓。迈克因法定强奸罪被捕，当成年人与18岁以下的未成年人发生任何性行为都会被认定构成该罪。迈克辩称，基于珍娜在成人酒吧玩耍，且其身份证显示其是25岁，以及她似乎拥有自己公寓的事实，他真诚地相信珍娜就是一位成年人。请分析这个案例。

---

〔1〕 Shima Baradaran Baughman, Richard G. Singer & John Q. La Fond, *Criminal Law: Examples and Explanations*, Wolters Kluwer, 2022, p. 151.

5. Section 19 of 2013 "Opinions on Punishing Crimes of Sexual Assault on Minors in Accordance with the Law" stipulates: "If a person knows or should know that the other party is a minor girl under the age of 14, and commits sexual assault such as rape, the actor shall be found to 'know' that the victim is a minor girl under 14 years old. For a victim under the age of 12, the actor who commits sexual assault such as rape shall been deemed to know that the other party is a minor girl. If a victim who has reached the age of 12 but less than 14 years old may appear to be a minor girl according to the observation of her physical development, speech and behavior, clothing characteristics, and rules of life and rest, the actor who commits sexual assault such as rape shall been deemed to 'know' that the other party is a minor girl." Some scholars argue that this section constitutes a strict liability clause, do you agree? Please explain your reasoning.

2013年《关于依法惩治性侵害未成年人犯罪的意见》第19条规定:"知道或者应当知道对方是不满十四周岁的幼女,而实施奸淫等性侵害行为的,应当认定行为人'明知'对方是幼女。对于不满十二周岁的被害人实施奸淫等性侵害行为的,应当认定行为人'明知'对方是幼女。对于已满十二周岁不满十四周岁的被害人,从其身体发育状况、言谈举止、衣着特征、生活作息规律等观察可能是幼女,而实施奸淫等性侵害行为的,应当认定行为人'明知'对方是幼女。"有学者认为该条款属于严格责任条款,你赞同吗?请阐释理由。

■ Curriculum Ideology and Politics(课程思政)

Anglo – American criminal law regards statutory rape as a crime of strict liability. If an actor engages in sexual intercourse with a minor girl below the legal age, the actor is deemed to have committed the crime of rape, regardless of whether the actor knows the minor's identity. Section 19 of the "Opinions on Punishing Crimes of Sexual Assault on Minors in Accordance with the Law" contains similar clause regarding the rape of a minor girl under the legal age. However, this does not necessarily indicate that China has a strict liability clause. As a norm of judicial interpretation, section 19 of the "Opinions" supplements and refines the crime of rape as outlined in section 236 of Chinese criminal law. Rape is an intentional crime, and the judicial interpretation norm is merely a presumption of the cognitive element of the crime of rape combined with common life experience, rather than a denial of the cognitive element of rape. Therefore, in comparative studies of criminal law within and outside the jurisdiction, one cannot selectively extract a foreign criminal law theory or concept and transplant it into Chinese criminal law without considering the systematic and logical nature of Chinese criminal law. It is essential to deeply understand the inherent logic of our country's criminal law to better advance the construction of the rule of law in our country.

英美刑法将奸淫幼女型的法定强奸罪视为严格责任犯罪,行为人与不满法定年龄的幼女发生性关系,无论行为人对幼女身份是否明知,一律判定其构成强奸罪。我国《关于依法惩治性侵害未成年人犯罪的意见》第 19 条对行为人奸淫法定年龄以下的幼女也有类似规定,那么,能否说明我国也有严格责任的规定?《关于依法惩治性侵害未成年人犯罪的意见》第 19 条作为司法解释规范,是对《刑法》第 236 条强奸罪的补充和细化,强奸罪是公认的故意犯罪,该司法解释规范是对强奸罪的认识因素结合生活常识和社会经验进行推定,而不是否认强奸罪中的认识因素。因此,在域内外刑法的比较研究中,不能片面地撷取某个域外刑法理论或概念,并将其移植于中国刑法之中,而无视中国刑法的系统性与逻辑性,应深刻认识到我国刑法的自有逻辑,以更好地推进我国的法治建设。

■ Summary(总结)

1. Mens rea is the term that describes the mental element required for the commission of a crime, representing the state of mind that an offender must possess during the actus reus. Under the provisions of the Model Penal Code, mens rea is categorized into four distinct levels: purpose, knowledge, recklessness, and negligence.

主观心态是用来描述犯罪中主观要件的术语,即犯罪者在实施犯罪行为的同时必须具备的主观心理状态。根据《模范刑法典》的规定,主观心态划分为蓄意、明知、轻率和疏忽 4 种类型。

2. A strict liability offense is one offense in which the prosecution is not required to prove the actor's mens rea. Public welfare crimes are generally regarded as strict liability crimes.

严格责任犯罪是指控方无须证明被告任何主观心态的罪行。公共福利犯罪通常被视为是严格责任犯罪。

3. Mistake refers to the actor's misunderstanding of the legal significance or factual circumstances of the act he has committed. Generally speaking, there are two types ofmistakes: mistake of the law (i. e. ignorance of the law) and mistake of the facts. Mistake of the law is generally not exempt from liability, and only affects criminal responsibility on special circumstances. Mistake of fact may constitute a denial of the

mens rea of an offence if it involves a fact that forms part of the actus reus. However, the mistake is not excusable if that part of the actus reus does not require a mental element, as is the case with strict liablity offenses.

认识错误是指行为人对自己实施行为的法律意义或者事实情况发生的认知错误。一般而言,认识错误分为两大类型:对法律的认识错误(对法律的无知)和对事实的认识错误。法律的认识错误一般不免责,只在较为特殊的情形下影响刑事责任。事实认识错误如果涉及构成犯罪行为一部分的事实,则可能构成对主观心态的否认。但是,如果该犯罪行为部分不需要主观要件,譬如严格责任犯罪,那么认识错误就不能成为免责理由。

4. Intoxication is defined as the disturbance of mental or physical capacities resulting from the introduction of any substance into the body. Intoxication can be divided into voluntary intoxication and involuntary intoxication. Voluntary intoxication is difficult to be excused, and pathological intoxication is usually excusable, but the excusability of other involuntary intoxication depends on the jury's judgment.

醉态是指由于将任何物质引入体内而使精神或身体能力受到干扰。醉态可以分为自愿醉态和非自愿醉态。自愿醉态是很难免责的。非自愿醉态中的病理性醉态通常可以成为免责理由,但其他非自愿醉态能否免责主要取决于陪审团的判断。

Chapter 5　Defenses to Criminal Liability: Justifications
第5章　刑事责任抗辩事由:正当化事由

■ The Learning Objective(学习目标)

1. to understand the concept of defenses to criminal liability.

了解刑事责任抗辩事由的概念。

2. to understand the criteria for distinguishing justifications and excuses.

了解正当化事由、可宽恕事由的区分标准。

3. to understand the constitutive elements of justification in the defense of criminal liability.

了解刑事责任抗辩事由中正当化事由的构成要件。

4. to be able to assess and apply the justification in judicial cases.

可以在司法案件中对正当化事由予以判断和运用。

5. To learn some terminologies related to the topic.

掌握本章的专业术语。

■ Chapter Outline(本章内容概要)

Justification, which is a kind of affirmative defence is an important defense to criminal liability. Justification is legally permissible and is not a criminal act. The main topic of this chapter is justification. We first introduce the criteria for distinguishing between justifications and excuses, and then explore the following concepts: justifications, including self-defense, defense of others, defense of home and property, the Castle Law, necessity, and consent of the victim.

正当化事由是重要的刑事责任抗辩事由,是积极抗辩事由。正当化事由是被法律许可的,不属于犯罪行为的情形。本章首先介绍了正当化事由、可宽恕事由的区分标准,然后对正当事由中的自我防卫、防卫他人、防卫住宅和财物、城堡法、紧急避险、被害人同意等进行介绍和阐述。

■ The Purpose of Curriculum Ideology and Politics for this Chapter (本章的课程思政目标)

Justifications for self – defense and necessities are found in the criminal laws in the UK and the US, as well as in many other countries. Although actions that can work as justifications bring harms, the seemingly harmful behaviour can be transformed into legitimate behavior for certain reasons except those caused by the actor. Therefore, actions that can be used as justifications are in nature justified. No matter which country's criminal law stipulates the justifications, these justifications share the same principle evil does not overpower righteousness and righteousness does not yield to evil. Therefore, an in – depth exploration of the legal basis and underlying value of the justifications can cultivate students' awareness of fairness.

英美刑法和其他国家的刑法一样,也有自我防卫、紧急避险等正当化事由。行为虽然造成了损害,但因行为人以外的其他原因,使具有危害的行为转变为具有正当性的行为。因此,从实质上看,具有正当化事由情形的行为本身具有正义性。无论哪个国家刑法规定的正当化事由,其本质与核心均依据的是邪不压正、正不屈于邪的原则。因此,深度探究正当化事由背后的这一法理依据和价值诉求,能培养学生的公正性意识。

In legitimate defense, whether it is a self – defense, defense of others, defense of property, or defense of home, citizens are granted the right to defend when their rights and interests are infringed upon. Therefore, legitimate defense is a right enjoyed by citizens. However, while citizens enjoying the right to defense, the law also sets conditions for the exercise of the right to defense. It means that the exercise of rights cannot exceed a certain limit and should be exercised within the scope of legitimacy. By analyzing and understanding the constitutive elements of legitimate defense, and uncovering the underlying reasons, students can cultivate an understanding of the rule, of law and an appreciation for rights.

在正当防卫中,无论是自我防卫、防卫他人、防卫财产,还是防卫住宅,均是法律赋予公民在自己权益遭受侵害时,进行防卫的权利。因此,正当防卫是公民享有的一种权利。但是,在国民享有防卫权的同时,法律又对防卫权的行使设置了条件。这意味着权利的行使不能超过一定的限度,且应在正当性的范畴内行使。通过对正当防卫构成要素的剖析和理解,发掘其背后的原因,能培养学生的法治精神和正确的权利意识。

■ Terminologies(专业术语)

affirmative defenses	积极抗辩事由
justifications	正当化事由
excuses	可宽恕事由
self - defense	自我防卫
deadly force	致命性武力
nonlethal force	非致命性武力
incomplete self - defense	不完全防卫
defense of others	防卫他人
defense of home and property	防卫住宅和财物
the castle laws	城堡法
the "new castle laws"	新城堡法
defense of habitation law	居所防御法
castle doctrine	城堡准则
choice of evils	两"害"相权取其轻
necessity	紧急避险
consent	被害人同意
Model Penal Code(MPC)	《模范刑法典》

5.1 Affirmative Defenses and Burden of Proof(积极抗辩事由和举证责任)

In criminal law, a criminal defense is a specific cause of action that can serve to relieve or mitigate guilt. Defenses can be divided into affirmative defenses and negative defenses. Negative defenses are related with the consitutive elements of the crime, and they are established when the constitutive elements of the crime are absent or are denied. Affirmative defenses include justifications and excuses, which are defenses that exist independently from the constitutive elements of the crime.

刑事抗辩事由是指在刑法上能够起到解脱或减轻罪责作用的特定事由。抗辩事由可以分为积极抗辩事由和消极抗辩事由。消极抗辩事由是从犯罪成立的构成要件出发,通过不具备或否定犯罪构成要件去抗辩犯罪的成立。积极抗辩事由具体包括正当化事由、可宽恕事由,是在犯罪构成要件之外提出的独立存在的抗辩事由。[1]

Among the affirmative defenses, justifications include self - defense, defense of others, defense of property, defense of the home and necessity. Excuses include mental illness, duress, battered woman syndrome and so on. Justifications and excuses are different: justifications are an evaluation of the behavior, while excuses are an evaluation of the actor. Justifications are permitted in law and are not a kind of criminal acts. Professor Robinson, an American scholar, points out: "Justifiable conduct is correct conduct that is encouraged, or at least tolerated. Excuses refer to the behavior that is legally wrong and undesirable. However, it is not appropriate to hold the actor criminally responsible because some characteristics of the actor have dissuaded society from punishing them." This chapter, focuses on justifications, and excuses will be discussed in chapter 6.

在积极抗辩事由中,正当化事由主要包括自我防卫、防卫他人、防卫财产、防卫住宅和紧急避险等;可宽恕事由主要包括精神病、胁迫、妇女综合征等。正当化事由和可宽恕事由是有区别的,其区别是:正当化事由是对行为的评价,可宽恕事由是对行为人的评价;正当化事由是被法律许可的,不属于犯罪行为。美国学者 Ribinson 教授指出:"正当化行为是被鼓励,至少是被容忍的正确行为。可宽恕事由表明行为在法律上是错误的和不受欢迎的,但是由于行为人的某些特征打消了社会处罚他的意愿,因此再追究刑事责任并不适当。"[2]本章主要讨论正当化事由,而可宽恕事由将在第6章进行阐述。

It is important to note that the differences between justifications and excuses have already received attention in the early English common law. However, the legal application the consequences of justifications and that of excuses are the same, leding to the waning interest of most scholars in the difference between the two in the 19th and 20th centuries. In light of this, it is not surprising that courts sometimes use the terms "justifications" and "excuses" interchangeably.

需要注意的是,早期的英国普通法就已经注意到了正当化事由与可宽恕事由之间的区分。但因为正当化事由与可宽恕事由的法律适用后果一致,所以19世纪到20世纪的多数学者对二者的差异兴趣减弱。鉴于此,法院有时交替使用"正当化事由"和"可宽恕事由"这两个用语。

---

〔1〕 参见夏勇:《英美刑法:五国刑法论要》,法律出版社2020年版,第56页。

〔2〕 Paul H. Robinson, *Criminal Law Defense*, Volume 1, West Publishing House, 1984, p. 100 - 101.

Most justifications and excuses are affirmative defenses, with a mechanism like this: defendants need to "provide some evidence in support" of their justification or excuse. We call this the burden of production.[1] It can be seen that the burden of proof for justifications and excuses, which are affirmative defenses, rests with the defendants. This is also in line with the general principle of the burden of proof in criminal proceedings, that is, the principle of "whoever claims, whoever proves".

大多数正当化事由和可宽恕事由都是积极抗辩事由,其运作方式是这样的:被告必须"通过提供一些证据来支持他们的正当化事由和可宽恕事由"。我们称为举证责任。由此可见,作为积极抗辩事由的正当化事由和可宽恕事由,是由被告方承担举证责任的。这也符合刑事程序举证责任的一般原则,即符合"谁主张,谁举证"原则。

Most defenses are perfect defenses; if they're successful, defendants are acquitted. A defense that does not constitute a perfect defense may lead to mitigation of criminal liability or a minor offense. For example, words, however insulting, cannot reduce murder to manslaughter in most states, but they might mitigate a death sentence to a life sentence without parole. So when a black man killed a white man in a rage due to the White man's relentless taunting of "nigger, nigger", the killing was still regarded murder but the taunting might mitigate the death penalty to a life sentence without parole.[2]

大多数辩护事由都是完美辩护:如果辩护成功,被告会被无罪释放。而不构成完美辩护的抗辩事由,则可能令被告获得减轻刑事责任或转为轻罪的处置。例如,在大多数州,无论多么具有侮辱性的言词都无法将谋杀罪减轻为过失杀人罪,但却可能将死刑减轻为无假释的终身监禁。因此,当一个黑人男子因白人男子无情地嘲讽他为"黑鬼,黑鬼"而愤怒地杀死一个白人男子时,杀人行为仍然是谋杀,但因为白人男子的嘲讽行为可以将黑人男子的刑罚从死刑减轻为终身监禁。

5.2 Self – Defense(自我防卫)

In contemporary U. S. criminal law, self – defense is an act of aggression by the actor against a wrongdoer to avoid the threat, when the actor reasonably believes that there is an imminent threat to his or her personal safety by the wrongdoing. Specifically, the act of self – defense can be further divided into two types: self – defence with deadly

---

[1] Joel Samaha, *Criminal Law*, 10th edition, Wadsworth Cengage Learning Press, 2011, p. 136.

[2] Joel Samaha, *Criminal Law*, 10th edition, Wadsworth Cengage Learning Press, 2011, p. 137.

force and self - defence with nonlethal force. For what is a reasonable measure of defense, in what circumstance deadly force can be used and in what circumstance only nonlethal force can be used, this criterion should be set with comprehensive consideration, and is not immutable. Self - defense is a defense to all crimes, including murder and treason. Below is a brief introduction to the constituent elements of self - defense.

在现在的美国刑法中,自我防卫是指行为人在合理地相信自己的人身安全面临紧迫的不法侵害威胁的情况下,为了避免威胁而对不法侵害者实施的必要的侵害行为。[1] 具体又可以将防卫行为划分为致命性武力和非致命性武力防卫两种。对于什么是合理的防卫措施,何时可以使用致命的暴力,何时只能采用非致命的暴力,这个标准要综合考虑,并非一成不变。自我防卫可以对所有犯罪进行抗辩,包括谋杀罪和叛国罪。下面将简单介绍自我防卫的构成要素。

5.2.1 Elements of Self - Defense(自我防卫的构成要素)

Generally speaking, self - defense consists of four elements: (1) *Unprovoked attack* The defender didn't start or provoke the attack. (2) *Necessity* Defenders can use deadly force only if it is necessary to repel an imminent deadly attack, namely one that is going to happen right now. (3) *Proportionality* Defenders can use deadly force only if the use of nonlethal force is not enough; excessive force is not allowed. (4) *Reasonable belief* The defender reasonably believes that it is necessary to use deadly force to repel the imminent deadly attack.[2]

These, four elements are further elaborated below.

一般而言,自卫包括4个要素:(1)无端攻击,防卫者没有发动或挑起攻击;(2)必要性,自卫者只有在有必要抵御迫在眉睫的致命攻击(眼下即将发生的攻击)时才能使用致命武力;(3)相称性,自卫者只有在使用非致命武力不够的情况下才可以使用致命武力,即不允许过度使用武力;(4)合理确信,自卫者必须合理地认为,有必要使用致命武力抵御迫在眉睫的致命攻击。

下面,将对无端攻击、必要性、相称性和合理确信这4个构成要素进行阐述。

5.2.1.1 Unprovoked Attack (无端攻击)

Self - defense is available only against unprovoked attacks. So it is not available to an initial aggressor; someone who provokes an attack cannot then use force to defend

---

[1] 参见刘士心:《美国刑法中的犯罪论原理》,人民出版社2010年版,第136页。

[2] Joel Samaha, *Criminal Law*, 10th edition, Wadsworth Cengage Learning Press, 2011, p. 138.

themselves against the attack they provoked. With one exception: according to the rule of withdrawal exception, if attackers completely withdraw from attacks they provoke, they can defend themselves from an attack by their initial victims. For example, in the case of State v. Good, a son threatened to shoot his father with a shotgun. The father went to a neighbor's house, borrowed the neighbor's shotgun, and came back. The son told him to "stop". When the father shot, the son turned and ran. However, the father continued to pursued the son. The son then turned back and shot his father dead. Although the son had become an initiral attacker due to his intent to kill his father, the son gave up his intent when the father came back to him. It means that the son had withdraw from his inital attack, and fled from the father in good faith of withdraw. Knowing that the defendant was endeavoring to withdraw, pursued the son and sought to kill him, or do him some grievous bodily harm, then the son's right of self - defense is revived, and the son's killing of his father is regarded as a self - defense.[1]

自卫的成立首先就是有无端攻击的发生。因此,最初的攻击者不能适用正当防卫;挑起攻击的人不能使用武力来抵御他挑起的攻击。但有一个例外:根据"撤出例外"规则,如果攻击者完全撤出了他挑起的攻击,就可以对最初受害者的攻击进行自卫。比如,在 State v. Good 这个案件中:一个儿子威胁要用猎枪射杀他的父亲。父亲去了邻居家,借了邻居的猎枪回来。儿子让他"住手"。父亲开枪后,儿子转身就跑,父亲追了上去。儿子转身向父亲开枪,杀死了父亲。尽管儿子可能是出于杀死父亲的意图而成了最初的攻击者,但后来父亲要加害他时,儿子已经放弃了他对父亲的加害。这意味着儿子已经"撤出"其最先进行的攻击,并为了"撤出"而真心地从父亲面前逃离。后来,在他父亲知道儿子正从这种冲突中解脱出来,但仍然追赶儿子并试图杀死他,或对他造成某种严重的身体伤害时,儿子可以进行自我防卫。因此,后面儿子杀死父亲的行为属于自我防卫。

5.2.1.2 Necessity(必要性)

Necessity refers to an imminent danger of attack and therefore a need for defense. Simply put, it means, "The time for defense is right now!" Necessity means that an attack is imminent and has created an imminent danger to personal rights. In other words, the attack is "in progress" and must be defended immediately. In such an emergency, the person attacked cannot wait for official authorities to protect his interests. In order to avoid the attack and minimize harm, they must act on their own.

---

[1] Joel Samaha, *Criminal Law*, 10th edition, Wadsworth Cengage Learning Press, 2011, p. 138.

Necessity does not limit the defender to the killing of someone who is going to kill. The defender can also kill an attacker whom they reasonably believe is right now going to grievely hurt them or someone else.[1] Under the Model Penal Code, physical force can be used to stop such behavior as long as the attack is real.[2]

必要性是指面对面对迫在眉睫的攻击危险,有必要进行防卫。简单地说,就是“现在必须立即进行防卫!”。必要性就是某种攻击迫在眉睫,并且已对人身权利产生紧迫的危险。换言之,攻击是“正在进行”,必须立即予以抵御。在这种紧急情况下,被攻击者不能等待官方来保护他的利益。为了避免被攻击,尽量减少伤害,他必须自己采取行动。必要性并不局限于杀死将要杀人的人,也可以杀死一个被合理相信现在会严重伤害防卫者或其他人的杀人者。根据《模范刑法典》的规定,只要攻击是现实存在的,就可以使用武力制止这种行为。

5.2.1.3 Proportionality(相称性)

The basic requirement of proportionality in United States criminal law is “be reasonably proportionate to the threatened harm which defender seeks to avoid”.[3] If the reasonable limit is the use of nonlethal force, deadly force cannot be used; deadly force cannot be used to counter non - deadly force. For example, a defendant who reasonably believes that another person is committing unlawful violence against him, and the force does not rise to the level of death or serious injury. Correspondingly, the defendant use non - deadly force in self - defense. If the defendant reasonably believes that another person is committing an unlawful killing or serious injury against him, they may use deadly force in self - defense.

美国刑法关于相称性的基本要求是“与防卫者试图避免的侵害威胁相称”。如果使用非致命的武力是合理的限度,就不能使用致命的武力,不能用致命武力反抗非致命的武力。例如,被告人合理相信另一个人正在对他实施非法暴力,但该暴力尚未达到死亡或严重伤害的程度,他就可以实施非致命的武力进行自卫。如果被告人合理相信另一个人正在对他实施非法的杀害或严重伤害,他可以使用致命的武力进行自我防卫。

However, some self - defense statutes go by allowing the use of deadly force in defense of “imminent” felonies even though they do not threaten life or cause grievous

---

[1] Joel Samaha, *Criminal Law*, 10th edition, Wadsworth Cengage Learning Press, 2011, p. 138 - 139.

[2] Model Penal Code § 3.04(1).

[3] Wayne R. Lafave & Austin W. Scott, Jr., *Substantive Criminal law*, volume 1, West Publishing Co., 1986, p. 651.

bodily harm. These felonies typically include rape, sodomy, child molestation, and armed robbery. They also include burglary and sometimes crimes against personal property.

不过,有些自卫法规甚至更进一步,允许使用致命武力防卫"即将"发生的但不会威胁到生命或引起严重身体伤害的重罪。这些重罪通常包括强奸、鸡奸、猥亵儿童和武装抢劫,甚至包括入室盗窃,有时还包括侵害个人财产的犯罪。

5.2.1.4 Reasonable Belief(合理确信)

Regardless of whether the above three elements of defense exist objectively, as long as the actor reasonably believes in their existence, a defense of self - defense can be established. In other words, "Reasonable Belief" works as a guidance serving as the basis fro evaluating other elements like "degree", "time" and "cause".

无论上述三种防卫的要素在客观上是否存在,只要行为人在主观上合理确信它们存在,就可以成立防卫的辩护理由。[1]换言之,"合理确信"条件具有统帅性,其是"限度""时间""原因"等条件的判断基础。

The reasonable belief of the actor has two fold meanings: (1) the actor actually believes; (2) the actor's belief is reasonable. Opinions on the criterion of "reasonableness" are divided, and two different positions have been developed, one objective and the other subjective. The objective criterion is: a reasonable person in the same situation would have believed that the attack was imminent, and that the need for force, and the amount of force used, were necessary to repel an attack.[2] If the actor had an honest but unreasonable belief in the circumstances, it cannot constitute self - defense. The subjective standard is the defender's criterion, which means that an actor has a reasonable belief if he/she believes it is necessary to use deadly force to protect himself or herself from imminent, unlawful, and deadly violence. This is also the standard adopted by the Model Penal Code and regulated by §3.04(1). However, the Model Penal Code limits the subjective standard through §3.09(2), which stipulates that the defendant may be convicted of reckless or negligent homicide if the defendant's subjective belief is found to be reckless or negligent. This additional provision can avoid extreme situations resulting from the application of the subjective standard, and can prevent the occurrence of injustice arising from the subjective standard.

行为人主观上的合理确信包含两个方面的含义:(1)行为人实际地相信

---

〔1〕 参见刘士心:《美国刑法中的犯罪论原理》,人民出版社2010年版,第141页。

〔2〕 Joel Samaha, *Criminal Law*, 10th edition, Wadsworth Cengage Learning Press, 2011, p. 139.

(actually believe);(2)行为人的相信是合理的(reasonable)。[1] 合理标准的判断有分歧,且形成了客观标准和主观标准两种不同的立场。客观标准是指:一个理性人在同样的情况下会相信攻击是迫在眉睫的,需要使用武力以及使用武力的程度是击退攻击所必需的。如果行为人对当时的防卫情况真诚地相信但相信理由不合理,就不能构成自我防卫。主观标准是防卫者标准,即行为人认为使用致命武力才能保护其自身避免遭受迫近的不法致命暴力的伤害,则行为人使用致命性武力对抗他人就具有合理确信。[2] 这也是《模范刑法典》采取的标准,且由§3.04(1)予以规定。但是《模范刑法典》通过§3.09(2)对此主观标准进行了限制:如果被告的主观确信存在轻率或者疏忽,则被告可能因其轻率或疏忽被定杀人罪。[3] 这一补充规定能避免适用主观标准导致的极端化情况,防止主观标准产生的不公正发生。

However, it should be mentioned that the standards, with regard to judging reasonable belief and adopted by many jurisdictions of common law system, are different from the subjective standard of the Model Penal Code. In short, although the Model Penal Code adopts subjective standard and many jurisdictions follow it, there are still many jurisdictions, in the common law system, that adopt objective standard.

但是,需要提及的是:针对合理确信的判断,普通法下的很多司法区域所采用的标准,是与《模范刑法典》的主观标准不同的。简言之,尽管《模范刑法典》采用了主观标准,且有很多司法管辖仿效之,但在普通法系,还是有很多司法管辖区采取了客观标准。

5.2.2 The Change of Retreat Rule(退让规则的变化)

In the justifiable defense of British and American criminal law, there used to be the principle of retreat. But as time passed by, this requirement was gradually eliminated. We will briefly introduce the development and changes of the principle of retreat, below.

曾经在英美刑法的正当防卫中,是有"退让原则"的。但随着时间的推移,这一要件逐渐被取消。

As far back as the thirteenth century, English common law punishes severely homicide resulting from self - defense. However, if the defendant can prove that he or she "has retreated to the wall", then self - defense can be established. The English common law "retreat to the wall" survived in a minority of American states. But one of

---

〔1〕 参见刘士心:《美国刑法中的犯罪论原理》,人民出版社2010年版,第141页。

〔2〕 参见[美]约书亚·德雷斯勒:《美国刑法纲要》,姜敏译,中国法制出版社2016年版,第187页。

〔3〕 参见[美]约书亚·德雷斯勒:《美国刑法纲要》,姜敏译,中国法制出版社2016年版,第187页。

the most important charges in American legal and social history occurred in the nineteenth century when the nation as a whole repudiated the English common - law tradition in favor of an American theme of "no duty to retreat": that one was legally justified in standing one's ground to kill in self - defense. Recognized at the time as a crucial change and as "American mind". Thus, the harsh "principle of retreat", which had existed for centuries in British self - defense system, was abolished and replaced by a more lenient self - defense system without the element of "retreat".〔1〕

早在13世纪,英国普通法就严厉惩罚自我防卫导致的杀人行为。但是,如果被告能证明自己已"退到墙角",则可以成立自我防卫而出罪。英国普通法中的"退到墙角"规则在美国少数州得以保留。但是在19世纪,美国法律和社会历史发生了重要的变革,整个国家抛弃了英国普通法传统,转而支持"无退却义务":一个人在自卫时站在原地杀人,其行为在法律上是正当的。这在当时被视为关键性转变,且被视为"美国人思想"。就这样,在英国自我防卫中存在长达数百年之久的严苛的"退让原则"被取消,取而代之的是不需要"退让"要素的更宽容的自我防卫规则。

Currently, most jurisdictions in America do not have a requirement of retreat in self - defense; the defender has no duty to retreat. So Judges and legislators generalized the right to self - defense into the majority stand - your - ground rule, namely that if the defender didn't start the fight, he could stand his ground and kill to "defend himself without retreating from any place he had a right to be".〔2〕

目前,美国大多数管辖区自我防卫并没有退让的要求。也就是说,防卫者没有退却的义务。也正是基于这个原因,法官和立法者将自卫权概括为多数人的站在原地原则:如果防卫者没有挑起冲突,他就可以站在原地实施防卫,以"保护自己不从他有权站立的地方撤退"。

A few jurisdictions provide that a non - attacker may not use deadly force to prevent/fend off an attack if they know that they can retreat to a place of complete safety, but a key exception exists: a defender is never required to flee his or her home. It is the content of the "defense of the home" (castle law) described below. According to this castle exception, when you're attacked in your home, you can stand your ground and use deadly force to fend off an unprovoked attack, but only if you reasonably believe the attack threatens death or serious bodily injury.〔3〕

---

〔1〕 Joel Samaha, *Criminal Law*, 10th edition, Wadsworth Cengage Learning Press, 2011, p. 143.

〔2〕 Joel Samaha, *Criminal Law*, 10th edition, Wadsworth Cengage Learning Press, 2011, p. 143.

〔3〕 Joel Samaha, *Criminal Law*, 10th edition, Wadsworth Cengage Learning Press, 2011, p. 143.

少数管辖区规定,如果非攻击者知道其可以退到一个完全安全的地方,则其不得使用致命的武力来排除侵害。但存在一个关键性例外:绝不能要求防卫者逃离其住所。[1] 这也就是下面介绍的"防卫住宅"(城堡法)的内容。根据城堡例外原则,当一个人在家中受到攻击时,其可以站在原地使用致命武力抵御无端攻击,但前提是他有理由相信该无端攻击会威胁到他的生命安全或对他造成严重的身体伤害。

■ Case study(案例学习)

UNITED STATES v. PETERSON, United States Court of Appeals. District of Columbia Circuit, 1973. 483F. 2d 1222. (美国诉彼得森案)[2]

Fact(基本案情)

The events immediately preceding the homicide are clear. Charles Keitt, the deceased, and two friends drove in Keitt's car to the alley in the rear of Peterson's house removing the windshield wipers from Peterson's wrecked car. While Keitt was doing so, Peterson came out of the house into the back yard to protest. After an altercation, Peterson went back into the house, obtained a pistol, and returned to the yard. In the meantime, Keitt had reseated himself in his car, and he and his companions were about to leave with his companison.

凶杀案发生前的事实清楚。死者查尔斯·基特和两个朋友开着基特的车来到彼得森家后面的小巷,从彼得森废弃的车上拆下雨刷器。在凯特这样做的时候,彼得森从房子里出来到后院抗议。经过一番言语交锋,彼得森回到屋内,拿起一把手枪后回到院子里。在此期间,基特在他的车里坐了下来,和他的同伴准备离开。

Upon his reappearance in the yard, Peterson paused briefly to load the pistol. "If you move", he shouted to Keitt, "I will shoot". Peterson walked to a point in the yard slightly inside a gate in the rear fence and, pistol in hand, said, "If you come in here I will kill you". Keitt alighted from his car, took a few steps toward Peterson and exclaimed, "What the hell do you think you are going to do with that?" Keitt then returned to his car and retrieved a lug wrench. With the wrench in a raised position, Keitt advanced toward Peterson, who stood with the pistol pointed toward him. Peterson warned Keitt not to "take another step" and, when Keitt continued onward shot him in

---

[1] 参见[美]约书亚·德雷斯勒:《美国刑法纲要》,姜敏译,中国法制出版社2016年版,第34页。

[2] Joshua Dressler & Stephen Garvey, *Cases and Materials on Criminal Law*, 6th edition, West Academic, 2012, p. 500 – 510.

the face from a distance of about ten feet. Death was apparently instantaneous.

当彼得森再次出现在院子里时,他短暂停顿了一下,给手枪上了子弹。"如果你敢动,"他对基特喊道,"我就开枪。"他走到院子里靠近后方围栏的门那里,手里拿着手枪,说:"如果你进来,我会杀了你。"基特从车上下来,朝彼得森走了几步,并喊道:"你以为你要用这个做什么?"然后基特转过身来,回他的车上拿了一把扳手。基特将扳手举起,朝彼得森走去。彼得森站在原地,用手枪对准基特,并警告他不要"再走一步",当基特继续前进时,彼得森从距离大约10英尺(约3米)的地方向基特的脸部开了枪,当场打死了基特。

Dispute(主要争议)

The first of Peterson's complaints centers upon an instruction that the right to use deadly force in self - defense is not ordinarily available to one who provokes a conflict or is the aggressor in it. The evidence is uncontradicted that when Peterson reappeared in the yard with his pistol, Keitt was about to depart the scene. The indisputable fact thar Keitt was leaving shows plainly that so far as he was concerned the confrontation was ended. It demonstrates just as plainly that even if he had previously been the aggressor, he no longer was.

彼得森的第一项控诉集中在自卫中使用致命武力的权利通常不适用于挑起冲突或在冲突中作为攻击者的人。当彼得森带着手枪再次出现在院子里时,基特正要离开现场。基特要离开这一不争的事实清楚地表明,对基特而言对抗已经结束了。换言之,即使基特先前是侵略者,但他现在已不再是攻击者了。

The second aspect of the trial judge's charge as to which Peterson asserts error concerned the undisputed fact that at no time did Peterson endeavor to retreat from Keitt's approach with the lug wrench. The judge instructed the jury that if Peterson could have safely retreated but did not do so, that failure was a circumstance which the jury might consider, together with all others, in determining whether he went further in repelling the danger, real or apparent, than he was justified in going. Peterson contends that this imputation of an obligation to retreat was error, even if he could safely have done so. He points out that at the time of the shooting he was standing in his own yard, and argues he was under no duty to move. The Appeals Court are persuaded to the conclusion that in the circum - stances presented here, the trial judge did not error in giving the instruction challenged.

彼得森认为,法官指控的第二个方面是错误的。这涉及一个无可争议的事实,即彼得森在整个过程中,根本就没有试图从基特拿着扳手的做法中退让。法官对陪审团说:如果彼得森可以安全地撤退但却没有这样做,陪审团应该把这点和其他要素同时考虑后,再决定他是不是在防卫危险时超过了必要限度。彼得森争辩说,即使他可以安全地撤退,但这种对退让义务的指责也是错误的。因为他认为,在枪击事件发生时,他正站在自己的院子里,他没有退让的义务。最后,上诉法院得出的结论是,在本案的情况下,初审法官的判决并没有错。

It should be noted that this case arises in the District of Columbia. Although the "castle" doctrine is almost universally accepted in the United States jurisdictions, its status in the District of Columbia has never been clearly established.

需要说明的是,本案发生于哥伦比亚特区。尽管城堡例外原则在提出这一观点的美国司法管辖区内几乎被普遍接受,但其在哥伦比亚特区的地位却从未得到明确的确立。

Conclusion(结论)

SPOTTSWOOD W. ROBINSON, III, CIRCUIT JUDGE:

Indicted for second – degree murder, and convicted by a jury of manslaughter as a lesser included offense, Bennie L. Peterson [appeals]. He complains that the judge twice erred in the instructions given the jury in relation to his claim that the homicide was committed in Self – defense. One error alleged was an instruction that the jury might consider whether Peterson was the aggressor in the altercation that immediately foreran the homicide. The other was an instruction that a failure by Peterson to retreat, if he could have done so without jeopardizing his safety, might be considered as a circumstance bearing on the question whether he was justified in using the amount of force which he did. The Court of Appeals affirm Peterson's conviction.

斯伯茨伍德 · W. 罗宾逊三世(Spottswood W. Robinson, Ⅲ)巡回法官认定:彼得森被指控犯有二级谋杀罪,并被陪审团判定犯有过失杀人罪,作为较轻的罪行。彼得森上诉称,关于他杀人是出于自卫的主张,法官给陪审团两次错误指示。其中一个错误指示是,关于陪审团考虑彼得森是否是凶杀案发生前争吵中的攻击者。另一个指示是,彼得森没有退让,如果彼得森在不危及自身安全的情况下可以退让,那么可以考虑他是否有理由使用他所使用的武力的问题。对于彼得森的行为,上诉法院维持原判。

Questions:1. Whether the case meets the proportionality requirement for self – defense?

本案是否符合正当防卫的比例要求?(Please scan the QR code on the right to get the answer)(答案请扫描右侧二维码获取)

2. Does Peterson have a duty to retreat?(The way to obtain the answer is the same as above)

彼得森是否有撤退义务?(答案获取方式同上)

5.3 Defense of Others(防卫他人)

In the United States, the defense of others means that a person can use reasonable force to keep another person from being harmed. The common law places more stringent limits on the right of defense of others. The elements of defense of others are essentially the same as those of self – defense: first, the defendant must have reasonably believed that the person being assisted was experiencing an unlawful invasion; second, the defendant's use of violence must be limited to stopping the unlawful invasion; and third, the defendant must have a reasonable belief that the person being assisted had the right to use self – defense.

在美国刑法中,防卫他人是指一个人可以使用合理的武力,保护另一个人免受不法侵害。普通法对防卫他人的权利进行了较为严格的限制。防卫他人的构成要件为:其一,被告人必须合理地相信被帮助者正在经受非法侵害;其二,被告人使用暴力要以制止非法侵害为限;其三,被告人必须合理相信被帮助者有权使用自我防卫。[1]

Issues requiring special attention include:

需要特别地注意的问题有:

1. The scope of "others". Most courts and statutes allow the defender's protection of the person of friends other than relatives, as well as strangers, but some courts limit the defense of others only to the protection of relatives. However, the modern view of the law, the tends to remove the restrictive scope of the object of protection, and the protection of relatives, friends, strangers, etc. , from unlawful invasion can be used as a criminal defense.

"他人"的范围。多数法院和制定法都允许防卫者对亲属之外的朋友以及陌生人的人身加以保护,但是,有一些法院仅将防卫他人的范围限制在亲属内。不过,现代法律的观点是倾向于取消保护对象的限制范围,保护亲属、朋友、陌生人等免受不法侵害,都可以作为刑事抗辩理由。

2. On the necessity of "retreat". According to the Model Penal Code, if it is possible for the assisted person to retreat first, the defender should help the other person

---

〔1〕 参见夏勇:《英美刑法:五国刑法论要》,法律出版社 2020 年版,第 117 页。

to retreat as much as possible, and cannot use deadly force directly. That means deadly force can be used only if the retreat is unsuccessful. However, the defender and the assisted person are not required to retreat first in residential and office premises.

关于“退让”的必要性。根据《模范刑法典》的规定,被帮助者如果有可能先退让,则防卫者应当尽可能地帮助他人退让,不能直接使用致命的暴力。也就是说,只有在退让不成功时防卫者才可以使用致命暴力。但是,在居民住宅和办公场所时,防卫者和被帮助人可以不先行退让。

3. Whether it is conditional on the “other person” objectively possessing the right of defense. For example, A and B got into a conflict and the defendant went to protect A because the defendant believed that A, whom he was protecting, was being wrongfully assaulted, but in fact B was a plainclothes police officer and B’s physical injury to A was lawful, and the defendant instead obstructed the police officer’s law enforcement activities. Does the defendant still establish a defense of defense of others? There are two different principles in American criminal law that deal with this issue: the reasonable - appearance rule; and the act - in - peril rule, also know as the “stands in the shoes” rule, or the “alter ego” rule. Traditionally, it has been evaluated according to the act - in - peril rule, which allows the defender to use violence to protect other person as long as the defender reasonably believes that the other person is experiencing an unlawful attack, even if the defendant’s judgment of unlawful violence is wrong. Currently, the provisions of the Model Penal Code are based on the “act - in - peril rule”.

是否以“他人”客观上拥有防卫权为条件。例如,A、B 双方起了冲突,被告人去保护 A,因为被告人认为他保护的 A 正在受到不法侵害,但实际上 B 是一名便衣警察,B 对 A 的人身伤害是合法的,被告人反而妨害了警察的执法活动。此时,被告人是否依然成立防卫他人的抗辩呢?关于这一问题,美国刑法中有两种不同的处理原则:一是表面合理原则(reasonable - appearance rule);二是实际处境原则(act - in - peril rule),其也被称为设身处地原则(stands in the shoes),还有人把其称为“另一个我”(alter ego)规则。[1] 传统的做法是根据实际处境原则进行评价,只要防卫者合理地认为他人正在经受非法侵害,就可以使用合理的暴力保护他人,即使防卫者对非法暴力的判断是错误的。目前,《模范刑法典》的规定采取的是实际处境原则。

---

〔1〕 参见刘士心:《美国刑法中的犯罪论原理》,人民出版社 2010 年版,第 145 页。

■ Case study(案例学习)

PEOPLE v. KURR, Court of Appeals of Michigan, 2002. 253 Mich. App. 317, 654 N. W. 2d 651.[1] **(检察官诉库尔案)**

Fact(基本案情)

The defendant stabbed Pena on October 9, 1999. According to a Kalamazoo police officer, the defendant told him that she and Pena had argued that day over Pena's cocaine use. The defendant told the officer that Pena subsequently punched her twice in the stomach and that she warned Pena not to hit her because she was carrying his babies. After the dispute when Pena came toward the defendant again, she stabbed Pena in the chest. Pena died as a result of the stab wound.

被告于1999年10月9日刺伤了佩纳。据一名卡拉马祖警官称,被告告诉他,她和佩纳当天因佩纳使用可卡因而发生争执。被告告诉警官,在发生争执后,佩纳在她的腹部打了两拳,被告警告佩纳不要打她,因为被告怀着佩纳的孩子。当佩纳再次向她走来时,她用刀刺向佩纳的胸部。佩纳因被刺伤而死亡。

Months before trial, the defendant moved for permission to present testimony and to argue that she killed Pena in defense of her unborn babies. The trial court concluded that a person could use the defense of others as a defense.

在审判前几个月,被告请求法院允许她提供证词并辩称她杀死佩纳是为了保护她未出生的孩子。审判法庭认为,一个人可以把防卫他人作为辩护理由。

Dispute(主要争议)

In this case, in order to determine whether the court should indeed have given the defense of others instruction, we must initially decide the purely legal question whether a nonviable fetus constitutes an "other" in the context of this defense. With certain restrictions, we conclude that it does.

在该案中,必须首先解决一个纯粹的法律问题:无法存活的胎儿在这种防卫中是否构成"他人"? 在某些限制条件下,胎儿是一个"他人"。

"In Michigan, the killing of another person in self-defense is justifiable homicide if the defendant honestly and reasonably believes that his life is in imminent danger or that there is a threat of serious bodily harm." Case law in Michigan also allows a person to use deadly force in defense of another. Traditionally, the "defense of others" concept

---

[1] Joshua Dressler & Stephen Garvey, *Cases and Materials on Criminal Law*, 6th edition, West Academic, 2012, p. 549-553.

applied solely to those persons with whom the defendant had a special relationship, such as a wife or brother. The defense now makes no distinction between strangers and relatives with to its application.

"在密歇根州,如果被告诚实和合理地认为他的生命处于迫在眉睫的危险中,或者其面对有严重的身体伤害的威胁,那么在自我防卫中杀死另一个人是正当的。"密歇根州的判例法也允许一个人在保卫他人时使用致命的武力。传统上,"保卫他人"的概念只适用于那些与被告有特殊关系的人,如妻子或兄弟。现在的防卫在适用上对陌生人和亲属没有区别。

The plain language of these provisions shows the Legislature's conclusion that fetuses are worthy of protection as living entities as a matter of public policy. Indeed, we note that a violation of one provision of the Act is punishable by up to life imprisonment, nearly the harshest punishment available in our state. Moreover, in enacting the fetal protection act, the Legislature did not distinguish between fetuses that are viable, or capable of surviving outside the womb, and those that are nonviable. In fact, the Legislature used the term "embryo" as well as the term "fetus" in describing the prohibited conduct.

立法机构的结论是,作为公共政策问题,胎儿值得作为生命实体受到保护。事实上,违反胎儿保护法的一项规定可被判处终身监禁,这几乎是密歇根州最严厉的惩罚。此外,在制定胎儿保护法时,立法机构并没有区分有生命力的胎儿,或有能力在子宫外生存的胎儿,以及没有生命力的胎儿。事实上,立法机构在描述被禁止的行为时,既使用了"胚胎"一词,也使用了"胎儿"一词。

Because the act reflects a public policy to protect even an embryo from unlawful assaultive or negligent conduct, we conclude that the defense of others concept does extend to the protection of a nonviable fetus from an assault against the mother. We emphasize, however, that the defense is available solely in the context of an assault against the mother. Indeed, the Legislature has not extended the protection of the criminal laws to embryos existing outside a woman's body, i. e. , frozen embryos stored for future use, and we therefore do not extend the applicability of the defense of others theory to situations involving these embryos.

由于该法案反映了保护胚胎免受非法攻击或过失行为的公共政策,因此法院的结论是,防卫他人的概念确实延伸到保护无法生存的胎儿免受对母亲的攻击。然而,法院强调,该辩护仅适用于针对母亲的攻击行为。事实上,立法机构并没有将刑法的保护范围扩大到妇女体外的胚胎,即为将来使用而储存的冷冻胚胎,因此法院并没有将为他人防卫理论的适用性扩大到涉及这些胚胎的情况。

Conclusion(结论)

METER, PRESIDING JUSTICE.

Defendant, who killed her boyfriend, Antonio Pena, with a knife, appeals from her conviction by a jury of voluntary manslaughter. The trial court sentenced her as a fourth – offense habitual offender to five to twenty years' imprisonment. Defendant argues on appeal that she should have been allowed a jury instruction regarding the defense of others because the jurors could have concluded that she killed Pena while defending her unborn children. We agree that a defense of others jury instruction was appropriate here and therefore reverse defendant's conviction and remand this case for a new trial.

该案主审法官认为,被告用刀杀死了她的男友佩纳,她对陪审团判定的故意杀人罪提出上诉。初审法院将她作为第四次犯罪的惯犯,判处 5 年至 20 年的监禁。被告在上诉中辩称,她应该有防卫他人的陪审团指令,因为陪审团成员可能会据此得出结论,她在保护她未出生的孩子时杀死了佩纳。法庭同意陪审团的防卫他人指示在这里是适当的,因此推翻了对被告的定罪,并将此案发回重审。

Note(注意)

Some states have enacted special statutes to deal with the issue. In 2009, for example, Oklahoma enacted the Use of Force for the Protection of the Unborn Act, which provides, in part:

美国的一些州已经制定了专门的法规来处理类似问题。例如,2009 年,俄克拉何马州颁布了《使用武力保护未出生婴儿法》,其中部分规定:

A. A pregnant woman is justified in using force or deadly force against another to protect her unborn child if:

在以下情况中,孕妇有理由对他人使用武力或致命武力来保护其未出生的孩子:

1. Under the circumstances as the pregnant woman reasonably believes them to be, she would be justified in using force or deadly force to protect herself against the unlawful force or unlawful deadly force she reasonably believes to be threatening her unborn child; and

在孕妇有理由相信她使用武力或致命武力的行为(保护自己免受有可能威胁其未出生孩子的非法武力或非法致命武力侵害的行为)是合法的;以及

2. She reasonably believes that her intervention and use of force or deadly force are immediately necessary to protect her unborn child.

她有理由相信她的干预和使用武力或致命武力对保护她未出生的孩子是立即必要的。

B. This affirmative defense to criminal liability does not apply to:

这种对刑事责任的肯定性辩护不适用于:

1. Acts committed by anyone other than the pregnant woman;

由孕妇以外的任何人所实施的行为;

2. Acts where the pregnant woman would be obligated to retreat, to surrender the possession of a thing, or to comply with a demand before using force in self – defense. However, the pregnant woman is not obligated to retreat before using force or deadly force to protect her unborn child, unless she knows that she can thereby secure the complete safety of her unborn child; or

孕妇在使用武力自卫前有义务退让、交出物品或服从要求的情况。然而,在使用武力或致命武力保护其未出生的孩子之前,孕妇没有退让义务,除非她知道她可以用退让确保其未出生孩子的完全安全;

3. The defense of human embryos existing outside of a woman's body.

对存在于妇女身体之外的人类胚胎的保护。

Questions:1. whether a nonviable fetus constitutes an "other" in the context of this case. (Please scan the QR code on the right to get the answer)

在这一案例中,无法存活的胎儿是否构成"他人"?(答案请扫描右侧二维码获取)

2. Does the defense of "embryos" apply only to assaults against the mother? Can the protection of criminal law be extended to a woman's embryos outside her body (frozen embryos stored for future use)? (The way to obtain the answer is the same as above)

防卫"胚胎"是否仅适用于针对母亲的攻击行为?是否能将刑法的保护范围扩大到妇女体外的胚胎(将来使用而储存的冷冻胚胎)?(答案获取方式同上)

3. Are pregnant women obligated to retreat before using force in self – defense? (The way to obtain the answer is the same as above)

孕妇在使用武力自卫前是否有义务退让?(答案获取方式同上)

5.4 Defense of Home and Property(防卫住宅和财物)

Defense of home and property means that a defendant may use violence to protect his or her property or to defend his or her home when a person's lawful property is illegally attacked or when another person illegally enters his or her real estate. In U. S. criminal law, some theoretical perspectives juxtapose the defense of home and the defense of property, while others separate them.

防卫住宅和财物是指当一个人的合法财物受到非法侵害,或者当他人非法进入自己的不动产时,被告人可以使用暴力保护自己的财物或防卫住宅。在美国刑法中,有的理论观点将防卫住宅和防卫财物并列,有的理论观点将其分开。

In the defense of property, the issues to be kept in mind are:

1. The limits of the use of violence. In the defense of property, there are limits to the use of violence, which should be limited to the preventing of actual damage to one's possessions. If it is possible to prevent other people's infringement on one's own property in ways other than the use of violence, there is no need to use violence, and deadly force generally cannot be used. Generally speaking, when one's own property faces unlawful infringement, one can use non - deadly force to protect one's own property; if the defender commits nonlethal force, and then the aggressor retaliates by physically assaulting him or her, in such a case, the defender can use deadly force in self - defense.

在防卫财物中,需要注意的问题有:

暴力使用的限度。在防卫财物的情形中,暴力的使用是有限度的,应当以防止自己的财物受到的实际损失为限度。如果能够以使用暴力之外的其他方式防止他人对自己财物的侵害,就没有必要使用暴力,且一般不能使用致命的暴力。一般来说,当自己的财物面临非法侵害时,可以使用非致命暴力保护自己的财物;如果防卫者实施了非致命的暴力,随后侵害者却进行人身攻击予以反击,这种情况下,可以使用致命暴力进行自我防卫。[1]

2. Is it permissible to take back property afterwards? In judicial practice, a situation often arises where personal property is acquired by another person on the spot, but the defender is not taking back his or her property on the spot, can it be a defense of property and constitute a criminal defense? In this regard, according to the U. S. Model Penal Code, a defendant may retrieve his or her property at any time, as long as he or she believes that another person is not entitled to a possession of his or her property. For example, if a defendant has his or her cell phone stolen and, a few days later, sees another person using the cell phone on the street, the defendant may use reasonable force

〔1〕 参见夏勇:《英美刑法:五国刑法论要》,法律出版社 2020 年版,第 118 页。

to retrieve his or her cell phone if he or she reasonably believes that the other person is the person who stole it. If the defendant believes that the person using the cell phone may have obtained it from the thief, he or she cannot use violence to retrieve the cell phone, but may also assert the right to return it.

是否允许防卫者事后夺回财物?在司法实践中,经常出现的一种情况是,个人财物被他人当场取得,但防卫者不是当场夺回自己的财物。这种情况能否属于防卫财物,构成刑事抗辩理由呢?对此,美国《模范刑法典》规定,只要行为人相信他人无权占有自己的财物,就可以在任何时间夺回自己的财物。例如,行为人的手机被盗窃,几天后,他在街上看到他人正在使用自己被盗窃的手机,如果行为人合理相信对方就是盗窃自己手机的人,则可以使用合理的暴力将自己的手机夺回。如果行为人认为,使用手机的人可能是从窃贼那里获得的,则不能使用暴力夺回手机,但他可以主张返还手机的权利。

3. For the defense of home, the other constituent elements are the same as the defense of property except that deadly force may be used. Under the Model Penal Code, a suspect's mere commission of the felony offense of breaking and entering does not ipso facto give the defendant the right to use deadly force, such as shooting a gun, and in order to inflict deadly force on an intruder, the defendant must reasonably believe that the intruder is armed or poses a danger to the safety of the occupants. This is known as the "dangerous felony" rule. The defense of the residence has changed considerably in recent centuries, and the defense of the residence in common law is not consistent with the norms of U. S. criminal law, as explained in detail in the following chapter.

对于防卫住宅而言,除了可以使用致命性暴力,其他构成要素与防卫财产相同。[1]《模范刑法典》的立场是,若闯入者仅实施了非法闯入的重罪,防卫者还不能当然地取得开枪等使用致命暴力的权利。要对闯入者施以致命的暴力,行为人必须合理相信闯入者持有武器或者对居住者的安全带来了危险。这被称为危险重罪(dangerous felony)规则。[2] 防卫住宅在近几个世纪以来发生了较大的变化,普通法中的防卫住宅与美国刑法中的规范也不一致,具体内容将在下节中予以详细梳理与阐释。

■ Curriculum Ideology and Politics(课程思政)

From above, it can be seen that the English and American criminal laws generally

---

〔1〕 参见刘士心:《美国刑法中的犯罪论原理》,人民出版社2010年版,第148页。

〔2〕 参见夏勇:《英美刑法:五国刑法论要》,法律出版社2020年版,第118页。

divide legitimate defense into different types based on the protected object, such as self - defense, defense of others, defense of property, and defense of residence, and set different constituent elements for different types. Different constituent elements mean different degrees of defense and different ways of exercising the right to defense. Corresponding to the different objects the defense rules carry different rights and values, as well as different damage outcomes, recovery possibilities, and so on.

从前面的内容来看,英美刑法一般是根据保护的对象,把正当防卫划分为防卫自我、防卫他人、防卫财产和防卫住宅等不同类型,并根据不同类型设置了不同的构成要素。不同构成要素意味着防卫权的大小、行使方式等不同。不同对象不仅意味着防卫规则承载了不同的权益和价值,更意味着其损害结果、恢复的可能性等有所差异。

5.5 The Castle Laws(城堡法)

The Castle Laws are actually the defense of home. In the United States, both the Model Penal Code, federal criminal law, or the U. S. state criminal laws distinguish between types of self - defense depending on the legal interest protected. Regardless of the type of defense, defense of the residence is a form of justifiable defense. The justifiable defense of the home is also known as the "castle law," after the phrase "a man's home is his castle".

城堡法其实就是防卫住宅。在美国,无论是《模范刑法典》、联邦刑法,还是美国的各州刑法,均根据保护法益的不同,对正当防卫类型进行了区分。无论对正当防卫的行为类型如何划分,防卫住宅都属于正当防卫。防卫住宅规则被称为"城堡法",取义于"一个人的住宅就是他的城堡"。[1]

5.5.1 The development of "castle laws"(城堡法的发展)

Castle law in the United States inherited the castle law in the common law but has evolved and changed considerably around the turn of the 21st century. The castle law before the beginning of the 21st century is called the "Old Castle Law" and the castle law after that is called the "New Castle Law". Here's the old castle law first.

美国的城堡法继承了普通法中关于城堡法的内容。21 世纪前后,"城堡法"发生了较大变化。在 21 世纪初之前的城堡法被称为"旧城堡法",21 世纪初之后的城堡法被称为"新城堡法"。下面先介绍旧城堡法的相关内容。

---

〔1〕 参见姜敏:《正当防卫制度中的"城堡法":渊源、发展与启示》,载《法学评论》2018 年第 5 期。

In the "old castle law," the right to defend home was not substantially different from the right to defend oneself and one's property in self - defense. The early castle law in the United States adhered to the common law principle of retreat and limited the use of force. The application of the defense of home is subject to certain restrictions, as follows: (1) Before using force in defense, one should retreat; [1] (2) the use of deadly force in defense is limited to violent crimes against the person committed in the home; (3) the 18th - century Castle Law also restricts the time of defense. The use of deadly force in defense is limited to wrongful invasions that occurred at night or a violent robberies that occurred during the day. [2]

旧城堡法中,防卫住宅的权利与正当防卫中防卫自身、财物等防卫权没有实质性差异。美国早期的城堡法坚持普通法中的退让原则并且限制使用武力。在适用防卫住宅时,要受到一定的限制,具体表现为:(1)在使用武力防卫之前,应当先行退让;(2)仅限于在住宅中的暴力性人身犯罪,防卫者才可以使用致命的暴力进行防卫;(3)18世纪的城堡法对防卫的时间也有限制,仅限于夜晚发生的不法侵害或者白天发生的暴力抢劫,防卫者才可以使用致命的暴力予以防卫。

As time progressed, the rights of the defender in the castle law also expanded. This was reflected in the loosening of the principle of retreat and the restriction on the use of force. In the late 19th century, there was the first movement to abandon the duty to retreat in the United States. At that time, however, the "duty to retreat" movement was not very effective. Then, in 1914, after the People v. Tomlinsa case, the "duty of retreat" in the Castle Law was really loosened. In 1876, the Ohio Supreme Court in Erwin v. State did not apply the duty to retreat. In 1877, the Indiana Supreme Court enforced the "American mentality" that Americans should not retreat in the face of aggression as the British did, but should go forward as Americans in Runyan v. State. [3] Thus, by the late 19th century, many states had already abolished the duty to retreat in their judicial practice and had adopted the defense of home as a new right on its own. In 1921, the U. S. Federal Court abolished the duty to retreat in Brown v. United States expressly. [4]

---

[1] Benjamin Levin, *A Defensible Defense ? Re - examing Castle Statues*, 47 Harvard Journal on Legislation 528(2010).

[2] Joel. Samaha, *Criminal law*, 10th edition, WADSWORTH Cengage Learning, 2011, p. 149.

[3] Joel. Samaha, *Criminal law*, 10th edition, WADSWORTH Cengage Learning, 2011, p. 529.

[4] 256 U. S. 335(1921).

随着时间的推移,城堡法中防卫者权利也有所扩张,具体表现为退让原则和限制使用武力的松动。19 世纪晚期,美国首度兴起放弃"退让义务"的运动。[1] 但此时,"退让义务"运动的效果不尽如人意。随后,在 1914 年 People. v. Tomlinsa 案后,城堡法中的"退让义务"才得到真正的松动。1876 年,俄亥俄州高等法院在尔文诉国家(Erwin v. State)案中,没有适用"退让义务"。1877 年,印第安纳州高等法院在鲁尼恩诉国家(Runyan. v. State)中,采用了"美国人思维",即法院认为美国人不应像英国人一样,在面临侵害时退却,而应该像美国人一样勇往直前。因此,在 19 世纪晚期,美国很多州已经在司法实践中废止了"退让义务",将防卫住宅作为一项新权利。1921 年,美国联邦法院在布朗诉美国案中,明确废止了"退让义务"。[2]

In addition, the reform of the Castle Law at the beginning of the 20th century changed the requirements for limiting the use of force. The restriction on the time of defense in the 18th century castle law was removed, and the time restriction was no longer limited to the night. Of course, the definition of "castle" differed greatly from region to region, but the term "castle" was generally considered to exclude the courtyard and the open space in the courtyard. The subject of defense was also expanded from the owner and servants of the house to the visitors of the house.

除此之外,20 世纪初美国法律对城堡法的改革,也改变了限制使用武力的要求。此时,美国法律取消了 18 世纪旧城堡法对防卫时间的限制,时间不再限制于夜晚的时间段。当然,不同地区对于何谓"城堡"的规定区别也较大,但一般而言,"城堡"不包括庭院和庭院的空地。防卫的主体也从住宅的主人和仆人,扩大到住宅的访问者等。

Until the end of the 20th century, the reform of the castle law was mainly focused on the above aspects. At the beginning of the 21st century, American legislation began to revise the law and expand the rights of defenders. Castle Law in this phase is also known as the "New Castle Law". In 2005, Florida amended its Castle Law, and Florida became the first state to do so. Since then, it has been followed by other states. In 2009, again amended its 2005 Castle Law and became the model for the contemporary New Castle Law. At this time, more than 40 states have passed or proposed similar legislation,[3] all of which were referred to as "New Castle laws".

---

〔1〕 Christine Catalfamo, *Stand Your Ground: Florida' S Castle Doctrine Foe The Twenty - First Century*, 4 RUTGERS J. L. & PUB. POL'Y 504(2007).

〔2〕 参见姜敏:《正当防卫制度中的"城堡法":渊源、发展与启示》,载《法学评论》2018 年第 5 期。

〔3〕 Joel. Samaha, *Criminal law*, 10th edition, WADSWORTH Cengage Learning, 2011, p. 149.

直到 20 世纪末期,城堡法的改革都主要是围绕着以上几个方面展开。在 21 世纪的初期,美国国家立法开始重新修改法条,扩张了防卫者的权利。这个阶段的城堡法也被称为"新城堡法"。2005 年,佛罗里达州第一次修改城堡法,其也成为第一个重新修订城堡法的州。此后,很多州效仿了佛罗里达州。佛罗里达州在 2009 年再次修改 2005 年的城堡法,并成为当代新城堡法的典范。此时,美国已有 40 多个州通过或者提议了相似的立法,均被称为新城堡法。

5.5.2 The changes in the new castle laws(新城堡法的变化)

Florida's New Castle Law is set forth in the Floria Personal Protection Law (2009). The main elements of new castle act are:

佛罗里达州的新城堡法被设置在《2009 年个人权利保护法》中。新城堡法的主要内容有:[1]

(1) Modifies the previous "reasonable person" standard to "actor reasonably (honestly) believed" under Florida law §776.012 and §776.013, and allows that the "actor reasonably (honestly) believed" can be judged by presumption.[2]

佛罗里达州法律 §776.012 和 §776.013 的规定修改以往的"理性人"判断标准,以"行为人合理(诚实)相信"作为判断标准,并且可以通过推定的方式对"行为人合理(诚实)相信"进行判断。

(2) Under the provision of Florida law §776.013, defense that use deadly force or cause serious bodily injury may be justified under certain circumstances. Such circumstances include, the intruder is entering or has entered unlawfully or compulsively into the dwelling, residence, or means of transportation used by another; and that the actor reasonably (and honestly) believes that the unlawful and compulsive intrusion has occurred or is occurring.

根据佛罗里达州法律 §776.013 的规定,防卫者可以在特定的情况下使用致命的暴力或严重的身体伤害予以防卫,这样的防卫具有正当性。这一情况具体包括,侵入者正在或者已经非法或强迫性地进入他人住所、居所或使用的交通工具中;行为人合理(诚实)地相信非法且强迫性的侵入行为已经发生或正在发生等。

(3) "Reasonable fear" can be presumed under the provision of Florida law §776.013(1)-(4). If an occupant is presumed to have a "reasonable fear", his or her use of force to resist the assault is justified.

---

〔1〕 参见姜敏:《正当防卫制度中的"城堡法":渊源、发展与启示》,载《法学评论》2018 年第 5 期。

〔2〕 Joel. Samaha, *Criminal law*, 10th edition, WADSWORTH Cengage Learning, 2011, p. 151.

佛罗里达州法律§776.013(1)—(4)规定,可以对“合理恐惧”予以推定。若居住者被推定为“合理恐惧”,其使用武力抵挡侵害的行为具有正当性。

(4) Unlawful or forcible entry into a dwelling, residence, or means of transportation in use is presumed to be “violent or unlawful by force” under Florida law §776.013(4). An intrusion is presumed to be “violent or wrongful by force” even if the intent is not to commit violence or wrongs by force.

根据佛罗里达州法律§776.013(4)的规定,非法或者强制性地进入他人住所、居所或使用中的交通工具行为,可以被推定为“暴力或武力不法”。即使侵入者入侵的意图不是为了实施暴力或者武力不法,也会被推定为“暴力或武力不法”。

(5) “Domicile,” “residence,” and “means of transportation” are defined in Florida law under §776.013(5) and §776.013.

佛罗里达州法律§776.013(5)和§776.013对“住所”“居所”和“交通工具”进行了定义。

In short, Florida's castle law accomplished the following: (1) abolished the duty to retreat rule; (2) charged the “reasonable person” requirement in common law; (3) extended the right to use deadly force outside the home to “any place you have a right to be”; (4) broadened the legitimate circumstances where deadly force applies, including threats to property and threats that are not imminent; (5) created blanket criminal and civil immunity for defenders using force permitted by the law. (This immunity is broader than law enforcement officers' immunity.)[1] It can be seen that the New Castle Law has largely expanded the rights of the defender.

简言之,佛罗里达州的城堡法革新有:(1)废除了撤退的义务规则;(2)更改了普通法中的“合理人”要求;(3)将在家庭之外使用致命武力的权利扩展到“你有权去的任何地方”;(4)扩大了使用致命武力的合法情况,包括对财产的威胁和非紧迫性的威胁,都可使用暴力防卫;(5)为任何使用法律允许的武力的防卫者创造了全面的刑事和民事豁免权,甚至这种豁免权比执法人员的豁免权更广泛。从这些变化可以看出,新城堡法在很大程度上扩大了防卫者的权利。

5.5.3 “Right to Defend” or “License to Kill”? (“防卫权”还是“杀人许可证”?)

The 2009 Florida provision on the New Castle Law has also been the subject of numerous challenges. The issue at stake is whether the castle law is a “right of defense” or a “license to kill”.

---

〔1〕 Joel Samaha, *Criminal Law*, 10th edition, Wadsworth Cengage Learning Press, 2011, p. 151 – 152.

2009年佛罗里达州关于新城堡法的规定,也曾遭到诸多质疑。其最具争议的问题是:城堡法到底是“防卫权”还是“杀人许可证”?

The main argument against thenew castle law is that the standards for the use of force by police officers in law enforcement are even higher than the standards for the use of force of the defenders under the New Castle Law. The negative effect of this is that the enforcement of the law by the police will also be affected, for example, the enforcement of the law by the police in the residence will be physically dangerous. Moreover, the application of the New Castle Law may lead to the killing of innocent people, and may lead to more violent crimes.

反对新城堡法的观点主要有,警察在执法时可使用武力的标准,甚至严格于“新城堡法”中防卫者使用武力的标准。这会导致警察执行法律会受到影响的负面效果出现,比如警察入户执行法律会有人身危险,从而影响法律的执行。除此之外,新城堡法的适用可能会导致无辜的人被杀害以及引发更多的暴力犯罪等问题出现。

There's no empirical research to help explain why so many states have followed the "new castle laws". But there's plenty of speculation as to why these laws have proliferated now. Two commonly mentioned reasons are Americans' heightened consciousness and concern about their security since 9/11 and the lack of enough police officers to protect the public in Amerian society.〔1〕

没有实证研究来帮助解释为什么这么多州都仿效了佛罗里达州的新城堡法。对于这些法律激增的原因,人们有很多猜测。通常提到的两个原因是,自“9·11”事件以来,美国人的安全意识和对安全的关注程度提高了,且美国社会缺乏足够的警察来保护公众。

Even though the opposing viewpoints question the value of the New Castle Law, the lawmakers still believe that the New Castle Law has theoretical and practical bases. The provisions of the New Castle Law are in line with the American way of thinking, reflecting the recognition and protection of individual rights and values, truly granting citizens the right to enjoy the protection of their bodies, lives, and property in their own homes without being violated, and granting them the right to live in peace without being violated or disturbed by others. For some vulnerable groups, expanding the right of defense in the castle law would give them the right to better protect themselves. Anyway, the provisions of the New castle law are consistent with the new environment

〔1〕 Joel Samaha, *Criminal Law*, 10th edition, Wadsworth Cengage Learning Press, 2011, p. 154.

of American society, the criminal justice system, and American thinking and values, and have important positive implications. So it's been widely followed.

即使反对观点质疑新城堡法的价值,但立法者依然认为新城堡法具有理论和现实根据。新城堡法的规定符合美国人的思维方式,其体现了对个人权利、个人价值的认同与保护,真正赋予公民在自己的住宅中享受不被侵犯,保护自身身体、生命、财产的权利,赋予公民享有不受他人侵犯,不受他人干扰平静生活的权利。对于一些弱势群体,扩大城堡法中的防卫权,可以使其更好地保护自身的权利。不论如何,新城堡法的规定符合美国社会的新环境、刑事司法制度以及美国人的思维和价值取向,所以被各州广泛仿效。

■ Curriculum Ideology and Politics(课程思政)

Defense of home (castle law) is a characteristic knowledge in English and American criminal law, which clearly reflects the "defender centered" ideology. Especially in the new castle law, it grants defenders greater rights, which enables citizens to better protect their rights. However, we need to take a critical perpective towards castle law. Firstly, the excessively inflated civil defense rights may lead to negative consequences. The controversy over whether it is a right of defense or a murder permit also shows the without constraining mechanisms legal risks will follow. In the United States, the constraining mechanism is its judicial system and jury system. Secondly, the civic consciousness reflected in the Castle Law can be accepted by American citizens. Students need to be guided with systematic and localized thinking to train their ability to think systematically and practically.

城堡法(防卫住宅)是英美刑法的一个特色知识,其明显地体现了"防卫者本位"思想。尤其是新城堡法赋予了防卫者更大的权利,使公民能更好地保护自己的权益。对此,仍要保持理性的认识。首先,过度膨胀的公民防卫权,有可能导致负面后果。从新城堡法引起的"是防卫权还是杀人许可证"的争议可见,如果没有机制予以制约,则有法治隐患。在美国,能对其进行制约的是司法制度和陪审团制度。其次,城堡法体现的公民权意识,能为美国公民接受。以系统化和本土化思维引导学生,训练学生的系统化和实践性思考问题的能力。

5.6 "Choice of Evils" (General Principle of Necessity)(两害相权取其轻:紧急避险一般原则)

Necessity means that a person, in an emergency situation, is faced with the dilemma of either complying with the norms of criminal law, resulting in a greater detrimental outcome, or violating the norms of criminal law, resulting in a lesser detrimental outcome. The doctrine of necessity is used as a criminal defense for public policy reasons when the law has to sacrifice a small interest to preserve a larger one. The legitimacy of necessity lies essentially in the lesser of two evils. It should also be mentioned that necessity is considered to be excuses precisely because it is justified as the lesser of two evils. But the Model Penal Code considers necessity to be a justification.

紧急避险是指一个人在紧急情况下,在面临两难的选择时,要么遵守刑法的规范,造成较大的损害结果,要么违反刑法的规范,造成较小的损害结果。当法律不得不牺牲小的利益来保全大的利益时,出于对公共政策的考虑,紧急避险被视为抗辩事由。紧急避险的正当性在于两害相权取其轻。在此还需提及的是,正因其正当性在于两害相权,所以紧急避险又被视为是可宽恕事由。但是,《模范刑法典》认为紧急避险是正当化事由。

In the case of necessity as a defense to criminal liability, the emergency must arise from the forces of nature, and from factors other than human conduct, for example, fire, earthquake, storm, etc. The emergency cannot originate from the duress of another person, and if the danger of the emergency originates from a coercion by others, a legal defense may be raised. However, the Model Penal Code extends the source of danger of necessity to human factors, blurring the line between necessity and duress.

在作为刑事责任抗辩事由的紧急避险中,紧急情况源于自然界以及行为人之外的其他因素。例如,火灾、地震、风暴等。紧急情况不能源于他人的胁迫行为,若产生紧急情况的危险源于他人的胁迫行为,可以进行合法的防卫。但是,《模范刑法典》将紧急避险的危险来源扩展到了人为因素,淡化了紧急避险与防卫之间的界限。

The main conditions for establishing necessity are:

成立紧急避险的条件主要有:

1. The defendant faces greater damage. There is no constraint on the damage here, including bodily injury or property damage. For example, one man took another's man's food to save his own life; such behaviour can constitute necessity.

被告人面临较大的损害。这里的损害没有限制,包括身体伤害或者财产损坏。例如,一个人为了挽救自己的生命,拿了另一个人的食物,则其行为可以成立紧急避险。

2. The damage is occurring or there's an urgency that greater damage may occur. Necessity is implemented in a situation of necessity, if the defendant could have had a

better choice at the time, it is not applicable to apply the defence of necessity. The reason is that necessity applies when complying with the norms of criminal law. resulting in a greater harm, or when violating the norms of criminal law. resulting in a lesser harm. If a third option exists, necessity cannot be applied. For example, a person who is only in a state of hunger and steals food from a store, such act cannot be defended by necessity. Because in a state of hunger, one can go elsewhere or obtain food by other means and so the act still constitutes the crime of theft.

正在发生或者具有发生较大损害的紧迫性。紧急避险是在行为人迫不得已的情况下进行的选择,如果行为人在当时可以有更好的选择,就不能适用紧急避险。因为紧急避险适用的情况是,要么遵守刑法的规范从而造成较大的损害,要么违反刑法的规范从而造成较小的损害,如果存在第三种选择,就不能适用紧急避险。例如,一个人只是处于饥饿的状态下而从商店里盗窃食物,不能作为紧急避险。因为处于饥饿状态,人们可以去其他地方或者通过其他途径获得食物。因此,该盗窃食物的行为仍然构成盗窃罪。

3. The greater damage was not caused by the defendant's act. In some cases, the source of the danger was attributed to the defendant's own actions, and the defense of necessity cannot be established. If the actor is subjectively negligent about the danger, he or she may also be criminally liable. For example, if A drives after drinking, his driving directly will hit B, and driving on the sidewalk will hit C. In this case, A's act can not constitute necessity, no matter which direction he chooses.

较大损害不是行为人导致的。在有些情况下,危险的来源是行为人自身的行为,此时不能成立紧急避险。如果行为人对危险在主观上具有过失,还可能承担刑事责任。例如,A 喝酒后驾车,直接行驶会撞倒 B,开到人行道上将会撞倒 C。这种情况下,A 无论选择哪个方向,都不能构成紧急避险。

4. Only the method that causes relatively minor damage can be used to avoid larger damage. In other words, the benefit preserved in the case of necessity is greater than the benefit sacrificed. As to how to judge the magnitude of the interest, it mainly depends on the opinion of the court (generally the court judges according to the standard of ordinary normal people); the court and the jury make a comprehensive judgment according to the principle of utilitarianism, ethical norms, and the specific circumstances of the case, etc., rather than from the view of the parties. For example, in the event of a fire, a person can choose whether to save another person or a painting; the person chooses to save the painting rather than the other person. The court finds that the value of the

person's life is higher than the value of the painting, and that he cannot use the defense of necessity. A prison inmate who escapes due to the poor sanitary conditions of the prison still constitutes the crime of escape; a person who kills another person in order to save his own life still constitutes the crime of intentional homicide, etc. Sometimes, more complex situations exist where no matter what choice the actor made, the damage could not have been avoided or involved the weighing of the value of different human lives. For example, A and B are both trapped in the sea, when a plank is available, but can only hold the weight of one person. Whether A or B get the plank, one person is bound to die. At this point, killing the other person to save his own life cannot constitute an necessity. Because, in law, life has equal value regardless of age, health, or status. Sacrificing a life of equal value is not protecting a greater interest at the expense of a lesser interest and, therefore, does not constitute necessities.

只能用造成相对较小损害的方法避免出现较大损害。也就是说,紧急避险情况下所保全的利益要大于牺牲的利益。至于如何对利益大小进行判断,主要取决于法院的意见(一般法院按照普通的正常人标准进行判断),法院和陪审团根据功利原则、伦理规范、案件的具体情况等方面进行综合判断,[1]而不是根据当事人的看法进行判断。例如,在火灾时,一个人可以选择救人还是救油画,在紧急情况下当事人进行了选择,他选择救油画而不是救人,法院认为人的生命价值高于油画的价值,因此他不能以紧急避险予以抗辩。监狱里的犯人由于监狱的卫生环境差而越狱的,依然构成逃脱罪;一个人为了保全自己的性命而杀死另一个人的,依然构成故意杀人罪。有时,情况更为复杂,无论行为人作何选择,都不能避免损害的发生,或者情况涉及不同的人生命价值的权衡。又如,A和B都被困在海里,此时有一块木板,但只能承受一个人的重量。无论是A还是B获得木板,都必然导致另一人死亡。这时,以保全自己的生命而杀死另一个人,不能构成紧急避险。因为,在法律上,无论年龄、健康、地位,生命都是具有同等价值的。牺牲一个同等价值的生命,不属于以牺牲较小的利益保护更大的利益,因此不构成紧急避险。

5. It is important to note that necessity only applies to situations where the law does not provide for it, and if the law has provided for it, it needs to be followed. For example, the law has already provided for whether the mother can have an abortion. At this point, there is no need to weigh the value, and it can be handled directly according to the law.

---

[1] 参见刘士心:《美国刑法中的犯罪论原理》,人民出版社2010年版,第154页。

紧急避险仅仅适用于法律没有规定的情形，若法律已经作出规定，就需要遵守法律的规定。例如，关于母亲是否能进行人工流产，法律已经作出了规定，就不需要再进行价值的权衡，直接按照法律规定处理即可。

6. The actor subjectively had the intent to avoid greater harm. If the actor subjectively lacked the intent to avoid greater harm, he or she cannot raise the defense of necessity even if he or she objectively avoided the occurrence of greater harm. This is true as long as the actor subjectively, sincerely and reasonably believed that there was an imminent danger and that there was no other way to avoid the danger than to take the necessity action. Generally speaking, the actor's motive does not affect the establishment of necessity.

行为人主观上具有避免更大损害的意图。若行为人主观上缺乏避免更大损害的意图，即使客观上避免了更大损害的发生，也不能提出紧急避险辩护。只要行为人主观上真诚而合理地相信存在紧迫的危险，并且除采取避险行为之外没有其他方法可以避免危险发生就可以。[1] 一般情况下，行为人的动机不影响紧急避险的成立。

In general, necessity may apply in these situations: a pharmacist dispenses medicine without a doctor's prescription in order to relieve the pain of a patient's emergency; a prisoner may escape from prison if he is coerced or raped by another person and it is too late to take other measures; property is destroyed in order to stop the spread of a fire; in case of storm a ship takes refuge in a port that it is not allowed to enter and the act of sailing is only to take refuge; a doctor performs an abortion for a raped young girl; an ambulance runs a red light; a police officer does a trick in gambling to gain the trust of others in order to catch a gambler; a captain of a ship or a captain of a plane abandons his cargo to protect his passengers, etc.

一般情况下，以下这些情况都可以适用紧急避险：为了缓解病人紧急情况的痛苦，药剂师在没有医生处方的情况下发药；囚犯在受到他人威逼、强奸等情况下，如果来不及采取其他措施，可以越狱；为了制止火势的蔓延而毁损财产；船只在遇到风暴时，驶入不得进入的港口避难，且驶入行为仅仅是为了避难；医生为被强奸的少女实施人工流产手术；救护车闯红灯；警察为了抓捕赌徒而在赌博时做手脚以获得他人的信任；船长或机长抛弃货物以保护乘客等。

---

〔1〕 参见刘士心：《美国刑法中的犯罪论原理》，人民出版社2010年版，第153页。

■ Case study(案例学习)

NELSON v. STATE, Supreme Court of Alaska, 1979. 597 P. 2d 977.[1](纳尔逊诉国家案)

Fact(基本案情)

Shortly after midnight on May 22, 1976, Dale Nelson drove his four – wheel drive truck onto a side road off the highway. His truck became bogged down in a marshy area about 250 feet off the highway. Nelson testified that he was afraid the truck might tip over in the soft ground. He and his two companions, Lynnette Stinson and Carl Thompson, spent an hour unsuccessfully trying to free the vehicle. At about 1:00, Nelson began walking with Stinson down the highway. An acquaintance drove by and offered to help, but was unable to render much assistance. He then drove Nelson and Stinson to a Highway Department Yard where heavy equipment was parked. The yard was marked with "no – trespassing" signs. After waiting several hours for someone to come by, they decided to take a dump truck and use it to pull out Nelson's vehicle. But then, the dump truck also became stuck.

1976 年 5 月 22 日午夜过后不久,戴尔·纳尔逊驾驶他的四轮驱动卡车驶入高速公路旁的一条小路。他的卡车在离高速路约 250 英尺(约 76.2 米)的沼泽地里陷了下去。纳尔逊作证说,他担心卡车会在柔软的地面上翻倒。他和他的两个同伴林内特·斯坦森和卡尔·汤普森花了 1 个小时时间试图把车辆拖出,但没有成功。大约凌晨 1 点,纳尔逊和斯坦森一起走在高速公路上。一位熟人开车经过并表示愿意提供帮助,但无法提供太多的帮助。然后,这位熟人开车将纳尔逊和斯坦森送到高速公路管理局的一个院子里,那里停放着重型设备。院子里有"禁止擅入"的标志。在等待了几个小时后(等待相关负责设备的人经过),他们决定用一辆翻斗车来拉出纳尔逊的车。但之后,这辆翻斗车也被卡住了。

At approximately 10:00 that morning a man identified only as "Curly" appeared. His vehicle was also stuck further down the highway. Curly offered to assist Nelson. They returned to the heavy equipment yard and took a front – end loader, which they used to free the dump truck. They then used the dump truck to free Curly's car. The dump truck was returned to the equipment yard, but when Nelson attempted to use the front – end loader to free his own truck the front – end loader also became bogged down.

---

[1] Joshua Dressler & Stephen Garvey, *Cases and Materials on Criminal Law*, 6th edition, West Academic, 2012, p. 560 – 565.

Frustrated and tired after twelve hours of attempting to free his vehicle, Nelson and his companions quit and went to sleep. Two of them slept in a tent. One of them went to sleep in the truck. They were awakened by a Highway Department employee, who placed them under citizen's arrest.

当天上午 10 点左右,一个留着卷发的人出现了。他的车辆也被卡在了公路的更远处。他提出要帮助纳尔逊。他们回到存放重型设备的院子,开了一台前端装载机,用来解救翻斗车。他们先用翻斗车拖出了卷发男子的车。翻斗车被送回存放设备的院子,但当纳尔逊试图使用前端装载机来拖出他自己的卡车时,前端装载机也陷了进去。尼尔森和他的同伴在尝试拖出他的车辆的第 12 个小时后,感到沮丧和疲惫,于是他们去睡觉了。其中两人睡在一个帐篷里,另一人在卡车上睡觉。他们被高速公路管理局的一名雇员叫醒,后者对他们进行了公民逮捕。

Dispute(主要争议)

The sole question presented in this case is whether the jury was properly instructed on the defense of necessity. Nelson requested an instruction which read: You are instructed that the defendant is allowed to use a motor vehicle of another person without permission if the use is for an emergency in the case of immediate and dire need.

该案的唯一问题是,陪审团是否得到了关于成立紧急避险的适当指示。纳尔逊要求的指示是这样的:陪审团得到的指示是,如果被告是为了紧急的、迫切的需要而使用他人的机动车,则允许被告未经许可而使用。

You are further instructed that once the defendant has raised the issue of emergency or necessity, the state must prove the lack of emergency or necessity beyond a reasonable doubt.

陪审团还被告知,一旦被告提出紧急情况或紧急避险的问题,州政府必须在排除合理怀疑的情况下证明没有紧急情况或紧急避险的情况。

Over Nelson's objection, the court gave an instruction on the necessity defense which read as follows:

在纳尔逊的反对下,法庭就紧急避险的辩护作出指示,内容如下:

You are instructed that it is a defense to a crime (the defense of necessity is established) such as joyriding or taking someone else's motor vehicle without his permission that the actor acted out of necessity in a case of immediate and dire need. However, such a defense exists only when natural forces create a situation wherein it becomes necessary for a person to violate the law in order to avoid a greater evil to himself or his property. The harm which is to be avoided must be the greater harm and it must be immediate and dire. Where a reasonable alternative other than violating the law is available in order to avoid the harm the defense of necessity is not applicable.

纳尔逊被告知,对于兜风或未经他人许可而占用他人机动车的犯罪行为,如果该行为人是在急需的情况下出于必要而行事,则可以作为辩护理由(成立紧急避险)。然而,只有在自然力量造成该情形的情况下,为了避免对自己或自己的财产造成更大的伤害,一个人有必要违反法律,这样的辩护才成立。所要避免的伤害必须是更大的伤害,而且必须是直接的和严重的。如果为了避免伤害,除了违反法律还有其他合理的选择,那么紧急避险就不适用了。

Nelson argues that the instruction received by the jury was erroneous because it allowed the jury to apply what he calls an "objective, after – the – fact" test of need and emergency, rather than a "subjective, reasonable man" test. Nelson means that he was entitled to have explained to the jury that they must view the question of necessity from the standpoint of a reasonable person knowing all that the defendant did at the time he acted.

纳尔逊认为,陪审团得到的指示是错误的,因为它允许陪审团应用所谓的"客观的、事后的"需要和紧急情况的测试,而不是"主观的、理性的人"测试。纳尔逊的意思是,他有权向陪审团解释,陪审团必须从一个理智的,知道被告在采取行动时的所有情况的人的角度来看待紧急避险的问题。

The court finally affirm the conviction.

法院最终维持有罪判决。

Commentators generally agree that there are three essential elements to the defense: (1) the act charged must have been done to prevent a significant evil; (2) there must have been no adequate alternative; (3) the harm caused must not have been disproportionate to the harm avoided.

该辩护有三个基本要素:(1)被指控的行为必须是为了防止重大的罪恶;(2)必须没有适当的替代方案;(3)造成的伤害必须与避免的伤害不相称。

Conclusion(结论)

Considerable damage was done to both the front – end loader and the dump truck as a result of Nelson's attempt to free his truck. Nelson was convicted in district court of reckless destruction of personal property in violation of AS 11. 20. 515(b) and joyriding in violation of AS 28. 35. 010. This conviction was affirmed on appeal to the superior court.

纳尔逊因试图拖出他的卡车,对前端装载机和翻斗车都造成了相当大的损害。

纳尔逊在地区法院被判违反 AS 11.20.515(b) 的规定,即构成破坏个人财产罪,以及违反 AS 28.35.010 的规定,即构成偷车罪。当上诉到上级法院时,上级法院维持了这一定罪。

It cannot be said that the harm sought to be avoided in this case—potential damage to Nelson's truck—was greater than the harm caused by Nelson's illegal actions. Even disregarding the actual damage to the equipment caused by Nelson's use, the seriousness of the offenses committed by Nelson were disproportionate to the situation he faced. The legislature has made this clear by making reckless destruction of personal property a crime punishable by imprisonment for up to one year and a $ 5,000 fine, and joyriding punishable by imprisonment for up to one year and a $ 1,000 fine. The equipment taken by Nelson was marked with no trespassing signs. Nelson's fears about damage to his truck roof were no justification for his appropriation of sophisticated and expensive equipment.

最后,不能说本案所要避免的伤害(纳尔逊卡车的潜在损害),比纳尔逊的非法行为所造成的伤害更大。即使不考虑纳尔逊的使用对设备造成的实际损害,纳尔逊所犯的罪行的严重性与他所面临的情况也是不相称的。立法机关已经明确了这一点,其规定破坏个人财产是一种犯罪,可被判处 1 年以下的监禁和 5000 美元的罚款,而偷车兜风可被判处 1 年以下的监禁和 1000 美元的罚款。纳尔逊开走的设备所在地有禁止擅入的标志。纳尔逊担心他的卡车车顶会受到损害,这并不能成为他盗用复杂和昂贵设备的理由。

Questions: **1.** Does Nelson have any other options in such a situation? (Please scan the QR code on the right to get the answer)

纳尔逊在这样的处境中是否还有其他选择?(答案请扫描右侧二维码获取)

2. The benefit preserved in the case of necessity is greater than the benefit sacrificed. How to judge the magnitude of the interest? Whether it mainly depends on the opinion of the court or according to the subjective judgment of the parties? (The way to obtain the answer is the same as above)

对于紧急避险情况下,所保全的利益要大于牺牲的利益。如何对利益大小进行判断,是主要取决于法院的意见还是按照当事人的主观判断进行判断?(答案获取方式同上)

5.7 Consent(被害人同意)

Victim consent means that a crime against oneself can be a defense for the defendant. Victim consent as a defense means whether the fact that the victim consented can exclude or reduce the criminal liability of the defendant. For consent, there are both similarities and differences between the legal norms in the UK and the US.

被害人同意是指针对被害人的某些犯罪行为可以成为行为人的抗辩事由。[1] 被害人同意作为抗辩事由是指被害人同意的事实,能排除或减轻被告人的刑事责任。对于被害人同意,英国和美国的法律规范既有相似之处,也有不同之处。

In England, the victim's consent can be a defense to the criminal responsibility of the defendant. For crimes such as assault, theft, criminal damage and rape, the defense of victim's consent is applicable. However, the defense of victim consent is not available for crimes such as murder and general homicide.

在英国,被害人同意可以作为被告人刑事责任抗辩的理由。对于侵害罪、盗窃罪、刑事损害罪、强奸罪等犯罪,都可以适用被害人同意这一抗辩。但是,对于谋杀罪、一般杀人罪等犯罪不能适用被害人同意这一抗辩。

In the United States, in general, victim consent does not preclude the defendant from criminal liability. Only in the case of rape, the conditions for the establishment of rope determine that the victim's consent can be a defense, since the lack of victim's consent is a constitutive element of the crime. In addition, the Model Penal Code stipulates that, victim consent can also be used as a defense to criminal liability if the victim's consent prevents the commission of the harm. For example, consent in competitive sports may preclude the commission of a crime.

在美国,一般情况下,被害人同意不能排除被告人的刑事责任。只有在强奸罪这类犯罪中,成立条件本身就决定了被害人同意可以作为抗辩事由,因为强奸罪缺乏被害人同意是犯罪构成的一个要件。除此之外,《模范刑法典》规定,如果被害人的同意阻止了伤害的实施,也可以将被害人同意作为刑事责任抗辩事由。例如,在竞技体育中的承诺,可以排除犯罪。

The English and American legal norms are similar in that victim consent is usually invalid if it is given under false pretenses. If the defendant believed in good faith that the victim consented, even that belief was false and contrary to the facts, the defendant's guilty intent may be negated.

---

〔1〕 参见夏勇:《英美刑法:五国刑法论要》,法律出版社2020年版,第64页。

英国和美国法律规范相同的地方是,对于被害人是由于受到欺骗而表示的同意,通常是无效的。如果被告人真诚地相信被害人予以同意,即使这种相信是错误的,与事实相悖的,但仍可以以此否定被告人的犯意。

5.8 Exercise(课后练习)(答案请扫描右侧二维码获取)

5.8.1 Test of Terminologies(术语考查)

①Justifications ②Excuses

③Self – Defense ④Defense of Others

⑤The Castle Laws ⑥Choice of Evils

⑦Consent ⑧Model Penal Code(MPC)

5.8.2 True or False(判断题)

1. Criminal liability defenses can be divided into affirmative defenses and negative defenses, with affirmative defenses distinguished between justifications and excuses.

刑事责任抗辩事由可以分为积极抗辩事由和消极抗辩事由,积极的抗辩事由有正当化事由与可宽恕事由之分。

2. A defender may use deadly force only if the use of non – lethal force is insufficient, i. e. , excessive force is not permitted.

防御者只有在使用非致命武力不足以应对的情况下才可以使用致命武力,即不允许过度使用武力。

3. There are differences between the laws of different jurisdictions under common law and the Model Penal Code with respect to the requirements for the establishment of justifiable defense. The differences are mainly found in the different requirements for the belief element of justifiable defense in the two.

普通法下不同地区的法律与《模范刑法典》对正当防卫的成立条件的规定存在差别,集中体现在对正当防卫的相信要件的不同要求。

4. Florida's Castle Act of 2009 abolished "the duty to retreat".

2009 年佛罗里达州的城堡法废除了退让义务规则。

5. Necessity can also be applied in situations not provided for by law, or if the law has been provided for, the law can be disregarded.

紧急避险也可以适用于法律没有规定的情形,若法律已经作出规定,也可以不遵守法律的规定。

5.8.3 Short – answer Questions (简答题)

1. What are affirmative defenses?

什么是积极抗辩事由?

2. What conditions must be met for self – defense?

自我防卫必须满足哪些条件?

3. Does defense of others include friends and strangers other than relatives?

防卫他人是否包括亲属以外的朋友和陌生人?

4. What are the changes in the new castle law?

新城堡法的变化是什么?

■ Summary(总结)

1. Self – defense is an important justification; it consists of four elements: (1) unprovoked attack; (2) necessity; (3) proportionality; (4) reasonable belief.

自我防卫是重要的正当化事由,其成立的要素包括:(1)无缘无故的攻击;(2)必要性;(3)相称性;(4)合理确信。

2. The defense of others is a type of defense against infringement of personal rights. In the early days, "others" in defense of others was generally limited to family members or other persons with whom one had a special relationship. In contemporary times, however, the category of "others" has been expanded to include strangers.

防卫他人是一种正当的针对侵害人身权利的防卫。早期的防卫他人的"他人"一般只包括家人或有特殊关系的其他人。但在当代,"他人"范畴扩大至陌生人。

3. The defence of property is a justification of defence against property that has been infringed upon. Unlike self – defence, in the defence of property, the use of violence is subject to harsher restrictions, i. e. , it should be limited to preventing actual damage to one's property.

防卫财物是一种对侵害财物行为进行防卫的正当化事由。不同于自我防卫,在防卫财物的情形中,暴力行为的使用受到更苛刻的限制,即应当以防止自己的财物受到实际损失为限度。

4. The defense of home is also known as the Castle Law. The castle law before the beginning of the 21st century was called the old castle law, and the castle law after that was called the new castle law. The New Castle Law began in Florida in 2009, and it greatly expands the rights of defenders.

防卫住宅又被称为"城堡法"。在 21 世纪初之前的城堡法被称为旧城堡法,21 世纪初之后的城堡法被称为新城堡法。新城堡法于 2009 年开始于佛罗里达州。新城堡法极大地扩大了防卫者的权利。

5. The main conditions for the establishment ofnecessity are: (1) the actor is facing greater damage; (2) greater damage is occurring or has the urgency of occurring; (3) the greater damage is not caused by the actor; (4) the greater damage can only be avoided by means of inflicting a relatively lesser damage; (5) the necessity applies only to situations not provided for by law; (6) the actor subjectively has the intent to avoid greater damage.

成立紧急避险的条件主要有:(1)行为人面临较大的损害;(2)正在发生或者具有发生较大损害的紧迫性;(3)较大损害不是行为人导致的;(4)只能用造成相对较小损害的方法避免较大损害;(5)紧急避险仅适用于法律没有规定的情形;(6)行为人主观上具有避免更大损害的意图。

6. Victim consent, which refers to the promise or consent of the victim when another person violates his or her interests, is an important defence to criminal liability. However, the victim consent defence is not always admitted. Only in a very small number of crimes can it provide a defence that reduces or exempts criminal liability.

被害人承诺是指被害人在他人侵害自己利益时表示允诺或者同意,是一种重要的刑事责任抗辩事由。但被害人承诺抗辩事由并不一定会获得认可,其只有在极少数犯罪中,才可以作为减少或免除刑事责任的抗辩事由。

Chapter 6 Defenses to Criminal Liability: Excuse
第 6 章 刑事责任辩护事由:宽恕事由

■ The Learning Objective(学习目标)

1. To have a basic understanding of the excuse defenses to criminal liability.

对刑事责任宽恕事由有基本了解。

2. To understand all kinds ofcriminal liability excuse defenses, including mental illness, diminished capacity of responsibility, age excuse, duress, intoxication, police entrapment and " syndrome " excuse defense, and to understand their concepts, formations and application.

了解各类刑事责任宽恕事由,包括精神病宽恕事由、责任能力降低宽恕事由、年龄宽恕事由、胁迫宽恕事由、醉态宽恕事由、警察圈套宽恕事由以及综合征宽恕事由,了解其概念、形成及具体适用。

3. To learn terminologies related to the topic.

掌握本章中的专业术语。

■ Chapter Outline(本章内容概要)

This chapter mainly introduces several excuse defenses of criminal liability. The first is the defense of insanity. Starting from the specific criteria of the judgment of mental illness, we discuss how it becomes a defense excuse of liability. It includes the "right - wrong Test", "irrepressible impulse Test", "substantial capacity Test" and "The Product - of - Mental - Illness Test". The second is capacity defense, that is, the defense of reducing responsibility. It is often applied to patients with mental disorders which are caused by recognized health conditions impairing the ability to understand the nature of behaviour, forming rational judgments and exercise self - control. The third is age excuse. Minors under a certain age do not have to bear criminal liability due to lack of relevant cognitive ability. The fourth is the duress defense, that is, the imminent threat of life can be a reason for excuse. The fifth is the argument of intoxication. Intoxication will make the actor lack the intention needed to commit a crime. The sixth is the police entrapment defense. The police entrapment defense must meet subjective or objective conditions. The seventh is the "syndrome" defense, typically battered woman syndrome and premenstrual syndrome.

本章主要介绍几种刑事责任的宽恕事由。一是精神病宽恕事由,从精神病判断的具体标准出发,讨论其如何成为责任的宽恕事由。具体包括精神病判断的"对—错标准""不可抑制冲动标准""实质能力标准""精神疾病产物标准"四个标准。二是责任能力降低宽恕事由,即减轻责任的宽恕。该宽恕往往适用于患有由公认病症引起的精神失常导致理解行为性质、形成理性判断以及行使自我控制的能力受损的病人。三是年龄宽恕事由,一定年龄以下的未成年人由于缺乏相关的认知能力而无须承担刑事责任。四是胁迫宽恕事由,迫在眉睫的生命威胁可以成为被宽恕的理由。五是醉态宽恕事由,醉酒会使行为人缺乏犯罪所需的意图。六是警察圈套宽恕事由,警察圈套宽恕必须满足主观或客观上的条件。七是综合征宽恕事由,典型的是受虐妇女综合征和经前期综合征。

■ The Purpose of Curriculum Ideology and Politics for this Chapter (本章的课程思政目标)

1. Through the study of this chapter, students should have a systematic understanding of the excuses of criminal liability in Anglo – American criminal law, and learn to think how the defense of criminal liability in Anglo – American criminal law relates to the modernization of social governance. The modernization of social governance needs to consider the special situation of individuals under special circumstances, and the causes of excuse are important special situations in extreme events. The good application of the causes of excuse is conducive to the overall governance of society.

通过本章内容的学习,使学生对英美刑法的刑事责任宽恕事由有系统的了解和认识,思考英美法系刑事责任宽恕事由如何与社会治理现代化相关联。社会治理现代化需要考虑个体在特殊情况下的特殊境况,而宽恕事由就是在极端事件中的重要特殊境况。应用好宽恕事由,有利于社会的全面治理。

2. To explore the differences between the excuses of criminal liability in Anglo – American criminal law and those in Chinese criminal law and understand on their diverse

characteristics and their reasonability, and to help us build a richer and more systematic system of the excuses of criminal liability. A richer and more systematic system of excuse causes can better meet China's current and future practical needs, and better help judicial practitioners pursue the unification of legal, social and political effects in complex case trials.

挖掘英美刑法的刑事责任宽恕事由与中国刑法的刑事责任宽恕事由的差异，了解其多样性特征及其合理之处。

3. To consider how the excuse defenses of criminal liability in Anglo – American criminal law match with the core values of a society, and keep developing. Various core values of society are related to different causes of excuse, which will affect the understanding, introduction and application of specific causes of forgiveness, and need to be specifically screened.

思考刑事责任宽恕事由如何与社会的核心价值观念相匹配，并不断发展。各种社会核心价值观念与不同的宽恕事由关联，会影响具体的宽恕事由的理解、引入和适用，需要我们对其具体地甄别。

■ Terminologies（专业术语）

defense of insanity	精神病宽恕事由
defendant	被告人
jurisdiction	司法管辖区
Model Penal Code（MPC）	《模范刑法典》
jury	陪审团
offender	罪犯，犯罪者
the right – wrong test of insanity	精神病判断的"对—错标准"
irresistible impulse	不可抑制的冲动
the substantial capacity test of insanity	精神病判断的实质能力标准
the product – of – mental – illness test	精神病判断的"精神疾病产物标准"
capacity	责任能力
defense of diminished capacity	责任能力降低宽恕事由
the excuse of age	年龄宽恕事由
mitigation	减轻罪刑
the court of appeals	上诉法院
probation	缓刑

rebuttable presumption	可反驳的推定
minimum chronological age	最低实足年龄
duress	胁迫
the defense of intoxication	醉态宽恕事由
circuit court	巡回法院
the subjective test of entrapment	警察圈套"主观论"
the objective test of entrapment	警察圈套"客观论"
battered women's syndrome	受虐妇女综合征
premenstrual syndrome(PMS)	经前期综合征
American Psychiatric Association(APA)	美国精神病学协会

The causes of defense are divided into two categories, and the one is the causes of justification, the other is the causes of excuse. The previous chapter is about justification, and this chapter is mainly about excuse. The excuse of criminal liability occupies an important position in the criminal law system of various countries. Due to the differences in culture and history of various countries, the system of the excuse of criminal liability in Anglo – American Criminal law is different from that in China, and each system has its advantages and disadvantages in content and division. The excuses in Anglo – American Criminal law include mental illness, reduced capacity of responsibility, age, coercion, intoxication, police entrapment and syndrome. Therefore, students should expand their international vision and deeply think about global common topics by learning the connotation and examples of the excuses of criminal liability in Anglo – American criminal law.

抗辩事由分为两类,一类是正当事由,另一类是辩解事由。前一章讲的是正当事由,本章主要讲的是辩解事由。刑事责任宽恕事由在各国刑法体系中都占据重要地位。由于各国文化及历史的差异,在内容和划分上各有优劣。英美刑法中的宽恕事由包括精神病、责任能力降低、年龄、胁迫、醉态、警察圈套以及综合征。通过学习英美刑法刑事责任宽恕事由的内涵和实例,学生可以拓宽国际视野,深度思考全球共性课题。

6.1 Defense of Insanity(精神病宽恕事由)

People's abilities to know the law and to choose under free will are necessary for criminal liability and punishment. Criminal law assumes people have these abilities, so it only recognizes insanity in a few strict instances. Insanity as an excuse inquires the personal capacity to know the law and choose. An insane individual cannot understand the immorality of the conduct or obey the law, so punishing such individual cannot prevent crimes and seems cruel. The insanity test assumes that the existing mental illness/disorder be not under control of the individual, important psychological functions be impacted, and the impacted function significantly affect the ability to understand and choose his/her behaviors.

人们对法律的认识和自由选择的能力是刑事责任和刑罚的必要条件。刑法假设人们具有这些能力,所以只在少数的情况下承认精神错乱。作为一种宽恕事由,精神错乱探究个人了解法律和作出选择的能力。一个精神失常的人不能理解行为的不道德或遵守法律,所以惩罚该人不但不能防止犯罪,而且看起来是残酷的。精神错乱标准假设个体存在的精神疾病/障碍不受控制,重要的心理功能受到影响,并且受影响的功能显著影响其理解和选择行为的能力。

During the trail of the case, experts will form an opinion on the defendant's mental state at the time of the crime and whether it meets the elements of the insanity test used in their jurisdiction, based on a variety of information, such as the defendant's mental health history, account of the crime, facts and circumstances surrounding the crime, as well as psychological and medical tests. There are different criteria for insanity in common law countries, especially in the United States. Next, several main insanity tests will be introduced.

在进行案件审理时,专家会根据各种各样的信息,如被告的精神健康史、对犯罪的叙述、与犯罪有关的事实和情况,以及心理和医学标准,就被告在犯罪时的精神状态,以及是否满足他们所在管辖区域范围内使用的精神失常标准的要素,形成意见。在英美法系国家,尤其是在美国,精神病判断有不同的标准。下面,将介绍几种主要的精神病判断标准。

6.1.1 The Right – Wrong Test of Insanity(精神病判断的"对—错标准")

The right – wrong test, also known as M'Naghten rules, provides an answer to the question of how to tell whether a person is mentally ill. If the person is completely out of his mind and does not know what he is doing, he will lack the mental elements necessary to commit a crime. The law still depended on the House of Lords' answer in M'Naghten (1843). Under the M'Naghten test,[1] a defendant cannot be convicted if

[1] M'Naghten's Case, 101 Cl. & F. 200, 8 Eng. Rep. 718 (H. L. 1843).

he was mentally ill at the time of the crime, and in fact did not know what he was doing, or did not know what he was doing was wrong in social sense. For the latter, mental illness almost impairs the actor's cognitive ability, so he is unable to exercise the moral understanding as a normal person. Without the ability to rationally recognize and evaluate the moral problems caused by his behavior, the criminal law cannot influence his choice of behavior. In 1992 in Canada, the insanity defense was renamed the Mental Disorder Defense, and the verdict of not guilty by reason of insanity was renamed the verdict of not criminally responsible for anything other than a mental disorder. The mental disorder defence now states that no actor is criminally liable for an act or omission committed while suffering from a mental disorder that prevents the person from understanding the nature and quality of the act or omission, or from knowing that it is wrong.[1] Each of these categories will be described below.

在如何判断一个人是否具有精神病这一问题上,"对—错标准"(又称"M'Naghten 规则")提供了一种答案。如果这个人完全失去理智,不知道自己在做什么,他的行为缺乏犯罪所必需的精神因素。法律仍然依赖于上议院对 M'Naghten 案(1843 年)的标准。根据"对—错标准",如果被告在犯罪时患有精神疾病,不知道自己事实上在做什么或不知道自己在社会意义上做错了,那么他就不能被定罪。在社会意义上,精神疾病几乎使行为人的认知能力丧失,因此他不能实现正常人的道德理解。如果没有理性地认识和评价自己行为所引起的道德问题的能力,刑法就无法影响他的行为选择。1992 年,在加拿大,精神错乱辩护被重新命名为精神障碍辩护,因精神错乱而无罪的判决被重新命名为因精神障碍而不承担刑事责任的判决。现在,精神障碍辩护规定:在行为人患有精神障碍,无法理解作为或不作为的性质和特性,或不知道它是错误的情况时,其对所实施的作为或不作为不负有刑事责任。下面分别对这些种类进行介绍。

The ability to understand the nature of an action is not simply the knowledge or recognition that the action is being performed. It involves the ability to measure and anticipate the consequences of actions. For instance, the special requirement in Canadian criminal law is "perception", the ability to perceive the effects and consequences of physical actions. The defendant may be aware of the physical nature of his act (asphyxiation, for example) but not necessarily have the capacity to recognize that, in nature and quality, the act will result in a person's death.[2] The court did not extend

---

〔1〕 Canadian Criminal Code, s 16(1).

〔2〕 (1979), 51 CCC (2d) 129 at 147 (SCC) [Cooper].

the defence to those who, because of a mental disorder, were emotionally unable to recognise the impact of their actions on the victim. A plea does not apply to the defendant who has the necessary understanding of the nature, characteristics and consequences of the act, but simply lacks an appropriate sense of the victim or lacks a sense of remorse or guilt for the act he has done. No doubt the absence of such feelings is a common feature of many who engage in repetitive and serious criminal behaviours.〔1〕 Inability to understand the penal consequences of an act because of mental illness does not render the defendant incapable of understanding the physical consequences of that act.〔2〕

理解行为性质的能力不仅要求对行为正在被实施具有认识或认知。它还包括衡量和预见行为后果的能力。例如,加拿大对此特有的要求是"感知",即一种感知身体行为的影响和后果的能力。此时,被告可能意识到他的行为的物理性质(如窒息),但不一定有能力认识到,该行为经由其性质和特性将导致一个人的死亡。因此,加拿大最高法院没有将辩护范围扩大到那些因精神障碍而在情感上无法认识到自己的行为对受害者的影响的人。宽恕事由不适用于那些对行为的性质、特征和后果有必要理解,只是缺乏对受害者适当的感知或缺乏对他所做行为的悔恨感或内疚感的被告。毫无疑问,这些感情的缺乏是许多从事重复和严重犯罪行为的人的共同特征。被告由于精神疾病不能理解某一行为的刑罚后果,并不影响被告不能理解该行为的物理后果。

Common law jurisdictions differ as to the meaning of "wrong". Some jurisdictions define wrong as legally wrong, meaning the defendant must be unaware that the act is against the law. Others in USA define wrong as "legally and morally wrong", meaning the defendant must also be unaware that the act is condemned by society. But both hold that the defendant needs to be unaware that his actions are legally wrong. If a defendant knew that an action was legally wrong, should this person obtain the insanity defense? This issue was controversial in the past. In Schwartz, The Supreme Court of Canada justices have disagreements, with the majority saying that a defendant whose defense is

〔1〕 R v Simpson (1977), 35 CCC (2d) 337 at 355 (Ont CA) [Simpson].

〔2〕 (1982), 68 CCC (2d) 394 at 405 - 6 (SCC) [Abbey].

insanity must not know that an action was legally wrong.[1] In R. v. Chaulk, the Supreme Court overturned the conclusion reached in Schwartz, holding that defendants should obtain an insanity plea if, because of mental illness, they were unable to know that an action was morally wrong, even if they were able to know that the action was legally wrong.[2] Subsequent cases have shown that the insanity defense does not apply

---

〔1〕 In 1973, Schwartz murdered Barbara Jean Blum and Edward Julius Merckle, and was charged with non-capital murder. Schwartz's main defense was insanity at the time of the alleged offences, which was rejected by the British Columbia Court of Appeal. When the case was appealed to the Supreme Court of Canada, the focus issue was summarized as how to understand the "wrong" in s. 16 (2) of the Canadian *Criminal Code*. In the opinion of the Court of Appeal, "wrong" meant "forbidden by law" which Schwartz was capacity to know, so he wasn't within the definition of insanity. The appellant's submission was that the word "wrong" means contrary to the ordinary standard of reasonable men. Even if a person who has committed a crime knew that his act was legally wrong, he would still be within the definition of insanity if he believed his action to be right according to the ordinary standard of reasonable men. The Supreme Court ultimately supported the views of the Court of Appeal and dismissed Schwartz's appeal. Schwartz v. R., (1977), 29 CCC (2d) 1 (SCC).

1973 年,Schwartz 谋杀了 Barbara Jean Blum 和 Edward Julius Mernickle,因此被指控犯非死刑谋杀罪,Schwartz 的主要辩护理由是在实施被指控犯罪时精神错乱,但未被不列颠哥伦比亚省上诉法院采纳。案件上诉至加拿大最高法院后,案件焦点为如何理解《加拿大刑法典》第 16(2)条的"错误"。上诉法院认为错误是指行为被法律禁止,Schwartz 能够认识到这一点,因此他不在精神错乱的范围内。上诉人认为"错误"意味着违背理性人的一般标准。即便犯罪的人知道其行为在法律上是错误的,但如果他认为自己的行为符合理性人的一般标准,那么依然属于精神错乱的范围内。最高院最终支持了上诉法院的观点,驳回了 Schwartz 的上诉。

〔2〕 On September 3, 1985, Chaulk and Morrissette entered a home in Winnipeg, plundered it for valuables and then stabbed and bludgeoned its sole occupant to death. They were convicted of first degree murder, and the only defense raised at trial was insanity. Expert evidence was given at trial that the appellants (Chaulk and Morrissette) suffered from a paranoid psychosis which made them believe that they had the power to rule the world and that the killing was a necessary means to that end; They knew the laws of Canada existed, but believed that the law was irrelevant to them. This defense was rejected by the jury and the Court of Appeal upheld the conviction. The Supreme Court of Canada held that the meaning of "wrong" used in s. 16 (2) of the Canadian *Criminal Code* should be interpreted to mean "morally wrong" and not "legally wrong" simply. Although the appeal was ultimately rejected by the Supreme Court, the meaning of "wrong" in mental disorders had actually changed. R. v. *Chaulk*, [1990] 3 SCR 1303.

1985 年 9 月 3 日,Chaulk 和 Morrissette 进入温尼伯的一处住宅,掠夺其贵重物品,然后用棍棒刺死了唯一的住户,他们被判定为犯一级谋杀,提出的唯一辩护理由是精神错乱。审判中的专家证据显示,上诉人(Chaulk and Morrissette)患有偏执狂精神病,他们相信自己有能力统治世界,杀人是实现这一目的的必要手段;尽管其知道加拿大的法律存在,但认为法律与他们无关。这一辩护理由被陪审团拒绝,上诉法院也维持了原判。加拿大最高法院认为,《加拿大刑法典》第 16(2)条中"错误"的含义应该被解释为道德上错误,而不仅仅是法律上错误。尽管上诉最终被最高法院驳回,但是精神错乱中"错误"的含义实际上已经发生改变。

to "a mentally ill person or a person who follows an abnormal moral code". Nor does the s. 16 defence of insanity apply if such a person is able to know that his or her actions are wrong in the eyes of society and chooses to carry them out despite such knowledge[1], and if the accused understands society's view of what is right and wrong, but believes, because of a delusion or mental disorder, that what he did was justified.[2]

英美法系各地区对"错误"的定义有所不同。美国的一些司法管辖区将错误定义为"法律上的错误",这意味着被告必须不知道该行为是违法的。美国其他管辖区将错误定义为"法律上和道德上的错误",这意味着被告也必须不知道该行为会受到社会的谴责。但这两者都认为被告需要不知道自己的行为在法律上是错误的。如果被告知道自己的行为在法律上是错误的,其是否能获得精神错乱辩护?这一问题曾经存在争议。在 Schwartz 案中,加拿大最高法院的法官产生了分歧,多数法官认为主张精神错乱抗辩的被告绝对不能知道某项行为在法律上是错误的。在 R. v. Chaulk 案中,最高法院推翻了 Schwartz 案得出的结论,其认为如果因为精神疾病使被告无法知道一个行为在道德上是错误的,那么他们就应该获得精神错乱宽恕,即使他们能够知道该行为在法律上是错误的。后续案例表明,精神错乱辩护不适用于"精神病患者或遵循异常道德准则的人"。如果这样一个人能够知道他的行为在社会看来是错误的,并且在知道后仍选择实施这些行为;如果被告理解社会对是与非的看法,但由于一种妄想或精神障碍,认为他所做的事情是正当的,那么《加拿大刑法典》第 16 条的精神病辩护也不适用。

6.1.2　The Irresistible Impulse Test of Insanity(精神病判断的"不可抑制冲动标准")

Reflection on the defects of the right - wrong test gave rise to the irrepressible impulse test. A criticism of the Right - Wrong text is that they only allow an assessment of the defendant's cognitive abilities. M'Naghten does not allow an assessment of the defendant's volitional incapacity. The narrowness of it has led to reforms in many jurisdictions in the United States. Suppose a person has some kind of "mental illness" that leads to an "irresistible urge" to commit a crime. In the United States, the concept of irresistible impulse is supported in the Model Penal Code, but with a certain change in language. To avoid giving the impression that an irresistible impulse must be sudden, the Model Penal Code uses the expression "capacity to conform his conduct to the requirements of law". The Model Penal Code states that "a person is not responsible for

---

〔1〕 R. v. Oommen (1994), 91 CCC (3d) 8 at 19 (SCC).

〔2〕 R. v. W(JM) (1998), 123 CCC (3d) 245 (BCCA); R. v. Ross, 200 9 ONCA 149.

a criminal conduct if at the time of such conduct as a result of mental disease or defect he lacks substantial capacity either to appreciate the criminality [wrongfulness] of his conduct or to conform his conduct to the requirements of law". A typical case is that John Hinckley tried to assassinate the hugely popular President Reagan in order to impress Yale freshman, actress Jodie Foster.[1] Hinckley argued for an insanity defense, claiming he was under irresistible compulsion from a mental illness or defect. Under the M'Naghten rule, Hinckley could not successfully defend himself because, while his thought process was clearly irrational, Hinckley knew that he was shooting at a human being and that such action was illegal and, in fact, that Hinckley intended to murder. But he successfully convinced the jury that he was legally insane under a lower irresistible impulse standard. In 1982, he was taken to St. Elizabeth's Hospital in Washington for treatment.[2] From this case, the irresistible impulse portion of the test has been criticized for protecting impulses that should and could be suppressed.[3] After Hinckley used the test to escape liability, most U. S. states reinstated the M'Naghten

---

〔1〕 On March 30, 1981, Hinckley attempted to assassinate the President of the United States, Ronald Reagan, in the driveway of the Washington Hilton Hotel, and wounded several people including the President. Hinckley was charged under federal law with attempted assassination of the President of the United States, assault on a federal officer, use of a firearm in the commission of a federal offense, and with attempted murder, multiple assault charges and a weapons charge under the District of Columbia Code. At his criminal trial, Hinckley presented evidence that he suffered from a mental disease or defect that was responsible for his conduct on the day of the shootings, and on June 21, 1982, the jury found him not guilty by reason of insanity. "As the consequence of a successful insanity defense is not freedom but an indeterminate detention in a mental hospital", Hinckley was committed to St. Elizabeths Hospital under D. C. Code § 24 – 301. Afterwards, he applied several times and was gradually granted and privileges of conditional releases, until June 15, 2022, when he was unconditional release from his commitment. United States v. Hinckley, 2021 WL 8200009.

1981 年 3 月 30 日,欣克利试图在华盛顿希尔顿酒店的车道上暗杀美国总统罗纳德·里根,他使用枪支打伤了包括总统在内的多人。根据联邦法律欣克利被指控企图暗杀美国总统、袭击一名联邦官员、在实施联邦犯罪中使用枪支,以及根据《哥伦比亚特区法典》被指控谋杀未遂、多项攻击指控和武器指控。在审判中,欣克利提出了证据,证明他患有精神疾病或缺陷,这要对他在枪击事件当天的行为负责,于是 1982 年 6 月 21 日陪审团认定他因精神错乱而无罪。"由于成功的精神错乱辩护的结果不是自由,而是在精神病院的不确定拘留",根据华盛顿特区法典 § 24 – 301,欣克利被交给圣伊丽莎白医院。之后他数次申请并被逐渐授予有条件释放特权,直到 2022 年 6 月 15 日才被无条件释放。

〔2〕 United States v. Hinckley, 672 F. 2d 115.

〔3〕 Stephen J. Morse, *Culpability and Control*, 142 U. Pa. L. Rev. 1587 (1994).

rule.[1]

对于“对—错标准”缺陷的反思催生了“不可抑制冲动标准”。对“对—错标准”的批评是,它们只涉及对被告认知能力的评估,而不涉及对被告无意志能力的评估。“对—错标准”的狭隘性使美国众多司法管辖区进行改革。假设一个人有某种“精神疾病”,导致其产生实施犯罪的“不可抗拒的冲动”。在美国,不可抗拒的冲动这个概念在《模范刑法典》中得到了支持,但在语言上有一定的变化。为了避免给人“不可抗拒的冲动”一定是突然发生的这种印象,该法典使用的是“按照法律的要求行为的能力”的表述。《模范刑法典》规定,“如果一个人在由于精神疾病或缺陷而实施犯罪行为时,缺乏理解其行为的犯罪性(不法性)或使其行为符合法律要求的实质能力,则其无须对犯罪行为负责”。一个典型案例是,约翰·欣克利为了给耶鲁大学一年级学生,演员朱迪·福斯特留下深刻印象,试图刺杀极受欢迎的里根总统。欣克利在审讯中主张精神错乱辩护,声称他处于精神疾病或精神缺陷带来的不可抗拒的强迫之下。若根据“对—错标准”,欣克利将不能辩护成功,因为虽然他的思维过程明显不合理,但他知道自己是在向一个人开枪,而且这样的行为是非法的,事实上,欣克利的确意图谋杀。他成功地使陪审团相信(根据“不可抑制冲动标准”),他是法律上的精神病患者。1982年,他被送往华盛顿圣伊丽莎白医院接受治疗。经由此案,精神病标准中不可抗拒的冲动部分因为保护了应该和可能被抑制的冲动而遭到批评。在欣克利利用“不可抑制冲动标准”摆脱罪责后,美国大多数州恢复了“对—错标准”。

Canadian courts have long refused to recognize "irresistible impulse" as a separate category of insanity defense.[2] At the same time, however, evidence of an irresistible impulse, such as evidence of delusion, may be relevant to determining whether a defendant qualifies for a mental disorder defense. The reason is that delusion can be a mental disorder. The argument of irresistible impulse has never been accepted as a sufficient defence in the law of England. It is mainly because people think irresistible impulses are unprovable.[3] A fatal objection is the inability to draw the line between an irresistible impulse and an impulse that is simply not resisted. Certain medical conditions may increase a person's desire or inclination to commit certain criminal acts, but such a person knows that he is doing the wrong thing, and he knows the nature of what he is

---

〔1〕 Lisa A. Callahan et al., *Insanity Defence Reform in the United States Post – Hinckley*, 11 Mental & Physical Disability L. Rep. 54 (1987).

〔2〕 The Queen v. Borg, 1969, CanLII 79 (SCC). R. v. Oommen, 1994 CanLII 101 (SCC).

〔3〕 R. v. Kopsch (1927) 19 Cr. App. R. 50 at 51.

doing. If any protection is to be given, it should be taken into account at the sentencing stage. The appropriate solution is to consider his condition as a mitigating factor when sentencing.

加拿大法院长期以来一直拒绝承认“不可抗拒的冲动”是精神错乱辩护的一个单独类别。然而,与此同时,不可抗拒的冲动的相关证据,如妄想的证据,可能与确定被告是否有资格进行精神障碍辩护有关。理由是,妄想可以是一种精神障碍。但在英格兰的法律中,不可抗拒的冲动从未被作为充分的辩护理由接受。这主要是因为人们认为不可抗拒的冲动是无法证明的。一个致命的反对意见是,人们无法在不可抗拒的冲动和仅仅是没被被告人抗拒的冲动之间划清界限。某些疾病的确可能会增加一个人实施某些犯罪行为的欲望或倾向,但这样的人知道他在做错误的事情,也知道他所做的事情的本质。如果要给予他任何保护,则应在量刑阶段予以考虑,即在量刑时将他的病情作为减刑因素。

6.1.3 The Substantial Capacity Test of Insanity(精神病判断的“实质能力标准”)

The substantial capacity test originated in McDonald v. United States Government (1962). The appellant was convicted of manslaughter and sentenced to imprisonment. In this case, the court required that juries be informed that mental illness or defect includes any abnormal state of mind that seriously impairs control of mental or emotional processes or actions.[1] This statement has an impact on the subsequent legislation. In

---

〔1〕 McDonald was convicted of manslaughter and sentenced to from five to fifteen years' imprisonment for aiding and abetting his employer, Davis, in the shooting of one Jenkins during an altercation. The defendant appealed and urged that the district court's charge to the jury was fatally defective in two respects. One was the court twice enumerated the alternative verdicts available to the jury, but both times it failed to include "not guilty because of insanity". Evidence including expert opinion evidence implied that McDonald had a "mental defect", because his I. Q. rating shown by various tests was below the "average" intelligence range of 90 to 110, and would lack the ability of normal persons to foresee the consequences of his acts. The Court of Appeal held a view, the jury should be told that a mental disease or defect includes any abnormal condition of the mind which substantially affects mental or emotional processes and substantially impairs behavior controls. Apparently, meaning of a verdict of not guilty by reason of insanity wasn't told to the jury. Consequently, McDonald's conviction was reversed. McDonald v. United States, 312 F. 2d 847 (D. C. Cir. 1962).

麦克唐纳因为协助和教唆他的雇主戴维斯在一次口角中枪杀了一个叫詹金斯的人而被判过失杀人罪,被判处5年至15年监禁。被告提出上诉,并主张地方法院对陪审团的指示在两个方面存在致命缺陷。其中一个缺陷是,法院两次列举了陪审团可以获得的替代判决,但两次都没有包括“因精神错乱而无罪”。包括专家意见证据在内的证据表明,麦克唐纳存在“精神缺陷”,因为各种测试显示他的智商低于90至110的“平均”智力范围,并且可能欠缺正常人具有的预见行为后果的能力。上诉法院认为,陪审团应该被告知,精神疾病或缺陷包括任何严重影响精神或情绪过程并严重损害行为控制的异常心理状况。显然,陪审团在当时没有被告知因精神错乱而无罪的含义。因此,麦克唐纳的判决被推翻。

drafting the provisions of the Model Penal Code on insanity, the American Law Institute cited the statement in M'Naghten and McDonald cases: "A person is not responsible for a criminal conduct if at the time of such conduct as a result of mental disease or defect he lacks substantial capacity either to appreciate the criminality [wrongfulness] of his conduct or to conform his conduct to the requirements of law."[1] The test is often described as having two "elements". (1) "Recognizing his actions as criminal" is a cognitive problem corresponding to M'naghten's formula for recognizing wrongdoing. The word "cognition" is thought to add an emotional element - the term refers to the ability to empathize with others and understand how your actions affect them. The term is also thought to contradict the M'Naghten language of understanding the "nature and consequences" of one's actions. (2) The phrase "to obey his conduct" is a volitionary equivalent to the "irresistible impulse" test.

"实质能力标准"源于1962年麦克唐纳诉美国政府案。上诉人被判过失杀人罪,判处监禁。该案中,上诉法院要求告知陪审团,精神疾病或缺陷包括任何严重削弱对精神、情绪过程或行为控制的精神异常状态。这个说法对后续立法产生了影响。在起草《模范刑法典》关于精神错乱的条款时,美国法学会引用了M'Naghten和McDonald案件中的说法:"如果一个人在由于精神疾病或缺陷而进行犯罪行为时缺乏充分的能力来认识其行为的犯罪性或使其行为符合法律要求,则他无须对该犯罪行为负责。"这种标准通常被描述为有两个"要素":(1)"认识到他的行为是犯罪"。这个要素其实就是指认知方面的能力,与"对—错标准"对不法行为的认识相一致。"认识"一词被认为添加了情感元素——这个词指的是对他人感同身受的能力,以及理解自己的行为如何影响他人的能力。"认识"这个术语也被认为与理解一个人行为的"性质和后果"的M'Naghten用语相抵触。(2)"遵从他的行为"这个短语与"不可抑制冲动标准"在意志方面相对应。

6.1.4 The Product - of - Mental - Illness Test(精神病判断的"精神疾病产物标准")

The product - of - mental - illness test is used only in New Hampshire and has been the established insanity defense in New Hampshire since the late 1800s. In 1869, New Hampshire, in its simplest form, instructed juries to acquit a defendant of a crime whenever it was "the offspring or product of mental illness."[2] If the offender's

---

[1] Model Penal Code § 4.01(1)(1962).

[2] State v. Pike, 49 N.H. 399, 402 (1870).

criminal behavior was the result of illness rather than out of a mind capable of choice, and the result of an uncontrollable impulse rather than one governed by one's motives and will, then the insanity defense applies.[1] However, the court failed to give definitions for product, mental disease, or mental defect. Thus, the product - of - mental - illness test is extremely difficult to apply.

精神病判断的"精神疾病产物标准"只在新罕布什尔州使用,19 世纪末以来一直是新罕布什尔州既定的精神错乱辩护理由。1869 年,新罕布什尔州以最简单的形式,指示陪审团无论何时,只要犯罪是"精神疾病的结果或产物",就应宣告被告无罪。如果罪犯的犯罪行为是疾病的结果,而不是出于有选择能力的心理;是一种无法控制的冲动的结果,而不是由一个人的动机和意志支配的结果,那么就适用精神病辩护。然而,法院未能给出产物、精神疾病或精神缺陷的定义。因此,精神病判断的"精神疾病产物标准"极难适用。

■ Case Study(案例讨论)

Case of Eugen with schizophrenia.[2](尤金精神分类案)

Fact(基本案情)

Eugene was diagnosed with schizophrenia at a young age. The illness lulled him into the illusion that his life was in danger. On many occasions, his illness led him to believe that his family was trying to kill him, to which he reacted violently to protect himself. He eventually went on medication, which, along with weekly counseling, allowed him to lead a relatively normal life for years. However, the drug made him not feel like himself, and he always hated it. One day, Eugene decided to stop taking his medication. Soon after, Eugene is at his desk, overcome by the belief that his colleague Alan is trying to kill him. When Alan approached Eugene in the cafeteria, Eugene mistakenly thought Alan was finally going to kill him. Fearing for his life, Eugene grabbed a steak knife and attacked Allen, stabbing him repeatedly in the chest. Several people pulled Eugene away, but in the confusion Eugene stumbled backwards and fell, hitting his head on the corner of the table and severely injuring his head and brain.

尤金在很小的时候就被诊断出患有精神分裂症。疾病使他产生了有生命危险的错觉。在很多情况下,尤金的疾病让他相信他的家人试图杀死他,尤金对此做出

---

〔1〕 Rogers v. Commonwealth, 48 Mass. 500, 503 (1843).

〔2〕 Shima Baradam Baughman, John Q. La Fond & Richard G. Singer, Criminal Law Examples and Explanations (Wolters Kluwer, 2022) 569.

了暴力反应以保护自己。尤金最终接受了药物治疗,以及每周的心理咨询,这让他多年来过上了相对正常的生活。然而,药物使尤金感觉他不像自己,所以一直讨厌它。有一天,尤金决定停止服药。不久之后,尤金在他的办公桌前,确信他的同事艾伦试图杀死他。当艾伦在自助餐厅接近尤金时,尤金误以为艾伦终于要把他杀死了。尤金担心自己的生命安全,便抓起一把牛排刀袭击艾伦,在他的胸部连续捅了几刀。几个人把尤金拉开,但在一片混乱中,尤金向后踉跄摔倒,头撞在桌子的角上,头部和大脑严重受伤。

6.2 Defense of Diminished Capacity(责任能力降低宽恕事由)

The general concept of "diminished responsibility" was borrowed from Scotland, where it developed as judge – made law. For murder, legislation is needed.

"责任能力减少"的一般概念借用自苏格兰,在那里它是作为法官制定的法律而发展起来的。但对于谋杀而言,"责任能力减少"的规则需要立法。

Section 2 of England's Homicide Act 1957 states:

英格兰 1957 年《杀人法案》第 2 条规定如下:

1. A person ("D") who kills or is a party to the killing of another is not to be convicted of murder if D was suffering from an abnormality of mental functioning which—

(1) arose from a recognised medical condition,

(2) substantially impaired D's ability to do one or more of the things and these things are ①understand the nature of D's act; ②form a rational judgment; ③self – contral exercise,

(3) provides an explanation for D's acts and omissions in doing or being a party to the killing.

1. D 杀死或是参与杀死他人,如果 D 患有以下情况的精神功能异常,则不应被控谋杀:(1)由公认的病症引起,(2)严重损害 D 做下列一件或多件事情的能力(这些事情是:①理解 D 行为的本质;②形成理性判断;③运用自我控制能力),以及(3)为D 的作为和不作为提供了解释。

2. On a charge of murder, it shall be for the defence to prove that the person charged is by virtue of this section not liable to be convicted of murder.

2. 在谋杀指控中,辩方须证明根据本条,被控人不成立谋杀罪。

3. A person who but for this section would be liable, whether as principal or as accessory, to be convicted of murder shall be liable instead to be convicted of

manslaughter.

3. 任何可能(如无本条规定)被判犯有谋杀罪之人,无论其作为主犯还是从犯,都应被判犯有过失杀人罪。

4. The fact that one party to a killing is by virtue of this section not liable to be convicted of murder shall not affect the question whether the killing amounted to murder in the case of any other party to it.

4. 杀人的一方根据本条不应被判犯有谋杀罪,这一事实不应影响任何其他的杀人方是否构成谋杀的问题。

Thus, he should have been convicted of murder, but because his abnormal mental functioning, stemming from a recognized medical condition, greatly impaired his ability to understand the nature of his actions, form rational judgments or exercise self - control, and provided an explanation for his acts and omissions, so he was convicted of manslaughter. This article, in turn, has been adopted by other countries in the common law world.

可见,本来应当被判处谋杀罪的,但因为他的精神功能异常源自一种公认的病症,极大地损害了他理解其行为本质、形成理性判断或自我控制的能力,为他的作为和不作为提供了解释,因此他会被判过失杀人。后来,本条规定也被普通法世界的其他国家采纳。

The law cannot prescribe a reduction of liability as a complete defence. Deminished capacity targets those who retain some degree of culpability ability. It's not just about protecting people who aren't capable of being guilty of anything. If the accused commits a proscribed act while in a proscribed mental state, it is against public policy to think he's totally incapable of responsibility and exempt him from responsibility and thus from all forms of social control.

法律不能规定责任的减少是一个完全辩护事由。减轻责任能力针对的是那些保留一定程度罪责能力的人。它的目的不仅是保护那些没有任何罪责能力的人。如果被告在一种被规定的精神状态下做出了被规定的行为,那么认为他完全没有责任能力而免除他的责任,进而免除一切形式的社会控制是违反公共政策的。

The diminished capacity defence requires that the defendant suffer from an abnormality of mental function resulting from a recognized health condition that significantly impairs the defendant's ability to understand the nature of his actions, form rational judgments, and exercise self - control. Abnormal mental function means that according to social standards, mental function is abnormal. If there is unassailable expert evidence that strongly demonstrates that the defendant meets the test of diminished capacity, the jury cannot ignore it. The jury must consider evidence that strongly supports defendant's diminished capacity. Basically, the jury decides whether the defendant's medical condition impairs his ability to comply with the criminal law. In most cases, the defendant will deny that he understands the nature of his actions or that he is able to form rational judgments. The jury will decide whether he is credible based on the medical evidence and the facts of the case.

减轻责任能力的辩护要求被告患有由公认的病症引起的精神功能异常,这种精神功能异常严重损害了被告理解自己行为的性质、形成理性判断、运用自我控制的能力。精神功能异常是指按照社会的标准,精神功能是不正常的。如果有不容置疑的专家证据,有力地表明被告符合减轻责任能力的标准,陪审团应当予以重视。陪审团必须考虑有力证明被告责任能力减弱的证据。基本上,陪审团会裁决被告的疾病是否削弱了他遵守刑法的能力。在大多数情况下,被告会否认他了解自己行为的本质或他能够形成理性的判断。陪审团将根据医学证据和案件事实来裁决被告是否可信。

Limiting the defence to those with a recognized medical condition aims to exclude emotions such as anger, fear, jealousy and hatred. It rules out the use of vague diagnoses that are not based on science for rasing a defence. For example, V had been suicidal for several months and had been begging her husband to help her kill herself. V thought she had a terminal illness, but she didn't. Still, she was afflicted by a number of other non – life threatening illnesses. One night, V took an overdose of medicine and attempted suicide. V told her 73 – year – old husband that if the pills didn't work, he should kill her. Her sleep became lighter, and the husband began to worry that V would wake up. As her sleep grew lighter, he smothered her to death. This is not a case of assisted suicide because the chain of causation was broken by The husband's deliberate intervention. The husband smothered V. The defendant raised a defence of diminished responsibility on the grounds that he suffered from an "adjustment disorder" brought on by the stress of caring for his mentally ill wife over a long period of time. He successfully pleaded mitigation, and the Court of Appeal commuted his two – year prison sentence to a 12 – month suspended sentence.[1] Here, the recognized adjustment disorder was found to reduce the defendant's capacity for responsibility, and the husband

[1] R. v. Webb [2011] EWCA Crim. 152.

was granted a reduced sentence.

将减轻责任能力辩护仅限用于那些有公认病症的人,目的是排除诸如愤怒、恐惧、嫉妒和仇恨等情绪。这种做法排除了不是基于科学的模糊诊断被用于提出辩护的情况。比如,V有自杀倾向已经好几个月了,她一直央求丈夫帮她自杀。V以为她得了绝症,但她没有。尽管如此,她还是被其他一些没有生命危险的疾病折磨着。一天晚上,V服用了过量的药物企图自杀。V告诉她73岁的丈夫,如果药片不起作用,他就应该杀了她。她的睡眠变浅了,丈夫开始担心V会醒来。当她的睡眠越来越浅时,他把她闷死了。这不是一个协助自杀的案例,因为因果链被丈夫的故意干预打破了,即丈夫闷死了V。被告人提出了责任减轻的辩护,理由是长期照顾患有精神疾病的妻子的压力导致他患有适应障碍。他成功地提出了减刑宽恕,上诉法院将他的2年监禁减刑为12个月缓刑。在此,公认的适应障碍被认定为减轻了丈夫的责任能力,所以丈夫获得了减刑的待遇。

Another situation in which capacity is reduced is that if a person's state of health causes him to drink heavily and his state of intoxication greatly reduces his ability to understand the nature of his behaviour, to form rational judgments and to exercise control, he may raise this defence.〔1〕

责任能力降低的另外一种情况是,如果一个人的健康状况导致他大量饮酒,而他的醉酒状态大大降低了他理解其行为性质、形成理性判断和行使控制的能力,他就可以提出该项辩护。

Defendants who successfully raise the defense face different legal consequences. Imprisonment remains a fairly common outcome, with custodial sentences imposed in most cases of diminished responsibility.〔2〕 However, many offenders are treated in hospitals and some are dealt without guardianship assistance. The forerunner of the general defence of diminished responsibility was the special rule on infanticide, which is still in force: section 1 of the Infanticide Act 1938 says if "at the time of the act or omission the balance of her mind was disturbed by reason of her not having fully recovered from the effect of giving birth to the child or by reason of the effect of lactation consequent upon the birth of the child", she "may for such offence be dealt with and punished as if she had been guilty of the offence of manslaughter of the child". Infanticide is as punishable as manslaughter, so judges have complete discretionary

---

〔1〕 R. v. Wood [2008] 2 Cr. App. R. 507. Cf. R. v. Tandy [1989] 1 W. L. R. 350.

〔2〕 Cf. R. v. Wood [2010] 1 Cr. App. R. (S) 6; R. v. Welsh (2011) 119 B. M. L. R. 21; cf. R. v. Drew [2003] 1 W. L. R. 1213.

power. In many cases, the result is always a hospital or probation order. In recent years, the woman has simply been released.[1]

成功提出减轻责任能力宽恕的被告,面临不同的法律后果。监禁仍然是相当普遍的结果,在大多数减轻责任能力的案件中被告人都会被判处监禁。然而,许多罪犯在医院接受治疗,有些人在没有监护协助的情况下被治疗。减少责任能力的一般性辩护的先驱是关于母亲杀婴的特别规则,该规则现在仍然有效:英国1938年《杀婴法》第1条规定,如果在该作为或不作为发生时,由于母亲尚未完全从分娩的影响中恢复过来,或由于分娩后哺乳的影响,她的精神平衡受到干扰,那么她的行为应认定为过失杀人。此时,杀婴应受与过失杀人罪一样的惩罚,因此法官有完全的自由裁量权。在许多情况下,结果总是一份入院令或缓刑令;但是近年来,杀婴的妇女只是简单地被释放了。

6.3 The Excuse of Age(年龄宽恕事由)

All actors are presumed capable of committing a crime from the time of arrest unless the law precludes criminal liability. The excuse of age is one of them. Infancy is an inborn incompetence. Most children do not have the intelligence, judgment, emotional maturity and moral capacity to make the rational choices required by criminal law. Therefore, the law does not hold very young children criminally liable, even if their actions were intended to cause serious harm. This is done by providing a plea of infancy also known as the excuse of age. The common law uses the actual age at the time of the crime to determine when a child is criminally responsible. At common law, (1) this is a complete defence to the charge that the accused was a child under the age of 7 at the time of the offence. The common law uses a conclusive presumption. It is irrefutably assumed that a child under the age of 7 cannot constitute the *mens rea* necessary to commit a crime. (2) For those between the ages of 7 and 14, there is a rebuttable presumption of incapacity. If the prosecution can show that the defendant understood that the crime was wrong, then this assumption can be overcome. Prosecutors bear the burden of proof and persuasion. (3) Children over the age of 14 are considered capable of committing a crime and can be tried as adult offenders unless insane. Every "child" eventually becomes an "adult" and takes responsibility for their actions. Criminal law takes an approach of different ages to determining when a child can no longer claim an

[1] R. D. Mackay, *The Consequences of Killing Very Young Children*, 21 Crim. L. R. (1993).

infantilism defense and may be criminally liable for their actions.

所有行为人自被捕时起都被推定具有犯罪能力,除非法律另有规定排除其刑事责任。年龄宽恕事由就是法定排除刑事责任的一种事由。在年龄宽恕事由中,未成年是一种天生的无行为能力事由。大多数儿童不具备智力、判断力、情感成熟度和道德能力,无法做出刑法所要求的理性选择。因此,法律不要求非常年幼的儿童承担刑事责任,即使他们的行为意在造成严重伤害。这是通过提供未成年的抗辩,即“年龄宽恕事由”来实现的。普通法使用犯罪发生时的实际年龄来确定儿童何时应承担刑事责任。在普通法中,(1)7 岁以下一般为完全无刑事责任年龄阶段。对于被告在犯罪时是 7 岁以下的儿童的指控,这是一个完全的辩护。普通法终局性推定 7 岁以下的儿童不可能具有构成犯罪所必需的犯罪意图。(2)7 岁至 14 岁为推定无刑事责任能力年龄阶段。其含义是对于年龄在 7 岁至 14 岁的人,一般被推定为无刑事责任能力。但是这一年龄阶段无刑事责任能力的推定可被推翻,也即如果控方能够证明被告明白犯罪行为是错误的,证明被告具有认识能力和控制能力,是具有刑事责任能力的,那么该推定可以被推翻。检察官承担提供证据和说服的责任。(3)14 岁以上的儿童被认为有犯罪能力。对于这个年龄阶段的人,除非精神失常,否则可以像成年罪犯一样受审。可见,刑法采取了不同年龄段的方法来确定儿童承担刑事责任的情况。

The common law determines the age of absolute irresponsibility mainly based on the physiological age and the relative age of criminal liability based on the psychological age, which has different emphasis in different jurisdictions. Many American states follow some version of the common law. Their statutes set a minimum age of criminal liability, usually 7 or 8 years old at the time of the offence. Children under a certain age are ultimately presumed to be incapable of committing a crime. This is an emphasis on biological age. Similarly, in Scotland, the defence of non - age stands for the principle that a child aged 7 or under is not liable for a criminal offence,[1] that a child aged under 12 cannot be prosecuted for a crime,[2] and that a child aged 12 or over cannot be prosecuted for an act committed when he or she was under 12.[3] This means that while children aged 8 to 11 are considered capable of committing a crime, offences committed by children of this age are not dealt with through the criminal courts. Instead, the child can be referred to the children's hearing system, where he or she can be dealt with on the

---

[1] Criminal Procedure (Scotland) Act 1995, s 41.

[2] Criminal Procedure (Scotland) Act 1995, s 41A(1).

[3] Criminal Procedure (Scotland) Act 1995, s 41A(2).

grounds of the offence or on other grounds depending on the circumstances. The Age of Criminal Resonponsibility is not only the rule of criminal procedure, but also the content of substantive law. A common law offence can only be established if the defendant has *mens rea*, and a child under the age of eight cannot have *mens rea*. Age of Criminal Liability (Scotland) Act 2019 changes the age of criminal liability in Scotland from 8 to 12 (see section 1). After the Act was implemented, harmful behaviour by children aged 8 to 11 would never be treated as a crime, but will be dealt with differently.

普通法这种根据生理年龄为主来确定绝对不负刑事责任年龄,根据心理年龄来确定相对负刑事责任年龄的做法,在不同的法域会有不同的侧重。美国许多州遵循相同版本的普通法,其法规规定了最低刑事责任年龄通常是犯罪时7岁或8岁。未满特定年龄的儿童最终被推定为没有犯罪能力,侧重生理年龄。同样,在苏格兰,未达年龄的宽恕事由所代表的原则就是7岁及以下年龄的儿童不对刑事犯罪负责,不满12岁的儿童不因犯罪被起诉,12岁或以上年龄的儿童不会因不满12岁时的行为被起诉。这意味着,虽然8岁至11岁的儿童被认为有犯罪能力,但这个年龄的儿童所犯的罪行不会通过刑事法庭处理。相反,该儿童可被转介到儿童听证系统,在那里他可根据犯罪或根据其他情况而受到处理。刑事责任年龄不仅是刑事程序规则,也是实体法内容。普通法上的罪行只有在被告有犯罪意图的情况下才能成立,而8岁以下的儿童不可能有犯罪意图。苏格兰《2019年刑事责任年龄法》第1条将苏格兰的刑事责任年龄从8岁改为12岁。在该法案实施后,8岁至11岁儿童的有害行为将确定不会被视为犯罪,但将以不同的方式被处置。

However, some states in America do not set a minimum chronological age. Instead, they assume that children under a certain age (like 14 in California) cannot commit a crime unless the state can prove that the child knew what he was doing and that it was wrong.[1] This requires "clear and convincing" evidence. Determining whether a child is capable of understanding what is wrong with his or her behavior is specific to the facts.[2] A number of factors are usually considered: (1) the nature of the offence, (2) the age and maturity of the child, (3) whether the child had a desire for confidentiality, (4) whether the child told the victim (if any) not to say, (5) whether the previous act was similar to the alleged act, (6) any consequences associated with the previous act, and (7) whether the child admitted that the act was wrong and could result

---

〔1〕 State v. Ramer, 86 P.3d 132, 114 (Wash. 2004).

〔2〕 State v. Ramer, 86 P.3d 132, 114 (Wash. 2004).

in detention.[1] This approach focuses on the child's "mental age" rather than his or her biological age. If convicted, he or she will receive the same severe punishment as an adult criminal. In particular, the nature and severity of the crime can determine whether the defendant is charged as an adult. Courts generally prefer to hold that if a juvenile's crime is violent and harmful to others, then he should be tried as an adult.[2]

然而,美国有些州没有设置最低年龄。相反,这些州假定未满一定年龄的儿童(如加利福尼亚州是14岁)是不能犯罪的,除非州政府能证明该儿童知道自己在做什么,而且这样做是错误的。这要求用"清晰且令人信服"的证据予以表明。判断一名儿童是否有能力理解其行为的错误之处,要根据具体事实而定。在确定这一问题时通常会考虑以下因素:(1)犯罪的性质;(2)儿童的年龄和成熟度;(3)儿童是否有保密的愿望;(4)儿童是否告诉受害者(如果有的话)不要说;(5)之前的行为与被指控的行为是否类似;(6)与之前的行为有关的任何后果;(7)儿童是否承认该行为是错误的,可能导致其被拘留。这种判断方法关注的是孩子的"心理年龄",而不是他的生理年龄。如果罪名成立,他将受到和成年罪犯一样严厉的惩罚。特别是,犯罪行为的性质和严重程度可以决定被告是否作为成年人被起诉。法院通常更倾向于认为,如果一名青少年的罪行是暴力的,并且对他人有害,那么他应该被当作成年人来审判。

Section 4.10 of the United States Model Penal Code provides a defence to immaturity. Simply put, no one under the age of 16 can be tried and convicted. Children who were 16 or 17 years old at the time of the crime may be tried in juvenile court or adult court if the juvenile court waives jurisdiction over the offender and agrees.

美国《模范刑法典》第4.10条规定了"不成熟"的辩护事由。16岁以下的人不能被审判和定罪。该条说明,犯罪时16岁或17岁的儿童可以在少年法庭受审,如果少年法庭放弃对罪犯的管辖权并同意,该儿童也可以在成人法庭受审。

6.4 Defense of Duress(胁迫宽恕事由)

Duress causes the actor to submit unwillingly to an illegal power and it is one of the important causes of excuses in the criminal law of the common law system. Typical cases of duress are the reluctant participation in riots and the supply of supplies to

---

[1] State v. Ramer, 86 P.3d 132, 114 (Wash. 2004). Com v. Martz, 118 A.3d 1175, 1183 (Penn. 2015). United States v. Ramirez, 297 *United States* F.3d 185, 193 (2d Cir. 2002).

[2] Ring v. State, 894 S.W.2d 944, 947 (Ark. 1995). United States v. Juvenile Male, 754 F. Supp. 2d 569, 575 (E.D.N.Y. 2010)

occupying forces.[1] In fact, some British authorities argue that treason is the only crime that can be exonerated by duress. A British judgment in 1838 did not grant immunity from duress.[2]

胁迫是指使行为人不情愿地服从非法的强制力，其是普通法系刑法中的重要宽恕事由之一。典型的胁迫案例是不情愿地参与暴乱和提供补给给占领军。胁迫为违法行为提供了宽恕的借口。事实上，一些英国权威论述认为，叛国罪是唯一可以因胁迫免责的罪行。但 1838 年英国的一项判决不认可胁迫为免责事由。

In one of the early U. S. treason prosecutions, the defendant was captured by the British during the Revolutionary War and then served in the British army. The judge instructed the jury that "nothing but fear of immediate death can justify joining the enemy", However, the jury acquitted him.[3] This shows that there were no clear rules in the early days. At the end of the 19th century, several judgments in the United States showed that duress could exonerate criminals in the face of imminent and inevitable threats to their lives. A Mississippi court wrote: "We can imagine that there may be circumstances in which, under compulsion to do something that would save him from committing a crime." However, this imminent danger must be present, imminent, and inescapable.[4] In 1893, an Alabama court, in an influential opinion, noted that at common law no one could justify killing an innocent person on the grounds of necessity or compulsion, but expressed doubt that the threat of future punishment would deter a perpetrator facing an immediate threat of death. The court therefore rejected the defendant's instructions on more narrow grounds, namely that the threats were not realised immediately when they were made and that the defendant had an opportunity to escape from his accomplices before arriving at the scene of the murder.[5]

在美国早期的一起叛国罪起诉中，被告在独立战争期间被英国人俘虏，然后在英国军队服役。法官指示陪审团，"除了对立即死亡的恐惧，没有任何理由可以为加入敌人的行为开脱"。然而，陪审团宣告其无罪。这说明早期并未形成明确的规则。在 19 世纪末，美国的几项判决表明，面对迫在眉睫和不可避免的生命威胁，胁迫可以作为被告辩护的宽恕事由。密西西比州的一个法院判决道："我们可以想象，被告

---

[1] Walter Harrison Hitchler, *Duress as a Defense in Criminal Cases*, 4 Va. L. Rev. 519 (1917).

[2] R. v. Taylor, 8 C & P 616 (1838).

[3] Respublica v. McCarty, 2 Dallas 86 (1781).

[4] Bain v. State, 67 Miss. 557 (1890).

[5] Arp v. State, 97 Ala. 5, 12 – 13 (1893); accord, People v. Repke, 103 Mich. 459 (1895).

人在某些情况下,可能会在被强迫的情况下……做出某种行为,从而使他免于犯罪的责任。”然而,胁迫当中的危险必须是现时存在的、迫在眉睫的、不可避免的。1893年,亚拉巴马州的一家法院在一份颇具影响力的判决书中指出,在普通法上,任何人都不能以必要或强迫为由为自己杀害无辜者的行为开脱,但面向未来的刑法惩罚的威慑,能否阻止直接面临死亡威胁的行为人屈从于他人的胁迫,法院对此表示怀疑。因此,法院以更狭义的理由拒绝了被告以胁迫进行的辩护,即威胁不是在发出时就立即生效的,被告在到达谋杀现场之前有机会逃离他的同伙。

The provisions of the Model Penal Code make duress conditional on the threat of unlawful force against any person, which in the case of the accused a person of reasonable firmness could not resist.[1] The defense must establish that a reasonable person in the defendant's position also would have committed the crime. This standard allows the jury to consider situational factors such as the relative strength and past interactions of the parties, as well as the availability of weapons, but does not take into account differences in maturity, courage, or independence.[2] In some cases, the duress defense fails. Article 2.09 of the Model Penal Code provides that a defendant cannot be defended if (1) he or she recklessly puts himself or herself at risk of duress; (2) there is no defence to a crime of negligence if he negligently puts himself in danger. The code also places the onus on the prosecution to prove that duress was not justified.

《模范刑法典》的条文把对他人使用非法武力的威胁规定为胁迫成立的条件,这种胁迫是有合理坚定立场的人在被告所处的情况下都无法抗拒的。辩方必须证明,一个处于被告地位的理性人也会犯下该罪行。这一标准允许陪审团考虑情境因素,如双方的相对实力和过去的互动,以及武器的可获得性,但不考虑成熟度、勇气或独立性的差异。在有的情形下胁迫辩护不成立。《模范刑法典》第2.09条规定:如果(1)被告鲁莽地将自己置于被胁迫的危险之中,则被告不能进行辩护;如果(2)他疏忽地将自己置于危险之中,则不能为过失犯罪辩护。法典同时规定控方有责任证明胁迫行为不成立。

Today, a significant minority of jurisdictions define duress along the lines recommended by the Model Penal Code. Of the 12 largest states, Texas, New York, Pennsylvania, and New Jersey apply duress for all crimes; using the threat of unlawful force as a plea so that a reasonable and determined person could not resist; this defense is prohibited for those who, regardless of the consequences, put themselves in danger of

---

〔1〕 Model Penal Code § 2.09 (1962).

〔2〕 Model Penal Code Commentaries, Part I, Sect. 2.09, at 372 – 377 (1985).

being duress.[1] Most other states require the threat of imminent great bodily harm as grounds for forgiveness of a crime. Many states bar defendants from this defense for at least some forms of homicide. Duress is not usually classed as justification. Normally, the burden is on the defendant to prove it by preponderance of evidence. But in a minority of jurisdictions, prosecutors bear the burden of overturning that justification.[2]

今天,美国有相当少数的司法管辖区按照《模范刑法典》建议的方针来界定胁迫行为。在美国12个最大的州中,得克萨斯州、纽约州、宾夕法尼亚州和新泽西州对所有犯罪都可用胁迫进行宽恕;非法的武力威胁,是该宽恕的成立条件,且该威胁要使一个理性坚定的人无法抵抗;对于那些不顾后果将自己置于被胁迫危险中的人,则禁止使用此辩护。其他大多数州都要求有即将遭受重大身体伤害的威胁作为犯罪宽恕理由的前提。许多州至少对某些形式的杀人罪禁止被告用胁迫进行辩护。胁迫通常不被归为正当事由。正常情况下,被告有责任通过优势证据来证明这一事由的成立。但在少数司法管辖区,检察机关承担了推翻这一正当事由成立的责任。

Jurisdictions that require an imminent threat may apply this requirement very differently. Anguish was accused of bank robbery. Four days prior to the bank robbery, two men threatened to harm Anguish and his family unless he robbed a bank. Anguish believed that these threats were related to his discovery of the FBI agent's extramarital affair and that the FBI agent and his lover conspired to kill the lover's husband. Two men's motive was to discourage him from conducting future investigations of the FBI agent or the agent's lover. After Anguish confronted the FBI agent, Anguish's home was burglarized, and he began receiving threatening phone calls. Although Anguish reported these incidents, law enforcement did not assist him. Anguish thought that reporting the threats would be futile given law enforcement's previous inaction. The Texas Court of Appeals addresses whether threats made four days before appellant committed the offenses constituted imminent threats and held that a threat is not rendered imminent solely because law enforcement agencies are unable to provide protection. An imminent threat has two components of immediacy. First, the person making the threat must intend and be prepared to carry out the threat immediately. Second, carrying out the

---

[1] N. Y. Penal Law § 40.00 (1968); Tex. Penal Code § 8.05 (1994) (however Texas requires a threat of imminent great bodily harm to excuse a felony); 18 Pa. C. S. § 309 (1973); N. J. Stat. § 2C:2-9 (1979).

[2] Fla. Std. Jury Instr. (Crim.) 3.6(k) Duress or Necessity (2014); Cal. Crim. Jury Instruction 3402 (2008).

threat must be predicated upon the threatened person's failure to commit the charged offense immediately. No evidence reflected that the persons making this threat either intended or were prepared to carry it out immediately. Further, there was no evidence that the persons making the threat required Anguish to immediately or at a certain time carry out the robbery. Actually, Anguish waited several days before robbing the bank. Therefore, the threat that appellant claimed compelled him to commit the robbery fails on both components of immediacy. The court of Appeals concluded that the alleged threat was not an imminent threat, and dismissed Anguish's appeal.〔1〕Another case involves a taxi driver named Contento – Pachon who was threatened by the cab owner to kill his wife and children unless he helped smuggle drugs into America. But he was denied a duress defense at trail on the grounds that the threatened harm was not immediate in time or space and that he could have avoided the crime by contacting the police. The Ninth Circuit concluded that the defendant had reason to fear that his family would soon be threatened in Colombia if he stopped cooperating en route to the United States. The court also considers Contento – Pachon's allegations of police corruption in Colombia to be a triable matter of fact. In the end, they argued, the possibility of the family escaping gang retribution was a matter of fact for the jury.〔2〕Here, whether to recognize the realization of the rule of law in a jurisdiction affects the judgment of whether the content of duress is imminent. The urgent great bodily harm standard appears to balance the seriousness of the threatened harm with the seriousness of the offence ordered. On the one hand, the threat of less than lethal force is excluded, and on the other, the crime of intentional and attempted homicide is excluded too. As such, it avoids excuses for intentionally inflicting more serious harm than is threatened.

要求威胁迫在眉睫的各司法管辖区对胁迫事由的适用可能截然不同。例如，Anguish 被指控抢劫银行。在银行抢劫案发生的四天前，两名男子威胁他说，如果他不抢劫银行，就会伤害他和他的家人。Anguish 认为，这些威胁与他发现 FBI 探员的婚外情有关，FBI 探员和他的情人密谋杀害情人的丈夫。这两名男子的动机是阻止他在未来对联邦调查局特工或特工的情人进行调查。在他与 FBI 探员对峙后，他的家被盗，他开始接到威胁电话。尽管他报告了这些事件，但执法部门并没有帮助他。他认为，鉴于执法部门此前的无所作为，报告这些威胁是徒劳的。得克萨斯州上诉法院讨论了在上诉人犯罪前四天发出的威胁是否构成必要的迫在眉睫的威胁，并认

〔1〕 Anguish v. State, 991 S. W. 2d 883 (1999).

〔2〕 United States v. Contento – Pachon, 723 F. 2d 691 (1984).

为威胁不会仅仅因为执法机构无法提供保护而变得迫在眉睫。迫在眉睫的威胁的迫切性有两个组成部分。第一,发出威胁的人必须打算并准备立即实施威胁。第二,实施威胁必须以受威胁的人未能立即犯下被指控的罪行为前提。没有证据反映威胁者有意或准备立即实施这一威胁。而且,也没有证据表明威胁者要求 Anguish 立即或者在某一时间实施抢劫。事实上,Anguish 在抢劫银行之前等了好几天。上诉人声称的迫使他实施抢劫的威胁,在迫切性的两个组成部分上都不成立。因此,上诉法院确定 Anguish 声称的威胁并不是迫在眉睫的威胁,驳回了 Anguish 的上诉。另一个案例是,出租车司机 Contento - Pachon 被出租车的所有人威胁要杀他妻儿,除非他帮助运毒到美国。他在审判中被驳回了胁迫辩护,理由是受到威胁的伤害在时间和空间上都不是立即发生的,他本可以通过联系警方来避免犯罪。但第九巡回法院的结论是,被告有理由担心,如果他在前往美国的途中停止合作,他在哥伦比亚的家人将很快受到威胁。法庭还认为 Contento - Pachon 对哥伦比亚警察腐败的指控是一个可审判的事实问题。最后,他们主张,对于陪审团来说,全家逃脱黑帮报复的可能性是一个事实问题。在此,是否承认某一法域实现了法治,影响了对胁迫的内容是否迫在眉睫的判断。紧急重大身体伤害标准似乎平衡了威胁伤害的严重程度与命令实施的罪行的严重程度,一方面,低于致命武力的威胁被排除了;另一方面,故意和企图杀人的罪行也被排除了。因此,它避免了为故意施加比威胁内容更严重的伤害提供免责事由。

As the above cases show, determining whether there is an imminent threat of violence, is very complex. The Model Penal Code does not require an imminent threat of violence. It requires only a threat of violence to overcome the resistance of people who have a reasonably firm stand in the circumstances facing the accused. An average person in a similar situation – for example, faced with corrupt or unresponsive law enforcement – would find it hard to resist the threat of a gang killing a family member. So there is a defense to duress in this case. Instead of prohibiting the defence of serious offences, the code incorporates the seriousness of the offence into normative judgments about the reasonableness of yielding to threats. Surely a sane and determined person would not kill to avoid a slap. At the same time, the standard of reasonable firmness does not take into account the defendant's exceptional mental ability to resist stress. Such incompetence can only be considered on the pretext of mental illness or defect (or underage, if the offender is a juvenile). Reasonable and firm standards focus on the threat of unlawful force and competitive pressure faced by the accused, namely the deterrent threat of punishment. It aims to exonerate the accused when the unlawful force threatened by the assailant is disproportionate to the punishment imposed for the crime, which is ineffective as a deterrent.

上面的案例表明,是否有迫在眉睫的暴力威胁的判断非常复杂。《模范刑法典》第2.09条并不要求有迫在眉睫的暴力威胁,它只要求暴力威胁能压制有合理坚定立场的人在被告所面对的情况下的抵抗。一个普通人在类似的情况下,例如面对腐败或反应迟钝的执法部门,会发现自己难以抵抗黑帮杀害家人的威胁。所以此种情况下的胁迫可以成立辩护事由。《模范刑法典》没有禁止对严重犯罪的辩护,而是将犯罪的严重程度纳入对屈服于威胁的合理性的规范性判断。想必一个理智坚定的人是不会为了躲避一巴掌而杀人的。同时,合理坚定立场的标准不考虑被告抵抗压力的异常心理能力。这种无行为能力只能以精神疾病或缺陷(或未成年,如果罪犯是青少年)这类宽恕事由予以考虑。合理坚定立场的标准着重于考察被指控者面临的非法武力威胁和被指控者面临的相反方向的压力,即刑事惩罚的遏制性威慑。适用这个标准的目的是在攻击者威胁的非法武力与刑法对罪行所施加的惩罚不成比例时为被告开脱,因为这种惩罚无法作为一种威慑起作用。

Section 17 of the Criminal Code of Canada states: A person who commits an offence under duress by threats of immediate death or bodily harm from a person who is present when the offence is committed is excused for committing the offence if the person believes that the threats will be carried out and if the person is not a party to a conspiracy or association whereby the person is subject to compulsion, but this section does not apply where the offence that is committed is high treason or treason, murder, piracy, attempted murder, sexual assault, sexual assault with a weapon, threats to a third party or causing bodily harm, aggravated sexual assault, forcible abduction, hostage taking, robbery, assault with a weapon or causing bodily harm, aggravated assault, unlawfully causing bodily harm, arson or an offence under sections 280 to 283 (abduction and detention of young persons). Therefore, there are many conditions for the defense to be established under the Canadian Criminal law, including (1) The first requirement, the threat of death or bodily harm was directed at the accused or a third party; (2) Second requirement, reasonable belief that the threat will be carried out; (3) Third requirement, there is no safe escape route; (4) Fourth requirement, there is a strong temporal link between the initiation of a threat and the harm of the threat; (5) Fifth requirement, the harm avoided is proportional to the harm caused; (6) Sixth requirement, the person is not a party to a conspiracy or association whereby the person is subject to compulsion.

《加拿大刑法典》第17条规定:一个人受到犯罪时在场的人以立即死亡或人身伤害的威胁胁迫而实施犯罪,如果该人认为威胁会被实施,并且该人不是使其受到强迫的共谋或组织的一方,可对该犯罪免责。但本节不适用犯下的罪行是重叛逆罪或叛国罪、谋杀、海盗行为、谋杀未遂、性侵犯、使用武器的性侵犯、威胁第三者或造成身体伤害、严重性侵犯、强迫绑架、挟持人质、抢劫、使用武器的攻击或造成身体伤害、严重攻击、非法造成身体伤害、纵火或第280条至第283条(绑架及拘留青少年)所规定的罪行。从这个规定看,加拿大刑法要求的该项辩护成立的条件有很多,包括:(1)第一项要求,死亡或人身伤害的威胁针对了被告或第三方;(2)第二项要求,合理地相信威胁将会被执行;(3)第三项要求,没有安全的逃生大道;(4)第四项要求,威胁发出和威胁的危害之间存在紧密的时间联系;(5)第五项要求,避免的伤害与造成的伤害是成比例的;(6)第六项要求,该人不是使其受到强迫的共谋或组织的一方。

■ Case Study(案例学习)

R v. Conway [1989] QB 290.(女王诉康威案)

Fact(基本案情)

Conway was arrested for reckless driving, contrary to Section 2 of the Road Traffic Act 1972. Conway recklessly drove away from the plainclothes officers. Conway's defence was that he had acted under duress and feared for his life and that of his passenger because of the circumstances: his passenger had been the victim of a shotgun attack in similar circumstances a few weeks earlier and had suffered serious injuries as a result. Conway was jailed for six months for reckless driving and banned from driving for 18 months. He appealed against the verdict.[1]

康威因违反1972年《道路交通法》第2条鲁莽驾驶而被捕。康威不顾一切地驾车逃离便衣警察。其辩护理由是,他是在胁迫下行事的,在当时的情况下,他很担心自己和乘客的生命安全:几周前,他的乘客在类似的情况下遭到了猎枪的袭击,并因此受了重伤。后来,康威因鲁莽驾驶被判入狱6个月,并被禁止驾驶18个月。他对判决提出上诉。

Question: Whether the circumstances led to a defence of duress? (Please scan the QR code on the right to get the answer)

本案中的情形存在胁迫事由吗?(答案请扫描右侧二维码获取)

---

[1] Conway [1989] QB 290.

6.5 The Defense of Intoxication(醉态宽恕事由)

According to the Model Penal Code, intoxication is "a disorder of mental or physical capacity caused by the entry of a substance into the body".[1] The causes of intoxication can be divided into alcohol, drug, and other substances. The most typical form of intoxication is voluntary drunkness. Most societies have enjoyed alcoholic beverages since ancient times, but alcohol can change the way many people behave. Alcohol's effect on the brain is inhibitory from the start. It can loosen the constraints of social rules and morality upon it, impair physical performance, and impair judgment. Due to the numbing of the higher centers of control (and gradually others as well), alcohol produces a kind of stimulative effect, thereby weakening or removing the inhibitions that normally keep us within the bounds of civilized behavior. It also impairs the ability to perceive, reason, and foresee consequences.

《模范刑法典》第2.08条认为,醉态是指"一种物质进入身体而引起的精神或身体能力的紊乱"。醉态的缘由可以分为醉酒、中毒以及其他情况。最为典型的醉态情况是自愿醉酒。大多数社会从古代就开始享受酒精饮料,但酒精会改变许多人的行为方式。酒精对大脑的功能从一开始就具有抑制作用。酒精的摄入可以让人们放松社会规则和道德对其的约束,并损害其体能,削弱其判断力。由于麻痹了高级控制中枢(也逐渐麻痹了其他中枢),酒精会产生一种刺激作用,削弱或消除通常使我们处于文明行为界限内的拘束。酒精也会损害人们感知、推理和预见后果的能力。

Types of intoxication can be divided into voluntary intoxication and involuntary intoxication. Voluntary intoxication is a conscious decision to introduce a substance into the body that causes a disturbance of mental or physical capacity, whereas involuntary intoxication is a disturbance of mental or physical abilities caused by the introduction of a substance into the body without one's knowledge or by someone else. Whether intoxication can be used to defense varies according to the type of intoxication.

醉态的类型可以分为自愿醉态和非自愿醉态。自愿醉态是在自己知情的情况下决定让某种物质进入身体引起精神或身体能力的紊乱,而非自愿醉态是在自己不知情的情况下或者他人强行让某种物质进入身体引起精神或身体能力的紊乱。醉态能否用于辩护因醉态的类型而异。

---

[1] MPC § 2.08(5)(a).

6.5.1　Voluntary Intoxication(自愿醉态)

In the past, voluntary intoxication was seen as an aggravating characteristic, but now it is seen as a potential defence. In some cases, the defendant is allowed to introduce evidence of intoxication to prove that he was too drunk to form the specific intent required to commit the crime. Specific intent refers to direct intent in its pure form: the purpose of defendant is to take some action in order to produce some result. The defendant had both the intent to not only commit the crime, but also to achieve a specific end result. A drunk can get away with murder in this way if his state of intoxication is sufficient to prevent him from forming a specific intent to murder.[1] If he didn't form intent, he can't be convicted of murder. If the evidence seems to show that he just accidentally bumped into another, the fact that he was drunk may reinforce any doubts the jury may have about his intentions and lead them to acquit him of murder (as well as wounding with intent). In such cases, the burden of proving intent is usually on the prosecution.[2] By the end of the 19th century, most U. S. jurisdictions allowed evidence of intoxication to be considered in determining whether the defendant was capable of forming a specific intent to commit the crime charged.[3]

在过去,自愿醉态被视为加重犯罪的特征,但现在它被视为一个潜在的宽恕理由。在某些案件中,被告被允许提出醉态的证据,以证明他醉得太厉害,以致于无法形成犯罪所需的具体意图。具体意图指的是纯粹形式的直接意图:被告人的目的是采取某种行为以产生某种结果。被告人不仅有实施犯罪的意图,而且有达到特定最终结果的意图。如果醉汉的醉态状态足以阻止他形成谋杀的特定意图,醉汉能以这种方式逃脱谋杀罪的指控。如果他没有形成具体意图,就不能被判谋杀。如果证据表明他只是无意中撞到了他人,那么他醉态的事实可能会加强陪审团对他形成具体意图的任何怀疑,并使他们判他不成立谋杀罪(以及故意伤害)。在这种情况下,控方通常要承担具体意图的举证责任。到19世纪末,大多数美国司法管辖区允许在确定被告是否有能力形成实施被控罪行的具体意图时考虑醉态事由是否成立的相关证据。

Evidence of intoxication might convince a jury that he lacked the intent or other mental factors normally required to commit a crime. A common law offence cannot be constituted by proof of conduct alone. In such offences, actual intent must at least be

---

〔1〕 R. v. Sheehan [1975] 1 W. L. R. 739; D. P. P. v. Beard [1920] A. C. 479.

〔2〕 R. v. Sheehan [1975] 1 W. L. R. 739.

〔3〕 Hall, *Intoxication and criminal liability*, 57 Harv. L. Rev. 1045 (1944).

established to commit the physical act involved in the alleged offence. Defendants are usually convicted of lesser crimes where recklessness or negligence is sufficient to satisfy the psychological element.[1] Although a defendant is acquitted on evidence of intoxication, there is usually an alternate offense that the prosecution can secure a conviction for because it is a crime of basic intent that cannot be overturned by evidence of intoxication. A drunk killer may be found not guilty of murder because he did not intend to kill; but he will be found guilty of manslaughter. The law of manslaughter is so broad that it applies even when a person kills another person while in a minimally conscious state. The defendant killed his lover under the influence of hallucinogenic drugs (LSD) (hallucinating that he was fighting snakes in the center of the Earth). Because he had committed an illegal act, he was found guilty of constructive manslaughter and sentenced to six years in prison. It was an attack, because his confused state of consciousness was the result of voluntary poisoning.[2] The perpetrator may be found not guilty of intentional injury, but may be found guilty of lesser crimes such as assault, unlawful injury, etc., because they are considered crimes of basic intent (intent to carry out the act associated with the crime without any additional motives, intentions, or purposes). All in all, he may be found not guilty of criminal damage with intent to endanger life, but for certain lesser charges. Evidence of intoxication usually does not help him.

醉态的证据可能使陪审团确信被告人缺乏犯罪通常所需的意图或其他主观因素。普通法上的罪行不能仅凭行为的证明就认为罪行成立。在这类罪行中,必须至少证实被告人具有被指控的罪行所涉及的身体行为的实际意图。即使被告因醉态证据而被宣告无罪,也通常会有一种控方可以确保定罪的替代罪名,因为这是一种基本意图不能被醉态证据推翻的犯罪。被告人通常会被判一些较轻的罪行,其中鲁莽或疏忽足以满足这些罪行的心理因素要求。一个醉态的杀人者可能被判谋杀罪不成立,因为他并没有杀人的意图;但他将被判过失杀人罪。过失杀人罪的法律适用范围是如此宽泛,甚至当一个人在意识极不清醒的状态下杀死了另一个人时,该法律也适用。例如,一被告人在迷幻药的作用下杀死了他的情人(其产生了以为自己在地球中心与蛇搏斗的幻觉)。由于该被告人实施了非法行为,他被判犯有过失杀人罪,并被判处6年监禁。虽然该被告人的行为是一种人身攻击,但他的混乱意

[1] R. v. Connor (1980) 146 C. L. R. 64 at 79.

[2] R. v. Lipman [1970] 1 Q. B. 152. Commissioner of Police of the Metropolis v. Caldwell [1982] A. C. 341.

识状态是自愿醉态的结果。行为人可能被判故意伤害罪不成立,但可能被判处攻击、非法伤害等较轻的罪行,因为这些罪行被视为基本意图犯罪,即被告人意图实施与犯罪有关的行为,基本意图犯罪是不需要被告人有任何额外的动机、意图或目的的犯罪。总而言之,醉态的被告人可能被判意图危害生命的损害罪不成立,但对于某些较轻的指控,醉态的证据通常对他没有帮助。这些较轻的罪行只需具有基本的意图即可。

In criminal policy, we cannot fully allow this kind of defense. However, convicting him, especially for a crime as serious as murder, may seem harsh. A person who commits a crime while drunk may have previously lived a blameless life. Drinking (or taking drugs) may have had an unexpected effect on him, and the behavior may not reflect his true character. On the other hand, the fact that many offenders had consumed alcohol before committing the criminal act cannot be a general defence. As a result of being drunk, a person actively impairs his self - control and the judgment. If his harmful behavior is likely to happen again, he must be brought under social control. The common law conclusion is that the act of drunkenness is itself a responsible act. As a result of the consumption of alcohol, the defendant acted "recklessly" about the negative effect that alcohol might have on him. Moral responsibility at least comes down to his decision to drink despite being aware of the effects of alcohol. Obviously, it would not be good for the safety of all of us if a judge declared that anyone could be absolved of criminal liability by getting drunk. Intoxication isn't acknowledged as a genral defense of excuse, this rule serves as a particular deterrent, ensuring that those who prove unable to control their violent impulses while voluntarily drunk go to jail.[1]

然而,在刑事政策上不能完全允许这种醉态辩护而给被告人定罪,尤其是像谋杀这样严重的罪行,这听起来可能很残酷。一个醉态犯罪的人,以前可能过着清白的生活,但饮酒(或吸毒)却对他产生了意想不到的影响,虽然这种行为可能并不能反映他的真实性格。另外,许多罪犯在实施犯罪行为之前已经饮酒,这说明醉态不能作为一般性的辩护理由。一个人通过喝醉主动地削弱自己的自控力和判断力。如果他的有害行为有可能再次发生,就必须将他置于社会控制之下。普通法的结论是,醉态行为本身就是一种有责的行为。由于饮酒,被告对酒精给自己带来的不利影响表现得"无所顾忌"。道德上的责任至少可以归结为他在意识到酒精影响的情况下还是决定喝酒。显然,如果法官宣布任何人都可以通过醉态来免除刑事责任,

---

〔1〕 Montana v. Egelhoff (1996) 518 U. S. 37 at 50.

这对所有人的安全都是不利的。醉态不被承认属于一般性的免责事由,这一规则起到了一种特殊的威慑作用,确保那些被证明在自愿醉态时无法控制暴力冲动的人进监狱。

The law was, and is, that evidence of intoxication is not a passport to acquittal. The fact that a person was drunk at the time of the crime is no excuse. Drinking may have loosened his inhibitions, made him more violent, and made him do terrible things that he would not have done sober; but none of these justifies his acquittal. Intentions under intoxication are still intentions. A child molester could not avoid conviction because the drugs had only served to lessen his self – control – he still intended to assault the boy.[1] A drunk person can decide to kill someone. If he lunged at the victim and stabbed him, the jury might conclude that he intended to kill. An affected person may be very capable of deciding to kill someone, but the evidence may show that he did not make such a decision. The simplest question for the jury is: Are you sure the defendant has the necessary state of mind? For this purpose, it is irrelevant to consider the fact of intoxication.[2] A special case is that if a person intentionally gets drunk to commit murder or other serious crimes for the sake of "drunken valor", he may be convicted, even if he is an "automatic machine" at the moment of the act.

无论是过去还是现在,法律都规定,醉态不是无罪释放的通行证。一个人在犯罪时喝醉了这一事实不能成为免责事由。喝酒可能放松了他的抑制,使他更加暴躁,使他做出在清醒时不会做的可怕的事情;但这些理由都不能使他获得无罪释放。醉态之下的意图仍然是意图。一个处于醉态之下的娈童者是无法避免被定罪的,因为其吸收的毒品只起到了减轻他的自控力的作用——但行为人仍然打算侵犯那个男孩。一个醉酒的人可以决定杀死某人。如果他冲向受害者并刺伤他,陪审团可能会得出他意图杀人的结论。一个受醉态影响的人可能也很有能力决定杀死某人,但证据却可能表明他没有做出这样的决定。对陪审团来说,最简单的问题是:你确定被告有构成犯罪所必要的主观状态吗?为了这个目的,考虑醉酒的事实是无关紧要的。一个特例是,如果一个人为了"酒后之勇"而故意喝醉,去实施谋杀或其他严重的罪行,那么他可能会被定罪,即使他在行动的那一刻是一台"自动机器"。

6.5.2 Involuntary Intoxication(非自愿醉态)

Different from intoxication mentioned above, involuntary intoxication may be the

---

〔1〕 R. v. Kingston [1995] 2 A. C. 355.

〔2〕 R. v. Sheehan [1975] 1 W. L. R. 739; R. v. Pordage [1975] Crim. L. R. 575; R. v. Hayes [2002] EWCA Crim. 1945.

result of the defendant's own actions, but is not considered self - induced - that is, the defendant was unaware that he was takinga substance having an anesthetic effect. Intoxication may occur involuntarily due to fraud (excessive drinking), accident (drug overdose), reasonable error (misinterpreting a doctor's order), duress, etc. In a crime of specific intent, the only problem is *mens rea*. In the crime of basic intent, involuntary intoxication's denial of criminal intent can be used as a defense.[1] Involuntary intoxication does not necessarily negate *mens rea*, it has a degree of requirement, that is, the degree of involuntary intoxication must in fact negate the defendant's criminal intent. In R. v. Kingston, a child molester with a penchant for young boys was drugged, after which he lost control and assaulted a boy. His coffee was laced with a powerful drug. Despite his love for young boys, he can usually keep his criminal urges in check. Although his intoxication was involuntary, he could not escape justice because it only weakened his self - control. He knew what he was doing and was found guilty because drunken intent is still an intent.[2]

与前已述及的醉态不同,非自愿醉态虽然可能客观上是被告自己行为的结果,但不被认为是自我招致的——也就是说,被告不知道他正在服用具有麻醉效果的物质。非自愿醉态可能是由于欺诈(饮酒过量)、意外(药物过量)、合理的错误(误解医生的指示)、胁迫等而非自愿情形发生。在具体意图犯罪中,唯一的问题是证明犯罪意图。在基本意图犯罪中,非自愿醉态能够否定犯罪意图,由此可以作为辩护事由。非自愿醉态并不是一定就能否定犯罪意图,其有程度上的要求,即非自愿醉态的程度必须事实上否定被告的犯罪意图。在女王诉金士顿案中,一个对小男孩有癖好的娈童者被下了药,此后他失去了控制,侵犯了一个男孩。他的咖啡里掺了强效药物。尽管他喜欢小男孩,但他通常能控制自己的犯罪欲望。他的醉态是不自愿的,但他无法逃避正义的审判,因为醉态只是削弱了他的自制力。他知道自己在做什么,醉态下的犯罪意图仍然存在,因此他被判有罪。

6.6　The Defense of Entrapment(警察圈套宽恕事由)

In some jurisdictions of America, entrapment is an active defense. The defendant must present evidence to support the defense, and it must be based on a majority of the evidence. In other jurisdictions, the defendant has the burden of evidence, but the prosecution must prove that the defendant was predisposed to commit a crime. If

[1] D. P. P. v. Majewski [1977] A. C. 443.

[2] R. v. Kingston [1995] 2 A. C. 355.

successful, the entrapment charge would bar prosecution.[1]

在美国的某些司法管辖区,警察圈套是一种积极的辩护。被告必须出示支持辩护的证据,而且必须以多数证据为依据。在其他司法管辖区例如英国,被告有提供证据的责任,但控方必须证明被告有犯罪倾向。警察圈套的相关指控如果成功,将禁止起诉相关罪行。

The emergence of entrapment stems from the need to fight crime. In criminal policy, since participants often have no incentive to notify the police when they commit these crimes, effective law enforcement often requires the involvement of undercover officers in these crimes in order to detect and arrest those who commit them. Not all crimes are reported to the police, especially so - called victimless crimes. These crimes often involve consensual activities that do not appear to involve the "real" victims. Prostitution, the sale or purchase of drugs, and gambling are common examples of "victimless" crime. UK courts acknowledged that consensual crimes (such as in the areas of sex, drinking, drugs and gambling) cannot usually be detected without some testing of suspects. As a result, in actions against relevant criminal organizations, criminal organizations often have to be infiltrated by police spies who must demonstrate a passion for offense.[2]

警察圈套的出现源于打击犯罪的需要。在刑事政策上,由于犯罪的参与者通常缺乏在犯罪同时通知警察的动机,所以有效的执法往往需要卧底警察参与这些犯罪行为,以便成功发现和逮捕那些犯罪分子。并不是所有的犯罪都有人向警方报案,尤其是所谓的无受害者犯罪。这些犯罪通常涉及合意活动,而这些活动似乎不涉及"真正的"被害人。卖淫、贩卖或购买毒品以及赌博是"无被害人"犯罪的常见例子。英国法院承认,如果不对犯罪嫌疑人进行一些测试,通常无法发现当事人合意的犯罪(如性、饮酒、毒品和赌博领域)。因此,在针对相关犯罪组织的行动中,经常由警察线人渗透进去,并且警察线人必须表现出对这项犯罪事业的热情。

The establishment of police entrapment as an excuse, and the impact on criminal liability after it, is more complex, and in different countries and different jurisdictions, the situation is different. At the same time, police entrapments occur in different situations. Police entrapments can be divided into subjective and objective standard. The legal consequences of the resulting police entrapment defense are different, which will be analyzed below.

---

[1] R. v. Sang [1980] A. C. 402; R. v. Jones [2010] 2 Cr. App. R. 69.

[2] R. v. Jones [2008] Q. B. 460. Cf. State v. Nero, 1 A. 3d 184 (2010).

警察圈套作为宽恕事由到底是否能成立,以及成立后对刑事责任的影响,是比较复杂的,且在不同的国家和不同的司法管辖区,情况也不尽相同。同时,警察圈套出现的情况也不同。针对警察圈套成立的标准可分为主观的标准和客观的标准,由此而产生的警察圈套抗辩,其法律后果是不同的,下面将对此进行分析。

6.6.1 The Subjective Test of Entrapment(警察圈套主观论)

The subjective test of entrapment means law enforcement pressures the defendant to commit the crime against his or her will. The federal government and most states recognize this kind of entrapment defense,[1] in which the perpetrator argues that he or she was not with "prior intent", but was actively instigated by the police or an undercover agent acting on their behalf.[2] If the facts show that the defendant was predisposed to commit a crime without the pressure of law enforcement, the defendant will not win the defense. The two - step approach, used by federal courts and most state courts, focuses both on the nature of police conduct and on the defendant's propensity to commit crime. (1) The government act induced the crime. As the Court pointed out, there is a fine line between merely offering criminals the opportunity to commit a crime and actually inducing innocents to do so.[3] As far as causation is concerned, criminal law usually considers only the final causal factor. The entrapment defense, however, effectively allows the defendant to argue that the government "caused" him to commit the crime. (2) The defendant is not predisposed to commit a crime. This factor shifts the analysis from what the government did to the character and criminal history of the accused. That allowed the government to argue that it was simply providing an opportunity for "careless criminals" to take the bait and commit crimes. The prosecutionmust prove that the defendant was predisposed to commit a crime and that his predisposition was not the product of government action. This was not proved in Jacobson v. United States: Jacobson had subscribed to a magazine which published child pornography. After the passage of a federal law criminalizing child pornography, the defendants stopped subscribing to the magazine. In order to explore his willingness to break the law, government agents kept mailing him materials, including one from a fake lobbying group that advocated for the law's repeal and criticized government censorship.

---

[1] Connecticut Jury Instruction on Entrapment, 2010.

[2] Soriano v. State, 248 P. 3d 381 (2011); U. S. v. Theagene, 565 F. 3d 911 (2009); Jacobson v. U. S., 503 U. S. 540 (1992).

[3] Sorrells v. United States, 287 U. S. 435.

Agents then sent him information about ordering magazines whose titles suggested they contained pornographic images of young boys. Twenty – six months after receiving these emails, Jacobson ordered two magazines containing pornographic material. After the controlled delivery to Jacobsonthe defendant, he was arrested, charged and convicted of possession of child pornography.[1] The Supreme Court held that the prosecution failed to establish beyond reasonable doubt that Jacobson was predisposed, prior to the Government acts intended to create predisposition, to commit the crime of receiving child pornography through the mails already. The evidence that Jacobson was ready and willing to commit the offense came only after the Government had devoted two and a half years to convincing him that he had or should have the right to engage in the very behavior proscribed by law. Accordingly, the Court of Appeals' judgment affirming the conviction of Jacobson was reversed.

警察圈套主观论是指执法人员迫使被告违背其意愿实施犯罪的情况。美国联邦政府和大多数州承认此种警察圈套抗辩,在这种情况下,行为人辩称并非“事先有意”,而是由警察或代表他们的卧底特工主动唆使的。如果事实表明被告在没有执法压力的情况下就有犯罪倾向,被告将无法在辩护中获胜。美国联邦法院和大多数州法院使用的两步走的判断方法,既关注警察行为的性质,也关注被告的犯罪倾向。警察圈套事由得以成立的主观论具有两个要素:(1)政府行为诱发了犯罪。正如法院所指出的,在仅仅为罪犯提供犯罪机会和实际上诱使无辜者犯罪之间,存在一条微妙的界线。就因果关系而言,刑法通常只考虑最后的因果因素。然而,警察圈套的辩护有效地允许被告辩称政府“导致”他犯罪。(2)被告原本没有犯罪的倾向。这一因素是指从警察的所作所为转移到被告的性格和犯罪历史上。这允许政府辩称,警察只是为“不小心的罪犯”提供了一个上钩并犯罪的机会。控方必须证明被告有犯罪的倾向,而且他的倾向不是警察行为的产物。而这个犯罪倾向不是警察行为的产物的要求,并没有在雅各布斯诉美国案中得到满足:雅各布斯曾订阅一份刊登儿童色情照片的杂志。在一项将儿童色情定为犯罪的联邦法律通过后,被告停止订购该杂志。为了考察雅各布斯是否有违反法律的意愿,政府特工不断给他邮寄材料,包括来自一个虚假游说组织的宣传材料,这个游说组织主张废除这项法律,并批评政府的审查制度。然后特工们向他发送了订购杂志的信息,这些杂志的标题表明它们含有年轻男孩的色情图片。在收到这些邮件 26 个月后,雅各布斯订购了两本载有色情内容的杂志。在警察控制下,杂志被交付给雅各布斯后,他被逮捕、指控并

[1] Jacobson v. United States, 503 U. S. 540 (1992).

被判持有儿童色情物品罪。最高法院认为,控方无法就雅各布斯在政府制造犯罪倾向的行为之前,已经倾向于犯下通过邮件接收儿童色情制品的罪行这一点,排除合理怀疑。在政府花了两年半的时间,说服他有权或应该从事法律禁止的行为后,才出现了雅各布斯准备并愿意犯罪的证据。因此,上诉法院对雅各布斯的定罪判决被推翻。

In liability theory, the entrapment defense might serve as a denial of true criminal intent, claiming that the defendant did not really choose to commit the crime. This theoretical understanding will affect the criminal's liability in the following situations: (1) Entrapment can be a mitigating issue if the perpetrator is not the prime mover of the scheme, and if he is not tempted, he may avoid committing any crime. Judges sometimes strongly object to the police using agents provocateurs,[1] in the sense that people should not cause crime. The role of the police is to detect and solve crime, not to create it or induce law - abiding citizens to commit it. According to this opinion, the Prosecutor General or the Public Prosecution Service may quash crimes that appear to have been instigated by agents provocateurs. One principle that has been clearly established is that if the way in which the informant was employed affected the "quality of the offence", that fact must be disclosed at trial.[2] (2) Entrapment does not even mitigate penalties if undercover agents simply pretend they are in the market for something like drugs or obscene publications without using special persuasion to overcome reluctance.[3]

在责任理论上,警察圈套主观论能帮助辩方否认存在真实的犯罪意图,即被告人个人并非真的选择犯罪。这个认识在以下情形中会影响犯罪人的责任:(1)如果犯罪者不是某个犯罪计划的主要推动者,即如果犯罪者没有受到警察的诱惑,他可能会避免犯下任何罪行,那么警察圈套可以作为一个减轻罪行的理由。法官有时强烈反对警察使用密探,因为在某种意义上说,人们不应该引发犯罪。警察的作用是侦查和侦破犯罪,而不是制造犯罪或诱使守法公民犯罪。根据这种观点,检察长或公诉机关可能撤销似乎是由密探唆使的罪行的指控。英国法院已经明文规定的一项原则是,如果警察线人的卧底方式影响了犯罪人所犯罪行的特性,控方必须在审判时披露这一事实。(2)如果卧底特工只是假装他们在市场上购买毒品或淫秽出版

〔1〕 Nottingham City Council v. Amin [2000] 1 W. L. R. 1071.

〔2〕 R. v. Birtles [1969] 1 W. L. R. 1047.

〔3〕 R. v. Thornton [2003] EWCA Crim. 919 at paras. 23 - 26; R. v. Mayeri [1999] 1 Cr. App. R. (S.) 304.

物之类的东西,而不使用特别的劝说来说服犯罪人犯罪的不情愿,那么警察圈套甚至不能减轻犯罪人的处罚。

6.6.2 The Objective Test of Entrapment(警察圈套客观论)

Objectivism focuses on law enforcement actions – tactics used by law enforcement that would induce a reasonable, law – abiding person, rather than the individual defendant, to commit a crime actively, then police entrapment is established. MPC §2.13 provides, if a government agent, in order to gather evidence that a crime has occurred, "induces or encourages another person to participate in (the crime), either by (a) knowingly making a false statement in order to induce the belief that such conduct is not prohibited; or (b) using persuasion or inducement that creates a substantial risk that the offence will be committed by someone other than the person preparing the offence." The defence of entrapment stands. Since the defendant's inclination is irrelevant, this approach can be summarized as the objective test of entrapment. This approach, adopted by the MPC and a few states, mostly looks at what the government does and assesses how it affects normal law – abiding people. Despite initial rejection, repeated solicitations over time, solicitations for sympathy, promises of excessive benefits, or other persuasion tactics that may tempt law – abiding people to commit crimes will support this proposition. It is less concerned with the criminal attitude or history of a particular offender and more about controlling the behaviour of the police. This formulation can be seen as an attempt to monitor how the police work. By providing a disincentive to police misconduct, this substantive criminal law defense serves the same general purpose as the rules of criminal procedure, as does the Miranda exclusion.

客观论关注的是执法行为,即如果执法部门使用的策略会诱使一个理性的、守法的人,而不是被告个人主动犯罪,那么警察圈套成立。《模范刑法典》第2.13条规定,如果一名政府特工为了收集犯罪发生的证据,"诱导或鼓励另一个人参与(犯罪),要么通过(a)故意作出虚假陈述,以诱导其相信这种行为是不被禁止的;或(b)采用劝说或诱骗方法,造成这种犯罪将由准备犯罪的人以外的人实施的重大风险",那么警察圈套辩护是成立的。由于被告的倾向与本案无关,这一方法可以被概括为警察圈套的客观论。《模范刑法典》和少数州采用的这种方法主要着眼于政府所做的事情,并评估它对正常守法的人会产生什么影响。警察卧底在最初被守法者拒绝后,在接下来的时间里仍旧使用反复怂恿、博取同情、承诺过多利益,以及其他可能诱使守法的人犯罪的劝说策略,都会支持警察圈套成立的这一主张。它不太关心特定罪犯的犯罪态度或背景,更多关注的是控制警察的行为。这种构想可以被看作是监督警察如何工作的一种尝试。通过对警察不当行为进行抑制,这种实质性的刑法辩护与刑事诉讼规则具有相同的一般目的,就像米兰达排除规则一样。

Entrapment defense can be regarded as a kind of criminal procedure rules regulating police investigation behavior. Courts will exclude evidence obtained by entrapment only in exceptional circumstances. The court can exclude evidence if in view of access to evidence, admission of evidence can adversely affect the fairness of the process.[1] Courts must balance the requirement that criminals should be caught and punished with the requirement that there should be no abuse of process. Entrapment is a defense that attempts to balance proper police undercover investigation and detection of crime with inappropriate police abetting of crime. The defense focused on what the police did and the defendant's propensity to commit a crime. If the abuse of process is serious, it brings the criminal justice system into disrepute.[2] The court will weigh a number of considerations to decide whether the police have gone overboard, including the nature of the offence (the police should prove that there was no other reasonable way to stop the alleged offence),[3] whether the police were acting in good faith (did they have probable cause against the accused? Or are they simply acting out of revenge?). It then draws conclusions about whether the police's actions would have induced a reasonable, law - abiding person to commit a crime.

客观的警察圈套宽恕事由可以被看作一种规范警察调查行为的刑事诉讼规则。法院只会在例外情况下排除通过警察圈套获得的证据。如果考虑到警察获取证据的情况,承认证据会对程序的公正性产生不利影响,法院可以排除相关证据。法院必须在罪犯应被抓获、被惩罚的要求与不应滥用诉讼程序的要求之间实现平衡。警察圈套是一种试图在适当的警察卧底调查和侦查犯罪与不适当的警察唆使犯罪之间取得平衡的辩护事由。该事由将重点放在警察的所作所为和被告的犯罪倾向上。如果滥用程序情节严重,则会使刑事司法系统名誉扫地。法庭会权衡多项考虑因素,以裁决警方是否过界,包括罪行的性质(警方应证明没有其他合理的方法来阻止被指控的罪行),警方是否出于善意(他们有合理的理由针对被告吗?或者他们的行为仅仅是为了报复?)。然后得出警方的行为是否会诱使一个通情达理、遵纪守法的人犯罪的结论。

The most important consideration, however, is the nature of police involvement in

---

〔1〕 Section 78(1) of the Police and Criminal Evidence Act 1984.

〔2〕 R. v. Latif [1996] 1 W. L. R. 104 at 112.

〔3〕 Re Attorney - General's Reference (No. 3 of 2000) [2001] 1 W. L. R. 2060 at 2079.

the crime (to what extent did the police encourage the accused to commit the crime?).[1] A useful guide on this point is to consider whether the police are simply offering the accused an ordinary opportunity to commit a crime. Generally, the test is whether the police's actions prior to the crime did not exceed what others might have expected in the circumstances.[2] Once the state goes beyond ordinary behavior, it is likely to increase the incidence of crime by artificial means.[3] The greater the temptation offered by the police, and the stronger or more persistent the offer, the easier it will be for the court to conclude that the police have overstepped the mark: that their behaviour is likely to cause a person who would normally avoid such a crime to commit it. In assessing the weight of police inducements, the defendant's circumstances, including his vulnerability, should be taken into account. This acknowledges that what may be an important temptation for one person may not be for another.

然而,最重要的考虑是警察参与犯罪的性质,即警察在多大程度上鼓励被告犯罪。关于这一点,一个有用的判断方法是考虑警方是否只是给被告提供了一个实施犯罪的普通机会,警察在犯罪人实施犯罪之前的诱导行为是否不超过在当时情况下其他人可能期望的行为。一旦国家警察的所作所为超越普通行为,警察就很可能以人为手段增加犯罪的发生率。警察提出的诱惑越大,提出的提议越强烈或越持久,法院就越容易得出警察越界的结论:警察的行为很可能导致一个通常会避免实施犯罪的人犯罪。在评估警方诱因的权重时,还应考虑到被告的情况,包括他的脆弱性。对一个人来说可能是重要的诱惑,对另一个人来说可能不重要。

Whether legally or illegally, if the police acted like an ordinary customer, it would generally not be considered objectionable to the defendant.[4] A police officer cannot be said to have caused the offence if he acted in the same way as the general public and merely provided the opportunity for the accused to commit the offence.[5] For example, Mr Amin owns a taxi, which is not licensed in Nottingham. Two plainclothes police officers saw him driving down a Nottingham street in the middle of the night and flagged him down. He stopped and agreed, upon request, to take them to their appointed destination. When they arrived, the police paid the fare and then charged him with

[1] Re Attorney – General's Reference (No. 3 of 2000) [2001] 1 W. L. R. 2060 at 2075.
[2] Re Attorney – General's Reference (No. 3 of 2000) [2001] 1 W. L. R. 2060 at 2069.
[3] McHugh J. in Ridgeway v. The Queen (1995) 184 C. L. R. 19 at 92.
[4] Re Attorney – General's Reference (No. 3 of 2000) [2001] 1 W. L. R. 2060 at 2070.
[5] Re Attorney – General's Reference (No. 3 of 2000) [2001] 1 W. L. R. 2060 at 2075.

hiring without a license. The policeman hailed the taxi like an ordinary citizen. They didn't wave £ 50 notes or pretend to be in pain.[1] If the police offer a suspected drug dealer a huge financial reward to start growing marijuana, they have crossed the line.

警方如果表现得像一个普通顾客,无论警方的行为本身是合法的还是非法的,法院一般不会认为被告可以提出警察圈套的异议。如果一名警察的行为与一般社会公众的行为相同,只是提供机会让被告犯下罪行,则不能说他导致被告犯下有关罪行。比如阿明有一辆在诺丁汉没有出租执照的出租车。两个便衣警察看到他半夜在诺丁汉的一条街上开车,示意他停下来。阿明停了下来,在警察要求下同意带警察去警察指定的目的地。当警察到达时,警察付了车费,然后控告他无照出租。警察像普通市民一样招呼出租汽车,没有挥舞 50 英镑的钞票,也没有假装很痛苦。然而,如果警方向一名涉嫌贩毒的人提供巨额经济奖励,以鼓励他开始种植大麻,警察就越界了。

6.7　The Syndromes Defense(综合征宽恕事由)

The syndromes defense is one of the "new groundsof excuses". The law can treat claims of "new grounds of excuses" in at least three ways: (1) it can exclude them altogether; (2) It may permit them as mitigation of guilt, but not as a complete exoneration; (3) They can be allowed to play a role in sentencing. The applicable path is different at different historical moments for different grounds of clemency, but it is not uncommon to start with the last approach and then "work your way up" to a full defense, that is, a defense of excuse.

综合征宽恕事由属于新宽恕事由的一种。对于综合征,有三种立场:(1)完全排除其作为宽恕事由;(2)作为减轻罪责事由,但不能完全免责;(3)作为量刑要素。对于不同的宽恕理由,在不同的历史时期,适用的路径是不同的,但在司法实践中,从最后一种作为量刑要素的路径开始,向上发展到全面辩护,成为宽恕事由,这并不罕见。

6.7.1　Women's syndrome(妇女综合征)

"Women's syndrome" is a more important syndrome. Prior to the 1970s, battered women who claimed self - defense described themselves as "temporarily insane" or "passionate", because the law did not recognize "battered spouse syndrome" as a scientific theory. Today, by contrast, every state in the United States allows evidence of

[1] Re Attorney - General's Reference (No. 3 of 2000) [2001] 1 W. L. R. 2060 at 2076.

battered spouse syndrome in such cases. Many who agree with battered spouse laws, however, caution against jumping rashly into new excuses, pointing to arguments about the progressive researches on XYY chromosome and premenstrual syndrome as proof of the effectiveness of the law's cautious pace.[1]

受虐妇女综合征是较为重要的综合征。在20世纪70年代之前,认为自己构成自卫的受虐妇女把她们自己描述为"暂时精神错乱"或"情绪激动",因为当时的法律还不承认受虐配偶综合征是一种科学理论。如今,相比之下,美国每个州都允许在反击配偶的案件中提供构成受虐妇女综合征的证据。然而,许多同意受虐配偶综合征相关法律宽待的人都警告说不要轻率地接受新的免责事由,他们指出有关XYY染色体和妇女经前期综合征的研究尚在进展之中的论据,证明了法律谨慎步伐的有效性。

"Battered women's syndrome" is a cycle of "learned helplessness". The "learned helplessness" factor argues that after a cycle of beatings, reconciliation and growing tension, wives come to believe there is no escape. "Cinderella complex" is said to make wives believe that they, not their husbands, are to blame for domestic abuse; If they were better wives, husbands would not beat them. As a result, a mixture of fear and guilt convinces these women to submit to intolerable abuse. Forty years ago, evidence of battered wife syndrome was rejected in almost all courts. Battered woman syndrome was first cited in 1980 in a New York case.[2] Today, all courts admit evidence of the syndrome objectively exist, and some state statutes now specify that such evidence is admissible, although there may be disagreements as to the exact point at which evidence is allowed.[3]

受虐妇女综合征,是一种"习得性无助"的循环。"习得性无助"因素主张,经过一段时间的循环(包括殴打、和解和关系日益紧张的循环),妻子们开始相信没有逃避的办法。据说,"灰姑娘情结"让妻子们相信,是她们自己,而不是丈夫,应该为家暴负责;如果她们是更好的妻子,丈夫就不会打她们。因此,恐惧和内疚的混合说服了这些妇女屈服于无法忍受的虐待。40年前,几乎所有法庭都不接受受虐妇女综合征的证据。1980年,在纽约的一起案件中,受虐妇女综合征第一次被引用。今天,所有的法院都承认该综合征的证据是客观存在的,一些州的法规现在明确规定,这些

---

[1] State v. Maraschiello (2000) 88 S. W. 3d 586.

[2] People v. Powell(1980) 102 Misc. 2d 775.

[3] Cal. Evid. Code §1107 (Deering 2008). See generally, Annot., 57 A. L. R. 5th 315; Annot., 58 A. L. R. 5th 749.

证据是可接受的,尽管在允许采纳该证据的确切视角上可能存在分歧。

Abused wives believe there is no realistic alternative to murder. They often point out that poor protection by the police and other government agencies is part of history. If beatings and "syndromes" are part of the rational person's background, then the necessity test isa rational battered woman who, suffering from learned helplessness, thinks it necessary. If the offence is committed multiple times over a considerable period of time, it will be difficult for the defendant to prove that she did not have a reasonable chance of escaping the harm threatened to cause.[1] The death of a batterer is a social good and should in any case be seen as justified or justified as a battered woman's choice. This is to treat it as a legitimate cause. In a non – adversarial setting, the abused spouse does not have an adequate claim of self – defense and may agree that her killing constituted "imperfect" self – defense, thereby reducing her culpable homicide liability. The elements of self – defense contain subjective and objective factors that focus, respectively, on the sincerity and reasonableness of the defendant's beliefs. Whether as an objective factor of the self – defense or imperfect self – defense, the defendant must actually believe in the need to defend oneself against imminent peril to life or great bodily injury. If the belief subjectively exists but is objectively unreasonable, there is imperfect self – defense; however, if the belief is objectively reasonable, perfect self – defense can be constituted and the defendant will be exonerated completely. Based on the evidence of battered woman syndrome, in the case above imperfect self – defense is accepted.[2]

被虐待的妻子们认为,除了谋杀,她们没有其他办法可以避免丈夫的继续加害。她们经常指出,警方和其他政府机构对她们的保护不力。如果遭受殴打和患上综合征是一个理性人的经历,那么认定构成综合征的必要性标准就是遭受习得性无助的理性受虐妇女认为谋杀是必要的。如果犯罪行为在相当长的一段时间内多次发生,被告将很难证明她没有其他合理的机会逃脱其配偶威胁要造成的伤害。施暴者的死亡是对社会有益的结果,在任何情况下都应被视为正当的或作为被虐妇女的选择而被正当化。这是将综合征视为一种正当事由。在非对抗性的环境中,被虐待的配偶虽不能主张其行为构成充分的自卫,但美国法院可能会同意她的杀人构成"不完美的"自卫,从而将其刑事责任从故意杀人减为过失杀人。自卫的要素包含主观和客观因素,分别关注被告信念的真诚和合理性。无论是作为完美自卫还是不完美自

〔1〕 R. v. Emery (1993) 14 Cr. App. R. (S.) 394 at 398.

〔2〕 People v. Jaspar (2000) 98 Cal. App. 4th 99.

卫的主观要素,被告都必须真正相信需要保护自己免受迫在眉睫的生命危险或重大身体伤害。如果这种信念主观上存在,但客观上不合理,则存在不完美的自卫;如果这种信念客观合理,那么成立完美自卫,被告可以免除罪责。基于受虐妇女综合征的证据,上述情况成立不完美的自卫是可以接受的。

Killings caused by loss of control due to fear (rather than anger) will establish a partial defence, reducing the killing to manslaughter. In rare cases, fear may cause a person to lose control. For example, a woman with battered woman syndrome may lose control because she is afraid to face further beatings.[1] The court held that the characteristics of battered woman syndrome could be taken into account in determining whether the defendant had reasonable grounds for giving in to threats. The evidence that the defendant suffered from battered woman syndrome as a result of the previous abuse was relevant to the jury's judgment as to whether she was under duress due to fear of serious harm to herself or her daughter, which was honest and reasonable in her circumstances. Such conditions may include a history of assault and battered woman syndrome.[2]

恐惧(而不是愤怒)引起的失控杀人将成立部分正当事由,将故意杀人罪责减轻为过失杀人。在极少数情况下,恐惧可能会导致一个人失去自我控制。例如,一个患有受虐妇女综合征的妇女可能会失去自我控制,因为她害怕面对进一步的殴打。美国法院认为,在确定被告是否有合理理由屈服于威胁时,可以考虑受虐妇女综合征的特征。如果有证据表明被告因之前的虐待而患有受虐妇女综合征,那么这将关涉陪审团对被告进行的判断,即在她的情况下她是否诚实、合理地因害怕自己或女儿遭受严重伤害而受到胁迫。这里所说的"她的情况"可能包括被殴打史和受虐妇女综合征。

6.7.2 Premenstrual Syndrome (经前期综合征)

Premenstrual syndrome is another type of physical condition that is said to affect behavior. While many women experience cramps, nausea, and other (often severe) discomfort prior to menstruation, the term PMS has always been limited to a small percentage (about 2% – 3%) of people who suffer from such distress and pain or mood swings that sometimes become severely violent. The woman who made the claim was forced to include it in the existing category of defence recognised by common law. For

---

[1] Elizabeth Sheehy et al., *Defences to Homicide Battered Women: A Comparative Analysis of Laws in Australia, Canada and New Zealand*, 34 Sydney L. Rev. 467 (2012).

[2] State v. B. H. (2003) 834 A. 2d 1063.

example, insanity, provocation and diminished responsibility. However, PMS is not considered a mental illness, and because it is not permanent, changes in insanity are often unmeasurable. So PMS cannot be linked to insanity as an excuse. Provocation defense is impossible because the victim may not have done anything provocative at all. Furthermore, a woman may lose control during her period, but such a condition affecting her general capacity for tolerance or self - restraint cannot be considered, since the accused's characteristic irritability, sensitivity or excitable nature does not affect questions concerning normal (female) persons' general capacity for self - control.

经前期综合征是另一种据称会影响行为的生理状况。虽然许多女性在月经前会经历痉挛、恶心和其他(通常是严重的)不适,但经前期综合征这个术语总是局限于一小部分(2%—3%)遭受这种痛苦(疼痛或者情绪波动,有时会变得严重暴力)的女性。主张经前期综合征的妇女被迫将经前期综合征纳入普通法承认的现有辩护事由的某个类别。例如,精神错乱、他人挑衅和责任减轻的事由。然而,经前期综合征不被认为是一种精神疾病,因为它不是一直存在的,由它引起的精神错乱的变化通常是不可测量的,所以经前期综合征难以适用精神病这种事由。她们的配偶构成挑衅也是不可能的,因为她们的配偶作为受害者可能根本没有做任何挑衅的事情。而且,虽然女性在经期可能会失去控制,但这种影响到她的一般容忍或自我克制能力的情况不能被纳入考虑,因为被告人特有的易怒、敏感或易激动性并不影响有关正常(女)人一般自我控制能力的判断。

However, if an acknowledged health condition affects defendant's general capacity for self - restraint, then the proper defence is a partial defence of diminished responsibility. In 1994, the American Psychiatric Association (APA) added premenstrual anxiety disorder (PMDD) - a severe premenstrual syndrome - to its list of depression in its Diagnostic and Statistical Manual (DSM - IV). This could mean that (1) other women will be excluded from PMS; (2) Women who claim anxiety disorder will be considered mentally ill and may be pardoned after a successful defense.[1] The defendant was able to invoke the diminished responsibility part of the defence because she suffered from premenstrual syndrome and postpartum depression.[2]

如果一种公认的健康状况影响了被告人的自我约束的一般能力,那么适当的辩

---

〔1〕 Connie Huang, *It's a Hormonal Thing: Premenstrual Syndrome and Postpartum Psychosis as Criminal Defenses*, 11 S. Cal. Rev. L. & Women's Stud. 345 (2002).

〔2〕 R. v. Reynolds [1988] Crim. L. R. 679.

护方向是责任部分减少了。1994年,美国精神病学协会(APA)在其《诊断与统计手册》(DSM－IV)中将经前焦虑症(PMDD)——一种严重的经前期综合征,列入抑郁症名单。这可能意味着(1)其他女性将被排除在经前期综合征之外;(2)主张经前焦虑症的女性将被视为患有精神疾病,在辩护成功后可能得到宽恕。被告人能够援引责任部分减轻的辩护,因为她患有经前期综合征和产后抑郁症。

■ **Curriculum Ideology and Politics: Analyze the theory of "syndrome" defense cause, improve the comprehensive comparative ability of analyzing the status of women in the family and learn to pay attention to the protection of women groups in the judiciary(课程思政:剖析妇女综合征宽恕事由理论,提升综合比较分析妇女在家庭中的境遇的能力,学会在司法中重视妇女群体的保护)**

By studying the specific connotation of battered woman syndrome, the students can critically analyze the differences between Anglo－American criminal law in dealing with similar problems. Anglo－American criminal law takes the psychological concept of battered woman syndrome as the defense reason of battered woman's killing husband, and combines the defense of justifiable defense, so as to broaden the legal defense space scope of such cases. But whether the psychological concept of battered women's syndrome can become a typed cause of defense in criminal law remains to be discussed, and further analysis and demonstration are needed.

通过学习受虐妇女综合征的具体内涵,学生能批判性分析英美刑法处理类似问题的差异。英美刑法将受虐妇女综合征这一心理学概念作为受虐妇女杀夫行为的宽恕事由,结合正当防卫的辩护事由,从而拓宽了此类案件的合法辩护范畴。但受虐妇女综合征这一心理学概念能否成为刑法上类型化的出罪事由仍有待商榷,需要进一步的分析论证。

6.8 Exercise(课后练习)(答案请扫描右侧二维码获取)

6.8.1 Test of Terminologies(术语考查)

①Mens rea ②Irresistible impulses
③Duress ④Entrapment
⑤Battered women's syndrome ⑥Premenstrual syndrome

6.8.2 True or False(判断题)

1. Surely insanity is an excuse.

毫无疑问,精神错乱是一种宽恕事由。

2. According to the right – wrong test of insanity, insane defendants can be sentenced to prison even if they don't understand what they are doing, as long as they realize they are committing a crime.

根据精神病判断的"对—错标准",精神错乱的被告即使不明白自己在做什么,只要他们意识到自己在犯罪,也可能被判入狱。

3. It is not valid for a person who unreasonably believes that he will be seriously injured to argue that he is under duress.

对于一个没有正当理由而认为自己会受重伤的人来说,辩称自己被胁迫是无效的。

6.8.3 Short – answer Questions(简答题)

1. In applying the excuse of insanity, what is the conclusion if the person completely loses their mind and doesn't know what they're doing?

在适用精神病事由时,如果一个人完全失去理智,不知道自己在做什么,其危害行为能否构成犯罪,为什么?

2. In applying the excuse of intoxication, would all of the drunkard charges go down?

在适用醉态事由时,对醉汉的所有指控都不会成立吗?

3. In dealing with an entrapment, according to the objective test, can the court suspend proceedings because of police entrapment abuses of process?

在处理警察圈套问题时,根据客观标准,法院是否可以因为警察圈套滥用程序而中止诉讼?

■ Curriculum Ideology and Politics: The Rule of Law Value of Defenses to Criminal Liability(课程思政:刑事责任宽恕事由的法治价值)

Through the study of the excuses of criminal liability, the learners of criminal law should establish the concept of fairness and justice. The excuses of criminal liability are for the protection of human rights and the maintenance of fairness and justice under the rule of law. Through the study of the excuses of criminal liability in Anglo – American criminal law, students should have a clearer understanding of the concepts and application of excuses of criminal liability. In the subsequent study and exploration and the practice of rule of law.

通过对刑事责任宽恕事由的学习,刑法学习者应树立公平正义的法治观念。刑事责任宽恕事由是对人权的保护,是对法治公平和正义的维护。学生通过对英美刑法的刑事责任宽恕事由的学习,对刑事责任宽恕事由等概念及适用将有更为清晰的认识,在之后的学习探索和法治工作实践中,能更好地落实人道主义和宽容精神。

■ Summary(总结)

1. Excuse defense is when a defendant admits to committing a criminal act, but argues that because there was no criminal intent, he or she cannot be held responsible. The excuses used in courts today are: mental illness excuse, diminished capacity excuse, age excuse, duress excuse, intoxication excuse, police entrapment excuse, and "syndrome" excuse.

宽恕事由是指被告承认实施了犯罪行为,但认为由于其不存在犯意,所以不能被追究责任的事由。目前在法庭上使用的宽恕辩护事由包括:精神病宽恕事由、责任能力降低宽恕事由、年龄宽恕事由、胁迫宽恕事由、醉态宽恕事由、警察圈套宽恕事由以及综合征宽恕事由。

2. The diminished responsibility defence requires that the defendant suffer from an abnormality of mental function resulting from a recognized health condition that significantly impairs the defendant's ability to understand the nature of his actions, form rational judgments, and exercise self - control. Abnormal mental function means that according to social standards, the defendant's mental function is abnormal.

责任能力降低宽恕事由要求被告患有由公认的健康状况引起的精神功能异常,这种精神功能异常严重损害了被告理解自己行为的性质、形成理性判断、运用自我控制的能力。精神功能异常是指按照社会的标准,被告的精神功能是不正常的。

3. Most children do not have the intelligence, judgment, emotional maturity and moral capacity to make the rational choices required by criminal law. Therefore, the law does not hold very young children criminally liable, even if their actions were intended to cause serious harm. The common law uses the actual age at the time of the crime to determine whether a child is criminally responsible.

大多数儿童不具备智力、判断力、情感成熟度和道德能力,无法做出刑法所要求的理性选择。因此,法律不要求非常年幼的儿童承担刑事责任,即使他们的行为意在造成严重伤害。普通法使用犯罪发生时的实际年龄来确定儿童是否应承担刑事责任。

4. The causes of intoxication can betaking alchohol, drug, and other substancs. Types of intoxication can be divided into voluntary intoxication and involuntary intoxication. In criminal policy, intoxication pleading is not entirely permissible.

醉态的缘由可以分为醉酒、中毒以及其他情况。醉态的类型可以分为自愿醉态和非自愿醉态。在刑事政策上,不完全允许醉态辩护。

5. The success of police entrapment as a cause of excuse, and the impact on criminal liability after success, is more complex, and in different countries and different jurisdictions, the situation is different. At the same time, police entrapments occur in different situations. The standards of establishing police entrapment have their own classification, which can be divided into subjective standard and objective standard.

警察圈套作为宽恕事由,到底是否能成立,以及成立后对刑事责任的影响,是比较复杂的,且不同的国家和不同的司法管辖区情况也不尽相同。同时,警察圈套出现的情况也不同。针对警察圈套成立的标准可分为主观的标准和客观的标准。

Chapter 7 Complicity and Vicarious Liability
第 7 章　共同犯罪和替代责任

■ The Learning Objective（学习目标）

1. To understand complicity and the elements of complicity.

理解共同犯罪和共同犯罪构成要件。

2. To understand vicarious liability, including corporate vicarious liability and individual vicarious liability.

理解替代责任,包括法人替代责任和个人替代责任。

3. To learn some terminologies in this chapter.

掌握本章中的专业术语。

■ Chapter Outline（本章内容概要）

This chapter covers two main topics: complicity, better known as accomplice liability, and vicarious liability.[1] This chapter focuses on the definition, types and importance of complicity and vicarious liability. Additionally, it uses some classic cases to elaborate on and explain these two topics.

本章涵盖两个主题:共同犯罪(共犯责任)和替代责任。本章重点介绍了共同犯罪和替代责任的定义、类型及构成要素,并借助一些经典案例予以阐述和说明。

■ The Purpose of Curriculum Ideology and Politics for this Chapter（本章的课程思政目标）

1. Enhancing students' international legal literacy and improving their knowledge

---

〔1〕 Jennifer L. Moore & John L. Worrall, *Criminal Law*, 2nd editon, Pearson Education Inc. ,2018, p. 97.

system of criminal law, this chapter primarily focuses on the professional knowledge of complicity and vicarious liability within Anglo – American criminal law, as well as the English expressions of relevant professional terms. By thoroughly and systematically studying the concepts of complicity and vicarious liability in Anglo – American criminal law, along with the English expressions of professional terms presented in this chapter, students can expand their understanding of criminal law and improve their proficiency in legal English. This approach fosters an international perspective and the ability to engage in international legal communication.

提升学生国际化素养,完善学生刑法知识体系。本章内容涉及英美刑法共同犯罪和替代责任的专业知识和刑法专业术语的英语表达。全面系统学习英美刑法共同犯罪和替代原则的基本内容及本章刑法专业术语的英语表达,既能拓展刑法知识体系,又能提升法律英语能力,培养国际视野及国际交往能力。

2. The establishment of complicity in Anglo – American criminal law requires meeting the basic elements: accomplice actus reus, accomplice mens rea, and the scope of accomplice liability, which is limited in certain aspects. By correlating the knowledge points of Anglo – American criminal law with their counterparts in Chinese criminal law and conducting a comparative analysis at more specific levels, we can cultivate students' critical thinking and analytical skills. Chinese criminal law also addresses complicity and the treatment of status offenders within the context of complicity. However, when examining specific countermeasures, there are significant differences between the approaches to complicity and the support of status offenders in Chinese criminal law and those in Anglo – American criminal law.

英美刑法的共同犯罪成立除了需要满足基本要素,共犯客观行为和共犯犯罪意图,还一定程度上受到其他限制。通过联系英美刑法知识点和中国对应的类似知识点并进行更具体层面差异的比较,能培养学生思辨和分析能力。中国刑法也有共同犯罪,也涉及身份犯的共同犯罪处置问题。但从具体对策层面看,中国刑法和英美刑法的共同犯罪对策,以及针对身份者的共同犯罪支持方法,还是有较大差异。

3. To explore the reasons underlying our understanding of criminal law and to cultivate the ability to think deeply and critically, we must delve into the philosophical foundations of legal principles, concepts of punishment, and precedents. When studying the knowledge points of criminal law, including those within Anglo – American jurisprudence, we should consider not only the laws themselves but also the underlying

rationales. For instance, vicarious liability may seem to contravene the principle of personal responsibility, yet it is a form of liability confined to specific relational contexts. We must consciously engage in deep thinking while studying criminal law in order to enhance our level of critical thought and cognitive abilities.

探寻刑法知识背后的缘由,培养深度思考和认知的能力,必须深入研究法律原则、惩罚理念和先例的哲学基础。学习包括英美刑法知识在内的刑法知识点,不仅要考虑法律本身,还要考虑其背后的理论基础。比如,替代性责任似乎是违背罪责自负原则,但替代责任是被限制在具有特殊关系情况下才施加的责任。学习刑法知识需要有意识地进行深度思考,才能提升思维层次和认知水平。

■ Terminologies (专业术语)

complicity	共同犯罪
principal	主犯
accomplice	共犯
accomplice liability	共犯责任
derivative liability	派生责任
accomplice actus reus	共犯客观行为
accomplice mens rea	共犯犯罪意图
nonproxyable offenses	不可代理的犯罪
abandonment	中止
vicarious liability	替代责任
corporate vicarious liability	法人替代责任
individual vicarious liability	个人替代责任

7.1 Complicity(共同犯罪)

Complicity is defined as a state of being an accomplice. An accomplice is one who knowingly, voluntarily and with common intent unites with the principal offender in the commission of a crime. Anyone, other than the primary offender, who participates before and during the commission of a crime is an accomplice. Complicity is a form of derivative liability, meaning that a second offender derives his or her liability from the primary individual with whom he or she associates.[1] Complicity consists of the actus reus and mens rea required for accomplice liability, and this liability is limited in certain aspects.

共同犯罪被定义为“作为共犯的一种状态”。共犯是指故意、自愿和有共同意图地与主犯联合实施犯罪的人。除主犯外,在犯罪前和犯罪过程中参与犯罪的人都是共犯。共犯是一种派生责任,这意味着共犯承担了与之有关联的主犯所衍生的刑事责任。共同犯罪是由共犯客观行为和共犯犯罪意图组成的,并且共犯责任在某些方面受到限制。

7.1.1 The Elements of Complicity(共犯要件的构成要素)

The actus reus and mens rea for accomplice liability constitute the elements of complicity, and each of these two main elements is described below.

共同犯罪的构成要件包括共犯的客观行为和共犯的犯罪意图,下面分别对这两个主要构成要素进行介绍。

7.1.1.1 Accomplice Actus Reus(共犯的客观行为)

The actus reus for accomplice liability is, at its most basic level, assistance. That is, a person who assists a principal in the commission of a crime has satisfied the actus reus of accomplice or accessory liability. According to Joshua Dressler, there are three means by which assistance is typically provided: (1) assistance by physical conduct; (2) assistance by psychological influence; and (3) assistance by omission (assuming in this latter case that the omitter has a duty to act).[2]

从最基本层面看,共犯责任的客观行为是协助。也就是说,协助主犯实施犯罪的人已满足共犯或从犯责任的客观行为要素。根据乔舒亚·德雷斯勒的观点,通常有三种提供帮助的方式:(1)身体行为的帮助;(2)心理影响的帮助;(3)不作为的帮助(在后一种情况下,假设不作为者有义务采取行动)。

Assistance by physical conduct is straightforward. For example, in Hensel v. State

[1] Jennifer L. Moore & John L. Worrall, *Criminal Law*, 2nd editon, Pearson Education Inc. ,2018, p.97 - 98.

[2] See Jennifer L. Moore & John L. Worrall, *Criminal Law*, 2nd editon, Pearson Education Inc. ,2018, p. 99.

of Alaska, [1] the defendant, Hensel, aided in the commission of a felony by providing dynamite and fuses that were used to blow up a storage bunker. According to the court, for accomplice liability to attach, the actus reus component requires that the defendant "aid, abet, assist, or facilitate the commission of the particular substantive crime for which the state seeks to hold the defendant liable as an accomplice". Hensel indeed satisfied this requirement. [2]

通过身体行为提供帮助是直接的。以亨塞尔诉阿拉斯加州案为例,被告亨塞尔

---

〔1〕 On December 5, 1973, the co – defendants, various members of a group broken into the storage bunkers in Eagle River and stolen a large quantity of explosives. The night of December 6, the group took the dynamite in two cars to a location of Hensel for deal. They arrived about midnight. Charon, alone, went upstairs and inside to speak with Hensel, while the others waited outside by the cars. Charon remained upstairs with Hensel for fifteen to twenty minutes. Charon eventually returned to the cars with Hensel. The car trunks were opened, Hensel inspected the explosives, and stated that he could "handle it all." After the co – defendants loaded the explosives into Hensel's Jeep, Charon asked Hensel if he had any fusing. Hensel stated that he had some out at his cabin. Charon, Cloud, and Hensel drove out to Hensel's cabin and unloaded the dynamite, storing it in the attic. At this time, according to the co – defendants' testimony, the subject of "bunkers" was mentioned. Charon and Cloud said they needed six sticks for six bunkers. Hensel brought down seven sticks from the attic, the extra stick being reserved for purposes of a demonstration. The defendants stated that they wanted fifteen minute fuses. Hensel said, "[f]ine, I can give you enough where you have more than enough time; with time to spare." Hensel then capped and fused each stick, explaining how to place the charges in each of the bunkers so that the concussion of the one stick would explode the entire bunker. Accompanied by Cloud and Charon, Hensel took the seventh stick of dynamite to a nearby field, where he exploded it as a demonstration. Cloud and Charon left Hensel and picked up the other co – defendants. On their way to the bunkers, they discovered that Hensel had fitted the charges with only six minute fuses. They agreed that this would not allow them enough time to blow up all six bunkers, so they decided to blow up only one. The co – defendants returned to Eagle River by car, placed the stick of dynamite in one of the bunkers as Hensel had directed, lit it, and fled. At the time of the explosion, Hensel was asleep.(1973 年 12 月 5 日,共同被告即一个犯罪团伙的多名成员闯入位于鹰河的一个装满炸药的储存掩体,盗走大量炸药。12 月 6 日晚,该团伙成员将炸药分别装在两辆汽车上,前往亨塞尔的住所进行交易。他们大约在午夜到达。查龙独自一人上楼找亨塞尔,其他人则在屋外车旁等待。查龙与亨塞尔在楼上待了 15 分钟到 20 分钟。然后,查龙与亨塞尔一起回到车旁。打开车的后备箱,亨塞尔检查了炸药,并表示他可以"处理所有事情"。在将炸药装入亨塞尔的吉普车后,查龙问亨塞尔是否有引信。亨塞尔表示在他的小屋里有一些。查龙、克劳德和亨塞尔开车前往亨塞尔的小屋,卸下了炸药,并将其存放在阁楼上。根据共同被告的证言,当时提到了"掩体"的话题。查龙和克劳德说他们需要 6 根炸药棒来炸 6 个掩体。亨塞尔从阁楼上拿下 7 根炸药棒,其中一根是为了演示而保留的。被告们表示需要 15 分钟的引信。亨塞尔说:"好的,我可以给你们足够的时间,让你们会有足够的时间逃走。"然后,亨塞尔对每根炸药棒加上盖帽和引信,并解释如何在每个掩体中放置炸药,以便一根炸药棒的冲击波会炸毁整个掩体。在查龙和克劳德的陪同下,亨塞尔将第 7 根炸药棒带到附近的田野,并演示如何进行爆炸。共同被告离开亨塞尔并接到其他共同被告后,发现亨塞尔只给炸药装上了 6 分钟的引信。他们认为这不足以让他们有足够的时间炸毁 6 个掩体,因此决定只炸毁 1 个。共同被告们驾车返回鹰河,按照亨塞尔的指示将炸药棒放入其中一个掩体中,点燃后逃离。爆炸时,亨塞尔正在睡觉。)

〔2〕 Jennifer L. Moore & John L. Worrall, *Criminal Law*, 2nd editon, Pearson Education Inc. ,2018, p. 99.

提供炸药和引信帮助他人实施一项重罪,这些炸药和引信被用来炸毁一个储存掩体。法院认为,亨塞尔要承担共犯责任,因为从共犯客观行为方面的要求看,其犯罪行为部分是要求被告实施了"帮助、教唆、协助或方便实施国家要求被告承担共犯责任的特定实质性犯罪"。而在亨塞尔诉阿拉斯加州案中,亨塞尔实施的行为确实满足这一要求。

Assistance by psychological influence generally requires a certain amount of coaxing, encouraging, persuading, or soliciting. Mere presence at the scene of the crime is not enough to satisfy the actus reus component of accomplice liability.[1] For example, here are the facts from a case in which Carl Pace appealed his conviction of being an accomplice in a robbery: appellant, his wife and two infant children were in a car driving from South Bend to LaPorte. Eugene Rootes was riding with them. The appellant was driving with his wife and one child in the front seat. Rootes and appellant's other child were in the back seat. While in South Bend, appellant after asking his wife for permission stopped to pick up a hitchhiker, Mr. Reppert, who sat next to Rootes in the back seat. Later Rootes pulled a knife and took Reppert's wallet. After driving further, Reppert got out of the car, Rootes then took his watch. The appellant said nothing during the entire period and they continued driving to LaPorte. After the incident, the appellant, Carl Pace, was accused of being an accomplice to the crime of robbery, but he appealed. The court decided that Pace was not an accomplice because "while he was driving the car, nothing was said nor did he act in any manner to indicate his approval or countenance of the robbery." In other words, the appellant merely "appeared at the scene of the crime", he passively acquiesced to the robbery and, therefore, could not be considered an accomplice.[2]

心理影响的帮助通常需要一定程度的哄骗、鼓励、劝说或恳求。但这不意味着,仅仅出现在犯罪现场就能满足共犯责任的归责要件。以上诉人卡尔·佩斯被指控的抢劫罪共犯案为例:上诉人、上诉人妻子、两个婴儿和尤金·根同乘一车,从南本德前往拉波特。上诉人开车,其妻和一个婴儿坐在前座位置,而尤金·根和另一个婴儿坐在后座位置。当车还行驶于南本德时,上诉人征得妻子同意,停车让里珀特搭车,里珀特坐在尤金·根身旁。而后尤金·根掏出一把刀,抢了里珀特的钱包。车行驶一段路程后,里珀特准备下车,此时,尤金·根又夺取他的手表。整个案发过

---

〔1〕 Jennifer L. Moore & John L. Worrall, *Criminal Law*, 2nd editon, Pearson Education Inc. ,2018, p. 99.

〔2〕 Jennifer L. Moore & John L. Worrall, *Criminal Law*, 2nd editon, Pearson Education Inc. ,2018, p. 99 – 100.

程,上诉人一言不发,继续开车前往拉波特。案发后,上诉人卡尔·佩斯被指控抢劫罪的共犯,但其不服,提出上诉。上诉法院认定卡尔·佩斯不成立共犯,因为“他开车时,没有说任何话,也没有以任何方式表明他赞成或支持抢劫”。换言之,上诉人仅仅是属于“出现在犯罪现场而已”,卡尔·佩斯被动地默许抢劫,不能被视为共犯。

In the case of accomplice liability, an omission will result in a conviction only if the omitter has a duty to intervene. For example, in State v. Walden, a mother stood by and did not attempt to intervene (or call for help) while her child was being assaulted. She was convicted as an accomplice because a North Carolina statute requires that parents have an "affirmative duty" to protect their children. In a related case, a mother knew that two men who lived with her repeatedly raped and sexually assaulted her two daughters. Consequently, the mother was accused of being an accomplice to the crimes of rape and sexual assault. The court noted that there was "no doubt" that the woman was aware of what was happening and did nothing to intervene or stop it.[1] She was convicted as an accomplice. The two mothers in the aforementioned cases had the legal duty to protect their children, yet they stood without taking intervention measures when their children were assaulted by a third party, and thus becoming accomplice to the third party's crime.

对于不作为的共犯责任案件,只有不作为者在有义务干预的情况下,不作为才会被定罪。例如,在北卡罗来纳州诉瓦尔登案中,一位母亲在她孩子被侵犯时袖手旁观,没有试图干预(或寻求帮助),被判构成共犯,因为北卡罗来纳州的法规要求父母有保护孩子的“积极义务”。另一个相关案件中,一位母亲知道与其同居的两名男子多次强奸和性侵犯她的两个女儿。其后,这位母亲被指控构成强奸罪和性侵罪的共同犯罪。法院指出,毫无疑问这位母亲知道发生了什么,却没有采取任何干预或阻止措施,因此,她被判构成共犯。可见,上述案件中的两位母亲都有保护自己孩子的法定义务,但在孩子遭受第三方侵害时却坐视不理,没有采取任何干预措施,因而构成第三方所实施罪行的共犯。

7.1.1.2 Accomplice Mens Rea(共同犯罪的犯罪意图)

An all-encompassing definition of accomplice mens rea is as follows:

(1) The intent to assist the primary party to engage in the conduct that forms the basis of the offense; and (2) The mental state required for commission of the offense.[2] The mens rea requirement for accomplice liability is a little more tedious than the mens

---

〔1〕 Jennifer L. Moore & John L. Worrall, *Criminal Law*, 2nd editon, Pearson Education Inc., 2018, p. 100.

〔2〕 Jennifer L. Moore & John L. Worrall, *Criminal Law*, 2nd editon, Pearson Education Inc., 2018, p. 101.

rea requirement for other crimes. For ordinary criminal liability, there is one type of mens rea(e.g. intent or knowledge). For accomplice liability, there are two levels of mens rea.[1]

共犯犯罪意图的全面定义一般包括两个方面的要素:协助主犯从事构成犯罪基础行为的意图和实施犯罪所需的犯罪意图。从这个两个要素看,共同犯罪责任的犯罪意图比其他犯罪的犯罪意图更显复杂。在普通刑事犯罪中,只有一种类型的犯罪意图(如蓄意或明知),而共同犯罪责任则有两级犯罪意图。

First, the accomplice must intend to assist. Second, assuming he or she intends to assist, criminal liability will attach as long as his or her mental state meets what the statute requires. If the statutory mens rea is defined in terms of negligence, then he or she will be held liable as an accomplice if he or she acted negligently. Similarly, if the statutory mens reais defined in terms of knowledge, then he or she will be considered an accomplice if he or she acted with knowledge.[2]

首先,共犯必须有协助的意图。其次,假设共犯有意协助,那么只要其犯罪意图符合该罪的法律规定,就得承担刑事责任。倘若该罪规定的犯罪意图是过失,如果共犯行为是过失实施的,那么他将作为过失共犯承担责任。同样,倘若该罪规定的犯罪意图是明知,如果共犯在明知的情况下实施该行为,那么也将被认定为是明知的共犯。

Consider the case of State of New Mexico v. Harrison. Harrison drove two friends, Thompson and Carter, to a parking lot where they stole a vehicle. Thompson and Carter attempted to rob a gas station attendant, but when they were unsuccessful, they fled the crime scene and were later arrested. Harrison was also arrested and charged as an accomplice to the robbery, even though he did not participate in the actual crime. He was convicted but appealed his conviction, arguing that the judge's instructions to the jury were flawed. The judge instructed the jurors as follows: The State does not have to offer evidence to prove that a man charged with a crime actually had a guilty intent. This is because a person is presumed to have intended to do the act he committed. Accordingly, until some credible evidence comes into the case tending to prove that because in the light of the circumstances as he honestly and in good faith believed them to be, the act he committed would appear to be lawful, or because the act was an

---

[1] Jennifer L. Moore & John L. Worrall, *Criminal Law*, 2nd editon, Pearson Education Inc. ,2018, p. 100.

[2] Jennifer L. Moore & John L. Worrall, *Criminal Law*, 2nd editon, Pearson Education Inc. , 2018, p. 101.

accident, until such credible evidence appears in the case, the State may rest upon the presumption that the accused intended to commit an act which he did commit.[1]

以新墨西哥州诉哈里森案为例。哈里森开车带着朋友汤普森和卡特到停车场偷了一辆车。汤普森和卡特试图抢劫一名加油站服务员，但未成功，后逃离犯罪现场时被逮捕。哈里森也被逮捕并被指控为抢劫罪共犯，尽管他并未参与抢劫罪。他被判有罪后提起上诉，辩称法官对陪审团的指示有缺陷。法官指示陪审团如下：国家无须提供证据证明被控犯罪的人实际上有犯罪的意图，这是因为人们被推定有意实施他们所做的行为。因此，除非案件出现可信证据足以证明被告诚实和真挚地相信自己所实施的行为似乎是合法的，或者该行为纯属意外。在这样的可信证据出现在案件中之前，国家可以推定被告有意实施其所做的行为，从而认定该犯罪是具备行为要素的。

Harrison further argued that this instruction put the burden on him to prove that he did or did not intend to see the robbery completed. However, this burden should fall on the prosecution. The Supreme Court of Connecticut agreed. Harrison's argument was successful, and he was given a new trial.[2]

但哈里森进一步辩护称，这一法官给陪审团的指示使其会承担责任证明自己是否蓄意看到抢劫行为实施完毕。然而，证明责任应由控方所承担。康涅狄格州最高法院对哈里森的这一辩护表示同意。因此，在上诉中，哈里森辩护成功，并得到一次重审机会。

Harrison's case dealt with the crime of robbery, for which intent to commit the crime was a specific element. But what if the mens rea requirement for the offense involves something less than outright intent, such as recklessness or negligence? How does this affect the mens rea calculation for accomplice liability? State v. Foster, another Connecticut case, offers an answer. Foster, who was convicted of being an accomplice, to criminally negligent homicide, argued in his appeal that there was no such crime because he could not intend for an unintended death to occur (negligent homicide is a homicide that generally can be foreseen). While his argument was certainly plausible, the Connecticut Supreme Court disagreed with it.[3] Thus it can be seen that the Anglo –

[1] Jennifer L. Moore & John L. Worrall, *Criminal Law*, 2nd editon, Pearson Education Inc., 2018, p. 100.

[2] Jennifer L. Moore & John L. Worrall, *Criminal Law*, 2nd editon, Pearson Education Inc., 2018, p. 101.

[3] Jennifer L. Moore & John L. Worrall, *Criminal Law*, 2nd editon, Pearson Education Inc., 2018, p. 101.

American criminal law affirms the existence of the concept of negligent accomplice.

哈里森案涉及抢劫罪,该罪的犯罪意图是具体故意。但是,如果某种罪行的犯罪意图不是直接故意,而是轻率或疏忽,那该怎么处理?这对共犯的犯罪意图有何影响?康涅狄格州诉福斯特案为此提供了答案。福斯特被判成立过失杀人罪的共犯,但他上诉辩称,不存在这样的罪行,因为他不可能有意地造成意外死亡(过失杀人罪是一种通常可以预见的杀人罪)。福斯特的论点显然是合理的,但康涅狄格州最高法院不同意他的观点。由此可见,英美刑法肯定过失共犯的存在。

7.1.2 Complicity Limitations and Defenses(共同犯罪限制和辩护)

Accomplice liability is limited in certain respects. Firstly, some offenses are what legal scholars call "nonproxyable", meaning that complicity is impossible because the crime can only be committed by a specific person or class of individuals. Secondly, a defense of abandonment could also be asserted. If successful, it acts as a bar to accomplice liability. Finally, legal immunity might also exist in certain situations, making a complicity conviction unlikely, if not impossible. This aspect will be discussed in more detail separately.

共犯的责任成立在某些方面受到限制。首先,某些罪行被法律学者称为"不可代理"的犯罪,这意味着不可能成立共犯,因为某种犯罪只能由一个特定的人或一类人实施。其次,共犯中止能成为一种辩护理由,如果以中止辩护成功,将成为共犯成立的障碍。最后,在某些情况下也可能存在法律豁免,使共犯成立的可能性减小。接下来将分而述之。

7.1.2.1 Nonproxyable Offenses(不可代理的犯罪)

A nonproxyable offense is one that can only be perpetrated by a designated person or class of persons. Such offenses introduce complications in the case of multiple offenders. For example, in People v. Enfeld, a woman fraudulently induced a public official into issuing a false certificate, a crime that only a public official can commit. Because the official was fraudulently induced to commit the crime, he did not meet the intentional conditions required for the establishment of the crime, and thus criminal liability did not attach.[1] The crime of issuing false certificates can only be committed intentionally by officials, however the woman, not having the status of an official, could not be an accomplice to the offense and was therefore not convicted. This means

[1] Jennifer L. Moore & John L. Worrall, *Criminal Law*, 2nd editon, Pearson Education Inc., 2018, p. 104.

that nonproxyable offense can only be committed by persons in a certain status, and a person who does not possess that status cannot constitute the crime.

不可代理的犯罪是只能由指定的人或某一类人实施的罪行。在涉及多名罪犯时,这会导致案情变得错综复杂。以人民诉恩菲尔德案为例,一名妇女欺诈性地诱使一名政府官员签发虚假证书,签发虚假证书罪是一种唯有政府官员才能实施的犯罪。而该名官员因被诱骗才签发虚假证书,不具备该罪成立的故意,因此不承担刑事责任。由于签发虚假证书罪只能由官员故意实施,[1] 但该女性不具有官员的身份,不可能成为该罪的共犯,也就没有获罪。这也说明,不可代理的犯罪只限于某种身份者才能实施,不具备身份者不能构成该罪。

7.1.2.2 Complicity Abandonment(共犯中止)

Complicity abandonment refers to the concept that one who assists in the commission of a criminal act may choose to withdraw from the collaborative effort or otherwise abandon his or her intent to participate in the crime. To succeed, though, the individual must notify the principal and neutralize the effects of any assistance offered to that point. For example, if someone provides a weapon for the principal to use in the crime, he or she must get it back. As an alternative, had that person's assistance gone only so far as an expression, then he or she must neutralize its effect. A statement along the lines of "Let's burglarize that house" could be neutralized by a statement to the effect of "Let's not—I changed my mind".

共犯中止是指协助实施犯罪行为的人可以选择退出合作,或以其他方式放弃参与犯罪的意图。然而,要想成功退出,协助者必须通知主犯,并消除其所提供帮助的影响。例如,如果有人提供武器给主犯使用,那么,他必须取回武器。作为一种选择,如果他的协助仅仅是一种口头表达,那么必须抵消其表达所造成的效果。诸如"我们去偷那栋房子吧"可以被"我们不要——我改变主意了"之类的话语否定。

Importantly, it is not enough for one who offers assistance before the commission of a crime to turn heel and leave as the crime is about to be committed. Again, there must be a bona fide effort to stop the crime or neutralize the assistance already provided. For

---

〔1〕 New York Penal Law 175.40 provides: A person is guilty of issuing a false certificate when, being a public servant authorized by law to make or issue official certificates or other official written instruments, and with intent to defraud, deceive or injure another person, he issues such an instrument, or makes the same with intent that it be issued, knowing that it contains a false statement or information.
《纽约州刑法典》第175.40条规定:任何人作为法律授权制作或签发官方证书或其他官方书面文书的公职人员,意图欺诈、欺骗或伤害他人,在明知该文书载有虚假陈述或信息的情况下签发或意图签发该文书,则该人犯有签发虚假证书的罪行。

example, in State v. Thomas, a man, Thomas, expressed his desire to two acquaintances to "shoot the police". When one of them pulled a gun on an officer, Thomas left. The officer was shot and killed. Thomas was convicted of aiding and abetting in the murder, and he appealed unsuccessfully.

重要的是,在犯罪之前提供帮助的人,在犯罪即将发生时仅转身离开是不够的。其必须做出真诚的努力来制止犯罪或抵消已经提供的帮助。例如,在州诉托马斯案中,一名叫托马斯的男子向两个熟人表达了"射杀警察"的愿望。当其中一人拿枪指着一名警官时,托马斯转身离开。这名警官被枪杀。托马斯也被判协助和教唆谋杀罪,他上诉未获得成功。

The reviewing court held: Defendant's own testimony at trial, taken at face value, indicates that he simply left when he saw Jennette take out his gun. Nothing in his testimony suggests that he communicated to Jennette that he was leaving or that he disapproved of the contemplated act, or that he otherwise sought to actively withdraw the support to the proposed event which his presence supplied. According to defendant, he merely left the scene within minutes before the shooting occurred. As a matter of law, such a spontaneous, unannounced withdrawal, without more, only briefly before the commission of the offense which had been previously encouraged by defendant's presence or other support, is insufficient to insulate the defendant from criminal liability as an aider and abettor.〔1〕

上诉法院裁定被告辩护不成立的理由为:从表面上看,被告法庭的证词表明被告看到珍妮特拿出枪时就离开了。在其证词中,没有任何迹象表明被告已经告知珍妮特自己准备离开现场,或者不赞成原定计划的行动,或者试图积极撤回对自己所提议事件的支持。根据被告的说法,他只是在枪击发生前几分钟离开了现场。作为一个法律问题,被告在犯罪之前通过在场或其他支持方式鼓励他人犯罪,而后又自发、未经宣布、没有更多地、只是简单地在犯罪之前退出,不足以使被告免除作为帮助者和教唆者的刑事责任。

7.1.2.3　Immunity from Conviction(定罪的刑事豁免)

Accomplice liability is not possible when one of the parties to a crime is supposed to be protected by the applicable statute. The best example is statutory rape. Statutory rape laws make it a crime to have sexual intercourse with a minor. So, assuming Clint, an 18 - year - old, has sex with his 17 - year - old girlfriend (and assuming the jurisdiction

〔1〕 Jennifer L. Moore & John L. Worrall, *Criminal Law*, 2nd editon, Pearson Education Inc., 2018, p. 104.

in which they are located treats 17 - year - olds as juveniles), he has committed statutory rape. His girlfriend was a party to the crime, but she was also protected by the statutory rape law. Thus, she cannot be considered an accomplice to her own rape. If she were to be considered an accomplice, it would undermine the purpose of the law.〔1〕

当犯罪的一方当事人应当受到适用法律保护时,共犯不可能成立。最为典型的例子就是法定强奸罪。法定强奸罪的法规规定,与未成年人发生性关系是犯罪行为。因此,假设18岁的克林特和其17岁的女友发生性关系(假设他们所在的司法管辖区将17岁的人视为未成年人),克林特就构成法定强奸罪。克林特女友则是参与犯罪的一方,但她也受到法定强奸罪法规的保护。因此,她不能被当作强奸罪的共犯。如果她被认定为共犯,就会破坏法律目的。

■ Curriculum Ideology and Politics(课程思政)

In the Anglo - American criminal law, it is generally accepted that the imposition of accomplice liability is subject to certain limitations. For instance, accomplice liability cannot be imposed for nonproxyable offenses. A nonproxyable offense is roughly equivalent to the status offense in Chinese criminal law, however, differences exist in the philosophy of punishment. The mainstream view in Chinese criminal law is that a person without a specific status cannot independently constitute a status offense because he or she lacks the specific status, but if he or she colludes with a person who possesses the specific status to commit a crime, he or she can be considered as an accomplice to a status offense. For instance, an ordinary person who is not a government official cannot independently constitute the crime of embezzlement. However, by colluding with a government official, he or she may become an accomplice to the crime of embezzlement. This is completely different from the treatment of nonproxyable offense in Anglo - American criminal law, and learners should gain a deep understanding of the similarities among these types of criminal phenomena, and also recognize the subtle differences.

英美刑法普遍认为共犯责任的施加要受到一定程度的限制,譬如不可代理的犯罪就不能施加共犯责任。不可代理的犯罪大致等同于中国刑法中的身份犯概念,但在惩罚理念上有差异。我国刑法主流观点认为,无身份者因缺乏某种特殊身份而不能独立构成身份犯,但如果其勾结有身份者共同实施犯罪,则可以构成身份犯的共

〔1〕 Jennifer L. Moore & John L. Worrall, *Criminal Law*, 2nd editon, Pearson Education Inc. ,2018, p. 105.

犯。譬如,普通人因不具备国家工作人员身份,无法单独构成贪污罪,但其可以和国家工作人员相互勾结,构成贪污罪的共犯。这和英美刑法不可代理犯罪处置是完全不同的,学习者应深度认识这类犯罪现象的相似性,但同时也要认识到细微之处的差异。

7.2 Vicarious Liability(替代责任)

Vicarious liability occurs when one person is held liable for the actions of another, and perhaps when the former person has no idea what the latter person's activities. Formally defined, vicarious liability is "the imposition of liability on one person for the actionable conduct of another, based solely on a relationship between the two persons". So, while vicarious liability involves two or more parties, there are two conditions that make it different from accomplice liability: (1) it takes only one party's actions to trigger liability, and (2) liability transfers from one of them to the other. For example, an employee may do something that is prohibited by law, but the employer will be held responsible for it.[1] In this section, we will introduce two of the more common forms: corporate vicarious liability and individual vicarious liability.

当一个人对另一个人的行为负有责任——也许前者不知道后者实施何种行为时,就发生了替代责任。根据正式定义,替代责任是"仅基于两人之间的关系,将一人的可诉行为的责任施加于另一人"。因此,虽然替代责任涉及两个或两个以上的当事人,但有两个条件使其与共犯责任不同:(1)只需要一方的行为即可触发责任;(2)责任从其中一方转移到另一方。例如,雇员可能会做法律所禁止的事情,但雇主将对此负责。本节将介绍两种比较常见的形式:法人替代责任和个人替代责任。

7.2.1 Corporate Vicarious Liability(法人替代责任)

Corporate vicarious liability refers to the liability of a corporation, no matter its size, for the criminal conduct of its employees. Its origins can be traced to the medieval doctrine of respondeat superior, Latin for "Let the master answer". And the master could be held to answer for the action of his agent. A few nineteenth century English court decisions also formed the basis for corporate vicarious criminal liability. However, the turning point in American history was the U. S. Supreme Court's decision in New York Central & Hudson River Railroad v. United States. At issue was whether a corporation could be held criminally liable for the issuance of illegal rebates by its agents and

---

[1] Jennifer L. Moore & John L. Worrall, *Criminal Law*, 2nd editon, Pearson Education Inc. ,2018, p. 107.

officers. The Court held, in part, "We see no valid objection in law, and every reason in public policy, why the corporation which profits by the transaction, and can only act through its agents and officers, shall be held punishable".[1]

法人替代责任是指无论法人规模如何,其对员工的犯罪行为负有责任。其起源可以追溯到中世纪的"respondeat superior"原则,拉丁语意为"让主人负责"。主人可以因为他代理人的行为而被追究责任。19 世纪英国法院的一些判决也为法人替代责任的发展奠定了基础。然而,美国历史的转折点是美国最高法院在纽约中央和哈德逊河铁路公司诉美国案中的判决。该案争议的焦点是,一个法人可否因其代理人和高管发放非法回扣而承担刑事责任。法院部分地表示:"我们在法律上看不到有效的反对意见,而在公共政策上,我们有充分的理由认为,那些从交易中获利并只能通过其代理人和高管行事的企业应该受到惩罚。"

The general rule today is that a corporation is criminally liable for the actions of its agents when (1) those agents act in the official scope of their employment and (2) for the benefit of the corporation. As one court put it, "An agent's knowledge is imputed to the corporation where the agent is acting within the scope of his or her authority and where the knowledge relates to matters within the scope of authority". Then, if an employee exploits his or her position for personal gain (such as by stealing inventory and selling it on the side), the corporation will most likely not be held liable. The second requirement—that the employee be acting with the corporation's interests at heart—is less clear. As one team of experts put it, it "is not necessary that the employee be primarily concerned with benefitting the corporation, because courts recognize that many employees act primarily for their own personal gain". In fact, some corporations have been held criminally liable for the actions of low - ranking employees who may have little to no knowledge about the parent company's structure or motives. And corporations have even been held criminally liable for their subordinates' actions after implementing policies and procedures intended to prevent misconduct.[2]

今天的一般规则是,法人对其代理人的行为负有刑事责任,如果:(1)这些代理人在其受雇的正式范围内;(2) 为法人的利益行事。正如一个法院所言,"代理人的明知归于法人,代理人在其职权范围内行事,并且该明知与职权范围内的事项有关"。如果一个员工利用其职位谋取个人利益(比如偷取库存货物并私下出售),很

[1] Jennifer L. Moore & John L. Worrall, *Criminal Law*, 2nd editon, Pearson Education Inc. ,2018, p. 107.

[2] Jennifer L. Moore & John L. Worrall, *Criminal Law*, 2nd editon, Pearson Education Inc. ,2018, p. 107 - 108.

可能不会被追究法人责任。第二项要求雇员行为必须以法人利益为重就不太明确，因为正如一些专家所言，“雇员主要关心法人利益是没有必要的，因为法院承认许多雇员主要是为了谋取个人利益”。事实上，某些法人已对低级别员工的行为承担了刑事责任，主要是员工可能对母公司的结构或动机知之甚少。法人在制定旨在防止不当行为的政策和程序之后，甚至还需对谋取个人利益而不是法人利益的员工行为承担刑事责任。

7.2.2　Individual Vicarious Liability(个人替代责任)

With individual vicarious liability, one person is held liable for another's behavior. Individual vicarious liability can be divided into two main categories, namely, parental liability for a child's behavior and principal – agent liability. In some states, parents can be held criminally liable for their kids' illegal activities. In addition, principals can also be held liable for the actions of their agents (an "agent" is one who acts on behalf of a principal).[1] Here's a brief explanation of the two categories:

个人替代责任是指个人对另一个人的行为负责。个人替代责任主要分为两大类，即父母对孩子行为的责任和委托代理责任。某些州规定父母应对孩子的非法活动承担刑事责任。此外，委托人也可以对其代理人的行为负责(代理人是代表委托人行事的人)。下面，对二者进行简单的阐述：

Firstly, parental liability for a child's behavior. There are two main types of statutes used to hold parents accountable for the actions of their children. First, every state penalizes "contributing to the delinquency of a minor". Known as CDM statutes, these can be used against basically anyone who contributes to a child's delinquency, not just parents. Second, many states have taken it a step further by enacting laws aimed specifically at the parents of children. The common thread running throughout the laws is that they punish parents for failing to intervene when their children act out in inappropriate ways.[2]

第一，父母对孩子行为的责任。根据两种主要类型的法规，父母应对孩子的行为负责。其一，每个州都会惩罚“助长未成年人犯罪”的行为。这些法规被称为CDM (contributing to the delinquency of a minor 助长未成年人犯罪)法规，其基本上被用来规制导致孩子犯罪的任何人，而不仅仅是父母。其二，许多州已经更进一步，

---

〔1〕 Jennifer L. Moore & John L. Worrall, *Criminal Law*, 2nd editon, Pearson Education Inc., 2018, p. 109.

〔2〕 Jennifer L. Moore & John L. Worrall, *Criminal Law*, 2nd editon, Pearson Education Inc., 2018, p. 109.

颁布了专门针对孩子父母的法律。贯穿这些法律的一个共同点是,当孩子表现出不恰当的行为时,法律就会惩罚未能干预的父母。

Secondly, principal – agent liability. Principal – agent liability is also commonplace. A principal is the individual who hires or oversees an agent; the agent acts on his or her behalf. Often, the principal is the employer and the agent is the employee, but this need not always be the case. To illustrate an employer – employee relationship, in one case, a bank in El Paso, Texas, hired a repossession company to recover Sanchez's vehicle because she defaulted on her loan. Two men who were dispatched to Sanchez's home found the vehicle in the driveway. Sanchez confronted the men as they were hooking the vehicle to a tow truck. Just as the men were getting ready to tow the vehicle away, Sanchez jumped inside it, locked the doors, and refused to get out. The men then towed the vehicle away with Sanchez inside. They parked the car in a fenced lot and left Sanchez inside while a Doberman pinscher guard dog wandered about the lot. She was later rescued by her husband and police. The court held that the bank had a duty to take precautions for safety and was responsible for the breach of peace committed by the repossession company agents. Not unlike corporations, then, individual principals can be liable (criminally and civilly) for the actions of their agents. And whether the principal is an employer or just an ordinary person is largely immaterial.〔1〕

第二,委托代理责任。委托代理责任也很常见。委托人是雇用或监督代理人的个人;代理人代表委托人行事。通常情况下,委托人是雇主,代理人是雇员,但情况并非总是如此。在此,举例说明雇主与雇员的关系,得克萨斯州埃尔帕索的某家银行雇用一家回收公司前去回收桑切斯的车辆,因为她拖欠贷款未还。被派往桑切斯家的两名男子在车道上发现了该车辆。当他们将车辆系上拖车时,桑切斯与他们对峙。就在这两名男子准备将车拖走之际,桑切斯跳进车内,锁上车门,并拒绝下车。随后,这两名男子就连人带车一齐拖走,并将车置于带有围栏的停车场里,停车场里还有只巡逻的杜宾犬。而后桑切斯被她丈夫和警察合力救出。法院认为,银行有责任采取安全预防措施,并对代理人所实施的破坏治安行为负责。与法人不同,个人委托人可以对其代理人的行为承担(刑事和民事)责任。至于委托人是雇主还是普通人则无关紧要。

〔1〕 Jennifer L. Moore & John L. Worrall, *Criminal Law*, 2nd editon, Pearson Education Inc., 2018, p. 110.

■ Case study(案例学习)

State v. Formella 960 A.2d 722 (N.H. 2008)(新罕布什尔州诉福迈拉案)

Fact(基本案情)

On the afternoon of Wednesday, June 13, 2007, Paul Formella (defendant), a junior at Hanover High School, and two friends were studying at thenearby library. After studying for a couple of hours, they went back to the school to pick up books from their lockers. Upon entering the school, they encountered another group of students who said they intended to steal mathematics exams from the third floor. The defendant and his companions were asked to serve as lookouts during the theft, which they agreed to do. They were instructed to yell something like "Did you get your math book?" up to the third floor as a code to alert the thieves if someone was coming. The defendant and his friends then proceeded to their second – floor lockers. The defendant testified that on their way to their lockers they looked around to "confirm or dispel" whether anyone was there. Once the defendant and his friends had retrieved their books, they "were all feeling like this was the wrong thing to do", and decided to head back down to the first floor to wait for the other group. On their way down the stairs, they encountered a janitor who told them that they ought to leave the school. The defendant and his friends left the school building, but waited in the parking lot for approximately five to ten minutes for the other group. Eventually, the other students exited the school with the stolen examinations, and all the students shared the exam questions. The next week, someone informed the dean of students that some students had stolen the exams. The police were called, and in connection with their investigation they interviewed the defendant, who admitted his involvement in the theft. The defendant was later charged and convicted of theft as an accomplice.

被告保尔·福迈拉是一名汉诺威高中三年级的学生,2007年6月13日星期三下午,他和两个朋友去学校附近的图书馆学习。学习了几小时后,他们打算去学校储物柜拿书。进入学校后,被告和朋友遇到了一群学生,这群学生说要去三楼偷数学试卷。被告和朋友同意帮他们望风。被告被指示如果有其他人过来,就向三楼大喊诸如"你拿到数学书没"之类的暗语作为提醒。被告随后前往二楼的储物柜。被告作证说,在前往储物柜的路上,他们环顾四周,"确认或排除"是否有人。当被告等人拿到书后,"都觉得这样做是错误的",于是决定回到一楼等待另外一些人。下楼时,遇到一位看门人,看门人告诉他们应该离开学校。被告们就离开学校大楼,在停车场等待另外一些人,等了5—10分钟。那群偷试卷的学生带着偷来的试卷离开了学校,最后,所有人都分到了试题。第二周,教务主任得知学生盗窃试卷之事后报警。警察调查询问时,被告承认参与盗窃。而后,被告被指控和判决成立盗窃罪的共犯。

Dispute(争议点)

The defendant contends that because he had been acting as a lookout, leaving the scene so as to no longer be "looking out" deprived his complicity of its effectiveness, and, therefore, findings regarding the timing of the offense were required.

被告辩称,由于他担任的是望风者,但由于离开了现场,不再"望风",就失去共犯效力,所以还需要对其犯罪的时间进行调查。

Conclusion(结论)

The court of appeal disagreed. While at the point he left the scene, he was no longer an effective lookout, the defendant did nothing to counter his prior complicity. According to the defendant, the principals had requested aid in committing the offense, he agreed to provide it, and he agreed to warn the principals if anyone approached, thus encouraging the act. Further, upon reaching the second floor, the defendant looked around to "confirm or dispel" whether anyone was around who might have apprehended the thieves or otherwise spoiled the crime. Thus, it was the complicity of agreeing to aid the primary actors and then actually aiding them that needed to be undone; silently withdrawing from the scene did not, in any way, undermine the encouragement the defendant had provided. As there was no evidence that the defendant had wholly deprived his complicity of its effectiveness, it was not error for the trial court to refuse to make findings on the timing of the offense because such findings would not have altered the result.[1]

上诉法庭不同意被告的辩护理由。因为被告离开现场,虽然不再是一个有效的望风者,但他没有做任何事情来抵消先前共犯的影响。根据被告的说法,主犯在实施犯罪时请求帮助,被告同意提供帮助,并同意如果有人靠近,就会提醒主犯,从而鼓励了盗窃行为。此外,在到达二楼之后,被告环顾四周以"确认或消除"是否附近有人可能会逮捕小偷或破坏犯罪。因此,他先是同意帮助主犯,而后实际帮助主犯,就成立共犯,这种影响需要被抵消。默默退出现场,无论如何都不会抵消被告所提供的鼓励。由于没有证据表明被告完全否定其共犯的效力,初审法院拒绝对犯罪时间作出认定是正确的,因为这种认定不会改变结果。

---

〔1〕 Jennifer L. Moore & John L. Worrall, *Criminal Law*, 2nd editon, Pearson Education Inc. ,2018, p. 105 - 106.

Questions:1. Did the defendant act as an "accomplice" to the crime, and if so, what were the critical factors in establishing accomplice liability? (Please scan the QR code on the right to get the answer)

被告是否成立该罪的"共犯",如果是,确定共犯责任的关键因素是什么?(答案请扫描右侧二维码获取)

2. What was the defendant's legal argument on appeal in this case? (The way to obtain the answer is the same as above)

该案中被告在上诉时的法律论据是什么?(答案获取方式同上)

3. Did the defendant effectively "abandon" his criminal plan in this case? (The way to obtain the answer is the same as above)

该案中被告是否有效地"放弃"了他的犯罪计划?(答案获取方式同上)

7.3 Exercise(课后练习)(答案请扫描右侧二维码获取)

7.3.1 Test of Terminologies(术语考查)

①complicity　②principal

③accomplice　④accomplice liability

⑤derivative liability　⑥accomplice actus reus

⑦accomplice mens rea　⑧nonproxyable offenses

⑨vicarious liability

7.3.2 True or False(判断题)

1. The actus reus for complicity is, at its most basic level, assistance.

在最基本的层面上,共同犯罪的客观行为是协助。

2. Accomplice liability is not possible when one of the parties to a crime is supposed to be protected by the applicable statute. The crime of statutory rape serves as an example.

当参与犯罪的一方当事人应当受到适用法律保护时,共犯责任是不可能成立的。法定强奸罪就是典例。

3. Vicarious liability transfers criminal responsibility from one party to another due to a special relationship. Consequently, vicarious liability may be imposed on the party even when he or she was not involved in the crime and had no actus reus and no mens rea.

替代责任基于特殊关系将刑事责任从一方转移到另一方。因此,即使一方没有参与犯罪,没有实施任何行为,也没有应受惩罚的心理状态,都有可能承担替代责任。

7.3.3 Short – answer Questions（简答题）

1. Explain the two levels of mens rea for the purposes of complicity.

请解释共同犯罪目的中所包含两个层次的犯罪意图。

2. Explain abandonment for purposes of accomplice liability.

请解释何谓共犯中止。

3. Explain three means by which assistance is provided in the context of complicity.

解释在共同犯罪情况下提供帮助的三种方式。

■ Curriculum Ideology and Politics(课程思政)

Vicarious liability in Anglo – American criminal law epitomizes the maintenance of social order and the protection of public interest. It underscores several key points: corporations must bear criminal liability for improper job – related actions by their employees; parents must bear criminal liability for illegal activities committed by their minor children; and principals are responsible for the actions of their agents. This doctrine encourages both corporations and individuals to exercise caution in their hiring practices or other relationships involving supervision, thereby fostering and promoting a sense of responsibility and social concern. Although vicarious liability may seem to contravene the principle of personal culpability, its underlying rationale is rooted in the special relationship between the surrogate and the person being replaced, such as the relationship between parents and their underage children or between employers and their employees. This special relationship imposes certain responsibilities, guardianship, or supervisory duties on the relevant party. If the surrogate fails to fulfill or neglects these duties or responsibilities, resulting in serious consequences, criminal law punishes them on the basis of the concept of vicarious liability. Setting aside the debate on whether it contravenes the principle of personal culpability, vicarious liability indeed emphasizes the importance of responsibility and accountability.

替代责任充分体现了英美刑法对社会秩序和公众利益的维护。因为其强调法人承担雇员不当职务行为的刑事责任、家长对未成年孩子的非法活动承担刑事责任以及委托人对其代理人的行为负责,这将激励法人或个人在雇用或其他关系中谨慎对待其所监管的对象,同时培养和促进法人或个人的责任意识和社会关怀。尽管从表象看,替代责任违反罪责自负原则,但从深层的依据看,替代责任依据是替代者和被替代者的特殊关系(比如父母和未成年儿童之间的关系,或雇主和雇员之间的关系等),且因这种特殊的替代关系赋予了相关一方一定的责任、监护或监管义务。但是,替代者并没有履行好或忽视了这种义务或责任,并导致了严重后果,刑法便以替代责任理念对其予以处罚。姑且无论其是否违背罪责自负原则,但其确实体现了对责任和担当精神的重视。

■ Summary(总结)

1. Complicity occurs when two or more offenders work together and commit a criminal act.[1]

当两个或两个以上的罪犯一起合作并实施犯罪行为时,就是共同犯罪。

2. An accomplice is one who knowingly, voluntarily, and with common intent unites with the principal offender in the commission of a crime.[2]

共犯是指明知、自愿及具有共同意图与主犯联合实施犯罪的人。

3. Accomplice liability is limited in three aspects: nonproxyable offenses, abandonment, and legal immunity.

共犯责任受到三个方面的限制:不可代理的犯罪、共犯中止和法律豁免。

4. Vicarious liability occurs when one person is held liable for the actions of another, and perhaps when the former person has no idea what the latter person is up to.[3]

当一个人对另一个人的行为承担责任时,也许前者不知后者实施何种行为,此时就会发生替代责任。

5. Corporate vicarious liability refers to the liability of a corporation, no matter its size, for the criminal conduct of its employees. The general rule today is that a corporation is criminally liable for the actions of its agents when (1) those agents act in the official scope of their employment and (2) for the benefit of the corporation.[4]

法人替代责任是指法人对其雇员的犯罪行为所承担的责任,无论其规模大小。今天的一般规则是,在以下情况下,法人对其代理人的行为负有刑事责任:(1)这些

---

〔1〕 Jennifer L. Moore & John L. Worrall, *Criminal Law*, 2nd editon, Pearson Education Inc., 2018, p. 111.

〔2〕 Jennifer L. Moore & John L. Worrall, *Criminal Law*, 2nd editon, Pearson Education Inc., 2018, p. 111.

〔3〕 Jennifer L. Moore & John L. Worrall, *Criminal Law*, 2nd editon, Pearson Education Inc., 2018, p. 112.

〔4〕 Jennifer L. Moore & John L. Worrall, *Criminal Law*, 2nd editon, Pearson Education Inc., 2018, p. 112.

代理人在其正式职业范围内;(2)为法人的利益行事。

6. With individual vicarious liability, one person is held liable for another's behavior,[1] typically when there is a specific relationship between them that justifies this legal imposition.

个人替代责任通常是指一个人因另一个人的行为而承担的责任,这通常发生在他们之间存在某种特定的关系时,这种关系使法律强加的责任是合理的。

[1] Jennifer L. Moore & John L. Worrall, *Criminal Law*, 2nd editon, Pearson Education Inc., 2018, p. 112.

Chapter 8 Inchoate Crimes: Attempt, Conspiracy, and Solicitation

第 8 章 未完成犯罪:未遂罪、共谋罪和教唆罪

■ The Learning Objective（学习目标）

1. To understand inchoate crimes.

理解未完成犯罪。

2. To understand attempt, conspiracy, and solicitation.

理解未遂罪、共谋罪和教唆罪。

3. To learn some terminologies in this chapter.

掌握本章中的专业术语。

■ Chapter Outline（本章内容概要）

This chapter covers three main types on inchoate crimes: attempt, conspiracy, and solicitation. This chapter focuses on the definition, types and constituent elements of attempt, conspiracy, and solicitation. Additionally, this chapter employs some classic case to illustrate and explain these three types of inchoate crimes.

本章涉及未完成犯罪的三大类:未遂、共谋和教唆。本章重点讨论未遂、共谋和教唆的定义、类型及各自的构成要素。同时,本章还使用了一些经典案例来阐述和解释这三类未完成犯罪。

■ The Purpose of Curriculum Ideology and Politics for this Chapter（本章的课程思政目标）

The criminal laws of many jurisdictions punish inchoate offenses, such as attempts and preparations to commit a crime. However, the models for punishment vary significantly across different legal systems and countries. By studying and mastering the patterns and unique features of how Anglo – American criminal law addresses inchoate offenses, students can identify common ground and analyze disparities, thereby enhancing their analytical, critical, and discerning abilities.

诸多国家的刑法均惩罚犯罪的未完成形态,如未遂、预备等。但不同法系、不同国家惩罚的处罚模式差异较大。通过学习和掌握英美刑法处罚未完成犯罪的模式及其独特之处,探寻共识并剖析差异,可以提升学生的分析能力、批判能力、辨析能力。

In Anglo – American criminal law, the establishment of inchoate crimes such as attempt, conspiracy, and solicitation all necessitate mens rea. The primary reason criminal law punishes inchoate offenses is that the perpetrator has already demonstrated mens rea. From this premise, students are guided to deeply consider the impact of subjective elements on human behavior and legal characterization, and are encouraged to foster a commitment to ethical conduct within themselves.

英美刑法未遂罪、共谋罪及教唆罪的成立,均需要主观心态。刑法之所以惩罚没有实施完毕的犯罪,主要是因为行为人已具备主观罪过。以此为切入,深度引领学生观察主观要件对人的行为及法律属性的影响,引导学生重视自己内心向善的追求。

■ Terminologies (专业术语)

inchoate crime	未完成犯罪
attempt	未遂
factual impossibility	事实上的不能犯
legal impossibility	法律上的不能犯
conspiracy	共谋
overt act	表征性行为
Wharton's rule	沃顿规则
solicitation	教唆

8.1 Inchoate crimes(未完成犯罪)

An inchoate crime is one that is "partial; unfinished; begun, but not completed". Inchoate crimes are also considered "incipient", meaning they often lead to one or more other crimes. Yet even though they are "incomplete", inchoate crimes are offenses in themselves. In other words, a person can be convicted of an inchoate crime even if he or she does not actually complete the crime he or she intended to commit. One who attempts a robbery can be found guilty of attempted robbery. Likewise, one who attempts to kill another can be found guilty of attempted murder. The three primary inchoate crimes are attempt, conspiracy, and solicitation.〔1〕From the perspective of the history of Anglo – American criminal law, there was no clear distinction between ancient criminal law and tort law. Consequently, the law at that time did not stipulate that perpetrators should be punished for failing to achieve the goal of their crime. With the development of the times, probably in the Middle Ages, the trend of private duels prevailed in Europe. Britain took the lead in stipulating the crime of duel to regulate this kind of behavior. This legislation not only punished actual duel behavior but also gradually began to punish those who attempted duels and those who instigated and assisted in planning duels in judicial practice. Circumstances such as attempt, conspiracy, and instigation were mixed in the same sentence, sharing the common feature that the typical crime of duel, with complete constituent elements, was inchoate. From the second half of the 17th century, the Court of Queen's Bench gradually changed the law, developing these three inchoate crimes. By the 19th century, each of these three categories of inchoate crime had its own constituent characteristics. Although there are differences between the three types of inchoate crimes, there is a similarity: despite the perpetrator not directly achieving the goal of the crime, their actions all demonstrated mens rea. The three inchoate crimes are described in turn below.

未完成犯罪是指部分的、未完成的、已开始但尚未完结的犯罪。未完成犯罪也被认为是犯罪的“萌芽状态”，这意味着由它们开始发展出一种或多种其他犯罪。然而，即使它们是“未完成的”，但其本身也是犯罪。换言之，某人即使没有实际完成其计划实施的罪行，也可以被判未遂罪。抢劫未遂者可被判抢劫未遂罪。同样，企图杀害他人者也可被判谋杀未遂罪。未完成犯罪主要有三种类型，即未遂、共谋和教唆。从英美刑法的历史来看，古代刑法与侵权法没作明确区分，因此，当时的法律并未规定处罚没有完成犯罪目标的行为人。随着时代发展，大概在中世纪时期，欧洲私人决斗之风盛行，英国率先规定决斗罪以规制这类行为，不仅处罚已经实际进行的决斗行为，而且逐渐在司法实践中开始惩罚未遂决斗者和唆使、协助策划决斗者。由是，未遂、共谋和教唆等情节混杂在同一判决中，它们的共同特点是：相对于典型的具有完备构成要件的决斗罪而言，其都是未完成形态的。大约从 17 世纪下半叶开始，王座法庭逐渐修改法律，发展出来这三种类型的未完成犯罪。但一直到

---

〔1〕 Jennifer L. Moore & John L. Worrall, *Criminal Law*, 2nd editon, Pearson Education Inc., 2018, p. 114.

19 世纪时,这三类未完成犯罪才各自具有独立的构成特征。[1] 尽管三种未完成犯罪类型有所差异,但还是有相似之处,即虽然行为人并没有直接实现犯罪目标,但其行为都彰显了主观罪过。下面将依次介绍这三种类型。

8.2 Attempt(未遂罪)

Attempt is the "intent to commit a crime coupled with an act taken toward committing the offense". There are four elements of attempt to commit a crime: (1) intent to commit it, (2) an overt act toward its commission, (3) failure of consummation, (4) and the apparent possibility of commission[2].

未遂罪是指"具有犯罪意图并采取了犯罪行动"。未遂罪有四个要素:(1)犯罪意图;(2)实施犯罪的表征性行为;(3)行动未能完成;(4)犯罪的明显可能性。

The first two elements are basically the mens rea and actus reus of attempt, respectfully. The last two elements are well judged. If the crime is consummated, or completed, then it is no longer just an attempt. "Apparent possibility" just refers to the possibility that the offender could have attempted the crime. If, for example, a defendant is charged with attempted burglary but was nowhere near the scene of the crime, then it is not apparent that he or she could have committed the offense. This is roughly analogous to an alibi defense.[3] Therefore, the first two elements will be highlighted in the following content.

前两个要素,即犯罪意图和客观行为,是未遂罪的两个基本要素。后两个要素是能够较好判断的。如果犯罪已经完成,或者已经既遂,那么就不再仅是"未能完成"。而"犯罪的明显可能性"则是指行为人有企图实施某罪的可能性。例如,如果被告被控夜盗未遂罪,却在案发时根本不在犯罪现场附近,那么其显然不可能实施夜盗罪。这大致也类似于"不在犯罪现场"这种辩护事由。因此,将在下面的内容中着重介绍前两个要素。

8.2.1 The Mens Rea of Attempt(未遂的犯罪意图)

There are two parts of the mens rea of attempt: to (1) intend the act and

---

[1] 参见储槐植:《美国刑法》,北京大学出版社 2005 年版,第 102 页;[英]丹尼斯·贝克:《格兰维尔·威廉姆斯刑法学教科书》,李立丰译,法律出版社 2023 年版,第 469 页。

[2] Jennifer L. Moore & John L. Worrall, *Criminal Law*, 2nd editon, Pearson Education Inc., 2018, p. 114.

[3] Jennifer L. Moore & John L. Worrall, *Criminal Law*, 2nd editon, Pearson Education Inc., 2018, p. 114.

(2) intend the result. To intend the act means the offender must intend to commit some sort of overt act toward completion of the offense. As to intending the result, the defendant must also intend for the substantive crime to occur. So, for example, if Brian intends to shoot Larry in the knee but does not intend for Larry to die, Brian has not satisfied the mens rea of attempted murder. Brian will likely be convicted of some other crime, however, as he certainly did something illegal (e. g., battery). Attempt is a specific intent offense. This is so even if the target offense is of the general intent variety. For example, "breaking and entering" is a general intent offense; it has no specific mens rea requirement. Nevertheless, to be found guilty of attempted breaking and entering, the defendant must specifically intend to break and enter. This adds yet another layer of complexity to the mens rea of attempt.[1]

未遂的主观要素包括两个部分:(1)故意实施行为;(2)故意造成结果。故意实施行为是指罪犯必须意图实施某种明显行为以完成犯罪。针对结果的故意是指,被告还必须有造成实质性犯罪的意图。举例来说明一下,如果布莱恩计划射击拉里的膝盖,但并不想致其死亡,那么布莱恩就不满足谋杀未遂的犯罪意图。然而,布莱恩很可能会被判其他罪名,因为他肯定实施了非法行为(如殴打)。未遂罪属于具体故意犯罪,即使目标犯罪属于概括故意犯罪也是如此。例如,"非法侵入"属于概括故意犯罪,且没有具体的犯罪故意要求。然而,要判定为非法侵入未遂罪,被告必须有非法侵入的具体意图。这又给未遂罪的犯罪意图增加了更多复杂性。

8.2.2 The Actus Reus of Attempt and the Criteria(未遂客观行为及认定标准)

There is no uniformly accepted definition of actus reus for the crime of attempt. There are two reasons for this. First, the actus reus of attempt falls somewhere between "preparation" and "perpetration". But deciding where preparation ends and perpetration begins is rather difficult, especially since no one crime is the same as the next. Second, there is a greater inclination to find intent when the substantive offense is of the serious variety. For example, if a murder fails, most would agree that holding the offender accountable for attempted murder is desirable. However, if a petty theft fails, would there be much point in going to the ends of the earth to convict someone of attempting the crime? Probably not. The courts have formulated six tests for gauging the presence of actus reus in attempt crimes. They are complex, they overlap to some extent, and

---

[1] Jennifer L. Moore & John L. Worrall, *Criminal Law*, 2nd editon, Pearson Education Inc., 2018, p. 115.

they still leave unanswered the core question at hand: What is the actus reus of attempt? There simply is no clear answer; the tests merely offer some guidance. Dressler calls attention to six such tests: the "last act" test, the "physical proximity" test, the "dangerous proximity" test, the "indispensable element" test, the "probable desistance" test, and the "unequivocality" test. Additionally Modle Penal Code stipulated a substantial step test. We will consider each of these tests below.[1]

关于未遂罪的犯罪行为,没有一个统一的被认可的定义,原因有二。首先,未遂罪的犯罪行为介于"准备"和"实施"之间。但判断"准备"何时结束、"实施"何时开始是相当困难的,尤其是每一次犯罪的具体情况都不会相同。其次,当实质性犯罪属于严重犯罪时,法律更倾向于查证犯罪意图。例如,如果谋杀未遂,大多数人会同意以谋杀未遂罪追究罪犯的责任,这是不会引起质疑的。然而,如果小偷小摸的行为没有得逞,即使不惜一切代价证明了行为存在也意义不大。法院已经制定六种检验标准来衡量未遂罪中是否存在犯罪行为。这些标准都很复杂,且在一定程度上相互重合,而且都没有回答当前的核心问题:什么是未遂的犯罪行为?虽然对这个问题根本就没有明确的答案,但这些检验标准还是提供了一些指导。约书亚·德雷斯勒提出要高度重视法院制定的六种标准,即最后行为检验标准、实际接近检验标准、危险接近检验标准、不可或缺要素检验标准、可能放弃检验标准和明确性检验标准。此外,《模范刑法典》还提出了实质性步骤标准。下面,会对这些标准逐一进行阐述。

8.2.2.1 The Last Act Test(最后行为检验标准)

According to the last act test, the actus reus of attempt is satisfied once the defendant has committed the last act necessary to complete the target crime. This test is advantageous because it is basically "black and white." Unfortunately, however, to wait until the very last moment undermines the intent of criminalizing attempt. As one court put it, "[T]he law of attempts would be largely without function if it could not be invoked until the trigger was pulled, the blow struck, or the money seized." For this reason, there is a preference to move back in time from the completed crime to some earlier act.[2]

根据最后行为检验标准,一旦被告实施了完成目标犯罪所需的最后行为,即满足了未遂罪的客观行为要素。这一检验标准的优势在于其基本是"泾渭分明"的。

---

〔1〕 Jennifer L. Moore & John L. Worrall, *Criminal Law*, 2nd editon, Pearson Education Inc. ,2018, p. 115 - 116.

〔2〕 Jennifer L. Moore & John L. Worrall, *Criminal Law*, 2nd editon, Pearson Education Inc. , 2018, p. 116.

然而,不幸的是,等到最后一刻才惩罚,削弱了将犯罪未遂视为刑事犯罪的意义。正如一家法院所言,“如果在扣动扳机、实施打击或扣押钱财之前都不能援引未遂罪法规,那么未遂罪法规在很大程度上就失去了作用”。因此,人们倾向于将未遂行为成立的时间从已完成的行为回溯到更早的行为。

8.2.2.2　The Physical Proximity Test(实际接近检验标准)

According to the physical proximity test, the actus reus of attempt is satisfied once the offender is nearly able to commit the target crime. Moreover, the offender must be physically close to the intended victim, hence the test's name. A few court decisions have offered explicit definitions of physical proximity. For example, the defendant's action must go so far that it would result, or apparently result in the actual commission of the crime it was designed to effect, if not extrinsically hindered or frustrated by extraneous circumstances.[1]

根据实际接近检验标准,一旦犯罪者几乎能够实施目标犯罪,即构成未遂罪。此外,犯罪者必须实际接近预定的受害者,这也是该检验标准名称的由来。一些法院判决对“实际接近”进行了明确定义,例如,被告的行为必须达到这样的程度,即如果没有外在情况的妨碍或阻挠,将会导致或明显导致实际实施其计划实施的罪行。

8.2.2.3　The Dangerous Proximity Test(危险接近检验标准)

According to this test, the actus reus of intent is satisfied once the individual's conduct is in dangerous proximity to success. Alternatively, an attempt is said to occur when the act is so near to the result that the danger of success is very great. The dangerous proximity test requires only a high degree of likelihood that the target offense will be completed.[2]

根据危险接近检验标准,一旦个人的行为危险地接近成功,即满足了犯罪意图支配下的行为性。或者说,当行为如此接近结果,以至于既遂的危险非常大时,就可以说是未遂。危险接近标准只要求目标犯罪完成的可能性很大。

8.2.2.4　The Indispensable Element Test(不可或缺要素检验标准)

The “indispensable element” test looks not at proximity to crime completion, but rather at what, if anything, is lacking such that the crime could not be completed. The tests focus on whether the defendant has control of everything that he or she needs to

---

〔1〕 Jennifer L. Moore & John L. Worrall, *Criminal Law*, 2nd editon, Pearson Education Inc., 2018, p. 116.

〔2〕 Jennifer L. Moore & John L. Worrall, *Criminal Law*, 2nd editon, Pearson Education Inc., 2018, p. 116.

complete the crime. For example, in State v. Addor, the defendants apparently intended to manufacture illegal liquor, but they lacked a still. Since the still was an indispensable element (liquor could not be made without it), the men were not guilty of attempting to manufacture illegal liquor.[1]

不可或缺要素检验标准不是看犯罪是否接近完成,而是看行为缺少哪些要素(如果有的话)会导致犯罪无法完成。该检验标准的重点是被告是否控制了完成犯罪所需的一切条件。例如,在州诉艾多案中,被告显然打算制造非法酒类,但他们缺少蒸馏器。由于没有蒸馏器就无法酿酒,对于制造非法酒类而言,蒸馏器是不可或缺的要素。因此,在该案中,被告制造非法烈酒未遂罪不成立。

8.2.2.5 The Probable Desistance Test(可能放弃检验标准)

This test looks at the likelihood of the offender stopping once the wheels have been set in motion. The American Law Institute came up with this test, noting that attempt occurs when "the actor... reached a point where it was unlikely that he would have voluntarily desisted from his effort to commit the crime". Understood differently, the probable desistance test looks at the proverbial point of no return. If the offender reaches it but fails to complete the target offense, attempt occurs. The Wisconsin Supreme Court put it this way: "The defendant's conduct must pass that point where most men, holding such an intention as the defendant holds, would think better of their conduct and desist." Unfortunately, it is difficult for juries to draw conclusions about the offender's subjective motivations. It is rarely clear to anyone exactly what is going on in the defendant's head, making this test somewhat limited.[2]

该检验标准考察的是犯罪者一旦开始行动就会停止的可能性。美国法学会提出了这一检验标准,并指出,当行为人达到不可能自愿放弃犯罪努力的程度时,即为未遂。从另一个角度来理解,可能放弃检验标准注重众所周知的"不归点"。如果罪犯抵达这一点,但未能完成目标罪行,就构成未遂。威斯康星州最高法院认为:"被告行为必须超过这样一个点,即大多数人在怀有与被告相同意图的情况下,会对自己行为做出更好的考虑并停止行动的临界点。"但遗憾的是,陪审团很难就罪犯的主观动机得出结论。很少有人能清楚地知道被告脑袋里究竟想些什么,使得这一检验标准具有一定的局限性。

---

〔1〕 Jennifer L. Moore & John L. Worrall, *Criminal Law*, 2nd editon, Pearson Education Inc., 2018, p. 116.

〔2〕 Jennifer L. Moore & John L. Worrall, *Criminal Law*, 2nd editon, Pearson Education Inc., 2018, p. 116.

8.2.2.6　The Unequivocality Test(明确性检验标准)

Simply put, the unequivocality test holds that attempt occurs when it is no longer ambiguous to an ordinary person what the would - be offender intends. That is, an attempt occurs when it becomes clear what the actor's intention is and when the acts done show that the perpetrator is actually putting his plan into action. As with the rest of the tests, this one is also ambiguous. It may not always be clear when an individual intends to commit a crime.[1]

简单地说,明确性检验标准认为,当一个普通人对潜在犯罪者的意图不再感到模棱两可时,未遂即成立。也就是说,当行为人的意图变得非常明显,其所实施的行为表明行为人实际上正在将其计划付诸实施时,未遂即成立了。与其他检验标准一样,这个检验标准也是模棱两可的。因为,一个人何时计划犯罪并不总是非常清晰。

8.2.2.7　The Model Penal Code Substantial Step(《模范刑法典》的实质性步骤检验标准)

The Model Penal Code's substantial step provision stipulates that to establish an attempt to commit a crime, the actor must have taken substantial steps towards the commission of the crime, which strongly indicates the defendant's criminal purpose. Examples of a "substantial step" include "lying in wait", "enticing or seeking to entice" the intended victim to a particular location, and unlawfully entering a structure in which the intended crime is to occur.[2]

《模范刑法典》的实质性步骤检验标准规定,要认定未犯罪未遂,必须是行为人已采取了实质性步骤,而且必须能充分地证实被告的犯罪目的。实质性步骤的例子包括埋伏、引诱或试图引诱预定受害人到达特定地点,以及非法进入预定犯罪发生的建筑物。

8.2.3　Defenses to Attempt(未遂罪的辩护理由)

One who is charged with a crime of attempt can assert almost any criminal defense. However, two defenses are unique to attempts: impossibility and abandonment. Both defenses are akin to those associated with accomplice liability, as discussed in Chapter 7, but they function differently within the context of attempt crimes. These defenses will

〔1〕 Jennifer L. Moore & John L. Worrall, *Criminal Law*, 2nd editon, Pearson Education Inc., 2018, p. 116.

〔2〕 Jennifer L. Moore & John L. Worrall, *Criminal Law*, 2nd editon, Pearson Education Inc., 2018, p. 116.

be elaborated upon below.[1]

被控未遂罪的人几乎可以提出任何刑事辩护。然而,有两个辩护理由是未遂罪所特有的:不能犯和中止犯。这两个辩护理由与第7章的共犯责任辩护理由相类似,但在未遂案件中它们的运作方式略有不同。下面,将对其分别予以阐述。

8.2.3.1 Impossibility(不能犯)

Impossibility refers to situations where it is impossible for a defendant to have committed the attempted crime in question. For example, if an adult male enters an Internet chat room and carries on a discussion with someone who he thinks is an underage female but is actually a law enforcement officer, then he sends obscene photographs of himself to the undercover officer, can he be guilty of attempted distribution of obscene materials to a minor? The answer is not cut - and - dried, but clearly the person who received the images in our hypothetical was not a minor. Such is the essence of the defense of impossibility.[2]

不能犯是指在某些情况下,被告不可能实施有关的犯罪未遂。例如,如果一名成年男子进入互联网聊天室,与其认为的某个未成年女孩聊天,但实际该女孩是由执法者假扮的,然后该男子将自己的淫秽照片发送给这位实际是卧底执法者的女孩,他是否会被判向未成年人传播淫秽物品未遂罪?答案并非没有争议,但在我们假想的案件中,收到照片的人显然不是未成年人。这就是其以不能犯辩护的实质理由。

The courts recognize two types of impossibility: factual impossibility and legal impossibility. Factual impossibility occurs when "extraneous circumstances unknown to the actor or beyond his control prevent consummation of the intended crime". A classic example of this is when a person reaches into the pocket of another to steal a wallet, but there is no wallet in the pocket. Legal impossibility is said to occur where the intended acts, even if completed, would not amount to a crime. Legal impossibility exists when: (1) The motive, desire, and expectation are to perform an act in violation of the law. (2) There is intention to perform a physical act. (3) There is a performance of the intended physical act. (4) The consequence resulting from the intended act does not amount to a crime.

法院承认两种不能犯即事实不能犯和法律不能犯。事实不能犯是指行为人未

[1] Jennifer L. Moore & John L. Worrall, *Criminal Law*, 2nd editon, Pearson Education Inc., 2018, p. 117.

[2] Jennifer L. Moore & John L. Worrall, *Criminal Law*, 2nd editon, Pearson Education Inc., 2018, p. 117 - 118.

知或无法控制的外在情况阻止预期犯罪的完成。典型的例子就是，某人将手伸进另一个人的口袋偷取钱包，但口袋里并没有钱包。法律不能犯是指预期行为即使完成也不会构成犯罪。法律不能犯成立的条件有：(1) 动机、愿望和期望是实施违法行为；(2) 有实施身体行为的意图；(3) 实施了意图实施的身体行为；(4) 意图行为造成的后果不构成犯罪。

Some examples of legal impossibility include the following: (1) If A takes an umbrella the he believes belongs to B, but that in fact is his own, his actions do not constitute a crime. It is not a crime to take your own umbrella. (2) If a man, mistaking a dummy in female dress for a woman, tries to ravish it, he does not have the intent to commit rape since the ravishment of an inanimate object cannot be rape. (3) If a man mistakes a stump for his enemy and shoots at it, notwithstanding his desire and expectation to shoot his enemy, his intent is to shoot the object aimed at, which is the stump.[1]

下面举三个法律不能犯的例子：(1) 如果 A 拿了一把自认为属于 B 的雨伞，但实际是 A 的雨伞，那么 A 的行为不构成犯罪，因为拿走自己的雨伞不构成犯罪。(2) 如果某男将一个穿着女士服装的假人误认为女人，并试图奸淫它。但此男没有强奸的故意，因为奸淫一个没有生命的物体不能构成强奸罪。(3) 如果某人将树桩误认为敌人并向其射击，尽管他渴望射杀敌人，但他的意图是射杀所瞄准的物体，即树桩。

Legal impossibility is often regarded as a defense to attempt, while factual impossibility is not. If, for example, a person commits an act thinking it is illegal when it is not, this is the textbook case of legal impossibility. Because there is no law criminalizing the act, it is legally impossible for it to occur. More difficult is the situation in which the intended result is a criminal act, but the actor's actions fall short. In Wilson v. State, Wilson was prosecuted for and convicted of forgery because he added a "1" to the amount on a check written to him for $2.50, making it $12.50. However, he did not alter the writing on the check. Under existing law at the time, he altered an "immaterial" part of the check; for forgery to have occurred, he must have also altered the written part, changing it from "Two and 50/100" to "Twelve and 50/

[1] Jennifer L. Moore & John L. Worrall, *Criminal Law*, 2nd editon, Pearson Education Inc., 2018, p. 118.

100"—or similar.[1] Therefore, Wilson appealed on this ground. The Court of Appeals upheld Wilson's defence, leading to the overturning of his conviction.

法律不能犯通常被视为未遂的辩护理由,而事实不能犯则不能。举例来说,如果一个人实施了一项行为,他认为它是非法的,但事实上其实施的行为并不构成犯罪,这就是法律不能犯的典型案例。因为没有法律将该行为规定为犯罪,所以在法律上不可能发生犯罪。更困难的情况是,预期的结果是犯罪行为,但行为人的行为没有达到预期结果。威尔逊诉州政府一案就属于这种情况,在该案中,威尔逊被起诉并被判犯伪造罪,因为他在一张写给他的 2.50 美元的支票上添加了一个"1",使金额变成了 12.50 美元。然而,他并没有更改支票上的文字。根据当时法律,他篡改的是支票上不重要的部分;如果要认定伪造,他还必须篡改书面部分,将其从"2 and 50/100"改为"12 and 50/100"或类似内容。因此,威尔逊以此为理由提出上诉。上诉法院认可了威尔逊的辩护事由,使威尔逊的定罪被推翻。

More difficult is what Dressler calls "hybrid legal impossibility". This occurs when an accused makes a factual mistake about the legal status of some detail of the crime. A classic example is when a person shoots a corpse, thinking it is alive. The factual mistake is thinking the corpse is a living, breathing person. The legal mistake is basically the same, because to be convicted of homicide, the key requirement is that a "human being" be killed. In cases like these, to keep things simple, courts will default to factual instead of legal impossibility and deny the defense. The reason should be clear. In our example, a person who shoots a corpse thinking it is a living person is intent on killing another person; to clear that person of any wrongdoing would undermine efforts to criminalize attempted wrongdoing.[2]

更困难的是德雷斯勒所说的"混合法律不能犯",也就是某种不能犯既是法律不能犯,也是事实不能犯。当被告对犯罪某些细节的法律地位存在事实认识错误时,就会出现这种情况。典型例子就是,某人以为一具尸体还活着,就开枪射击尸体。事实错误是将尸体误认为是活人。法律认识错误基本是一样的,因为要被判定构成杀人罪,关键要求是"人"被杀死。此类案件中,为了使事情简单化,法院会默认其是事实不能犯而不是法律不能犯,并拒绝接受辩护。理由应该很清楚:在我们的例子中,某人射杀了一具误以为是活人的尸体,此人就是蓄意杀害他人;为其洗脱罪行会

---

〔1〕 Jennifer L. Moore & John L. Worrall, *Criminal Law*, 2nd editon, Pearson Education Inc., 2018, p. 118.

〔2〕 Jennifer L. Moore & John L. Worrall, *Criminal Law*, 2nd editon, Pearson Education Inc., 2018, p. 119.

破坏将未遂不法行为定为刑事犯罪的努力。

Factual impossibility, on the other hand, is generally not regarded as a defense to the crime of attempt. For example, just because an abortionist (assuming abortion is illegal in the jurisdiction in question) attempts to remove a fetus from a nonpregnant woman, should we absolve that person of all guilt? Clearly, there was intent to commit the crime. Alternatively, if a wouldbe killer points a gun at his intended victim, pulls the trigger, and then realizes it is not loaded, should he be cleared of any wrongdoing? Probably not, as he certainly had the intent—and tried—to kill. However, in some cases, especially when it is an "inherent impossibility", the courts of some states consider it a defence. What if a would - be terrorist tries to bring down a skyscraper with a firecracker? Would it be sensible to find him guilty of an attempt crime? According to at least one state (Minnesota), the answer is no. Minnesota recognizes a defense of inherent impossibility, which is a form of factual impossibility. If the actor "uses means which a reasonable person would view as completely inappropriate to the objectives sought", that person can successfully assert a factual impossibility defense. But the courts in every other state take the opposite approach, which the Nevada Supreme Court summarized in this way,〔1〕 even though the actual commission of the substantive crime is impossible because of circumstances unknown to the defendant, he is guilty of an attempt if he has the specific intent to commit the substantive offense, and under the circumstances, as he reasonably sees them, he does the acts necessary to consummate what would be the attempted crime. It is only when the results intended by the actor, if they happened as envisaged by him, would fail to consummate a crime, then and only then, would his actions fail to constitute an attempt.〔2〕

另外,事实不能犯一般不被视为未遂罪的辩护理由。例如,仅仅因为堕胎者(假设堕胎在有关司法管辖区是非法的)试图从未孕妇女体内取出胎儿,我们就应该免除此人的所有罪责吗?显然不能,因为此人有犯罪意图。反过来说,如果一个杀人犯把枪口对准目标受害人,扣动扳机,然后发现枪里没有子弹,他是否就可以洗脱罪名呢?也许不能,因为他肯定具有杀人的意图,而且试图杀人。但在某些情况下,尤其是事实不能犯是属于"固有的不可能"的事实时,有些州的法院则认为其可作为抗

〔1〕 Jennifer L. Moore & John L. Worrall, *Criminal Law*, 2nd editon, Pearson Education Inc., 2018, p. 119.

〔2〕 Jennifer L. Moore & John L. Worrall, *Criminal Law*, 2nd editon, Pearson Education Inc., 2018, p. 119.

辩事由。如果一个潜在的恐怖分子试图用鞭炮炸毁一座摩天大楼呢？认定他构成未遂罪是明智的吗？至少有一个州，即明尼苏达州认为答案是否定的。明尼苏达州坚持“固有的不可能性”这一辩护理由，规定其为事实不能犯的一种形式。如果行为人“使用了一个有理智的人会认为与所追求的目标完全不相称的手段”，那么此人就可以以“事实不能犯”作为辩护理由，且该辩护事由会获得认可。但其他各州的法院则采取相反的做法，比如内华达州。内华达州认为：最高法院对此进行总结，即使因被告所未知的情形导致其不可能实际完成实质性犯罪，但如果他有实施实质性犯罪的具体故意，在其能理性认识到的某些情况下，他实施了对于完成企图实施犯罪而言必需的行为，那么被告就成立未遂罪。只有当行为人期盼的结果即使按照其所设想的发生也将无法完成犯罪时，其行为才不构成未遂罪。

8.2.3.2 Abandonment（中止犯）

If a would – be offender abandons his or her attempt to commit a crime, should he or she be cleared of any wrongdoing? In general, the answer is no; most courts do not recognize a defense of abandonment in the attempt context. But there are exceptions. For example, if the defendant completely and voluntary has a change of heart, the defense may succeed. Consider the facts as explained by the court in Pyle v. State:

如果潜在的罪犯放弃其犯罪企图，是否应免除其任何不法性？一般来说，答案是否定的；在未遂的语境下，大多数法院是不承认中止抗辩事由的。但也有例外，例如，如果被告彻底地自愿改变主意，那么辩护就可能成功。下面以法院在“派尔诉州政府”一案中对事实的解释对此进行说明。

At 1:15 p. m. on October 7, 1981, the appellant arrived at a residence occupied by Mary and Sally. Mary was his former girlfriend. After being invited to enter, he pulled a gun on the women and ordered Mary to wrap and padlock chains around herself. Thereafter, he ordered Mary to handcuff Sally to a bannister. He then forced Mary into his van and drove away with her. Sally liberated herself 15 minutes later and called the police. Meanwhile, the appellant spent the next six hours driving to Defiance, Ohio, and then back to Fort Wayne, Indiana. During the trip, he repeatedly told Mary that if the police stopped the van, he would empty six bullets into her head. Eventually, a police car signaled the van to stop. Consequently, the appellant exclaimed, “we're caught”, and proceeded to pull over to the side of the road. Subsequently, he grabbed the gun, said “good bye Mary”, and shot her in the chest. He then surrendered to the police.

1981 年 10 月 7 日下午 1 时 15 分，上诉人来到玛丽和莎莉的住所。玛丽是他的前女友。上诉人应邀进入住所后，用枪指着两位女士，命令玛丽在自己身上缠上铁链并挂上锁。随后，又命令玛丽将莎莉铐在栏杆上。然后，强迫玛丽上了他的面包车，并开车带她离开。15 分钟后，莎莉挣脱锁铐并报警。与此同时，上诉人花了 6 个小时驾车前往俄亥俄州迪芬斯，然后又返回印第安纳州韦恩堡。途中，他多次告诉玛丽，如果警察拦下面包车，他将用六颗子弹打爆她的头。最后，一辆警车示意面包车停下。于是上诉人大喊"我们被抓了"，将车停在路边，拿起枪，说了声"再见，玛丽"，就朝玛丽胸部开了一枪。随后，上诉人向警方自首。

Mary did not die but, rather, suffered a serious wound. The defendant was found guilty of attempted murder. He appealed, claiming that he did not intend, at the last minute, for Mary to die and only wanted to inflict a superficial wound. The court did not accept his argument and affirmed his conviction, noting that he evidenced no "rising revulsion for the harm intended". Likewise, if a would - be offender abandons his or her attempted crime in the face of victim resistance, he or she will not succeed with an abandonment defense, as it is not voluntary. For an abandonment claim to succeed, then, the offender must genuinely and completely withdraw from his or her efforts to break the law—and convince a jury of it.[1]

玛丽并没有死亡，只是受了重伤。被告被判谋杀未遂。他提出上诉，声称自己在最后一刻并没有打算让玛丽死亡，只是想造成皮外伤。法院对被告的说法并不买账，并且指出他没有表现出对伤害意图的强烈反感，因此被告的中止抗辩没成功，法院维持原判。同样，如果犯罪嫌疑人是因被害人的反抗而放弃自己的犯罪企图，那么其中止辩护也不会成功，因为这不是自愿的。因此，犯罪中止辩护要想成功，罪犯必须真正地、完全地放弃其非法行为，并获得陪审团的认同。

■ Curriculum Ideology and Politics（课程思政）

The essence of punishing attempted crimes in Anglo - American criminal law is to penalize the mens rea of those who have not completed the crime. Similarly, the punishment of conspiracy and solicitation is fundamentally based on the presence of mens rea. Therefore, imposing criminal liability for attempts, conspiracies, and solicitations is aimed at crime prevention, which holds positive significance. Consequently, students are guided to expand the depth of their professional knowledge and improve their ability

---

[1] Jennifer L. Moore & John L. Worrall, *Criminal Law*, 2nd editon, Pearson Education Inc. ,2018, p. 119 - 120.

to discern through the cognition of appearances and main intentions.

英美刑法处罚未遂犯,究其本质,就是处罚未完成犯罪者的主观罪过。而后文所讨论的共谋罪和教唆罪之所以被惩罚,实质上也依据的是主观可责罚性。因此,给未遂罪、共谋罪及教唆罪施加刑事责任,旨在预防犯罪,这具有积极意义。由此,引导学生通过对表象和主要旨意的认知,扩展其专业知识的深度和提升辨析的能力。

8.3 Conspiracy(共谋罪)

Conspiracy is a type of inchoate crime, but it also closely resembles complicity because one person (or multiple people) can be held criminally liable for the actions of someone else. Under common law, a conspiracy was defined as an agreement between two or more persons to commit a criminal act. The early common law's approach was "bilateral", in reference to the minimum requirement that two or more people be involved in the conspiracy. Thus, if one person entered into an agreement with an undercover police officer to break the law, there was no conspiracy because there were not two guilty parties. Modern statutes, however, take a "unilateral" approach, which permits the conviction of any person who agrees with another to commit a crime, even if only one party to the agreement breaks the law.

共谋是一种未完成犯罪,但它也与共同犯罪非常相似,因为一个人(或多人)可能要为其他人的行为承担刑事责任。在普通法中,共谋被定义为两人或多人之间达成的实施犯罪行为的协议。早期的普通法的做法是双边的协议,即至少要求两人或多人参与共谋。根据这种观点,如果一人与卧底警官达成违法协议,则不存在共谋,因为没有两个有罪方。现代立法采用"单边"协议,允许对与他人达成犯罪协议的任何人定罪,即使协议中只有一方违法。

Under common law, nothing other than the agreement was necessary. Under modern statutes, however, it is often required that the prosecutor prove that those who entered into the agreement actually took some step in furtherance of the agreement—called an overt act. For example, if Susan and Margie agreed on a plan to kill Mike, this would be conspiracy under common law. If they went one step further and acquired a gun, then this is the "overt act" part of modern conspiracies. There are exceptions to the overt act requirement, however. On the one hand, the United States Supreme Court has held, with respect to federal drug laws, that an overt act is not necessary for a conspiracy to be completed. On the other hand, some states require a "substantial act", which is more significant than an overt act. This is the difference between the common law and the modern law on conspiracy. In terms of its constituent elements, conspiracy is composed of the mens rea of conspiracy and the actus reus of conspiracy, and these basic components are described next in turn.

普通法规定,除协议外无须其他证据就可成立共谋。然而,现代立法则通常要求检察官证明达成协议的人实际上采取了某些步骤来推进协议,即具有表征性行为。例如,苏珊和玛吉就杀死迈克的计划达成一致意见,根据普通法,这就是共谋。如果他们更进一步,购买了枪支,那么这就是现代立法中的共谋的表征性行为部分。不过,表征性行为要求也有例外。一方面,美国联邦最高法院在联邦毒品法方面认为,共谋完成并不需要表征性行为。另一方面,一些州要求实质性行为,这比表征性行为要求更高。这就是普通法和现代立法对共谋的不同规定。

从构成要素来看,共谋是由共谋的犯罪意图和共谋的客观行为两大部分组成的,接下来将依次介绍这些基本组成部分。

8.3.1 The Mens Rea of Conspiracy(共谋的犯罪意图)

Under common law, conspiracy was a specific intent crime. Today, it is regarded in basically the same fashion. First, the defendant must intend to enter into an agreement with one or more others to commit a crime. Second, the defendant must have intended to commit the target offense. Note the similarity between conspiracy mens rea and complicity mens rea. There is some question about what intent means. Is it the defendant's conscious objective to commit the target crime? Or is it sufficient if the defendant simply knows it is likely to happen? At the risk of casting too wide a net, courts typically prefer to equate intent with purpose. However, knowledge may suffice. For example, in Direct Sales Co. v. United States, the defendant, a drug wholesaler, sold morphine to a physician in quantities 300 times higher than those that would have been required for lawful purposes. The court held, that the evidence, from which it could be inferred that the seller not only knew the physician was selling the drug illegally but intended to cooperate with him therein, was sufficient to sustain the seller's conviction of conspiracy. In another case, the court held that defendants who sold sugar, an important ingredient in whisky, to persons who they knew were manufacturing illegal whiskey had their convictions affirmed. So, while the defendants in these cases may not have intended for customers to break the law, they surely knew what the buyers were doing.[1] This means that as long as there is "knowledge", there is a subjective guilt of conspiracy.

普通法规定,共谋是一种具体意图犯罪。如今,人们对它的看法基本相同,尽管对于客观行为要素有些分歧。对于主观罪过方面,需要进一步探讨。首先,被告必须故意与一人或多人达成犯罪协议。其次,被告必须故意实施目标罪行。注意共犯犯罪意图与共谋犯罪意图的相似性。对于故意的含义存在一些疑问。被告是否有意地以实施目标罪行为目的?还是被告仅仅明知有可能发生就足矣?冒着扩大惩罚范围的风险,法院通常倾向于将故意等同于蓄意。然而,这导致仅具有明知就可能足以构成犯罪。以直销公司诉美国案为例,被告是一名药品批发商,向一名医生出售吗啡的数量比合法用途所需的数量足足高出300倍。法院认为,出卖方不仅知道医生非法销售药物,而且还打算与医生合作的证据足以支持对卖方予以共谋定罪。在另一起案件中,法院认为,被告明知顾客制造非法威士忌,而仍然向其销售一种制作威士忌所需的重要原料(白糖),因此判其有罪。尽管这些案件的被告可能没有让顾客触犯法律的故意,但他们肯定明知买家的所作所为。这意味着,只要具备"明知",就具备了共谋罪的主观罪过。

8.3.2 The Actus Reus of Conspiracy

The actus reus of conspiracy consists of two parts. First, and most importantly, there must be an agreement to commit a crime. Second, in a number of states, it is also necessary that the parties to the conspiracy commit an "overt act" in furtherance of the agreement. Once again, common law did not require this second actus reus element, but modern statutes frequently do.[2]

共谋的犯罪行为由两部分组成。首先,也是最重要的一点,必须有一项犯罪协议。其次,在一些州,共谋各方还必须实施表征性行为以推进协议。同样,普通法并不要求第二个行为要素,但现代法规经常要求必备第二个要素。下面,将对这两个要素分别进行简要阐述。

8.3.2.1 The Agreement (犯罪协议)

The agreement to commit a crime between two or more people can take a number of forms. It may be an express agreement. For example Jim could say to John, "Let's kill Bob". It may also be an unspoken agreement. John could look at Jim, nod his head in

---

[1] Jennifer L. Moore & John L. Worrall, *Criminal Law*, 2nd editon, Pearson Education Inc. ,2018, p. 122.

[2] Jennifer L. Moore & John L. Worrall, *Criminal Law*, 2nd editon, Pearson Education Inc. ,2018, p. 122 – 123.

Bob's direction, and then be present when Jim kills Bob. Indeed, John may be nowhere around and still be convicted of a crime because he gave an earlier order to Jim that he "take care of Bob". In this instance, a "conspiracy may exist even if a conspirator does not agree to commit or facilitate each and every part of the substantive offense". For example, that Jim decides to hire his own "hit man" to kill Bob. Even though John is arguably not aware of this, he is a party to a conspiracy because of that simple order to "take care of Bob".〔1〕

二人或多人之间的犯罪协议有多种形式。可以是一种明确的协议,比如,吉姆对约翰说:我们杀了鲍勃吧。也可以是一种无言的协议,比如,约翰看着吉姆,朝鲍勃的方向点点头,然后也留在吉姆杀死鲍勃的现场。事实上,约翰可能根本不在现场,但仍被判有罪,因为他早先曾命令吉姆杀死鲍勃。在这种情况下,即使共谋者不同意实施或协助实质性犯罪的每一部分,共谋也可能成立。例如,吉姆决定雇佣杀手杀死鲍勃。尽管约翰可能并不知道吉姆雇凶杀人这件事,但由于他下达"解决鲍勃"的简单命令,所以他也是共谋的一方。

Most conspiracies are relatively secret, at least beyond the parties to the agreement. This, it would seem, could make it difficult for a prosecutor to prove the presence of a conspiracy. After all, how could a prosecutor prove the existence of something that no one besides the parties to the agreement knows about? Fortunately, the courts are quite flexible in terms of the evidence that can be used to prove the existence of an agreement to commit a crime. As one court observed, "[B]ecause of the clandestine nature of a conspiracy and the foreseeable difficulty of the prosecution's burden of establishing the conspiracy by direct proof, the courts have permitted broad inferences to be drawn... from evidence of acts, conduct, and circumstances."〔2〕 Hearsay, circumstantial evidence, and the like are admissible. Yet the government must also ensure that defendants' due process rights are not violated in its zeal to prove the presence of conspiratorial agreements.〔3〕

大多数共谋都是相对秘密的,至少对于协议各方之外的其他人而言是如此的。这似乎会使检察官难以证明共谋的存在。毕竟,除了协议各方之外,检察官是难以

〔1〕 Jennifer L. Moore & John L. Worrall, *Criminal Law*, 2nd editon, Pearson Education Inc., 2018, p. 123.

〔2〕 People v. Persinger, 363 N. E. 2d 897 (Ⅲ. App. Ct. 5th Dist. 1977).

〔3〕 Jennifer L. Moore & John L. Worrall, *Criminal Law*, 2nd editon, Pearson Education Inc., 2018, p. 123.

证明不为人知的事情是存在的。幸运的是,法院对于证明存在犯罪协议的证据方面采取了相当灵活的方法。正如一家法院所指出的,由于共谋的秘密性质以及控方通过直接证据证明共谋责任的显而易见的困难,法院允许根据行为、举止和情节的证据中进行广泛的推断。甚至道听途说、间接证据等均可采纳。然而,政府也必须确保被告的正当程序权利不会因热衷于证明存在共谋协议而受到侵犯。

8.3.2.2 The Overt Act(表征性行为)

The overt act requirement for the actus reus of conspiracy is relatively recent in its origins. Not every jurisdiction requires proof of an overt act, but logic for such a requirement is straightforward; it offers evidence that a conspiracy has moved beyond the "talk stage" and is actively being carried out. There is no requirement that the overt act be illegal. Indeed, it can be perfectly legal. The example we offered is purchasing a gun. Assuming there is no law against doing so (or the person is barred by law from buying a gun), there is nothing criminal about such an act. There is also no requirement that all parties to a conspiracy commit an overt act. If one party to a larger conspiracy commits the overt act, no other action is necessary. What exactly is an overt act? In jurisdictions that require an overt act, any act will suffice. No matter how trivial the action, it will meet the overt act requirement. For example, Steve and Mary agree to kill Sandy. If Steve calls Sandy to see if she is home, he has committed an overt act taken in furtherance of the agreement. Although the phone call is far more innocuous than, say, buying a gun. Nevertheless, Steve did something in furtherance of the agreement, which is all it takes.[1]

共谋犯罪的表征性行为要求起源较晚。并非每个司法管辖区都要求提供表征性行为的证据。但这一要件的逻辑简单明了;根据它提供的证据,证明共谋已经超越了谈论阶段,并且共谋者正在积极实施计划。没有要求表征性行为必须是非法的,事实上,"表征性行为"完全可以是合法的。以购买枪支为例,假设没有法律禁止购买枪支(或法律禁止个人购买枪支),那么这种行为就属于合法行为。同时,也没有要求共谋的所有各方都实施表征性行为。如果具有很多共谋犯的一方实施了表征性行为,则无须其再采取其他行动。究竟什么是表征性行为?"表征性行为"其实是一个模糊的概念,这导致在把其作为要件的司法管辖区,任何行为都足以构成共谋。无论多么微不足道的行为,都能满足表征性行为的要求。例如,史蒂夫和玛丽同意杀死桑迪,如果史蒂夫打电话给桑迪询问她是否在家,他就实施了促进协议的

---

〔1〕 Jennifer L. Moore & John L. Worrall, *Criminal Law*, 2nd editon, Pearson Education Inc., 2018, p. 123.

表征性行为,即便这个电话比买枪等行为要无害得多。史蒂夫打电话的行为就是推进共谋杀人协议的表征性行为,构成共谋罪。

As mentioned at the outset of this section, some jurisdictions require a substantial act or a substantial step in lieu of an overt act. For example, Washington State's conspiracy statute reads, in part, that a person is guilty of criminal conspiracy when, with intent that conduct constituting a crime be performed, he or she agrees with one or more persons to engage in or cause the performance of such conduct, and any one of them takes a substantial step in pursuance of such agreement. Just what, then, is a substantial step? One court defined it as conduct that is strongly corroborative of the actor's criminal purpose. Moreover, the substantial step need not be the last proximate act prior to the consummation of the offense. This definition is clearly subjective, meaning that courts decide what constitutes a substantial step on a case – by – case basis. For example, Mike, who mistakenly believed that an off – duty police officer was the person who previously threatened him, pointed a shotgun in the officer's direction and threatened to blow his head off. This action constituted a substantial step in furtherance of the crime. On the other hand, some jurisdictions have deemed preparatory acts, such as casing a building, as substantial steps. Clearly, there is much room for interpretation.[1]

如本节开头所述,一些司法管辖区要求以实质性行为或实质性步骤代替表征性行为。例如,华盛顿州的共谋成文法规定:"如果某人意图实施构成犯罪的行为,他或她与一人或多人达成从事或导致实施该行为的协议,且其中任何一人为履行该协议采取了实质性步骤,该人即犯有共谋罪。"但何为实质性步骤?一家法院将其定义为:"强烈佐证行为人犯罪目的"的行为。此外,实质性步骤"不一定是犯罪完成之前的最后一个近似行为"。这一定义显然是主观的,这意味着法院要根据具体案件来决定什么是实质性步骤。例如,迈克误以为一名下班的警官就是之前威胁他的人,于是用猎枪指着警官,威胁要"打爆他的头"。这一行为构成了进一步实施犯罪的实质性步骤。除此之外,一些司法管辖区认为预备行为也是实质性步骤,如对建筑物进行踩点。显然,"实质步骤"的判断标准,也是有很大争议的。

---

[1] Jennifer L. Moore & John L. Worrall, *Criminal Law*, 2nd editon, Pearson Education Inc. ,2018, p. 123 – 124.

8.3.3 Conspiracy Defenses（共谋的辩护理由）

There are four defenses to conspiracy. As you will recall from earlier in this chapter, two of them—abandonment and impossibility—are also defenses to attempt. The others—withdrawal and Wharton's rule—are somewhat unique to conspiracy.[1]

共谋有四种辩护理由。这四种辩护事由包括前述提及的中止、不能犯、脱离原则和沃顿规则。其中，中止、不能犯在前面的未遂罪中已有论及，但脱离原则和沃顿规则却是共谋所特有的辩护理由。

8.3.3.1 Abandonment（中止）

Since the essence of conspiracy is an agreement, once the agreement is made, the proverbial horse has already left the barn. In other words, once a crime has been committed, it cannot be "undone". For this reason, there is usually no abandonment defense to a conspiracy charge. This is true regardless of whether an overt act is a requirement for a conspiracy conviction. That said, abandonment may work as something of a defense to charges for subsequent crimes arising from a conspiratorial agreement; if one party to a conspiracy withdraws and then finds himself or herself charged with conspiracy for crimes committed after such withdrawal, then the defense may succeed.[2]

由于共谋的本质是一种协商，一旦协议达成，就如同俗话所言的，"木已成舟，米已成炊"。基于此原因，被告通常不能以中止共谋为辩护理由。无论表征性行为是否是共谋定罪的必要条件，都是如此。尽管如此，中止可以作为某些辩护理由，可以作为因共谋协议而引起的后继犯罪的辩护。如果共谋的一方撤销协议，然后发现自己因撤销协议后所犯的罪行而被控共谋，则中止辩护理由可能成立。

The Model Penal Code calls this defense "renunciation." For it to apply, two conditions must be met. First, the defendant must have thwarted the success of the conspiracy. Second, the abandonment must have been complete and voluntary. For example, Larry is a party to a murder conspiracy with Frank and tells police that he can no longer see it through, he may succeed with the defense if the police are able to prevent Frank (such as by arresting him) from committing the crime.[3]

---

〔1〕 Jennifer L. Moore & John L. Worrall, *Criminal Law*, 2nd editon, Pearson Education Inc., 2018, p. 127.

〔2〕 Jennifer L. Moore & John L. Worrall, *Criminal Law*, 2nd editon, Pearson Education Inc., 2018, p. 127.

〔3〕 Jennifer L. Moore & John L. Worrall, *Criminal Law*, 2nd editon, Pearson Education Inc., 2018, p. 127.

《模范刑法典》将这种辩护称为“放弃”。若要适用,必须满足两个条件。第一,被告必须“阻止了共谋的完成”。第二,放弃的成立必须是“完全自愿的”。例如,拉里是与弗兰克共谋杀人的一方,但后面拉里告诉警方他无法再“坚持到底”,那么如果警方能够阻止弗兰克(如逮捕他)实施犯罪,其后若拉里以“放弃了共谋”作为辩护事由,他就可以成功辩护。

8.3.3.2　Impossibility(不能犯)

Although impossibility rarely comes up in a conspiracy context, it is a possible defense in certain contexts. Assume that Jack and Jill just bought a new mattress to replace their tired, worn – out one. They notice on the side of the mattress a tag that says, “Under penalty of law, this tag may not be removed”. They decide to tear it off, thinking they have committed a crime. They fail to notice, however, that the tag also says, “except by the consumer”. They have not committed a crime, even though they think they have. Such is the essence of impossibility—particularly legal impossibility. In substance, Jack and Jill’s actions belongs to legal impossibility. This means that in the context of conspiracy, legal impossibility can be a defence. However, factual impossibility cannot be used as a defence. Assume once again that Frank and Larry decide to commit murder. One of them buys a gun. They then agree to break into John’s house in the middle of the night and shoot him. Unbeknownst to Frank and Larry, John died of a heart attack earlier that night while he was sleeping. Frank pulls the trigger and shoots John. It is impossible for him to murder John because John is already dead. This does not mean, however, that Frank and Larry will go free. If caught, they will likely face conspiracy charges for attempted murder.[1]

虽然不能犯很少出现在共谋语境之中,但在某些情况下,它也是一种可能的辩护理由。假设杰克和吉尔刚买了一张新床垫,以替换原先那张破旧不堪的床垫。他们注意到床垫侧面有一个标签,上面写着“根据法律规定,此标签不得撕下”。他们决定撕掉标签,并以为自己犯罪。然而,他们没有注意到,标签上还写着“消费者除外”。因此,根据法律的规定,作为消费者的杰克和吉尔并没有犯罪,尽管他们认为自己已经犯罪。这就是不能犯的本质,尤其是法律不能犯。从实质看,杰克和吉尔的行为属于法律不能犯。这意味着在共谋罪的语境下,法律不能犯是可以作为抗辩事由的。但共谋罪的事实不能犯却不能作为抗辩事由。比如,弗兰克和拉里决定实施谋杀,其中的一人买了一把枪。然后他们商定半夜闯入约翰家并枪杀他。但弗兰

〔1〕 Jennifer L. Moore & John L. Worrall, *Criminal Law*, 2nd editon, Pearson Education Inc., 2018, p. 127.

克和拉里并不知道,当晚早些时候,约翰在熟睡时已死于心脏病。弗兰克扣动扳机射击约翰。尽管事实上弗兰克已经不可能谋杀约翰,因为约翰已经死了,但这并不意味着弗兰克和拉里就可以逍遥法外。如果被抓,弗兰克和拉里很可能面临谋杀未遂罪的共谋指控。

8.3.3.3 Withdrawal(犯罪脱离)

Withdrawal is similar to abandonment, but it is not the same. First, abandonment requires that the defendant seek to defeat the conspiracy. There is no such requirement with withdrawal. Also, the withdrawal defense is more widely available than abandonment. Withdrawal is similar to abandonment, however, as it starts the clock on the statute of limitations; the statute of limitations starts at the point of withdrawal, not at some subsequent point in time if another crime is committed that the defendant did not agree to or participate in. The Model Penal Code also contains a withdrawal defense, which requires that the defendant either advise his co – conspirators that he is no longer involved in it or inform police about the conspiracy.[1] Moreover, the co – conspirators eventually completed the conspiratorial crime.

犯罪脱离与犯罪中止相似,但并不相同。首先,犯罪中止要求被告设法阻止共谋犯罪的既遂。而犯罪脱离则无此限制。其次,犯罪脱离的辩护比犯罪中止的辩护更广泛些。然而,犯罪脱离与犯罪中止相似,因为它启动了诉讼时效;诉讼时效从犯罪脱离时开始计算,而不是从被告没有同意或参与的另一项犯罪发生后的某个时间点开始计算。《模范刑法典》还包含一项犯罪脱离辩护,要求被告告知共谋者他不再参与共谋,或将共谋情况告知警方,且共谋者最终还是完成了共谋的犯罪。

8.3.3.4 Wharton's Rule(沃顿规则)

Recall that one of the key purposes of conspiracy laws is to give authorities some extra tools to address the dangers of group criminality. However, conspiracy is limited in some exceptional circumstances. Certain crimes, however, cannot be completed without two people. Adultery is one such (common law) crime; it cannot be completed without two people. A drug sale works in the same way; it requires a buyer and a seller. Does it make sense to use conspiracy laws to target such crimes? In general, no, and Wharton's rule offers some protection. The rule provides that a conspiracy cannot occur when two persons are required for the commission of a crime. The intentions of Wharton's rule are noble, but this rule also frustrates law enforcement. Why? Strictly

[1] Jennifer L. Moore & John L. Worrall, *Criminal Law*, 2nd editon, Pearson Education Inc., 2018, p. 127.

applied, if two parties entered into an agreement for one to sell and the other to buy drugs, prosecutors could do nothing until the sale was attempted. Instead of being able to prevent the crime, the authorities would have to wait until it was nearly completed. For this reason, courts often limit Wharton's rule to cases in which the intended crime has been completed or attempted.[1]

设立共谋法的主要目的之一是为司法机关提供一些额外工具来应对集团犯罪。但是,共谋罪在某些特殊情况下是受到限制的,某些罪行必须具备两人时才能完成。通奸就是这样一种(普通法)犯罪;没有两个人是无法完成的。毒品销售也是如此,需要有买方和卖方。在这种至少需要两个才能实施的犯罪中,再附加以共谋罪进行制裁,是没有意义的。沃顿规则就是对此进行限制的规则。该规则规定,当实施犯罪需要两个人时,共谋不能成立。沃顿规则的初衷是崇高的,却对执法有很大的阻碍。严格来说,如果双方达成协议,其中一方销售毒品,另一方购买毒品,那么在销售未遂之前,检察官则无计可施。当局非但不能阻止犯罪,反而要等待犯罪接近完成。因此,法院通常将沃顿规则限制在预期的犯罪已经完成或未遂的案件中。

So, in our example, both parties could be charged with conspiracy to sell drugs—even in the face of Wharton's rule. Wharton's rule is also limited in other ways. First, if more than the minimum number of offenders is involved (e. g., a third person in our drug sale example), the rule will not apply. Likewise, if there are two parties to an agreement, but they are not the two parties necessary to complete the crime, then the rule does not apply. For example, two men conspire for one of them to sell drugs to a third person, then the rule does not apply because the buyer was not a party to the agreement. The Supreme Court has limited Wharton's rule such that it is widely regarded as no more than a presumption in the absence of contrary legislative intent. If, for example, a law permits a conspiracy charge in the context of a two - party crime, then the rule will be ignored by the court.[2]

因此,在我们所举的例子中,即使面对沃顿规则,双方都有可能被控共谋贩卖毒品。沃顿规则在其他方面也有其限制。第一,如果这些行为的犯罪人超过最低人数(例如,我们所举例的毒品销售案件涉及第三人),该规则将不适用。第二,如果协议有双方,但他们不是完成犯罪所必需的双方,那么该规则也不适用。例如,两名男子

---

〔1〕 Jennifer L. Moore & John L. Worrall, *Criminal Law*, 2nd editon, Pearson Education Inc., 2018, p. 127 - 128.

〔2〕 Jennifer L. Moore & John L. Worrall, *Criminal Law*, 2nd editon, Pearson Education Inc., 2018, p. 128.

共谋让其中一人将毒品卖给第三人,那么该规则就不适用,因为买方不是协议的一方。最高法院对沃顿规则进行了限制,在没有相反立法意图的情况下,该规则被广泛认为只是一种推定。如果法律允许在双方犯罪的情况下指控共谋,那么该规则将被法院忽略。

8.4 Solicitation(教唆罪)

Solicitation occurs when a person entices, advises, incites, orders, or otherwise encourages someone else to commit a crime. There is no requirement that the crime actually be completed. Solicitation is typically limited to felonies or misdemeanors that involve either obstruction of justice or breach of peace. Under common law, solicitation was a misdemeanor. Under the Model Penal Code and many state statutes, it is a crime of the same grade and degree as the most serious crime solicited. Some states, however, still treat solicitation as less serious than the target offense.〔1〕

当某人引诱、建议、煽动、命令或以其他方式怂恿他人犯罪时,其行为即构成教唆罪。但是,在教唆罪中,并不要求行为人实际完成犯罪。教唆罪的成立受到一些限制,其通常仅限于涉及妨碍司法公正或破坏治安的重罪或轻罪。根据普通法规定,教唆属于轻罪。但根据《模范刑法典》和许多州的法律规定,教唆罪与被教唆的最严重罪行属于同一等级和程度的罪行。不过,有些州仍将教唆罪视为比目标犯罪更轻的罪行。

8.4.1 Solicitation Under common law(普通法规定的教唆罪)

Under common law, solicitation was a specific intent crime, meaning that solicitor must have intended for the solicited person to commit a particular crime. Much the same holds true today. For example, Leroy says to Bubba, "Wouldn't it be cool if you blew up Cletus's trailer?" he has merely joked about having Bubba commit a crime. He has not satisfied the mens rea element of solicitation. However, if Leroy offers Bubba $100 and says, "I'll let you keep this if you blow up Cletus's trailer", then arguably he intends for a crime to be committed.〔2〕

根据普通法规定,教唆是一种具体故意犯罪,这意味着教唆者必须有让被教唆者实施某种特定犯罪的故意。今天的情况也大致如此。例如,勒罗伊对巴布说:"如

〔1〕 Jennifer L. Moore & John L. Worrall, *Criminal Law*, 2nd editon, Pearson Education Inc., 2018, p. 128.

〔2〕 Jennifer L. Moore & John L. Worrall, *Criminal Law*, 2nd editon, Pearson Education Inc., 2018, p. 128.

果你炸毁克莱图斯的拖车，是不是很酷啊？"他只是开玩笑而已，没有满足教唆罪的犯罪故意要件。但是，如果勒罗伊向巴布提供 100 美元，并说："如果你炸毁克莱图斯的拖车，这些钱就是你的啦"，那么勒罗伊就是诱使巴布故意实施特定的犯罪。

A solicitor may hire someone to commit a crime, which is what we typically think of with respect to solicitation, but there is no requirement that money change hands. Also, there is no requirement that any steps be taken toward completion of the target crime. That is, there is no "overt act" requirement, as with conspiracy. A simple agreement between two people that one will commit the crime for the other suffices. This is true even if the solicited party refuses to commit the crime or says he or she will do so but does not really mean it.[1]

教唆者还可以雇用他人实施犯罪，这是通常所言的教唆行为，不过法律并不要求雇凶所需的钱财易手。不仅如此，教唆罪的成立也不要求为完成目标犯罪采取任何步骤。也就是说，无须像共谋罪那样有表征性行为的要求。还需注意的是，即使被教唆者拒绝实施犯罪，或者虚情假意地说会如教唆那般行事而没行事，都不影响教唆罪的成立。

One key limitation is that if the solicitor's message never reaches the solicited person (or if it cannot be known whether it reaches the solicited person), the actus reus requirement has not been satisfied. For example, a prison inmate sent letters to his wife on the outside, soliciting various criminal activities. There was no evidence the letters actually reached his wife, so the inmate could not be convicted of solicitation.[2]

教唆罪的成立受到限制：如果教唆者的信息从未到达被教唆者（或者无法得知信息是否到达被教唆者），则没有满足教唆行为的要求。例如，一名囚犯寄信给监狱外的妻子，在信中教唆其妻进行各种犯罪活动。但没有证据表明这些信件确实到达其妻手中，因此不能判定这名囚犯构成教唆罪。

8.4.2 Solicitation under the Model Penal Code（《模范刑法典》规定的教唆行为）

In general, as defined by the Model Penal Code Section 5.02, solicitation requires that (1) a person commands, encourages or requests another person to engage in an illegal act with (2) the purpose to promote or facilitate it. The Code treats solicitation as seriously as the target offense, and it does not limit solicitation to felonies. Even an

---

〔1〕 Jennifer L. Moore & John L. Worrall, *Criminal Law*, 2nd editon, Pearson Education Inc., 2018, p. 128.

〔2〕 Jennifer L. Moore & John L. Worrall, *Criminal Law*, 2nd editon, Pearson Education Inc., 2018, p. 128.

attempted solicitation is considered solicitation under the Model Penal Code. However, the Model Penal Code does offer a defense of "renunciation". A person is not guilty of solicitation if he or she (1) completely and voluntarily renounces his or her criminal intent and (2) either persuades the other party not to offend or blocks the crime's commission.[1]

通常而言,根据《模范刑法典》第5.02条的定义,教唆需要满足(1)一个人命令、鼓励或请求另一个人从事非法行为,并且(2)目的是促进或便利该行为。《模范刑法典》将教唆视为与目标犯罪同等严重的行为,并且不将教唆限制在重罪范围内。即使是教唆未遂,也被视为《模范刑法典》所规定的教唆。然而,《模范刑法典》确实提供了一种"放弃"的辩护理由。如果一个人(1)完全且自愿地放弃了其犯罪意图,并且(2)要么说服对方不要犯罪,要么阻止了犯罪的实施,那么其行为就不构成教唆罪。

■ Curriculum Ideology and Politics(课程思政)

Chinese criminal law addresses uncompleted crimes through provisions for attempt, abandonment, and preparation. Correspondingly, in Anglo – American criminal law, abandonment is a defense to the offenses of attempt, conspiracy, or solicitation. Consequently, Chinese criminal law and Anglo – American criminal law have adopted different approaches to handling "abandonment". Students are guided to recognize these differences, and in doing so, their analytical and cognitive skills are cultivated.

在未完成犯罪中,中国刑法规定了未遂、中止和预备。与之对应,在英美刑法中,中止是作为未遂罪、共谋罪或教唆罪的抗辩事由。因此,中国刑法和英美刑法对"中止"采取了不同的处置模式。引导学生认知此差异,培养学生的辨析和认知能力。

■ Case study (案例学习)

People v. Lubow 29 N. Y. 2d 58, 272 N. E. 2d 331 (纽约州诉鲁博案)

Fact (基本案情)

Defendants were convicted after trial for solicitation to commit a felony. They were in the jewelry business and owed Silverman $30,000 for diamonds on unpaid notes.

---

[1] Jennifer L. Moore & John L. Worrall, *Criminal Law*, 2nd editon, Pearson Education Inc., 2018, p. 129.

when Silverman approached the defendants for payment. Instead of making payment, the defendants suggested that they all get together and participate in a scheme to declare bankruptcy and obtain money payments. Silverman reported the matter to the police, and a trial ensued.

经审判,被告被判犯有教唆重罪。被告从事珠宝业务,拖欠西尔弗曼 30,000 美元的钻石货款。西尔弗曼要求被告付款。被告人没有付款,而是建议他们共同参与某个申请破产并获取钱款的欺诈计划。西尔弗曼向警方报案,然后法院对被告进行了审判。

Dispute(争议点)

Is the evidence sufficient to support the punishment of the defendant for solicitation to commit a felony under New York law.

根据纽约法律规定,证据是否足以支持对被告以实施重罪的教唆进行惩罚?

Conclusion(结论)

The crime of solicitation does not require an overt act; it is complete when the solicitation is made, even if the object of the solicitation is never consummated. The communication itself with the intent that the other person engage in the unlawful conduct, is sufficient and requires no corroboration.

教唆罪并不需要有表征性行为;教唆行为一旦发生,教唆罪就已完成,即使教唆的目的没有实现。故意促使他人从事非法行为的交流本身就足以构成教唆罪,不需要实际协作。

Question: To constitute the crime of solicitation, is it necessary for the solicited party to commit the crime? (Please scan the QR code on the right to get the answer)

要构成教唆罪,被教唆方是否需要实施犯罪行为?(答案请扫描右侧二维码获取)

8.5 Exercise(课后练习)(答案请扫描右侧二维码获取)

8.5.1 Test of Terminologies(术语考查)

①inchoate crime ②attempt

③factual impossibility ④legal impossibility

⑤conspiracy ⑥overt act

⑦Wharton's rule ⑧solicitation

8.5.2 True or False(判断题)

1. Attempt, conspiracy, and solicitation, are finished crimes.

未遂、共谋和教唆,属于已完成的犯罪。

2. Abandonment is when the defendant, completely or partially, voluntarily withdraws from commission of the offense before it is consummated.

犯罪中止是指被告人在犯罪实现之前完全或部分地自愿退出犯罪行为。

3. Solicitation to commit a felony doesn't constitute a crime when the person solicited either refuses to commit it or fails to do so.

对于教唆他人犯重罪,如果被教唆的人拒绝或者简单地未能实施,不构成犯罪。

4. Solicitation may occur even when an individual mistakenly asks another person to commit a crime.

即使个人错误地要求他人犯罪,也构成教唆。

5. Solicitation is limited to the forms of a request, suggestion, or encouragement to complete the crime.

教唆只能采取请求、建议或鼓励他人完成犯罪的形式。

8.5.3 Short－answer Questions (简答题)

1. Explain both components of the mens rea of attempt.

解释未遂罪的犯罪意图的两个组成部分。

2. Summarize the elements of conspiracy.

简要概述共谋的构成要素。

3. Please provide a comparative analysis of whether this example constitues legal impossibility from the perspective of Chinese and Anglo－American criminal law: If a man mistakes a stump for his enemy and shoots at it, does this constitue legal impossibility or factual impossibility? And, is this impossibility considered an attempt?

如果某人把树桩误认为是敌人并向它开枪,请问行为人的行为是属于法律不能犯还是事实不能犯?并且,这种不能犯是否是未遂罪?请依据中国和英美刑法分别进行回答。

■ Summary(总结)

1. An inchoate crime is one that is partial, unfinished, or begun and not completed. Inchoate crimes include attempt, conspiracy, and solicitation.

未完成犯罪是指部分犯罪、未完成犯罪或已开始但未完成的犯罪。未完成犯罪包括未遂、共谋和教唆。

2. Attempt is the intent to commit a crime coupled with an act taken toward committing the offense.

未遂罪是指具有犯罪意图,并采取了犯罪行动的犯罪。

3. Multiple tests are used to determine the presence of actus reus in the attempt context.

在未遂情况下,证明客观行为的存在有多种不同的标准。

4. Under common law, a conspiracy was defined as an agreement between two or more persons to commit a criminal act.

根据普通法的定义,共谋为二人或多人达成的实施犯罪行为的协议。

5. There are two parts to the mens rea of conspiracy. First, the defendant must intend to enter into an agreement with one or more others to commit a crime. Second, the defendant must have intent to commit the target offense.

共谋罪的犯罪意图由两部分组成。第一,被告必须故意与一人或多人达成犯罪协议。第二,被告必须有实施目标罪行的故意。

6. The actus reus of conspiracy consists of two parts. First, and most importantly, there must be an agreement to commit a crime. Second, in some jurisdictions the parties to the conspiracy must commit an "overt act" in furtherance of the agreement.

共谋罪的客观行为由两部分组成。第一,也是最重要的一点,必须有实施犯罪的协议。第二,在某些司法管辖区,共谋各方必须实施表征性行为以推进协议。

7. Solicitation occurs when a person entices, advises, incites, orders, or otherwise encourages someone else to commit a crime.

当某人引诱、建议、煽动、命令或以其他方式鼓励他人犯罪时,其行为即为教唆。

Chapter 9 Crimes Against Persons Ⅰ: Murder and Manslaughter
第9章 人身侵害犯罪Ⅰ:谋杀罪和非预谋杀人罪

■ The Learning Objective(学习目标)

1. To understand the historical evolution of homicide.
了解杀人犯罪的历史流变。

2. To have a basic understanding of what are murder and other types of homicide.
了解谋杀等杀人犯罪的定义。

3. To understand the types of homicide.
了解杀人犯罪的分类。

4. To understand the elements and punishments of homicide.
了解杀人犯罪的构成与处罚。

5. To learn some terminologies related to the topic.
掌握本章的专业术语。

■ Chapter Outline(本章内容概要)

Homicide is the most fundamental, standard, and important type of crimes. The three main functions of criminal law (namely regulating behavior, determining responsibility, and measuring punishment[1]) are all most typical manifestations and explanations in the homicide. This chapter intends to combine the historical changes of homicide with specific cases to introduce the historical changes of typical homicide, such as murder in the English and American criminal laws. By doing so, it will explain the definition and classification of homicide in the common legal system, deeply explore the

---

〔1〕 See Paul H. Robinson, *A Functional Analysis of Criminal Law*, 88 Nw. U. L. Rev. 857 (1994).

elements and punishment of homicide and help students master relevant professional terminology.

杀人罪是最基础、最标准、最重要的犯罪类型。刑法的三种主要功能(规范行为、认定责任以及公正量刑)都在杀人罪中得到了最典型的体现与说明。本章结合杀人犯罪历史流变,通过具体判例,对英美刑法中谋杀等典型杀人犯罪的历史流变加以介绍,借此阐释普通法系中谋杀等杀人犯罪的定义、杀人犯罪的分类,深入探讨杀人犯罪的构成与处罚,帮助学生掌握相关的专业术语。

■ The Purpose of Curriculum Ideology and Politics for this Chapter (本章的课程思政目标)

1. One of the classic Marxist writers went straight to the heart of the matter that the most obvious and extreme manifestation of contempt for social order is the crime. From this perspective, it can be further argued that the most obvious and extreme crime is contempt for the lives of people who form social relationships. The criminal laws of common law countries also stipulate the crime of homicide, which protects individual lives. Everyone should respect the lives of others, cherish and protect one's own life.

马克思主义经典作家一针见血地指出:"蔑视社会秩序的最明显、最极端的表现就是犯罪。"而其中最明显、最极端的犯罪就是对于组成社会关系的人的生命的犯罪。英美国家的刑法规定了杀人罪,对个体生命进行保护。每个人应尊重他人的生命,也爱惜和保护好自己的生命。

2. The crime of homicide, as a traditional crime stipulated earlier in common law, has been continuously improved over a long historical development process, ultimately forming a highly complex system of charges and penalties. The legislative provisions, such as distinguishing between first and second degree murder, in the common law countries are highly distinctive in relevant judicial practices. Understanding the above characteristics can help students deeply understand the crime of homicide in the common law system, further expand their knowledges of criminal law, and objectively evaluate the relevant legislation and practice of English and American criminal laws.

杀人罪作为普通法中较早规定的传统犯罪,在漫长的历史发展过程中被不断完善,最终形成了高度复杂的罪名体系与刑罚制度。普通法区分一级和二级谋杀,相关司法实践均极具特色。对于上述特色的了解,可以帮助学生深度理解普通法系中的杀人犯罪,进一步拓展刑法视野,更为客观地评价英美刑法的相关立法与实践。

■ Terminologies(专业术语)

slayer	杀人者
homicide	杀人犯罪
murder	谋杀
manslaughter	非预谋杀人
viability	生存力
feticide	杀婴
human being	人类
abortion	堕胎
foreseeability	可预见性
remoteness	接近性
express malice	明示的恶意
implied malice	默示的恶意
reckless indifference	轻率的无所谓心态
depraved heart murder	丧心病狂的谋杀

9.1 the Historical Evolution of the Homicide(杀人犯罪的历史流变)

Homicide, especially murder, which leads to the death of others', even of fetuses', is considered the most serious crime. In Exodus, it is explicitly stated that the doctrine of "Thou shalt not kill". And this has always been regarded as the fundamental values and moral bottom line of British and American society. In fact , the United States , as the only country in the west hemisphere that reating the death penalty , applies exclusively the death penalty in certain jurisdictions to murder case besides to treason crime.

杀人,因为导致了他人,甚至胎儿的死亡,被视为最为严重的犯罪。《出埃及记》中,就明确规定了"汝不能杀戮"之类的教义,而这也一直被奉为英美社会基本价值观与道德底线。事实上,作为西方几乎唯一保留死刑的国家,美国目前某些司法管辖区的死刑,除叛国罪之外,几乎仅适用于谋杀案件。[1]

In the 13th century, homicide was essentially a civil issue in English law. The perpetrator was called a "slayer", roughly equivalent to the "killer" in modern

〔1〕 与此相关的介绍,可参见李立丰:《上帝与死囚:基督教视野中的美国死刑问题》,载《世界宗教研究》2010 年第 5 期。

vocabulary. The perpetrator needed to pay compensation to the victim's family, but did not need to bear criminal sanctions. At the same time, it was legal to seek revenge against the perpetrator, which was even an appropriate form of relief. In earlier times, those who secretly killed strangers were called "murdrum", which seemed to be the etymology of "murder". The concept of "murdrum" in common law was originated during the Norman Conquest of England in the 11th century. During this period, a large number of assassinations occurred in the English region targeting invaders. In order to prevent similar situations from escalating, the ruler of the time, William I, announced that if a French person was killed and there was no culprit responsible for it, one hundred British people would need to pay a fine, and this punishment was called "murdrum". On the other hand, if a British person was killed but the perpetrator was not caught, there was no need to impose similar punishment on the French side. Of course, this kind of punishment, as it occurred between the government and individuals, appeared to be somewhat different from the current punishment. Although this story is not related to the contemporary understanding of murder, which is an illegal killing based on "prior malice", historians believe that even if "murdrum" is understood as a fine, it represents a secret act of murder, especially the so - called "lying in wait" murder. Murder committed through secret means is often considered more evil than other types of murder, so the term "murdrum" later referred to the most serious part of murder.

在13世纪的英国法中,杀人还基本属于民事问题。杀人者被称为"slayer",大致相当于现代语汇中的"凶手"。凶手需要向受害人家属支付赔偿金,但不需要承担刑事制裁。同时,向凶手复仇是合法的,甚至被视为天经地义的救济方式。更早的时候,秘密杀死陌生人者,被称为"murdrum",这似乎也可以被视为是"谋杀"(murder)的词源。普通法中的"murdrum"概念,起源于11世纪诺曼联军征服英格兰时期。这个时期,针对入侵者,英格兰地区出现了大量的暗杀行为。为了防止类似的情况愈演愈烈,当时的统治者威廉一世(William Ⅰ)[1]宣布,如果有法国人被杀,而没有罪魁祸首对此负责,就需要有一百名英国人为此支付罚金,这种罚金刑,就被称为"murdrum"。而如果有英国人被杀,但凶手没有落网的,对法国人则无须作出类似的惩罚。当然,这种惩罚因为发生在政府与个人之间,看起来多少和现在

---

〔1〕 威廉一世(William Ⅰ),1027—1087年,英国国王,原为法国诺曼底公爵。其在作为自己的表亲的英王爱德华死后,借口无嗣的爱德华曾经许诺死后让自己继位,遂渡海侵入英国,并击败已经登记的英王哈罗德二世,自封为王,称威廉一世,之后重用并分封土地给诺曼人,压制盎格鲁-撒克逊贵族。

的刑罚有些不同。虽然这个故事和当代通常意义上理解的谋杀,即基于“事先恶意”实施的非法杀人无关。但历史学家相信,即便将“murdrum”理解为罚金,其也针对的是一种秘密杀人的行为,尤其是所谓“埋伏”(lying in wait)杀人。通过秘密方式实施的杀人,往往被认为比其他类型的杀人更邪恶。因此“murdrum”这一术语为指代杀人罪中最为严重的类型。[1]

Another force that greatly influences the development of homicide in common law comes from efforts to limit the scope of application of the death penalty. Even after a hundred years of French conquest of England, all murderers still needed to be executed. But in the late 15th century, the so - called “manslaughter” began to emerge, with the aim of ensuring that not all homicide was a death penalty crime. Famous historians have verified that the French term homicide is a type of concept, that is, a superior concept, while murder and manslaughter are the two subordinate concepts of this type of concept. In addition, at that time, there was another legal norm to reduce criminal responsibility for murder, but it mainly applied to clergy, which ensured that clergy were not subject to secular justice in similar situations. It is worth mentioning that at that time, because most people were illiterate and only priests had received education, murderers could prove their priestly identity by reciting a certain paragraph of the Bible. Of course, this rule was later abused by some cunning criminals. Correspondingly to the above viewpoint, some scholars believe that the development direction of murder in common law is precisely because the fines imposed on the perpetrator or have become increasingly heavy, making it impossible for them to bear them, which later lead to murder being seen as a crime against the government. Since then, the government has taken on the responsibility of punishing the killers. Anyway, the evolution of the concept of murder in common law may seem like a linguistic transformation and evolution, but in reality it represents conflicts between different cultures, entanglements between secular and religious beliefs, a balance between hatred and compensation, and a transition between barbarism and civilization. Early common law did not distinguish the specific types of homicide and treated all homicide crimes equally. But in the late 18th and early 19th centuries, most judicial districts abolished this practice and instead classified the death penalty into different types. For example, in 1794, Pennsylvania classified homicide through precedent, which mainly attempted to exempt some murderers with lower

〔1〕 相关内容,可参见李立丰:《美国刑法评解》(下册),社会科学文献出版社 2023 年版,第 784 页。

culpability from the death penalty. Although California does not use first - degree murder and second - degree murder as the sole rule to distinguish between death row murder and non - death row murder. But there are still other reasons to distinguish between first degree and second - degree murder. It is undeniable that the crime of homicide in criminal laws of various jurisdictions in the United States, taking the judicial practice in California as an example, still largely maintains the aforementioned rheological characteristics of homicide in common law. Similar to other jurisdictions, murder in California is a representative of the occasional development of common law and lacks a unified concept. For example, according to the current California Code, homicide refers to the act of a person illegally killing another person. Murder can be further divided into two types: murder and negligent homicide. Compared to murder, manslaughter is a relatively minor crime. Of course, if there are legitimate grounds for excuse or justification, the act of depriving others' lives may also be legal, and the actor is not a criminal.

另外一种极大影响普通法中杀人罪发展的力量,来自限制死刑适用范围的努力。即使在法国人征服英格兰100年之后,所有杀人犯仍然都需要被处死。但在15世纪后期,“非预谋杀人”(manslaughter)开始出现,其设立目的在于保证并非所有杀人罪都是死刑犯罪。经历史学者考证,“杀人犯罪”(homicide)这一法语词汇,是一种类概念,即所谓上位概念。而谋杀和非预谋杀人,则是这一类概念的两个下位概念。除此之外,在当时,还存在另外一种减轻杀人罪刑事责任的法律准则。但该准则主要适用于教士,即在发生类似情况的时候,保证教士不受世俗司法的审判。值得一提的是,当时因为大部分人都是文盲,只有教士接受过教育,因此,杀人犯可以通过诵读《圣经》的某个段落,来证明自己的教士身份。当然,这一规则后来也被某些狡猾的罪犯滥用。[1] 普通法中杀人罪的发展方向与上述观点相互对应。有学者认为,恰恰是因为凶手或杀人者无力负担越来越重的罚金,才导致杀人转而被视为对政府的犯罪。自此之后,政府承担起惩罚杀人者的责任。[2] 无论如何,普通法中杀人罪概念的流变,表面上看虽然是一种语言的转化与演变,但实际上却代表着不同文化之间的冲突,代表着世俗与宗教的纠葛,代表着仇恨与补偿的平衡,代表着野蛮与文明的过渡。早期普通法不区分杀人罪的具体类型,对所有杀人犯罪同等处

[1] See Martha G. Duncan, *Beauty in the Dark of Night: The Pleasures of Form in Criminal Law*, 59 Emory L. J. 1203 (2010).

[2] See John Rockwell Snowden, *Second Degree Murder, Malice, and Manslaughter in Nebraska: New Juice for an Old Cup*, 76 Neb. L. Rev. 399 (1997).

理。但在18世纪末19世纪初,大部分司法管辖区就废除了这种做法,转而将杀人犯罪分为不同类型。[1] 例如,1794年,宾夕法尼亚州通过判例将杀人分级,主要是对一些可责性较低的杀人犯不适用死刑。加利福尼亚州虽然并没有将一级谋杀和二级谋杀作为是否适用死刑的唯一标准,但仍将其作为重要的参考因素。[2] 不可否认,目前美国各司法管辖区刑事成文法中的杀人罪,仍然在很大程度上保持了普通法中杀人罪的上述特征。但和其他司法管辖区类似,加利福尼亚州杀人罪是普通法偶发式发展的代表,缺乏统一的理念。例如,根据现行《加利福尼亚州法典》,杀人罪是指一个人非法杀死另外一个人的行为。杀人又可以进一步分为谋杀与"非预谋杀人"两种类型。较于谋杀,非预谋杀人相属于程度较轻的犯罪。[3] 当然,如果存在合法的免责事由或者正当化事由,剥夺他人生命的行为也可能合法,行为人并不犯罪。[4]

9.2 the Legal Definition of the Beginning and End of Human Being("人"的生与死的法律界定)

Traditionally, the common law adheres to the principle of "being born alive" when it comes to being human. This guideline is based on medical technology in the 16th and 17th centuries. According to this principle, regardless of how many weeks pregnant the woman is, as long as the baby is being born alive will be ok. This is because at that time, technology and medical methods made it difficult to distinguish the cause of fetal death. This means that in law, killing an unborn fetus is not considered a homicide, let alone murder. This view persisted until the 18th century. Until around 1850, some states in the United States began to expand the scope, believing that killing a fetus could be a object of murder if the fetus being born alive and later died. For example, in the *Williams v. Maryland*, the defendant had a conflict with a neighbor, during which the defendant swung a bow and arrow, which shot through the body of a nearby pregnant woman. The pregnant woman died immediately, but the fetus in her womb was born and survived for seventeen hours before dying. The defendant was charged with two counts of manslaughter. The defendant filed an appeal, arguing that the death of the fetus

---

〔1〕 See Stephen J. Morse, *Undiminished Confusion in Diminished Capacity*, 75 J. Crim. L. & Criminology 1 (1984).

〔2〕 See Charles L. Hobson, *Reforming California's Homicide Law*, 23 Pepp. L. Rev. Iss. 495 (1999).

〔3〕 See People v. Antick, 15 Cal. 3d 79 (1975).

〔4〕 相关内容,可参见李立丰:《美国刑法评解》(下册),社会科学文献出版社2023年版,第784页。

should not constitute a crime. The superior court held that manslaughter is a serious crime in the common law and according to common law and judicial practice in other states, the "born alive" rule should be adopted, because the victim infant in this case was born alive and later died due to injury caused by the defendant. Therefore, it was determined that the defendant should also bear criminal responsibility for manslaughter for the death of the fetus. This common law's tradition continues to this day, and currently, there are still eighteen states in the United States that apply the "being born alive" rule through legislation or judiciary. Ten states, including Alabama, Alaska, Colorado, Hawaii, Montana, Nebraska, Oregon, Texas, and Idaho, have explicitly defined the starting point of "human" as being born alive in their written laws, while eight states, including Maine, Connecticut, Kentucky, Maryland, New York, North Carolina, Vermont, and West Virginia, adopt a judicial model by case law.

传统上，普通法对何时为人，秉持"出生时为活体"准则。这一准则建立在 16、17 世纪医学科技的基础上。根据这一原则，无论孕妇怀孕几周，只要胎儿出生的时候是活体就属于法律意义上的"人"。这是因为当时的科技与医学手段，很难区分胎儿的死亡原因。[1] 这就意味着，在法律上，杀死未出生的胎儿，不属于杀"人"，更不被视为谋杀。这一看法，一直持续到 18 世纪。直到 1850 年前后，美国有些州开始扩充这一准则，认为针对胎儿实施杀伤行为，如果胎儿生下来时存活，之后死亡的，胎儿亦可成为谋杀的对象。[2] 例如，在威廉诉马里兰州案（Williams v. State）[3] 中，上诉人威廉与邻居发生冲突，在此过程中上诉人挥舞手中的弓箭，弓箭击发，射穿了旁边的一个孕妇的身体。该孕妇随即死亡，但其腹中的胎儿脱离母体后生存了 17 个小时才被宣告死亡。被告人被指控犯有两起非预谋杀人罪（分别针对孕妇与新生儿）。被告人提起上诉，认为对胎儿的死亡不应该成立犯罪。上诉法院认为，非预谋杀人属于一种普通法意义上的重罪，根据普通法以及其他州的司法实践，应当采用"出生为活体"规则。本案中的受害婴儿在出生的时候是活体，之后才因为被告人所造成的伤害死亡。因此，认定被告人对胎儿的死亡，也应当承担非预谋杀人罪的刑事责任。这一普通法传统延续至今，目前，全美仍有 18 个州通过立法或司法，适用"出生时为活体"规则。亚拉巴马州、阿拉斯加州、科罗拉多州、夏威夷州、蒙大

---

[1] Clarke D. Forsythe, *Homicide of the Unborn Child: The Born Alive Rule and Other Legal Anachronisms*, 21 Val. U. L. Rev. 563 (1987).

[2] See Stephanie Ritrivi McCavitt, Note, *The "Born Alive" Rule: A Proposed Change to the New York Law Based on Modern Medical Technology*, 36 N. Y. L. Sch. L. Rev. 609(1991).

[3] See Williams v. State, 550 A. 2d 722(Md. 1988).

拿州、内布拉斯加州、俄勒冈州、得克萨斯州、爱达荷州等多个州在成文法中,明确将"人"的界定起点,定义为出生时为活体,缅因州、康涅狄格州、肯塔基州、马里兰州、纽约州、北卡罗来纳州、佛蒙特州、西弗吉尼亚州等8个州则通过司法判例的方式对此加以界定。[1]

However, the subsequent evolution of the rule of "being born alive" faces two unresolved issues. Firstly, what should be done if malicious harm is carried out against the fetus about to be delivered, resulting in fetal death in the womb, or if the output is a dead body? For example, in *Keeler v. Superior Court*, Keeler, the Petitioner, intercepted his ex-wife, who was in the advanced state of pregnancy, and shoved his knee into her abdomen following his exclamation that he was going to stomp the fetus out of her. As a result, the fetus was delivered stillborn with a fractured skull. Keeler was charged with murder of the fetus under California's Penal Code which provides that "murder is the unlawful killing of a human being, with malice aforethought". Keeler moved to set aside the charge based on his contention that a fetus is not a human being as contemplated by the murder statute. But the California Supreme Court, by a vote of 5-2, determined that the child had died at birth. According to the "being born alive" rule applicable under California law at the time, a fetus is considered a human only if being born alive. Keeler's behavior should be considered as killing the fetus, which is not a statutory crime and does not constitute murder. This judgment is clearly unreasonable. A poll once asked whether those who attack pregnant women should face additional charges of harming unborn children. More than 80% of people answered that the perpetrator should face additional charges of murder. Therefore, the California legislature amended written law to include fetuses, along with "human being" as objects of murder.

"出生为活体"规则面临两个无法解决的问题。首先,如果针对即将生产的胎儿实施恶意伤害行为,导致胎死腹中,或者产出时为死体的,该如何处理?例如,在凯勒诉加利福尼亚州上诉法院案[2]中,分居中的丈夫和怀了别人孩子的妻子不期而遇,丈夫猛击孕妇的腹部,并告诉自己的妻子:"我听说你怀孕了,你弄清楚了,我就是要把它给打掉!"当时,受害人已经怀孕35周,胎儿因为头部骨折,导致死产。虽然检方指控被告人犯有谋杀罪,但加利福尼亚州最高法院以5:2的表决结果,认定孩子出生时已经死亡,因此不构成杀人罪。根据加利福尼亚州法当时适用的"出生时为活体"规则,胎儿只有在出生后为活体的,才算是人。被告人的行为,不属于杀

---

[1] 相关内容,可参见李立丰:《美国刑法评解》(下册),社会科学文献出版社2023年版,第784页。

[2] See Keeler v. Superior Court, 470 P. 2d 617 (Cal. 1970).

"人",应被视为杀害"胎儿"而不是"人",因此其不构成谋杀罪。这一判决明显不合理。曾有民调就"攻击孕妇的人,是否应当面临另外伤害未出生儿童的指控"这一问题做出调查,超过80%的人回答,犯罪人应当面临另外的谋杀指控。[1] 因此,加利福尼亚州立法机关修改了成文法,将胎儿也包括进来,和"人"一道,被列为谋杀罪的对象。[2]

The further evolution of the "being born alive" rule still get some problem needed to be solved. During pregnancy, at which stage can a fetus obtain the same legal value and status as a human being? For example, in the U. S., Arkansas has a twelve week rule. Missouri, Pennsylvania, Louisiana, North Dakota, Illinois, Minnesota, and Wisconsin protect the entire stage from implantation to birth. Some states, such as Arizona, North Dakota, and Utah, only stipulate criminal acts against fetuses that should be punished, but do not establish standards for identifying fetuses. Finally, there are also those states mentioned earlier that apply the "being born alive" rule, treating pregnant women, not fetuses, as victims of homicide. In California alone, after the Keeler case, the California Supreme Court, based on newly amended legislation, made infants over seven weeks old the subject of murder. Meanwhile, the California Supreme Court rejected the so - called "viability" standard, which refers to the further development of understanding of the fetus and the legal definition of the developmental stage of the fetus with the development of contemporary medicine. In *Roe v. Wade*, the Supreme Court of the United States defined the "viability" rule as the ability of a fetus to survive independently from the uterus at the end of the second stage of pregnancy. At present, Indiana, Tennessee, Massachusetts, Oklahoma, and South Carolina consider the viability of the fetus as a prerequisite rule for becoming a target of murder. The so - called "viability" standard established in the *Roy v. Wade* is roughly the sixth month of pregnancy, and it is generally believed that from then on, the fetus can survive independently outside the mother's body. Ironically, the proposal of the "viability" rule is also aimed at the previously considered unscientific identification criteria. Prior to the application of the "viability" rule, the commonly recognized standard is the

---

〔1〕 See Marjorie M. Shultz, *Abortion and Maternal—Fetal Conflict: Broadening Our Concerns*, 1 S. Cal. Rev. L. & Women's Stud. 80 (1992).

〔2〕 See Cal. Penal Code § 187. 除加利福尼亚州之外,还有11个州通过立法规定,胎儿必须达到了特定的发展阶段,才能被视为谋杀罪的对象。在加利福尼亚州,胎儿必须经过胚胎期,大约发展到7周或8周,才属于刑法所保护的对象。See April Walker, *From State of California v. Scott Peterson* to *State of Utah v. Mark Hacking Will More States Adopt Fetal Protection Laws*, 4 Crim. L. Brief 46 (2009).

"Quickening" rule, which defines fetal movement as the mother's first sensation of a child's activity in the uterus, typically occurring between the 16th and 18th weeks of pregnancy. Once fetal movement occurs, the common law begins to protect the fetus. Florida, Michigan, Mississippi, Nevada, Rhode Island, and Washington state, according to this standard, punish the act of killing a fetus. Georgia specifically treats this situation as "infanticide". Overall, the development of medical technology has not led to the determination of the legal identity of the fetus in written law. According to incomplete statistics, approximately 60% of statues in various jurisdictions in the United States refer to the legal identity of a fetus as "Human Being" rather than "Person". Some states, such as Georgia mentioned above, simply treat the act of killing a fetus as an independent crime beyond murder and manslaughter.

如果将"人"的成立时点从出生向前推,仍然无法明确其起点。十月怀胎,哪个阶段的胎儿才可以获得与"人"相同的法律价值与法律地位?例如,阿肯色州规定的是12周。密苏里州、宾夕法尼亚州、路易斯安那州、北达科他州、伊利诺伊州、明尼苏达州,以及威斯康星州规定的是从胚胎着床到胎儿出生的全阶段。还有一些州,如亚利桑那州、北达科他州以及犹他州,仅仅规定了对胎儿的犯罪行为该当惩罚,但是没有规定对胎儿的认定标准。最后,还有之前提到的那些州,适用"出生为活体"规则,将孕妇,而非胎儿,视为杀人罪的对象。[1] 单就加利福尼亚州而言,在凯勒诉加利福尼亚州上诉法院案之后,加利福尼亚州最高法院根据新修改的立法,将7周以上的婴儿作为谋杀罪的对象。同时,加利福尼亚州最高法院否定了"生存力"(viability)标准。[2] "生存力"标准,是指随着当代医学的发展,对胎儿的认识,以及对胎儿生成阶段法律界定的进一步发展结果。联邦最高法院在罗伊诉韦德案[3]中,将"生存力"标准界定为孕期的第二阶段结束时,这个时候的胎儿可以离开子宫独立存活。目前有印第安纳州、田纳西州、马萨诸塞州、俄克拉何马州以及南卡罗来纳州,将胎儿的生存力,视为是否成为杀人罪对象的前提标准。罗伊诉韦德案所确立的"生命力"标准,大致为孕期的第6个月,一般认为,从此之后,胎儿可以在母体外独立生存。颇为讽刺的是,"生存力"标准的提出,也是针对之前被认为不科学的认定标准所提出的。在"生存力"标准适用之前,通用的认定标准是"胎动"(quickening)标准,"胎动"被定义为母亲第一次感觉到孩子在子宫里的活动,基本上

[1] See Hilary A. Converse, *Note and Comment: The Fetal Homicide Fallacy: A Comparison of California's Inconsistent Statutes to Other States*, 25 T. Jefferson L. Rev. 451(2003).

[2] See People v. Davis, 872 P.2d 591(Cal. 1994).

[3] See Roe v. Wade, 410 U.S. 113(1973).

出现在孕期第16周到第18周。一旦胎动发生，普通法就开始保护胎儿。[1] 佛罗里达州、密歇根州、密西西比州、内华达州、罗得岛以及华盛顿州，根据这种标准，惩罚杀害胎儿的行为。佐治亚州更专门将这种情况作为杀婴罪处理。[2] 总体来说，医学科技的发展，并未导致成文法中胎儿的法律身份得到确定。据不完全统计，美国各司法管辖区当中，大约60%的成文法将胎儿的法律身份称为“人类”（human being），而不是“人”（person）。[3] 有些州，如上面提到的佐治亚州，干脆将杀害胎儿的行为作为谋杀和非预谋杀人之外的独立犯罪加以处理。[4]

In the trial of a murder case, in addition to other elements, the prosecution must also prove that someone has passed away. At first glance, human death is usually easy to prove. However, with the widespread application of life support facilities and advances in medicine, it has become possible to artificially prolong circulation and respiratory function, while also making it difficult to construct the time of death. Now, the law provides two alternative definitions of death, aiming to reduce uncertainty in the judicial determination of death. Firstly, when the actor experiences irreversible damage to the circulatory and respiratory systems, it is considered a legal death. Secondly, the perpetrator is considered to have died legally when their entire brain, including the brainstem, experiences irreversible loss of function, which is considered legal death. The California court generally holds that death refers to the end of life, cessation of existence, and the doctor's determination that blood circulation throughout the body, arteries, and veins, such as respiratory pulse, will determine death. For example, the California Court of Appeals, based on the common law definition of death, states that victims of brain death may be legally alive. It is generally believed that the reason why judicial practice tends towards this standard is mainly from a pragmatic perspective, that is, the significance of organ transplantation.

在杀人案件的审理过程中，除其他要素之外，检方还必须证明有人死亡。乍看起来，人的死亡通常是容易证明的。然而，随着生命维持设施的普遍适用，医学的进步使人工延续循环与呼吸功能变得可能，同时也使死亡的时间很难确定。现在，法

[1] See Sandra L. Smith, *Note*, *Fetal Homicide*: *Woman or Fetus as Victim? A Survey of Current State Approaches and Recommendations for Future State Application*, 41 Wm. & Mary L. Rev. 1845 (1999).

[2] See Clarke D. Forsythe, *Homicide of the Unborn Child*, 21 Val. U. L. Rev. 563(1987).

[3] See Carolyn B. Ramsey, *Restructuring the Debate over Fetal Homicide Laws*, 67 Ohio St. L. J. 721 (2006).

[4] 相关内容，可参见李立丰：《美国刑法评解》（下册），社会科学文献出版社2023年版，第784页。

律规定了两种具有替代性的死亡定义,力图减轻对死亡司法认定方面的不确定性。首先,行为人在循环与呼吸系统出现不可逆的损害时,即为法定死亡。其次,行为人被认为法律上的死亡,当其整个脑部,包括脑干出现不可逆的功能丧失,就是法律上的死亡。[1] 加利福尼亚州法院一般认为,死亡是指生命的终结,停止作为"人"的存在,医生认定,如果一个人全身,包括动脉和静脉的血液停止循环,呼吸脉搏停止,就可认定其死亡。[2] 例如,加利福尼亚上诉法院根据普通法对死亡的界定,认为脑死亡的受害人可能在法律上是存活的。[3] 一般认为,司法实践之所以倾向这一标准,主要是从实用主义角度,即从器官移植方面出发的考量。[4]

■ Curriculum Ideology and Politics(课程思政)

The determination of the begining and ending points of a person, as well as the disagreement on whether a "fetus" belongs to a person, is not only a controversial issue in British and American criminal laws, but also a controversial issue in other countries' criminal laws, including Chinese criminal law. Therefore, this is still a practical and theoretical issue without consensus. For these difficult problems, a spirit of in – depth research should be cultivated to provide intelligence for the solution of these problems.

针对人之起点和终点的确定,以及"胎儿"到底是否属于人的分歧问题,不仅是英美刑法中的有争议的问题,而且也是包括中国刑法在内的其他国家刑法中的有争议的问题。这还是一个没有共识的实践和理论问题。对于这些疑难问题,应培养深度研究的精神,以为这些问题的解决提供智识。

9.3 the Types of Homicide and Their Definitions(杀人犯罪的分类及相关定义)

Homicide is the killing of one human being by another. Murder and Manslaughter are two types of homicide. Manslaughter is a lesser offense to murder. A homicide can be lawful or unlawful. If a person kills with a legally valid excuse or justification, the killing is lawful and he or she has not committed a crime. If there is no legally valid excuse or justification, the killing is unlawful and, depending on the circumstances, the person is guilty of either murder or manslaughter.[5] Hereby after, by using relevant

---

[1] Cal. Health & Safety Code § 7180.

[2] See Thomas v. Anderson, 96 Cal. App. 2d 371(1950).

[3] See People v. Mitchell, 132 Cal. App. 3d 389(1982).

[4] 相关内容,可参见李立丰:《美国刑法评解》(下册),社会科学文献出版社 2023 年版,第 784 页。

[5] CALCRIM No. 500.

legislation and judicial practice in California as an example, the chapter will illustrate the specific types and related elements of homicide in the common law system.

杀人犯罪,是指杀人者杀死了受害人的犯罪,杀人犯罪的具体类型包括谋杀和非预谋杀人。后者相比于谋杀罪更轻。杀人可以是合法的,也可以是非法的。如果基于合法的免责事由或正当化事由杀人,则不具有违法性,杀人者亦不构成犯罪。如果不具备合法的免责事由或正当化事由,则杀人是非法的。根据具体情况,杀人者构成谋杀罪或非预谋杀人罪。下面的内容结合美国加利福尼亚州相关立法与司法实践,对普通法世界中杀人犯罪具体类型及相关构成加以举例说明。

9.3.1 Murder(谋杀罪)

California Penal Code provide that , murder is the unlawful killing of a human being, or a fetus, with malice aforethought. However, according to the Therapeutic Abortion Act, such crimilization will be shall not apply to any person who commits an act that results in the death of a fetus if the act is committed by a holder of a physician's and surgeon's certificate, as defined in the Business and Professions Code, in a case where, to a medical certainty, the result of childbirth would be death of the mother of the fetus or where her death from childbirth, although not medically certain, would be substantially certain or more likely than not. *Judicial Council of California Criminal Jury Instructions* (CALCRIM) stipulates, if it is determined that the defendant has committed murder, the prosecution must prove beyond reasonable doubt that the defendant has committed an act that resulted in the death of another person or the fetus, and, when the defendants acts, they have a mentality known as "malice aforethought", When the defendants claim that their actions are justifiable or excusable, the prosecution also bear the burden to prove such justifications or excuses dose not stand. In view of this, combined with relevant academic summaries, the elements of murder are summarized as follows.

《加利福尼亚州刑法典》规定,谋杀是指基于事先恶意,非法杀人或杀害胎儿的行为。但是根据《医疗性堕胎法》实施的堕胎,为了挽救孕妇必要实施的堕胎以及得到孕妇要求、批准、帮助或同意的堕胎除外。[1]《加利福尼亚州司法委员会刑事陪审法律指导意见》规定,如果要认定被告人实施了谋杀犯罪,检方必须排除合理怀疑地证明:被告人实施了导致他人,或胎儿死亡的行为;并且,被告人行为时,具有被称为"事先恶意"的心态;在被告人提出其行为具有正当性或可免责时,检方还需要证

〔1〕 See Cal. Penal Code § 187.

明行为人在没有免责事由或正当化事由的情况下实施了杀人行为。[1] 有鉴于此，结合相关学界总结，[2]对谋杀罪的构成要素进行介绍。[3]

As mentioned earlier, the differentiation of homicide in the California Penal Code is mainly based on the basis of Mens rea. But in addition to mental states, specific means and methods of committing killing are also considered. Based on comprehensive evaluation, murder can be further divided into two categories: first degree murder or second degree murder.

如前所述，《加利福尼亚州刑法典》对杀人罪的区分主要建立在犯意基础上。但除了犯意，实施杀人的特定手段、方法等也被考虑进来。综合评价，谋杀又进一步分为两类：一级谋杀或二级谋杀。[4]

California Penal Code provides, the actor is guilty of first degree murder if the People have proved that the acted willfully, deliberately, and with premeditation. The actor acted willfully if perpetrator intended to kill. The actor acted deliberately if actor carefully weighed the considerations for and against perpetrator's choice and, knowing the consequences, decided to kill. The perpetrator acted with premeditation if perpetrator decided to kill before completing the acts that caused death. The length of time the person spends considering whether to kill does not alone determine whether the killing is deliberate and premeditated. On the one hand, the amount of time required for deliberation and premeditation may vary from the circumstances. A decision to kill made rashly, impulsively, or without careful consideration is not deliberated and premeditated. On the other hand, a cold, calculated decision to kill can be reached quickly. The test is the extent of the reflection, not the length of time.[5]

《加利福尼亚州刑法典》规定，如果检方已经证明行为人的行为是有意的、蓄意的和有预谋的，那么行为人就犯有一级谋杀罪。"有意"杀人，是指行为人意图实施杀人行为。"蓄意"杀人，是指犯罪者仔细权衡利弊，并在明知后果的情况下决定杀人。"预谋"杀人，是指犯罪者在完成导致死亡的行为之前就已经决定杀人。并不能单独根据行为人考虑是否杀人的时间长短来判断杀人是蓄意的还是有预谋的。一方面，蓄意和预谋所需的时间可能因情况而异。鲁莽、冲动或未经深思熟虑而做出

---

〔1〕 See CALCRIM No. 520.

〔2〕 See Shiva Shirazi Davoudian, *Developments in California Homicide Law*: *Introduction*: *The Basic*, 36 Loy. L. A. L. Rev. 375(2003).

〔3〕 相关内容，可参见李立丰：《美国刑法评解》(下册)，社会科学文献出版社2023年版，第784页。

〔4〕 See Cal. Penal Code § 189.

〔5〕 See CALCRIM No. 521.

的杀人决定，并非蓄意和预谋。另一方面，行为人也可以很快便做出冷静斟酌、深思熟虑的杀人决定。应当采取的检验标准应该是反思的程度，而非反思时间的长短。

Besides the mens rea mentioned above, in judicial practice, if the prosecution has proved that the perpetrator murdered by torture, or the perpetrator murdered while lying in wait or immediately thereafter, or the perpetrator murdered by using a destructive device or explosive, or the perpetrator murdered by using a weapon of mass destruction, or the perpetrator used ammunition designed primarily to penetrate metal or armor to commit the murder and the perpetrator knew that the ammunition was designed primarily to penetrate metal or armor, or the perpetrator murdered by shooting a firearm from a motor vehicle, or the perpetrator murdered by using poison. It should be emphasized here that the prosecution has the burden of proving beyond a reasonable doubt that the killing is first degree murder rather than a lesser crime. If the People have not met this burden, you must find the perpetrator not guilty of first degree murder and the murder is second degree murder.[1]

除上述犯意外，在司法实践中，如果检方已经证明行为人通过残忍手段杀人，或在埋伏期间或之后立即实施杀人行为，或犯罪人被使用破坏性装置或爆炸物实施谋杀，或使用大规模杀伤性武器实施谋杀，或使用主要用于穿透金属制品或防弹衣的弹药且犯罪者明知此类弹药主要用于穿透金属制品或防弹衣，或行为人从机动车辆上开枪杀人，或罪犯使用毒药实施谋杀，都可以认定构成一级谋杀。这里应该强调的是，检方有责任排除合理怀疑地证明上述谋杀是一级谋杀，而不是较轻的罪行。如果无法履行上述证明责任，就必须认定犯罪者并未犯有一级谋杀罪，而是二级谋杀。

Second degree murder is known as "fill in the gaps" type of murder, which means that although similar to first degree murder, if the defendant lacks malice aforethought or is not classified as a serious felony murder, it should be considered as second degree murder. As mentioned earlier, second degree murder includes three types, namely killing without malice aforethought or premeditation; killing with implied malice (from a reverse perspective, without provocation, it can be inferred that the behavior is malicious, and the defendant's behavior often constitutes second degree murder. The existence of provocation can refute this presumption); and felony murder with inherent danger.

---

[1] See CALCRIM No. 521.

二级谋杀被称为"补漏"型谋杀犯罪,也就是说,其虽然类似一级谋杀,但被告人缺乏事先恶意心态,或者不属于法定类型的重罪谋杀,就应被认定为二级谋杀。如前所述,二级谋杀包括三种类型,即没有事先恶意或事先恶意的故意杀人;基于默示恶意的谋杀(从反向来看,缺乏"挑衅"就可推定行为是恶意的,被告人的行为往往构成二级谋杀。可以通过证明存在挑衅来反驳这种推定)以及具有内在危险性的重罪谋杀。[1]

9.3.2 Manslaughter(非预谋杀人罪)

In early common law, manslaughter was not an independent crime. It evolved from the effort to punish someone who is accountable but not culpable of the death penalty. Initially, there was no difference in punishment between murder and manslaughter. Both were serious crimes and had been sentenced to death. However, in early common law, lower levels of homicide beyond murder could be punished with general pardon. One way to avoid the harsh effects of common law was the "benefit of clergy". Later, the law extended this privilege to the general public. This has led to the transfer of certain crimes within the privileges of the church. Therefore, according to common law, the standard of whether a church should be considered a privilege mainly examines whether it should be subject to the death penalty. Judicial practice distinguishes murder with malice aforethought and excludes other crimes from the privileges of the church. The illegal killing, which is considered a privilege of the church, does not apply the death penalty. For this kind of homicide, the common law has constructed a new concept of "manslaughter" because it distinguishes between the death penalty and non - death penalty with malice aforethought. The common law defines manslaughter as illegal homicide without prior malicious intent. The difference between different types of homicide is a factual, non - legal distinction.

在早期普通法中,非预谋杀人并不是独立的犯罪类型,其是从惩罚某种具有可责性但又不该当死刑的犯罪行为的两难处境中演化而来。最初,在谋杀和非预谋杀人之间的刑罚并无差别。两者都是重罪,且都被处以死刑。然而,在早期普通法当中,谋杀之外的较低层级的杀人罪,可以被处以"大赦"(general pardon)。避免普通法严苛效果的做法之一,便是"教士特权"(The benefit of clergy)。后期,法律将这种特权扩展至普罗大众。这导致教会特权中的某些犯罪被转移出来。因此,在普通法中,是否适用教会特权的标准,主要考察其是否适用死刑。司法实践区分了基于事

[1] See Cal. Penal Code § 189.

先恶意的杀人,将其他的犯罪从教会特权中排除出去。被认为适用教会特权的非法杀人,不适用死刑。对此类杀人罪,普通法建构了一种全新的概念,即“非预谋杀人”[1]。因为杀人者是否具有事先恶意关乎是否对其适用死刑,所以根据普通法,非预谋杀人往往被理解为没有事先恶意的情况下实施的非法杀人行为。[2]

In England, the ingredients of manslaughter are supposed to be the same as that of murder, except that the requirements of oblique intention or actual intention as to killing are omitted. In fact, the two crimes differ in a further respect, that certain exceptions from murder(loss of self control, diminished responsibility, suicide pacts, infanticide), not stated in the traditional definition, and the crime can reduce to manslaughter. Manslaughter falls into two categories: voluntary manslaughter occurs when the perpetrator with the requisite fault for murder kills the victim, but successfully raises the partial defense of loss of control, or with the requisite fault for murder kills the victim, but successfully raises the partial defense of diminished responsibility, or where the perpetrator and victim agree to take their lives as a part of a suicide pact. “loss of control” “diminished responsibility” and “suicide pact” are legal defenses that can be a raised against a murder charge, but do not necessarily allow the defendant to go free. The judge has the usual wide discretion in sentencing for manslaughter. Besides, involuntary manslaughter covers gross negligence manslaughter; constructive manslaughter(otherwise known as unlawful dangerous act manslaughter, subjective recklessness manslaughter and corporate manslaughter).[3]

在英国法当中,非预谋杀人罪的构成要件被认为与谋杀罪的构成要件相同,但其省去了针对杀人的间接故意或者实际故意的要求。事实上,这两种罪行还有一点不同,传统定义中没有规定的某些谋杀的例外(丧失自我控制、减少责任、相约自杀、杀婴),可将罪行减轻为非预谋杀人。非预谋杀人被分为两类:自愿实施的非预谋杀人和非自愿实施的非预谋杀人。自愿实施的非预谋杀人,首先包括被告人基于谋杀所要求的罪过心态杀害了被害人,但成功地提出了“失去控制”等抗辩事由。其次,被告人基于谋杀所要求的罪过心态杀害了被害人,但成功地提出了“减轻责任”的抗辩事由。最后,被害人甲与被害人乙相约自杀。“失去控制”“减轻责任”“相约自杀”是可以针对谋杀指控提出的法定抗辩事由,但不一定使被告人获得无罪开释。

---

[1] See Francis B. Sayre, *Mens Rea*, 45 Harv. L. Rev. 975(1932).

[2] 相关内容,可参见李立丰:《美国刑法评解》(下册),社会科学文献出版社 2023 年版,第 784 页。

[3] Dennis J. Baker, *Glanville Williams' Textbook of Criminal Law*, 4th edition, Sweet & Maxwell (2015).

这种形式的非预谋杀人,被称为"自愿实施的非预谋杀人",因为被告人故意实施了杀人行为,或以其他方式具有谋杀罪的主观要件。法官对非预谋杀人的量刑通常有一般自由裁量权。除此之外的非自愿实施的非预谋杀人罪,主要包括严重的非预谋杀人以及推定非预谋杀人(又称实施非法危险行为所导致的非预谋杀人、主观轻率非预谋杀人以及法人实施的非预谋杀人)。[1]

■ Case study(案例学习)

People v. Washington [1976] 58 Cal. App. 3d 620; 130 Cal. Rptr. 96(加利福尼亚州诉华盛顿案)

Facts(基本案情)

In the case appellant was found guilty of second – degree murder. Victim was shot by appellant, his homosexual partner, while the two were riding in the victim's car. The killing resulted from a lover's quarrel. Appellant argued that in defining heat of passion, the Court should modify the standard of "an ordinarily reasonable person of average disposition" to account for his homosexuality.

本案中,上诉人被判犯有二级谋杀罪。受害人被上诉人,即他的同性恋伴侣所枪杀,当时两人同在受害者的车里,因为感情问题发生激烈争吵。上诉人辩称,在定义激情冲动时,法院应该对"普通的理性人"的标准加以修改,以涵盖他所具有的同性恋身份。

Issues(争议焦点)

What the appropriate standard should be for a heat of passion defense.

激情冲动抗辩的适当认定标准应该为何。

Held(法官意见)

Affirmed.

To be sufficient to reduce a homicide to manslaughter, the heat of passion must be such as would naturally be aroused in the mind of an ordinary, reasonable person, under the given facts and circumstances, or in the mind of a person of ordinary self control. No defendant may set up his own standard of conduct and justify or excuse himself because in fact his individual passions were aroused.

维持原判。

---

〔1〕 参见[英]丹尼斯·贝克主编:《格兰维尔·威廉姆斯刑法学教科书:典型罪编》,李立丰译,法律出版社2023年版,第144页。

为了将杀人罪减为非预谋杀人罪，激情冲动的强度必须是在既定的事实和情况下，在一个普通的理性人的脑海中，或者在一个具有自我控制的人的头脑中自然激发出来的。任何被告都不能因为他个人的激情冲动实际上被激发出来而确立自己的行为标准并将其作为自己的抗辩或免责事由。

Decision（上诉判决）

The Court found that the appropriate standard was in use. Under Appellant's suggested standard, each individual defendant would have the ability to set up a standard that would account for their individual personalities. The current reasonable person standard ensured that no man of extremely violent passion could justify killing.

法院认定正在使用的标准具有适当性。因为根据上诉人提出的标准，每个被告都可以制定一个标准来解释他们的个人特质。目前的理性人标准可以确保没有任何具有极端激情冲动的行为人能够据此为其所实施的杀人行为提供正当性抗辩。

Questions：1. If the standard of an ordinarily reasonable person of average disposition cannot consider the special attributes of homosexuality, can race, gender, education level, intelligence, or other personal traits be included?（Please scan the QR code on the right to get the answer）

如果普通理性人标准不考虑行为人系同性恋这一个人特质，那么是否可以纳入种族、性别、受教育程度、智商或者其他个人特质？（答案请扫描右侧二维码获取）

2. What's the difference between second degree murder and manslaughter?（The way to obtain the answer is the same as above）

二级谋杀与非预谋杀人之间的区别是什么？（答案获取方式同上）

■ Curriculum Ideology and Politics for this Chapter（课程思政）

In the common law and the continental criminal law, there is the so - called reasonable person standard. The reason for this is not only to limit the discretion of judges, but more importantly, to highlight the essential attributes of criminal law, that is, to give moral condemnation to illegal acts marked as crimes. In this condemnation process, it is necessary to cite the so - called reasonable person standard representing public opinion.

无论是普通法系刑法学，还是大陆法系刑法学，均存在所谓理性人标准，究其原因，除借此限制法官的自由裁量权之外，更为重要的是均意在凸显刑法的本质属性，即对于被标识为犯罪的违法行为给予道德的否定评价，而在这个否定过程中，必然需要援引代表社会公众意见的所谓理性人标准。

9.4 Exercise(课后练习)(答案请扫描右侧二维码获取)

9.4.1 Test of Terminologies(术语考查)

①slayer ②homicide
③murder ④manslaughter
⑤viability ⑥feticide
⑦human being ⑧abortion
⑨embryonic man ⑩foreseeability
⑪remoteness ⑫express malice
⑬implied malice

9.4.2 Short - answer Questions(简答题)

1. Why distinguish murder with manslaughter?

为什么要区分谋杀与非预谋杀人？

2. Assuming that at the time of committing the murder, the defendant sincerely believed that the victim had passed away. The defendant stabbed the victim with the intention of killing and believed that the victim had already been killed. The defendant then threw the victim off a cliff or into the river, resulting in the destruction of the body. However, medical evidence shows that the victim was either thrown to death or drowned. Does this defendant guilty of murder?

假设在实施杀人行为的时候，被告人由衷认为被害人已经死亡，比如被告人捅了被害人，意图杀死对方，并相信自己已经将其杀死，之后将被害人扔下悬崖，或扔进河里，从而毁尸灭迹。但医学证据显示，被害人是被摔死或淹死的。在这种情况下，被告人的行为是否构成谋杀？

■ Curriculum Ideology and Politics(课程思政)

Common law countries have developed a relatively complex system of criminal responsibility and punishment for homicide, and have continuously improved it through precedents in judicial practice. This combination of legislation and precedents can better achieve substantive justice. From this, it can be seen that the organic combination of judicial precedents and legislation in punishing crimes not only has more flexibility, but also enables the integration of law and practice, and can better achieve goals and justice.

普通法国家针对杀人犯罪制定了相对复杂的罪责体系与刑罚制度,并且在司法实践中通过判例得到了不断完善。这种立法和判例相结合的方式,更能实现实质正义。由此可以看出,对于惩罚犯罪,司法判例和立法的有机结合,不仅更具有灵活性,而且也更能使法律与实践相融合,更好地实现公平正义。

■ Summary(总结)

1. French term homicide is a type of concept, that is, a superior concept, while murder and manslaughter are the two subordinate concepts of this type of concept.

杀人犯罪这一法语词汇,是一种类概念,也就是上位概念,而谋杀和非预谋杀人,则是这一类概念的两个下位概念。

2. The "Viability" standard, which refers to the further development of understanding of the fetus and the legal definition of the developmental stage of the fetus with the development of contemporary medicine. In *Roe v. Wade*, the Supreme Court of the United States defined the "Viability" rule as the ability of a fetus to survive independently from the uterus at the end of the second stage of pregnancy.

"生存力"标准是指随着当代医学的发展,对胎儿的认识以及对胎儿发展阶段法律界定的进一步发展结果。在罗伊诉韦德案中,美国联邦最高法院将"生存力"标准界定为孕期的第二阶段结束后,这个时期的胎儿可以离开子宫独立存活。

3. If it is determined that the defendant has committed murder, the prosecution must prove beyond reasonable doubt that the defendant has committed an act that resulted in the death of another person or the fetus; And, when the defendant acted, they had a mentality known as "malice aforethought"; When the defendant claimed that their actions are justifiable or excusable, the prosecution also bore the burden to prove such justifications or excuses dose not stand.

如果要认定被告人实施了谋杀犯罪,检方必须排除合理怀疑地证明:被告人实施了导致他人或胎儿死亡的行为;并且被告人行为时,具有被称为"事先恶意"的心态;被告人提出其行为具有正当性或可免责时,检方还需要证明其在没有免责事由或正当化事由的情况下,实施了杀人行为。

Chapter 10 Crimes Against Persons Ⅱ: Sex offences, Bodily Injury, and Crimes of Personal Restraint

第 10 章 人身侵害犯罪Ⅱ:性犯罪、人身伤害犯罪和限制人身犯罪

■ The Learning Objective(学习目标)

1. To understand the historical evolution of the sex offenses.

了解性犯罪的历史流变。

2. To have a basic understanding of what is rape and its types and elements.

了解强奸罪的定义、类型与构成。

3. To understand the criminalization of domestic violence in western countries.

了解西方国家对家庭暴力行为的犯罪化。

4. To understand the typcial crimes against persons.

了解人身伤害类的主要犯罪。

5. To understand the elements and punishing of crimes of stalking.

了解缠扰罪的构成与处罚。

6. To learn some terminologies related to the Chapter.

掌握本章的专业术语。

■ Chapter Outline(本章内容概要)

If the punishment for homicide represents a society's emphasis and protection of its own existence, then the criminal protection of sexual and physical rights represents a society's level of civilization and moral dilemmas. This chapter mainly discusses the sexual offences, bodily injury, and crimes of restricting personal freedom in British and American criminal law through specific cases, including the historical changes, constituent elements, and types and levels of sexual offences; rape in sexual offences; typical crimes such as assault, battery, domestic violence, and stalking that infringe upon personal rights.

如果说对于杀人犯罪的惩罚,代表一个社会对于自身存续的重视与保护,那么对于性权利与身体权利的刑法保护,则代表着一个社会的文明程度与道德困境。本章主要结合具体案例讨论英美刑法中的性犯罪、人身伤害犯罪和限制人身犯罪,具体包括性犯罪的历史流变、构成要素、类型层级;性犯罪中的强奸罪;侵犯人身权的殴打罪、攻击罪、家庭暴力犯罪、缠扰罪等典型犯罪。

■ The Purpose of Curriculum Ideology and Politics for this Chapter (本章的课程思政目标)

1. The criminal laws of common law countries have stipulated many crimes against persons, such as sexual offences, assault, battery, and stalking. The reason why criminal law is used to protect the rights and interests of citizens is because it has significant implications for human survival and development, and even for the development of society. We should cultivate the character of respecting the personal rights and interests of others'.

英美法系国家刑法规定了诸多针对人身权的犯罪,如性犯罪、攻击罪、殴打罪和缠扰罪等。之所以用刑法保护公民的这些权益,是因为其对人的生存和发展,甚至对社会的发展等,具有重大意义。作为一个文明社会的公民,应养成尊重他人人身权益的品格。

2. Compared with China and other countries, the criminal laws of common law countries not only prohibit acts or protect rights, but also have significant differences in the constituent elements of crimes, such as targeted crimes and crimes that harm personal rights and interests. Understanding the patterns of such crimes in the common law system, makes students realize the diversity of criminal laws in various countries around the world.

英美法系国家刑法针对性犯罪、伤害人身权益等犯罪的规定,和中国或其他国家相比较,不仅禁止的行为或保护的权益等有差异,在犯罪构成要素上也有很大差异。了解英美法系这类犯罪的样态,使学生认识到世界各国刑法的多样性。

■ Terminology(专业术语)

wrongful intent	错误意图
knowledge	了解

dolus eventualis	间接故意
substantial sexual conduct	实质性行为
annoy	骚扰
molest	猥亵
prurient interest	淫欲
distribute	传播
pimping	淫媒
prostitute	拉客
pandering	迎合
battery	殴打罪
assault	攻击罪
the crime of fornication	通奸罪
Megan's Law	梅根法
Jessica's Law	杰西卡法
sexual assault	性攻击
marital rape	婚内强奸
aggravated sexual abuse	加重型性虐待
earnest resistance	真诚抵抗
reasonable resistance	合理抵抗
oral copulation	口交
sodomy	鸡奸
remoteness	(证据的)疏远性
sexual penetration	性器插入
lewd and lascivious act	淫行法
unlawful sexual intercourse	不法性交
a threat to retaliate	威胁报复
advance consent	事先合意

10.1 Sex Offenses(性犯罪)

According to statistics, in the United States, a sexual assault occurs every two minutes. To address this situation, since the 1970s, rape laws in various jurisdictions in the United States have begun to expand. This directly led to the passage of the Violence Against Women Act in the United States in 2013. From the perspective of the development of criminal law theory, the significant changes in the U. S. criminal law over the past few decades which are related to sex offenses. Firstly, the scope of crackdown on rape crimes has significantly expanded; For example, including California, the vast majority of jurisdictions in the United States have abandoned the traditional views represented by the Model Penal Code and recognized the criminality of marital rape. Secondly, there is a clear trend towards increased civil and criminal liability for sex offenders. For example, for sex offenders, at the end of the 20th century, various versions of *the Megan's Law* and *Jessica's Law* have been introduced in various states in the US, which not only increase penalties for sex offenders, but also add civil obligations such as a residence registration system, GPS tracking, and others. The legislative body attempts to legislate in this way to combat heinous and cruel sexual offences, particularly those against minors.

据统计,在美国,每两分钟就会发生一起性侵事件。为了应对这一情况,自从 20 世纪 70 年代开始,美国各司法管辖区的强奸成文法开始扩展。[1] 这也直接导致 2013 年美国联邦通过《针对妇女实施的暴力行为法案》。[2] 从刑法理论的发展脉络来看,晚近美国刑法中变化较大的部分当属与性犯罪相关之规定。首先,强奸犯罪的打击范围出现了显著的扩张。例如,包括加利福尼亚州在内,美国绝大多数司法管辖区已经放弃了《模范刑法典》[3] 所代表的传统观点,承认婚内强奸的犯罪性。[4] 其次,性犯罪者的民事责任与刑事责任苛重化倾向明显。例如,20 世纪末,美国联邦与各州纷纷设定各种版本的"梅根法"[5] 和"杰西卡法"[6],除了对性犯罪

[1] See Kathleen Daly & Brigitte Bouhours, *Rape and Attrition in the Legal Process: A Comparative Analysis of Five Countries*, 39 Crime& Just. 565 (2010).

[2] 42 U. S. C. § 13701 to § 14040.

[3] See MPC § 213.1.

[4] See Michelle J. Anderson, *Marital Immunity, Intimate Relationships, and Improper Inferences: A New Law on Sexual Offenses by Intimates*, 64 Hastings L. J. 1465 (2003).

[5] "梅根法",1994 年,殁年 7 岁的美国小女孩梅根·坎卡被住在她家附近的一名性犯罪分子绑架并遭其奸杀。1996 年 5 月 17 日,克林顿总统签署了"梅根法",根据该法,被正式建档的性犯罪案件资料,包括被释放的性犯罪人信息将放到网上公开。

[6] "杰西卡法",是指 2005 年佛罗里达州率先通过的儿童性犯罪保护法,该法案规定,性侵 14 岁以下儿童,最低刑期为 25 年,最高无期或死刑。不得假释,不得担保。前科犯必须终身佩戴 GPS 监控装置,每 6 个月回警局报告一次,并且禁止接近学校 600 米以内等,随后,大多数州均通过了类似的法案。

人加重刑罚,还增加了诸如住所登记制度、GPS 追踪以及其他民事义务。[1] 立法机构试图通过此类立法来抗制那些手段残忍、令人发指的严重性犯罪,特别是针对侵害未成年人的性犯罪。[2]

10.1.1 Context of Sex Offenses(性犯罪的背景)

Overall, in the context of U. S. criminal law, sexual offenses refer to a cluster or bundle of crimes primarily related to rape. In some states, the term "sexual assault" can be used interchangeably with "rape". New Jersey and other states define rape as a specific "sexual assault" crime, highlighting the violent nature of rape and other sexual offences, transforming the long - standing unjust and harsh punishment of rape on victims, and placing more emphasis on the behavior of the defendant. However, generally speaking, the difference between rape and so - called "sexual assault" or "assault" crimes is that the latter includes a series of sexual offenses that do not include the insertion of instruments, while rape does. In addition, in some states, the establishment of rape requires the perpetrator to use violence, while sexual assault only implies sexual intercourse without consent. Some scholars even believe that the concept of "sexual assault" was created mainly because the feminist movement that emerged in the 1960s in the United States hoped to convey a signal that rape was not a sexual crime, but a violent crime. Understanding sexual offenses requires special attention to the following points. Firstly, the incompleteness of the gender binary system. Indeed, based on gender dualism, the use of expressions such as "violence against women" is often criticized for being biased, lacking inclusiveness, and facing criticism from experience, theory, politics, and practice. Especially from the perspective of dualism, it is evident that men find it difficult to become victims of sexual abuse. Even from the perspective of rape, the most typical sexual crime, male victims can be found. In addition, the binary opposition between genders is facing new challenges in today's society the typical issue among these is that of transgender individuals. From the perspective of historical trends, in addition to maintaining strict punishment for sex offenses in the United State, there has also been a technological transformation from moral negation to behavioral control.

---

〔1〕 See David A. Singleton, *Sex Offender Residency Statutes and the Culture of Fear: The Case for More Meaningful Rational Basis Review of Fear—Driven Public Safety Laws*, 3 U. St. Thomas L. J. 600 (2006).

〔2〕 相关内容,可参见李立丰:《美国刑法评解》(下册),社会科学文献出版社 2023 年版,第 858 页。

总体来说,美国刑法语境中的性犯罪,是指以强奸罪为主的一个犯罪集群或犯罪束。在某些州,所谓"性侵"或"性攻击"与"强奸"一词可以互换使用。新泽西州等州将强奸罪界定为一种具体的"性攻击"犯罪,从而凸显强奸等性犯罪所蕴含的暴力属性,转变长久以来强奸罪对受害人的不当苛责,更多侧重被告人的行为的做法。[1] 但一般来说,强奸与所谓"性侵"或"性攻击"犯罪的区别在于:后者包含一系列并不包括性器插入的性犯罪,而强奸则不然。另外,在某些州,强奸的成立要求行为人使用暴力,而性侵仅仅意味着在非同意情况下的性交行为。甚至有学者认为,"性侵"作为一个概念之所以被创制出来,主要是因为20世纪60年代兴起的美国女权运动希望借此表达这样一种信号:强奸不是一种肉欲犯罪,而是一种暴力犯罪。[2] 对性犯罪的理解,需要特别注意如下几点:首先是性别两分法的不完整性。的确,基于性别二元论,使用"对女性的暴力"的这类表述方式,往往被批判为具有偏见性,缺乏包容性,面临经验、理论、政治和实践的批评。特别是从二元论出发,男性很难成为性侵害的受害者。[3] 即使就作为典型的性犯罪,即强奸罪而言,也可以发现男性受害人的身影。除此之外,性别的二元对立在当今社会面临全新挑战。从历史发展的趋势与潮流来看,美国性犯罪刑罚处遇除了一如既往地保持严苛[4],还呈现出从道德否定到行为控制的技术性转型特征。[5]

10.1.2　Nature of Sex Offenses(性犯罪的本质)

Although sexual offenses represented by rape touch upon one of the most cherished "rights" of humanity, the criminal law regulations related to it exhibit a strange instability. The definition of sexual offenses varies greatly among different judicial regions in the United States, and there is also much controversy within specific jurisdictions regarding the connotation and extension of sexual offenses, which has not yet reached a very certain level of certainty. The fundamental reason for the emergence of this situation is largely due to the multiple legal interests infringed upon by sexual offenses, which have constantly evolved and proliferated with the development of the

---

〔1〕 See Joshua Dressler, *Where We Have Been, and Where We Might Be Going: Some Cautionary Reflections on Rape Law Reform, The Sixty—Eighth Cleveland—Marshall Fund Lecture*, 46 Clev. St. L. Rev. 409 (1998).

〔2〕 See Myka Held & Juliana McLaughlin, *Rape & Sexual Assault*, 15 Geo. J. Gender & L. 155(2014).

〔3〕 See Julie Goldscheid, *Gender Neutrality, the "Violence Against Women" Frame, and Transformative Reform*, 82 Umkc L. Rev. 623(2014).

〔4〕 See Guy Goldberg & Gena Bunn, *Balancing Fairness & Finality: A Comprehensive Review of the Texas Death Penalty*, 5 Tex. Rev. Law & Pol. 49(2000).

〔5〕 相关内容,可参见李立丰:《美国刑法评解》(下册),社会科学文献出版社2023年版,第858页。

times. Essentially, sexual offenses can be classified as violence against sexual freedom/autonomy and non violent infringement of sexual freedom/autonomy. Although it can be classified into these categories, its essence is an infringement of sexual freedom.

尽管以强奸为代表的性犯罪所触及的是人类最为珍视的权利之一,但与之相关的刑法规制却呈现出明显的不稳定性,美国各个司法管辖区对强奸罪的定义差异悬殊,在特定司法管辖区内部,围绕强奸犯罪的内涵与外延也多有争议,远未达到十分确定的程度。[1] 导致这一局面出现的根本原因,在很大程度上在于性犯罪侵害的多元法益正随着时代的发展不断蜕变与增生。从本质上可以将性犯罪分为对性自由的暴力侵害、对性自由的非暴力侵害等不同种类。尽管可以分为这些种类,但其本质是对性自由的侵害。[2]

Firstly, Violence against sexual freedom/autonomy. According to the common law's tradition in the UK, the establishment of rape requires the perpetrator to use violence or threaten to use violence against the victim. During this period, rape in British law was defined as knowingly engaging in sexual activity against a woman's will. For a long period of time, the legislation also largely adopted this definition. The logic behind this definition is that the mainstream values of the common law society at that time believed that if the object of rape protection was seen as a woman's chastity, then if a female wanted to have sex with someone other than her husband, she would become impure and not belong to "true rape". This can also explain why historically, the judicial determination of rape often requires the victim to objectively implement "maximum resistance". Especially at that time, there was no so-called sexual autonomy. If sexual activity occurred outside of marriage, the court would suspect that the victim claimed to have been raped in order to evade criminal responsibility for incest or adultery. Nowadays, most states have criminalized male rape, same-sex rape, and other forms of sexual assault (such as forced oral and sodomy), while abolishing the elements of resistance and passing rape victim protection laws. About half of the states in the US have criminalized forced sexual intercourse within marriage.

第一,对性自由的暴力侵害。根据英国普通法传统,强奸罪的成立要求正犯对受害人使用暴力或以暴力相威胁,即将其理解为"明知违背妇女意志,仍强行与其发

---

〔1〕 See Nicole Fusill, *Note: New York State of Mind: Rape and Mens Rea*, 76 St. John's L. Rev. 603 (2002).

〔2〕 相关内容,可参见李立丰:《美国刑法评解》(下册),社会科学文献出版社2023年版,第858页。

生性行为”。早期美国法也在很大程度上沿用了这一定义。[1] 这一定义背后的逻辑在于,普通法社会主流价值观认为,如果将强奸保护的对象视为女性的贞操,那么倘若一个女人想与她丈夫之外的其他人发生性行为,就变得不贞洁,不属于“真正的强奸”。这也可以解释为什么从历史上来看,强奸罪的司法认定,往往要求强奸犯罪的被害人客观上实施了“最大限度的抵抗”。特别是在性自主权还未出现的情况下,如果发生婚外性行为,法院会怀疑受害人之所以主张自己遭到强奸,是为了逃避乱伦或通奸的刑事责任。时至今日,美国大多数州都已将男性强奸、同性强奸以及其他形式的性侵犯(如强迫口交和肛交)犯罪化。同时,废除了反抗要件,通过了强奸被害人保护法。美国约一半的州完成了婚内强制性交的犯罪化。

Seccondly, non violent infringement of sexual freedom/autonomy. The so - called non violent infringement of sexual freedom refers to the situation where, in addition to using violence and coercion, the victim is presumed to have no intention of having sexual intercourse when they are young or fall into an unconscious or erroneous state of understanding. For example, the Model Penal Code stipulates that in cases where the victim is under ten years old, even if the defendant has a reasonable error towards the victim being over ten years old, it cannot be used as a defense against sexual assault. In other words, the Model Penal Code recognizes strict liability for the age of the victim as an element. In addition to the application of consensual fiction for sexual offenses against minors, most states in the United States also criminalize sexual activity between powerful perpetrators and subservient victims. The term “powerful” refers to the defendant’s opportunity to exercise their dominant position over the victim, such as employers and employees, doctors and patients, pastors and believers, caregivers and caretakers, teachers and students. As of now, only eight states in the US do not have similar regulations.

第二,对性自由的非暴力侵害。对性自由的非暴力侵害是指除使用暴力、胁迫手段之外,利用受害人年幼,或受害人陷入无意识或认识错误状态,推定其不具有发生性关系的合意的情况。例如,《模范刑法典》规定在被害人不满10周岁的情况下,即使被告人对受害人已满10周岁具有合理的错误认识也不可以作为性侵犯罪的抗辩。换句话说,对受害人年龄这一要素,《模范刑法典》承认严格责任。[2] 除了针对

---

〔1〕 See Matthew R. Lyon, *Comment, No Means No?: Withdrawal of Consent During Intercourse and the Continuing Evolution of the Definition of Rape*, 95 J. Crim. L. & Criminology 277 (2004).

〔2〕 See Kenneth W. Simons, *When is Strict Criminal Liability Just*, 87 J. Crim. L. & Criminology 1075 (1997).

未成年人的性犯罪适用合意拟制,美国大多数州还将具有一定权势的行为人与屈从的受害人之间发生的性行为加以犯罪化。[1] "权势",是指被告人有机会对受害人实施其主导地位,适例如雇主与雇员、医生和病人、牧师和信徒、被照顾者和照顾者、老师和学生。截至目前,美国只有 8 个州没有类似的规定。

10.1.3 Crime of Rape(强奸罪)

In general, the provisions in Common law are divided into two categories based on whether the target of infringement is specifically targeted at minors. Common sexual offenses that do not consider the age group of the target include rape, oral copulation, sodomy, sexual penetration, lewd and lascivious acts, etc. Sexual offenses targeting minors only include illegal sexual intercourse, oral sex, sodomy, genital insertion, sexual assault, and other illegal activities. In addition to the criteria for dividing by the age of the victim, there are also some special types of sexual offences, such as crimes involving pornographic materials, prostitution, illegal acts committed in public, incest, and sexual abuse of animals. Hereby after will only take the crime of rape in California Penal Cod as an example to briefly introduce the sexual offenses stipulated in US criminal law. From a legislative perspective, rape in California Penal Code mainly refers to the act of a perpetrator engaging in vaginal intercourse with a female in the absence of or presumed absence of consent. It can be further subdivided into two categories: typical rape and atypical rape.

概括来说,英美刑法中性犯罪的规定,以侵害对象是否专门针对未成年人为界,大体分为两类:普通性犯罪和针对未成年人的性犯罪。其中,不考虑对象年龄段普通性犯罪包括强奸、口交、鸡奸、性器插入、淫行罪等,仅针对未成年人的性犯罪包括违法性交、口交、鸡奸、性器插入、淫行罪及其他违法行为。除以被害人年龄进行划分的标准之外,还存在一些特殊的性犯罪类型,如涉及淫害物品的犯罪,容留介绍卖淫、卖淫、乱伦及性虐待动物。这里仅以强奸罪为例,简要介绍以加利福尼亚州法为代表的美国刑法中规定的性犯罪。从立法角度来看,加利福尼亚州法律规定中的强奸,主要是指在不具备,或推定不具备合意的情况下,行为人与女性发生阴道性交的行为。[2] 而其又进一步可以被细分为典型强奸与非典型强奸两大类。[3]

Firstly, let's introduce the typical crime of rape. The so – called typical rape refers

[1] See John F. Decker & Peter G. Baroni, "*No*" *Still Means* "*Yes*": *The Failure of the* "*Non—Consent*" *Reform Movement in American Rape and Sexual Law*, 101 J. Crim. L. & Criminology 1081(2011).

[2] People v. Kelly, 1 Cal. 4th 495(1992).

[3] 相关内容,可参见李立丰:《美国刑法评解》(下册),社会科学文献出版社 2023 年版,第 858 页。

to rape and marital rape carried out through force, fear, or threat. In this regard, the prosecution needs to prove that the perpetrator engaged in sexual intercourse with a female through specific means in the absence of consent. Sexual intercourse refers to the act of inserting the penis into the female vagina or external genitalia in any form, regardless of the degree of penetration or ejaculation required. The specific means used here generally include three situations in judicial practice. Firstly, it refers to the situation where the defendant accomplished the intercourse by force, violence, duress, menace, or fear of immediate and unlawful bodily injury to the female or to someone else; Secondly, it refers to the situation where the defendant accomplished the intercourse by threatening to retaliate in the future against the female or someone else when there was a reasonable possibility that the defendant would carry out the threat. A threat to retaliate is a threat to kidnap, falsely imprison, or inflict extreme pain, serious bodily injury, or death. Thirdly, it refers to the situation where the defendant accomplished the intercourse by threatening to use the authority of a public office to incarcerate, arrest, or deport someone. A public official is a person employed by federal, state, or local government who has authority to incarcerate, arrest, or deport. The female must have reasonably believed that the defendant was a public official even if he was not. The violence in the crime of rape does not have a special meaning, and the court does not need to define it. Coercion refers to the direct or indirect threat to use force, violence, create danger, or retaliate, causing rational individuals to act against their will or submit. When determining whether there is coercion, it is necessary to comprehensively examine all the circumstances, including the age of the victim and their relationship with the perpetrator. If the victim is genuinely and reasonably afraid, or if the victim's concerns are genuine but unreasonable, but the perpetrator knows and takes advantage of this, it is considered coercive sexual intercourse. Same as above. The perpetrator can create fear through false or deceptive statements, leading rational individuals to act against their will and engage in consensual sexual behavior. The situation of obtaining agreement through coercion or intimidation does not include objective violence or coercion.

首先,对典型强奸罪进行介绍。典型强奸是指通过暴力、恐吓或胁迫实施的强奸及婚内强奸。[1] 对于该罪,其客观行为是行为人通过特定手段在女性缺乏合意

[1] See Cal. Penal Code, §261(a)(2), (6)&(7).

的情况下与其性交。而性交是指以任何形式将阴茎进入女性阴道或外生殖器的行为，不考虑进入程度，不要求射精。[1] 这里的特定手段，在司法实践当中一般包括三种情况。第一，行为人对受害女性或第三方实施强制、暴力、胁迫、或威胁立即实施非法身体伤害；第二，行为人威胁将来对受害女性或第三方实施报复，且行为人未来有合理可能实施该威胁（"威胁报复"包括威胁绑架、非法拘禁，实施足以造成严重身体痛苦、伤害或死亡的行为）；第三，具有公权者身份的行为人威胁使用公权力监禁、逮捕或驱逐某人。公权者是指受雇于联邦、州或地方政府，有权决定监禁、逮捕或驱逐的人。即使行为人并非上述人员，但如果被害人合理确信的，同样适用于这种情况。需要指出的是，根据相关司法实践，如果行为人使用的强制力足以压制受害女性的意志，就属于通过暴力实施性交。而强奸罪中的暴力，也不具有特殊的含义，法庭无须对其加以界定。[2] 对此，加利福尼亚州最高法院曾指出，对"暴力"一词的通常理解，或者强奸罪的立法规定本身，不需要再指控强奸罪时使用的暴力，和合意性行为中通常伴生的暴力存在实质性的差别。[3] 相反，长期以来，强奸罪中的暴力，检方只需证明行为人实施了违反受害女性意志的性交行为即可。[4] 胁迫是指直接或间接威胁使用强力、暴力、制造危险或实施报复，导致理性人不得不违心去做或屈服。在判断是否存在胁迫的时候，需要综合考察所有情节，包括受害女性的年龄及其与行为人的关系。如果受害女性真诚且合理害怕，或者虽然受害女性的担心是真诚但不合理的，而行为人明知并利用了这一点，都属于胁迫性交。行为人可以通过虚假或欺骗性表述制造恐惧，从而使理性人在违反其意志的情况下行事，合意发生性行为。通过胁迫或恐吓的方式获得合意的情形，并不包括客观的暴力或强制。[5]

Particularly noteworthy is, whether female victims have a willingness to engage in sexual intercourse becomes the key to their judicial determination. "against the will" refers to a lack of agreement. It is generally believed that as a prerequisite for the existence of consensus, women must be aware of the essence of their behavior and be able to act freely and voluntarily. It should be emphasized that in California's judicial practice, it is recognized that women have the right to withdraw their consent at any time regarding whether and how they engage in sexual intercourse. In other words, even

[1] See CALCRIM No. 1000.

[2] See People v. Griffin, 33 Cal. 4th 1015(2004).

[3] See People v. Cicero, 157 Cal. App. 3d 465(1984).

[4] See People v. Young, 190 Cal. App. 3d 248(1987).

[5] See People v. Cardenas, 21 Cal. App. 4th 927(1994).

women who initially agreed to have sex can change their minds during the sexual intercourse process. If such changes occur, according to relevant laws, sexual intercourse will be considered to have been carried out in a non consensual manner if the following conditions are met: a female expresses her opposition to sexual intercourse to the perpetrator and attempts to stop the behavior. This opposition expressed through words and actions is enough to make a rational person understand that she lacks consent during sexual intercourse. In this case, the perpetrator still disregards the opposition of the victim and forcibly continues sexual intercourse. The timing at which a victim expresses opposition to sexual intercourse is not important, but rather the information conveyed to the perpetrator. In the crime of rape, resistance from the victim is not required, and any legal guidance on this requirement is incorrect. Generally speaking, because there is often no third party presenting during sexual intercourse, judicial authorities often need to refer to indirect evidence when determining whether the victim is consensual. For the typical vertical pattern of rape, as long as the perpetrator's genitalia is inserted into the female vagina, regardless of the degree, it is considered a complete rape. Because there is no issue of the number of crimes in U. S. criminal law similar to that in continental law, each entry can be considered as a separate offense. For the typical horizontal pattern of rape, there is a problem of determining accomplices. It should be emphasized that in California judicial practice, rape accomplice is a separate crime and not an aggravating circumstance. The distinction between accomplices in California Penal Code also starts with distinguishing between perpetrators and instigators and accomplices. If the perpetrator personally commits rape and voluntarily collaborates with other accomplices or instigators to commit rape, or if the perpetrator voluntarily assists or instigates the perpetrator to commit rape in person, it constitutes an accomplice to the crime of rape. Overall, the mainstream practice in California's judicial system still believes that accomplices in rape can only be based on rape committed through forced and violent means. On the other hand, the establishment of an accomplice in rape does not require the accomplice to commit the act of rape. For example, even if the perpetrator did not personally commit the rape act, it can still constitute an accomplice in rape when it appears at the scene of the rape crime. For example, a perpetrator who points a gun at the victim's family in another room constitutes an accomplice in rape. However, currently the California Supreme Court has not resolved whether individuals who provide assistance to the crime but do not appear at the overall crime scene constitute accomplices to rape, such as those who provide relevant information to rapists but do not appear at the crime scene, constitute accomplices to rape.

特别需要注意的是,女性受害人对性交的发生是否具有合意,是司法认定的关键。"违反意愿"即缺乏合意。一般认为,作为合意存在的前提,女性必须明知行为的本质,且可以自由并自愿行动。需要强调的是,加利福尼亚州司法实践中一般认为,女性对是否及如何进行性交,存在随时撤回合意的权利。换句话说,即使起初合意性交的女性,也可在性交过程中改变主意。如果发生此类改变,根据相关法律,在满足下列条件的情况下,性交将被视为在非合意情况下进行:女性向行为人表达自己反对性交行为,并试图停止该行为;这种通过言行所表达的反对,足以使理性人理解其对性交缺乏合意;在这种情况下,行为人仍不顾受害女性反对,就是属于强行继续性交。[1] 受害女性表达反对性交的时间点并不重要,重要的是其向行为人表达了这一信息。[2] 强奸罪的成立并不要求受害女性的抵抗都是错误的。一般来说,因为性交行为发生时往往没有第三方在场,因此,司法机关在认定受害女性是否具有合意时,往往还需要参考间接证据。对典型强奸的犯罪来说,只要行为人的性器插入女性阴道,无论进入程度如何,都视为强奸的既遂。因为美国刑法中并不存在类似于大陆法系的罪数问题,因此,每次进入,都可以视为单独成立一次犯罪。[3] 对典型强奸来说,还存在共犯的认定问题。需要强调的是,加利福尼亚州司法实践中,强奸共犯是单独的犯罪,不是加重情节。[4] 加利福尼亚州成文法对共犯的区分,也是从区分实行犯和教唆、帮助犯入手的。如果行为人亲自实施了强奸,并且自愿与其他帮助犯或教唆犯实施强奸,或者行为人自愿帮助、教唆亲自实施强奸的行为人,都构成强奸罪的共犯。[5] 总体来看,目前加利福尼亚州司法实践的主流做法还是认为强奸共犯只能建立在通过强制、暴力手段实施的强奸基础上。除此之外,强奸共犯的成立,并不要求共犯实施强奸的实行行为。例如对出现在强奸犯罪实施的现场的共犯,即使其并没有亲自实施强奸行为依然可以构成强奸共犯。在另外一个房间用枪指着受害人家人的行为人,也构成强奸共犯。[6] 但是,目前加利福尼亚州最高法院并没有解决那些为犯罪提供帮助,没有出现在整体犯罪现场的行为人是否构成强奸共犯的问题。[7]

---

〔1〕 See CALCRIM No. 1000.

〔2〕 See In re John Z, 29 Cal. 4th 756(2003).

〔3〕 See People v. Harrison, 48 Cal. 3d 321(1989).

〔4〕 See People v. Ramirez, 189 Cal. App. 3d 603(1987).

〔5〕 See CALCRIM No. 1001.

〔6〕 See People v. Champion, 9 Cal. 4th 879(1995).

〔7〕 See People v. Champion, 9 Cal. 4th 879(1995).

Secondly, the so – called atypical rape refers to the act of the perpetrator inserting the penis into the female vagina or external genitalia in any form, knowing that the sexual partner is unable to make a valid agreement. Atypical rape, specifically manifested as rape through rape, refers to rape where the victim is in a state of intoxication or marital rape. This situation refers to the act of the perpetrator illegally entering the victim's vagina or external genitalia in any form while the victim is in a state of intoxication. In this regard, the prosecution must prove that the effects of intoxication, anesthesia, and controlled substances make it impossible for the victim female to resist, and that the perpetrator knew or reasonably knew that the effects of the intoxication, anesthesia, and controlled substances would make it impossible for the victim female to resist. Atypical rape also includes rape where the victim is in a state of unconsciousness or marital rape. This situation refers to the act of the perpetrator illegally entering the female vagina or external genitalia in any form without considering the degree of entry or requiring ejaculation, without the victim's understanding of the essential attributes of the behavior. Therefore, California judicial practice generally requires the prosecution to prove that the female victim is unable to resist because she has no understanding of the essence of the behavior, and that the perpetrator is aware that the female victim is unable to resist because she has no understanding of the essence of the behavior. In other words, the law guarantees women's sexual autonomy throughout the entire process of sexual activity. In addition, atypical rape also includes rape where the victim is a disabled woman. This situation refers to the act of the perpetrator illegally entering the vagina or external genitalia of a female with psychological or physiological defects in any form, without considering the degree of entry or requiring ejaculation. In California's judicial practice, it is believed that the prosecution needs to prove that the perpetrator and the female victim were not married during sexual intercourse, and also need to prove that the female victim has intellectual disabilities, developmental disabilities, or physical disabilities, making it impossible for them to reach a legal agreement. The perpetrator knew or should have known that the female had intellectual disabilities, developmental disabilities, or physical disabilities, making it impossible for them to reach a legal agreement. Of particular note is the so – called rape by fraud. This situation refers to the behavior of the perpetrator entering the female vagina or external genitalia in any form, without considering the degree of entry or requiring ejaculation. The perpetrator and the female are not married during sexual intercourse, and the victim agrees to have sexual intercourse because she believes that the perpetrator is her husband; And the perpetrator deceived the victim by lying or hiding information from them, thereby making them believe that they are in a marital state. According to the general judicial practice in the United States, if the victim agrees to sexual intercourse due to a factual error, in other words, the victim is deceived and does not understand that the consent is for sexual intercourse with the perpetrator, then this consent is invalid. The perpetrator's actions violate the victim's free will. But if the victim knows that they want to have sexual intercourse with the other party, but the reason for the sexual intercourse is due to the perpetrator's false statement, causing them to fall into a state of cognitive error, then it cannot be considered that the victim lacks consent for sexual intercourse based on this. Scholars have cited that if a doctor falsely claims to insert surgical instruments into a woman's vagina, but in reality inserts the doctor's penis, it constitutes rape. But if a doctor falsely claims that having sexual intercourse with oneself can cure a disease and leads the victim to believe that they have had sexual intercourse with him/her, it cannot be considered as rape.

非典型强奸,是指行为人明知性交对象无法作出有效合意,仍以任何形式将阴茎插入该女性阴道或外生殖器的行为。非典型强奸具体表现为迷奸,即受害女性处于迷醉状态下的强奸或婚内强奸。[1] 这种情况是指行为人违法在受害人处于迷醉状态的情况下,以任何形式将阴茎进入受害女性阴道或外生殖器的行为。对此,检方必须证明迷醉、麻醉、管制物品的效果使受害女性无法反抗,并且行为人明知或合理知道该迷醉、麻醉、管制物品的效果将会导致受害女性无法反抗。[2] 非典型强奸还包括受害女性处于无认识状态下的强奸或婚内强奸。这种情况是指行为人违法在受害人对行为的本质属性无认识的情况下,以任何形式将阴茎进入女性阴道或外生殖器的行为,不考虑进入程度,不要求射精。为此,加利福尼亚州司法实践一般要求检方必须证明受害女性因为对行为本质无认识,因此无法抵抗,同时行为人明知受害女性因为对行为的本质无认识因此无法抵抗。换言之,法律保障女性在性行为全过程的性自主权。[3] 除此之外,非典型强奸还包括受害女性属于残疾人的强奸。这种情况是指行为人违法以任何形式将阴茎进入心理或生理存在缺陷的女性阴道或外生殖器的行为,不考虑进入程度,不要求射精。加利福尼亚州司法实践中认为,对此检方需要证明行为人与受害女性在性交时没有结婚,同时还需要证明受害女性

[1] See CALCRIM No. 1002.
[2] See Cal. Penal Code § 222.
[3] See CALCRIM No. 1003.

罹患智障、发育不良或生理残疾,使其无法作出法律意义上的合意,行为人明知或合理应当知道该女性罹患智障、发育不良或生理残疾,使其无法作出法律意义上的合意。[1] 特别值得一提的是骗奸,[2]这种情况是指行为人以任何形式将阴茎进入女性阴道或外生殖器的行为,不考虑进入程度,不要求射精,行为人与该女性在性交时并没有结婚,但受害女性因为相信行为人是其丈夫才同意发生性关系;并且行为人欺骗了受害人,向受害人撒谎或向其隐藏信息,从而使其相信彼此处于婚姻状态。根据美国的一般司法实践,如果受害人因为陷入事实认识错误而同意性交,换言之,受害人因为受到欺骗,并不了解自己同意的事项是与行为人发生性关系,那么这种同意就是无效的。行为人这样做违反了受害人的自由意志。但如果受害人知道自己要和对方发生性关系,但发生性关系的理由是因为行为人的虚假陈述,导致其陷入认识错误的状态,则不得据此认为受害人缺乏性交的合意。有学者举例称,如果医生谎称将外科手术用具插入女性阴道,实际上插入的是该医生的性器官,就构成强奸。但如果医生谎称和自己性交可以治病,导致受害人信以为真与其发生性关系,就不得认定其构成强奸。[3]

■ Curriculum Ideology and Politics(课程思政)

Although sexual offences in common law countries have weakened gender distinctions in their historical evolution, they still primarily focus on protecting women. Moreover, in practice, sexual offences mainly target women. Women play an important role in society or families, and even in modern society, they have made tremendous contributions to the development of politics, economy, culture, education, and more. Protecting women's sexual autonomy from infringement through sexual offences and other means reminds citizens and society to respect women.

尽管英美法系国家的性犯罪在历史的演化中削弱了性别区分,但其还是以保护女性为主。而且从实践情况看,性犯罪也主要是以女性为侵害对象。女性在社会或家庭中发挥着重要作用,在现代社会,女性对政治、经济、文化、教育等发展作出了巨大贡献。法律通过性犯罪等罪名保护女性的性权利不受侵犯,倡导公民和社会尊重女性。

---

〔1〕 See CALCRIM No. 1004.

〔2〕 See CALCRIM No. 1005.

〔3〕 相关内容,可参见李立丰:《美国刑法评解》(下册),社会科学文献出版社 2023 年版,第 858 页。

10.2 None Fatal Offense against the Person(侵犯人身权犯罪)

The reason why crimes that infringe on personal bodies are special is because they are closely related to various crimes that infringe on the right to life, freedom, property, and even sexual freedom, and more importantly, because of their long - standing historical roots as a crime in the sense of natural law.

侵害人身权的犯罪之所以特殊,不仅在于其与侵犯生命权、自由权、财产权乃至性自由权的各种犯罪关系密切,更在于其作为一种自然法意义上的犯罪所具有的悠久历史根源。

10.2.1 History(相关历史)

In the common law tradition, intentional injury (including physical harm to others) has always been a serious crime similar to murder, rape, robbery, and arson, and after the 13th century, serious crimes typically involve hanging. Prior to this, in addition to hanging, the King of England sometimes poked eyes or cut off hands and feet of felon. Since the 19th century, courts have emphasized the principle of conditional intent, which means that the defendant proposes that if the victim does not meet specific requirements - such as engaging in specific actions or omissions - to commit harm, this conditional intent can be used as a possible proof that it may ultimately carry out the harmful behavior it objectively threatens.

在普通法传统中,故意伤害(包括残害他人肢体)一直是和谋杀、强奸、抢劫以及纵火类似的重罪。在13世纪之后,重罪通常会执行绞刑。而在此之前,除了绞刑,英国国王有时还会对重罪罪犯处挖眼或者砍掉手断脚的刑罚。[1] 而从19世纪开始,法院就开始强调条件性犯意原则,也就是说,被告人提出如果被害人不满足特定要求,比如不满足从事特定的作为或不作为而实施伤害,就可将这种条件性犯意作为其最终可能实施其所威胁的危害行为的一种可能性证明。[2]

In early English common law, when a person maliciously deprives others of body parts used for attack or defense, or thereby reduces the opponent's ability to attack or defend, it leads to a situation of maim. As pointed out by the renowned jurist Blackstone, the main purpose of establishing the crime of victimization is not simply to protect the victim, but to prevent the permanent loss of labor and even combat

---

〔1〕 See David J. Seippa, *The Distinction Between Crime and Tort in the Early Common Law*, 76 B. U. L. Rev. 59(1996).

〔2〕 See Samuel E. Peckham, *Holloway v. United States: The United States Supreme Court Examines "Conditional Intent" in the Anti Car Theft Act of*, 30 Seton Hall L. Rev. 602(2000).

effectiveness caused by acts of victimization, endangering the entire royal family and even society. Based on this foundation, only injuries with disabilities can become the basis of crime. For example, when the victim cuts off their finger or makes their hands disabled. For example, common law precedents believe that the act of the perpetrator scalding the victim's feet with hot water, causing the victim's toes to stick together and thereby losing combat effectiveness, constitutes the crime of cruelty, and when piercing the eyes or knocking out front teeth, it may cause harm. Castration also constitutes harm. On the contrary, cutting off the victim's nose, lips, or ears does not constitute a crime of cruelty, as the victim's combat effectiveness will not be compromised as a result. According to a series of British regulations implemented in 1403, the scope was expanded to include other injuries that do not directly affect the victim's combat ability. Later, in the 1760s, it further expanded to the act of simply destroying a person's appearance. It is generally believed that this is related to the incident in the 1760s when Lord Coventry was deliberately disfigured and had his nose cut off by thugs in the streets for expressing his views in the British Parliament. Therefore, in the late 18th century, the definition of the crime of harm in English law was: "The crime of harm is the act of maliciously causing disability or disfigurement of a person's appearance." This means that the legislative purpose of the crime of harm during this period has evolved to protect the integrity of the natural state and the normal appearance of the face and body. But the change raises the question of whether the consequence of harmful behavior needs to be permanent or irreparable. Initially, the punishment for perpetrators of the crime of cruelty was to damage the same amount and body parts as the victim. According to Blackstone, this "eye for eye" form of punishment was abolished because it was not enough for multiple criminal acts, and "because for a repeated crime, punishment cannot be repeated". Imprisonment, rather than physical injury, had already become an acceptable punishment for the crime of cruelty before the Blackstone era. After the Coventry Act, more punishments were provided for intentional disability, including the possibility of imposing property penalties. In traditional common law, the crime of harm requires the permanence of harm. Therefore, temporary loss of function of body parts or cutting of lips without leaving permanent harm will not constitute the crime of cruelty. When the criminal cut off the latter's hand at the request of his companion, allowing his friend to become a higher income beggar, the defendant committed the crime of cruelty. On the other hand, with the patient's consent, when cutting off a limb in order to save the patient's life, the doctor clearly does not constitute the crime of cruelty.

在早期英国普通法中,当一个人恶意剥夺他人用于进攻或防御的身体部位,或借此减少对手的进攻或防卫能力时,就会导致残害的情形。[1] 正如著名法学家布莱克斯通所指出的那样,规定残害罪的主要目的,不单单保护受害者,更是防止残害行为造成劳动力乃至战斗力的永久丧失,危及整个王室乃至社会。根据这一基础,只有残疾性质的伤害才能成为犯罪的基础。例如,行为人切下受害者的手指,或使其手残疾。又如,普通法判例认为,行为人用热水烫伤受害人的脚,使受害人的脚趾粘连,进而丧失战斗力的行为构成残害罪[2];戳瞎眼睛或敲掉前牙,可能会造成残害,阉割也构成残害。相反,切下受害者的鼻子、嘴唇或耳朵并不构成残害罪,理由在于受害人的战斗力不会因此受到损害。根据 1403 年开始施行的一系列英国法规,残害罪的范围扩大到包括其他不直接妨碍受害者战斗能力的伤害。后来,又在 17 世纪 60 年代,该罪进一步扩展至单纯毁人容貌的行为。一般认为,这与 17 世纪 60 年代考文垂勋爵因在英国议会发表政见被暴徒当街蓄意毁容、割掉鼻子的事件有关。由此,在 18 世纪后期,英国法律对残害罪的定义是:"残害罪是恶意致残或恶意毁人容貌的行为。"这意味着,这一时期残害罪的立法目的,已经演变为保护自然状态的完整性和正常人脸及身体的正常外观。但这一改变引起的问题是残害行为结果是否需要具有永久性,或者不可恢复性。最初,对犯有残害罪罪犯的惩罚是损坏其与受害者所遭受的一样数量及位置的身体部位。根据布莱克斯通的观点,"以眼还眼"形式的惩罚之所以被废除,是因为"对一个重复的罪行,惩罚不能重复"。监禁而不是肢体伤害,早在布莱克斯通时代之前,就已经成为残害罪可被接受的刑罚。考文垂法案后,英国司法实践对故意致残施加了更严厉的惩罚,包括可能判处财产刑。在传统普通法中,残害罪要求伤害的永久性。因此,暂时性使身体部位丧失机能,或者划破嘴唇但不会留下永久伤害的行为,将不构成残害罪。被告应同伴的要求切断了后者的手,以便让其依靠身体残疾在行乞时获得更高收益,被告犯有残害罪。不过,经病人同意,为了保住病人的生命而切掉其肢体时,医生显然是不构成残害罪的。[3]

10.2.2 Overview of Battery and Assault in the United States(美国刑法中殴打罪与攻击罪概说)

Offences such as battery are common, frequent and diverse in types, with significant differences in specific types and the constitution. This will be elaborated in

[1] See State v. Johnson, 58 Ohio St. 417 (1898).

[2] See State v. McDonie, 89 W. Va. 185(1921).

[3] 相关内容,可参见李立丰:《美国刑法评解》(下册),社会科学文献出版社 2023 年版,第 953 页。

the following text. But in addition, there are also some related situations that urgently need to be summarized.

攻击、伤害类犯罪常见、多发且类型多样，其具体类型、构成区分也比较大。对此，将在后文详述。但除此之外，还有一些相关情况亟须概说。

Firstly, considering the legalization of gun ownership in the United States, it is necessary to explain one of the aggravating factors of the crime of assault, which is the use of dangerous or lethal weapons. Generally speaking, lethal weapons are not necessary for such crimes. If a firearm is pointed at the victim and direct violent injury occurs, it constitutes aggravated assault. The essential purpose of this attack is to use weapons. If the defendant does not have any other form of injury other than holding a weapon, then if the defendant does not use the weapon they hold and has no intention of using it, it does not constitute an aggravating crime of injury. In summary, considering the specific factual circumstances of the case, in the practice of criminal justice in the United States, cars, teeth, dogs, telephones, simulation guns, pens, rulers, sticks, hunting knives, folding knives, chisels, large stones, bottles, sticks, and even plastic chairs have been identified as lethal weapons.

首先，考虑到美国持枪合法化的现实情况，需要对攻击伤害罪的加重事由之一，即使用危险的或致命的武器加以说明。一般来说，致命武器对此类犯罪而言并不是必要的。如果用枪支指向受害者，并出现了直接暴力损伤，则构成加重攻击罪。这种进攻的本质是使用武器。如果被告人除持有武器外不存在其他形式的伤害结果，那么若被告人没有使用其所持有的武器，也没有使用的打算，则不构成伤害的加重罪。总之，考虑到案件的具体事实情况，美国刑事司法实践中，曾将汽车、牙齿、恶犬、电话、仿真枪、钢笔、尺子、棍子、猎刀、折叠刀、凿子、大石头、瓶子、棒子乃至塑料椅子等作为致命武器加以认定。[1]

Secondly, it is necessary to consider the situation of human rights violations such as abuse related to domestic violence. Domestic violence involves mental or physical violence and even control behavior between individuals with special relationships. Domestic violence may occur in marital relationships, common law relationships, or equal dating relationships, and may affect people of different ages, races, religious beliefs, educational backgrounds, income, or sexual preferences in various industries. In the United States, over one million women suffer from deadly violence against them

〔1〕 See Mary G. Leary, *Criminal Defense*: *Assault and Battery Cases*, 92 Am. Jur. Trials 1 (2016).

every year by those closely related to them. At least one – third of adult women have experienced more than one physical attack by other family members. The prevalence of elderly abuse is a serious problem in the United States. According to the United States Attorney General's estimate, 200,000 elderly people in California become victims of abuse every year. Abusing the elderly can bring devastating damage. This group of people will face weakened coordination, visual, auditory, and motor functions, as well as other physiological and psychological barriers due to their limited age, health, disability, and resources. In addition, in 1995, the United States reported one child abuse incident every ten seconds. When determining whether to assume criminal responsibility, the usual focus of the defense is on the purpose of corporal punishment and the harm caused to the body. But the intensity of corporal punishment cannot cause permanent or serious physical harm, and can also cause psychological harm. Therefore, parental discipline defenses must provide limited protection to parents who use corporal punishment. Only nonviolent corporal punishment, such as specifically defined spanking, should be within the allowable range of defense. In addition to the so – called corporal punishment and discipline, there are many behaviors of physical abuse of children, such as female circumcision, which are not explicitly prohibited by laws in the United States. Although specific laws such as child abuse can be used to punish them, related cases are very rare. It is worth mentioning that the United States has not participated in torture treaties. The latest report of the Committee against Torture recommends that the United States should enact and implement federal laws to prohibit acts of torture committed outside of its jurisdiction. The committee also urges the United States to pass clear laws that absolutely prohibit torture. Therefore, when discussing crimes of assault, injury, and other violations of personal rights in U. S. criminal law, we must pay attention to the above background knowledge.

其次,需要考虑与家庭暴力有关的虐待等侵犯人权犯罪状况。家庭暴力涉及关系特殊人群之间的精神或身体暴力乃至控制行为。家庭暴力可能发生在婚姻关系、普通法关系或平等的约会关系中,可能影响不同年龄、种族、宗教信仰、教育背景、收入或性偏好的各行各业的人。在美国,每年有超过100万妇女遭受与她们关系密切的人对其实施的致命暴力。至少1/3的成年女性曾经历过其他家庭成员实施的一次以上的人身攻击。虐待老人较为普遍,这在美国是一个严重的问题。据美国联邦司法部长估计,在加利福尼亚州,每年有20万老年人成为虐待的受害者。虐待老人会给老人带来毁灭性的损害。老人会因为自身年龄、健康、残疾和资源等方面的有限性,面临协调性、视觉、听觉、运动机能等方面的弱化,以及其他生理和心理障碍。[1] 此外,1995年,美国每10秒钟就会报告一例儿童虐待事件。在确定施虐者是否承担刑事责任时,通常的抗辩重点是对儿童体罚的目的和对其身体造成的伤害。体罚施加的力度不可能造成永久性或严重的身体伤害,但却可以引起心理伤害。因此,管教抗辩只能对实施体罚的父母提供相对有限度的保护。[2] 除了体罚管教,对于儿童的身体虐待还有很多,如女性割礼等行为在美国尚无明确禁止的法令,虽然可以通过虐待儿童等具体法律加以处罚,但相关个案却十分罕见。值得一提的是,美国并未参加酷刑条约,禁止酷刑委员会的最新报告建议美国颁布和实施联邦法令,禁止在美国司法管辖区之内犯下的酷刑行为,同时,该委员会还敦促美国通过明确的法律绝对禁止酷刑。[3] 因此,当我们讨论美国刑法中的攻击、伤害等侵犯人身权犯罪时,必须注意到上述背景知识。

10.2.3 Types and Elements of Battery and Assault(殴打罪与攻击罪的类型与构成)

10.2.3.1 Battery(殴打罪)

The crime of battery in American criminal law generally refers to the use of violence against others, resulting in harmful or offensive physical contact. Therefore, it covers a wide range and even includes physical contact for sexual purposes. Although, the crime of ordinary battery is only a minor offense in common law, it is generally necessary to subdivide the crime of aggravated battery based on the different objects of battery. We will explain the basic and aggravated forms of the crime of battery, taking into account relevant legislative provisions in California, United States, as well as relevant provisions in CALCRIM as below.

美国刑法中的殴打罪,一般是指对他人使用暴力,导致危害或冒犯性身体接触的行为。因此,其涵盖范围较广,甚至还包括基于性目的的身体接触。虽然在普通法当中,普通殴打罪仅仅属于一种轻罪,但基于殴打对象的不同,需要对加重型殴打罪加以细分。下面的内容就结合美国加利福尼亚州相关立法规定,以及《加利福尼亚州司法委员会刑事陪审法律指导》的相关规定,对殴打罪的基本样态及其加重

---

[1] See Arthur Meirson, *Prosecuting Elder Abuse: Setting the Gold Standard in the Golden State*, 60 Hastings L. J. 431 (2008).

[2] Kimberlie Young, *An Examination of Parental Discipline As a Defense of Justification: It's Time for A Kinder, Gentler Approach*, 46 Naval L. Rev. 1 (1999).

[3] See Julianne Harper, *Defining Torture: Bridging the Gap between Rhetoric and Reality*, 49 Santa Clara L. Rev. 823 (2009).

样态加以说明。[1]

According to relevant laws and judicial precedents in California, it is generally believed that the establishment of ordinary battery requires the defendant to intentionally and illegally engage in dangerous or aggressive contact with victims who do not have a special identity. The intention here only refers to the intentionality of the actor's contact behavior. It is not required to prove that the defendant wishes to gain any benefits through contacting with the victim. And the so - called contact does not require degree, but it requires danger or aggression, in other words, even the slightest contact is enough to constitute battery. Contact does not necessarily cause any form of pain or injury, and can also be carried out by others or objects, such as through the victim's clothing. In addition, there is also the so - called "sexual battery". According to relevant California laws, the basic form of ordinary sexual battery crime refers to the behavior of the defendant, in order to obtain sexual excitement, sexual satisfaction, or sexual abuse for special purposes, violating the defendant's wishes and touching their private parts. To establish this crime, it is required that the defendant must have the subjective mentality of direct intention mentioned above, and must also have contact with the victim's private parts.

加利福尼亚州相关法律[2]及司法判例一般认为,普通殴打罪的成立,要求被告人故意且非法地以危险或有攻击性的方式接触不具有特殊身份的被害人。这里的故意,仅指行为人对自己接触行为的有意性。并不要求证明被告人希望通过接触被害人获得任何好处。而所谓接触,并不要求程度,只要求具有危险性或攻击性即可,[3]换句话说,哪怕是最轻微的接触都足以构成殴打。[4] 接触不一定造成任何形式的疼痛或伤害,还可以借由他人或物体实施,例如隔着受害人的衣物。除此之外,还存在"性殴打",根据加利福尼亚州相关法律规定[5],基本形态的普通性殴打犯罪,是指被告人为了获得性兴奋、性满足或性虐待的特殊目的,违背被告人意愿,接触其私密部位的行为。成立本罪,要求被告人必须具有上述直接故意的主观心态,同时必须接触受害人的私密部位。[6]

---

[1] 相关内容,可参见李立丰:《美国刑法评解》(下册),社会科学文献出版社 2023 年版,第 953 页。

[2] Pen. Code, § §242.

[3] See People v. Martinez, 3 Cal. App. 3d 886 (1970).

[4] See People v. Myers, 61 Cal. App. 4th 328 (1998).

[5] Pen. Code, §243.4(e)(1).

[6] See People v. Elam, 91 Cal. App. 4th 298 (2001).

10.2.3.2 Assault(攻击罪)

In U. S. criminal law, assault is generally understood as a preparatory offense tobattery. However, based on the basic principle of one action, one evaluation, and one charge, the crime of assault should be independently convicted and punished. However, even if the perpetrator did not intend to physically assault, as long as the victims reasonably feel that they may have been assaulted, it may still constitute this crime. Overall, unless targeting specific targets or if the perpetrator is a repeat offender, ordinary aggressive behavior is only considered a minor offense. Its criminal standard is relatively low, and in most judicial districts in the United States, it is sufficient to make the victim reasonably feel that they may have suffered physical harm. But there are some differences in legislation between different judicial regions. Here, we will only use California's relevant regulations as an example to illustrate this crime.

在美国刑法中,攻击罪一般被理解为殴打罪的预备罪。但基于一行为一评价一罪名的基本原则,攻击罪该当独立定罪处罚。即便行为人本身并没有殴打的故意,但只要让被害人合理感觉到自己可能遭到殴打,其依然可能构成本罪。整体而言,除非针对特定对象,或者行为人系累犯,普通的攻击行为仅仅属于轻罪。攻击罪成立标准较低,在美国大多数司法管辖区,只要受害人合理感觉自己可能遭受身体伤害即可成立该罪。但不同司法管辖区的立法又多少存在差别。下面仅以加利福尼亚州相关规定作为范例,对此加以说明。[1]

According to the relevant provisions of California Penal Code, the common offense of assault refers to the intentional act of the defendant that directly or potentially leads to violence against someone. On the one hand, the defendant should subjectively realize that their behavior will essentially lead a rational person to believe that it will directly and confidently lead to the use of violence against someone. This crime does not require the actor to have a reasonable understanding of the illegality of their actions. The prosecution does not need to prove that the defendant did intend to use violence against someone during the act. In other words, the crime of assault belongs to the category of generalized criminal intent or indirect intentional crime. On the other hand, objectively speaking, the defendant has the ability to use violence against others when carrying out the aforementioned actions. The term "the use of violence" means coming into contact with someone in a dangerous or an aggressive manner. If done in a rude or an irritable

〔1〕 相关内容,可参见李立丰:《美国刑法评解》(下册),社会科学文献出版社2023年版,第953页。

manner, the slightest contact is sufficient. Contacting with others can be achieved through someone's clothing. Contact is not necessary to cause any pain or injury. Contact can be indirectly achieved by causing an object or other person to come into contact with another person, and the prosecution does not need to prove that the defendant actually made contact with someone. In addition to the use of violence, ordinary assault crimes can also be committed through conditional threats. Those who have no right to do so intentionally threaten to use violence against others and force them to immediately carry out the actions requested by the defendant. Subjectively, the defendant does not need to intentionally harm others or gain benefits based on indirect intentional threat behavior. Objectively, when the defendant makes a threat, they have the ability to use the threatened violence against others. No matter how offensive language or non threatening behavior may be, it cannot be used as a legitimate reason for an attack or fight. In addition to the common offense of assault, there are also offenses committed using lethal and non – lethal weapons.

根据加利福尼亚州刑法相关规定[1],普通攻击罪是指被告人故意实施直接或可能导致对某人施加暴力的行为。一方面,被告人在实施该行为时,主观上应意识到其行为本质上会使一个理性人认为将直接且盖然地导致对某人使用暴力。本罪不要求行为人对自己行为的违法性具有合理认识。检方无须证明被告人在实施行为时确实意图对某人使用暴力。换句话说,攻击罪属于概括犯意或间接故意犯罪。[2] 另一方面,客观上被告人在实施上述行为时有能力对他人使用暴力。“暴力的施加”或“施加暴力”一词意味着以危险或有攻击性的方式接触某人。如果以粗鲁或者暴躁的方式完成,最轻微的接触就足够。通过某人的衣服就可以达到与他人接触。接触不必要造成任何疼痛或伤害。接触可以通过使物体或其他人接触到另一个人来间接地完成,检方不需要证明被告人实际接触了某人。[3] 除施加暴力之外,普通攻击罪还可以通过附条件威胁的方式实施,也就是说,无权这样做的行为人故意威胁对他人使用暴力,迫使他人立即实施被告人要求的行为。主观上,被告人基于间接故意实施威胁行为,并不需要意图违法伤害他人或获得利益。客观上,当被告人作出威胁时,其有能力对他人使用其所威胁的暴力。无论多么冒犯的语言和不具有威胁性的行为,都不能成为攻击或殴斗的正当化理由。[4] 除了普通攻击罪,

---

〔1〕 Pen. Code, § 240.

〔2〕 See People v. Lee, 28 Cal. App. 4th 1724 (1994).

〔3〕 See CALCRIM No. 915.

〔4〕 See CALCRIM No. 917.

还存在使用致命性武器及非致命性武器实施的攻击罪。[1]

10.3 False Imprisonment(非法拘禁罪)

In addition to the crimes of assault and battery, the third type of crimes against person is false imprisonment. false imprisonment usually involves exerting force on the body, thus also is equivalent to physical assault. However, if someone who is already in the room is illegally locked inside, even if it does not involve an assault, it still constitutes false imprisonment. Although on the surface, such behavior should not be regarded as a crime against person, it is still considered a crime against person in the common law.

除攻击和殴打罪之外,第三种传统意义上的侵犯人身罪便是非法拘禁。非法拘禁通常涉及对身体施加强力,因此也相当于身体攻击。但是,行为人非法将已经在房间里的人锁在里面,虽然不涉及攻击行为,也构成非法拘禁。虽然从表面上来看,这种行为不应被视为侵犯人身,但其仍然被视为普通法意义上的侵犯人身权犯罪。[2]

One thing that needs to be clarified is the connection and differences between false imprisonment and the common law crime known as "kidnapping". The latter generally refers to taking the victim away without someone's consent. In the case of *R. v. D*, the House of Lords believed that the crime of kidnapping includes four constituent elements: the victim being taken away by someone else; need to be implemented through strong or fraudulent means; without the consent of the victim being taken away and without justifiable reasons. It can be considered that kidnapping is the most serious form of false imprisonment, but in judicial practice, the difference in degree between the two gradually disappears. To this day, the only characteristic of kidnapping compared to false imprisonment is that it serves as an aggravating factor, and kidnapping must involve taking the victim away from their hiding or desired place through force or threat (now expanded to deception). Although the maximum punishment for kidnapping is the same as false imprisonment, the declared sentence for kidnapping is generally more severe and may be subject to life imprisonment.

需要明确的一点是非法拘禁与被称为"绑架"的普通法犯罪之间的联系与区别。

---

[1] See Pen. Code, §§ 245(a)(1)-(4), (b).

[2] 参见[英]丹尼尔·贝克:《格兰维尔·威廉姆斯刑法学教科书:典型罪编》,李立丰译,法律出版社2023年版,第426页。

后者一般指未经某人同意而将受害人带走。在“女王诉 D 案”(*R. v. D*)[1]中,英国上议院认为绑架罪包括四个构成要素:被害人被他人带走,需要以强力或欺诈手段实施,未经被带走的受害人同意以及无正当理由。可以认为,绑架是最为严重的非法拘禁,但在司法实践当中,二者在程度上的差异逐渐消弭,时至今日,绑架相较于非法拘禁的唯一特质在于其作为加重处罚情节,绑架必须涉及通过强力或以强力相威胁(法律现已将其扩大到通过欺骗手段)将被害人从其隐匿或想停留的地方带走。虽然绑架罪的最高刑罚与非法拘禁相同,但绑架罪的宣告刑一般更为严厉,有可能被适用终身监禁。

■ Case study(案例学习)

Cullison v. Medley [1991], 570 N. E. 2d 27(科里森诉麦德雷案)

Facts(事实)

Plaintiff Cullison met 16 – year – old Sandy Medley in a grocery store parking lot, invited her to have a soda with him and to come to his home to talk further. A few hours later he was awoken by a knock at his door. He was confronted by Sandy Medley, her father Ernest, her brother, brother – in – law, and mother. Ernest had a revolver in a holster strapped to his thigh. Sandy called him a pervert and her mother berated him. Ernest kept grabbing and shaking the gun while still in the holster and threatening to jump astraddle of him if he did not leave Sandy alone. Although no one ever touched Cullison, he feared he was about to be shot because Ernest kept grabbing the gun as if to draw it from the holster while threatening him. As a result of this incident, Cullison sought psychological help to deal with nervousness, depression, sleeplessness, inability to concentrate, and impotency. He sued the Medleys for assault, among other torts. The trial court granted a summary judgment in favor of defendants on all claims, the appeals court affirmed, and the Indiana Supreme Court reversed on the assault count.

原告科里森在一家杂货店的停车场遇到了时年 16 岁的女孩珊迪·麦德雷,于是上前搭讪,邀请其喝饮料,进而邀请其和自己回家深入交谈。几个小时后,科里森被敲门声吵醒。找上门来的是珊迪·麦德雷,她的父亲欧内斯特,她的兄弟、姐夫和母亲。欧内斯特大腿上绑着一把左轮手枪。珊迪称科里森为变态,她的母亲也对其大肆斥责。欧内斯特则抓着枪套里的枪,不停摇晃着枪柄,并威胁说,如果科里森继

---

[1] R. v. D [1984] A. C. 778 at 801. 在英美刑法实践中,对于需要保护个人隐私的被告人姓名,通常用“被告人”(defendant)英文的首字母,即 D 代表。

续骚扰珊迪,就要“让他好看”。虽然并没有人与科里森发生任何肢体接触,但科里森担心自己会被枪杀,因为欧内斯特在威胁他时一直抓着枪,好像随时都会拔枪。由于这一事件,科里森不得不寻求心理帮助,以应对紧张、抑郁、失眠、无法集中注意力甚至阳痿等问题。他起诉麦德雷一家侵犯他的隐私权。一审法院作出了对被告有利的判决,并且得到了上诉法院的支持。印第安纳州最高法院推翻了原审判决。

Issue(争议问题)

Whether threatening language coupled with a holstered pistol rises to the level of assault.

威胁性语言加上挥舞带枪套的手枪是否会达到构成攻击罪的程度。

Held(判决)

Yes. Assault occurs when one intentionally creates the reasonable apprehension of imminent harmful or offensive contact in another. It is a touching of the mind, if not the body, and as such, the damages which are recoverable are for mental trauma and distress. It is assault to shake a fist under another's nose, to aim or strike at him with a weapon or to hold it in a threatening position, or to surround him with a display of force. Additionally, the apprehension must be one that would be aroused in the mind of a reasonable person. In this case, a jury could reasonably conclude that the Medleys intended to frighten Cullison by surrounding him in his trailer and verbally threatening him with bodily harm while one of them was armed with a holstered revolver. Accordingly, the Indiana Supreme Court reversed the summary judgment on the assault count.

达到了攻击罪的程度。当一个人故意制造对另一个人即将发生的有害或攻击性接触的合理担忧时,就会发生攻击。在这种情况下,触及的即使不是身体,也是心灵。因此,可以弥补的损害是精神创伤和痛苦。在他人眼皮底下挥舞拳头,用武器瞄准或攻击他人,或将其置于威胁性位置,或用武力包围他人,都是攻击。此外,这种担忧必须是一个理性的人会想到的。在本案中,陪审团可以合理地得出结论,麦德雷一家将科里森包围在拖车,并口头威胁要对他进行身体伤害,以此来恐吓科里森,而其中一人还携带带枪套的左轮手枪。因此,印第安纳州最高法院推翻了原审判决。

Discussion(讨论)

It is important to note that typically words alone do not rise to the level of assault, unless together with acts or circumstances they put the other in a reasonable apprehension of imminent harm. Moreover, the imminence element does not mean that the harm must be immediate, but that there will be no significant delay in effectuating the harm.

需要注意的是,在通常情况下,言语本身不会上升到攻击的程度,除非与行为或其他情节一起,使对方对迫在眉睫的伤害有合理的担忧。此外,迫在眉睫的因素并不意味着伤害必须是立即的,而是在实现伤害方面不会有显著的延迟。

Questions: 1. Assault is both tort and crime, so what is the substantive difference between tort and crime in the Anglo American law system? (Please scan the QR code on the right to get the answer)

攻击既是侵权,也是犯罪,在英美法律体系中,侵权与犯罪的实质性区别为何?(答案请扫描右侧二维码获取)

2. What's the difference between assault and false imprisonment? (Please scan the QR code on the right to get the answer)

攻击罪与非法拘禁罪的区别为何?(答案请扫描右侧二维码获取)

10. 4 Stalking(缠扰罪)

In the late 1980s, taking the opportunity of actress Rebecca Schaffer being subjected to long - term attempted harassment by a crazy fan and ultimately being brutally murdered, the issue of tailgating officially entered the public eye. Under public pressure, California was the first to introduce legislation, and the California Criminal Code defined tailgating as any person who willfully, maliciously, and repeatedly follows or harasses another person and who makes a credible threat with the intent to place that person in reasonable fear for his or her safety, or the safety of his or her family members. Other states in the United States followed the legislative pace of California, and by 1993, almost all jurisdictions had established similar legislation. It is worth mentioning that Canada, Australia, England, and Wales have successively passed legislation with similar purposes. Some European countries are considering or preparing such legislation. In less than a decade, major western countries have constructed a completely new category of crime, and it is in this sense that stalking have aroused widespread interest among scholars.

20 世纪 80 年代末,以女演员丽贝卡·谢弗遭遇疯狂粉丝长期未遂骚扰并最终惨遭杀害为契机,缠扰问题正式进入公共视野,迫于公众压力,加利福尼亚州率先出台立法,《加利福尼亚州刑法典》把缠扰罪定义为“故意、恶意、反复跟踪或骚扰他人,并发出可信威胁,意图使该人对其安全或其直系亲属的安全感到合理恐惧的行为"。[1] 美国其他州紧随加利福尼亚州的立法步伐,截至1993年,几乎所有司法管辖区均设立了类似立法,更值得一提的是,加拿大、澳大利亚、英格兰和威尔士,都相继通过了目的大致相似的立法。一些欧洲国家正在考虑或准备这类立法。在不到10年的时间里,主要西方国家纷纷建构出同一种全新的犯罪类别,正是在这个意义上,缠扰罪才引起了研究者的普遍兴趣。[2]

So far, most studies on stalkers have focused on the types of mental disorders that this group of people suffer from. Although the gender, age, and mental state of stalkers is quite complex, they can still be divided into three categories: the erotomania or delusional stalker, the domestic violence stalker, and the nuisance stalker.

迄今为止,对缠扰者的大部分研究都集中在这一类人群所罹患的精神障碍类型之上。虽然缠扰者的性别、年龄、精神状态等情况相当复杂,但还是可以将其分为三大类:色情狂或妄想缠扰者、家庭暴力缠扰者和骚扰型缠扰者。[3]

In judicial practice, in order to prove the guilty of the crime of stalking, the prosecution needs to exclude reasonable doubt that the defendant willfully and maliciously harassed or willfully, maliciously, and repeatedly followed another person and made a credible threat with the intent to place the other person in reasonable fear for his/her safety or for the safety of his/her immediate family. It should be emphasized that a credible threat may be made orally, in writing, or electronically or maybe implied by a pattern of conduct or a combination of the statement and conduct. Harassing means engaging in a knowing and willful course of conduct directed at a specific person that seriously annoys, alarms, torments, or terrorizes the person and that serves no legitimate purpose. A course of conduct means two or more acts occurring over a period of time, however short, demonstrating a continuous purpose.[4]

在司法实践中,如果要证明缠扰罪成立,检方需要排除合理怀疑地证明被告人故意、恶意骚扰或者故意、恶意、多次尾随他人;以及被告发出可信的威胁,意图使他人出于其本人的安全或其直系亲属的安全的合理担忧。其中,可信的威胁是指使威胁目标合理地担心其安全或其直系亲属的安全的威胁,以及威胁制造者似乎能够实

---

[1] See Pen. Code, § § 646.9(a), (e) - (h).

[2] Paul E. Mullen & Michele Pathe, *Stalking*, 29 Crime & Just. 273 (2002).

[3] Carol E. Jordan, Karen Quinn & Bradley Jordan eds., *Stalking: Cultural, Clinical and Legal Considerations*, 38 Brandeis L. J. 513(2000).

[4] See CALCRIM No. 1301.

施的威胁。可信的威胁可以通过口头、书面或电子方式发出,也可以通过行为模式或声明与行为的组合暗示。骚扰是指对特定的人进行明知且故意的行为,严重激怒、折磨或恐吓该人,且没有正当目的。行为过程是指在一段时间内发生的2次或2次以上的行为,无论多么短暂,都表明了一个持续的目的。

■ Curriculum Ideology and Politics(课程思政)

In common law countries and other countries, criminal law has criminalized stalking, which is of great significance for protecting the personal rights and peaceful life of individuals. Whether from the perspective of crime prevention or protecting the rights and interests of citizens, the legislative practice of criminalizing stalking is still of great significance.

英美法系国家和其他国家的刑法把“缠扰行为”进行了犯罪化,这对于保护个体的人身权和生活安宁具有重要意义。无论是从预防犯罪,还是从保护公民权益角度看,把缠扰行为犯罪化的立法实践,是具有重要的意义的。

10.5 Exercise(课后练习)(答案请扫描右侧二维码获取)

10.5.1 Test of Terminologies(术语考查)

①rape ②sexual assault
③marital rape ④aggravated sexual abuse
⑤oral copulation ⑥sodomy
⑦sexual penetration ⑧dolus eventualis
⑨annoy ⑩molest
⑪prurient Interest ⑫distribute
⑬pimping ⑭prostitute
⑮pandering ⑯hate crime
⑰battery ⑱assault

10.5.2 Short – answer Questions(简答题)

1. Give an example to illustrate the situation where “fraud” constitutes rape.
举例说明“骗奸”构成强奸的情况。

2. Briefly describe the concept and types of Stalking.
简述缠扰罪的概念及类型。

■ Curriculum Ideology and Politics(课程思政)

The legislatures of western countries such as the United States and the United Kingdom have basically abandoned the moral attributes that punishment should have when formulating criminal law, especially when setting up crimes. In addition, their definition of crime is merely a formality, one – sided pursuit of the interests and demands of specific groups, ultimately leading to a lack of theoretical depth in their criminal theory system, a lack of internal logic in the legislative regulation of charges and statutory penalties, and the inability to achieve good judicial results. The above issues are very evident in traditional criminal fields, including sexual offences, as well as emerging criminal fields represented by tail crimes.

英美等国家立法机构在制定刑法,特别是设立犯罪时,基本上放弃了刑罚本应具有的道德属性,加之其对犯罪的定义流于形式,片面追求特定群体的利益诉求,最终导致其犯罪论体系缺乏理论深度,罪名及法定刑的立法规制缺乏内在逻辑,无法取得良好的司法效果。上述问题在包括性犯罪在内的传统犯罪领域,以及以缠扰罪为代表的新兴犯罪领域都体现得十分明显。

■ Summary(总结)

1. Overall, in the context of American criminal law, sexual offenses refer to a cluster or bundle of crimes primarily related to rape.

总体来说,美国刑法语境中的性犯罪,是指以强奸罪为主的一个犯罪集群或犯罪束。在某些州,“性侵”或“性攻击”与“强奸”一词可以互换使用。

2. Essentially, sexual offenses can be classified as violence against sexual freedom/autonomy and non – violent infringement of sexual freedom/autonomy. Although it can be classified into these categories, its essence is an infringement of sexual freedom.

从本质上可以将性犯罪分为对性自由的暴力侵害、对性自由的非暴力侵害等不同种类。尽管性犯罪可以被分为这些种类,但其本质都是对性自由的侵害。

3. The crime of battery in American criminal law generally refers to the use of violence against others, resulting in harmful or offensive physical contact. Therefore, it covers a wide range and even includes physical contact for sexual purposes. Although in common law, the crime of ordinary battery is only a minor offense, it is generally necessary to subdivide the crime of aggravated battery based on the different objects of battery.

美国刑法中的殴打罪,一般是指对他人使用暴力,导致危害或冒犯性身体接触的行为。因此其涵盖范围较广，甚至还包括基于性目的的身体接触。虽然在普通法当中，普通殴打罪仅仅是一种轻罪，但基于殴打对象的不同，一般需要对加重型殴打罪加以细分。

4. In addition to the crimes of assault and battery, the third type of crimes against person is false imprisonment. False imprisonment usually involves exerting force on the body, thus also equivalent to physical assault. However, if an actor illegally locks someone who is already in the room inside, even if his act does not involve an assault, it still constitutes false imprisonment. Although on the surface, such behavior should not be regarded as a violation of personal right, it is still considered a crime against person in the common law.

除了攻击和殴打罪，第三种传统意义上的侵犯人身罪便是非法拘禁。非法拘禁通常涉及对身体施加强力，因此也相当于身体攻击。但是，行为人非法将已经在房间里的人锁在里面，虽然不涉及攻击行为，也构成非法拘禁。虽然从表面上来看，这种行为不应被视为侵犯人身，但其仍然被视为普通法意义上的侵犯人身权犯罪。

Chapter 11　Property Crimes
第 11 章　财产犯罪

■ The Learning Objective(学习目标)

1. To have a basic understanding of what are property crimes.

了解财产犯罪的定义。

2. To understand the historical evolution of property crimes.

了解财产犯罪的历史流变。

3. To understand the types of property crimes.

了解财产犯罪的分类。

4. To understand the elements and punishments of property crimes.

了解主要财产犯罪的构成与处罚。

5. To learn some terminologies related to the topic.

掌握本章的专业术语。

■ Chapter Outline(本章内容概要)

"Property and the law are born and must die together."[1] Any organized society has a law that contain at least some basic property crimes. In different cultures, the formation of ownership is extremely diverse. The actors' various ways of committing torts and the development of criminal law and civil law in this area make the property offenses in the criminal law system the most conceptually complex and structurally diverse. Almost everyone will at some point in their lives have been the victim of crimes such as theft, fraud, robbery, or burglary.[2] This chapter will introduce and analyze

---

[1] John Bowring, *The Works of Jeremy Bentham*, William Tait, 1838, p. 307.

[2] Markus D. Dubber & Tatjana Hörnle, *The Oxford Handbook of Criminal Law*, Oxford University Press, 2014, p. 768.

the definition, classification, evolution, and punishment of property crimes in common law system, with specific cases.

"所有权与法律同生共死。"[1]在任何一个组织有序的社会的法律中,都至少包含某种形式的财产犯罪。在不同文化中,所有权的形成方式极其多元。行为人千奇百怪的侵权方式,加上在这一领域各国刑法与民法的不断发展,都使刑法体系中的财产犯罪概念变得最为复杂、结构最为多样。事实上,几乎每个人都会在一生中的某个时刻成为盗窃、欺诈、抢劫或入室盗窃等犯罪的受害人。[2] 鉴于此,本章将结合具体案例,介绍、分析普通法系中财产犯罪的定义、分类、流变以及惩罚等问题。

■ The Purpose of Curriculum Ideology and Politics for this Chapter (本章的课程思政目标)

1. Marxist criminal law theory holds that the economic base is the sum of production relations that are compatible with the level of productivity in a certain social and historical stage. Its main content is the form of ownership of means of production and the forms of production, distribution, and circulation that are linked to the form of ownership of means of production. The current form of ownership of means of production in China is dominated by public ownership of means of production, with multiple forms of ownership coexisting, and on this basis, a socialist market economy is implemented. Correspondingly, the protection of the economic base in China's criminal law is also the protection of multiple forms of ownership dominated by public ownership and the socialist market economy. It is in this context that studying property crimes in various countries, especially in common law system, has comparative law reference value and significance.

马克思主义刑法理论认为,经济基础是与一定社会历史阶段的生产力水平相适应的生产关系的总和,其主要内容是生产资料所有制形式以及与生产资料所有制形式相联系的生产、分配、流通的形式。我国现阶段的生产资料所有制形式是以生产资料公有制为主,多种所有制并存,并在此基础上实行社会主义市场经济;相应地,我国刑法对经济基础的保护也就是对以公有制为主的多种所有制和社会主义市场经济的保护。[3] 正是在这个意义上,研究各国,特别是普通法系财产犯罪,才具有

[1] [英]边沁:《道德与立法原理导论》,时殷弘译,商务印书馆 2000 年版,第 216 页。

[2] 参见[加]马库斯·杜博、[德]塔蒂安娜·霍恩雷主编:《牛津刑法手册》,李立丰译,上海三联书店 2023 年版,第 829 页。

[3] 刑法学编写组:《刑法学》(上册·总论),高等教育出版社 2023 年版,第 54 页。

了比较法上的参考价值与意义。

2. The protection of private property has long been regarded as the basic system of capitalism. That's the reason why, in the long process of historical development, western countries have developed highly complex and comprehensive legal system to protect private property, including strict criminal legislation and a wide range of property crimes. Only by systematically understanding it can we objectively evaluate the nature of the property protection system in western countries from the perspective of historical materialism.

私有财产保护,一直以来都被视为资本主义的基础制度。正因如此,在漫长的历史发展过程中,西方国家发展出了高度复杂、完备的法律制度,包括严密的刑事立法以及种类繁多的财产犯罪以保护私有财产。只有对其系统了解,才能从历史唯物主义出发,对西方国家财产保护制度的本质进行客观评价。

3. For property crimes, they can be classified into different types according to different standards. In addition, in capitalist countries, there is a connection and distinction between property crimes and white - collar crimes. In socialist countries, there is a connection and distinction between property crimes and economic crimes. Only through accurate understanding of property crimes in western contries represented by the common law system can we correctly recognize the above differences and form our own independent judgments, avoiding following others' opinions without criticism.

对于财产犯罪,可以根据不同标准进行分类。除此之外,在西方国家,存在财产犯罪与白领犯罪之间的联系与区分,在社会主义国家,存在财产犯罪与经济犯罪的联系与区分。唯有通过对以普通法系为代表的西方国家财产犯罪的精准认知,才能正确认知上述问题并形成自己的独立判断。

■ Terminologies(专业术语)

agreement to sell	买卖合意
animus furandi	窃取的意图
asportation	窃取他人动产
assume	侵吞
breaking bulk	盗窃托管物品罪
choses in action	诉讼中的物
embezzlement	侵吞
false accounting	伪造账目罪

false pretenses	欺诈
ferae naturae	不属于私产的
fraudulent conversion	欺诈性侵占罪
information	起诉书
intangible property/Incorporeal property	无形财产
involuntary bailee	非自愿的受托人
King Edmund's Code	《埃德蒙国王法典》
klopanie	盗窃癖
larceny	侵财犯罪
larceny by bailee	受托人盗窃罪
let the buyer beware	买者当心
misappropriation	侵吞
movables/Chattels	动产
obtaining by false pretences	虚构事实骗取财物罪
obtaining credit by fraud	骗取贷款罪
occupy Wall Street Movement	占领华尔街运动
offence of dishonesty	有悖诚信犯罪
Personal Identification Number, PIN	个人识别码
real property/Reality	不动产
res nullius	无主物
retail crimes	零售犯罪
Squatter	擅自占用空置物业者
The Middlesex Session	中庭法院
the Offence of making off without paying	逃单罪
trespassory caption	侵害遗失物之诉
trover	侵入性获取
withe Collar Offenses	白领犯罪

11.1 What are the Property Offenses(财产犯罪的定义)

While the term property crimes or crimes against property provides a convenient shorthand, it is more accurate to speak of "crimes affecting persons' rights and interests in property". Different property crimes affect different sticks in the bundle of property rights in different ways. Trespass, joyriding, and unauthorized use of a movable consist of temporarily using other's property without permission—a kind of temporary dispossession, but without any requirement of damage to property. Besides vandalism and criminal damage, typically involve damage to the owner's property, but no dispossession.[1]

虽然财产犯罪或侵犯财产罪这一概念的表述相对简单明了,但更准确的说法应该是"影响人的财产权益的犯罪"。不同的财产犯罪以不同的方式影响着财产权属中的不同具体权利。比如,非法侵入、偷开他人机动车和未经授权使用动产(包括未经许可临时使用他人财产,只需临时剥夺他人权益即可构成犯罪,并不要求对财产造成任何损害)。此外,破坏公物和刑事损害通常涉及对物权所有人财产的损害,但不涉及转移占有。[2]

Whether a given crime is classified as a property offense in the first place will tend to reflect underlying assumptions about the values and interests an offense regime is meant to further. For example, rape was once thought of as a property offense, reflecting the view that the rapist had harmed "property" belonging to the female victim's husband or father.[3] Nowdays, it is invariably classified as a crime against the person. Kidnapping was also once viewed as a property offense, and was understood as involving a wrong done to the "property" of the parent of the kidnapped child, or to a slave owner.[4] It too is now viewed as a crime against the person. Conversely, arson, once viewed primarily as an offense against the person, is now typically classified as an offense against property.[5] Back in the history, some scholars define crime as "acts of force or fraud undertaken in pursuit of self - interest". This wide - ranging definition, inspired by the classic principles of Roman law, presents the advantage of easily generating consensus. However, from a comparative law perspective, the main challenge is to identify the operational definitions of crime used across time and space. From that perspective, property offenses are particularly problematic. Even if the basic

〔1〕 Markus D. Dubber & Tatjana Hörnle, *The Oxford Handbook of Criminal Law*, Oxford University Press, 2014, p. 768.

〔2〕 参见[加]马库斯·杜博、[德]塔蒂安娜·霍恩雷主编:《牛津刑法手册》,李立丰译,上海三联书店2023年版,第831页。

〔3〕 Patricia J. Williams, *On Being the Object of Property*, in Katharine T. Bartlett and Rosanne Kennedy eds., Feminist Legal Theory: Readings in Law and Gender, Westview Press, 1991, p. 165.

〔4〕 Melburn N. Washburn, *Kidnapping as a Military Offense*, 21 Military LR 1, 2(1963).

〔5〕 Markus D. Dubber & Tatjana Hörnle, *The Oxford Handbook of Criminal Law*, Oxford University Press, 2014, p. 768.

principle remains the same—taking something that belongs to someone else against his or her will—the concepts of property and its distribution across the population has undergone so many changes.[1] It is easy to tell that compared with socialist criminal law that emphasizes the substantive feature of social harm, property crimes in the common law system are often confined to specific formal characteristics.

特定的犯罪是否被归类为财产犯罪,一般会反映出立法者希望借此推行的特定价值观和利益分配关系。例如,强奸曾经被认为是一种财产犯罪,这反映了强奸犯损害了属于女性受害人丈夫或父亲的"财产"的观点。如今,强奸被归类为侵害人身的犯罪。绑架也曾被视为一种财产犯罪,其被理解为对被绑架儿童的父母或奴隶主的"财产"实施的错误行为。现在也被视为侵犯人身权的犯罪。相反,纵火一度被主要视为对人的犯罪,现在通常被归类为对财产的犯罪。[2] 回溯历史,有学者将犯罪定义为"为追求自身利益而采取的暴力或欺诈行为"。这一定义受到罗马法基本原则的启发,较为宽泛,具有容易达成共识的优势。然而,从比较法的角度来看,主要的挑战是如何能够赋予犯罪以超越时空条件限制的且具有现实操作的定义。从这个角度来看,财产犯罪的确很难定义。即使财产犯罪的本质,即违背所有者的意愿拿走属于他的东西保持不变,但财产的概念以及财产在整个人群中的分配,也已经历了很大变化。[3] 由此不难看出,和强调社会危害性这一犯罪实质特征的社会主义刑法相比,普通法系中的财产犯罪往往窠臼于具体的形式特征。

While there are various competing theories concerning the source of property rights and what constitutes their fair distribution, and that the state should, to some degree, protect people's interests in property through a combination of civil and criminal methods. And our law does in fact include a vast range of devices designed to protect property rights of one sort of another, in a wide range of contexts. Indeed, much of the civil law—including the law of contract, tort, agency, and inheritance—has as one of its primary goals just that. Determining when property rights should be protected by the criminal law rather than, or in addition to, civil law invites complex questions of criminalization. Sometimes, the line between crimes and civil wrongs will depend on the magnitude or intensity of harm. For example, insider trading, tax evasion, and illegal

---

〔1〕 Paul Knepper & Anja Johansen, *The Oxford Handbook of the History of Crime and Criminal Justice*, Oxford University Press, 2016, p. 63.

〔2〕 参见[加]马库斯·杜博、[德]塔蒂安娜·霍恩雷主编:《牛津刑法手册》,李立丰译,上海三联书店2023年版,第831页。

〔3〕 参见[英]保罗·克内珀、[英]安贾·约翰森主编:《牛津犯罪及刑事司法史手册》,李立丰译,上海三联书店2024年版,第63页。

downloading, when performed on a large scale, are more likely to be treated as crimes than when performed on a small scale. Similarly, trespass to land is normally a crime only when it involves actual injury to property. Theft and other property crimes can be thought of as causing harm in at least two senses. First, they are harmful in the narrow sense that they limit or deprive a property owner of a thing that saves him labor, from which he derives pleasure, or which generates income for him. Secondly, property crimes are harmful in the sense that they undermine the very reason we have a system of property rights in the first place—presumably, to facilitate the creation and preservation of wealth that makes many forms of human endeavor possible. Widespread theft, vandalism, and arson all tend to have a destabilizing effect on neighborhoods and on the economy more generally. In this broader sense of harm, what matters is not that the specific theft or trespass itself undermines the institution of property ownership but that they are actions that jeopardize the property system if they proliferate and go unpunished.[1]

关于财产权的来源和公平分配的构成,存在各种不同的理论。的确,国家应该在某种程度上,通过民事和刑事相结合的方式保护人民的财产利益。事实上,各个国家的法律基本上都包含了一系列旨在保护财产权的方法,其范围很广,包括刑事手段以及非刑事手段。许多民事法律,包括合同法、侵权法、代理法和继承法,其主要目标之一就是保护财产权。确定财产权何时应当受到刑法,而不是民法的保护,或还应同时受到民法的保护,引发了复杂的犯罪化问题。有时,犯罪与民事过错之间的界限取决于行为危害的程度或强度。比如,内幕交易、偷税漏税、非法下载等,如果情节严重,就要比情节轻微危害不大时更容易被视为犯罪。同样,侵入他人土地,通常只有在造成实际财产损害时才是犯罪。一般来说,财产犯罪可以被认为至少在两种意义上造成了危害。首先,从狭义上来讲,财产犯罪因为限制或剥夺财产所有人的劳动、福祉或收入,因此具有危害性。其次,财产犯罪因为破坏了财产权制度创建的初衷,大概是为了促进创造和保存财富,使许多形式的人类努力成为可能。盗窃、故意破坏和纵火行为如果多发,势必会对社区和更普遍的经济产生不稳定的影响。在这种更广泛的危害意义上,重要的不是具体的盗窃或非法侵入本身破坏了财产所有权制度,而是如果其泛滥且不受惩罚的话,这种行为会对财产制度造成

〔1〕 Markus D. Dubber & Tatjana Hörnle, *The Oxford Handbook of Criminal Law*, Oxford University Press, 2014, p. 769 - 770.

危害。[1]

Even so, it is still possible to summarize and generalize the meaning of the so-called property, which is the object of property crimes in common law countries. Property is defined for the purpose of theft in section 4(1) of the Theft Act 1968: "Property includes money and all other property, real or personal, including things in action and other intangible property." "Real property" (otherwise called "reality") means freehold land. "personal property" (otherwise called "personalty") means all other property, including leasehold land, movables ("chattels"), and money. At common law the thing has to have some value, but the rule is so interpreted that it has practically no effect, except in wholly artificial applications. Anyway, it is not repeated in the Theft Act. One may steal, for example, a commercially worthless piece of paper, because there are many pieces of paper that people want to keep, even though they have no market value. If a thing is derisively worthless, like a used matchstick, the prosecution could not establish dishonesty.[2]

即便如此,还是可以对于普通法系国家财产犯罪的对象,即财物的含义加以总结与概括。例如,根据英国1968年《盗窃法》第4(1)条,财产犯罪中的财物被定义为:财物包括金钱和所有其他财物,即不动产和个人财物,包括"权利动产"和其他无形资产。其中的"不动产"是指自由保有土地。而"个人财物"是指所有其他财物,包括租赁土地、"动产"以及货币。在普通法中,作为财产犯罪对象的物品必须具有一定价值,但除了某些人为拟制的情况,这种定义形同虚设。总之盗窃法中并没有重复这条规则。比如说,可以盗窃没有商业价值的纸片,因为有很多纸片,即使没有市场价值,但人们还是会敝帚自珍。如果物品被视为一文不值,就像用过的火柴棒,就不能将其作为财产犯罪的对象来加以保护。[3]

11.2 Typical Property Crimes(典型财产犯罪)

Most criminal law systems today contain a wide range of offenses that are classified as "property crimes". The U. S. Department of Justice's Bureau of Justice Statistics includes within its category of property offenses a relatively limited collection of crimes:

---

〔1〕 参见[加]马库斯·杜博、[德]塔蒂安娜·霍恩雷主编:《牛津刑法手册》,李立丰译,上海三联书店2023年版,第830页。

〔2〕 Dennis J. Baker, *Glanville Williams' Textbook of Criminal Law*, 4th edition, Sweet & Maxwell, 2015, p. 1233.

〔3〕 参见[英]丹尼斯·贝克主编:《格兰维尔·威廉姆斯刑法学教科书:典型罪编》,李立丰译,法律出版社2023年版,第212页。

household burglary, motor vehicle theft, and property theft. The influential U. S. Model Penal Code identifies a much longer list of "offenses against property": arson, criminal mischief, and other property destruction; burglary and other criminal intrusion (including criminal trespass); robbery; theft and related offenses (including blackmail, receiving stolen property, unauthorized use of vehicles, failing to return lost property, and theft by deception); and forgery and fraudulent practices (including writing bad checks, deceptive business practices, and commercial bribery). To these lists, we might add more novel property offenses such as carjacking, insider trading, misappropriation of trade secrets, criminal copyright infringement, trademark infringement, identity theft, and a wide range of frauds.[1] We will briefly introduce several leading common law property crimes as following.

目前大多数刑法体系,都包含一系列被归类为"财产犯罪"的犯罪。例如,"美国司法部司法局"在统计数据时,在财产犯罪类别中包含了一系列范围相对有限的犯罪:入户实施夜盗、盗窃机动车和盗窃财产。影响力巨大的美国《模范刑法典》中包括的"侵犯财产罪"数量更多:纵火、寻衅滋事和其他破坏财产的行为;夜盗和其他犯罪行为(包括非法侵入);抢劫;盗窃及相关犯罪(包括勒索、收受赃物、擅自使用他人车辆、不归还遗失物、骗盗等);伪造和欺诈行为(包括开空头支票、欺骗性商业行为和商业贿赂)。除此之外,还涌现出了很多全新的财产犯罪,如劫车、内幕交易、盗用商业秘密、侵犯著作权犯罪、侵犯商标权、冒用身份以及各种各样的欺诈行为。[2] 下面,就几项较为典型的普通法系财产犯罪简要加以介绍。

11.2.1 Theft(盗窃罪)

Theft is certainly one of the oldest crimes, hailing back to King Edmund's Code in the tenth century and further still to more ancient law codes.[3] The law of theft that emerged from this history was a highly complex one: a wide array of theft and theft-related offenses were viewed as more or less distinct crimes, with distinct labels, elements, defenses, and punishments. But starting in the late nineteenth century, in both the United States and England, there was considerable skepticism about the value of this

---

〔1〕 Markus D. Dubber & Tatjana Hörnle, *The Oxford Handbook of Criminal Law*, Oxford University Press, 2014, p. 769–771.

〔2〕 参见[加]马库斯·杜博、[德]塔蒂安娜·霍恩雷主编:《牛津刑法手册》,李立丰译,上海三联书店2023年版,第830页。

〔3〕 Paul Knepper & Anja Johansen, *The Oxford Handbook of the History of Crime and Criminal Justice*, Oxford University Press, 2016, p. 156.

scheme. A number of then – influential commentators pointed out that the law of theft was too complex for prosecutors, judges, juries, and the public at large to understand; it involved esoteric legal concepts like breaking bulk, asportation, trespassory caption, animus furandi, and ferae naturae, as well as elusive distinctions between possession, title, and custody, and between larceny by trick and false pretenses. And these concepts were not merely confusing: it was said that they allowed defendants to escape conviction unfairly by arguing that their conduct fell into the gap between offenses, or that rather than committing the form of theft charged, they had actually committed a different form of theft. By the mid – twentieth century, the reformers finally had their opportunity to rewrite the law of theft. In the United States, theft reform became a primary goal of the American Law Institute, in drafting its Model Penal Code, first promulgated in 1962. And in England, theft reform became an early goal of the Criminal Law Revision Committee, the precursor to the Law Commission of England and Wales, which drafted what would become the Theft Act 1968. Both efforts led to Criminal Code that eliminated supposedly archaic distinctions such as those between larceny, embezzlement, and false pretenses, and replaced them with a more or less consolidated offense of "theft", incorporating what had previously been the separate common law theft offenses, while at the same time retaining robbery, burglary, and writing bad checks as distinct offenses.〔1〕In comparison, the merger of theft in the Model Penal Code is particularly widespread. Within the scope of the crime of theft, there are several types of behaviors: theft committed through illegal removal or disposal, theft committed through fraudulent means, theft committed through extortion, theft involving lost, forgotten, or mistakenly delivered items, acceptance of stolen property, theft of entrusted funds not handled as required, theft of unauthorized use of cars and other vehicles. In comparison, the merger model adopted by the UK, Canada, and Australia is less extreme.

盗窃,无疑是最古老的罪行之一,可以追溯到10世纪《埃德蒙国王法典》,或更为古老的法律规定。〔2〕在漫长的历史发展过程中,盗窃法的立法规定变得非常复杂:与盗窃或盗窃相关的犯罪各种各样,类型种类纷繁复杂,具有不同的行为标签、构成要件、抗辩事由和处罚措施。但从19世纪末开始,在美国和英国,人们开始质

〔1〕 Markus D. Dubber & Tatjana Hörnle, *The Oxford Handbook of Criminal Law*, Oxford University Press, 2014, p. 772.

〔2〕 参见[英]保罗·克内珀、[英]安贾·约翰森主编:《牛津犯罪及刑事司法史手册》,李立丰译,上海三联书店2024年版,第138页。

疑上述做法的价值。若干极具影响力的学者指出，盗窃法过于复杂，检方、法官、陪审团和公众都无法理解；相关立法涉及一些深奥的法律概念，如盗窃托管物品罪、窃取他人动产、侵入性获取、窃取的意图和不属于私产的；占有、所有权和监护权之间难以捉摸的区别，以及使用欺诈手段盗窃和“欺诈”之间的区别。这些概念不仅令人困惑，还被认为会导致被告不公平地逃避定罪。在司法实践中，被告往往辩称法律对自己的行为并无明确禁止，或者说他们实施的是未被法律所明确禁止的盗窃行为。到了20世纪中期，改革者终于有机会改写盗窃法。在美国，盗窃罪改革成为美国法律学会起草1962年首次推出的《模范刑法典》的首要目标。在英格兰，盗窃改革成为英格兰和威尔士法律委员会的前身，即刑法修订委员会的早期改革目标，该委员会起草了1968年的《盗窃法》。这两项努力都使英格兰的刑法典消除了盗窃罪、侵占罪和诈骗罪等被认为是过时的区别，取而代之的是或多或少的“盗窃罪”的合并，合并了以前单独的普通法盗窃罪，同时保留了抢劫罪、夜盗罪和开空头支票等明显独立的犯罪行为。[1] 相较而言，《模范刑法典》中盗窃罪的合并尤其广泛。在盗窃罪的范围内，有下列几种行为：以非法拿走或者处分的方式实施的盗窃，欺诈方式实施的盗窃，勒索方式实施的盗窃，涉及遗失物、遗忘物、误递物的盗窃，收受被盗财产，未按要求处理委托资金的盗窃，未经授权使用汽车和其他车辆的盗窃。[2] 相较而言，英国、加拿大和澳大利亚采用的合并模式并不那么极端。

We will take the theft legislation in British criminal law as an example to explain the constituents of theft.

下面，仅以英国刑法中的盗窃罪相关立法，对盗窃罪的构成要素加以说明。

The offence of theft created by the section 1(1) of the Theft Act 1968 is defined as "A person is guilty of theft if he dishonestly appropriates property belonging to another with the intention of permanently depriving the other of it; and 'thief' and 'steal' shall be construed accordingly." The actus reus of theft may be discussed under five propositions: (1) There must be property. (2) The property must belong to another. (3) The thief must appropriate the property. (4) It is immaterial that the owner is induced by fraud, threats and undue influence to consent to parting with the title to the property. (5) but in other case it is doubtful how far theft can be committed if the act of appropriation is lawful in civil law.

---

〔1〕 参见[加]马库斯·杜博、[德]塔蒂安娜·霍恩雷主编：《牛津刑法手册》，李立丰译，上海三联书店2023年版，第832页。

〔2〕 参见[美]美国法学会编：《美国模范刑法典及其评注》，刘仁文等译，法律出版社2005年版，第158页。

英国1968年《盗窃法》第1(1)条规定了盗窃的定义:“基于永久剥夺他人财物的故意,有悖诚信地取得属于他人的财物,则构成盗窃罪;‘小偷’和‘偷窃’应作相应的解读。”可以认为,盗窃罪的犯行认定可以从以下5个方面进行:(1)必须存在财物。(2)该财物必须属于他人。(3)行为人必须将财物占为己有。(4)所有权人在欺诈、威胁和不正当影响的诱使下同意放弃财物的所有权并不重要。(5)但是,在其他案件中,如果侵占行为在民法上是合法的,那么该行为能在多大程度上构成盗窃罪是值得怀疑的。

We may extract from the aforementioned definition of theft of its mental element: (1) At the time of appropriation the thief must intend to deprive another person permanently of his property. (2) The appropriation must be dishonest. The phrase formerly used to describe the mental element in stealing was animus furandi. For the sake of speaking English (even though rather peculiar English) we shall speak of it as theftous intent. Its two elements are the intent to deprive the owner permanently, and dishonesty. The two elements are independent. One may dishonestly appropriate property intending to deprive the owner temporarily ("borrowing" another's lawn – mower when the taker knows that the owner does not wish the taker to do so), but this is not theft.[1]

在此基础上,可以从上述关于盗窃的定义中提取一系列规则,其中关于主观要素的认定规则包括:(1)盗贼在侵占时,必须意图永久剥夺他人的财物。(2)侵占一定是有悖诚信的。以前用来形容偷窃中的主观要素是盗窃的意图。而其两个要素是永久剥夺物权人财物的意图,以及有悖诚信。这两个要素相互独立。人可以有悖诚信地侵占财物,但目的是暂时剥夺物主的权利(如“借用”他人的割草机,而窃取者知道物主不希望出借)时,并不属于盗窃。[2]

11.2.2 Burglary(夜盗)

Burglary was first defined in Coke's Institutes in 1641. The offense of burglary is peculiar to the common law countries. However, even in the common law countries, it has been criticized on several grounds. First is the fact that burglary has sometimes been used as a means to prosecute preparatory conduct that cannot be reached by the law of attempt. As such, it suffers from exactly the kinds of defects identified with other kinds

---

[1] Dennis J. Baker, *Glanville Williams' Textbook of Criminal Law*, 4th edition, Sweet & Maxwell, 2015, p. 1233.

[2] 参见[英]丹尼斯·贝克主编:《格兰维尔·威廉姆斯刑法学教科书:典型罪编》,李立丰译,法律出版社2023年版,第212页。

of "pre – inchoate" offenses, in that it denies people who have only just started down a criminal path the opportunity to change their minds, and gives undue power to the police to make stops and arrests. Another problem with burglary is that it invites a policy of "double dipping": whereas attempts invariably merge with the completed crime, burglars can be prosecuted for both the entry with intent to commit a crime and the crime that is actually committed once the offender is inside the target structure. Despite the criticisms of burglary, modern Anglo – American criminal codes' such as the Model Penal Code and the Theft Act 1968 (as amended by the Criminal Justice Act 1991) have retained the offense. The Model Penal Code Commentary states that the decision to do so "reflects a considered judgment that especially severe sanctions are appropriate for criminal invasion of premises under circumstances likely to terrorize occupants." At the same time, the commentary acknowledges that the offense has been retained out of what it calls "deference to the momentum of historical tradition"—a position that is virtually impossible to reconcile with the Code's radically revisionist attitude toward the theft offenses.[1]

夜盗这一概念,最早于1641年在柯克的研究中被加以界定。如前所述,夜盗罪是英美法系国家所特有的。但即便在普通法系国家,该罪名也受到了多方面的批评。首先,夜盗罪有时被用作起诉未遂法无法打击的预备行为的手段。因此,夜盗罪存在与其他类型的"不完整罪"一样的缺陷,因为其相当于剥夺了刚开始犯罪的人改弦更张的机会,并让警察掌握了不当滥捕的权力。夜盗罪存在的另一个问题是,立法者相当于采取了"双重打击"的刑事政策:尽管犯罪既遂总是可以包含未遂,但根据现在的立法,对基于实施犯罪意图进入特定建筑物的行为人,以及进入特定建筑物之后才产生特定犯意的行为人,均可提起夜盗罪的指控。尽管对夜盗的批评声不绝于耳,但现代英、美两国刑法,如《模范刑法典》和1968年《盗窃法》(经1991年《刑事司法法》修订)却都保留了这一罪行。《模范刑法典》评注指出,这样做的决定"反映出以下慎重的判断,即特别严厉的制裁在可能恐吓居住者的情况下发生的刑事入侵行为是适当的"。[2] 评注承认,保留这一罪行是出于"对于历史传统的尊重"——这一立场几乎无法与《模范刑法典》对盗窃罪的激进修正主义态度相

---

[1] Markus D. Dubber & Tatjana Hörnle, *The Oxford Handbook of Criminal Law*, Oxford University Press, 2014, p. 779.

[2] 参见[美]美国法学会编:《美国模范刑法典及其评注》,刘仁文等译,法律出版社2005年版,第153页。

协调。[1]

We will take the theft legislation in British criminal law as an example to explain the constituents of burglary below.

下面,仅以英国刑法中的夜盗罪相关立法,对夜盗罪构成要素加以说明。

Section 9 of the Theft Act 1968 runs as follows—

1968 年《盗窃法》第 9 条规定:

(1) A person is guilty of burglary if—

(1)下列情况属于夜盗罪:

(a) he enters any building or part of a building as a trespasser and with intent to commit any such offence as is mentioned in subsection (2) below; or

(a)以侵入者身份进入任何建筑物或建筑物的任何部分,并意图犯本条第(2)款所述的任何罪行;或

(b) having entered any building or part of a building as a trespasser he steals or attempts to steal anything in the building or that part of it or inflicts or attempts to inflict on any person therein any grievous bodily harm.

(b)以侵入者身份进入任何建筑物或建筑物的任何部分后,偷窃或企图偷窃该建筑物或建筑物的某一部分中的任何物品,或造成或企图造成其中任何人任何严重身体伤害。

(2) The offences referred to in subsection (1) (a) above are offences of stealing anything in the building or part of a building in question, of inflicting on any person therein any grievous bodily harm therein, and of doing unlawful damage to the building or anything therein…

(2)上文第(1)(a)款所述罪行,是指偷窃该建筑物或建筑物的某一部分中的任何物品、对其中任何人造成任何严重身体伤害,以及非法毁坏该建筑物或其中任何物品。

(4) References in subsections (1) and (2) above to a building, shall apply also to an inhabited vehicle or vessel, and shall apply to any such vehicle or vessel at times when the person having a habitation in it is not there as well as at times when he is.

(4)上文第(1)款及第(2)款所述建筑物,亦适用于有人居住的车辆或船只,即使居住者当时并未在场。

Section 10 creates an offence of aggravated burglary, punishable with imprisonment

---

[1] 参见[加]马库斯·杜博、[德]塔蒂安娜·霍恩雷主编:《牛津刑法手册》,李立丰译,上海三联书店 2023 年版,第 532 页。

for life, if the burglar has with him at the time of the burglary any firearm, any weapon of offence, or any explosive. Furthermore, burglary of a dwelling house is also treated as an aggravated form of burglary. Burglary of a dwelling – house (whether anyone is there at the time or not) is rightly regarded as much more serious than simple theft from other buildings. Whereas most offences under the Theft Act 1968 are triable either way, the more serious ones are purely indictable: robbery, assault with intent to rob, blackmail, and some forms of burglary. The precise rule for burglary is somewhat complicated, and it is enough to say that ordinary burglary simply for the purpose of theft is triable either way, whereas burglary involving an intention to commit an offence which can only be tried on indictment or burglary in a dwelling involving violence is triable only on indictment.[1]

《盗窃法》第 10 条规定了夜盗的加重犯,即发生夜盗时,窃贼随身携带任何火器、任何犯罪武器或任何爆炸物,都可被判处终身监禁。此外,进入住宅夜盗也被视为夜盗的加重犯。进入住宅夜盗(无论当时是否有人)被视为比进入其他建筑物实施的简单盗窃要严重得多。尽管 1968 年的《盗窃法》规定的大多数犯罪都是两可审犯罪,但更严重的犯罪只能循公诉程序定罪,包括:抢劫,基于抢劫意图的攻击、勒索和某些形式的夜盗。关于夜盗的精确规则有点复杂,但只需记住:仅仅为了盗窃目的的普通夜盗可自诉,而涉及实施只能检控审理的犯罪意图的夜盗或者涉及暴力的在住宅内的夜盗只能通过检控方式加以审理。[2]

11.2.3　Fraud(欺诈)

A related issue here arises out of divergent views about the relationship between theft and fraud. In most U. S. states, fraud tends to be viewed as a subset of theft, equivalent to the early statutory offense of false pretenses—essentially, theft by deception. In other jurisdictions, however, including England, various civil countries, and under some U. S. federal statutes, the concept of fraud refers to a wide variety of "dishonest" behavior, including schemes not just to obtain money or property, but also to achieve an "unjust advantage" or to "injure the rights or interests of another". Viewed in this broader sense, fraud sometimes functions as something other than a

---

〔1〕 Dennis J. Baker, *Glanville Williams' Textbook of Criminal Law*, 4th edition, Sweet & Maxwell, 2015, p. 1368.

〔2〕 参见[英]丹尼斯·贝克主编:《格兰维尔·威廉姆斯刑法学教科书:典型罪编》,李立丰译,法律出版社 2023 年版,第 336 页。

property crime.[1]

在美国大多数州，欺诈往往被视为盗窃犯罪的下位概念，相当于早期的法定欺诈罪，本质上是欺骗盗窃。然而，在其他司法管辖区，包括英国、大陆法系国家和一些美国联邦法规，欺诈的概念是指各种各样的"不诚实"行为，包括不仅是为了获得金钱或财产的计划，同时也是为了获得"不正当的利益"或"损害他人的权利或利益"。从这个更广泛的意义上看，欺诈有时不属于财产犯罪。[2]

We will take the fraud legislation in British criminal law as an example to explain the constituents of fraud below.

虽然如此，下面仍以英国刑法中的欺诈罪相关立法，对欺诈罪构成要素加以说明。

Section 1 of the Fraud Act 2006 outlines the three core fraud offences –

英国 2006 年《欺诈法》第 1 条规定了 3 项核心欺诈罪行为：

"(1) A person is guilty of fraud if he is in breach of any of the sections listed in subsection (2) (which provide for different ways of committing the offence).

(1)如果某人违反第(2)款中列出的任何条款(其中规定了不同的犯罪方式)，即属欺诈。

(2) The sections are –

(a) section 2 (fraud by false representation),

(b) section 3 (fraud by failing to disclose information), and

(c) section 4 (fraud by abuse of position).

(2)这些条款是：(a)第 2 条(虚假表示欺诈)；(b)第 3 条(未披露信息欺诈)；(c)第 4 条(滥用职权欺诈)。

Most acts of fraud, if not all, result from false representations. Therefore, it is of no surprise that the lead offence in the Fraud Act 2006 is fraud by false representation. Section 2 provides:

大多数欺诈行为(如果不是全部)都是由虚假表示造成的。因此，2006 年《欺诈法》中的主要罪行是通过虚假表示进行的欺诈。该法第 2 条规定：

(1) A person is in breach of this section if he –

(a) dishonestly makes a false representation, and

---

[1] Markus D. Dubber & Tatjana Hörnle, *The Oxford Handbook of Criminal Law*, Oxford University Press, 2014, p. 777.

[2] 参见[加]马库斯·杜博、[德]塔蒂安娜·霍恩雷主编：《牛津刑法手册》，李立丰译，上海三联书店 2023 年版，第 532 页。

(b) intends, by making the representation – (i) to make a gain for himself or another, or (ii) to cause loss to another or to expose another to a risk of loss.

(1)任何人违反以下条文,如果——(a)有悖诚信地做出虚假表示;(b)意图通过虚假表示——(i)为自己或他人谋取利益;(ii)给他人造成损失或使他人遭受损失的风险。

(2) A representation is false if –

(a) it is untrue or misleading, and

(b) the person making it knows that it is, or might be, untrue or misleading

(2)如果满足以下条件,则表示为虚假:(a)不真实或具有误导性;(b)做出表示的人知道该表示是或者可能是不真实或误导性的。

(3) Representation means any representation as to fact or law, including a representation as to the state of mind of –

(a) the person making the representation, or

(b) any other person.

(3)表示是指关于事实或法律的任何表示,包括关于以下主体心理状态的表示:(a)做出表示的人;(b)其他任何人。

(4) A representation may be express or implied.

(4)表示可以是明示或暗示的。

(5) For the purposes of this section a representation may be regarded as made if it (or anything implying it) is submitted in any form to any system or device designed to receive, convey or respond to communications (with or without human intervention).

(5)就本条规定而言,如果将表示(或暗示)以任何形式提交给旨在接收、传达或响应通信(有或没有人的介入)的任何系统或设备,均可被视为做出该表示。

The actus reus of this offence is the making of a false representation, express or implied. The most straightforward example of fraud by false representation is where defendant expressly makes a false representation about an existing fact. Absent an intent to make a gain or to cause a loss, or risk of loss to another, a false representation per se will not be enough to ground a conviction for fraud. In addition, the defendant must make the representation knowing it is false or knowing it might be false. If a person makes a false representation with an intent to gain or cause a loss, it is necessary to show that he knows as a matter of fact that his representation is false or might be false.[1]

---

〔1〕 Dennis J. Baker, *Glanville Williams' Textbook of Criminal Law*, 4th edition, Sweet & Maxwell, 2015, p. 1448.

在这个意义上，可以认为该罪的犯罪行为是做出虚假的表示，无论明示或暗示。通过虚假表示进行欺诈的最直接的例子是：被告人对现有事实以明示方法做出虚假表示。虚假表示型欺诈罪的犯意，可以被理解为：如果没有获利或给他人造成损失，或给他人造成损失风险的意图，虚假表示本身就不足以构成欺诈罪。此外，做出虚假表示的被告人必须明知相关意思表示是虚假的或可能是虚假的。如果行为人做出虚假表示，意图获得收益或造成损失，有必要证明他事实上知道自己的表示是虚假的或可能是虚假的。[1]

11.3　Punishment for Property Crimes（财产犯罪的处罚）

Generally speaking, the punishment for property crimes is slightly lighter than for violent crimes. For example, in the UK, the maximum sentence for theft is 7 years in prison.[2] Section 9 the Theft Act 1968 provides: A person guilty of burglary shall on conviction on indictment be liable to imprisonment for a term not exceeding—(1) where the offence is committed in respect of a building or part of a building which is a dwelling, fourteen years; (2) in any other case, ten years. Section 1 of the Fraud Act 2006 provides: A person who is guilty of fraud is liable – (1) on summary conviction, to imprisonment for a term not exceeding 12 months or to a fine not exceeding the statutory maximum (or to both); (2) on conviction on indictment, to imprisonment for a term not exceeding 10 years or to a fine (or to both).

一般来说，侵犯财产犯罪的处罚相较于暴力犯罪略轻，例如，在英国，盗窃罪的最高刑期是 7 年监禁。英国 1968 年《盗窃法》第 9 条规定，夜盗罪经循公诉程序定罪，可判处监禁：(1) 如果在作为住宅的任何建筑物或建筑物的任何部分中犯罪，刑期不超过 14 年；(2) 在任何其他情况下，刑期不超过 10 年。而根据该国 2006 年《欺诈法》第 1 条第 3 款，犯有欺诈罪的人应承担责任：(1) 一经简易程序定罪，可处以不超过 12 个月的监禁或不超过法定最高金额的罚金（或两者并处）；(2) 一经公诉程序定罪，可处以不超过 10 年的监禁或罚金（或两者并处）。

Andrew Ashworth has recently taken the position that imprisonment should essentially be abolished for (pure) property offenses. He believes that "the deprivation of the basic right to liberty of the person, being the most severe sanction available, should be reserved for the most serious offences [such as robbery, burglary, sexual

---

〔1〕 参见［英］丹尼斯·贝克主编：《格兰维尔·威廉姆斯刑法学教科书：典型罪编》，李立丰译，法律出版社 2023 年版，第 412 页。

〔2〕 Section 176 of the Anti – social Behaviour, Crime and Policing Act 2014.

offenses, and violence] and not imposed for a type of offence much lower on the scale." Ashworth would thus exempt from imprisonment not only larceny, but also repeat pickpocketing, embezzlement by public officials and "captains of industry", major frauds, handling stolen goods, and benefit fraud and tax evasion. In his view, all of these offenses can be addressed more efficiently and justly through non-prison sanctions. The only possible exception would be cases in which there are "exceptional circumstances that render the offence so extraordinarily serious that no sentence lower than custody would meet the justice of the case". A possible example would be "theft or fraud targeting an elderly or disabled victim, the exploitative element—combined with the theft or fraud of a significant sum or item—taking the offense above the usual combination of factors". There are potential problems with Ashworth's proposal. Empirical studies suggest that, unlike many violent offenses, the majority of property crimes is committed by a relatively small number of repeat career criminal offenders, who are motivated primarily by the desire for monetary gain. These are just the kind of offenders for whom threatened imprisonment might actually serve as an effective deterrent. Without the threat of prison time, the alternative sentence—presumably, some form of restitution and money damages—might become nothing more than a cost of doing business. The deeper issue concerns the apparent assumption that nonviolent property offenses are per se less blameworthy than violent offenses. Think about the extreme situation, the case of Bernard Madoff, the Ponzi-scheming investment advisor who defrauded investors of a sum estimated at more than $50 billion, depriving individuals of their retirement accounts and institutions of their endowments, and arguably contributing to the financial crisis of 2008. How should the blameworthiness of Madoff's acts be compared to, a violent assault? It is far from clear that the assault, for which incarceration would be the norm, is necessarily the more blameworthy act. Moreover, insofar as property offenders tend to be more privileged than violent offenders who come from the low strata of society, enjoying more social resources and rights. Thus, exempting them entirely from incarceration might result in class bias.[1]

安德鲁·阿什沃思提出,对于(纯粹的)财产犯罪,基本上应当废除监禁。他认为,"剥夺人身自由的基本权利,是现有最严厉的制裁措施,应当适用于最严重的犯罪(如抢劫、夜盗、性犯罪)",因此,阿什沃思认为,不仅可以免除盗窃罪的监禁,而

---

〔1〕 Markus D. Dubber & Tatjana Hörnle, *The Oxford Handbook of Criminal Law*, Oxford University Press, 2014, p. 787.

且可以免除重复扒窃、公职人员和“工业领袖”的侵占、重大欺诈、销赃、欺诈和逃税的监禁刑。他认为,这些违法行为都可以因为采取了非暴力手段而通过非监禁刑得到更有效、更公正的解决。当然,“有一些特殊情况使罪行非常严重,任何低于监禁刑的判决都不符合公正的原则”。可能的例子如“除了与盗窃和诈骗严重性相关的数额,还存在针对老年人或残疾人以及剥削性等加重因素”。阿什沃思的提议存在潜在问题。实证研究表明,与暴力犯罪不同的是,大多数财产犯罪往往由相对较少的职业累犯所犯,他们的动机主要是为了金钱利益。对这些罪犯来说,威胁监禁实际上可能起到有效的威慑作用。如果无须面对牢狱之灾的威胁,行为人就会将赔偿经济损失当作生意的成本。更深层次的问题在于,一般认为,相较于暴力犯罪,非暴力型财产犯罪的可责性较弱一些。想想看,在极端的情况下,从事庞氏骗局的策划投资顾问伯纳德·麦道夫,骗取投资者的金额估计超过 500 亿美元,洗劫个人退休账户和机构的捐赠,说他是 2008 年国际金融危机的罪魁祸首也不为过。麦道夫所作所为的可责性应该如何与暴力袭击相比?目前尚不清楚的是,通常情况下攻击犯罪该当的监禁,是否必然适用于更为严重的危害行为。此外,相较于大多出身社会底层的暴力犯罪人,财产犯罪人往往占据更多社会资源、享有更多权利,如果对其彻底免除监禁刑,可能会导致更为实质意义上的阶级偏见。[1]

11.4 Distinguishing Property Crimes from other Crimes(财产犯罪与相关犯罪的区别)

In order tofurther understand property crimes in the common law system, it is necessary to briefly examine the differences between property crimes and related crimes, especially between white - collar crimes and economic crimes.

为了更好地了解普通法系中的财产犯罪,有必要简要考察财产犯罪与相关犯罪,特别是白领犯罪和经济犯罪之间的区别。

11.4.1 Economic Crimes(经济犯罪)

Economic crimes, namely crimes that disrupt economic activities or economic relations, are commonly seen in socialist countries, such as the in former Soviet Union. For example, In the USSR, due to replacement of private ownership of the means of production by state ownership, crimes against state property were punished more severely than crimes against private property. Crimes against state property were really

〔1〕 参见[加]马库斯·杜博、[德]塔蒂安娜·霍恩雷主编:《牛津刑法手册》,李立丰译,上海三联书店 2023 年版,第 534 页。

"economic" crimes, and indirect crimes against the state. Thus, § 79 CC (1926) punished non - aggravated destroying or damaging of property of government agencies or enterprises by deprivation of liberty of up to one year, whereas the same act against private property was punishable by only up to six months' deprivation of liberty [§ 175 CC(1926)]. Theft of private property was punishable by up to three months' deprivation of liberty but theft of state property could be punished by up to five years' deprivation of liberty [§ 162(a,d,e) CC (1926)]. The original version of the CC - RSFSR (1960) continued this differentiation between crimes against socialist property and private property. After the Russian Revolution, the act of "buying and selling to make a profit" was immediately criminalized. § § 99, 99 - 1 CC (1926) punished by up to two years the acquisition of products or fish with the intent of selling them for profit. § 107 CC (1926) punished sale of agricultural products for profit. After NEP, however, Soviet codes provided for criminal punishment for entrepreneurial activity up until perestroika. See § 153 CC - RSFSR (1960). Besides, there was also criminalization of common labor infractions in the USSR. Once upon a time, missing or leaving work subjected conscripted workers would face a criminal charge of "labor desertion" under the CC (1922). During WWII, the legislation criminalized common labor infractions, such as quitting and shirking, and raised to new levels punishments for hooliganism, petty theft at factories, and production of defective goods. Such offenses were responsible for more than two - thirds of all criminal convictions in 1940, more than one - half in 1945, and over 40% even in 1949. Any employee of a state firm who quit a regular job without permission was subject to a term of imprisonment of two to four months. The edict also prohibited the firing of workers who shirked. Any shirker who missed all or part of a day at work faced a punishment of one to six months' corrective work with a deduction from earnings of up to 25%. To prevent workers from stealing something small from their factory in order to get fired so that they could find better work, a decree was issued on August 10, 1940, imposing a mandatory one - year prison sentence for petty theft at factories.[1]

经济犯罪,即破坏经济活动或经济关系的犯罪,多见于苏联等社会主义国家。例如,在苏联,由于生产资料的私有制被国有制取代,侵犯国有财产罪比侵犯私有财产罪该当更严厉的惩罚。危害国有财产罪实际上被作为经济犯罪,即间接危害国家

---

〔1〕 Markus D. Dubber & Tatjana Hörnle, *The Oxford Handbook of Criminal Law*, Oxford University Press, 2014, p.321.

的犯罪。因此,1926 年《俄罗斯苏维埃联邦社会主义共和国刑法典》第 79 条规定对非加重型破坏或损坏政府机构或企业财产的行为可以处以最多 1 年的剥夺自由,而对私人财产的同样行为能处以最多 6 个月的剥夺自由(1926 年《俄罗斯苏维埃联邦社会主义共和国刑法典》第 175 条)。盗窃私人财产可处以最多 3 个月的剥夺自由,但盗窃国家财产可处以最多 5 年的剥夺自由(1926 年《俄罗斯苏维埃联邦社会主义共和国刑法典》第 162 条)。1960 年《俄罗斯苏维埃联邦社会主义共和国刑法典》的原始版本延续了对侵犯社会主义财产罪和侵犯私有财产罪的区分。此外,苏俄革命后,"买卖牟利"行为被定为刑事犯罪,不过这一规定在新经济政策期间被取消,取而代之的是反垄断法或定价法。1926 年《俄罗斯苏维埃联邦社会主义共和国刑法典》第 99 条等规定对以营利为目的收购农渔产品的行为处以 2 年以下监禁的处罚。该法第 107 条处罚以牟利为目的销售农产品的行为。在新经济政策之后,直到 20 世纪 80 年代末,苏联刑法典一直将具有创业性质的活动作为犯罪加以刑事处罚。此外,在苏联,还曾一度出现过将常见劳动违法行为犯罪化的现象。例如,1922 年《俄罗斯苏维埃联邦社会主义共和国刑法典》规定了劳工逃避罪,对其加以刑事指控。这一规定后来被 1926 年《俄罗斯苏维埃联邦社会主义共和国刑法典》废除。卫国战争期间,苏联将诸如辞职、偷懒等常见的劳动违法行为定为犯罪,并将流氓行为、在工厂实施的小偷小摸行为和生产次品行为的惩罚提高到新的水平。1940 年,这类犯罪占全部刑事定罪的 2/3 以上,1945 年占 1/2 以上,甚至在 1949 年也超过 2/5。国营公司的任何雇员未经允许辞去正常工作,将被处以 2 个月至 4 个月的监禁。法令还禁止解雇逃避责任的工人。任何逃避工作的人如果错过了 1 天的全部或部分工作时间,将面临 1 个月到 6 个月的改造劳动处罚,并且在此期间其收入将减少 1/4。[1]

11.4.2 Economic Crimes(白领犯罪)

The term "white - collar crime" was introduced to the public arena by Edwin H. Sutherland in his 1939 presidential address to a joint meeting of the American Sociological Society and the American Economics Association. Sutherland later defined it as "crime committed by a person of respectability and high social status in the course of his occupation". From this definition and his other writings, five key features stand out in regard to Sutherland's view of white - collar crime. First, the offenders were, by definition, individuals of high social status and respectability. Second, the offenses were

---

〔1〕 参见[加]马库斯·杜博、[德]塔蒂安娜·霍恩雷主编:《牛津刑法手册》,李立丰译,上海三联书店 2023 年版,第 239 页。

committed within an occupational context. Third, the offenses were committed in a particular way—that is, through the "violation of delegated or implied trust". Fourth, the offenses involved massive financial and other costs. Fifth and finally, civil and administrative violations could be counted as white - collar crimes because civil law often deals with practices that are fundamentally similar to those proscribed by criminal law and because many illegal practices can be sanctioned under either criminal or civil law and often both. Although Sutherland's approach to defining white - collar crime is the one that resonates best with popular stereotypes of white - collar offenders, a competing conceptual approach emerged only a few decades after his address. This approach focuses on the nature of the offense rather than the offender. The most influential offense - based definition was promulgated by Edelhertz, who defined white - collar crime as "an illegal act or series of illegal acts committed by nonphysical means and by concealment or guile, to obtain money or property, to avoid the loss of money or property, or to obtain business or personal advantage". Edelhertz's definition differs from Sutherland's in important ways. It makes no reference to the social status of the actor or to the occupational location of the act. Rather, it focuses entirely on the means by which the illegal act is committed. Thus, for Edelhertz, any illegal act that is committed by "nonphysical means and by concealment or guile" for economic or personal advantage is a white - collar crime. Offense - based definitions enlarge the conceptual boundaries of white - collar crime far beyond the high - powered corporate executives that so concerned Sutherland.〔1〕

1939 年,埃德温·萨瑟兰在美国社会学学会和美国经济学会的一次联席会议上发表主旨演讲,将"白领犯罪"一词首次引入公共视野。萨瑟兰后来将其定义为"富有声望和社会地位较高的人在其职业生涯中犯下的罪行"。从这一定义和其他著作来看,萨瑟兰的白领犯罪观具备如下 5 个关键特征。第一,根据定义,白领犯罪系社会地位较高的个人。第二,白领犯罪是在职业背景下犯下的。第三,白领犯罪是以一种特殊的方式,即通过"违反委托或默示信托"实施的。第四,白领犯罪涉及巨大的经济和其他成本,例如社会关系。第五,民事和行政违法行为可以被视为白领犯罪,因为民法通常处理的做法与刑法禁止的做法基本相似,而且诸多非法行径往往可以同时根据刑法或民法予以制裁。尽管萨瑟兰定义白领犯罪的方法最符合大众心目中对白领犯罪人的刻板印象,但在他发表演讲几十年后,一种与之竞争的界定

〔1〕 Shanna R. Van Slyke, Michael L. Benson & Francis T. Cullen, *The Oxford Handbook of White - Collar Crime*, Oxford University Press, 2016, p. 3 - 7.

方法便悄然出现。这种方法侧重犯罪的性质,而不是罪犯。最具影响力的基于犯罪的定义由埃德尔赫茨提出。他将白领犯罪定义为“通过非物质手段和隐瞒或欺骗,以获得金钱或财产,避免金钱或财产损失,获得商业或个人利益而犯下的不法行为或一系列不法行为”。埃德尔赫茨的定义与萨瑟兰的定义在某些重要方面有所不同。前者没有提及行为人的社会身份或行为的职业属性,反倒完全侧重于实施不法行为的手段。因此,对埃德尔赫茨来说,任何为了经济或个人利益而“通过非物质手段、隐瞒或欺骗”实施的不法行为都是白领犯罪。基于犯罪的定义扩大了白领犯罪的概念界限,远远超出了萨瑟兰所关注的位高权重的企业高管。基于犯罪的定义,通常包括任何涉及坑蒙拐骗的财产犯罪,导致白领犯罪的数量大大高于基本犯罪人定义所估计的数量,后者仅包括社会地位较高个体犯下的与其职业相关的犯罪。[1]

■ Case study(案例学习)

R v Ryan [1996] Crim LR 320; (1996) 120 JP 610(女王诉瑞安案)

Facts(基本案情)

The defendant, Ryan, was discovered in the early hours of the morning stuck inside the window of an elderly person's house and had to be removed by the fire brigade. He had managed only to get his head and one arm inside the window. He was convicted with burglary and subsequently appealed against his conviction to the Court of Appeal.

案发当天凌晨,被告瑞安被发现卡在一位老人住家的窗户里,最后不得不出动消防队才将其解救出来。事后查明,意图实施入室盗窃的瑞安被卡住时,只将头和一只胳膊伸进了窗户。因为被判犯有夜盗罪,瑞安向上诉法院提出上诉。

Issues(争议焦点)

Under s. 9(1) Theft Act 1968, a person commits burglary: (a) they enter a building or part of a building as a trespasser with intent to commit any of the offenses described in paragraph (2) of this article, or (b) inflict grievous bodily harm on any person therein, when they enter a building or part of a building as a trespasser. The defendant argued that he had not been capable of stealing anything from the building because he was firmly stuck in the window. He also argued that he had not “entered” a building as he was partially outside it.

1968 年《盗窃法》第 9 条规定:(1)下列情况属于夜盗罪:(a)以侵入者身份进入

[1] 参见[美]尚娜·范·斯莱克、[美]迈克尔·本森、[美]弗朗西斯·卡伦主编:《牛津白领犯罪手册》,李立丰译,上海三联书店 2024 年版,第 3 页。

任何建筑物或建筑物的任何部分,并意图犯本条第(2)款所述的任何罪行;或(b)以侵入者身份进入任何建筑物或建筑物的任何部分后,偷窃或企图偷窃该建筑物或建筑物的某一部分中的任何物品,或造成或企图造成其中任何人任何严重身体伤害。被告辩称,因为被牢牢地卡在窗户里,自己没有能力从住宅里偷任何东西。瑞安还辩称,他根本没有"进入"任何建筑物,因为他的大部分身体还在该建筑物的外面。

Decision / Outcome(上诉结果)

The fact that nothing was stolen was only because he had gotten stuck. In any case it was irrelevant whether anything was actually stolen or not. The defendant' partial presence within the building amounted to entry under s. 9(1) of the 1968 Act. The court applied*R v Brown* [1985] Crim LR 212 and stated that a person could enter a building if only a part of his body with actually inside the premises. The court agreed with the trial judge's finding that it was up to a jury to decide whether there was entry or not based on the facts of the case.

事实上,本案中什么都没有丢的原因,只是瑞案被卡住了身体。而且,在任何情况下,是否有东西真的被盗都与其是否构成犯罪无关。根据1968年《盗窃法》的规定,被告部分进入大楼相当于进入。对此,上诉法院援引了女王诉布朗案,表示如果一个人的身体只有一部分确实在建筑物内,就可以被认定进入了该建筑物。上诉法院同意一审法官的裁决,即由陪审团根据案件事实决定瑞安是否进入了事发时的建筑物。

Question: Is it an entry to get only part of your torso across the threshold? (Please scan the QR code on the right to get the answer)

是不是只要求部分躯干越过门槛就可以认定进入了该建筑物?(答案请扫描右侧二维码获取)

11.5 Exercise(课后练习)(答案请扫描右侧二维码获取)

11.5.1 The test of Terminologies(术语考查)

①animus furandi ②asportation

③breaking bulk ④choses in action

⑤embezzlement ⑥false accounting

⑦false pretenses ⑧fraudulent conversion

⑨information ⑩intangibleproperty/incorporeal property

⑪klopanie ⑫larceny

⑬larceny by bailee ⑭misappropriation

⑮movables/chattels
⑯obtaining by false pretences
⑰obtaining credit by fraud
⑱personal identification number, PIN
⑲res nullius
⑳retail crimes
㉑The Middlesex Session
㉒trespassory caption
㉓withe collar offenses

11.5.2 Short – answer Questions(简答题)

1. Why the prosecution could not establish property crime if a thing is derisively worthless, like a used matchstick?

为什么无价值的物品不能成为财产犯罪的对象?

2. Why that imprisonment should not essentially be abolished for property offenses. ?

为什么不应废除财产犯罪的监禁刑?

■ Curriculum Ideology and Politics(课程思政)

Cultivate objective understanding of the development context and typical characteristics of property crimes, clarify the composition and punishment of typical property crimes in common law countries, understand the connections and differences between property crimes, economic crimes, and white – collar crimes. During the teaching process, students should consciously base themselves on the Chinese position, objectively evaluate the advantages and disadvantages of property crimes in common law countries, and be able to start from a positive attitude of being useful to themselves.

培养客观认知财产犯罪的发展脉络与典型特征,明确普通法系国家典型财产犯罪的构成与处罚,理解财产犯罪与经济犯罪、白领犯罪的联系与区别应当自觉立足于中国立场,客观评价普通法系国家财产犯罪的优缺点。

■ Summary(总结)

1. Any organized society has a law did contain at least some basic property crimes. The extraordinary diversity in ownership is reflected across cultures, the sheer ingenuity that offenders use to infringe such rights, and the substantial overlap that has developed between the criminal law and civil law in this area make the property offenses among the most conceptually complex and structurally varied offenses in our system of criminal law.

任何一个组织有序的社会,其法律至少都包含一些基本的财产犯罪。在不同文化中,所有权的形成方式极其多元,犯罪者所实施的相当独特的侵权方式,以及各国刑法与民法在这一领域不断发展的实质性重叠,都使财产犯罪成为刑法体系中概念最为复杂、结构最为多样的犯罪之一。

2. Widespread theft, vandalism, and arson all tend to have a destabilizing effect on neighborhoods and on the economy more generally. In this broader sense of harm, what matters is not that the specific theft or trespass itself undermines the institution of property ownership but that they are actions that would jeopardize the property system if generally proliferated and unpunished.

盗窃、故意破坏和纵火行为如果多发,势必会对社区和更普遍的经济产生不稳定的影响。在这种更广泛的危害意义上,重要的不是具体的盗窃或非法侵入本身破坏了财产所有权制度,而是如果其泛滥且不受惩罚的话,这种行为会对财产制度造成危害。

3. Generally speaking, the punishment for property crimes is slightly lighter than for violent crimes.

一般来说,财产犯罪的处罚相较于暴力犯罪略轻。

4. Economic crimes, namely crimes that disrupt economic activities or economic relations, are commonly seen in socialist countries such as the Soviet Union.

经济犯罪,即破坏经济活动或经济关系的犯罪,多见于苏联等社会主义国家。

Chapter 12 Crimes against Public Order
第 12 章 侵犯公共秩序犯罪

■ The Learning Objective(学习目标)

1. To have a basic understanding of basic categories of crimes against public order, the ambiguity of its scope and its dynamic development.

了解公共秩序犯罪的主要类型,理解其范围的不明确性及其动态发展性。

2. To understand main offences against public life order.

了解扰乱公共生活秩序犯罪的主要罪行。

3. To understand main offences against public administrative order.

了解扰乱公共管理秩序犯罪的主要罪行。

4. To understand common law offences against public order.

了解扰乱公共秩序的普通法罪行。

5. To learn terminologies related to the topic.

掌握本章的专业术语。

■ Chapter Outline(本章内容概要)

This chapter examines public order offences, mainly the creation of new offences relating to public order, the control of public processions, assemblies and the maintenance of public order in public places, the prohibition of the wearing of uniforms for political purposes and private maintenance of associations of a military or similar nature, and further discusses the dynamics of public order offences at common law.

本章探讨公共秩序犯罪,主要内容包括与公共秩序有关的新罪行的设立,对公共游行、集会及在公共场所维持公共秩序的管控,对为政治目的穿着制服及私人维持军事性或类似性质团体的禁止,以及对普通法中公共秩序犯罪的动态的进一步讨论。

The Purpose of Curriculum Ideology and Politics for this Chapter (本章的课程思政目标)

Understand the relationship between public order and people's aspiration for a better life. The development and changes of public order crimes in modern times reflect people's attention to the close relationship between life order and life quality, as well as the pursuit of a convenient, comfortable and tranquil life, so criminal legislation and criminal justice constantly update the scope of crimes of public order crimes.

认识公共秩序与人民群众对美好生活向往的关系。公共秩序犯罪在近现代的发展变化,体现了人们对生活秩序和生活质量之间的密切关系的重视,以及对便利、舒适和安宁生活的追求,所以刑事立法和刑事司法不断更新着公共秩序犯罪的罪行范围。

Consider the dynamic balance between the exercise of citizens' basic rights and the maintenance of public order. The exercise of fundamental rights, such as association, assembly and procession, is in tension with public order and needs to be dynamically balanced according to specific circumstances. On the one hand, the constitutions or constitutional documents of most countries clearly stipulates that citizens, in exercising their individual rights and freedoms, should take into account the interests of others, society and the state. On the other hand, while the criminal prohibition of violations of public order is intended to protect the good life of citizens, this means may also impede the exercise of their fundamental rights. Legislators should prudently maintain the balance between the two when setting up crimes.

思考公民基本权利行使和公共秩序维护之间的动态平衡关系。结社、集会、游行等基本权利的行使与公共秩序具有紧张关系,需要根据具体的情况予以动态平衡。一方面,多数国家的宪法或宪法性文件均明文规定,公民在行使个人权利和自由时,应当考虑他人的、社会的和国家的利益。另一方面,虽然对侵害公共秩序行为的刑事禁止是为了保护公民美好的生活,但这种手段也可能妨碍公民行使其基本权利。立法者在进行罪名设置时,应审慎维护二者的平衡。

Terminologies(专业术语)

public order	公共秩序
riot	暴乱
violent disorder	暴力骚扰
affray	斗殴

fear or provocation of violence	引起人们对暴力的恐惧或煽动暴力
intentional harassment, alarm or distress	故意造成他人烦扰、惊恐或痛苦
contamination of or interference with goods	污染或处理商品
advance notice of public processions	公共游行的提前通知
imposing conditions on public processions	公共游行的条件施加
prohibiting public processions	禁止公共游行
imposing conditions on public assemblies	公共集会的条件施加
prohibition of uniforms in connection with political objects	与政治目标相关制服的禁止
prohibition of quasimilitary organisations	准军事组织的禁止
public nuisance	滋扰公众
outraging public decency	破坏公众体统

12.1 Crimes against Public Life Order(扰乱公共生活秩序罪)

The offences in this subchapter are those that directly disturb the order of public life under Sections 1 to 5 of the Public Order Act 1986. These crimes are the most typical public order crimes, directly disturbing the order of people's daily life.

本节罪行主要为英国《1986 年公共秩序法》第 1 条至第 5 条规定的直接扰乱公共生活秩序的罪行。这些犯罪是最为典型的公共秩序犯罪,直接扰乱了人们的日常生活秩序。

12.1.1 riot(暴乱罪)

Section 1 of the Public Order Act 1986 prohibitsriot, which reads as follows:

《1986 年公共秩序法》第 1 条规定了暴乱罪,其规定的内容如下:

(1) Where 12 or more persons who are present together use or threaten unlawful violence for a common purpose and the conduct of them (taken together) is such as would cause a person of reasonable firmness present at the scene to fear for his personal safety, each of the persons using unlawful violence for the common purpose is guilty of riot.

(1)凡在场的 12 人或以上为共同目的而使用非法暴力或以非法暴力相威胁,而他们的行为(综合在一起被认为)会令在场具有适当坚定意志的人担心其人身安全,则为共同目的而使用非法暴力的每一名人均犯暴乱罪。

(2)It is immaterial whether or not the 12 or more use or threaten unlawful violence simultaneously.

(2)12 人或以上是否同时使用非法暴力或以非法暴力相威胁,无关紧要。

(3) The common purpose may be inferred from conduct.

(3)共同目的可由行为推知。

(4) No person of reasonable firmness need actually be, or be likely to be, present at the scene.

(4)不需要此种具有适当坚定意志的人实际在场,或可能在场。

(5) Riot may be committed in private as well as in public places.

(5)暴乱可在私人及公共场所发生。

(6) A person guilty of riot is liable on conviction on indictment to imprisonment for a term not exceeding ten years or a fine or both.

(6)任何人犯暴乱罪,一经指控程序定罪,可处不超过 10 年的监禁或罚金,或两者并罚。

Section 6 of the Public Order Act 1986 states the mental element of riot: a person is guilty of riot only if he intends to use violence or is aware that his conduct may be violent. But this does not affect the determination of the number of persons who use or threaten violence.

《1986 年公共秩序法》第 6 条规定了暴乱罪的主观因素:只有当一个人故意使用暴力或意识到他的行为可能是暴力的,他才会犯暴乱罪。但这并不影响确定使用暴力或以暴力相威胁者的人数。

Section 7 of the Act states a procedure issue of prosecution: no prosecution for an offence of riot or incitement to riot may be instituted except by or with the consent of the Director of Public Prosecutions.

该法第 7 条规定了起诉的程序:除非由总检察长发起或经其同意,否则不得就暴乱或煽动暴乱罪行提出检控。

12.1.2　violent disorder(暴力骚扰罪)

Section 2 of the Public Order Act 1986 prohibits violent disorder, which reads as follows:

《1986 年公共秩序法》第 2 条规定了暴力骚扰罪,内容如下:

(1) Where 3 or more persons who are present together use or threaten unlawful violence and the conduct of them (taken together) is such as would cause a person of reasonable firmness present at the scene to fear for his personal safety, each of the persons using or threatening unlawful violence is guilty of violent disorder. In judicial practice, the jury acquitted the two defendants named in the indictment, but found Maloof guilty. There are sufficient allegations in the indictment, and although no others

are named, there is evidence before the jury that three people, though not necessarily those named in the indictment, were involved in the criminal conduct.

(1)凡在场的3人或以上共同使用非法暴力或以非法暴力相威胁,而他们的行为(综合在一起被认为)会令在场具有适当坚定意志的人担心其人身安全,则使用非法暴力或以非法暴力相威胁的每一人均属暴力骚扰罪。在司法实践中,陪审团宣布起诉书中提到的2名被告无罪,但判马鲁夫有罪。[1] 起诉书中有充分的指控,并且虽然没有提到其他人的名字,但陪审团面前有证据表明,有3个人参与了犯罪行为,尽管他们不一定是起诉书中提到的人。[2]

(2)It is immaterial whether or not the 3 or more use or threaten unlawful violence simultaneously. The Court held that the simultaneous use or threat of violence by three or more persons in the same place, whether for the same or different purposes, is capable of creating a daunting prospect for those who may encounter them, as they represent a breakdown of law and order, the consequences of which are unpredictable. Simultaneous presence does not imply cooperation between those who use or threaten violence; All it takes is for them to be in the same place at the same time.

(2)3人或以上是否同时使用非法暴力或以非法暴力相威胁,无关紧要。法院认为,3个或3个以上的人在同一地点同时使用暴力或以暴力相威胁,无论是出于同一目的还是不同目的,都能够使那些可能遇到他们的人感到可怕的前景,因为他们代表着法律和秩序的崩溃,这种崩溃的后果是不可预测的。同时在场并不是暗指使用暴力或以暴力相威胁者间存在合作;其仅要求他们在同一时间出现在同一地点,仅此而已。[3]

(3)No person of reasonable firmness need actually be, or be likely to be, present at the scene.

(3)不需要此种具有适当坚定意志的人实际在场,或可能在场。

(4)Violent disorder may be committed in private as well as in public places.

(4)在私人场所和公共场所都可能发生暴力骚扰。

(5)A person guilty of violent disorder is liable on conviction on indictment to imprisonment for a term not exceeding 5 years or a fine or both, or on summary conviction to imprisonment for a term not exceeding 6 months or a fine not exceeding the statutory maximum or both.

---

[1] Mahroof (1988) 88 Cr App R 317.

[2] Lemon [2002] EWCA Crim 1661.

[3] NW [2010] 1 WLR 1426 [19].

(5)任何人如经指控程序定罪,可处不超过5年的监禁或罚金,或两者并罚;如经简易程序定罪,可处不超过6个月的监禁或罚金,或两者并罚。

Section 6 of the Act states the mental element of this crime: a person is guilty of violent disorder only if he intends to use or threaten violence or is aware that his conduct may be violent or threaten violence. Unlike rioting crimes, having a common purpose among those present is not a part of the definition of violent disorder.

该法第6条规定了本罪的主观因素:只有当一个人故意使用暴力或以暴力相威胁,或意识到他的行为可能是暴力或威胁使用暴力时,他才会犯暴力骚扰罪。与暴乱犯罪不同的是,在场的人有共同的目的并不是暴力骚扰定义的一部分。[1]

12.1.3 affray(斗殴罪)

Section 3 of the Public Order Act 1986 prohibits affray, which reads as follows:

《1986年公共秩序法》第3条规定了斗殴罪,内容如下:

(1) A person is guilty of affray if he uses or threatens unlawful violence towards another and his conduct is such as would cause a person of reasonable firmness present at the scene to fear for his personal safety.

(1)任何人对他人使用非法暴力或以非法暴力相威胁,而其行为会使在场具有适当坚定意志的人对其人身安全感到恐惧,即属斗殴罪。

(2) Where 2 or more persons use or threaten the unlawful violence, it is the conduct of them taken together that must be considered for the purposes of subsection (1) In practice, although affray is an ongoing offence, it is best to bring separate charges in different incidents and not all defendants are accused of being involved in every incident.

(2)基于第1款的目的,如果2人或以上使用非法暴力或以非法暴力相威胁,那么必须考虑他们的共同行为。在实践中,虽然斗殴是一种持续的罪行,但最好是在不同的事件中分别提出指控,并且不是所有被告都被指控参与每一起事件。[2]

(3) For the purposes of this section a threat cannot be made by the use of words alone. In practice, it usually involves a group of people who may yell, struggle, threaten, brandish weapons, throw objects, exchange and threaten beatings. Again, typically, it involves a continuous course of conduct whose criminal character depends on the general nature and effect of the whole act, rather than on the particular events and events that may occur in the course of that conduct. If reliance is placed on such a

---

〔1〕 NW [2010] 1 WLR 1426.

〔2〕 Flounders [2002] EWCA Crim 1325.

continuous course of conduct, there is no need for the court to identify and prove specific events.

(3)就本条而言,威胁不能仅以言语作出。实践中,它通常涉及一群人,他们可能大喊大叫、争斗、恐吓、挥舞武器、投掷物品、互殴和威胁殴打。此外,通常情况下,它涉及一个连续的行为过程,其犯罪性质取决于整个行为的一般性质和效果,而不是取决于特定事件和该行为过程中可能发生的事件。如果确信存在这种连续的行为过程,则法院没有必要查明和证明特定事件。[1]

(4) No person of reasonable firmness need actually be, or be likely to be, present at the scene. In practice, the question is not whether a person in the same situation as (the victim) would fear for his personal safety, but whether this hypothetical person, in the room, seeing (the defendant's behavior toward the victim), would be so worried… [The offence] was to protect bystanders. This is a violation of public order. There are other offences under the criminal code that protect the person against whom violence is directed. Magistrates wrongly found the defendant guilty of affray because she threatened to kill her long - term partner while drunk and with a knife in the bathroom, in an otherwise unoccupied house. The hypothetical bystander could not have feared for his safety because the exchanges were private and limited to turbulence between the couple, and therefore could not have raised fears of unlawful violence by others.

(4)不需要此种具有适当坚定意志的人实际在场,或可能在场。实践中,问题不在于一个处于(受害者)同样处境的人是否会担心他的人身安全,而在于这个假想的人,在房间里,看到(被告对受害者的)行为,是否会如此担心……[该罪行]是为了保护旁观者。这是违反公共秩序的行为。刑法上还有保护暴力所针对的人的其他罪行。[2] 地方法官错误地判定被告犯有斗殴罪,因为她在浴室里,在一所除他们外无人居住的房子中,酒后拿着刀威胁要杀死她的长期伴侣。假想的旁观者不可能担心他的安全,因为这些交流是私人的,仅限于这对夫妇之间的冲突,因此不可能引起对于他人非法暴力的恐惧。[3]

(5) Affray may be committed in private as well as in public places.

(5)斗殴既可以在私人场所进行,也可以在公共场所进行。

(6) A constable may arrest without warrant anyone he reasonably suspects is committing affray (repealed by Serious Organised Crime and Police Act 2005).

---

[1] Smith [1997] 1 Cr App R 14 at p. 16.

[2] Sanchez (1996) 160 JP 321.

[3] Leeson v DPP [2010] EWHC 994 (Admin).

(6)警察可以在没有逮捕证的情况下逮捕他有理由怀疑正在斗殴的任何人(被《2005年严重有组织犯罪和警察法》废除)。

(7) A person guilty of affray is liable on conviction on indictment to imprisonment for a term not exceeding 3 years or a fine or both, or on summary conviction to imprisonment for a term not exceeding 6 months or a fine not exceeding the statutory maximum or both.

(7)任何人犯斗殴罪,一经指控程序定罪,可处不超过3年的监禁或罚金,或两者并罚;如经简易程序定罪,可处不超过6个月的监禁或不超过法定最高限额的罚金,或两者并罚。

Section 6 states the mental element of this crime: a person is guilty of affray only if he intends to use or threaten violence or is aware that his conduct may be violent or threaten violence. This does not affect the determination of the number of persons who use or threaten violence.

第6条规定了本罪的主观因素:只有当一个人打算使用暴力或以暴力相威胁,或意识到他的行为可能是暴力或威胁使用暴力时,他才会犯斗殴罪。这并不影响确定使用暴力或以暴力相威胁者的人数。

12.1.4 Fear or provocation of violence(引起暴力恐惧或煽动暴力罪)

Section 4 of the Public Order Act 1986 prohibits fear or provocation of violence.

《1986年公共秩序法》第4条禁止引起人们对暴力的恐惧或煽动暴力。

(1) A person is guilty of an offence if he—

(a) uses towards another person threatening, abusive or insulting words or behaviour, or (b) distributes or displays to another person any writing, sign or other visible representation which is threatening, abusive or insulting, with intent to cause that person to believe that immediate unlawful violence will be used against him or another by any person, or to provoke the immediate use of unlawful violence by that person or another, or whereby that person is likely to believe that such violence will be used or it is likely that such violence will be provoked.

(1)如果一个人:

(a)对另一个人使用威胁性、辱骂性或侮辱性的言语或行为,或(b)向另一个人发布或展示任何威胁性、辱骂性或侮辱性的文字、标志或其他可见的表现,以使该人相信有人会立即对其或其他人使用暴力,或煽动该人或其他人立即使用暴力,或因此使该人有可能相信此种暴力会被使用,或使这种暴力可能被挑起,即属犯罪。

(2) An offence under this section may be committed in a public or a private place,

except that no offence is committed where the words or behaviour are used, or the writing, sign or other visible representation is distributed or displayed, by a person inside a dwelling and the other person is also inside that or another dwelling. Accordingly, the offence was not committed in that dwelling if the only person against whom the words or acts were directed was also in that dwelling or in another dwelling. In practice, if the common parts (common platforms) are the means to access the living dwelling, they are not part of the dwelling, even if accessed through the entrance telephone system, nor are they part of the living area or home.

(2)本条所指的罪行可在公共或私人场所犯下,但如有人在一所住宅内使用有关言语或行为,或发布或展示有关文字、标志或其他可见的表现,而另一人亦在该住宅或另一所住宅内,则不构成本罪行。因此,如果该言语或行为所针对的唯一对象也在该住宅或另一住宅内,则该罪行不属于在该住宅内犯下。[1] 实践中,如果公共部分(公共平台)是进入生活住所的手段,那么它们不是住宅的一部分,即使需通过入口电话系统才能进入,它们也不是生活区域或家的一部分。[2]

(3) A constable may arrest without warrant anyone he reasonably suspects is committing an offence under this section (repealed by Serious Organised Crime and Police Act 2005).

(3)警察可以在没有逮捕证的情况下逮捕他有理由怀疑正在犯本条罪行的任何人(被《2005 年严重有组织犯罪和警察法》废除)。

(4) A person guilty of an offence under this section is liable on summary conviction to imprisonment for a term not exceeding 6 months or a fine not exceeding level 5 on the standard scale or both.

(4)任何人犯了本条所订罪行,一经简易程序定罪,可处不超过 6 个月的监禁或不超过标准等级第 5 级的罚金,或两者并罚。

Section 6 of the Act states the mental element of this crime: a person is guilty of an offence under section 4 of the Public Order Act 1986 only if he intends his words or behaviour, or the writing, sign or other visible representation, to be threatening, abusive or insulting, or is aware that it may be threatening, abusive or insulting.

该法第 6 条规定了本罪的主观因素:只有当一个人想要他的言语或行为,或文字、标志或其他可见的表现具有威胁性、辱骂性或侮辱性,或意识到其可能具有威胁性、辱骂性或侮辱性时,他才会犯本法第 4 条所规定的罪行。

---

〔1〕 Atkin v DPP (1989) 89 Cr App R 199.

〔2〕 Rukwira v DPP [1993] Crim LR 882.

Section 7 of the Public Order Act 1986 states a procedure issue: on the trial on indictment of a person charged with violent disorder or affray, if the jury find him not guilty of the offence charged, they may [without prejudice to section 6(3) of the Criminal Law Act 1967] find him guilty of an offence under section 4 of the Act.

该法第7条规定了一个该罪的程序问题:如果在对被控暴力骚扰或斗殴的人的起诉审判中,陪审团认定他没有犯所控罪行,他们可以[在不违背1967年《刑事法》第6(3)条的情况下]认定他犯了本法第4条规定的罪行。

12.1.5 intentional harassment, alarm or distress(故意造成烦扰、惊恐或痛苦罪)

Section 4A of the Public Order Act 1986 was inserted by Criminal Justice and Public Order Act 1994, and it prohibits intentional harassment, alarm or distress, which reads as follows:

1994年《刑事司法和公共秩序法》插入了第4A条,该条规定了故意造成烦扰、惊恐或痛苦罪,具体内容如下:

(1) A person is guilty of an offence if, with intent to cause a person harassment, alarm or distress, he—

(1)如果一个人故意造成某人烦扰、惊恐或痛苦而实施以下行为,则其行为属于:

(a) uses threatening, abusive or insulting words or behaviour, or disorderly behaviour, or (b) displays any writing, sign or other visible representation which is threatening, abusive or insulting, thereby causing that or another person harassment, alarm or distress.

(a)使用威胁性、辱骂性或侮辱性的言语或行为,或扰乱秩序的行为,或(b)展示任何威胁性、辱骂性或侮辱性的文字、标志或其他可见的表现,从而造成该人或他人烦扰、惊恐或痛苦。

(2) An offence under this section may be committed in a public or a private place, except that no offence is committed where the words or behaviour are used, or the writing, sign or other visible representation is displayed, by a person inside a dwelling and the person who is harassed, alarmed or distressed is also inside that or another dwelling.

(2)本条所指的罪行可在公共或私人场所犯下,但如有人在一所住宅内使用有关言语或行为,或展示有关文字、标志或其他可见的表现,而感到烦扰、惊恐或痛苦的人也在该住宅或另一所住宅内,则不构成本罪行。

(3) It is a defence for the accused to prove—

(3)被告可证明以下事实作为辩护:

(a) that he was inside a dwelling and had no reason to believe that the words or behaviour used, or the writing, sign or other visible representation displayed, would be heard or seen by a person outside that or any other dwelling, or (b) that his conduct was reasonable. In practice, the accused posted a notice at the Sikh temple condemning the people running the temple, calling them hypocrites and liars. He successfully argued that his actions were reasonable given his right to free speech.

(a)他在一所住宅内,没有理由相信他所使用的言语或行为,或所展示的文字、标志或其他可见的表现,会被该住宅或任何其他住宅外的人听到或看到,或(b)他的行为是合理的。实践中,被告在锡克教寺庙张贴了一份告示,谴责管理寺庙的人,称他们为伪君子和骗子。他成功地辩称,考虑到他的言论自由权,他的行为是合理的。[1]

(4) A constable may arrest without warrant anyone he reasonably suspects is committing an offence under this section (repealed by Serious Organised Crime and Police Act 2005).

(4)警察可以在没有逮捕证的情况下逮捕他有理由怀疑正在犯本条罪行的任何人(被《2005 年严重有组织犯罪和警察法》废除)。

(5) A person guilty of an offence under this section is liable on summary conviction to imprisonment for a term not exceeding 6 months or a fine not exceeding level 5 on the standard scale or both.

(5)任何人犯本条所订罪行,一经简易程序定罪,可处不超过 6 个月的监禁或不超过标准等级第 5 级的罚金,或两者并罚。

The High Court described harassment, alarm or distressfor this offence as relatively strong words appropriate for crimes that could result in a prison sentence or a substantial fine, and held that the word "distress" in this penalty scale context required emotional disturbance or upset.

高等法院将本条中的烦扰、惊恐或痛苦描述为相对强烈的词语,使其与可能导致监禁或巨额罚款的罪行相称,并认为在这种刑罚幅度的语境下,"痛苦"一词要求情绪困扰或心烦意乱。[2]

12.1.6 harassment, alarm or distress(造成烦扰、惊恐或痛苦罪)

Section 5 of the Public Order Act 1986 prohibits harassment, alarm or distress,

[1] Dehal v CPS (2005) 169 JP 581.

[2] R (R) v DPP (2006) 170 JP 661.

which reads as follows:

《1986 年公共秩序法》第 5 条规定了造成烦扰、惊恐或痛苦罪,具体内容如下:

(1) A person is guilty of an offence if he

(1) 如果某人:

(a) uses threatening [or abusive] words or behaviour, or disorderly behaviour, or (b) displays any writing, sign or other visible representation which is threatening [or abusive], within the hearing or sight of a person likely to be caused harassment, alarm or distress thereby. In practice, delivering an envelope with insulting or insulting words hidden inside, sent through someone else's letterbox, does not constitute a "display".

(a) 使用威胁性[或辱骂性]的言语或行为,或骚乱行为,或(b)在可能因此而感到烦扰、惊恐或痛苦的人的听力或视线范围内展示任何具有威胁性[或辱骂性]的文字、标志或其他可见表现,则构成犯罪。实践中,通过别人的信箱投递一个内含侮辱或侮辱性文字的信封,不构成"展示"。[1]

(2) An offence under this section may be committed in a public or a private place, except that no offence is committed where the words or behaviour are used, or the writing, sign or other visible representation is displayed, by a person inside a dwelling and the other person is also inside that or another dwelling. In practice, the delivery of a letter to a person in his or her own home, while he or she reads the letter at home and is shocked or distressed by its contents, cannot constitute an offence under section 5. Such conduct would constitute an offence contrary to Section 1 (1) of the Malicious Communications Act 1988.

(2) 本条所指的罪行可在公共或私人场所犯下,但如某人在一所住宅内使用有关言语或行为,或展示有关文字、标志或其他可见的表现,而另一人亦在该住宅或另一所住宅内,则不构成本罪行。实践中,对身处他/她自己家中的某人递送信件,尽管他/她在家中阅读此信并对其内容感到震惊或痛苦,也不能构成第 5 条所规定的罪行。这种行为将构成违反 1988 年《恶意通信法》第 1(1)条的罪行。[2]

(3) It is a defence for the accused to prove

(3) 被告可以证明以下事实,作为无罪的辩护:

(a) that he had no reason to believe that there was any person within hearing or sight who was likely to be caused harassment, alarm or distress, or (b) that he was inside a dwelling and had no reason to believe that the words or behaviour used, or the

---

[1] Chappell v DPP (1988) 89 Cr App R 82.

[2] Chappell v DPP (1988) 89 Cr App R 82.

writing, sign or other visible representation displayed, would be heard or seen by a person outside that or any other dwelling, or (c) that his conduct was reasonable.

(a)他没有理由相信在听觉或视觉范围内有任何人可能被造成烦扰、惊恐或痛苦,或(b)他在一所住宅内,没有理由相信其所使用的言语或行为,或文字、标志或其他可见表现,会被该住宅或任何其他住宅以外的人听到或看到,或(c)他的行为是合理的。

A typical case is: a protester who for years has been protesting the use of weapons of mass destruction and opposing U. S. military policies defaced an American flag at a U. S. air Force base with the words "Stop Star Wars" written on the flag's stripes, walked up to a car, placed the flag in front, and then stood on it. U. S. service members and/or their families felt varying degrees of distress over her actions. On appeal to the District Court, she argued that her conduct was reasonable within the meaning of section 5(3)(c). Her conviction was quashed on the grounds that insufficient weight was given to the issue of proportionality when considering whether her conduct was reasonable.

一个典型案例是:一名多年来一直抗议使用大规模杀伤性武器和反对美国军事政策的抗议者在美国空军基地的美国国旗上涂污,在国旗条纹上写下"停止星球大战",走到一辆汽车前,把国旗放在前面,然后站在上面。美军人员和/或他们的家人对她的行为感到不同程度的痛苦。在向地区法院提出上诉时,她辩称她的行为在第5(3)(c)条的意义范围内是合理的。法院对她的定罪被撤销的理由是,在考虑她的行为是否合理时,对相称性问题没有给予足够的重视。[1]

(4) A constable may arrest a person without warrant if—(a) he engages in offensive conduct which the constable warns him to stop, and (b) he engages in further offensive conduct immediately or shortly after the warning (repealed by Serious Organised Crime and Police Act 2005).

(4)在下列情况下,警察可以无须逮捕令而逮捕某人:(a)该人从事冒犯性行为,而警察警告他停止,且(b)该人在警告发出后立即或不久从事进一步冒犯性行为(被《2005年严重有组织犯罪和警察法》废除)。

(5) In subsection (4) "offensive conduct" means conduct the constable reasonably suspects to constitute an offence under this section, and the conduct mentioned in paragraph (a) and the further conduct need not be of the same nature (repealed by

〔1〕 Percy v DPP (2002) 166 JP 93.

Serious Organised Crime and Police Act 2005).

(5)在第(4)款中"冒犯性行为"指警察合理怀疑构成本条所订罪行的行为,而(a)段所述的行为与其后的行为无须具有相同性质(被《2005 年严重有组织犯罪和警察法》废除)。

(6) A person guilty of an offence under this section is liable on summary conviction to a fine not exceeding level 3 on the standard scale.

(6)凡犯本条所订罪行的人,一经简易程序定罪,可处不超过标准等级第 3 级的罚金。

Section 6 of the Act states the mental element: a person is guilty of an offence under section 5 of the Act only if he intends his words or behaviour, or the writing, sign or other visible representation, to be threatening [or abusive], or is aware that it may be threatening [or abusive] or (as the case may be) he intends his behaviour to be or is aware that it may be disorderly.

该法第 6 条规定了本罪的主观因素:一个人只有在他想要他的言语或行为,或文字、标志或其他可见的表现具有威胁性(或辱骂性),或意识到它可能具有威胁性(或辱骂性),或(视情况而定)他想要或意识到他的行为可能是骚乱的情况下,才会犯本法第 5 条所规定的罪行。

Section 6 also states that, for the purposes of this subchapter, a person whose awareness is impaired by intoxication shall be taken to be aware of that of which he would be aware if not intoxicated, unless he shows either that his intoxication was not self-induced or that it was caused solely by the taking or administration of a substance in the course of medical treatment. "Intoxication" means any intoxication, whether caused by drink, drugs or other means, or by a combination of means.

第 6 条还规定,就本节的上述罪名而言,意识因醉态而受损的人,应被视为已意识到他在未醉情况下会意识到的事情,除非他证明他的醉态不是自己引起的,或完全是由于在医疗过程中服用或使用某种物质而引起的。"醉态"是指任何昏醉状态,无论是由饮酒、药物或其他手段引起的,还是由多种手段共同引起的。

In addition to this, sections 7 and 8 of the Public Order Act 1986 set out its procedures and explain the relevant terms. Specifically, section 7 provides that for the purposes of the rules against charging more than one offence in the same count or information, each of sections 1 to 5 creates one offence. Section 8 explains "dwelling", "structure" and "violence", and it states that in this subchapter, "dwelling" means any structure or part of a structure occupied as a person's home or as other living accommodation (whether the occupation is separate or shared with others) but does not include any part not so occupied; "structure" includes a tent, caravan, vehicle, vessel or other temporary or movable structure; "violence" means any violent conduct (a) except in the context of affray, it includes violent conduct towards property as well as violent conduct towards persons, and (b) it is not restricted to conduct causing or intending to cause injury or damage but includes any other violent conduct (for example, throwing at or towards a person a missile of a kind capable of causing injury which does not hit or falls short).

除此之外,《1986年公共秩序法》第7条和第8条还规定了其程序,并对相关用语进行了解释。具体而言,第7条规定:基于禁止以相同的事项或信息指控多项罪行的规则,第1条至5条每条均构成一项罪行。第8条解释了"住宅"、"构筑物"和"暴力",其规定,在本节中,"住宅"是指作为一个人的家或其他生活场所而被占用的任何构筑物或构筑物的一部分(无论该占用是单独的还是与他人共享的),但不包括任何未被如此占用的部分。"构筑物"包括帐篷、大篷车、车辆、船只或其他临时的或可移动的构筑物。"暴力"是指任何暴力行为:(a)除了在斗殴的情况下,它既包括对财产的暴力行为,也包括对人的暴力行为,并且(b)它不仅限于造成或意图造成伤害或损害的行为,还包括任何其他暴力行为(例如,向人投掷一种能够造成伤害但未击中或未达到的飞弹)。

12.1.7 contamination of or interference with goods with intention of causing public alarm or anxiety(污染或处理商品意图引起公众恐慌、焦虑罪)

Section 38 of the Public Order Act 1986 prohibits contamination of or interference with goods with intention of causing public alarm or anxiety, which reads as follows:

1986年《公共秩序法》第38条规定了污染或处理商品意图引起公众恐慌、焦虑罪,具体内容如下:

(1) It is an offence for a person, with the intention—

(1)任何人在有以下故意的情况下,即属犯罪:

(a) of causing public alarm or anxiety, or (b) of causing injury to members of the public consuming or using the goods, or (c) of causing economic loss to any person by reason of the goods being shunned by members of the public, or (d) of causing economic loss to any person by reason of steps taken to avoid any such alarm or anxiety, injury or loss, to contaminate or interfere with goods, or make it appear that goods have been contaminated or interfered with, or to place goods which have been contaminated or interfered with, or which appear to have been contaminated or interfered with, in a place where goods of that description are consumed, used, sold or otherwise supplied.

(a)引起公众恐慌或焦虑,或(b)给消费或使用商品的公众造成伤害,或(c)由于公众回避该商品而给任何人造成经济损失,或(d)经由有关方面采取避免任何上述诸类恐慌或焦虑、伤害或损失的措施,而给任何人造成经济损失,污染或处理商品,或使商品看起来已被污染或处理,或将已被或看起来已被污染或处理的商品放置在该商品被消费、使用、销售或以其他方式供应的地方。

(2) It is also an offence for a person, with any such intention as is mentioned in paragraph (a), (c) or (d) of subsection (1), to threaten that he or another will do, or to claim that he or another has done, any of the acts mentioned in that subsection.

(2)任何人在具有第(1)款(a)、(c)或(d)段规定故意的情况下,以他或第三者将要作出该款所规定的行为进行威胁,或声称他或三者已经作了该款规定的任何行为,亦属犯罪。

(3) It is an offence for a person to be in possession of any of the following articles with a view to the commission of an offence under subsection (1)—

(3)任何人管有以下任何物品,以犯第(1)款所订罪行,即属犯罪:

(a) materials to be used for contaminating or interfering with goods or making it appear that goods have been contaminated or interfered with, or (b) goods which have been contaminated or interfered with, or which appear to have been contaminated or interfered with.

(a)用作污染或处理商品或使商品看起来已被污染或处理的原料,或(b)已被污染或处理的商品,或看起来已被污染或处理的商品。

(4) A person guilty of an offence under this section is liable: (a) on conviction on indictment to imprisonment for a term not exceeding 10 years or a fine or both, or (b) on summary conviction to imprisonment for a term not exceeding six months or a fine not exceeding the statutory maximum or both.

(4)凡犯本条所订罪行的人:(a)经指控程序定罪,可处不超过10年的监禁或罚金,或两者并罚;或(b)经简易程序定罪,可处不超过6个月的监禁或不超过法定最高限额的罚金,或两者并罚。

(5) In this section "goods" includes substances whether natural or manufactured and whether or not incorporated in or mixed with other goods.

(5)本条中的"商品"包括无论是天然的还是人造的,也无论是否与其他商品附合或混合的物质。

(6) The reference in subsection (2) to a person claiming that certain acts have been

committed does not include a person who in good faith reports or warns that such acts have been, or appear to have been, committed.

(6)第(2)款所提到的声称某些行为已被作出的人,并不包括出于好意而报告或警告该等行为已被或看起来已被作出的人。

A typical case is: an offender admitted that he contaminated food by inserting pins, needles or nails into various items in the supermarket. His behavior continued for three months, and some customers who bought the contaminated products suffered minor injuries. There is no rational explanation for the offender's actions and no financial motive, but medical treatment is not recommended. The appeal court upheld the three - year prison sentence.

一个典型案例是,罪犯承认,他在超市里把大头针、针或钉子插入各种物品,污染了食品。他的这种行为持续了3个月,一些购买了受污染产品的顾客受到了轻微的伤害。罪犯的行为没有合理的解释,也没有经济动机,但强制医疗的意见并没有得到推荐。上诉法院维持了3年监禁的原判。[1]

12.2 Crimes against Public Administration Order(扰乱公共管理秩序罪)

Offences against public administration order are mainly those relating to processions and assemblies under part 2 of the Public Order Act 1986, as well as uniform offences relating to political objectives and quasimilitary organization offences under the Public Order Act 1936. These crimes were introduced in order to better balance the public order and the citizens' rights.

扰乱公共管理秩序的罪行主要是《1986年公共秩序法》第2节里面关于游行和集会的罪行,以及《1936年公共秩序法》里与政治目标有关的制服罪行、准军事组织罪行。这些罪行的出台是为了更好地平衡公共秩序和公民权利。

12.2.1 Advance notice of public processions(违反公共游行提前通知罪)

Section 11 of the Public Order Act 1986 provides for advance notice of public processions. Subsections 1 to 6 set out the requirements for prior notice:

《1986年公共秩序法》第11条规定了公共游行的提前通知。该条第1款到第6款规定了提前通知罪的构成要件:

(1) Written notice shall be given in accordance with this section of any proposal to hold a public procession intended—

---

[1] Cruickshank [2001] 2 Cr App R (S) 278.

(1)如拟举行具有以下目的的公共游行,须按照本条发出书面通知——

(a) to demonstrate support for or opposition to the views or actions of any person or body of persons, (b) to publicise a cause or campaign, or (c) to mark or commemorate an event,

(a)表明支持或反对任何个人或团体的观点或行动,(b)宣传某项事业或活动,或(c)标志或纪念某一事件,

unless it is not reasonably practicable to give any advance notice of the procession.

除非事先发出游行通知并非合理可行。

(2) Subsection (1) does not apply where the procession is one commonly or customarily held in the police area (or areas) in which it is proposed to be held or is a funeral procession organised by a funeral director acting in the normal course of his business. Assuming that Article 11 applies, a mass cycling event held every month in the same place and at the same time without a predetermined route is a procession normally or habitually held within the meaning of Article 11, paragraph 2, and is therefore not required to give notice.

(2)第(1)款不适用于通常或习惯上在拟举行游行的警区举行的游行,或由殡仪承办人在其正常业务过程中组织的殡仪游行。假定适用第11条,那么每月在同一地点、同一时间举行但没有预定路线的大规模骑自行车活动,是第11条第(2)款所指的通常或习惯上举行的游行,因此无须发出通知。[1]

(3) The notice must specify the date when it is intended to hold the procession, the time when it is intended to start it, its proposed route, and the name and address of the person (or of one of the persons) proposing to organise it.

(3)通知必须列明拟举行游行的日期、拟开始游行的时间、拟举行游行的路线,以及拟组织游行的人(或其中一人)的姓名和地址。

(4) Notice must be delivered to a police station—

(4)通知必须送达以下警区内的警署:

(a) in the police area in which it is proposed the procession will start, or (b) where it is proposed the procession will start in Scotland and cross into England, in the first police area in England on the proposed route.

(a)拟举行游行的警区,或(b)如果游行拟从苏格兰开始,然后进入英格兰,则为该拟定路线上的第一个英格兰警区。

---

[1] R. (Kay) v. Commissioner of Police of the Metropolis [2008] 1 WLR 2723.

(5) If delivered not less than 6 clear days before the date when the procession is intended to be held, the notice may be delivered by post by the recorded delivery service; but section 7 of the Interpretation Act 1978 (under which a document sent by post is deemed to have been served when posted and to have been delivered in the ordinary course of post) does not apply.

(5)如通知书在拟举行游行的日期前不少于6个整天送达,通知书可透过记录派递服务以邮递方式送达;但不适用《1978年解释法》第7条(该条款规定,以邮寄方式发送的文件被视为在邮寄时已送出,并在正常邮寄过程中送达)。

(6) If not delivered in accordance with subsection (5), the notice must be delivered by hand not less than 6 clear days before the date when the procession is intended to be held or, if that is not reasonably practicable, as soon as delivery is reasonably practicable.

(6)如通知书没有按照第(5)款送达,则通知书必须在拟举行游行的日期前不少于6个整天由专人送达,或这样做并非合理可行,则应在合理可行的情况下尽快交付。

It is clear from the foregoing that, although public processions are authorized, they must comply with the requirements of section 11 (1) to (6) of the Public Oreler Act 1986, failing which a public procession is an offence or even constitutes a crime.

从前述规定可以看出,尽管公共游行是被许可的,但其必须符合《1986年公共秩序法》第11条第1款到第6款的要求,否则公共游行就是违法行为,甚至构成犯罪。

Subsections 7 to 10 set out the penalties for failure to meet above requirements. From the content of subsections 7 to 10, subsection 7 provides for the essential elements of the crime, and mainly provides for the objective behavior constituting the crime, paragraph 8 and 9 provide for the defense of the crime, and subsection 10 provides for the statutory punishment of the crime.

该条第7款到第10款规定了不满足上述要求的相关罪刑内容。从第7款到第10款规定的内容看,第7款规定的是该罪的本体要件,且主要规定的是构成犯罪的客观行为,第8款和第9款规定的是该罪的抗辩事由,第10款规定的是该罪的法定刑。

(7) Where a public procession is held, such as—

(7)凡举行公共游行,如:

(a) the requirements of this section as to notice have not been satisfied, or (b) the date when it is held, the time when it starts, or its route, differs from the date, time or route specified in the notice.

(a)本条关于通知的要求未获满足,或(b)游行的举行日期、开始时间或路线与通知所指明的日期、时间或路线不同,则每名组织游行的人即属犯罪。

(8) It is a defence for the accused to prove that he did not know of, and neither suspected nor had reason to suspect, the failure to satisfy the requirements or (as the case may be) the difference of date, time or route.

(8)若被告能证明他不知道,并且从没有怀疑或没有任何理由怀疑,其所进行的游行不符合法律规定的日期、时间或路线,则这可作为抗辩事由。

(9) To the extent that an alleged offence turns on a difference of date, time or route, it is a defence for the accused to prove that the difference arose from circumstances beyond his control or from something done with the agreement of a police officer or by his direction.

(9)如果被指控的罪行是由于日期、时间或路线的不同引起的,那么若被告可证明这种不同是由他无法控制的情况或在警务人员的同意或指示下所做的事情造成的,则这可作为辩护事由。

(10) A person guilty of an offence under subsection (7) is liable on summary conviction to a fine not exceeding level 3 on the standard scale.

(10)凡犯第(7)款所订罪行的人,一经简易程序定罪,可处不超过标准等级第 3 级的罚金。

12.2.2　Imposing conditions on public processions(违反公共游行条件罪)

In addition to stipulating that public processions must be carried out in accordance with the approved time and route, the Public Order Act 1986 also stipulates that governments officals like police officers can attach certain conditions to approved public processions to ensure that public processions will not cause disorder. Section 12 of the Public Order Act 1986 goes to great lengths to elaborate on this, and it is also an offence if a person or an organisation breaches these additional conditions.

《1986 年公共秩序法》除规定公共游行必须按照批准的时间、路线等内容进行外,还规定了警务人员等政府人员可对批准的公共游行附加一定的条件,以保证公共游行不会引起混乱。《1986 年公共秩序法》第 12 条花了大量的篇幅对此进行了详细的规定,且若相关人员或组织违反这些附加条件,也构成犯罪。

First, section 12 (1) of the Public Order Act 1986 sets out the circumstances under which conditions may be imposed by police officers, which reads as follows:

首先,《1986 年公共秩序法》第 12 条的第(1)款规定了警务人员可附加条件的情况,其规定的内容如下:

(1) If the senior police officer, having regard to the time or place at which and the circumstances in which any public procession is being held or is intended to be held and to its route or proposed route, reasonably believes that—

(1)如高级警务人员在考虑到举行或拟举行公众游行的时间或地点及情况,以及游行的路线或拟定的路线后,合理地相信:

(a) it may result in serious public disorder, serious damage to property or serious disruption to the life of the community,

(a)可能造成严重的公共骚乱、严重损坏财产或严重扰乱社会生活;

(aa) in the case of a procession in England and Wales, the noise generated by persons taking part in the procession may result in serious disruption to the activities of an organisation which are carried on in the vicinity of the procession,

(aa)就在英格兰及威尔士举行的游行而言,参加游行的人所产生的噪声可能会严重干扰在游行附近进行的组织的活动;

(ab) in the case of a procession in England and Wales—

(ab)在英格兰和威尔士的游行中:

(i) the noise generated by persons taking part in the procession may have a relevant impact on persons in the vicinity of the procession, and

(i)参加游行的人所产生的噪声可能对游行附近的人有有关的影响;及

(ii) that impact may be significant, or

(ii)该影响可能是重大的,或

(b) the purpose of the persons organising it is the intimidation of others with a view to compelling them not to do an act they have a right to do, or to do an act they have a right not to do, he may give directions imposing on the persons organising or taking part in the procession such conditions as appear to him necessary to prevent such disorder, damage, disruption [F2, impact] or intimidation, including conditions as to the route of the procession or prohibiting it from entering any public place specified in the directions.

(b)组织游行的人的目的是恐吓他人,以迫使他人不做他们有权做的行为,或做他们有权不做的行为,他可发出指示,对组织或参加游行的人施加他认为必要的条件,包括游行路线的条件,或禁止游行进入指示所指明的任何公众场所,以防止这种混乱、损害、破坏[F2 条,影响]或恐吓。

From the content of subsection 1, it is mainly to guarantee the public parade not to disturb the order, not to cause public panic, not to affect the normal life of the public. Subsection (4) and (5) then set out the circumstances in which the violation of these conditions constitutes an offence and also the circumstances in which a defence may be mounted.

从第(1)款规定的内容看,其主要是为了保证公共游行不扰乱秩序,不引起公众的恐慌,不影响公众的正常生活。接着第12条第(4)款和第(5)款规定了触犯这些条件构成犯罪的情况,还规定了可进行辩护的情况。

Subsections (4) and (5) stipulate that the relevant organization and participation constitute a crime: a person who organizes or takes part in a public procession and... fails to comply with a condition imposed under this section is guilty of an offence, but it is a defence for him to prove that the failure arose from circumstances beyond his control.

第(4)款和第(5)款的规定是,组织、参与行为构成犯罪:组织或参与公共游行的人……不遵守根据本条施加的条件即属犯罪;但是,他如能证明不遵守是由他无法控制的情况引起的,便可作为辩护。

Of course, the provisions of section 12 (4) and (5) of the Public Order Act 1986 have changed over time due to the additional provisions of the Police, Crime, Sentencing and Courts Act 2022. Police, Crime, Sentencing and Courts Act 2022 inserted subsection 5A, to further state that a person is guilty of an offence under section 12(4) or (5) of the Public Order Act 1986 only if—

当然,随着时间的变化,《1986年公共秩序法》第12条第(4)款和第(5)款的规定,因《2022年警察、犯罪、量刑和法院法》增加的相关规定而有所变化。《2022年警察、犯罪、量刑和法院法》插入了第5A条,规定任何人只有在以下情况下才会犯《1986年公共秩序法》第12条第(4)款或第(5)款所指的罪行:

(a) in the case of a public procession in England and Wales, at the time the person fails to comply with the condition the person knows or ought to know that the condition has been imposed;

(a)就英格兰及威尔士的公共游行而言,该人知道或应该知道该条件已被施加却没有遵守该条件;

(b) in the case of a public procession in Scotland, the person knowingly fails to comply with the condition.

(b)就苏格兰的公共游行而言,该人明知其没有遵守该条件。

A comparison of the old and new laws shows that the Public Order Act 1986 does not provide for the subjective element, but the provisions of section 5A inserted in the Police, Crime, Sentencing and Courts Act 2022 define the subjective element of the offence, namely: in Wales and England, the subjective aspect is "knowing or ought to know"; In Scotland it is "knowing".

对新旧法进行对比从可以看出,《1986 年公共秩序法》没有规定主观方面的要素,但从《2022 年警察、犯罪、量刑和法院法》插入的第 5A 条的规定看,其限定了构成该罪的主观要素,具体就是:在威尔士和英格兰,其主观方面是明知或应当明知;在苏格兰是明知。

12.2.3 Prohibition of public processions(违反公共游行禁令罪)

Although section 12 of the Public Order Act 1986 provides for the conditions of public procession and the offence of contravening the conditions of public procession, in some cases these conditions imposed by, for example, conditions imposed on the participants of procession by the chief officer of police cannot be complied with and other means must be relied upon to maintain public order. Accordingly, section 13 of the Public Order Act 1986 also provides for the prohibition of public processions and the offences resulting from the violation of these prohibitions.

尽管《1986 年公共秩序法》第 12 条规定了公共游行的条件以及违反公共游行条件罪,但在某些情况下,警务长等人对游行施加的条件并不能得到游行人员的遵守,因此还必须依靠其他的手段才能维护公共秩序。所以,《1986 年公共秩序法》第 13 条又规定了公共游行的禁令,以及违反这些禁令导致的犯罪。

Section 13 (1) of the Public Order Act 1986 sets out the circumstances in which the chief officer of police may prohibit a public procession: if at any time the chief officer of police reasonably believes that, because of particular circumstances existing in any district or part of a district, the powers under section 12 will not be sufficient to prevent the holding of public processions in that district or part from resulting in serious public disorder, he shall apply to the council of the district for an order prohibiting for such period not exceeding 3 months as may be specified in the application the holding of all public processions (or of any class of public procession so specified) in the district or part concerned.

《1986 年公共秩序法》第 13 条第(1)款规定了警务处处长可禁止公共游行的情况:如警务处处长在任何时候合理地相信,由于任何地区或地区的部分存在特别情况,第 12 条下的权力不足以防止在该地区或地区的部分举行公共游行而导致严重的公共骚乱,他须向该区议会申请发出命令,禁止在该申请书所指明的不超过 3 个月的期间内,在该区或有关部分举行所有公众游行(或被如此指明的任何类别的公众游行)。

A breach of the foregoing prohibition may amount to an offense. This is provided for in section 13 (7) and (8) of the Public Order Act 1986, which provides that a person who organizes or takes part in a public procession the holding of which he knows is prohibited by virtue of an order under this section is guilty of an offence.

如果违反了前述禁令,就可能构成犯罪。该内容由《1986 年公共秩序法》第 13 条第(7)款和第(8)款进行规定,即任何人如组织或参与其明知为基于本条所作出的命令而禁止举行的公共游行,即属犯罪。

12.2.4 Imposing conditions on public assemblies(违反公共集会条件罪)

Section 14 of the Public Order Act 1986 provides for the circumstances in which conditions may be imposed on public assemblies and for offences against the conditions of public assemblies. Its paragraph (1) sets out the circumstances in which a public assembly can lead to the imposition of conditions, specifically:

《1986 年公共秩序法》第 14 条规定了公共集会施加条件的情况,以及违反公共集会条件犯罪的情况。其第(1)款规定了公共集会能导致施加条件的情况,这些情况具体为:

(1) the senior police officer, having regard to the time or place at which and the circumstances in which any public assembly is being held or is intended to be held, reasonably believes that—

(1)高级警务人员在考虑到举行或拟举行公共集会的时间或地点及情况后,合理地相信:

(a) it may result in serious public disorder, serious damage to property or serious disruption to the life of the community,

(a)该集会可能造成严重的公共骚乱、严重损坏财产或严重扰乱社会生活;

(aa) in the case of an assembly in England and Wales, the noise generated by persons taking part in the assembly may result in serious disruption to the activities of an organisation which are carried on in the vicinity of the assembly,

(aa)就在英格兰及威尔士举行的集会而言,参加该集会的人所产生的噪声可能会严重干扰在该集会附近进行的组织活动;

(ab) in the case of an assembly in England and Wales—

(ab)就在英格兰及威尔士举行的集会而言:

(i) the noise generated by persons taking part in the assembly may have a relevant impact on persons in the vicinity of the assembly, and

(i)参加集会的人所产生的噪声可能对集会附近的人产生相关影响,且

(ii) that impact may be significant, or

(ii)该影响可能是重大的,或

(b) the purpose of the persons organising it is the intimidation of others with a view to compelling them not to do an act they have a right to do, or to do an act they have a right not to do;

(b)组织该集会的人的目的是恐吓他人,以迫使他人不做他们有权做的行为,或强迫他们做他们有权不做的行为;

(1A) In response to the foregoing, a senior police officer may impose the following conditions on persons organizing or participating in an assembly: (a) in the case of an assembly in England and Wales, such conditions as appear to the officer necessary to prevent the disorder, damage, disruption, impact or intimidation mentioned in subsection (1);

(1A)针对前述情况,高级警务人员对组织或参加集会者可以规定以下条件:(a)就在英格兰及威尔士举行的集会而言,在该人员看来,为防止第(1)款所述的混乱、破坏、影响或恐吓所必需的条件;

(b) in the case of an assembly in Scotland, such conditions as to the place at which the assembly may be (or continue to be) held, its maximum duration, or the maximum number of persons who may constitute it, as appear to the officer necessary to prevent the disorder, damage, disruption or intimidation mentioned in subsection (1)(a) or (1)(b).

(b)就在苏格兰举行的集会而言,在该人员看来为防止第(1)(a)款或第(1)(b)款所述的骚乱、破坏、破坏或恐吓所必需的,有关该集会可能举行(或继续举行)的地点、集会的最长持续时间或可能构成该集会的最大人数的条件。

If organizations or individuals continue to violate the above conditions, it may constitute a crime. Subsections (4) and (5) stipulate that who organises or takes part in a public assembly and... fails to comply with a condition imposed under this section is guilty of an offence, but it is a defence for him to prove that the failure arose from circumstances beyond his control.

若依然有组织或个人违反前述条件,则可能构成犯罪。第(4)款、第(5)款规定了相关组织行为、参与行为构成犯罪:组织或参加公共游行的人……不遵守根据本条施加的条件即属犯罪。但他如能证明不遵守条件是由他无法控制的情况引起的,

便可作为辩护。

The aforementioned Police, Crime, Sentencing and Courts Act 2022 has also adjusted and even added new offences in the assembly category. The specific content is: Police, Crime, Sentencing and Courts Act 2022 inserted Section 14ZA, imposing conditions on one – person protests. Criminal Justice and Public Order Act 1994 inserted Section 14A, prohibiting trespassory assemblies, and Section 14B on offences in connection with trespassory assemblies and arrest therefor, and Section 14C, stopping persons from proceeding to trespassory assemblies.

前述提及的《2022 年警察、犯罪、量刑和法院法》也对集会类的犯罪进行调整，甚至增加了新罪。具体内容就是:《2022 年警察、犯罪、量刑和法院法》插入了第14ZA 条,对一人抗议施加了条件。《1994 年刑事司法和公共秩序法》插入了第 14A 条,禁止非法侵入性集会,第 14B 条规定了与非法侵入性集会有关的罪行和逮捕,以及第 14C 条,禁止人们进行非法侵入性集会。

12.2.5 Uniforms in connection with political objects(在公共场所穿戴与政治目标相关的制服罪)

Section 1 of the Public Order Act 1936 prohibits uniforms in connection with political objects.

《1936 年公共秩序法》第 1 条规定了在公共场所穿戴与政治目标相关的制服罪。

(1) Subject as hereinafter provided in subsection (1), any person who in any public place or at any public meeting wears uniform signifying his association with any political organisation or with the promotion of any political object shall be guilty of an offence.

第(1)款规定了罪行的实体内容:除下文另有规定外,任何人在任何公共场所或在任何公共公众集会上穿着表明他与任何政治组织或任何政治目标的宣传有联系的制服,即属犯罪。

In addition to this, however, the article also provides for situations that do not constitute an offence, i. e. it also provides that: provided that, if the chief officer of police is satisfied that the wearing of any such uniform as aforesaid on any ceremonial, anniversary, or other special occasion will not be likely to involve risk of public disorder, he may, with the consent of a Secretary of State, by order permit the wearing of such uniform on that occasion either absolutely or subject to such conditions as may be specified in the order.

但除此之外，该条还规定了不构成犯罪的情况，即其还规定：如警务处处长信纳在任何仪式、周年纪念或其他特别场合穿着上述任何制服都不会涉及扰乱公众秩序的危险，他可在获得国务大臣同意后，以命令的形式准许在该场合中不受限制地或依命令指明的条件穿着该等制服。

In judicial practice, whether a place is a public place depends on an assessment of the factual status of the place at the critical moment. A store parking lot can't be a public place when it closes at 11:30 p. m. If, at a critical moment, members of the public do have access to the premises as members of the public and not under any other legal provision, then section 9 provides that the premises is a public place, even though certain persons may be denied access.

在司法实践中，一个地方是否为公共场所，取决于对关键时刻下该场所事实地位的评估。商店的停车场在晚上 11 点半关门的时候不可能是公共场所。[1] 如果在关键时刻，公众确实可以仅作为公众成员而不根据任何其他法律规定进入该场所，则根据该法第 9 条规定，该场所为公共场所，即使某些人可能被拒绝进入。[2]

Section 9 also states that "public meeting" includes any meeting in a public place and any meeting which the public or any section thereof are permitted to attend, whether on payment or otherwise; "public place" includes any highway [or in Scotland any road within the meaning of the Roads (Scotland) Act 1984] and any other premises or place to which at the material time the public have or are permitted to have access, whether on payment or otherwise.

第 9 条还规定，"公共集会"包括在公共场所举行的任何集会，以及公众或其任何部分人士获准以付费或其他方式出席的任何集会；"公共场所"包括任何高速公路，或苏格兰《1984 年道路(苏格兰)法》所指的任何道路，以及在重要时间内，公众可以或被允许通过付款或其他方式进入的任何其他场所或地点。

Subsection 7(2) provides that where any person is charged before any court with an offence under this section, no further proceedings in respect thereof shall be taken against him without the consent of the Attorney – General except such as are authorised by section 6 of the Prosecution of Offences 1979. Thus, that if that person is remanded in custody he shall, after the expiration of a period of eight days from the date on which he was so remanded, be entitled to be [released on bail] without sureties unless within

---

〔1〕 Marsh v. Arscott, (1982) 75 Cr App Rep 211.

〔2〕 Hooper David Ormerod, *Blackstone's Criminal Law Practice* 2012, Oxford University Press, 2011, 652.

that period the Attorney – General has consented to such further proceedings as aforesaid.

第7条第(2)款规定了诉讼程序:任何人在任何法院被指控犯有本条所规定的罪行,未经总检察长同意,不得就该罪行对其进行进一步的诉讼,但《1979年刑事检控法》第6条授权的诉讼除外。因此,如果该人被还押拘留,他应在自他被还押之日起的8天期限届满后,有权在没有担保的情况下获得保释,除非在此期间总检察长同意上述进一步的诉讼程序。

Section 7(2) stipulates the penalty for this offense: any person guilty of [any offence under this Act other than an offence under section 2 ...] shall be liable on summary conviction to imprisonment for a term not exceeding three months or to a fine not exceeding [level 4 on the standard scale], or to both such imprisonment and fine.

第7条第2款规定了本罪的处罚:任何人犯有本法规定的任何罪行,[但第2条规定的罪行除外……]一经简易程序定罪,可处监禁不超过3个月或罚金不超过[标准等级第4级],或同时处监禁及罚金。

12.2.6 Organising, Training or Equipping Quasimilitary organisations(组织、训练或武装准军事组织罪)

Section 2 of the Public Order Act 1936 prohibits quasimilitary organisations.

《1936年公共秩序法》第2条规定了组织、训练或武装准军事组织罪。

(1) Subsection 1 stipulates the substantive content of the crime: if the members or adherents of any association of persons, whether incorporated or not, are—

第(1)款规定了罪行的实体内容:如果任何团体的成员或追随者,不论是否,

(a) organised or trained or equipped for the purpose of enabling them to be employed in usurping the functions of the police or of the armed forces of the Crown; or

(a)若经组织、训练或武装,以使其能够被用于篡夺警察或王国武装部队的职能;或

(b) organised and trained or organised and equipped either for the purpose of enabling them to be employed for the use or display of physical force in promoting any political object, or in such manner as to arouse reasonable apprehension that they are organised and either trained or equipped for that purpose; then any person who takes part in the control or management of the association, or in so organising or training as aforesaid any members or adherents thereof, shall be guilty of an offence under this section.

(b)经组织和训练或组织和武装,以使其能够被用于使用或展示武力来促进任

何政治目标,或以这种方式引起合理的担忧,即他们是为此目的而组织和训练或武装的;那么,任何参与控制或管理该团体的人,或如上所述组织或培训其任何成员或追随者的人,即属犯本条所订罪行。

However, in addition to providing for the aforementioned acts constituting an offence, subsection (1) also provides for the defence provided that in any proceedings against a person charged with the offence of taking part in the control or management of such an association as aforesaid it shall be a defence to that charge to prove that he neither consented to nor connived at the organisation, training, or equipment of members or adherents of the association in contravention of the provisions of this section.

但第(1)款除了规定前述构成犯罪的行为,其还规定了辩护事由:在对被控参与控制或管理上述社团的人进行的任何法律程序中,证明该人既不同意也不纵容违反本条的规定组织、训练或武装该社团的成员或信徒,即可作为该指控的抗辩理由。

(6) Subsection 6 also stipulates the circumstances for excluding the exclusion of crimes: nothing in this section shall be construed as prohibiting the employment of a reasonable number of persons as stewards to assist in the preservation of order at any public meeting held upon private premises, or the making of arrangements for that purpose or the instruction of the persons to be so employed in their lawful duties as such stewards, or their being furnished with badges or other distinguishing signs.

该条第(6)款还规定了排除排除犯罪的情况:本条的任何规定均不得解释为禁止雇用合理人数的人作为管事,以协助维持在私人处所举行的任何公共集会的秩序,或基于该目的作出安排,或指示如此受雇的人履行其作为该等管事的合法职责,或为他们配发徽章或其他区分标志。

Section 9 provides the explanation of terms: "meeting" means a meeting held for the purpose of the discussion of matters of public interest or for the purpose of the expression of views on such matters; "Private premises" means premises to which the public have access (whether on payment or otherwise) only by permission of the owner, occupier, or lessee of the premises. Subection (2) provides that no prosecution shall be instituted under this section without the consent of the Attorney – General.

该法第9条对术语进行了解释:"集会"指为讨论有关公众利益的事项或就该等事项发表意见而举行的集会;"私人处所"是指公众只有在该处所的拥有人、占用人或承租人的许可下才能(无论是以付款还是其他方式)进入的处所。本条第(2)款规定了未经司法部长同意,不得根据本条进行起诉。

Subsection 7(1) provides the penalty: any person who commits an offence under section two of this Act shall be liable on summary conviction to imprisonment for a term not exceeding six months or to a fine not exceeding one hundred pounds, or to both such imprisonment and fine, or, on conviction on indictment, to imprisonment for a term not exceeding two years or to a fine not exceeding five hundred pounds, or to both such imprisonment and fine.

该法第7条第(1)款规定了本罪的处罚:任何人犯本法第2条规定的罪,一经简易定罪,可处不超过6个月的监禁或不超过100英镑的罚金,或同时处上述监禁和罚金,或经指控程序定罪,可处不超过2年的监禁或不超过500英镑的罚金,或同时处上述监禁和罚金。

■ Curriculum Ideology and Politics(课程思政)

Objectively understand the relationship between the exercise of basic rights and the maintenance of public order. Public order cases may involve the issue of fundamental rights, especially in the context of the exercise of citizens' fundamental rights, which directly involve the conflict and balance between the maintenance of public order and the exercise of fundamental rights. Many countries have adopted criminal laws to penalize acts that disrupt public order and have attempted to strike a proper balance between the maintenance of public order and the protection of citizens' fundamental rights by, for example, specifying restrictions. The proper management of the relationship between the two requires the ability to judge the limitations and prohibitions on the exercise of rights and the level of law enforcement to be improved.

客观认知基本权利行使和公共秩序维护之间的关系。公共秩序犯罪可能涉及基本权利议题,特别是在行使公民基本权利的场景下,其直接涉及公共秩序维护和基本权利行使之间的冲突和平衡问题。诸多国家通过刑法惩罚扰乱公共秩序的行为,并试图通过明确限制条件等方式在维护公共秩序和保护公民基本权利之间实现恰当的平衡。处理好二者的关系需要提高限制和禁止权利行使的判断能力和执法水平。

12.3 Common Law Crimes against Public Order(扰乱公共秩序的普通法犯罪)

The common law crimes of disturbing public order mainly refer to the crime of public nuisance and the crime of outraging public decency. They have a long history and cover a wide range of public disorder, but they are not systematic and clear enough, and legal reform is needed. The following is a brief introduction to these two offences respectively.

普通法上的扰乱公共秩序犯罪主要是指滋扰公众罪和破坏公众体统罪。这些罪历史悠久,囊括了形形色色的扰乱公共秩序的行为,但其面临不够系统、不够明确的问题,需要进行法律改革。下面,分别对这个两个罪进行简要介绍。

12.3.1 Public nuisance(滋扰公众罪)

A traditional definition of public nuisance is: A person is guilty of a public nuisance (also known as common nuisance), who (a) does an act not warranted by law, or (b) omits to discharge a legal duty, if the effect of the act or omission is to endanger the life, health, property or comfort of the public, or to obstruct the public in the exercise or enjoyment of rights common to all Her Majesty's subjects.

滋扰公众罪的传统定义是:当一个人(a)做了未经法律授权的行为,或(b)不履行法律义务,如果该作为或不作为的后果是危及公众的生命、健康、财产或舒适,或阻碍公众行使或享受女王陛下所有臣民共有的权利,则他/她犯了滋扰公众罪(也称共同妨害罪)。[1]

Examples of public nuisance include: (1) obstructing the highway; (2) blasting and quarrying near built - up areas; (3) allowing land to be used as a dump, creating a dangerous or noxious environment; (4) noisy parties and "raves"; (5) bomb hoaxes and false calls to the emergency services; (6) hanging from motorways and bridges, for example in political demonstrations; (7) keeping pumas in a domestic garden; (8) gang activity involving drug dealing in an urban area.

滋扰公众的例子包括:(1)阻碍高速公路;(2)在建成区附近爆破和采石;(3)允许将土地用作垃圾场,造成危险或有害的环境;(4)吵闹的聚会和"狂欢";(5)炸弹吓诈和虚假呼叫紧急服务;(6)悬挂在高速公路和桥梁上,例如在政治示威中这样做;(7)在家庭花园里养美洲狮;(8)在市区从事涉及毒品交易的帮派活动。[2]

A scholar thinks the offence is so wide and the definition is so fluid that it lacks the certainty required of a criminal offence. Almost all examples of public nuisance are now covered by specialised statutory offences. Therefore, the scholar thinks the offence should be abolished, or the offence should be replaced by a narrower offence of doing a major hazard to the physical safety or health of the public.

---

[1] 2010 edition of Archbold's Criminal Pleading, Evidence and Practice, para 31 - 40; Rimmington and Goldstein, [2006] 1 AC 459 (HL), discussed para 2.17 below.

[2] Simplification of Criminal Law: Public Nuisance and Outraging Public Decency (2010) Law Commission Consultation Paper No 193, para. 2.2.

有学者认为,这一犯罪范围太广,定义也太不确定,缺乏刑事犯罪所需的确定性;现在几乎所有滋扰公众的例子都被专门的法定犯罪所涵盖。所以,该学者主张废除这一罪行,或者以更狭窄的犯罪,即实施了对公众人身安全或健康造成重大危害的犯罪取代。[1]

The Law Commission's 2010 consultation report made interim recommendations: (1) to replace the offence in statute law; (2) to introduce a intention or reckless element to strengthen the fault element of the offence. The 2015 Law Commission report formally considered the continued existence of the offence beneficial, but recommended that the offence be restated in the statute. The report, reiterating the importance of the crime and perfecting and clarifying its constituent elements, suggested that the external elements of the offence should include: (1) the voluntary act of the accused (including omission, if the accused is under an obligation at common law or statute law). (2) causing: (a) serious harm to the public or a portion of the public; or (b) prevent the public or sections of the public from exercising or enjoying rights common to the general public. Serious harm to a person means: (1) death, personal injury or disease; (2) loss of or damage to property; (3) severe distress, annoyance, inconvenience or loss of amenity; Or at risk of these things.

2010 年法律委员会的咨询报告给出了临时建议:(1)在成文法中取代这项罪行;(2)引入故意或疏忽的要件,以加强罪行的责任要件。[2] 2015 年法律委员会的报告正式认为该罪的继续存在是有益的,但建议在法规中重述这一罪行。[3] 该报告重申了该罪的重要性,并对该罪的构成要素进行了完善和明晰,建议该罪的外在要件应包括:(1)被告的自愿行为(包括不作为,如果被告在普通法或成文法上有义务)。(2)造成:(a)对公众或部分公众造成严重损害的;或(b)妨碍公众或部分公众行使或享受一般公众共有的权利。[4] 对人造成严重损害,是指:(1)死亡、人身伤害或者疾病;(2)财产灭失或者损坏;(3)严重痛苦、烦恼、不便或者丧失安乐的,或者

---

〔1〕 J R Spencer, *Public Nuisance—a critical examination* 55 CLJ 83(1989).

〔2〕 Simplification of Criminal Law: Public Nuisance and Outraging Public Decency (2010) Law Commission Consultation Paper No 193, para. 7. 3.

〔3〕 Simplification of Criminal Law: Public Nuisance and Outraging Public Decency (2015) Law Commission Paper No 358, para. 3. 3.

〔4〕 Simplification of Criminal Law: Public Nuisance and Outraging Public Decency (2015) Law Commission Paper No 358, para. 3. 48.

有遭受这些事情的风险。[1]

The report recommends that the offence should include an element of liability, including intentionally causing or recklessly causing: (1) serious harm to the public or a section of the public; (2) impeding the public or part of the public from exercising or enjoying rights common to the general public. "Intent" means that the defendant acted with a view to causing the danger or obstruction; A jury or other tribunal of fact may also find that the defendant intended to cause danger or obstruction if they are satisfied that he or she was aware that if the defendant began to do what he or she intended to do, the danger or obstruction was certain (unless there is special intervention). "Reckless" means: (a) the defendant was aware that his or her conduct would create a risk of danger or obstruction, and (b) it was unreasonable to take that risk in the circumstances as in the knowledge or belief of the defendant.

该报告建议该罪应包含责任因素,包括故意造成或疏忽造成:(1)对公众或部分公众造成严重伤害;(2)妨碍公众或者部分公众行使或者享受一般公众共有的权利。[2] "故意"指被告的行为是为了造成该危险或阻碍;陪审团或其他事实审裁处也可认定被告有意制造危险或妨碍,如果他们确信他或者她意识到,如果被告开始做了他或她打算做的事情,造成危险或妨碍是肯定的(除非有特别的干预)。"疏忽"意指:(a)被告意识到他或她的行为可能造成危险或阻碍的风险,以及(b)在被告明知或确信的情况下,承担该风险是不合理的。[3]

Besides, the report recommended that public nuisance should include the defence of reasonableness. The defendant is not liable if he or she can show that reasonable care or due care was used, which enables the defendant to show that he or she could not reasonably have foreseen or taken reasonable care to avoid the injury or hindrance caused.

除此之外,该报告建议滋扰公众罪应包含合理性的抗辩。如果被告能证明,合理的注意或应有的审慎已被使用,这使被告能够证明他或她不能合理地预见或采取

[1] Simplification of Criminal Law: Public Nuisance and Outraging Public Decency (2015) Law Commission Paper No 358, para. 3.49.

[2] Simplification of Criminal Law: Public Nuisance and Outraging Public Decency (2015) Law Commission Paper No 358, para. 3.58.

[3] Simplification of Criminal Law: Public Nuisance and Outraging Public Decency (2015) Law Commission Paper No 358, para. 3.59.

合理的谨慎措施来避免所造成的伤害或阻碍，被告不承担责任。[1]

12.3.2　Outraging public decency（破坏公众体统罪）

Outraging public decency is also a common law offence and used to be considered a form of public nuisance. The offence of outraging public decency would appear to be any indecent activity carried out in a place or manner which more than one member of the public is likely to witness and dislike. The judgement of the leading modern case on the offence says："if the offence of outraging public decency were to be proved, it was necessary to prove two elements. (i) The act was of such a lewd character as to outrage public decency; this element constituted the nature of the act which had to be proved before the offence could be established. (ii) it took place in a public place and must have been capable of being seen by two or more persons who were actually present, even if they had not actually seen it." The judgement also says："there is no reason why in principle the nature of the act cannot be witnessed in another way such as hearing; we therefore accept the argument of the prosecution that the nature of the act can be capable of being witnessed by means other than seeing."

破坏公众体统罪亦属普通法罪行，过去被视为滋扰公众罪的一种形式。破坏公众体统罪表现为在一名以上的公众可能目睹的地方，实施令人生厌或进行任何不雅的行为。该罪行在现代的指导性案例认为："如果要证明破坏公众体统的罪行，就必须证明两个要素。(i)该行为具有如此下流的性质，以致将破坏公众体统；这一构成行为性质的要素必须在确立犯罪之前加以证明。(ii)该行为在公共场所发生，并且必须能够被2名或2名以上实际在场的人看到，即使他们实际上并没有看到该行为。"[2]也有判决认为："原则上，没有理由不能以听到等其他方式来证明行为的性质；因此，我们接受控方的论点，即该行为的性质可以通过看到以外的手段加以证明。"[3]

The traditional forms of the offence involve either exposing oneself (either simply, or in the act of performing a sexual activity) or creating an indecent display, for example of pictures. Examples are as follows. (1) Indecent exposure. (2) Performing sexual activities in public. (3) Nude bathing in inhabited areas. (4) Disinterring a corpse for dissection. (5) Exhibition of sculpture consisting of human head with freeze -

[1] Simplification of Criminal Law: Public Nuisance and Outraging Public Decency (2015) Law Commission Paper No 358, para. 3.63.

[2] Hamilton, [2007] EWCA Crim 2062, [2008] QB 224 para 21 (CA).

[3] Hamilton, [2007] EWCA Crim 2062, [2008] QB 224 para 34 (CA).

dried human foetuses as earrings. (6) Urinating on a war memorial while drunk.

该罪行的传统形式包括(单纯地或是在进行性活动的行为过程中)暴露自身,或展示淫亵事物,例如照片。示例如下:(1)暴露狂;(2)在公共场所进行性行为;(3)在有人居住区裸泳;(4)挖出尸体进行解剖;(5)展览以冻干人类胎儿作为耳饰的人头组成的雕塑;(6)酒后在战争纪念碑上小便。[1]

The act or display must have been intentionally carried out by the defendant. But beyond that, there is no requirement for fault. The defendant need not have knowingly or believed, or recklessly believed, that the conduct or display was indecent. Nor does the defendant need to know, believe, or expect that someone will witness or be provoked or actually be present. As with the offence of public nuisance, the Law Commission's 2010 consultation report provisionally recommended that the offence be restated in the enactment law with the addition of a provision that the accused should intentionally or regardless of the risk that others would be provoked.

此等行为或展示必须是被告故意进行的。但除此之外,没有对主观责任的其他要求。被告不需要已明知、确信或疏忽地确信其行为或展示是不雅的。[2] 被告也不需要知道、相信或期望有人会目睹或被激怒或真的有人在场。[3] 与滋扰公众罪一样,法律委员会在2010年的咨询报告中,暂时建议在制定法中重新制定该罪行,并增加一项规定,即被告应对他人会被激怒的风险持故意或疏忽的心态。[4]

The Law Commission's official report in 2015 concluded that there was a need for an offence against public decency, but that the existing common law offence should be replaced with a statutory offence. The report focuses on the nature of the conduct rather than its possible consequences. It proposes that in the new offence of public decency, the following conduct or display be required: (1) indecent or disgusting; (2) to a degree sufficient to violate the minimum standards of public decency judged by a jury in contemporary society. In the new offence against public decency, it should be stipulated that the conduct or display must be carried out in a place accessible or visible to the public. However, the new offence should not contain a requirement for the presence of two persons. The report does not recommend introducing a provision that a defendant's

---

〔1〕 Simplification of Criminal Law: Public Nuisance and Outraging Public Decency (2010) Law Commission Consultation Paper No 193, para. 3. 2.

〔2〕 Gibson and Sylveire, [1990] 2 QB 619, 627.

〔3〕 Bunyan and Morgan, (1844) 1 Cox CC 74.

〔4〕 Simplification of Criminal Law: Public Nuisance and Outraging Public Decency (2010) Law Commission Consultation Paper No 193, para. 5. 52.

conduct is likely to cause public disgust or annoyance.

法律委员会2015年的正式报告认为,有必要设立一项破坏公众体统的罪行,但现行的普通法罪行应以一项法定罪行取代。[1] 该报告侧重于行为的性质,而非行为可能造成的后果。它建议,在触犯公共礼仪的新罪行中,须对行为或展示有下列要求:(1)下流或令人厌恶;(2)其程度足以违反当代社会陪审团所判断的公众体统的最低标准。[2] 在新的破坏公众体统罪行中,应规定有关行为或展示必须在公众可接近或能看到的地方进行。[3] 但新罪行不应包含对2人同时在场的要求。[4] 该报告也不建议引入另一项规定,即被告的行为有可能引起公众的厌恶或烦恼。[5]

The proposed elements of fault in the report also focus on the objective nature and condition of the conduct as recognized by the perpetrator, rather than the likely consequences of the conduct as recognized by the perpetrator. The report recommends that offences against public decency should include an element of fault. The requirement of fault for a crime against public decency should be that the defendant: (1) knew the nature of the act or display, or was reckless to whether the act or display was of that nature; And (2) knew or intended that the act or display was or would be performed in a place accessible or visible to the public, or acted recklessly in the circumstances. The "nature" of the conduct or display refers to those features, facts, and circumstances that in fact make it obscene or objectionable (whether or not the defendant finds the conduct indecent or believes that the conduct would violate generally accepted standards of propriety). "Reckless" means: (1) the defendant was aware that the conduct or display might have a risk of that nature, or (as the case may be) that the conduct or display might be located in a place accessible or visible to the public, and (2) it was unreasonable for the defendant to assume the risk when he knew or believed it existed.

报告中提议的过错要素亦侧重于行为人认识到的行为的客观性质和状况,而非行为人认识到的行为可能造成的后果。报告建议破坏公众体统的罪行应包括过错

---

[1] Simplification of Criminal Law: Public Nuisance and Outraging Public Decency (2015) Law Commission Paper No 358, para. 3. 111.

[2] Simplification of Criminal Law: Public Nuisance and Outraging Public Decency (2015) Law Commission Paper No 358, para. 3. 118.

[3] Simplification of Criminal Law: Public Nuisance and Outraging Public Decency (2015) Law Commission Paper No 358, para. 3. 125.

[4] Simplification of Criminal Law: Public Nuisance and Outraging Public Decency (2015) Law Commission Paper No 358, para. 3. 130.

[5] Simplification of Criminal Law: Public Nuisance and Outraging Public Decency (2015) Law Commission Paper No 358, para. 3. 134.

要素。破坏公众体统罪的过错要素应该是被告:(1)明知行为或展示的性质,或对该行为或展示的性质具有疏忽的过错;及(2)明知或意图该行为或展示是在或将会在公众可接近或可见的地方进行,或对情况是否如此行事疏忽。[1] 行为或展示的性质是指那些事实上使其成为淫秽或令人厌恶的特征、事实和情况,无论被告是否认为该行为不雅或认为该行为会违反普遍接受的得体标准。"疏忽"意指:(1)被告意识到该行为或展示可能具有该性质的风险,或(视情况而定)该行为或展示可能位于公众可接近或可见的地方,以及(2)在被告知道或认为存在的情况下,承担该风险是不合理的。[2]

■ Case study(案例学习)

Hamilton, [2007] EWCA Crim 2062, [2008] QB 224 (汉密尔顿案)

Fact(基本案情)

Hamilton took upskirt photos.

汉密尔顿实施了偷拍裙底的行为。

Dispute(争议点)

What offence is upskirt photography as in the case of Hamilton suspected of and can it be decriminalized by reference to the defence under Section 5 of Public Order Act 1986?

汉密尔顿案中的摄影裙底行为涉嫌什么罪名,该行为可以参照《1986 年公共秩序法》第 5 条中的抗辩事由予以出罪吗?

Conclusion(结论)

Upskirt photography is suspected of committing a crime against public decency, as it is against the public decency and may cause anger. The defense grounds for offence in section 5 of the Public Order Act 1986 are ambiguous. This defense focuses on the existence of a reason to believe, rather than the actual belief. Does "likely to cause anger" mean "likely to cause anger if he or she sees or hears the behavior or display" or "likely to see or hear and feel anger"? This form of defense could well exclude liability in an unseemly case like Hamilton's: the defendant could argue that there was no reason to believe that anyone within hearing or sight would have been provoked, because the

---

[1] Simplification of Criminal Law: Public Nuisance and Outraging Public Decency (2015) Law Commission Paper No 358, para. 4. 15.

[2] Simplification of Criminal Law: Public Nuisance and Outraging Public Decency (2015) Law Commission Paper No 358, para. 3. 160.

defendant took every precaution to ensure that no one would have seen his or her behavior.

摄影裙底涉嫌破坏公众体统罪,因为它破坏了公众体统且可能引起愤怒。《1986年公共秩序法》第5条中的辩护理由是模棱两可的。该辩护关注的是有理由相信,而不是实际相信。可能引起愤怒是指"如果他或她看到或听到行为或展示,可能会引起愤怒"还是"可能看到或听到并感到愤怒"?在像汉密尔顿这样的不雅案件中,这种形式的辩护完全可以排除责任:被告可以辩称,没有理由相信任何在听力或视力范围内的人会被激怒,因为被告采取了一切预防措施,以确保没有人会看到他的行为。

Questions:1. In a reasonable defense against public decency, should the defense focus on whether there is reason for the defendant to believe that there is no danger?(Please scan the QR code on the right to get the answer)

在破坏公众体统罪的合理性辩护中,辩方是否应当关注是否存在理由让被告去相信其不会造成危险?(答案请扫描右侧二维码获取)

2. Which focus is more likely to get a defendant acquitted?(Please scan the QR code on the right to get the answer)

哪一个关注点更容易让被告脱罪?(答案请扫描右侧二维码获取)

12.4 Exercise(课后练习)(答案请扫描右侧二维码获取)

12.4.1 Test of Terminologies(术语考查)

①public place ②public meeting

③a person of reasonable firmness at the scene

④public nuisance ⑤public decency

12.4.2 True or False(判断题)

1. The front garden of a house was not a public place in the sense of Public Order Act 1986.

《1986年公共秩序法》认为,房子的前花园不是公共场所。

2. In the determination of the crime of riot, it does not matter whether 12 or more people simultaneously used or threatened to use unlawful violence.

在暴乱罪的认定中,12个或更多的人是否同时使用或威胁使用非法暴力并不重要。

3. The law on processions and assemblies leads inevitably to the following

question：can（and if so，how）group activities be related to public order?

关于游行和集会的法律不可避免地导致以下问题:群体活动能否、如何与公共秩序相关联?

4. Harassment can be caused by threatening, abusive or insulting words, behaviour or display that can also cause alarm or distress (thus also a problem of breaching inner peace), but harassment can also be caused by disorderly behaviour that may not at the same time cause alarm or distress (thus external peace also should be protected by itself).

烦扰可由能造成惊恐或痛苦的威胁性、辱骂性或侮辱性的言语、行为或展示引起,因此其也是破坏内心平静的问题,但烦扰也可由可能不会同时造成惊恐或痛苦的扰乱治安行为引起,因此外部安宁本身也应该得到保护。

12.4.3 Short – answer Questions(简答题)

1. What is unlawful violence in riot crime?

暴乱罪中的非法暴力指的是什么?

2. Does the POA 1986 altogether excludes 'private dwellings' from the scope of public order?

《1986 年公共秩序法》是否将私人住宅一概排除在公共秩序的范围之外?

3. Can intrusive begging constitute a crime against public order?

不文明乞讨是否可能构成扰乱公共秩序犯罪?

4. Spreading terror hoaxes, throwing fake dangerous substances, threatening to set fire, to blast or to throw dangerous substances, are all to the alarm of the public. Is this kind alarm not a real public safety concern and thus the actor cannot be convicted of a public safety crime?

散布恐怖恶作剧,投掷假冒危险物品,以放火、爆炸、投掷危险物品相威胁,都会引起公众的惊恐。但造成这种惊恐不是真正的公共安全问题,行为人因此不会被判危害公共安全罪,对吗?

■ Curriculum Ideology and Politics(课程思政)

Understand the relationship between the rights and interests that citizens enjoy in their daily lives and the promulgation of relevant public order laws by the state. The people's aspiration for a better life is the pursuit of the country. Citizens in modern society enjoy the right and interest to be free from unnecessary harassment, alarm or distress in daily life, so acts that intentionally or negligently cause unnecessary harassment, alarm or distress to others should be punished by law. The judgment of "necessary" should balance the legal and legitimate social life rights and interests of the actor.

理解公民所享有的日常生活权益和国家出台的相关公共秩序法律之间的关联。人民对美好生活的向往就是国家的追求。现代社会的公民在日常生活中享有免于不必要的烦扰、惊恐或痛苦的权利和利益，所以故意或者过失导致他人不必要的烦扰、惊恐或痛苦的行为要受到法律的制裁。是否"必要"的判断要平衡行为人合法、正当的社会生活权利和利益。

■ Summary（总结）

1. The Public Order Act 1986 abolished a number of common law offences, including rioting, unlawful assembly and affray, and replaced them with statutory offences such as rioting, violent disorder, affray, threatening behaviour and disorderly conduct. It extended control over parades and created control over open - air gatherings. It provides for the prohibition of certain offenders from attending sporting events, in particular association football matches. This chapter also deals with the remaining offences under the Public Order Act 1936 and the common law offences of public nuisance and public decency.

《1986 年公共秩序法》废除了若干普通法罪行，包括暴乱、非法集会和斗殴，代之以暴乱、暴力骚扰、斗殴、威胁行为和扰乱治安等法定罪行。《1986 年公共秩序法》扩展了对游行的控制，并对露天集会进行了管制。《1986 年公共秩序法》规定禁止某些违法者参加体育赛事，特别是足球协会比赛。本章亦涉及《1936 年公共秩序法》规定的其他罪行及普通法上的滋扰公众罪行和破坏公众体统罪行。

2. The law provides for a large number of less serious public order offences that, although considered public order offenses, can be committed in private areas. It is important to pay attention to the public order basis of these offences when they occur in private areas, and they cannot be regarded as crimes against individuals alone. And the legislation does not provide for these offences in order to protect general public safety.

法律规定了大量不严重的公共秩序犯罪，尽管这些犯罪被视为公共秩序犯罪，但它们却会发生在私人领域。应该注意到发生在私人领域的这些犯罪的公共秩序根据，不能把其仅仅视为是针对个人的犯罪。立法规定这些犯罪，也并不是为了保护一般性的公共安全。

3. Insults directed against a person are arguably a species of crime against the

person, but these may also be the crime against public order when the criminal law does not directly protect the dignity of an individual, but otherwise protects them from insulting conduct in public life.

针对一个人的侮辱可以说是一种针对人的犯罪,但当刑法不直接保护个人的尊严,而是以其他方式保护个体免受公共生活中的侮辱行为时,这些行为也可能是针对公共秩序的犯罪。

Chapter 13 Crimes Against the State
第 13 章 侵害国家犯罪

■ The Learning Objective(学习目标)

1. To understand what crimes against the state are included in U. S. criminal law.
了解美国刑法中有哪些侵害国家的犯罪。
2. To understand the history of different crimes against the state.
了解不同侵害国家犯罪的历史沿革。
3. To understand the criminal components of different crimes.
了解不同罪名的犯罪构成。
4. To learn terminologies related to the topic.
掌握本章的专业术语。

■ Chapter Outline(本章内容概要)

This chapter is about crimes against the state in the U. S. criminal law, especially the historical origins and criminal composition of the key crimes, which include the crime of betrayal of the country, the crime of incitement, the crime of sabotage, the crime of espionage and the crime of counter – terrorism. This chapter will introduce the definition, origin and classic cases of each crime.

本章节主要内容是美国刑法中的侵害国家犯罪,尤其是重点犯罪的历史来源、犯罪构成,包括背叛国家罪、煽动罪、破坏罪、间谍罪和反恐怖主义罪。本章将会介绍各个犯罪的定义、来源以及相关的经典案例。

■ The Purpose of Curriculum Ideology and Politics for this Chapter (本章的课程思政目标)

1. By understanding the provisions of the United Kingdom and the United States on

crimes against the state, we can build citizen awareness of safeguarding national security. National security is closely related to the basic rights of citizens. Only by firmly ensuring national security can we effectively promote the steady development of various national undertakings.

通过了解英美两国关于侵害国家犯罪的规定,树立维护国家安全的公民意识。国家安全与公民的基本权利息息相关,只有牢牢保障国家安全,才能有效地促进国家各项事业的稳步开展。

2. Expanding students' horizons of professional knowledge in criminal law. The legislation of crimes against the state in the United States has become a model for relevant criminal legislation in many countries. By studying this chapter, students can understand the provisions of crimes against the state in other countries in the world, and then cultivate their international visions.

拓展学生的刑法专业知识视野。美国的侵害国家犯罪立法成为许多国家相关刑事立法的典范,通过本章的学习,可以了解世界其他国家关于侵害国家犯罪的规定,进而培养自身的国际化视野。

3. Understand the value of protecting human rights in penalty/punishment. National security crimes are felonies, and the punishment for such crimes must be very cautious and cannot be arbitrarily convicted. Although the United States has established a complete crime system, the punishment rate for related crimes is not high. Therefore, it is necessary to deeply understand the balance between punishing crimes and protecting human rights.

了解刑罚中的保障人权的价值。国家安全犯罪是重罪,对于这类犯罪的惩处一定要十分谨慎,不能肆意入罪。美国虽然建立了完善的罪名体系,但相关的犯罪惩处率并不高。因此,要深度认知惩罚犯罪与保护人权之间的平衡问题。

■ Terminologies(专业术语)

treason	背叛国家罪
sedition	煽动罪
sabotage	破坏罪
espionage	间谍罪
terrorism Crimes	恐怖主义犯罪
national emergency	国家紧急状态
war materials	战争物资

Smith Act	《史密斯法案》
terrorist organizations	恐怖组织
weapon of mass destruction	大规模杀伤性武器
joint enterprise	共同犯罪体
jurisdictional	有管辖权的
assault with dangerous weapon	持危险武器袭击
international terrorism	国际恐怖主义
domestic terrorism	国内恐怖主义

13.1 Treason(背叛国家罪)

13.1.1 Treason Laws and the American Revolution(背叛国家罪和美国革命)

Treason is essentially a violation of social loyalty. In the historical changes of many legal systems, the definition of "treason against the state" is sometimes so broad that it covers the entire criminal law. This is particularly obvious in British law. England was a barbaric land before the Roman Conquest, but the Romans established their own government and legal system in England. Therefore, in England, as in Rome, treason was not much defined, and it was understood only as a crime against society. It was not until the reign of Edward Ⅲ (1327 - 1377) that this situation changed.[1]

背叛国家罪本质上是对社会忠诚的侵犯。在诸多法律体系的历史流变中,"背叛国家行为"的定义有时非常广泛,以至于涵盖了整个刑法中规定的行为,这一点在英国法律中表现得尤为明显。在罗马征服英格兰以前,英格兰一直是一片野蛮的土地,但罗马人在英格兰建立了自己的政府和法律体系。因此,在英格兰,背叛国家罪就如在罗马一样,并无太多的定义,它只被理解为一种危害社会的罪行。直到爱德华三世统治时期(1327—1377 年),这一情况才有所改变。

Early in the reign of Edward Ⅲ, a knight forcibly held a man until he paid £ 90. Because the knight tried to exercise royal power, he was convicted of treason. This judgment made the defintion of treason confused and triggered widespread condemnation in society. A few years later, the famous Statue of Treason of 1352 was promulgated, which defined the scope of treason and abolished the local court's pawer to freely interpret treason. right. According to the requirements of the new decree, every British

[1] See Willard Hurst, *Treason in the United States? I. Treason down to the Constitution*, 58 Harvard Law Review 229 (1944).

subject should be loyal to the king in exchange for the king's protection. The laws of Edward III divided breaches of this allegiance into two degrees, namely petty treason and treason. Petty treason was a minor violation of private, family beliefs, but true treason occurred when a subject became so disloyal that he attacked the king himself.[1]

在爱德华三世统治的早期,一名骑士强行扣押了一名男子,直到该男子支付了90英镑。由于这名骑士试图行使王权,他被认定为叛国罪。这一判决所反映出的叛国罪界定的混乱引发了各界的声讨。几年后,著名的爱德华三世《1352年叛逆法令》颁布,[2]该法令对叛国罪的归责范围进行了界定,废除了地方法院行使的对叛国罪的自由解释权。根据新法令的要求,每一位英国的臣民都应该对国王效忠,以换取国王对他的保护。爱德华三世的法律将违反这种效忠的行为分为两级,即轻微叛国罪和叛国罪。轻微叛国罪是指对私人、家庭信仰的轻微违反,但当一个臣民变得十分不忠以至于攻击国王本身时,就会构成真正的叛国罪。

Since then, treason has been increasingly abused throughout British history. The most serious period was the reign of Henry Ⅷ (1509 – 1547). Under his rule, both the description of crimes and the severity of punishments for criminals were very different from those in the past. In the regulations he formulated, any words or deeds that may affect the dignity of the royal family will be sentenced to treason and corresponding imprisonment: People were required to pledge their obedience by taking an oath, and anyone who refused was liable to a state crime. After that, Edward Ⅵ abolished the severe treason laws of Henry Ⅷ and re – adopted and improved the Statue of Treasons of 1352 of Edward Ⅲ. Contrary to the laws of Henry Ⅷ's time, the statute again provided for some necessary public act or behavior, adding that two witnesses were required to make a determination.[3] Following Queen Mary's sucession, she quickly overturned

---

[1] High treason, by which the forfeiture of escheats went to the king, was defined as: to compass or imagine the death of the king, queen, or heir; to violate the king's eldest daughter or the wife of the king's heir; to levy war against the king; to adhere to the king's enemies or give them aid and comfort; to counterfeit the king's seal or money; and to slay the chancellor, treasurer, or king's justices. Petit treason, by which forfeiture of escheats went to the lord of the fee, was defined as: a servant slaying his master; a wife slaying her husband; and a religious man slaying his prelate. 25 Edw. 3, st. 5, c. 2 (1350).
叛国罪是指以下行为:唆使或想象国王、王后或继承人死亡;侵犯国王的长女或国王继承人的妻子;对国王发动战争;支持国王的敌人或给予他们帮助和安慰;伪造国王的印章或货币;以及杀害大法官、财务官或国王的法官。轻微叛国罪的定义是:仆人杀死主人;妻子杀死丈夫;宗教人士杀死牧师。

[2] 爱德华三世第25年法令是指爱德华三世执政第25年颁布的《1352年叛逆法令》。

[3] 1 Edw. 6, c. 12 (1547).

everything her brother Edward Ⅵ had done for the Reformation, abolishing all religious laws passed during her brother's reign. , and placed the Church in the same position which it had held at the end of the reign of Henry Ⅷ. A later act provided that all treason trials should be conducted at common law, and the judges condued that this meant treason trials no longer required the testimony of two witnesses.

自此之后,叛国罪在英国的历史中开始逐渐被滥用。最严重的时期是亨利八世统治的时期(1509—1547 年)。在他的统治下,无论是对罪行的描述还是对罪犯惩罚的严厉程度较之以往都有很大的不同。在他制定的法规中,可能影响王室尊严的一切言行都将被判处叛国罪并施以相应的监禁之刑。人们必须通过宣誓来表达自己的服从,任何拒绝的人都会被判以叛国罪。此后爱德华六世废除了亨利八世严厉的叛国法,重新采用并完善爱德华三世《1352 年叛逆法令》。与亨利八世时期的法律相反,该法令再次规定了一些必要的公开行为或举动,并补充规定需要 2 名证人才能对行为做出判定。玛丽女王(1553—1587 年)继位后,迅速推翻了其兄爱德华六世为宗教改革所做的一切,废除了在其兄统治时期通过的所有有关宗教的法律,并将教会置于与亨利八世统治末期相同的地位。后来的一项法案规定,所有对叛国罪的审判都应按照普通法进行,法官们认为这意味着不再需要 2 名证人。

When the pioneers immigrated from England and settled on the American continent, they retained the legal concepts that had prevailed in England and placing little emphasis on the protection of individual liberty.[1] But with the outbreak of the American Revolutionary War, new loyalists began to emerge. The framers of the U. S. Constitution began to focus on respect for the new sovereignty and the protection of civil liberties. At the U. S. Constitutional Convention held in 1787, the majority of people approved the inclusion of a clause in the Constitution to restrict the crime of treason. Among them, James Wilson and James Madison made the most outstanding contributions. They all agree with the concept of state supremacy and advocate the use of checks and balances to prevent arbitrary legislation and administrative tyranny. It was largely through the work and ideas of these two men that American treason was fundamentally transformed from that in the UK. In the United Kingdom, for centuries, treason has been used as a tool to punish political opponents and gain power by inserting anything remotely resembling the inclusion of a king's death into the clause. However, the Framers of the United States left no way for the courts and the Congress to create constructive treason, and no one

---

〔1〕 See Willard Hurst, *Treason in the United States? I. Treason down to the Constitution*, 58 Harvard Law Review 226 (1944).

should worry that electing a brutal leader of a different faith or belief would cost his life, family, or fortune.[1]

当拓荒者从英格兰移民,定居在美洲大陆时,他们保留了在英格兰盛行的法律观念,并不重视对个人自由的保障。但随着美国革命战争的爆发,新的效忠派开始出现。美国宪法制定者开始重点关注对新主权的尊重与公民自由的保障。在1787年召开的美国制宪大会上,宪法设立限制叛国罪的条款得到大多数人的赞同。其中,詹姆斯·威尔逊与詹姆斯·麦迪逊的贡献最为突出。他们都赞同国家至上的观念,主张通过制衡手段来防止立法肆意和行政暴政的现象出现。通过这两个人的研究和思考,美国的叛国罪与英国的相比,已得到了根本性的改变。在英国,几个世纪以来,叛国罪一直被当作惩罚政敌和掌权的工具,只要在该条款中插入任何与国王之死类似的内容即可。然而,美国制宪者没有给法院和国会留下任何“推定”叛国的途径,没有人会担心因选举一个有不同信仰或信念的残暴领导人而失去生命、家庭或财富。

13.1.2 Treason Law since the Adoption of the U. S. Constitution(美国宪法中背叛国家罪)

Treason in American law is not enshrined in the criminal code, but in the Constitution. This crime is also the only crime stipulated in the U. S. Constitution. Since the crime of treason threatens the survival of the country, it is regarded as the most serious crime and is stipulated in Article 3(3) of the Federal Constitution. And the Constitution grants the Congress the power to determine the punishment for treason. However, the United States does not legally stipulate that the killing or injury of the head of state is an act of treason. In the United States. only two forms of treason originate from British law but are different in content from British law.

美国法律中的叛国罪并没有规定在刑法中,而是规定在宪法中。该罪也是美国宪法中规定的唯一犯罪。由于背叛国家罪威胁国家的生存,所以被视为最严重的犯罪规定在《美国联邦宪法》第3条第(3)款中,宪法授予国会决定惩治叛国罪之刑罚的权力。但是,美国并未将对国家首脑个人的杀害或伤害作为叛国行为的一种在法律上规定下来。在美国的叛国罪中,只有两种叛国行为源自英国法律但又在内容上有别于英国法律。

According to Article 3(3) of the U. S. Federal Constitution: Treason against the

[1] See Michael Head. *Crimes Against the State*: *From Treason to Terrorism*, Taylor & Francis Group, 2011, p. 101.

United States, shall consist only in levying war against them, or in surrendering to their enemies, giving them aid and comfort. No person shall be convicted of treason unless on the testimony of two witnesses to the same overt act, or on confession in open court.

《美国联邦宪法》第3条第(3)款的规定:只有对美国发动战争,或投降于它的敌人,予敌人以帮助及便利者,方构成叛国罪。无论何人,如非经由2个证人证明其外在的叛国行为,或经由本人在公开法庭认罪者,均不得被判处叛国罪。

It can be seen from this that the elements of treason in the U. S. Constitution include two elements: (1) waging war against the United States; (2) surrendering to the enemy and giving aid to the enemy. In terms of understanding the former the "war" stipulated in American law does not require the condition of "being within the territory" like British law. It can include civil war and external war. As long as it is a war against the United States, all constitute the crime of treason. So – called waging a war does not necessarily require a formal declaration of war or actual fighting, but the intention to attack must be proven. The act of gathering people for the purpose of realizing a plan of armed rebellion also constitutes waging war. If there is only a plan to gather people for the purpose of carrying out armed rebellion, but no actual gathering of people, it does not constitute waging war, but is only a "conspiracy to wage war". However, a private riot that does not have the goal of overthrowing the government or obstructing the implementation of laws is not an act of treason.

据此可以看出,美国宪法中的叛国罪包括两个行为类型:(1)对美国发动战争;(2)归附敌人和给敌人以援助。就对前者的理解而言,美国法律里规定的"战争",并未像英国法律一样要求"在领土内"这一条件,它可以包括内部战争和外部战争,只要是反对美国的战争,都属于叛国罪行。所谓发动战争,不一定要正式宣战或实际作战,但必须证明有攻击的意图。为实现武装叛乱计划而纠集人员的行为,也构成发动战争。如果仅有纠集人员实行武装叛乱的计划,但并未实际纠集人员的,不构成发动战争,仅属"密谋发动战争"。不以推翻政府或阻碍法令的实施为目标的私人性质的暴动,不属叛国行为。

Giving aid and comfort to the enemy refers to behaviors such as providing intelligence, arms, equipment to the enemy, and providing prisoners and deserters to the enemy during the war, indicating that he has the intention of being disloyal to the United States or sympathizing with the enemy. As far as an individual is concerned, merely expressing sympathy, approval or support for the enemy, or being disloyal to one's own country's policies and interests, without the actual behavior listed above, is not enough to constitute treason. The external act of aiding the enemy must be for the purpose of rebelling against the United States, and any non – intentional act cannot constitute treason. An act shall constitute treason, whether it contributes to or attempts to strengthen the force of treason, or whether it causes or attempts to cause the degradation of the offensive or defensive capabilities of the Government of the United States.

归附敌人和给敌人以援助,是指发生在战争期间,表明行为人怀有对美国不忠诚的目的或对敌国同情的意图的行为,比如向敌人提供情报、军火、装备以及给敌人提供战俘、逃兵等。就个人而言,仅仅对敌人怀有同情,表示赞同或支持,或者对本国政策、利益怀有不忠,并不具有上列实际行为的,并不足以构成叛国罪。援助敌人这一外在行为必须以反叛美国为目的,任何非故意的行为都不能构成叛国罪。无论上列行为是否有助于或企图加强叛国的力量,或其是否导致或企图导致美国政府攻击或防御能力的下降,均构成叛国罪。

■ Case study(案例学习)

Kawakita v. United States, 343 U. S. 717 (1952)(川北诉美国案)

Facts(基本案情)

The case was a U. S. Supreme Court case. In the case, Tomomi Kawakita was born in California to Japanese parents, lived in Japan when the war broke out, and remained there until the end of the war. Upon his return to the United States, he was arrested and charged with treason for abusing American prisoners of war, had his U. S. citizenship revoked, and was sentenced to death. In 1953, President Eisenhower commuted his sentence to life in prison. Ten years later, President Kennedy ordered his release on condition that he would be deported and barred from re – entering the United States.

该案是美国最高法院审理的一个案件。在该案中,川北友弥出生于加利福尼亚州,父母是日本人。战争爆发时在日本居住,并一直待在日本直到战争结束。返回美国后,他因虐待美国战俘而被捕并被控叛国罪,其美国公民身份被取消,并被判处死刑。1953 年,艾森豪威尔总统将他的刑期减为无期徒刑。10 年后,肯尼迪总统下令释放他,条件是将他驱逐出境并禁止他再次进入美国。

Dispute(主要争议)

In that case, Kawakita claimed that he had effectively renounced his U. S. citizenship during his time in Japan and therefore could not be tried for treason. It further argued that a person with dual nationality could be guilty of treason only against the country of his or her residence and not against another country of which he or she was a national. However, the U. S. Constitution does not stipulate territorial limits for treason, and the court found that Kawakita should be loyal to the United States in Japan, so he was found guilty.

在该案中,川北声称在日本期间,他实际上已经放弃了美国公民身份,因此不能因叛国罪而受到审判。他进一步辩称,具有双重国籍的人只能对其居住国犯有叛国罪,而不能对声称其为本国国民的其他国家犯有叛国罪。然而,美国宪法对叛国罪没有规定领土限制,法院认定川北在日本期间应当效忠美国,故而进行了有罪的认定。

Conclusion(结论)

After the United States declared war on Japan, the mistreatment of prisoners of war demonstrated Kawakita's opposition to the American state, and American legislation included the United States' war with outsiders into "waging war against the United States." In addition, Kawakita's abuse of American prisoners of war had the intention of attacking the United States, and Kawakita's dual nationality was the real reason why he was ultimately sanctioned for treason by the United States.

在美国对日本宣战之后,虐待战俘的行为表明了川北对美国的反对,而美国的立法将美国与外部的战争也纳入了"发动反美战争"中。此外,川北虐待美国战俘的行为,具有对美国的攻击意图,川北的双重国籍身份正是其最终受到美国叛国罪制裁的真正原因。

Questions: **1.** Why is Kawakita's behavior considered an act of treason?(Please scan the QR code on the right to get the answer)

为什么川北的行为会被认定为叛国的行为?(答案请扫描右侧二维码获取)

2. What are the grounds for treason in the United States?(Please scan the QR code on the right to get the answer)

美国的叛国罪中存在哪些出罪事由?(答案请扫描右侧二维码获取)

■ Curriculum Ideology and Politics(课程思政)

Citizens' loyalty to their motherland is an inevitable requirement of a modern country governed by law. Looking at the path of treason in the United States from its origin in English law to independent legislation, it generally shows a substantial and rational identification of treason. In fact, the criminal laws of many countries in the world stipulate the crime of betrayal of the country and regulate acts of disloyalty by citizens to their countries. National security involves the vital interests of every citizen, and every citizen should love his motherland from the bottom of his heart.

国民忠于自己的祖国是现代法治国家的必然要求。纵观美国叛国罪,其来源于英格兰法,但后面也走向了自主立法的道路。从总体上看,其呈现出对叛国行为的实质与理性的认定。其实,世界上很多国家的刑法都规定了背叛国家罪,以规制国民不忠于祖国的行为。国家安全涉及每一个公民的切身利益,每一位公民都应该发自内心热爱自己的祖国。

13.2 Sedition, Sabotage, and Espionage(煽动罪、破坏罪和间谍罪)

13.2.1 Sedition(煽动罪)

Sedition refers to conspiracy or preparatory conduct intended to incite rebellion or minor insurrection against the government, as well as the act of advocating, instigating, or intending to encourage or likely to incite the imminent occurrence of illegal actions. In the United States, sedition has always been considered a classic crime. In 1798, a Federalist administration led by John Adams feared that the ideas of the French Revolution would infiltrate the new Republic, even potentially leading to its early demise. To prevent this, he and the federalist Congress passed the Alien and Sedition Acts, which stated, "if any persons shall unlawfully combine or conspire together, with intent to oppose any measure or measures of the government of the United States, which are or shall be directed by proper authority, or to impede the operation of any law of the United States, or to intimidate or prevent any person holding a place or office in or under the government of the United States, from undertaking, performing or executing his trust or duty, he or they shall be deemed guilty of a high misdemeanor..." The Democratic – Republican administration, led by Thomas Jefferson, which beat Adams and the Federalist party in elections in 1800 repealed the acts while in office.

煽动是指意图鼓动叛乱或反对政府的轻微暴乱的共谋或预备行为,以及鼓吹、唆使意图或可能鼓动非法行为即将发生的行为。在美国,煽动行为一直都被视为一种典型的犯罪行为。1798 年,约翰·亚当斯领导的联邦党政府担心,激进的法国大革命思想会渗透到新的共和国,甚至有可能导致其提前灭亡。为了防止这种情况发生,他和联邦制国会通过了《外侨与煽动叛乱法》,其规定:"如果任何人非法联合或共谋,意图反对美国政府或应由适当当局指示的任何措施,或阻碍美国任何法律的实施,或恐吓或阻止任何在美国政府内或在美国政府下担任职务或办公室的人承担、履行或执行义务,则他或他们应被视为犯有严重轻罪。”由托马斯·杰斐逊领导的民主共和党政府在1800年的选举中击败了亚当斯和联邦党,其执政期间废除了这些法案。

Afterwards, during the First World War, there was great turmoil in American society. In 1918, the United States' Sedition Act considered any act of "knowingly publishing, printing, writing, or publishing anything disloyal, blasphemous, or vulgar or abusive to the government of the United States". to be illegal. This means that any criticism of the U. S. government would be considered a crime under the law. After the law was enacted, the Schenck v. United States case[1] triggered discussions on freedom of speech and government regulation, and on whether the Sedition Act violated the U. S. Constitution.[2] In that case, Schenck distributed leaflets to urge men of draft age to resist enlistment on the grounds that the draft constituted involuntary servitude. And he was eventually convicted of violating the Espionage Act. In 1921, most the provisions of the Espionage Act and the Sedition Act were repealed, leaving only laws that prohibited foreigners from engaging in espionage activites in the United States and allowed military review of sensitive material.

此后,在第一次世界大战期间,美国社会出现了巨大的动荡局面。1918年,美国的《煽动叛乱法》将“故意发表、印刷、撰写或出版任何有关对美国政府的不忠诚、亵渎、粗俗或辱骂性语言”的行为都认定为非法行为。这意味着根据该法的规定,任何批评美国政府的行为都会被认定为犯罪。在该法颁布之后,申克诉美国政府案引发了关于言论自由与政府监管,以及《煽动叛乱法》是否违背美国宪法的讨论。在该案中,申克分发传单敦促达到征兵年龄的男性抵制入伍,理由是征兵构成非自愿奴役。他最终被判违反《间谍法》。1921年,《间谍法》与《煽动叛乱法》的大部分内容被废除,只留下了禁止外国人在美国从事间谍活动并允许对敏感材料进行军事审查的法律。

The current crime of incitement in the United States originates from the Smith Act enacted in 1940, which was later revised several times and incorporated into Section 2385 of Chapter 18 of the United States Code. This section provides for a total of three incitement offences. Among them, the first paragraph of this section, "Directly inciting subversion of the government", stipulates: "Whoever knowingly or willfully advocates, abets, advises, or teaches the duty, necessity, desirability, or propriety of overthrowing

[1] Schenck v. United States, 249 U. S. 47 (1919).

[2] See McCloskey R, *Free Speech, Sedition and the Constitution*, 45 American Political Science eview 662 (1951).

or destroying the government of the United States or the government of any State, Territory, District or Possession thereof, or the government of any political subdivision therein, by force or violence, or by the assassination of any officer of any such government" constitutes this crime;[1] Paragraph 2 of this section "The crime of publishing or distributing publications that incite subversion of the government" stipulates: "Whoever, with intent to cause the overthrow or destruction of any such government, prints, publishes, edits, issues, circulates, sells, distributes, or publicly displays any written or printed matter advocating, advising, or teaching the duty, necessity, desirability, or propriety of overthrowing or destroying any government in the United States by force or violence, or attempts to do so" shall constitute this crime;[2] Paragraph 3 of this section "The crime of establishing or joining an organization that incites subversion of the government" stipulates: "Whoever organizes or helps or attempts to organize any society, group, or assembly of persons who teach, advocate, or encourage the overthrow or destruction of any such government by force or violence; or becomes or is a member of, or affiliates with, any such society, group, or assembly of persons, knowing the purposes thereof", constitutes this crime.[3]

美国现行的煽动罪源于1940年制定的《史密斯法案》,该法后来几经修改,被编入《美国法典》第18章第2385节中。该节一共规定了三个煽动犯罪。其中,本节第1款"直接煽动颠覆政府罪"规定:"任何人明知或者故意地宣传、唆使、劝导或指导以武力或者暴力或者暗杀政府官员的手段推翻或者毁坏美国政府、美国州政府、管辖领土、地区或者财产,或者任何政治分支组织的政府的职责、必要性、愿望或合适性的",构成本罪;本节第2款"出版、发行煽动颠覆政府的出版物罪"规定:"任何人以引起推翻或毁坏政府为目的,印刷、出版、编辑、发表、流通、出售、发行或者公开展览任何宣传、劝导或教导以武力或暴力推翻或毁坏位于美国领土范围内政府的职责、必要性、愿望或者合适性的出版物,或者试图实施前述行为的",构成本罪;本节第3款"建立或者加入煽动颠覆政府的组织罪"规定:"任何人组织、帮助或者试图组织任何劝导、宣传、鼓励以武力、暴力推翻或毁坏前述政府机构的社团、集团或个人集会的,或者在明知这些组织或分支机构的目的后仍然成为原创成员或者后来加入的成员的",构成本罪。

---

[1] 18 U. S. Code, § 2385.
[2] 18 U. S. Code, § 2385.
[3] 18 U. S. Code, § 2385.

13.2.2　Sabotage(破坏罪)

The crime of sabotage in the United States mainly focuses on attacks on relevant military infrastructure. The relevant crimes are provided in Sections 2151 – 2156 of Chapter 105 of the United States Code. Article 2151 explains the terms "war materials", "war utilities" and "war public utilities". For example, the words "war material" include arms, livestock, forage, forest products and standing timber, stores of clothing, air, water, food, fuel, munitions, and all articles, parts or ingredients, which intended for, adapted to, or were suitable for the use of the United States or any associate nation, in connection with the conduct of war or defense activities.[1]

美国的破坏罪主要关注的是对相关军事基础设施的攻击行为,相关犯罪规定在《美国法典》第 105 章的第 2151—2156 条中。第 2151 条对"战争物资""战争场所""战争公用事业"等词语进行了说明。例如,"战争物资"一词包括武器、牲畜、饲料、林产品和林木、衣物储备、空气、水、食品、燃料、弹药以及所有物品、零件或成分,供应、适应或适合美国或任何伙伴国在进行战争或国防活动时使用。

Article 2152 provides for penalties for acts of sabotage of fortifications, harbor defences or defensive sea areas. This article stipnlates: Whoever willfully trespasses upon, injures, or destroys any of the works or property or material of any submarine mine or torpedo or fortification or harbor – defense system owned or constructed or in process of construction by the United States; or Whoever willfully interferes with the operation or use of any such submarine mine, torpedo, fortification, or harbor – defense system; or Whoever knowingly, willfully, or wantonly violates any duly authorized and promulgated order or regulation of the President governing persons or vessels within the limits of defensive sea areas, which the President, for purposes of national defense, may from time to time establish by executive order—Shall be fined under this title or imprisoned not more than five years, or both.[2]

第 2152 条规定的是对破坏防御工事、港口防御或防御海域行为的处罚。该条的规定:"故意侵入、损害或破坏美国所有、建造或正在建造的任何潜艇、水雷、鱼雷或工事或港口防御系统的任何工程、财产或材料的;或故意干扰此类潜艇水雷、鱼雷、工事、港防系统的操作或者使用的;或凡明知、故意或肆意违反总统正式授权和颁布的、总统为国防目的随时以行政命令建立的、针对防御海域范围内人员或船舶的命令或规定的人,应被处以罚金或 5 年以下监禁,或两者并罚。"

---

〔1〕 105 U. S. Code, § 2151.

〔2〕 105 U. S. Code, § 2152.

Article 2153 stipulates the penalties for destroying war materials, war premises, and war utilities, that is: (a) Whoever, when the United States is at war, or in times of national emergency as declared by the President or by the Congress, with intent to injure, interfere with, or obstruct the United States or any associate nation in preparing for or carrying on the war or defense activities, or, with reason to believe that his act may injure, interfere with, or obstruct the United States or any associate nation in preparing for or carrying on the war or defense activities, willfully injures, destroys, contaminates or infects, or attempts to so injure, destroy, contaminate or infect any war material, war premises, or war utilities, shall be fined under this title or imprisoned not more than thirty years, or both. (b) If two or more persons conspire to violate this section, and one or more of such persons do any act to effect the object of the conspiracy, each of the parties to such conspiracy shall be punished as provided in subsection (a) of this section.[1]

第2153条规定的是对破坏战争物资、战争场所、战争设施行为的处罚，即“(a)任何人在美国处于战争状态或总统或国会宣布国家紧急状态时，意图伤害、干扰或阻碍美国或任何伙伴国或进行战争或防御活动，或者有理由相信其行为可能损害、干扰或阻碍美国或任何伙伴国或进行战争或防御活动，故意伤害、破坏、污染或感染，或企图伤害、毁坏、污染或感染任何战争物资、战争房舍或战争设施的，应处以罚款或不超过30年的监禁，或两者并罚。(b)如果两个或两个以上的人共谋违反本节，并且其中一个或多个人采取任何行动来实现共谋的目的，则共谋的每一方均应按照第(a)款的规定受到惩罚。”

Article 2154 punishes the production of defective war materiel, war premises or war utilities. This article stipulates—

(a) Whoever, when the United States is at war, or in times of national emergency as declared by the President or by the Congress, with intent to injure, interfere with, or obstruct the United States or any associate nation in preparing for or carrying on the war or defense activities, or, with reason to believe that his act may injure, interfere with, or obstruct the United States or any associate nation in preparing for or carrying on the war or defense activities, willfully makes, constructs, or causes to be made or constructed in a defective manner, or attempts to make, construct, or cause to be made or constructed in a defective manner any war material, war premises or war utilities, or

---

[1] 105 U. S. Code, § 2153.

any tool, implement, machine, utensil, or receptacle used or employed in making, producing, manufacturing, or repairing any such war material, war premises or war utilities, shall be fined under this title or imprisoned not more than thirty years, or both. (b) If two or more persons conspire to violate this section, and one or more of such persons do any act to effect the object of the conspiracy, each of the parties to such conspiracy shall be punished as provided in subsection (a) of this section.[1]

第2154条是对生产有缺陷的战争物资、战争房舍或战争公用设施行为的处罚。该条规定:(a)任何人在美国处于战争状态或总统或国会宣布的国家紧急状态时,意图伤害、干扰或阻碍美国或任何伙伴国准备或进行战争防御活动,或有理由相信其行为可能损害、干扰或阻碍美国或任何伙伴国准备或进行战争或防御活动,故意制造、建造或导致以有缺陷的方式制造或建造,任何战争物资、战争房舍或战争公用设施,或任何工具、机器、器具或制造、生产、制造或修理任何此类战争物资、战争房舍或战争公用设施时使用或使用的容器的,应处以罚款或不超过30年的监禁,或两者并罚。(b)如2人或2人以上合谋违反本条,且其中1人或多人作出任何行为以实现合谋的目标,则该合谋的每一方均应按本条第(a)款的规定受到处罚。

Section 2155, however, extends the range of the sabotage provisions far into activies during peacetime. It provides: Whoever, with intent to injure, interfere with, or obstruct the national defense of the United States, or willfully injures, destroys, contaminates or infects, or attempts to so injure, destroy, contaminate or infect any national - defense material, national - defense premises, or national - defense utilities, shall be fined under this title or imprisoned not more than 20 years, or both, and, if death results to any person, shall be imprisoned for any term of years or for life.[2]

第2155条将破坏罪的处罚范围扩展到和平时期的活动。它规定:任何人意图伤害、干扰或阻碍美国的国防,故意伤害、破坏、污染或感染,或企图如此伤害、破坏、污染或感染任何国防材料,国防设施或国防公用设施的,应处以罚款或不超过20年的监禁,或两者并罚,如果导致任何人死亡,应处以任何年限的有期徒刑或终身监禁。

Section 2156 regulates the production of defective defense materials, defense sites or defense installations. It provides: (a) Whoever, with intent to injure, interfere with, or obstruct the national defense of the United States, willfully makes, constructs, or attempts to make or construct in a defective manner, any national - defense material, national - defense premises or national - defense utilities, or any tool, implement,

〔1〕 105 U. S. Code, § 2154.
〔2〕 105 U. S. Code, § 2155.

machine, utensil, or receptacle used or employed in making, producing, manufacturing, or repairing any such national – defense material, national – defense premises or national – defense utilities, shall be fined under this title or imprisoned not more than ten years, or both. (b) If two or more persons conspire to violate this section, and one or more of such persons do any act to effect the object of the conspiracy, each of the parties to such conspiracy shall be punished as provided in subsection (a) of this section.[1]

第2156条规制的是生产有缺陷的国防材料、国防场所或国防设施的行为。该条规定:(a)任何人意图伤害、干扰或阻碍美国国防,故意制造、建造或试图以有缺陷的方式制造或建造任何国防材料、国防房舍或国防公用事业,或用于制作、生产、制造或修理任何此类国防材料、国防房舍或国防公用事业的任何工具、工具、机器、器具或容器的,应处罚金或10年以下有期徒刑,或两者并处。(b)如果两个或两个以上的人共谋违反本条,并且其中一个或多个人采取任何行动来实现共谋的目的,则共谋的每一方均应按照第(a)款的规定受到惩罚。

13.2.3 Espionage(间谍罪)

Espionage refers to the criminal act of conducting espionage or secret surveillance on individuals, companies, governments, etc. in order to collect secret information or detect illegal activities and transfer this information to another organization or country. Therefore, espionage crimes are typical crimes endangering national security.

间谍行为是指为了收集秘密信息或侦查不法行为,并将这些信息转移给另一个组织或国家,而对个人、公司、政府等进行间谍活动或秘密监视的犯罪行为。因此,间谍犯罪属于典型的危害国家安全的犯罪。

Chapter 18, Section 794 of the United States Code stipulates two types of espionage crimes, namely "peacetime espionage" and "wartime espionage." According to the provisions of this article, the crime of peacetime espionage refers to: "directly or indirectly delivering U. S. defense information to a foreign government, group, military force, or its agent for the purpose of or having reason to believe that it will be used to harm the United States or to assist a foreign country." Human behavior. "It does not matter whether the intelligence receiving country is recognized by the United States or whether it is a friend or an enemy of the United States. "Wartime espionage" refers to "the act of collecting, recording, spying, and transmitting information on the actions, quantity, type, status, and deployment of U. S. military forces that may be used by the

[1] 105 U. S. Code, § 2156.

enemy for the purpose of handing over to the enemy during the war".[1] It can be seen that compared with wartime espionage legislators have given higher subjective proof conditions to peacetime espionage.

《美国法典》第 18 章第 794 条规定了两种间谍罪，即平时间谍罪与战时间谍罪。该条的规定，平时间谍罪是指："为了或者有理由相信将会被用以损害美国或者助力外国，而直接或者间接把美国国防情报交给外国的政府、团体、军事力量或者其代理人的行为。"至于情报接受国是否得到美国的承认、是美国的朋友还是敌人，都在所不问。战时间谍罪是指："在战争期间，为了交与敌人，而收集、记录、刺探、传送美国军事力量的行动、数量、种类、状态、部署等可能为敌人所用的信息的行为。"由此可见，相较于战时间谍罪而言，立法者赋予了平时间谍罪更高的主观证明条件。

■ Case study（案例学习）

United States v. Albury, 18 – cr – 0067 (WMW)（美国诉奥尔伯里案）

Facts（基本案情）

Terry J. Albury is a former FBI agent who was charged with leaking classified state documents to The Intercept.

奥尔伯里是一名美国前联邦调查局特工，他因向"The Intercept"网站泄露国家机密文件，而被受到起诉。

Dispute（主要争议）

How to balance the relationship between citizens' freedom of speech and national interests in the determination of espionage crime?

在间谍罪的认定中，如何平衡公民言论自由与国家利益之间的关系？

Conclusion（结论）

Citizens' freedom of speech cannot override the basic interests of the state. If a citizen discloses secrets related to national interests that he or she comes to know in the course of his or her work to the public, it will also constitute a crime of espionage.

公民的言论自由不能超过国家的基本利益。公民将工作过程中知悉的与国家利益有关机密向社会公开，也会构成间谍罪。

Question: What was the root cause of Albury's prosecution? (Please scan the QR code on the right to get the answer)

奥尔伯里被起诉的根本原因是什么？（答案请扫描右侧二维码获取）

---

[1] 18 USC Ch. 37: Espionage and Censorship.

■ Curriculum Ideology and Politics(课程思政)

Sedition, sabotage and espionage can cause damage to the security and stability of the country and directly violate the interests of the country. Therefore, these crimes are serious crimes in the criminal laws of various countries around the world. The United States has strict regulations on crimes here, and it can be said that it has established a strict legal network. However, at the same time, the United States often adopts the attitude of restrictive application towards related crimes. All countries in the world attach great importance to citizens' concern for national security, and citizens should cultivate national security awareness, which is also an important civic awareness..

煽动罪、破坏罪和间谍罪会对国家的安全与稳定造成破坏而直接侵犯国家的利益,因此,这些犯罪在世界各国的刑法中都是重罪。美国对这方面的犯罪进行了严格的规定,可以说是布下了严密的法网。但与此同时,美国对相关犯罪的理解往往采取限缩适用的态度。世界各国均重视公民对国家安全的关注,而公民也应当培养自身的国家安全意识,这是一种重要的公民意识。

13.3 Anti – Terrorism Crimes(反恐怖主义罪)

Terrorism is a crime that uses intimidation and violence to pursue political goals. It greatly violates national security and citizens' right to life. The United States faces severe terrorism challenges, and typical crimes include four anti – terrorism crimes. They will be briefly described below.

恐怖主义是一种以恐吓和暴力为手段,来追求政治目的的犯罪,它极大地侵犯了国家安全和公民的生命权。美国面临着严峻的恐怖主义挑战,典型罪名包括 4 个反恐怖主义犯罪。下面将对其分别进行简述。

13.3.1 The Use of Weapons of Mass Destruction(使用大规模杀伤性武器罪)

Weapons of mass destruction are nuclear, radioactive, chemical, biological or other devices designed to harm large numbers of people. Because the use of weapons of mass destruction will lead to uncontrollable situations, the United States has stipulated two types of crimes in its code, namely: the act of using weapons of mass destruction against U. S. nationals or nationals within the United States, and the act of U. S. citizens using weapons of mass clestruction outside the United States.

大规模杀伤性武器是指旨在伤害大量人员的核、放射性、化学、生物或其他装置。由于使用大规模杀伤性武器会导致不可控的局面,美国在其法典中一共规定了两类犯罪行为,即针对美国国民或美国境内国民使用大规模杀伤性武器的行为,以及美国公民在美国境外使用大规模杀伤性武器的行为。

For the former, US legislation has established a total of four different types. The first type is: the use, threat, attempt, or conspiracy to use weapons of mass destruction against a U. S. national while that national is outside the United States without lawful authorization. The second category is the use, threat, attempt, or conspiracy to use weapons of mass destruction against any person or property within the United States without lawful authority and (a) Using the mail or any interstate or foreign commerce facility to facilitate crime; (b) Such property is used in interstate or foreign commerce or in activities affecting interstate or foreign commerce; (c) Any offender travels or causes others to travel in interstate or foreign commerce in furtherance of a crime; or (d) The conduct or results of a crime affects, or under the threat, attempt, or conspiracy to affect, interstate or foreign commerce. The third category is the use, threat, attempted, or conspiracy to use weapons of mass destruction without lawful authority against any property owned, leased, or used by the United States or any department or agency of the United States, whether the property is located within or outside the United States. the behavior of. The fourth category is the use, threat, attempted, or conspiracy to use weapons of mass destruction against any property owned, leased, or used by a foreign government within the United States without lawful authority. The said act shall be punishable by imprisonment for any term or for life, and if death is caused, by death or by imprisonment for any term or for life, as provided in the Code.[1]

就前者而言,美国立法一共规定了 4 种不同的行为类型。第一种类型是:未经合法授权,使用、威胁、试图或密谋使用大规模杀伤性武器,针对美国国民,而该国民在美国境外的行为。第二种类型是:未经合法授权,使用、威胁、试图或密谋使用大规模杀伤性武器,针对美国境内的任何人或者任何财产,且(a)使用邮件或任何州际或国外商业设施来促进犯罪;(b)此类财产用于州际或国外商业或影响州际或国外商业的活动;(c)任何犯罪者在州际或外国商业中旅行或促使他人在州际或外国商业中旅行以促进犯罪;或者(d)犯罪行为或犯罪结果影响州际或外国商业,或者在威胁、企图或共谋的情况下,会影响州际或外国商业的行为。第三种类型是:未经合法授权,使用、威胁、试图或密谋使用大规模杀伤性武器,针对美国或美国任何部门或机构拥有、租赁或使用的任何财产,无论该财产位于美国境内还是境的行为。第四

[1] 18 U. S. Code § 2332a.

种类型是:未经合法授权,使用、威胁、试图或密谋使用大规模杀伤性武器,针对外国政府在美国境内拥有、租赁或使用的任何财产的行为。对于上述行为,根据法典规定,应处以任何年限的有期徒刑或终身监禁,如果导致死亡,应处以死刑或任何年限的有期徒刑或终身监禁。

13.3.2 Acts of Terrorism Transcending National Boundaries(跨国恐怖主义犯罪)

Chapter 18 of the United States Code, Section 2332b, stipulates the crime of transnational terrorism from seven aspects: prohibited conduct、jurisdiction、punishment、evidence requirements, extraterritorial jurisdiction, investigative agency, and concept definition.

《美国法典》第 18 章第 2332b 条从禁止行为、管辖权、处罚、举证要求、治外法权、调查机构、概念这 7 个方面,对跨国恐怖主义犯罪进行了规定。

In summary, this article mainly regulates the following three types of criminal activities: (1) Killing, kidnapping, serious injury, assault causing serious injury, and assault with dangerous weapons against people in the United States; (2) Destroying buildings in the United States, Vehicles or other movable and immovable property, and seriously endangering the personal safety of others; (3) Threaten to commit, attempt to commit, or conspire to commit acts (1) or (2), and the person intending to infringe is a federal official or public official, and the property intended to be violated is the property of the United States or its citizens, such as buildings and vehicles, and the criminal act involves the use of interstate or international commercial facilities such as postal services.

概括而言,本条主要规制以下三种犯罪活动:(1)对美国境内的人实施杀害、绑架、重伤、袭击致人重伤、持危险武器袭击的行为;(2)毁坏美国境内的建筑、车辆或者其他动产与不动产,严重危及他人人身安全的行为;(3)威胁实施、企图实施或者共谋实施(1)或(2)的行为,且意图侵害者是联邦官员或公职人员,意图侵害的建筑、车辆等财产是美国或其公民的财产,犯罪行为使用了邮政等跨州或者国际商业设施等条件的行为。

For the above - mentioned acts, in accordance with the provisions of S 2332b. (c) of the Federal Penal Code, the maximum penalty for killing or causing the death of a victim is the death penalty or life imprisonment, and the maximum penalty for kidnapping is life imprisonment. The maximum penalty is 35 years in prison for maiming. The maximum penalty is 30 years imprisonment for assault causing serious bodily injury or assault with a dangerous weapon. The maximum penalty is 25 years imprisonment for causing property damage or destruction.[1]

对于上述行为,按照《联邦刑法典》S 2332b.(c)的规定,犯跨境恐怖活动罪杀害或者致被害人死亡的最高处死刑或者终身监禁,绑架他人的最高处终身监禁,重伤他人身体的最高处 35 年监禁,袭击致人重伤或者持危险武器袭击的最高处 30 年监禁,造成财产损坏或毁灭的最高处 25 年监禁。

13.3.3 Harboring or Concealing Terrorists(窝藏或隐藏恐怖分子罪)

These wrongful acts are contained in Title 18, United States Code, Section 2339. The specific provisions are:(a) Whoever harbors or conceals any person who he knows, or has reasonable grounds to believe that the person, has committed, or is about to commit, an offense under section 32 (relating to destruction of aircraft or aircraft facilities), section 175 (relating to biological weapons), section 229 (relating to chemical weapons), section 831 (relating to nuclear materials), paragraph (2) or (3) of section 844(f) (relating to arson and bombing of government property risking or causing injury or death), section 1366(a) (relating to the destruction of an energy facility), section 2280 (relating to violence against maritime navigation), section 2332a (relating to weapons of mass destruction), or section 2332b (relating to acts of terrorism transcending national boundaries) of this title, section 236(a) (relating to sabotage of nuclear facilities or fuel) of the Atomic Energy Act of 1954 (42 U. S. C. 2284(a)), or section 46502 (relating to aircraft piracy) of title 49, shall be fined under this title or imprisoned not more than ten years, or both. (b) A violation of this section may be prosecuted in any Federal judicial district in which the underlying offense was committed, or in any other Federal judicial district as provided by law.

这些不法行为规定在《美国法典》第 18 卷第 2339 条中。具体规定如下:(a)任何人窝藏或隐匿其认识或有合理理由相信已犯下或即将犯下第 32 条(有关毁坏航空器或航空器设施)、第 175 条(有关生物武器)、第 229 条(有关化学武器)、第 831 条(有关核材料)、第 844(f)条第(2)款或第(3)款(有关可能造成伤亡的针对政府财产的纵火和爆炸)、第 1366(a)条(有关破坏能源设施)、第 2280 条(有关针对海上航行的暴力)、第 2332a 条(有关大规模毁灭性武器)或第 2332b 条(有关超越国界的恐怖主义行为)、1954 年《原子能法》(42 U. S. C. 2284(a))第 236(a)条(有关核设施或燃料的破坏)或第 49 卷第 46502 条(有关飞机海盗行为),应处以罚款或不超过

[1] 18 U. S. Code § 2332b.

10 年的监禁,或两者并罚。(b)违反本条规定的行为可在犯罪发生的任何联邦司法管辖区或法律规定的任何其他联邦司法区受到起诉。

13.3.4 Providing "Material Support" to Terrorists and/or Terrorist Organizations (实质帮助恐怖分子或恐怖分子集团罪)

This crime was stipulated in the Anti – Terrorism and Effective Death Penalty Act of 1996 and was later incorporated into the Patriot Act. This crime is currently stipulated in Section 2339 – B of Chapter 18 of the United States Code, which covers prohibited activities, civil penalties, injunctions, extraterritorial jurisdiction, investigation, confidential information for filing civil lawsuits, definition of concepts, etc. stipulated.

该罪是 1996 年《反恐怖及有效执行死刑法》中规定的罪名,后被纳入《爱国者法案》之中。该罪现规定于《美国法典》第 18 章第 2339 条之 B 款中,分别从禁止的活动、民事处罚、禁止令、域外管辖权、调查、提起民事诉讼的机密信息、概念等几个方面进行了规定。

According to the provisions of this article, the crime of substantively assisting terrorists refers to giving material or financial support to terrorists, or concealing it, knowing that it will be used to prepare, commit, or cover up terrorist criminal activities and escaping after committing a crime, or intending to use it for the aforementioned acts and disguising the nature, location, source or ownership of funding. The crime of substantively assisting terrorist groups refers to knowing that they are foreign terrorist organizations and providing them with money, financial services, housing, etc. Notably, the act of providing medical and religious materials was excluded.

该条规定,实质帮助恐怖分子罪是指明知将用于准备、实施、掩盖恐怖犯罪活动以及犯罪后逃跑,或者意图使其用于前述行为,而给予恐怖分子物质或者金钱资助,或者隐瞒、掩饰资助的性质、地点、来源或者所有权的行为。实质帮助恐怖分子集团罪是指明知是外国恐怖组织,而给予其金钱、金融服务、用房等帮助的行为。值得注意的是,提供医疗和宗教材料的行为被该罪排除在外。

■ Case study(案例学习)

United States v. Hammoud, 2:03 – cr – 80992, (E. D. Mich.)(美国诉哈穆德案)

Facts(基本案情)

In 1992, Hamoud, a Lebanese citizen, obtained permanent resident status by marrying a U. S. citizen. In the late 1990s, Hamoud, his wife, and brother participated in a cigarette smuggling operation involving approximately $7. 5 million worth of cigarettes, which resulted in the state of Michigan undercollecting $3 million in tax revenue. In 1996, Hamoud began leading Shia Muslims in weekly prayers at his home. During these events, Hamoud met Hezbollah's general secretary Hassan Naserallah, spiritual leader Sheikh Fadlallah, and Hezbollah's senior military commander Sheikh Abbas al – Khalaq. He has since urged attendees not only to donate to Hezbollah and transfer money to Halak, but also to transfer his own money to Hezbollah. It is understood that Hezbollah is an organization established by Lebanese Shia Muslims in response to the Israeli invasion of Lebanon in 1982. Hezbollah provided various forms of humanitarian aid to Lebanese Shiite Muslims. At the same time, the Middle East was strongly opposed to organizations in Western countries, especially the existence of Israel and the activities of the US government in the Middle East. In the end, the jury found Hamoud guilty of 14 counts, including providing "Material Support" to terrorist organizations.

1992 年,黎巴嫩公民哈穆德通过与美国公民结婚而获得永久居民身份。20 世纪 90 年代末期,哈穆德及其妻子、兄弟参与了香烟走私活动,涉及价值约 750 万美元的香烟,导致密歇根州少收取了 300 万美元的税收。1996 年,哈穆德开始带领什叶派穆斯林每周在其家里进行祈祷活动。在这些活动中,哈穆德认识了黎巴嫩真主党的总书记哈桑·纳瑟拉拉、精神领袖谢赫·法德拉拉,以及真主党高级军事指挥官谢赫阿巴斯·哈拉克。此后,他不仅敦促与会者向真主党捐款,将钱转给哈拉克,还将自己的钱转给真主党。据了解,真主党是黎巴嫩什叶派穆斯林为应对 1982 年以色列入侵黎巴嫩而成立的组织。真主党向黎巴嫩什叶派穆斯林提供各种形式的人道主义援助,同时,中东地区强烈反对西方国家的组织,尤其反对以色列的存在和美国政府在中东的活动。最后,陪审团判定哈穆德犯有 14 项罪行,其中包括实质帮助恐怖分子集团罪。

Dispute(主要争议)

Hamoud argued that Section B of 2339 of the United States Code is so broad and the definition of "material support" is vague, so it is unconstitutional and has no legal force. Moreover, even if it is believed that Hamoud provided funds to Hezbollah, it is not necessarily assumed that the money was definitely used for terrorism, but it may also be used for humanitarian financing.

哈穆德认为《美国法典》第 2339 条之 B 款的规定过于宽泛,对于"物质支持"的定义相当模糊,因而这个条款违反宪法,没有法律效力。而且,即便认为哈穆德向真主党提供资金,也未必能够认定这笔钱一定用在恐怖主义上,因为它也可能用于人道主义的资助上。

Conclusion(结论)

The jury found that Hamoud's conduct substantially contributed to the development of a terrorist group and should constitute an offence.

陪审团认为,哈穆德的行为实质地促进了恐怖主义集团的发展,应当构成犯罪。

Questions:1. What is the key to what Hammoud is considered to constitute a crime?(Please scan the QR code on the right to get the answer)

哈穆德被认为构成犯罪的关键是什么?(答案请扫描右侧二维码获取)

2. What is the maximum penalty for the offence of providing "Material Support" to terrorists and/or terrorist organizations?(Please scan the QR code on the right to get the answer)

实质帮助恐怖分子或恐怖分子集团罪的最高刑是多少?(答案请扫描右侧二维码获取)

13.4 Exercise(课后练习)(答案请扫描右侧二维码获取)

13.4.1 Test of Terminologies(术语考查)

①American Revolution ②terrorist organizations

③blameability ④national emergency

⑤war materials

13.4.2 True or False(判断题)

1. In the crime of treason in the United States the "waging of war" to must reach the level of declaration of war.

美国叛国罪中所指的"发动战争"必须要达到宣战的程度。

2. The crime of sabotage in the United States mainly focuses on attacks on relevant military infrastructure, and does not include civilian facilities.

美国的破坏罪主要关注的是对相关军事基础设施的攻击行为,不包括民用的设施。

3. Espionage crimes in the United States include both peacetime espionage and wartime espionage. Among them, the proving conditions for peacetime espionage are more stringent.

美国的间谍罪既包括平时间谍罪,也包括战时间谍罪。其中,构成平时间谍罪的证明条件更加严苛。

4. The scope of the U. S. crime of using weapons of mass destruction does not include acts committed outside the United States.

美国使用大规模杀伤性武器罪的规制范围不包括在美国境外实施的行为。

5. Sentencing for transnational terrorism crimes in the United States includes the death penalty.

美国跨国恐怖主义犯罪的量刑中包括死刑。

13.4.3 Short – answer Questions(简答题)

1. What is the difference between the crime of treason in the United States and the crime of treason in the UK?

美国的背叛国家罪与英国的背叛国家罪有何不同?

2. What specific crimes are included in U. S. Anti – Terrorism Crimes?

美国的反恐怖主义罪包含哪些具体的罪名?

3. Please briefly introduce the origin and composition of the crime of sedition in the United States.

请简要介绍美国煽动罪的来源和构成。

■ Curriculum Ideology and Politics(课程思政)

Facing serious threats from terrorist crimes, the United States has established complete crimes to punish terrorist crimes. The crime of terrorism in the United States is very inclusive. When combined with the same crime, it can include terrorism crimes composed of various different crimes. The United States has not adopted preventive criminalization legislative techniques. It pays more attention to the actual harm of terrorist crimes to national security, which makes the sentencing of terrorist crimes in the United States heavier.

Terrorist crime is a global organized crime. Every citizen should objectively understand its harm to national security and world security.

因面临严峻的恐怖主义犯罪的威胁,美国建立了完善的罪名来惩治恐怖主义犯罪。美国的恐怖主义犯罪的罪名包括性很强,在同一个罪名的统合下,包含各种不同犯罪构成的恐怖主义犯罪。美国未采取预防性犯罪化的立法技术,其更加重视恐怖主义犯罪对国家安全的实际危害,这使美国的恐怖主义犯罪量刑较重。

恐怖主义犯罪是全球性的有组织犯罪,每一位公民都应当客观认识其对国家安全以及世界安全的危害。

■ Summary(总结)

1. The crime of treason in the United States has extremely high requirements for evidence, that is, each act must be proven by at least two witnesses, or the defendant must admit it in open court, otherwise it cannot be convicted.

美国的背叛国家罪对证据有着极高的要求,即要求每个行为都必须至少有2位证人证明,或者被告人在公开法庭上做出承认,否则该证据不能被认定。

2. U. S. federal law divides terrorism into two types: “international terrorism” and “domestic terrorism”. The former refers to terrorist activities that occur outside the territory of the United States and target the United States, while the latter refers to terrorist activites that occurs within the territory of the United States.

美国联邦法律把恐怖主义划分为国际恐怖主义与国内恐怖主义两种。前者是指发生在美国领土之外以美国为目标的恐怖活动,而后者则是指发生在美国领土之内的恐怖活动。

3. The U. S. criminal law stipulates two types of espionage crimes, namely “peacetime espionage” and “wartime espionage”. Peacetime espionage refers to: “the act of directly or indirectly handing over U. S. defense information to a foreign government, group, military force, or its agent for the purpose of or having reason to believe that it will be used to harm the United States or assist a foreign country”. “Wartime espionage” refers to: “during a war, for the purpose of handing over to the enemy, the act of collecting, recording, spying, and transmitting information on the actions, quantity, type, status, and deployment of U. S. military forces that may be used by the enemy”.

美国刑法中规定了两种间谍罪,分别为平时间谍罪与战时间谍罪。平时间谍罪是指:“为了或者有理由相信将会被用以损害美国或者助力外国,而直接或者间接把美国国防情报交给外国的政府、团体、军事力量或者其代理人的行为。”战时间谍罪是指:“在战争期间,为了交予敌人,而收集、记录、刺探、传送美国军事力量的行动、数量、种类、状态、部署等可能为敌人所用的信息的行为。”

4. The United States has a relatively strict publishing censorship system. According to the crime of publishing and distributing publications that incite subversion of the government: “Whoever, with intent to cause the overthrow or destruction of any such government, prints, publishes, edits, issues, circulates, sells, distributes, or publicly displays any written or printed matter advocating, advising, or teaching the duty, necessity, desirability, or propriety of overthrowing or destroying any government in the

United States by force or violence, or attempts to do so".

美国有较为严格的出版审查制度,根据出版、发行煽动颠覆政府的出版物罪的规定:"任何人以引起推翻或毁坏政府为目的,印刷、出版、编辑、发表、流通、出售、发行或者公开展览任何宣传、劝导或教导以武力或暴力推翻或毁坏位于美国领土范围内政府的职责、必要性、愿望或者合适性的出版物,或者试图实施前述行为的",都构成犯罪。